KU-164-397

The Media Student's Book

Second Edition

GILL BRANSTON
and
ROY STAFFORD

London and New York

First published 1996
by Routledge
11 New Fetter Lane, London EC4P 4EE

Simultaneously published in the USA and Canada
by Routledge
29 West 35th Street, New York, NY 10001

Reprinted 1996 (twice), 1997, 1998

Second edition first published 1999 by Routledge
Reprinted 2000 and 2001 (three times)
Routledge is an imprint of the Taylor & Francis Group

© 1996, 1999 GILL BRANSTON and ROY STAFFORD

Typeset by 𝍢 Tek-Art, Croydon, Surrey
Printed and bound in Great Britain by Butler & Tanner Ltd, Frome and
London

All rights reserved. No part of t
reproduced or utilised in any fo
mechanical, or other means, no
invented, including photocopyi
information storage or retrieval
writing from the publishers.

WORCESTERSHIRE COUNTY COUNCIL	
133	
Cypher	28.10.01
302.23	£15.99

British Library Cataloguing in P
A catalogue record for this bool

Library of Congress Cataloguing in Publication Data
The media student's book/Gill Branston and Roy Stafford. – 2nd ed.
p. cm.
Includes bibliographical references and index.
1. Mass media. I. Stafford, Roy. II. Branston, Gill. III. Title.
P90.B6764 1999
302.23—dc21   98–42027

ISBN 0–415–17307–8 (hbk)
ISBN 0–415–17308–6 (pbk)

The Media Student's Book

Second Edition

The Media Student's Book is a comprehensive introduction for students of media studies on A-Level, City and Guilds, BTEC, GNVQ and undergraduate courses. It covers all the key topics you will encounter in media studies and provides a detailed and accessible guide to concepts and debates. The new edition of this highly successful book has been thoroughly revised and updated throughout with up-to-the-minute examples and expanded coverage of important issues in media studies.

It has been written by a lecturer and a freelance teacher, writer and chief examiner in the area, both aware of the needs of media students levels.

The Media Student's Book, Second Edition, has been specially desi be easy to use and to understand, with:

700021511334

- marginal key terms and references and a useful glossary
- follow-up activities, suggestions for further reading and resource centres
- clear explanations, whether of practical skills or theory with examples provided from a rich range of media forms including advertising, films, radio, television, newspapers, magazines, photography and the Internet.

Gill Branston is a Lecturer in Journalism, Media and Cultural Studies at Cardiff University. **Roy Stafford** is a Freelance Lecturer in Media Education and Training.

What readers said about the first edition of *The Media Student's Book*:

'Imaginative, accessible, comprehensive and shrewd – all textbooks should be like this. No student could read it without coming away thoroughly prepared for the pleasures, pitfalls and challenges of Media Studies, and no teacher in the field could fail to find it a superb and timely source of ideas.' Andy Medhurst, *Lecturer in Media Studies, University of Sussex*

'An exemplary textbook for Media Studies, especially but not exclusively at undergraduate level . . . they write in a lively, engaging style . . . they offer a strong sense of argument, debating the ideas of referenced authorities by asserting their own sense of where their positions lie. . . . They deal with the widest imaginable, exhaustive and enviable range of references . . . they are not frightened to explore the most difficult theories and they do so with enviable explanatory skill, constant references and exemplification. . . . An extraordinary feat of writing for an audience at this educational level. I've no doubt future publications will be judged by the standards it sets.' David Lusted, *English and Media Magazine no 35, Autumn 1996*

What readers said about the second edition:

'A book which no college or first-year undergraduate student of media studies can afford to ignore . . . indispensable.' Andrew Beck, *Coventry University*

'An essential introduction to the subject. . . . Easy to use and lively to read, this second edition offers an up-to-the-minute guide for beginning Media Studies. The writing of all new sections is clear and concise, the selection of material very contemporary and accessible to younger students.' Jonathan Bignall, *University of Reading*

'An outstanding book that will be valuable as a resource for both students and teachers.' David Carr, *Weald College, Middlesex*

'Finally! A textbook especially designed for a critical introductory course in media studies. . . . It is the perfect introduction to complex concepts and the authors do a wonderful job of explaining key critical theories in terms accessible to undergraduate students. I am a passionate fan of the book.' Clemencia Rodriguez, *University of Texas, San Antonio*

'A model textbook, one which never stops encouraging its readers to go further, to develop their ideas through independent thought and study. It is very attractively presented and accessibly written but never talks down - or dumbs down. A wide range of important terms, concepts and approaches are introduced to students without any skating over of complexities and difficulties. . . . But most of all it is the intellectual excitement that the book conveys and transmits to readers that makes it such an invaluable learning resource.' Professor Jeremy Hawthorn, *Norwegian University of Science and Technology, Trondheim*

Contents

Acknowledgements

Thanks to assorted helpers and challengers: Stuart Allan, Will Brooker, Rod Brookes, Cindy Carter, Jack Carter, Alison Charles, Val Hill, Malcolm Hoddy, Editor of the *Keighley News*, Tim Holmes, Simon Horrocks, Sara Jones, Nick Lacey, Daniel Meadows, Adrian Sales, Mike Ungersma, Wowo Wauters, Granville Williams.

To the readers and contributors to *in the picture* magazine.

To Rebecca Barden, Chris Cudmore, Alastair Daniel, Katherine Hodkinson and Moira Taylor for their rare combination of enthusiasm and patience during the lengthy process of making this second edition.

And of course, to Lauren Branston, Lucy Branston, Marion Pencavel and Rob Seago for many virtues, not least tolerating the authors.

Finally, and emphatically, none of this would have been possible without the help of all the students and teachers and media practitioners with whom we have worked over many years.

Figure acknowledgements

The following figures were reproduced with the kind permission of their rights holders and sources. Routledge has made every effort to trace copyright holders and to obtain permission to publish illustrated material. Any omissions brought to our attention will be remedied in future editions.

FIGURE ACKNOWLEDGEMENTS

5.11	*Battle of Algiers*, copyright Battaglia, source the Kobal Collection
5.12	*The Wild Bunch*, copyright Warner Bros, source the Kobal Collection
5.14	Preparing to lay down sound effects, Lucasfilms
6.2	*Se7en*, copyright New Line, source the Kobal Collection
6.3	Tender document, BBC
6.4	Studio production, Solihull College © Simon Derry
6.5	Stint before the microphone, Solihill College © Simon Derry
6.6	Editing suite, Roy Stafford
7.1	*Becky Sharpe*, copyright RKO, British Film Institute
7.2	*How Green Was My Valley*, source the Kobal Collection
8.1	Retail sales by Genre, BVA Yearbook 1997
8.2	*Titanic*, copyright Twentieth Century Fox and Paramount Pictures, photo by Merie W. Wallace, source the Kobal Collection
8.3	*The Roaring Twenties*, British Film Institute
9.1	*Tank Girl*, from issue no 2. of Deadline Magazine, Deadline Publications Ltd
9.2	*Men in Black*, The Ronald Grant Archive
9.3	*Mars Attacks!*, copyright 1996 Warner Bros, source the Kobal Collection
9.4	*X-Files Game*, copyright Twentieth Century Fox
10.1	Illustration Dick Bruna, copyright Mercis b.v. 1978
10.2a	Post-feminist postcard, copyright Leeds Postcards
10.2b	Lara Croft, Tomb Raider. Lara Croft and all likenesses are the copyrighted possession of Core Design Limited. Tomb Raider © and ™ 1997 Core Design Limited. Copyright and published 1997 Eidos Interactive Limited. All rights reserved
10.3	What Does She Have to do to Get a Job?, Commission for Racial Equality
10.4	Cotton pickers, Mary Evans Picture Library
10.5	Spastics ad, reproduced by kind permission of SCOPE (formerly The Spastics Society)
10.6	NUJ codes on race reporting, courtesy NUJ Equality Council
11.1	*Gone With the Wind*, British Film Institute
11.2	Thick Paddies postcard, copyright Leeds Postcards
12.1	Children's mobile library, from *Small World*, Intermediate Technology
12.2	Learn to Make This Last Longer, Wallis Tomlinson Limited
12.3	Get in Lane postcard, copyright Leeds Postcards
12.4	Posy Simmonds cartoon, reprinted by permission of Peters, Fraser and Dunlop
12.5	Thanks to the debt ad, reprinted by permission of Christian Aid
12.7	The Cooperative Bank ad, Chase Creative Consultants
12.8	The pleasures of reassurance?, BBC News and Current Affairs Department

FIGURE ACKNOWLEDGEMENTS

22.1   Diagram from *Anatomy of the Movies*, David Pirie (ed.) by permission of D. Services, London: Windward

22.2   Trends in UK cinemagoing, Roy Stafford

23.1   Media corporations, Roy Stafford

23.2   Screen grab from TCI, courtesy of TCI

23.3   Screen grab from The Lagardere Group/Matra-Hachette

24.1   Rupert Murdoch, courtesy News International

24.2   News Corporation, copyright News Corporation

25.1   Rita Hayworth, by permission of the National Archive and Records Administration, USA

25.2   Jodie Foster in *Contact*, 1997 Warner Bros, source the Kobal Collection

25.3   Jodie Foster by E. Robert, Sygma Agency

26.1   Audrey Hepburn by *Picture Post* photographer Bert Hardy, May 1950, courtesy Hulton Getty Picture Library

26.2   ITC screen grab from web page, courtesy Independent Television Commission; FCC screen grab from web page, courtesy FCC

26.3   *Welcome to Sarajevo*, copyright Channel 4/Miramax, source Kobal Collection

27.1   Channel 4's policy statement on its website, by permission of Channel 4

27.2   BBC logos used by permission of the BBC. These are trade marks of the British Broadcasting Corporation and are used under licence

27.3   ARD logo by permission of ARD, Germany

28.1   The South Bank Show logo, copyright LWT

28.2   Orson Welles on the set of *Citizen Kane*, copyright RKO

28.3   *Un chien andalou*, copyright Buñuel–Dali, source the Kobal Collection

28.4   Maya Deren in *Meshes of the Afternoon*, permission of Anthology Film Archives

28.5   *A bout de souffle*, copyright Oasis Films

29.1   Julie Dash, by permission of Julie Dash, Geechee Girls Multimedia, Inc.

29.2   Sally Potter in *The Tango Lesson*. Photo: Moune Jamet. Courtesy Adventure Pictures (Tango) Ltd 1996

29.3   Mathieu Kassovitz, courtesy of the Ronald Grant Picture Library, the Cinema Museum

29.4   *Chunking Express*, courtesy ICA Projects Limited

30.1   The flapper, courtesy Martin Pumphrey

30.4   Gold Leaf tobacco ad, photo of billboard taken and supplied by Roy Stafford

30.5   Ronaldo of the Brazilian world cup team, 1998, courtesy of Nike (UK) Limited

31.1–2   *Keighley News* front page, 'Wired' details, readership details, *Keighley News*

31.3   JICREG figures, *Keighley News, courtesy* JICREG

31.4   *KN* website, courtesy *Keighley News*

Introduction

Media Studies is now an established area of work in further and higher education. Yet there are very few books designed to help students through a subject which *both*

- relates very intimately to the sharpest contemporary cultural pleasures, *and*
- has to draw on a range of difficult theories to understand these experiences.

We have all grown up in environments saturated with media experiences. 'The media' are familiar and one of our first aims will be to make them 'strange' – to allow you to distance yourself from something you know, in order to look at it differently. This familiarity, and the expectations it arouses, also creates problems for a Media Studies textbook. Television, from children's programmes, through educational television, to the vast range of broadcast material, has probably taught you a great deal, in ways which books cannot hope to emulate. You may also have quite sophisticated experience of computers, at home and at college, including interactive forms like CD-ROMs and the Internet.

Such ways of learning have real implications for anyone setting out to write a textbook. We've tried to produce a guide which allows us to develop quite complicated arguments, where this needs to be done, in longish chapters. But we've also recognised that you will need to make all kinds of connections between ideas and will wish to exploit the possibilities of following links as you might on a website. You will therefore find plenty of cross-references and key terms, shown in **bold**, which can be traced through the glossary. Information is offered in different sized chunks and formats. We hope you'll like and use the jokes and quotes in the margins, the case studies, the activities and the feel of a book which is trying to work with a mixture of materials.

Modern technologies have dazzling capacities. It is now possible, using **digital imaging**, to make it seem as though Marilyn Monroe and Brad Pitt are playing a scene together or that the Earth can 'morph' into an apple before our eyes; to broadcast such scenes simultaneously across

Figure 0.1　Times Square, New York, 1997

continents; and to accompany them with music created entirely by computer. The Internet has been touted, like many earlier technologies, as a kind of utopian space where information about 'the universe and everything' is readily available and all questions can be answered. There are two potential dangers attached to this view:

- The ease of use of technologies – 'just push the button' – can make theories and histories seem irrelevant.
- Technologies are not equally distributed, nor are they accessible or affordable for everyone.

Terms in Media Studies

Some students have problems in Media Studies because of its terminology. Words which have fairly straightforward meanings in everyday life (like '**sign**' or '**closed**'), outside the subject, take on rather different ones within it. This can be confusing and we've tried, wherever possible, to warn you of such likely misunderstandings.

The development of Media Studies has been quite often 'driven' by developments in higher education. From the 1960s onwards, many academics, trying to get modern media taken seriously as objects for study, had to present arguments couched in very specialised language.

Along with an excitement with theoretical developments such as **structuralism** and **semiotics**, which seemed to promise radical political possibilities, this produced a very difficult set of theoretical terms – especially for those who had not been involved in the years of struggling through, applying and familiarising themselves with these terms.

Now the dust has settled, the real gains of some of these approaches can be brought into study of the media. Other parts of what has become almost the official language of the subject in higher education, we feel, are less useful, and often depend on such a huge amount of study that we have left them out.

Yes, the technologies are terrific – exciting and disturbing at the same time. But we hope you find useful our sections on their histories, distribution and ways of working, rather than a tedious diversion from the delights of simply celebrating 'virtual reality'. However convincingly you have Marilyn and Brad in the same frame together, however much information is at your fingertips on the Internet, you can't rely on virtual decisions about what dialogue they will speak, or how they will be lit, framed and directed to move. Nor can you make use of the Internet without some sense of *what* information you need.

Media Studies is still a young subject area and the syllabuses – the official definitions – offered by the various examining bodies are still being developed. We hope we've covered all the basic *concepts* you will encounter and quite a few of the *debates* or issues which are addressed by Media A Levels, GNVQ Advanced in Media: Communication and Production, BTEC and City & Guilds Media courses, and by Access courses and many undergraduate media units as well. Media theories have also influenced work in other subjects including Sociology, English and Cultural Studies. *Media production practice* increasingly spills over into Art, Design and Photography. Our 'target audience' includes many different groups of students and so don't be surprised if you find things that aren't on *your* syllabus. Dip into them anyway – we hope you'll find that they increase your understanding of the key concepts (and they may well be required for the next course you take).

We haven't included any essay questions as such, because no one particular syllabus is targeted and we would rather try to support your basic understanding of concepts and debates. We have suggested a wide range of 'activities', some very simple and others more complex. Most of these you can pursue on your own. We hope they are all enjoyable and worthwhile in their own right rather than dry 'exercises'.

This new edition has new or heavily revised chapters and case studies on:
- Digital publishing and the Internet
- Globalisation
- The international music industry
- Postmodernisms
- *Pulp Fiction*
- Science fiction
- The languages of media
- Ideologies and discourses
- Public service broadcasting
- Independent film-making

and, of course, all the other sections have been updated and revised.

The two of us have worked in most levels of further and higher education, and in media education generally for twenty years or so. We 'entered the field' because we enjoyed popular culture in all its forms and we recognised its importance in contemporary society. We hope that our enthusiasm comes through in the writing – Media Studies should be challenging *and* fun. Whatever your interest, in passing an exam or simply understanding the 'media society', enjoy reading and working with the book and let us know, by writing to the publishers, about your ideas for improving it. Even better, e-mail us direct with your comments. If you look on page 199 you'll find some advice about searching for our e-mail addresses.

How the book is organised

There are two types of material in the book. The main chapters carry the key theoretical ideas and concepts which are explained and contextualised in general terms. The case study chapters allow us to explore applications of theory or more specialised theoretical points in detail.

Case studies are distinguished by page design. Chapters use a single column and a margin for extra material, but case studies are presented in two columns without margins. We expect you will need to keep 'dipping in' to the main chapters, but that you might read the case studies straight through.

Finding material

The book isn't organised like a 'set text' – there is no correct way to use it. Instead, it is designed for your support, so it is important that, whatever you need, you can find it easily. At the start of all chapters and case studies is a list of main headings. In chapters the appropriate headings are repeated in a computer-style menu at the top of each page. 'Running heads' at the top of each page always let you know where you are.

If you want to find a **key term**, look in the glossary for a quick definition and in the index for specific page references. The first time a key term appears in a chapter it will be presented in **bold type**.

References

As all media researchers will tell you, good references are invaluable. They provide evidence of the origins of material and they point to further sources which could be used. We've adopted a number of strategies. Whenever we quote another writer, we have placed a name and a date in the text e.g. (Barthes 1972). This refers you to a book written by Barthes and published in 1972. The full reference (which includes title and publisher) is then given at the end of the chapter or case study. You should learn to list this full reference, for any books you use, at the end of your essays.

The list at the end of a chapter includes the sources we have used and perhaps some other material we think relevant. Some of our sources are quite difficult, both to obtain and to read, so we don't always expect you to go to them direct. At the end of the book we have included a 'selected' list of important (and accessible) texts which we recommend you do look at.

The titles of films, television and radio programmes, newspapers and magazines are usually given in *italics*. Again, this is a convention that you might usefully copy, especially if you word-process your work. It makes it much easier to read essays. We have given the country of origin and the date of release of films to help you find them in reference sources. We have tried to use film examples which are well-referenced, so, even if you've never heard of them, you should be able to find out more.

1 The languages of media

The media are not so much a 'thing' as a place most of us inhabit. Their pleasures and messages flow around and through us most of the time, and few have any trouble understanding or enjoying them. Yet many feel that our processes of response to media, and the visual and verbal languages they use, are worth studying seriously as a key part of the modern world.

Modern media are often thought of as a kind of conveyor belt of meaning between, or in the middle of, 'the world' and audiences, producing images 'about' this or that debate or event. This chapter, by contrast, will challenge assumptions that modern media work as simple channels of communication, as 'windows on the world'. Instead, it will argue, they actually *structure* the very realities which they seem to 'describe' or 'stand in for'. In particular we want to give you a grasp of **semiotics**, the study of how meaning is socially produced through various languages or codes, such as colour, gesture, photography and fashion as well as words.

The word 'media' comes from the Latin word *medium* = middle.

The chapter is not an easy read; you need to spend a bit of time with it. The *semiotic terms* you'll be trying out are not explicitly used, all the time, in media analysis, and have been qualified and criticised in recent years. But *semiotic approaches* are now very much part of the subject area, and indeed of mainstream television, press and fashion, with their frequent discussions of style differences and signs. You may find you already know more about them than you at first imagine!

Semiotics

When the media were first seriously studied, in the late 1950s, existing methods of literary and art criticism were applied to them. But it soon became clear that simply to discuss a film or television programme by such methods (valuing 'good dialogue' or 'convincing characters' or 'beautiful compositions') was not enough. People began to question the critical terms used and to ask: 'good' or 'convincing' or 'beautiful' according to what criteria? For whom? At the same time a whole body of ideas, now known as **structuralism** and **semiotics**, had developed which asked radical questions of how meanings are constructed in language, and applied these to the audio-visual workings of media. These approaches try to 'hold off' questions of the value of different stories or images in order to explore the ways that meaning is constructed.

Semiotics is also called 'semiology', and is the study of **signs**, or of the social production of meaning by **sign systems**, of how things come to have significance. Drawing largely on the work of the linguists **Saussure**, **Peirce** and **Barthes**, semiotics argues that verbal language is just one of many systems of meaning. These include clothing, gesture, haircuts, etc. which can be studied like verbal languages.

But how do these languages or 'codes', visual or verbal, work? At the time when semiotics was first developed, there were two main models for understanding language:

- Language as a *reflection* of the world, where meaning itself is already fixed ('the Truth') and lies in events, people, objects waiting for language to try to 'get at' or 'express' it (in 'realistic' photographic or film styles for example).
- Language as based in the *intentions* of the author or speaker; language as predominantly the way in which we each express ideas, feelings which are unique to ourselves (this approach would value much more eccentric styles of photography and film).

Of course there is a lot of point to both these positions (language trying to 'capture' the real outside the speaker, and language use as always unique and individual). But semiotics rejected both these models and took a third line:

- Language is *constructed* by people using it within cultures to produce meanings. Things and events in themselves do not have meaning. It is the ways that cultures, through their changing use of language, have 'agreed' to name things and events that determines how they get defined. And this social agreement means we cannot ever produce completely private languages of our own, however characteristic our individual language use will be, whether that be in words or fashions or the photos we take.

Further, semiotics used the term signs to describe the way meanings are socially produced. Signs have several characteristics:

- First, a sign has physical form (words, either in the form of marks on paper (R-O-S-E) (Figure 1.1), or sounds in the air; a haircut; a fingerprint; a traffic light). This is called the **signifier**.
- Second, a sign refers to something other than itself. This is called the **signified** and is a concept, not a real thing in the world. Though it's very hard to separate the sounds of 'rose' when you hear them from

Roland Barthes (1913–80) French linguist who pioneered semiotic analysis of cultural and media forms. Most famous for *Mythologies* (1957), a collection of essays applying his theories wittily to ads, wrestling, Greta Garbo's face and so on. (See later for **Saussure** and **Peirce**.)

Figure 1.1 A rose by any other name?

your concept of a rose, semiotics emphasises this distinction, and adds a third term, that of the **referent**, which is what both the signifier and the signified refer to: real roses, in all their different colours and shapes, which may differ from the single, rough and ready concept any one of us conjures up when we see or hear the word.

Plants, for example, are rigorously divided into those called 'weeds' and those called flowers, herbs or vegetables by gardeners. (If you live in a council block, the council's gardeners define all non-grass growth as 'weeds'.)

- Third, semiotics emphasised that our perception of reality is itself *constructed and shaped* by the words and signs we use, in various social contexts. By dividing the world into imaginative *categories*, rather than simply labelling it, language crucially determines much of our sense of things. The most famous example is snow – whereas English mostly uses only two nouns, snow and sleet, to distinguish snowy weather, the Inuit language makes subtle and detailed distinctions between different kinds of snow (which English can only describe with adjectives such as 'light', 'soft', 'packed', 'waterlogged', 'shorefast' and so on).

It could be argued that our culture, by contrast, has a huge range of words with which to signify or differentiate between motor vehicles. Can you list any of them?

snow		ice	siku
blowing —	piqtuluk	— pan, broken —	siqumniq
is snowstorming	piqtuluktuq	— ice water	immiugaq
falling —	qanik	melts — to make water	immiuqtuaq
— is falling — is snowing	qaniktuq	candle —	illauyiniq
light falling —	qaniaraq	flat —	qaimiq
light — is falling	qaniaraqtuq	glare —	quasaq
first layer of — in fall	apilraun	piled —	ivunrit
deep soft —	mauya	rough —	ivvuit
packed — to make water	aniu	shore —	tugiu
light soft —	aquluraq	shorefast —	tuvaq
sugar —	pukak	slush —	quna
waterlogged, mushy —	masak	young —	sikuliaq
— is turning into *masak*	masaguqtuaq		
watery —	maqayak		
wet —	misak		
wet falling —	qanikkuk		
wet — is falling	qanikkuktuq		
— drifting along a surface	natiruvik		
— is drifting along a surface	natiruviktuaq		
— lying on a surface	apun		
snowflake	qanik		
is being drifted over with —	apiyuaq		

Figure 1.2   Inuit terms for snow and ice, from Hall 1997, pp. 22–3

You can try to apply these terms to the process called 'signing' for hearing-impaired viewers on television, for example, where verbal language is signified through gesture. What seem to be the reasons for the choice of particular signed gestures?

ACTIVITY 1.1

- Jot down and read a list of four or five words (e.g.: cat, television, banana, wide). First focus simply on the actual marks on the paper (the signifiers) which make them up, trying to separate off any meaning they have for you – perhaps by repeating them over and over.
- How difficult is it to make this separation between signifier and signified?
- Why do you think this is?
- Now read the list, concentrating on the meanings of the words (i.e. as full signs, unifying signifier and signified).
- Now put the list away and mentally conjure up the things listed. Concentrate on your concept or image of them (the signifieds on their own).
- Now try to explain what you've just done to someone else, using the terms 'sign', 'signifier' and 'signified'.

These categories, into which verbal and other media languages divide the world, work by means of **differences**, an emphasis which semiotics shared with *structuralism*.

Structuralism

This is a set of ideas and positions which broadly emphasised two things.

First, all human organisation is determined by large social or psychological structures with their *own* irresistible logic, independent of human will or intention. **Freud** and **Marx** in the nineteenth century had begun to interpret the social world in this *structured* way. Freud argued that the human psyche (especially the unconscious mind) was one such structure, making us act in ways of which we're not aware, but which are glimpsed in the meanings of certain dreams, slips of the tongue and so on. **Marx** argued that economic life, and particularly people's relationship to the means of production (do they own them, or do they work for the owners of them?), was another, which determined political sympathies, taste etc.

Second, structuralism argued that meanings can be understood only within these systematic structures. For example, structuralist **anthropology** might study how a culture organises its rules on food as a system:

- by rules of exclusion (the English see eating frogs and snails as a barbaric French custom)
- by signifying oppositions (savoury and sweet courses are not eaten together)

Sigmund Freud (1856–1939) Austrian founder of **psychoanalysis** or the theory and practice of treating neuroses, and the theories of 'normal' unconscious mental processes obtained from its procedures.

Karl Marx (1818–83)   German political intellectual and activist, analysing and seeking to overthrow by revolutionary means the emerging industrial capitalist social order of nineteenth-century Europe.

Anthropology   the study of human groups, usually of other cultures than that of the researcher.

- by rules of association (steak and chips followed by ice cream: OK; steak and ice cream followed by chips: not OK).

ACTIVITY 1.2

Jot down other examples of these structures in food systems, for example Chinese or Indian food.

- Can you list any such oppositions or rules of combination in the way you and your friends dress?

Lévi-Strauss was a structuralist anthropologist whose work has had a great influence on semiotics. He emphasised the importance of *structuring oppositions* in myth systems and in language (also sometimes called **binary oppositions** because the qualities can be grouped into pairs of opposites).

Claude Lévi-Strauss (b. 1908) French anthropologist (not the inventor of the jeans). Most active from the 1950s, studying myths, totems and kindship systems of tribal cultures in North and South America.

Many familiar mythic and religious systems work with dual oppositions as a key part of their structure: God and the Devil or Good and Evil in Christian thought; Yin and Yang in Chinese Taoist thought; male and female in many systems. These in turn often structure popular stories and entertainments, often through opposed formal pairings: black/white (hats in early Westerns); night/day; East/West; hairy/smooth; brunette/blonde; female/male and so on.

PURE SMIRNOFF. THE DIFFERENCE IS CLEAR.

Figure 1.3   Advertisers depend largely on successfully claiming difference for their products from other, very similar, products in the market. Here the distinction claimed for this vodka is constructed visually through gender (male/female); historical (pre-humankind/human); biological (human/non-human) and textural (smooth/rough) differences

Saussure applied this to the ways that language produces meanings, often through defining things in terms of being the opposite of something else: black/white; hot/cold; 'man' as opposed to 'boy', or to 'woman', or to a 'god' or even to a 'beast'.

Ferdinand de Saussure (1857–1913)   French linguist who pioneered the semiotic study of language as a system of signs, organised in codes and structures.

He distinguished between *langue* as a system of speech (which children, for example, need to learn) and *parole* as acts of speaking. These may be much more various and creative than the rules of the langue might suggest. See Culler 1976.

Post-structuralists take these 'constructionist' positions even further. They argue that no shared meanings are possible because *everything* is understood *only* through difference. It's important to note however that meaningful differences (e.g. black/white) *differentiate* things that *share* certain qualities: here as parts of the colour spectrum. See Andermahr et al.

Example: Titanic

To deconstruct an ad or a film in semiotic terms involves trying to see which parts of it seem to be in systematic opposition. For example the narrative of *Titanic* (US 1997) works partly by contrasts such as upper-deck/lower-deck; upper-class/lower-class; American/European, which are worked through in signifiers of types of music, of dress, of colours, of sets etc.

In many semiotic analyses a further step is to explore the extent to which one side of an opposition is always valued less than the other. In this case, the lively, egalitarian 'lower-deck/lower-class' passengers, represented by Jack/DiCaprio, are valued more highly by the film than the upper classes on the upper decks. This set of oppositions is part of why Rose/Winslet's development and decisions through the plot are given more than romantic weight: the character is constructed as throwing in her lot with a more democratic future through this system of difference. (You might like to think about the connotations of characters' names in this context.)

Another example is advertising campaigns. In planning meetings there will often be 'brain storming' sessions where the qualities which will be attributed to the product (or celebrity to be associated with it) are contrasted, in a classic list of binary oppositions, to qualities which are 'not-Levi's' or 'not-BMW' or 'not-Coca-Cola' (see 'Narratives', Chapter 3, on syntagmatic and paradigmatic systems for a fuller discussion).

ACTIVITY 1.3

See if you can apply this method to an ad, or the most recent film you have seen.
- Chart those qualities, colours, music, kinds of settings etc which seem systematically grouped together, and in contrast or opposition to others, in your chosen ad or film.

This structuralist emphasis on oppositions or difference explains semiotics' insistence that signs are fully understood only by reference to their difference from other signs in their particular language system.

For example, once colour becomes possible in cinema or photography, the potential meaning of black and white is changed. It then signifies differently to produce a photo or a film in black and white (like *Schindler's List* (US 1993)) since black and white can then signify 'seriousness' or 'pastness' or even just quirkiness.

Once you grasp the extent to which visual and verbal languages are composed of such material signs, working partly through differences, it becomes easier to see that signs have relationships among themselves, as well as in the ways they *represent* the world. Words can rhyme, colours can be echoed (or 'rhymed'?) across a film, a pop video, an ad.

ACTIVITY 1.4

The arbitrariness of words and signification show up when we remember our misunderstandings of language as children – one person disappointed as a child at not getting warmer by standing next to what he'd been told was a Warm Air-orial (but was, in fact, a War Memorial). Another, an ex-childhood fan of the radio programme *Dick Barton: Special Agent*, spoke of her years of fascination with Asian British people, because she had thought the programme was called *Dick Barton: Special Asian*.

● Do you have any such memories? Have you ever misunderstood the lyrics of a pop song, which can be similar?
● What do they tell you about signification, and how meaning is produced in words?

Denotation and connotation: colours

Signs, then, signify or name or **denote** different aspects of our experience, the world. The word 'red' denotes a certain part of the colour spectrum, differentiated by language from other parts (such as 'blue' or 'pink') in what is in fact a continuous spectrum.

But signs also **connote**, or link as well as define things. They may link things by association with broader cultural concepts and values, or with meanings from personal history and experience. Let's take the codes which signify colours.

The word 'red' *denotes* a part of the colour spectrum. Broadly, it can be used to describe blood, fires, sunsets, blushing complexions – which perhaps indicates why, in certain cultures, the colour and the word have gathered *connotations* of fierceness, passion, danger. In *Pretty Woman* (US 1990) there is a scene where Vivien/Julia Roberts wears a red, quite formal dress (after her multicoloured hooker's gear in the first scene, and before a black, even more formal dress, in a later scene). At this point in the film it seems to signify a growing confidence and passion in her feelings about her relationship with Edward/Richard Gere. But 'red' does this both by means of its 'passionate' *associations* and also partly through its *difference* from her other costumes – and from the cultural awareness of readers that red is unlikely in this film to denote 'communism' or 'STOP' – as it might in other fictional structures.

The word 'gold' denotes either a certain part of the colour spectrum, or a particular metal. But it has connotations within certain cultures (deriving partly from its prizing for jewellery, special ceremonies, and as a currency) which are much wider, as in such phrases as 'golden opportunity', 'good as gold' and so on. In cigarette ads, under conditions of severe censorship for health, it can work as part of a structure signifying 'Benson & Hedges'.

1909 - 1911

1912 - 1936

1937 - 1938

1939 - 1945

1946 - 1955

1955 - 1973

1973 - 1996

1997

Figure 1.4   Evolution of the RAC image

ACTIVITY 1.5

Look at these logos for the RAC (Royal Automobile Club, a club selling services to motorists which began life as an exclusive social and sports club).

- Why do you think the logos have changed over the years?
- What kind of connotations seem to be attempted in the latest logo?
- Can you describe the connotations of the different designs?

Iconic, indexical, arbitrary and symbolic signs

Charles Sanders Peirce (1839–1914)   American pioneer of semiotics, usually quoted for his distinctions between different kinds of sign: *iconic, indexical, arbitrary* and *symbolic*.

Let's look in more detail at how semiotics has explored visual language systems, as well as words. A key distinction is made (initially by **Peirce**) between **iconic**, **indexical**, **arbitrary** and **symbolic signs**. Verbal language, spoken and written, is mostly composed of arbitrary signifiers in the sense that there is no necessary resemblance between the black marks on the page: 'daffodil' and those plants in the rest of the world that share the name 'daffodil'. Any pronounceable combination of letters could have been originally decided on to signify 'daffodils'.

Iconic signifiers, on the other hand, always resemble what they signify. There is a physical similarity between a photo, or a good drawing, of a daffodil and most people's experience of those flowers, and for this reason the photo is called an iconic signifier. Such distinctions are especially useful in drawing attention to the ways that photographs, film, television images and so on, though often seeming to be a record or even a trace of the real, are as constructed as verbal (arbitrary) accounts. They only seem like 'a window on the world'.

Indexical is used to describe signifiers that act as a kind of evidence: smoke of a fire; sweat of effort; spots of measles and so on. Or to use the distinction (see 'Technologies', Chapter 14) of analogue and digital, thermometers and sundials are indexical signs of heat or of time passing, whereas digital technologies (which use numbers to store and display physical properties) act like arbitrary signs.

Symbolic is used of visual signs (as opposed to words, which are usually 'arbitrary') that are arbitrarily linked to referents. The diamond hats often worn by monarchs, for example, are called crowns, and symbolise monarchy. Years ago the road sign to warn drivers about a school was the image of the 'torch of learning' (see Figure 1.5(*a*)): it was meant to stand as symbol of the place where that learning happened. But this conventional (i.e. socially agreed) meaning became unfamiliar, and the sign was changed to the 'two children crossing' sign (see Figure 1.5(*b*)). In other words, it was changed to a more iconic sign.

Icon originally referred to visual emblems or portraits of saints, rather than their written or spoken names. Confusingly though, global stars like Madonna are sometimes called 'icons', partly to suggest that they are like saints in a very visual culture.

Figure 1.5(a)

Figure 1.5(b)

Arbitrary and shared codes

There are important senses, then, in which signs, far from 'naturally' just 'labelling' things, are arbitrary. The choice of 'green' for the traffic sign meaning 'GO' could be replaced by 'pink', if that were the agreed colour for 'GO', just as words in different languages ('chien' in French and 'dog' in English) can refer to the same signified.

The only exceptions are spoken words called 'onomatopoeic', where a sound resembles what it signifies: like 'rumble' or 'hiss'.

Figure 1.6   Geri Spice – Cool Britannia?

Polysemy (from the Greek, *poly* = many, *semeion* = a sign): having many meanings.

But it's worth emphasising the need for cultural/social *agreement* for meaning to be produced, as well as its arbitrariness or slipperiness. We learn to read *arbitrary* signs in different kinds of combinations or **codes** which by definition have to be broadly *shared*. In this process of being socially used and therefore shared by many people, however, the meanings of signs are inevitably neither fixed or single, but **polysemic**, or capable of having several meanings.

Signs are inherently ambiguous or unstable because they have to be employed by 'readers' or 'users', to produce meanings at all. The Union Jack has stood as symbol of the unity of the United Kingdom, and the monarchy that rules it. But for Republican groups in Wales, Ireland or Scotland, it will be used and understood in quite other ways. The 1998 'Cool Britannia' campaign (Figure 1.6) tried to shift the connotations of this flag in yet other ways.

One way in which control will be attempted over this potentially disruptive **polysemy** or *ambiguity* of visual images is through the use of captions. This is called **anchoring**, a process which tries to select and therefore control the meanings which could be made by a reader. (Think of it as similar to the way that an anchor will try to limit the movements of a boat or ship in the sea.) Captions for adverts or newspaper photos will often act like this.

ACTIVITY 1.6

Take three photos, either from the press or from your family album.
- Devise captions for them which will anchor their connotations very differently from the way either the original press or family album setting had done.

ACTIVITY 1.7

- Cut out a few pictures at random from a paper or magazine.
- Cut out the same number of phrases, again at random, from the same sources.
- Mix them all up and pick out, face down, one picture and one phrase, at random. See whether the phrase, even though randomly chosen, seems to have a kind of authority as 'caption' anchoring the meaning of the picture. However 'wild', most captions seem to make a kind of sense of a picture.

Such shifting cultural 'agreements' on meanings mean that signification is never 'secure' or fixed – not even for the makers of this book! Such shifts also mean that struggles can take place over signification, over how a sign is to be 'officially' read. For example:

ACTIVITY 1.8

Look at the front and back covers of this book, and of a book you consider very different.

- What do you think the designers were trying to signify? What particular signs and connotations are your evidence?
- Is there any slippage between what seem to have been their intentions and the meanings you take from the designs?

- In the 1960s the centuries-old connotations of the word 'black' in western cultures was challenged by the US Civil Rights movement with the slogan 'Black is Beautiful'.
- The words 'cool', 'wicked', 'hectic' and 'bad' have, in some contexts, completely lost or even reversed their previous meanings in the last few years: a 'slippage' has occurred as slang terms have entered more mainstream circulation.
- The traffic sign for 'Caution, older people crossing the road' signified by stooped, stereotypical figures of 'the old' (Figure 1.7) has been objected to (a 'struggle over the sign' begun) by some groups of older people.

Figure 1.7

- Television and print newsrooms sometimes debate how they should describe certain acts: are they performed by terrorists? Freedom fighters? Patriots? Is an announcement about redundancies in a particular industry to be worded as 'massive job losses', 'rationalisation', 'downsizing' or 'slimming down the workforce'?

  Overall, semiotics has been enormously useful in rethinking the key human activity of meaning making. But semiotic and post-structuralist emphases have often been taken up as part of a crippling sense of powerlessness in the face of modern political and social developments. Language has been emphasised as being *only* untrustworthy, slippery, and

ACTIVITY 1.9

Make notes on the next news headlines or lead stories you encounter with an eye to such constructions. (They can also be visual: which of many possible photos of a celebrity or politician has been chosen?)

● Think how *else* particular events could be signified through different word or image choices. You might even build up a collection of pictures and alternative words for further news work.

of very limited use in understanding the world, let alone helping to change it.

As a result, several key questions have been posed of semiotic approaches (see Strinati 1975, and Hall 1997):

● Does its heavy emphasis on meaning as constructed (by codes) *over*emphasise the arbitrariness of signs, and *under*emphasise the extent to which they have to be shared in order to produce meaning at all? This has important implications for the sarcastic way in which many semioticians will dismiss such notions as 'identification' or 'empathy' or even 'politics'.

● Why privilege the latent or 'deep' over the surface meanings?

● Why presume that, once the preferred meaning is discovered, there are no more meanings to be found which are even more 'hidden'?

● How far can such slippery matters as interpretation and meaning be systematically and scientifically mapped?

● Do its methods of deconstruction use the language of exploration and discovery, but actually always find what they set out to find?

● Though semiotics has 'held off' questions of value and intention in the effort to show how meanings are always constructed, is there nevertheless a place for such debates, once the *shared* as well as the *arbitrary* nature of meaning is admitted?

● Is semiotics right to be quite so uninterested in **empirical** research into what actual audiences make of 'texts'?

Bear these questions in mind as you test out the usefulness of these approaches. The rest of this book tries to help you apply them, and takes them into much wider arenas of power, and the responses of audiences.

'Texts' (and their '**readers**') in ordinary life refer to written work, often holy, or official. In Media Studies they refer to anything capable of being read for meanings, whether written or not, highly valued or not (e.g. an ad, a piece of graffiti). Some have argued that this linguistic emphasis blurs the distinction between texts like songs or ads, and the 'thing-ness' of some social actions (also, misleadingly, called 'texts').

Empirical   relying on observed experience as evidence for positions. A controversial word, often caricatured by opponents to imply an approach opposed to any kind of theory and relying on sense experience or simplistic facts alone.

References

Andermahr, Sonya, Lovell, Terry and Wolkowitz, Carol (1997) *A Concise Glossary of Feminist Theory*, London and New York: Arnold.

Barthes, Roland (1957) *Mythologies* (trans. 1972), London: Paladin.

Culler, Jonathan (1976) *Saussure*, London: Fontana.

Hall, Stuart (ed.) 1997 *Representation: Cultural Representations and Signifying Practices*, London, Thousand Oaks and New Delhi: Sage (to which this chapter is indebted).

Further reading

Bignell, Jonathan (1997) *Media Semiotics: An Introduction*, Manchester and New York: Manchester University Press (from which several activities in this chapter are adapted).

Briggs, Adam and Cobley, Paul (eds) (1998) *The Media: An Introduction*, Harlow: Longman.

Corner, John (1998) *Studying Media: Problems of Theory and Method*, Edinburgh: Edinburgh University Press.

Eagleton, Terry (1983) *Literary Theory: An Introduction*, Oxford: Blackwell (esp. ch. 3).

Myers, G. (1994) *Words in Ads*, London and New York: Arnold.

Strinati, Dominic (1995) *An Introduction to Theories of Popular Culture*, London: Routledge.

Williams, Raymond (1976) *Keywords: A Vocabulary of Culture and Society*, London: Fontana/Croom Helm.

Williamson, Judith (1978) *Decoding Advertisements: Ideology and Meaning in Advertising*, London: Marion Boyars.

2 / Case study: Analysing images

This case study takes images from advertising and photojournalism, and tries to give you confidence in analysing them, using semiotic terms. We also introduce a less familiar area of **signification**: voices in sound media.

Sleau lunch

The 'Sleau lunch' Perrier mineral water ad was the first of a series used from 1995 onwards (Figure 2.1). At a **denotative** level the ad seems baffling: what is this snail made from green glass with a half hidden label stuck on it doing in a drink ad? Let's list the **connotations** of its signifiers and its technical and institutional **codes**:

- The skilfully crafted, clear, clean glass (a subdued green colour in the original, in perfect focus and probably computer generated), full of tiny bubbles, might *signify* a pleasantly leisurely meal and the drinks to go with it. It also offers broader cultural connotations of 'green': from summer countryside to ecological politics. (Think

Figure 2.1

how different it would look using brown coloured glass, actually closer to the average colour of the real-world **referent**: snails.)

These signifiers of 'green', along with the use of a small creature, seem to be asserting the 'naturalness' of this highly manufactured product. Even given the quality of drinking water in big cities, some people still object to paying for bottled water, and the ad has to take such possible objections to the 'manufactured' as part of its working context.

- The caption 'Sleau lunch' will signify 'witty play on words' to a readership that has basic French (which may be assumed of those the agency has tried to reach by placing the ad in papers such as the *Guardian*: arguably an institutional code).

- It also signifies *'Frenchness'*, since the French are stereotypically known for eating these creatures, and one of the clearest ways of differentiating between national cultures is often by means of what foods are taboo within them.

The Perrier label is another signifier of Frenchness. The full name 'Perrier' is not shown, though a few descriptive French words are visible in large billboard versions of the ad — flattering for an audience who are assumed to be able to pick up the reference. Clearly, for xenophobes or racists viewing the ad, even the connotations of 'Frenchness as sophistication' will not be positive or even available. For them the French are 'those Others who do fancy/barbaric things like eating frogs and snails'.

The snail itself seems used partly to signify a leisurely, slow meal (snails are known for their low land speed

ACTIVITY 2.1

Explore a range of *language connotations* within visual forms like ads.

- How many cosmetics and fashion brand names can you list which trade on the connotations of Frenchness as sophistication?
- Make up your own name for the brand you find least 'sophisticated'.
- How is 'Australianness' signified in such products as lager (and some shampoos)?
- What words would you use to make a product sound 'cool' as the twentieth century closes?

records. And the shape may remind some readers of the amiable Brian in *The Magic Roundabout*.)

But, unless you have been very unlucky in your choice of cafés, snails have little real-world connection to clean water. The snail seems used here partly to attract attention by its unexpectedness: what product could be advertising with a glass snail? This puzzling of an audience is a common strategy of advertisers in a crowded image environment. (It is worth remembering that for readers in locations where snails are unfamiliar, the ad would have very different meanings.)

When such *horizons of meaning* are brought into play, the work of the ad in trying to cut off possibly unpleasant connotations (or **anchor** the meaning of the

snail) becomes clear. This work is partly attempted by the way the ad is styled, photographed, gently coloured (cool clear glass rather than dark sticky slime), but also in the appeal, through its placement in particular newspapers, magazines, hoardings, to a metropolitan or city-dwelling audience who are expected to relish such an unexpected play of signifiers.

The next ad in the series is shown in Figure 2.2. See if you can make a similar analysis of this image and caption.

Tiananmen Square

Figure 2.3

The famous photograph in Figure 2.3 is from the June 1989 demonstrations of students and workers for democracy in Tiananmen Square, Beijing, China.

Figure 2.2

ACTIVITY 2.2

Make notes on the photo using your knowledge of *codes* (both technical and cultural) such as:

- *photographic technical and institutional codes*: lighting; the use of a certain kind of film stock (tricky for you since the original is in colour and we cannot afford that here); camera angle, distance from subject, and kind of focus; any evidence of an amateur or professional photographer etc.
- *codes related to broad cultural and aesthetic frames of reference*: framing, composition etc.

This is at one and the same time:

- an **iconic** sign (it is a photograph of a real person and military tanks in the Square: the sign visually resembles its referent and as such is vivid in ways that written accounts cannot be).

- an **indexical** sign. The light and shadows in the scene act as a kind of evidence (telling us the time of day, the weather); the photo (and video footage taken at the same time) was used as a kind of *political* evidence too.

- a **symbolic** sign. The photo was widely circulated; interpretations offered of who this unknown figure is, and for a time it became a symbol of 'western democracy/consumer society versus totalitarian communism'.

The pattern of the five tanks' advance, of the lines on the road (especially the one suggesting that a turn could be made at precisely the point where the demonstrator stands) all seem, by some kind of strange accident, to intensify the central *meaning/opposition* of 'lone human protest against inhuman military oppression'. The size of the tanks, and the absence of any human figures in or on them, as opposed to the human figure, and his simple protest in the face of them suggests a grossly unequal contest, and perhaps makes the protest all the more moving. A key *signifier* here is the bags being carried (for shopping?). In such a charged context (the street cleared of other activities; the bus, signifier of civilian life, whatever its actual function on that day, pulled over to one side) it seems to allow meanings around 'consumer society versus totalitarian communism' to be made. Many different headlines tried to *anchor* such interpretations.

ACTIVITY 2.3

Try to devise your own newspaper captions for the picture, across a wide range of meanings, from ones which try to *anchor* its meanings in sympathy for the protester to ones which take a pro-military line on the image.

Headlines in turn had to rely on other accounts for their meanings (written accounts of the political context for example). It is important both to use the methods of semiotics *and* to go beyond them in understanding how images are 'read' or used. The fact that western democracies made very little long-lasting protest at these events is a point which can be made in later *written* accounts, but which cannot be represented in such a moment of *photojournalism*.

In terms of *documentary codes*, the far-from-ideal distance from which the photo is shot is something (like the blurred quality of other photos) we have learnt to read, as a kind of *evidence* (of difficulty, of conditions of censorship) through familiarity with *technical codes* and signifiers. The key 'person/tank opposition' section of this photo was cropped and circulated, in very blurred form, over and over, as were moments in a CNN broadcast.

Some readers may simply see such technical qualities of blurring or distance as 'truthful-because-not-polished-looking' (following the evidence of numerous pieces of dangerously obtained pieces of photojournalism). But this quality can be faked or constructed, as in several notorious examples of 'arranged' war footage, or, more recently, in television codes such as the deliberately awkward, documentary 'snatched'-looking filming of *ER* or *Homicide* (see 'Realisms and the television police series', Case Study 17) – or through computer-generated imagery.

Here we enter fascinating areas of how we read *'realist' codes*: what do we take as (indexical) evidence that something 'really' happened? To some extent (and especially in an era of computer-fakeable imagery) we have to rely on evidence from outside the photo, or 'text' to answer these questions. (In fact, owing to the danger of those days, three western photographers were confined to their hotel room and managed to catch this moment from its window, with fairly long-lens cameras.) The video footage is slightly different in its impact, since the tank swerves to avoid the protester, who then crawls over it in a slightly comic way, and resumes his stance.

Q What does this suggest about the ways different media can signify the same event simply by virtue of their nature as video, or photograph etc.?

Reading a voice

Finally, 'images' need not always be visual. Sound is coded, and signifies, in ways as complex as photographic images, though, after decades of developed analysis, the visual image is more readily recognised as 'made up'. Sound is more difficult to discuss: we can't offer you a sound 'text' on the page, for one thing, and have had to ignore music, sound effects etc. But to ignore sound, for *audiovisual media* like television and cinema, can mean that a whole dimension is missing from analysis and appreciation.

You can't see a person, but you can hear their voice. What does this tell you about them? What codes are at play in this process of speaking and listening?

- pitch: is the voice 'high' or 'low'?
- volume: 'loud' or 'quiet'?
- texture: 'rough' or 'smooth', 'soft' or 'hard'?
- shape: 'round' or 'flat'?
- rhythm or cadence: does the voice rise and fall or keep a continuous tone?

Key components of voices will be in play:

- *accent*, which usually refers to pronunciation (and often rhythm, cadence) and inflection. British voices are particularly characterised by accents: flattened or extended vowels, missed consonants.
- *dialect*: everyone in the UK speaks a dialect, a sub-language which differs from a notional 'standard English'. So-called 'received pronunciation' or 'BBC English' is the dialect of the southern English middle class. All dialects have vocabulary and syntax as well as pronunciation differences. In the UK dialect and accent are key signifiers of class origin.
- *language register*: most of us are capable of changing the vocabulary and syntax we use to suit particular circumstances.

ACTIVITY 2.4

Take a cassette recorder and a good-quality external microphone and tape several different people talking in a variety of situations (in the classroom, in the pub, at home). Play back the recordings and try to ignore what they say, just listen to the sound of the voices.

- Can you recognise any of the codes listed above?
- Use them to describe the sound of any one voice.
- Can you relate it to the age or gender of the person? Surprisingly some 'old' voices sound 'young' and vice versa – perhaps it is something else which confirms the 'old person's voice'.
- Do some voices sound more attractive, more interesting? Why? Could you imagine any of them on the radio? Doing what?

Unlike the voices we encounter at college or at home, the *technical quality* of radio voices has been coded by radio. What we hear is a *reproduction* of the original voice, dependent on:

- the acoustics of the studio: a room with hard, shiny surfaces will produce a harsh, 'bright' edge to the voice; a studio with absorbent surfaces will soften the voice
- the choice of microphone
- the engineer's processing of the signal.

These *institutional and technical codes* are tremendously important on radio. How does Radio 5, for example, differ from Radio 4? Is it partly through the voices of the presenters, and callers, especially those with distinctive regional accents?

ACTIVITY 2.5

Run up and down the array of stations on your radio dial. Stop briefly at each voice you hear.

- Do you recognise the station immediately? Through the combination of cultural codes?
- Does BBC local radio use more recognisably 'local' voices? Are commercial stations more likely to be

staffed by presenters with an all-purpose 'music radio' voice?

● Why do you think this might be so?

This takes us into **realism** debates. Just like the blurred photographic image, the overlapping of voices on radio (i.e. everyone talking at once) on discussion programmes often signifies 'authentic lively debate' – and of course can be constructed, or faked, as can other aural signifiers.

ACTIVITY 2.6

Listen to a radio play or serial and make notes on how the signifiers (of 'childishness' or 'heated discussion' or 'danger' etc.) are constructed.

We hope these brief introductory ideas about a 'semiotics of sound' will help you think about voices in audiovisual forms, and in your approaches to recording voices for your own productions.

Further reading

Barker, Martin and Brooks, Kate (1998) *Knowing Audiences: Judge Dredd, Its Friends, Fans and Foes*, Luton: University of Luton Press. Provides useful discussion of these approaches.

Branston, Gill (1995) 'Viewer, I Listened to Him', in P. Kirkham and J. Thumim (eds) *Me Jane*, London: Lawrence & Wishart.

Crisell, Andrew (1994, 2nd edition) *Understanding Radio*, London: Routledge.

Myers, G. (1994) *Words in Ads*, London and New York: Arnold.

Scannell, Paddy (1996) *Radio, Television and Modern Life*, Oxford : Blackwell.

Wells, Liz (ed.) (1996) *Photography: A Critical Introduction*, London and New York: Routledge.

Wilby, Peter and Conroy, Andy (1994) *The Radio Handbook*, London: Routledge.

Williamson, Judith (1978) *Decoding Advertisements: Ideology and Meaning in Advertising*, London: Marion Boyars.

www.rab.co.uk for material on radio advertising.

3 Narratives

- Making narratives, or stories, is a key way in which meanings get constructed in the media – and outside them.
- Both factual and fiction forms are subject to this shaping.

Most of us tell stories all the time: gossiping about friends; telling jokes; filling family photo albums with appropriate events and some highly constructed characters: the proud graduate (never the hard-pressed student); the happy (never fraught) groups on holiday. All cultures seem to make stories as an involving and enjoyable way of creating sense and meanings in the world. Two points are worth bearing in mind as we attempt a systematic study of narrative in modern media:

- narrative theory suggests that stories in whatever media and whatever culture share certain features
- but particular media are able to 'tell' stories in different ways.

General theories of narrative

Narrative theory studies the devices and conventions governing the organisation of a story (fictional or factual) into sequence. The names of **Propp**, Barthes, **Todorov** and Lévi-Strauss, working mostly with myths and folk tales, are ones you will come across in discussion of media narrative processes. Here are the bare bones of their influential **structuralist** approaches to narrative.

Like most semiotic approaches, these *isolate* texts from their context and uses for the purpose of analysis. Of course very few of us see a film or television programme without any kind of knowledge of its genre, star or reviews.

Tzvetan Todorov Bulgarian structuralist linguist publishing influential work on narrative from the 1960s onwards.

Vladimir Propp (1895–1970) Russian critic and folklorist whose influential book on narrative, translated as *The Morphology of the Folk Tale*, was first published in 1928.

Propp

Propp examined hundreds of examples of one kind of folk tale, the 'heroic wondertale', to see whether they shared any structures. He argued that, whatever the surface differences, it was possible to group characters and actions into:

- eight character roles (or 'spheres of action' as he called them – to indicate how inseparable are character and action)
- thirty-one functions (such as 'a prohibition or ban is imposed on the

hero' or 'the villain learns something about his victim') which move the story along, often in a highly predictable order. For example 'the punishment of the villain' always occurs at the end of a story, and the 'interdiction' or forbidding of some act, always comes at the beginning. What is apparently the same act can function in different ways for different narratives. For example, the 'prince' may build a castle as:

- preparation for a wedding
- defiance of a prohibition
- completion of a task set.

Roles or spheres of action, Propp argued, make sense of the ways in which many very different figures (witch, woodcutter, goblin etc.), could be reduced to eight character roles – not the same as the actual characters since one character can occupy several roles or 'spheres of action'. These are:

1 the *villain*

2 the *hero*, or character who seeks something, motivated by an initial lack. ('Hero' is one of those terms that does not mean the same within theory as it does in life outside, where 'hero' and 'heroic' have moral connotations of 'admirable' or 'good'. Here it's much closer to describing an active way of carrying the events of a story.)

Figure 3.1

Diana, Princess of Wales, could be seen as having had her life 'told' through different narrative media constructions. An early narrative 'ended' at her wedding in 1981, and was a classic fairy tale, where her 'lack' (unhappy childhood, loss of her mother, desire to 'fit in', few formal educational qualifications) was resolved by the magical transformation of 'becoming a princess'. At the time this was signified by the kiss on the balcony of Buckingham Palace, repeated over and over in the media (Figure 3.1) (see Geraghty 1998).

To be continued …

3 the *donor* who provides an object with some magic property
4 the *helper* who aids the hero
5 the *princess*, reward for the hero (see above) and object of the villain's schemes
6 her *father*, who rewards the hero
7 the *dispatcher*, who sends the hero on his way
8 the *false hero*.

Such work on stories is inevitably bound up with the times and social orders which produced them. For example, it's worth noting tht the hero can now often be a female character, as in *Blue Steel* (US 1990), especially since the word 'heroine' (Propp's 'princess') implies a character who hangs around looking decorative until the hero is ready to sweep her away. (Many commentators prefer to use 'the sought-for person' instead of 'princess'.)

Yet since fairy tales, or versions of them (like *Pretty Woman* (US 1990) or the *Star Wars* series), are still familiar to most of us, Propp's approach continues to be influential. It tries to uncover structures beneath the surface differences of such widely circulated, popular forms. It reminds us that, though characters in stories may seem very 'real' (especially in cinema and television), they must be understood as constructed characters, who have roles to play for the sake of the story and who often get perceived very quickly as 'hero', 'villain', 'helper' and so on, with many accompanying expectations. We feel it very sharply when the person we thought was the hero or helper turns out to be the villain, as in *The Usual Suspects* (US 1995) or *Psycho* (US 1960) where, to the shock of its first audiences, the female hero (and star) is killed off a third of the way through the film, and the shy young man who seemed to be a helper turns out to be something very different.

Other narrative forms, such as the *Mahabharata* from Indian culture, or indeed western forms such as the musical, take pleasure in much less

Figure 3.2 Xena: Warrior Princess

The very terms 'prince' and 'princess' are much more than job descriptions. They come to us loaded with narrative expectations and connotations.

Q How are these expectations played with in the series *Xena: Warrior Princess*?

We do not have space to go into the many ways in which other cultures make narratives, from the 'magic realism' of Latin American forms to the ways in which Aboriginal culture tells its tales. If you can research them it will give you an idea of both how universally *shared* and how *differentiated* is this human activity.

action-driven narratives, using instead convoluted patterns (often circular) and several climaxes, with scenes of spectacle and humour given real narrative weight.

'This was Nature at her most unforgiving …' (BBC News reporter on floods in Italy, May 1998). What kind of a 'character', and narrative, is being evoked in such words?

ACTIVITY 3.1

Check that you can identify narrative roles in a favourite *fictional* media text. Then try watching for the way that media language will often attribute narrative roles and thus construct 'characters' even in *non-fiction* forms. *Weather forecasts* will sometimes characterise, or even narrativise, natural forces: winds, isobars and so on may be called 'the villain' or 'to blame'; a warm front is 'coming to the rescue'.

- Does *language used to describe illness or disease* often construct it in dramatically villainous, malign terms? (There is much medical debate about whether such 'imaging' is helpful or destructive for the sufferer.)
- Or in *crime programmes*, what difference does the word 'villains' make, instead of 'criminals'?
- What narrative images might it evoke?

Todorov

Todorov argued that all stories begin with an '**equilibrium**' where any potentially opposing forces are 'in balance'. This is disrupted by some event, setting in train a series of other events, to close with a second but different 'equilibrium' or status quo. His theory may sound just like the cliché that every story has a beginning, a middle and an end. But it's more interesting than that. His 'equilibrium' labels a state of affairs, a status quo, and how this is 'set up' in certain ways and not others. 'Workers today decided to reject a pay offer of 1%' for instance, begins a news story with a disruption to an equilibrium, but we know only about one side of that balance. We don't know who has offered the pay rise, for what kinds of conditions, after what negotiations. How, where and when *else* could the story have begun are always good questions to ask.

'Magnet [the kitchen manufacturers] have imposed all the conditions they were demanding when the strike began, including cuts in bereavement and paternity leave, and the scrapping of the pension scheme. I shouldn't say "demanded" because, as we know, workers "demand" and employers "offer" ' (Jeremy Hardy, reversing the usual narrative shape, *Guardian*, 2 May 1998).

Princess Diana's life, in its second period, was often 'told' by the media in terms of a 'new story' which begins with the question: what does her presence in the British royal family mean? What kind of 'disruption' to that set-up was it: breath of fresh air, or neurotic selfishness, like 'Fergie's'? The *Panorama* interview can be seen as an attempt by her to 'tell her own story': as one of moral virtue (see Geraghty 1998).

END OF THE FAIRY TALE

Figure 3.3   Even the participants in such events can experience them as a story. Here 'the fairytale' ends unhappily. Later Diana said of her divorce: 'it was just very, very sad. The fairytale had come to an end' (Princess Diana, *Panorama*, November 1997)

Barthes

Barthes suggested that narrative works with five different **codes** which activate the reader to make sense of it. Of particular interest is the idea that an enigma code works to keep setting up little puzzles to be solved (and not only at the beginning of the story), to delay the story's ending pleasurably: e.g. how will Tom Cruise get out of this predicament? What is in the locked room? An action code will be read by means of accumulated details (looks, significant words) which relate to cultural knowledge of our (often stereotypical) models of such actions as 'falling in love' or 'being tempted into a robbery'.

> The five codes are: the *action or proairetic*; the *enigma or hermeneutic*; the *semic*; the *symbolic* and the *cultural or referential* code. For more detail see Barthes (1977).

Such approaches have been applied not just to fiction forms but also to long-running news stories to see whether narrative structuring 'sets up' certain expectations and puzzles. ITN News teases us with enigmatic summaries of stories before the ad break. Newspaper billboards work in similar ways. In the stories themselves, disruption to the status quo (say in a war, or strike) is often narratively attributed to one group or person, rather than to others, whose actions before the 'story' started might have been equally provocative, but are less often tied into a story opening (see examples below). This can mean that historical and political explanations are structured out of the story-telling, both at the beginning and in the final 'equilibrium'.

Lévi-Strauss

Lévi-Strauss argued that an abiding structure of all meaning-making, not just narratives, was a dependence on **binary oppositions**, or a conflict between two qualities or terms. Less interested in the order in which events were arranged in the plot (called **syntagmatic** relations), he looked 'beneath' them for deeper or **paradigmatic** arrangements of themes. This theory was applied to the Western genre in the 1970s. Writers suggested

> **Paradigm**   a class of objects or concepts. **Syntagm**   an element which follows another in a particular sequence. Imagine choosing from a menu. Paradigmatic elements are those from which you choose (starters, main courses, desserts). The syntagm is the sequence into which they are arranged. Sometimes these are thought of as 'horizontal' and 'vertical' sets of choice.

Figure 3.4 Saint Diana?

Figure 3.5 Diana shrine outside Harrods, 1997

that the different sheriffs, outlaws and Native Americans not only existed in Proppian narrative terms but could be seen as making up systematic oppositions, among others:

homesteaders	Native Americans
Christian	pagan
domestic	savage
weak	strong
garden	wilderness
inside society	outside society

Applying these theories

Let's apply the work of these four theorists:

- Though news is a 'factual' form, it's striking how, especially in radio and television, the programmes themselves take on a narrative shape. Watch the start of the evening news programme on BBC or ITV for signs of a kind of 'once-upon-a-time-ness' in: the studio set-up, title music, signs of authority in newscasters' dress, voice, bearing, position and so on.

- Once a 'story', or an individual life, is closed (as with Princess Diana's death in 1997, or the singer Michael Hutchence's drug overdose in 1998), events before it will be told in the light of that ending as narrative **closure**, and often seen as 'leading up to it', as tragically unexpected or 'just what he deserved'.

There have been many claims made on an authoritative interpretation of Diana's story through readings of its ending. Immediately after, theories on the Internet tried to 'fix' the meaning of the car crash into conspiracies. 'Sick' jokes and critical questions (e.g. about her will and its absence of any donations to charity) played up her privileged and often frivolous lifestyle. Others claimed saintliness for her, in the flowers and messages on the site of the Paris car crash, Harrods etc. (Figure 3.5).

Other characters in versions of the story, such as Prince Charles, have since shifted function from 'villain' to 'hero', in his role as father to 'Will' and 'Harry', 'the little princes'.

Figure 3.6

- Reporters are trained in how to **construct** a 'good story'. This, especially for **tabloid** forms, involves shaping along the lines of suspense, a clear beginning and ending, and heroes and villains.
- Certain kinds of **close-up**, particular words or emphases in the reporter's account ('he *seems* distraught at the prospect ...'; 'looking radiant, she announced ...') will often signal parts of Barthes's action or enigma codes.
- Longer news stories are even more interesting. When an event is first constructed as news, it can be 'run' in a number of ways, without clear hero or villain roles. But if it goes on for long enough, it is often structured into a narrative. In the process, complex historical events and motives are often left out for the pleasures of a good story, and references to fictional film and TV forms.

Applying Todorov

However outrageous Saddam Hussein's invasion of Kuwait was, the way many news organisations treated it meant that other factors motivating his behaviour were structured out of the story (e.g. the power of the big western oil companies, the previous price-fixing which threatened catastrophe for Iraq's economy, and the military support that oil-hungry western powers had given to other despotic but oil-rich regimes). Much better, for story and war purposes, was an emphasis on individual villainy or despotism as prime cause of the war.

Later the war, like all wars, finished – but as a narrative ending the media will often structure such endings (the 'new equilibrium') so as to leave out certain stubborn elements that in fact don't end but go on happening (post-traumatic stress syndrome; long recovery from injuries; the continuing arms trade etc.). So deep are the satisfactions of 'the happy ending' that newsrooms will try hard to find signifiers of some happy foreign or domestic event, suggesting a return to normality – very like 'And so they all lived happily ever after'. The tanks roll home, the soldiers talk of their pleasure at a job well done, and eventually there is the welcome home by the women and children to shape this narrative ending.

Applying Propp

In fact, 'Saddam' was structured very clearly in the 'villain' role, with 'Stormin' Norman' (the US General Schwartzkopf) and the Allied Forces together carrying the hero role (John Major as 'helper'?). Of course, this does not exist in isolation from other processes of meaning construction. Long-standing stereotypes constructing 'the Orient' as full of cruel despots, patterns of censorship during wartime, and the difficulty of constructing a big story around pictures of night-time bombing raids, could also be said to contribute to this particular narrative emphasis.

Applying Lévi-Strauss

It is often possible to group together, in two opposing lists, the qualities which get structured into the story's conflict. For the Gulf War these might include:

East	West
barbarism	civilisation
despotism	democracy
Scud missiles	Patriot missiles
backward 'dirty' technology	futuristic 'clean' technology
the past	the future

'This goal makes it a happy ending for Newcastle ...' 'Owen, the hero of the match ....' 'Giant-killers Keighley ...'

Q Can you work out how camera placing, freeze frames, action replays and commentary tend to work with such narrative underpinnings?

Figure 3.7

ACTIVITY 3.2

Take any story, preferably a long-running one, from recent news and consider:

- How has the initial equilibrium, the 'once-upon-a-time-ness', been set up?
- How has the disruption to that ('something has happened') been constructed?
- How do you think this narrative will 'end' or 'close'?
- What may be left out of that ending?
- How else could the story have begun, with what other 'equilibrium', from whose point of view?
- Have any of the people involved been constructed as characters with narrative roles such as hero, villain, donor etc.?
- Are there any signs of 'action' or 'enigma' codes being set up?

Sports programmes also work with narrative forms, with 'stories-so-far' of stars which we're invited to bring to bear on particular performances. The processes of winning and losing, so central to sport, are told as narratives.

Narration, story and plot

The term **narration** describes how stories are told, how their material is selected and arranged in order to achieve particular effects with their audiences.

Plot and **story** are key terms here, though another useful distinction is the one used by Russian theorists in the 1920s between **syuzhet** and **fabula**. (These foreign terms are used instead of plot and story because the meanings of plot and story are often slippery, and often confused with each other.)

Story, or fabula, is helpfully defined by Bordwell and Thompson, who argue that 'the set of all the events in the narrative, both the ones explicitly presented and those the viewer infers, compose the *story*' (Bordwell and Thompson 1997, p. 66). This would include routine events, like a daily shave, which we assume carry on happening during a story, but would be tedious as part of the plot. It may also include material we find out only by the end of the story, having been busy trying to piece things together throughout, such as Norman's mental condition in *Psycho*.

'The term plot is used to describe everything visibly and audibly present in the film before us' (Bordwell and Thompson 1997, p. 67). Other writers have explored this area in terms of the knowledge which the 'reader' has compared to the characters: is it the same, or more? When? How much more?

Soap operas often work in terms of secrets, of knowledge, often kept from all other characters – but not the viewer.

Q How might this affect the pleasures of narrative suspense for viewers? What pleasures might take its place? (see Buckingham 1987).

For example, we should feel at the end of a good detective story or thriller that we have been pleasurably puzzled, so that the 'solution', our piecing together of the story in its proper order out of the evidence offered by the plot, will come as a pleasure. We should not feel that the plot has cheated; that parts of the story have suddenly been revealed which we couldn't possibly have guessed at. The butler cannot, at the last minute, suddenly be revealed to have been a poisons expert.

One of the pleasures of Sherlock Holmes or *Inspector Morse* stories is that though we can never be as brilliant as Holmes or Morse, we can catch up through Dr Watson or Lewis, and enjoy the satisfaction of feeling that we will never be that 'slow'.

ACTIVITY 3.3

Take one of your favourite stories and tell it in flashback form.

- What effect does this have on how you get to find things out, how your sympathies flow?

One example might be the story of Red Riding Hood:

- Who would have to be speaking, and to whom, to tell this story in flashback? The wolf in 'A Wolf's Afterlife'? Red Riding Hood herself?
- What effects would this have on suspense?

Figure 3.8 Nineteenth-century illustration to 'Little Red Riding Hood'. **What if the story began here?**

1912: two polar bears see a newspaper headline about the (real) sinking of the *Titanic*. One says to the newsvendor :'My friend wants to know: what happened to the iceberg?'

Another part of the construction of narratives involves the 'voice' telling the story. A first-person narration will use 'I' as the voice of the teller, and should not give the reader access to events that 'I' could not have witnessed, or known of.

A third-person or impersonal narration refers to a story which seems to 'get itself told', as in 'Once upon a time there was a kingdom …'. Though cinema and many television or video narratives begin with a

Spectacular cheats are possible: *Sunset Boulevard* (US 1950) uses a first-person narrator to tell the story who is in fact dead in the story's 'present'. And *The Usual Suspects* (US 1995) relies for its surprise on a long, misleading flashback.

ACTIVITY 3.4

Look at a few ads from television. Ask yourself of each:

- Is this a narrative? Does it 'begin' rather than just 'start', and 'end' rather than 'stop'?
- How do I know? Are the people in it constructed as 'characters'? How is this done?
- Or is it simply a list of claims or prices, or an image of a situation in which the product seems attractive?

'voice-over' telling us the story from a personal point of view, they usually settle into the mode of impersonal narration, just seeming to unfold before us.

Using narrative form, an ad will often:

- group its events in cause and effect order. Non-narrative ads won't do this. They may simply consist of a set of claims about a product, as in supermarket ads which list prices, or ads setting up a mood linked to the product, like the Anchor butter dancing cows.
- even in a few seconds, create a sense of characters and action or enigma codes through economical use of signs and stereotypical traits.

These work as Propp suggests: the same traits that help us build up a sense of them as 'real people' are simultaneously crucial for the action, the furthering of the plot. There will be a discernible 'hero' (you may feel this is usually the product).

There will be, as Todorov suggests, some sense of an initial situation, which is disrupted or altered and then happily resolved at the end; usually, of course, through the magical intervention of the product being sold.

You will also probably be able to distinguish syuzhet and fabula. Even if flashback is not used, try to imagine the same events told differently, from the point of view of another character, for example, or with different amounts of time, and therefore emphasis, given to different segments of the narrative (Figure 3.8).

Applying Lévi-Strauss's approach, television ads can often be analysed so as to show a systematic grouping of recurring signs, situations or characters in opposition to each other. Levi's jeans ads, for example, often group qualities as the following sets of oppositions.

Check to see if the latest Levi's ads are still using them, or if they have shifted.

young	old
hip	uncool
young generation	parental figures
sexy	asexual
rule-breaking	rule-enforcing
Levi's jeans	not Levi's

Narratives in different media

These broad structures, which seem to govern all story-making and story-telling, have to work differently in different media, and for different cultures. Consider this if you're involved in a project which asks you to *choose* a medium in which to make a story: what can *x* medium do (strip cartoon, say) that *y* cannot, and vice versa? These differences are partly due to the nature of different media.

Photography

This might seem an odd example of a narrative form, since it deals in frozen moments of time (like stained-glass windows, or cartoons). But often the impact of a powerful news or advertising photo lies in what it makes us imagine has gone before, or is about to happen. In this sense narrative is often signalled, depending on angle, information given, construction of imagined characters – and whether or not black and white film stock is involved. The difference between black and white and colour often signals 'pastness' and 'presentness' in the story.

ACTIVITY 3.5

Look for ads which use the black and white/colour contrast in the way suggested above.

● How do they set in play narrative expectations and knowledge?

Comic strips

Comic strips (and by extension animation) tell their stories by a compelling combination of:
● words (including thought bubbles)
● line drawings. These can streamline characters and events more than even the highest budget movie. You never have to worry about spots on the star's face, or problems with lighting in comic strip or animation.
● flashpoint illustrations of key moments involving extreme angles and exaggerations.

Cinema

Like video and audio recordings, this is a 'time-based' medium, manipulating time and space rather than image or words alone. The average feature film length of about two hours, and the way audiences pay to see it all at one sitting, can give it some of the intensity of a short story. It may lead to a different experience from that of longer fictions like novels, or soaps, read or viewed over days, weeks, years while we do many other things in between.

Early cinema soon shed the assumption that all the camera needed to do was to film actions as though they were theatre, from a fixed position in the stalls. Film-makers quickly elaborated an audiovisual language using **shots**.

A **shot** is a series of frames produced by the camera uninterruptedly. It can be as short as a few frames or as long as there is film in the camera. Try watching a film on television and tapping every time you spot a **cut** where shots are combined by editing.

> Try to develop an awareness of this, and avoid talking about characters in a film as though they were either real people or characters in a novel, where dialogue and description are supremely important. On the other hand, it's worth emphasising here the importance of script and basic story design. Much comment on cinema or television, wanting to distinguish it from literature, has downplayed the role of the writer. You certainly need to spend as much time as possible on the *writing* stage of audiovisual story projects, as well as thinking about their *audiovisual* qualities.

See also Chapter 5, Production Techniques, for ideas about technical codes of lighting, lenses etc. and other ways of organising narrative space.

Figure 3.9 shows some of the ways cameras can be moved to manipulate 'narrative space', often to invite the viewer into the action of the story. These allow for the **framing** of characters and objects. Camera movement became an important way of telling stories and involves choices around how much audiences see of a character or situation. The most familiar example is probably the tight framing on a character's hand opening the door to the mysterious darkened room in a horror film: the audience knows Something Nasty is waiting, and half wants to see it, but the film-maker deliberately frames so as to withhold that knowledge. This is both pleasurably frightening, and may pull our identification towards the character doing the exploring.

Mise en scène, or the setting up of a scene, is another term for discussing how stories are told in cinema and television. It originated in theatre (around the staging of a scene) and is used to describe many of the ways in which audiovisual media differ from literary forms. Some writers use it to describe all the visual elements, including camera movement, which make up shots (Figure 3.10). Others, more helpfully, use separate terms to include discussion of production design and costume (see Bruzzi 1997) as well as camera movement and choices around **colour balance**, lens, angle, etc.: **cinematography** (see 'Production techniques', Chapter 5).

If you think of your favourite scene from a movie, and the role of mise en scène within it, you will find that it has been an important part of your sense of the narrative. Or take a film like *Fatal Attraction* (US 1987). The mise en scène repeatedly constructed the 'good wife' in glowing, warm, soft colours, in comfily cluttered domestic spaces, with the actress's hair softly framing her face. The 'evil woman' however was given a flat next to a slaughterhouse,

CAMERA MOVEMENTS and POSITIONS

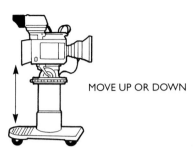

MOVE UP OR DOWN

The height of the camera position dictates the *viewpoint* – perhaps of a character looking at something or someone. It also provides the viewpoint of the audience on the action.

The convention is that the height of the camera will correspond to the 'eye-line' of characters on screen (whose eyes will usually be in the top third of the screen). Cutting from one character to another will usually require an '*eye-line match*'. Forgetting to raise or lower the camera during shooting is a common mistake of student operators.

The camera can move up or down as characters rise or sink to their knees, maintaining the same eye-line.

A *tilt* of the camera can give the impression of looking down (into a well?) or upwards (to the top of a tower?) – the *angled framing* of which may suggest the inferiority or superiority of the viewer to the subject.

Not to be confused with a *tilted frame*, in which the camera 'lists' to left or right.

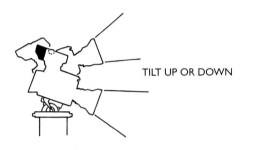

TILT UP OR DOWN

A common movement is the **pan**, when the camera swivels on its axis to describe an arc which displays a 'panorama'. The arc is usually not more than 270° – a full 360° pan is quite disorientating. Pans are usually slow and smooth, but a very fast 'whip pan' can be effective in action sequences.

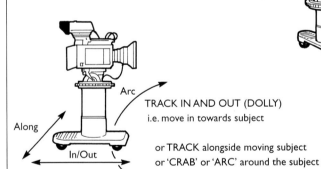

CAMERA 'PANS' LEFT OR RIGHT

Arc

Along

In/Out

TRACK IN AND OUT (DOLLY)
i.e. move in towards subject

or TRACK alongside moving subject
or 'CRAB' or 'ARC' around the subject

One of the most exhilarating experiences for audiences is when the camera physically moves across terrain, drawing the viewer into the action. Traditionally, this was done with a camera on a wheeled device running on tracks – thus a *tracking shot*. In a studio, cameras might be on a trolley able to move in different directions – known as a 'dolly' – or on a 'crane' able to rise way above a scene and 'swoop' down.

In recent years, cameras have been freed from restraints and can be carried by the operator, almost anywhere, with a smooth action thanks to the **Steadicam**.

With a 'STEADICAM', a camera operator can move with the camera in any direction

Figure 3.9

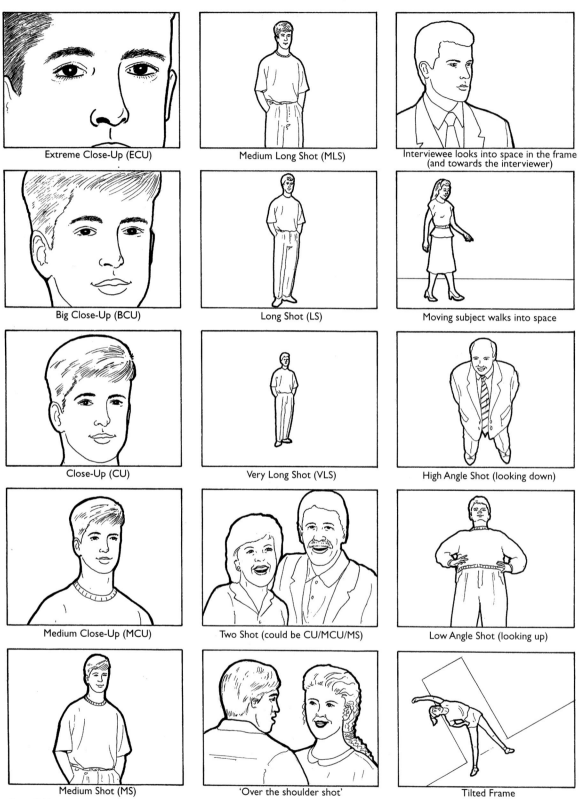

Extreme Close-Up (ECU)

Medium Long Shot (MLS)

Interviewee looks into space in the frame
(and towards the interviewer)

Big Close-Up (BCU)

Long Shot (LS)

Moving subject walks into space

Close-Up (CU)

Very Long Shot (VLS)

High Angle Shot (looking down)

Medium Close-Up (MCU)

Two Shot (could be CU/MCU/MS)

Low Angle Shot (looking up)

Medium Shot (MS)

'Over the shoulder shot'

Tilted Frame

Figure 3.10

minimally decorated in white, harshly lit, unwelcoming, while the actress playing her, Glenn Close, was given a hairstyle evoking serpent tails, and was repeatedly shot and lit in hard, angular ways.

Narrative time and space, then, can be manipulated (for the purposes of suspense, identification, withholding of knowledge etc.) by:

- the initial script and story
- the choices made in *design and cinematography* (*mise en scène*)
- editing.

Unwritten rules of editing (the combination of shots) soon developed, and came to be called **continuity editing** (because they gave a continuous flow to the narratives being 'told'). These involve the following:

- A section of a film or television fiction usually begins with an **establishing shot** which sets up the whole space in which the next part of the narrative will happen, helping us to identify where figures are in relation to each other, what significant 'marks' are, and so on.

- The camera tends to stay on one side of an imaginary '180° **line of action**' which can be drawn through any scene (e.g. a car chase or two people walking towards each other, see Figure 3.11). Again, this is intended to draw us into the story by minimising the effort needed to imagine ourselves within its space. And when cutting between two

> Actors in film and television are helped to position themselves correctly for each shot set-up by means of marks on the floor: hence '**hitting the mark**'.

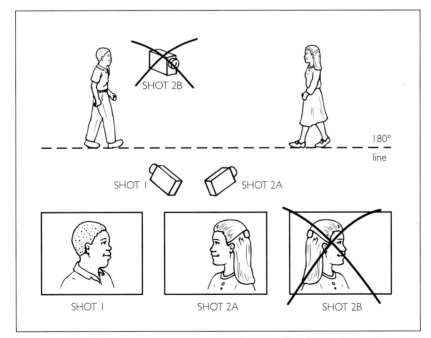

SHOT 2B

180°
line

SHOT 1   SHOT 2A

SHOT 1   SHOT 2A   SHOT 2B

> In this example if the camera position 2B is used, a cut from Shot 1 to Shot 2B would make it appear that both characters were walking in the same direction and therefore unlikely to meet. Try this out yourself with a video camera.

Figure 3.11 The 180° rule is designed to prevent confusing transitions by not allowing the camera to 'cross the line'

people looking or moving towards each other, failure to observe the rule can mean they will seem to be looking in the same direction.

- A change from one shot to another requires a transition. The most common kind of a **cut** is the abrupt replacement of one shot by another. Careful framing can disguise a cut's abruptness and aid the audience's absorption into the narrative. For example, conversations will be filmed by the '**shot/reverse shot**' system. Here, once the 180° line has been set up, the camera will cut back and forth from one end of that line to the other, involving, in a conversation, for example, a position close to one character, looking at the second, then with the second character looking at the first.

You will sometimes spot a 'break' with continuity rules. The most common example is a **jump cut.** If shots with the same content and very similar framings (e.g. two 'medium close-ups' of a face) are linked by a simple cut, the transition will be very obvious. The solution is to cut to a shot of the same content, but a different framing (e.g. a medium-shot), or a shot of a different but related content – a **cutaway**. You will probably learn this when you begin to edit your own narratives.

- **Cross cutting** is another way of telling a story through the manipulation of space in editing. It refers to the placing together of shots which actually belong to different spaces of the narrative. Audiences have learnt to read these as happening simultaneously – as in scenes above and below decks on the *Titanic*.
- The passage of longer amounts of time in editing will be signified by a **dissolve** or **mix** (video term) – the effect of one shot dissolving into the next – or by fades: one shot fades out to black, and the next gradually 'fades up'. Flashbacks, so useful in the arrangement of syuzhet or plot, can be economically signalled by them.

    Common in modern cinema is the development of framing possibilities which can replace a transition – the use of a **zoom** lens. The very fast, but continuous, zoom in or out is disorientating for viewers, especially in the 'digitally enhanced' zooms used in science fiction films like *Star Trek: First Contact* (US 1996).

    Though the continuity system never became a formal set of rules, it is powerfully entrenched in our expectations of cinema and television. One way of becoming aware of the rules is to watch them being broken in comic films or television parodies like those of French and Saunders.

    A further, much underestimated part of film is sound. This will be as carefully organised as images and editing to serve the narrative. Sounds can continue across visual cuts, thus 'carrying' the audience, making editing less obvious and therefore the narrative less disjointed. A useful, if very unfamiliar, term is **diegesis**, meaning the space constructed by the narrative. This can be used to specify whether sounds are emerging from that constructed space, or from outside it, as with atmospheric music.

A quick way of remembering this: imagine a film story using a group climbing to the top of a high mountain. The diegesis is unlikely to contain an orchestra up there, but the coding of non-diegetic triumphant music will very likely be used. See Mel Brooks's *High Anxiety* (US 1977) for the breaking of this and other codes.

ACTIVITY 3.6

Take any scene from a recent film or television fiction; or you could look at a television ad. Take notes on:

- how it has been edited;
- how the mise en scène contributes to the narrative.

Now examine the sound track:

- What are the components of this track: music? voices? noises? sound effects including distortion? How have they been chosen and arranged? Are some louder than others? Why do you think each has been included? Do any seem accidental?
- How have they been shaped around the action, or talk in that scene? How close do the voices seem, how have they been chosen, or constructed? How does all this help to construct the narrative?

Radio

This medium uses sounds and silence, which affects the way it can handle narrative, constructing through voices, noises, sound effects and silence the illusion of space between characters, and time between segments. It cannot give up much narrative time to features on which cinema might want to spend time (say the display of visual special effects). Characters cannot stay silent for long periods of time (like the Tim Roth character, mostly silent, dying 'onstage' in *Reservoir Dogs* (US 1992)), since they would seem to have 'disappeared'. Since radio's signifiers are relatively cheap and easy to produce, it is free to construct the most bizarre and exotic stories, from time travel to a play about memories flashing through the head of a drowning woman.

Institutions and narratives

Differences between the ways stories get told in different media are partly, then, to do with the *material* (sound, celluloid, line drawings, image and sound, words alone) of that medium. But they are also to do with *institutional or industrial demands*.

' "The Royals" is the longest-running soap opera in Britain … the long running story of an extremely wealthy and powerful family … The fact that "The Royals" is loosely based on reality only adds to its fascination' (Coward (1984), p. 163).

The following chart suggests differences in how closed and open narratives work in those different media institutions, 'cinema' and 'television'.

Closed narrative, e.g. cinema

1 'Tight' reading involved, with audience aware it's watching a two-hour story and therefore reading with the likely end in mind.

2 Relatively few central characters; huge range of 'depth' of audience knowledge, even interior voice-overs giving characters' thoughts, hallucinations etc.

3 Characters arranged in a 'hierarchy' (central, cameo, supporting roles, extras etc.).

4 Often with audience invited to make 'verdicts' on them, identifying narrative roles, as in Propp: hero, villain, donor.

5 Time usually very compressed: two hours of screen time constructs events as happening over months, years, sometimes centuries.

6 Time and events are usually special to this particular story, and need have no resemblance to the viewer's world. Flashbacks and even flashforwards are possible.

7 Reader or viewer usually has evidence about the characters only from this single text, plus star, publicity and genre expectations.

Open narrative, e.g. soap opera

1 Casual reading, without the sense of an ending. Soaps proceed as though they could go on for ever.

2 Many more characters, naturalistically represented and producing a *multi-strand plot.*

3 Characters not usually in a marked hierarchy but shift in and out of prominence.

4 Characters shift also in and out of narrative function. Today's villain may be next week's helper.

5 Time usually corresponds to 'real world time' *within the segments of each episode,* though across it time is compressed, as in cinema. Flashbacks are rare.

6 The differences between time in the serial and outside it are blurred. Episodes may make reference to real-life events going on at the same time, such as elections, Christmas.

7 Audiences are assumed to have different kinds of memory, and knowledge of a long-running soap. Magazines and the press often speculate about the fate of actors' contracts, and thus the characters they represent. Many different kinds of reading are therefore available.

| 8 The same audience can be assumed to watch the film from beginning to end. | 8 Each episode has to try and address both experienced and new viewers. |
| 9 Often elaborate visual image, and music as integral part of the narrative. | 9 Relatively rare use of music, especially in British soaps, and relatively simple visual image. |

The open-ended serial form (soap opera) developed first on US radio in the 1930s as a cheap way of involving housewives, whose buying choices the detergent manufacturers wanted to influence. Later it seemed an ideal form for commercial television, keen to sell to advertisers the promise of audiences' regular attention, and for the BBC, wanting to boost its early evening audiences. This is partly in the hope they will stay with the channel that evening, and also to help the BBC produce large audience numbers when it makes its arguments for the level of the next licence fee.

Though soap opera is one of the most familiar and discussed forms of media, it is not just 'one thing': even on British television there are Australian, American and British soaps, and these in turn divide into high- and low-budget forms, and have different relationships to documentary, glamour, sitcom, romance, regional identities and male audiences. Nevertheless, we can generalise that one of British soap's attractions for its producers is that costs can be kept down and the narrative can be centred on a few key locations (e.g. the hotel, pub or cafe). These are meeting places; one of the staples of the narrative, and also key to soaps' economies and production needs. Even though a soap has to go out for two or three nights a week, particular storylines swing in and out of prominence, allowing:

- time for rehearsals, holidays, pregnancies, the covering of illnesses etc.;
- a wide appeal through several stories happening at once so as to involve different sections of the audience. If you're impatient with one 'strand', you know that another, which interests you more, will probably be along in half a minute or so.

Soap narratives may also change as a result of attempts to shift the composition of their audiences – and advertisers. Over the last few years several soaps have moved 'upmarket' involving sets, situations and some character types which are part of the attempt to sell more expensive ad slots.

Q Can you detect this having happened, or happening, to any serial you watch?

After the success of *Brookside*, other soaps tried to attract male audiences to this traditionally female form by means of 'tough' storylines and characters as in *The Bill*, which falls between a soap (continuous production, never a 'closed' ending to an episode) and a series (self-contained storylines each week, like *The X-Files*; *Casualty*). Serials (including 'classic' serials) and 'mini-series' (often a pilot project) are other narrative forms designed to meet particular scheduling needs.

Soap operas now have websites, e.g. *Coronation Street* is covered by several sites, one of which is a database of all the actors and characters who have appeared since 1960.

ACTIVITY 3.7

Make notes on an episode of your favourite soap.

- How many storylines does that episode contain?
- To which sections of the audience might they appeal?
- Which are the main storylines? The same as a few weeks ago? Why do you think this is?
- How is time managed in the episode?
- How many sets are used? Why have these places been chosen?
- Are there any rumours circulating about the fate of particular characters or actors, in the press, on television or in fanzines?
- How does your knowledge of these affect your viewing? Does it add to your pleasure? How?
- How does the soap story try to address both experienced and new viewers? How are repeated use of characters' names, repeated updatings of the storylines and so on managed so as to inform new viewers, yet not bore regular ones?
- If it's on a commercial channel, what do the ads before, during and after suggest about the expected audience?

ACTIVITY 3.8

Explore the process of how you 'read' a film or ad for narrative sense in your next viewing. Then note how it relates to the kinds of knowledge usually available *before* entering a cinema or renting a video or watching ads.

- Have you ever seen a film or ad without any knowledge at all (generic, poster in cinema foyer, friends' comments) of what to expect?
- See 'Genres', Chapter 8, on how these expectations are prepared.

References

Barthes, Roland (1977) *Introduction to the Structural Analysis of Narratives*, London: Fontana.

Bordwell, David and Thompson, Kristin (1997, 5th edition) *Film Art: An Introduction*, London and New York: McGraw-Hill.

Bruzzi, Stella (1997) *Undressing Cinema: Clothing and Identity in the Movies*, London and New York: Routledge.

Buckingham, David (1987) *Public Secrets: EastEnders and its Audience*, London: BFI.

Coward, Ros (1984) *Female Desire: Women's Sexuality Today*, London: Paladin.

Geraghty, Christine (1991) *Women and Soap Opera: A Study of Prime Time Soaps*, London: Polity Press.

Geraghty, Christine (1998) 'Story' in 'Flowers and Tears: The Death of Diana, Princess of Wales', *Screen* vol. 39, no. 1, spring.

Lévi-Strauss, Claude (1972) 'The Structural Study of Myth', in R. and F. De George (eds) *The Structuralists from Marx to Lévi-Strauss*, New York: Doubleday Anchor.

Propp, Vladimir (1975) *The Morphology of the Folk Tale,* Austin: University of Texas Press.

Todorov, Tzvetan (1977) *The Poetics of Prose,* Oxford: Blackwell.

Further reading

Eagleton, Terry (1983) *Literary Theory: An Introduction,* Oxford: Blackwell (esp. ch. 3).

Perkins, Victor (1990) *Film as Film,* London: Penguin.

Turner, Graeme (1993) *Film as Social Practice,* London: Routledge (esp. ch. 4).

4 / Case study: *Psycho* (1960)

Psycho (US 1960) is one of the most celebrated films ever made, which is why we chose it for this case study. At the time of writing (1998) trailers are appearing for a second, colour 'Karaoke' version of the film, directed by Gus van Sant, using the identical script, with a rumoured change to the ending, and Anne Heche in the Janet Leigh role. This will obviously be a key point of comparison for you, especially in terms of how 'the same' shots can signify and structure narrative differently forty years on. However, if you have somehow missed seeing the original *Psycho*, directed by Alfred Hitchcock, read this synopsis of its plot.

Synopsis

Marion Crane (Janet Leigh) and her lover Sam (John Gavin) meet in her lunch break in a hotel room, as happens whenever he can come to Phoenix. He is divorced, working in a hardware store, and, since he's paying maintenance to his ex-wife, and for his father's debts, he feels they cannot afford to get married. She goes back to her work as a secretary, where her boss entrusts her with $40,000 in cash, asking her to bank it.

Later, she drives out of Phoenix with the money. After being stopped by a patrolman and exchanging her car to evade detection, she stops at a motel, run by Norman Bates (Anthony Perkins) whose mother can be glimpsed and heard in the house nearby. Unbeknown to Marion, Bates watches her undressing through a concealed hole in the wall. She seems about to return to Phoenix to confess to the theft and return the money, but is brutally stabbed to death in the shower. Norman, finding her body, puts it into a car (unwittingly

also putting the money with her) which he pushes into a swamp.

Lila, Marion's sister, arrives at Sam's workplace and they begin the hunt for Marion, at the same time as Arbogast, a private detective investigating the missing $40,000, arrives on the scene. Arbogast questions Norman, who at first denies Marion's visit to the motel. Returning later to investigate further, Arbogast is brutally stabbed to death.

When he fails to return, Lila persuades Sam to accompany her to the deputy sheriff, who tells them Mrs Bates has been dead for ten years, having poisoned the man she was involved with when she discovered he was married, and then killing herself. The bodies were found by Norman. We hear Norman speaking to his mother and insisting on taking her down to the cellar.

Lila and Sam check into the motel and begin to search it. Lila is shocked to discover a woman's stuffed corpse in the cellar and Norman, dressed in old-fashioned woman's clothing, enters, trying to stab her. Later, a psychiatrist explains that the now incarcerated Norman is schizophrenic, and had murdered his possessive mother two years after his father died, as he was jealous of her lover. He had then taken on her personality, especially at times when he was attracted to a woman, as he had been to Marion.

ACTIVITY 4.1

How different is this verbal account to the movie itself?

- Do you have any disagreements with particular emphases?

- Begin writing your own synopsis. How would you do it? Where would you begin?
- How much knowledge would you release to your reader? When?

The Internet Movie Database is full of plot summaries of other films, if you want to try the exercise on one of them.

Applying Todorov, Propp, Barthes and Lévi-Strauss to *Psycho*

Q How would you describe the initial situation or equilibrium in the film (i.e. after Todorov)?

A It consists of a secretary and her lover (Marion and Sam) who want to marry but cannot afford to.

Q And the disruption to this?

A Marion's decision to steal the $40,000 her boss asks her to bank.

We are partly prepared for this (Barthes's action codes), not just by the lovers' conversation about money but also by the dates which are superimposed on the film's opening shots:

PHOENIX, ARIZONA, FRIDAY, DECEMBER THE ELEVENTH, TWO FORTY-THREE P.M.

This plays with narrative construction, and also generic film markers such as the precise time – often signalled in films where a crime like a theft is important. It's a kind of visual cheat, since by the end of the film the theft has ceased to matter at all. It was a 'red herring', though important in character terms for our sense of Marion's change of mind just before she's murdered. When, to our surprise, this happens, a second equilibrium is set up. The surprise is partly one that would occur in whatever medium the narrative were told. Using Propp, Marion was the hero or central figure (with her boss as dispatcher) and we expect her to carry that role for most of the story.

But Marion/Leigh's death is also a play with the conventions of cinema: Janet Leigh, who plays Marion, is the star of the film and we expect stars to play in the film to the end. After her death, the hero role is split between Sam and Lila (with Arbogast as helper). The audience's attitude towards Norman probably changes, but is always partly formed as Propp and Barthes suggest.

Viewers or readers do seem to try to make sense of characters by exactly the kinds of 'spheres of action' which Propp offers:

- Is Norman going to turn out to be a helper/victim, as the scene clearing up the shower suggests?
- Is he the false hero for a while, when we may suspect he's clearing up after his mother's killing, and we anticipate the film may turn out to be about his defence of his mad mother?

Psycho, like any detective or mystery fiction, depends on setting up characters, codes of enigma, and codes of action which mislead the audience. These will work with stereotypical features of characters' actions (and within particular genres, and depending on the status of the film). Does Norman's angular appearance, accentuated by lighting and camera angles in his encounters with Marion, signify 'shy young man' or 'strange neurotic'? We busily read the signs or clues, as Barthes suggests, puzzling about what's going on, what will happen next, and expecting, as Todorov suggests, the pleasure of solution with the final equilibrium or closure. In the case of *Psycho*, this consists of:

- Norman incarcerated and diagnosed by the psychiatrist as criminally insane
- Lila and Sam safe, but knowing now Marion is dead
- an unknown number of bodies, including those of Marion and Arbogast, in the swamp, as well as the $40,000, which the audience has probably forgotten about.

Story and plot in *Psycho*

Q Think back to the initial equilibrium. What changes would occur to the narrative if this were constructed around Norman?

A Sympathy, knowledge and identification would be affected: the illusion that Mrs Bates is still alive would have to go, and Norman's madness would have to be signified. Sympathy and identification would be affected by this rearranged knowledge: for example, the plot or syuzhet could hardly begin with the arrival of Marion at the motel, since she would not yet be a character known to us, and her death would not therefore invite as much identification, and horror.

'Norman Bates heard a noise and a shock went through him. It sounded as though somebody was tapping on the windowpane … ' Thus begins the novel on which the film *Psycho* was based. How would you continue from here? How would you preserve suspense, especially around the mother's identity?

To focus on plotting and time shifts, we need to make notes on moments when the film goes into 'real time' (i.e. when the length of time taken by events on screen corresponds almost exactly to the length of time they would take in real life). When does this happen, and why do you think it happens?

One example: when Norman discovers Marion's body, and begins to clean up the bathroom. The scene begins with his cry 'Mother! Oh God! Mother, Mother! Blood, blood!' over shots of the house and his running from it towards the motel. This comparatively long scene seems partly constructed to allow audiences to recover from the shock of the killing. The audience reaction was much more extreme when the film was first released, indeed, according to Anthony Perkins, the entire scene in the hardware store following the shower murder was usually inaudible thanks to leftover howls after the shower scene. Hitchcock is even said to have asked Paramount to allow him to remix the sound to allow for the audience's reaction (see Rebello 1991).

The scene also swings suspicion away from this 'nervous young man'. If audiences suspected too early on that he was the killer, it might spoil some of the 'finding out' pleasures of this mystery/thriller/horror movie.

Clearly the careful arrangement of events in the plotting is crucial to most films, even ones that don't

proceed by flashback. Here, if the plot's ordering of events corresponded exactly to that of the story, we'd have a quite different kind of film, something like a psychological study of Norman. Our point of view would be affected: we'd be 'with' Norman at the beginning, and he could less easily function as the 'monster' in a horror movie, outside understanding and sympathy (a narrative role the word 'psycho' evokes in newspaper headlines).

Instead we'd be offered the pleasures of a developing understanding of this 'case history'. Knowledge, sympathy and of course possible styles of filming would be affected. In other stories using flashback, the moments when the plot goes into the past often try to elicit sympathy. In Emily Brontë's novel *Wuthering Heights*, for example, much is revealed about Heathcliff's childhood towards the end of the narrative, by which time he seems almost monstrous, and the insight into his treatment in childhood suddenly swings our sympathies right round, back to him for a while (see Figure 4.1).

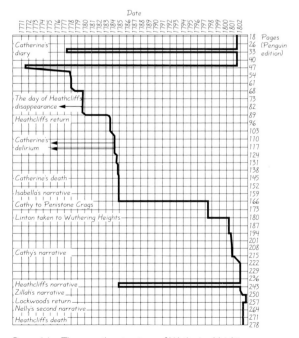

Figure 4.1   The narrative structure of *Wuthering Heights*

ACTIVITY 4.2

- Try to draw a graph or chart which will show how *Psycho* has been plotted in terms of time shifts. Draw a line that runs across the top of the graph to represent the actual time covered by the story (i.e. from Norman's childhood to his monologue in the police station. We're told he killed his parents ten years previously).
- Then draw, as the side of the graph, a line roughly representing plot or syuzhet time. This, of course, will be much less than the ten to fifteen years of the story. Try to proportion it according to the sections of the film, e.g. Lila and Sam set out about halfway through.
- When does the film go into flashbacks? Remember that events can be represented verbally in a film narrative, through conversations.
- What effects might these have on audience knowledge of events, or sympathy towards certain characters?

Applying Lévi-Strauss

Lévi-Strauss is less interested in the chronological plotting of a story than repeated elements and their systematic relationship, usually across many stories.

ACTIVITY 4.3

Jot down any repeated oppositions which strike you in this film, such as: dead/alive; mother/son; the past/the present; dark/light.

- Do they seem to fall into a pattern that might help to account for the movie's power?

Comment Lévi-Strauss's approach has been fruitfully applied to film and television so as to reveal their underlying patterns over a series, or whole genre (the Western; *Star Trek*; the gangster movie). It is more problematic when applied to a single film such as this. Still, you may feel it helps you to understand how the plot has been structured. Does it support the feeling that Mother is set up as the 'real' villain? She's the only main character (remember they can be constructed offscreen, by verbal accounts) whose story, or presence, or point of view we're not given. We only know her through the psychiatrist's account (very sympathetic to Norman), with phrases like 'His mother was a clinging, demanding woman' and 'Matricide is probably the most unbearable crime of all – most unbearable to the son who commits it'. Pretty uncomfortable for the mother too, but the film's plot gives us little room to feel this. Lévi-Strauss might help us see whether mothers, or the malign powers of dead women, are constructed in this way in other films by Hitchcock.

Psycho as a film narrative

Like most movies, this one is told in an 'impersonal' way. The camerawork and plotting do not position us with any one character's point of view. (Try to imagine it told from the point of view of Marion, or Norman, or Lila. See whether the new version does this.) And, working in the classic continuity system, events mostly just seem to unfold.

There are a few exceptions which prove the rule, when the camera seems to be telling the story in a more emphatic way. In the scene just after Marion has been entrusted with the $40,000, we see her dressing, the money lying on the bed. The camera, with suspenseful music on soundtrack, moves from the money to her handbag and back again, as though to offer her temptation. It's like the moment after the murder, when Norman takes a last look round the bedroom and the camera tells the story, reminding us of the money lying wrapped in a newspaper.

Though different media tell stories in different ways (**Q**: what would be the literary equivalent of these shots?) some narrative effects can be shared by different media.

- The repetition of certain compositions, or musical themes, or phrases in film and television. In *Psycho* Bernard Herrmann's score works with two main repeated themes, one signifying flight and pursuit, the other resembling a series of screams (most famously in the shower scene). These are an important part of how we read the 'clues' of the narrative. They also provide formal pleasures over and above that, as we register 'a story well told', as a joke can be well or badly told.

- The repeated use of certain compositions (such as a full-screen menacing face in *Psycho*) is both a narrative and a broader formal device, rather like the use of rhyme in poetry to point up connections and contrasts, or like refrains in songs.

It may be that when we see the full-screen face of Mother near the end, it's disturbing partly because it is reminiscent of the face of the traffic policeman, his eye sockets replaced by huge sunglasses, who gives Marion (and the audience) a nasty shock early on in the movie. It's also reminiscent of Norman's face, when lit so as to hollow out his eye sockets. The two sets of associations or connotations are brought together in the final shots of the film where, if you look carefully, you will see Norman's face merge with Mother's mummified one, then both dissolve into the image of a car being lifted from the swamp.

Critics have suggested the final shots are particularly satisfying because at the end of such a puzzling narrative we suddenly have explanation, and also an image of something coming into the light of day after so much repression and darkness. At any rate, it is a very visual narrative moment.

Figure 4.2

ACTIVITY 4.4
Look at other ways in which film and television construct narratives (such as lighting, costume, music, cutting, voices) and see how they work in this movie in a particular scene. How would you represent this scene, and these elements within it :
- on radio?
- in written form?
- in comic strip form?

ACTIVITY 4.5
Look at the poster for the re-release of the 1960 film (Figure 4.2) and say what expectations you think audiences might have had as they began to watch the film.
- What is your evidence for arguing this?

ACTIVITY 4.6
If available, look at the poster for the film's 1998 remake.
- What expectations does it want to arouse in a 1990s audience?
- What does the studio seem to feel are the key selling points of this remake?
- If so, how is Hitchcock's image being deployed?

References

Internet Movie Database on `http://uk.imdb.com`

Rebello, S. (1991) *Alfred Hitchcock and the Making of Psycho*, New York: Harper Perennial.

Further reading

Cook, Pam (ed.) (1985) *The Cinema Book*, London: BFI (section on Narrative).

Kapsis, Robert E. (1992) *Hitchcock: The Making of a Reputation*, Chicago University of Chicago Press.

Modleski, T. (1988) *The Women Who Knew Too Much*, London: Methuen.

Williams, Linda (1994) 'Learning to Scream', *Sight and Sound*, December 1994.

5 Production techniques

This chapter is intended both as an extension of 'Production organisation' (Chapter 6) and as a complement to 'The languages of media' (Chapter 1), 'Analysing images' (Case study 2) and 'Narratives' (Chapter 3). There is also a discussion of production techniques in 'Realisms' (Chapter 16).

This chapter will help you to make informed choices when you select and use materials and equipment for media projects. It should also help you to read other media texts in terms of their technical codes.

Technical codes

In Chapter 1 **codes** are defined as *systems* of signs – allowing meanings to be communicated. **Technical codes** are the choices that can be made in selecting or using materials and equipment on the basis of the technical qualities of the **format** or the technical qualities of the sound image or visual image created. For example you can select paper for printing a magazine on the basis of its colour, weight (thickness) and porosity (the extent to which the ink is absorbed). The quality of presentation of the text or photograph printed on the page will depend on the settings of the printer in terms of resolution, number of colours etc.

A good example of restrictive technology is the development of film and video cameras and lighting techniques which suit European skin tones and which are therefore not ideal for showing darker skin.

Look at some of the issues in 'Institutions' and 'Technologies', Chapters 26 and 14. Technology may be 'value-free' but it is used in value-laden institutional contexts, e.g. there are relatively few women cinematographers or sound editors.

You won't make your production choices in isolation, but in the context of a specific brief and mindful of the **cultural codes** of the content of your programme. Sometimes, the association of specific technical decisions with particular subjects has become conventionalised so that stylistic or aesthetic decisions have developed to signify a certain mood or atmosphere – the low-key lighting of a *film noir*, the jaunty music of a television quiz show; a particular format or shape has been adopted for a specific function – the small portrait photo for a passport. The strength of the technical or cultural connection is revealed when conventions are broken – in comedy texts for example. Technical codes are helpful in providing a convenient shortcut for presenting conventional texts, but they can also provide an excuse for institutionalised texts which are restrictive – where the technology is allowed to dictate the creative decision.

This chapter concentrates on the technical decisions which you as producer are going to make, mindful that in your proposal you have identified a purpose, a target audience and a genre or style.

Technical codes in print products

A print product requires ink and paper. There are many different kinds of paper and several different ways of getting ink on to them. Try to begin a print production with a sort through paper samples and possibly a discussion with a print professional about what kinds of paper are available.

Paper

Weight Paper is classified in 'grams per square metre' or 'gsm'. Standard photocopying paper is 80 gsm. Glossy brochures might use 120 gsm. Above about 150 gsm, paper becomes more like thin card. Weight is important for a number of reasons. At a very practical level, heavier paper means a heavier product and if it is going to be mailed out this could mean greater postal costs (heavier paper is already more expensive to buy). However, heavier paper can feel more luxurious. Thinner paper can suffer from 'see-through' or 'bleed' – if it is printed on both sides, heavy black text or illustrations will be visible through the paper and perhaps spoil the visual appeal of the page. This is also affected by coatings (see below).

Paper is usually purchased by the **ream** – 500 sheets.

Coated or uncoated? The cheapest paper (e.g. newsprint) is 'uncoated' and porous. This means that it feels a little rough between the fingers (ask a printer about paper and she or he will perhaps rub it between the thumb and first finger). It also means that, when ink is applied, it will tend to spread, because it is absorbed by the fibres. You will see this if you use cheap paper on an inkjet printer – the problem is exacerbated because the ink is very wet. Better-quality papers are coated with a layer of non-porous material (or are treated to have the same qualities). Ink is far less likely to spread and coated papers give much better reproductions of photographs, as well as feeling smoother. You can choose between 'glossy' or 'shiny' and 'matt' or 'velvet', according to taste (and what you think your readers will like).

The paper used in this book is 90 gsm, coated. This was changed from the first edition, which was felt to be slightly too heavy.

Texture, colour and other qualities Some expensive papers have a textured feel like old parchment or cloth-based paper. These can be absorbent, but can also look stylish. Paper doesn't have to be white. Different colour ranges are possible, including pastel shades, strong colours and fluorescent colours. If you are a real print fanatic, you may even consider the smell of the paper – it could signify luxury or suggest that it is only a 'throwaway' product. Another technical consideration will be the form of binding. If pages are glued together along one edge and the publication has a flat spine, it is known as 'perfect-bound'. Other methods 'stitch' or staple double-page spreads along the central fold, and another option is to 'spiral bind' with a strip of flexible plastic or coated wire.

Size and shape UK paper sizes are now standardised into the 'A' and 'B' series. You will be familiar with the A4 standard for photocopy paper and A5 for leaflets. The equivalents in the 'B' series are slightly larger. Books and magazines may use older sizes such as 'quarto' or 'royal'. Newspapers are usually **tabloid** (slightly smaller than A3) or **broadsheet** (slightly smaller than A2). Depending on your computer software, you may be offered templates for American paper sizes, which are noticeably different.

Often, you will make a decision about size and shape based on purely functional criteria – A5 for a booklet, A4 for a magazine. If you are printing on your school or college inkjet or laser printer, A4, or possibly A3, paper can be folded to give four pages of A5 or A4. If you go to a professional printer, who uses rolls of paper, there are fewer restrictions, and you can use an 'odd' size or shape. This could mean your product stands out. A4 magazines tend to signify an academic or 'amateur' product – a good example of an institutional sign? (see also the comments about tabloid and broadsheet newspapers in 'Institutions', Chapter 26). Most print products are 'portrait' (height greater than width), but some are 'landscape' (width greater than height). Some could be square and others very tall and narrow. They don't have to open as double pages – they could have two or more folds. All of these considerations will affect the way the product is 'read'.

Half A4 is A5. Twice A4 is A3. Using A4 sheets you can work up or down to see what A1, A2, A6 and A7 might look like.

ACTIVITY 5.1

Decisions on paper types

Collect a wide variety of magazines and books and try to distinguish between them in terms of paper size, shape, colour, weight etc. What conclusions do you come to about the institutional conventions – the 'rules' which enable a product to address a particular audience? Are there examples of products you immediately like or dislike because of the paper choices? If you can find examples, try to compare the same advertisement on different paper stock (e.g. in the matt newsprint format of weekend magazines like the *Guardian* or *Independent* and in a shiny, glossy style magazine).

Text and images

It helps to think about the printed page as a single image. Forget about what the words say for a moment: think about text in terms of shapes on the page. This will lead you into consideration of *typography* and **typesetting**, as well as **grids** and **white space**.

Typography As a 'print designer' you have the choice of hundreds of different **fonts**. A computer font will comprise up to 256 alphabetic, numerical and punctuation characters plus various symbols and accented characters. Fonts come in 'families' of different weights and styles, such as **bold**, light, roman ('upright'), *italic* etc. The family name is sometimes referred to as a **typeface**.

There are four main categories of typefaces. The main two, used for **body text**, to be read in small sizes, are known as **serif** and **sans-serif**. The serif is the bar across the ends of the 'arms and legs' of the character. Typefaces used primarily for posters and signs are known as **display** and may be ornate and therefore unsuitable for sustained reading. Typefaces classified as **script** are based on styles of handwriting.

Some typefaces are very old, dating back centuries. Others were designed last week. Classic faces like Gill, designed by Eric Gill in the 1920s, have moved in and out of fashion. If you are interested, there are several good catalogues or dictionaries of typography in reference libraries. You will find your own favourite faces, but you need to be aware of some typography conventions before you start to experiment, even if you want to break with them. Most typefaces are available in different formats for Macintosh (Postscript) and Windows (TrueType).

- Serif faces are said to be best for long runs of body text, because the serif helps to distinguish the characters in a block of text and makes sustained reading easier.
- Sans-serif faces are commonly used for headings where immediacy and clarity are important.
- In any single document, you should not use more than two typefaces for body text and headings. (You can use display fonts in adverts and you can make use of different styles and weights within the two typeface families you select.)

Typesetting With a desktop publishing programme like PageMaker or Quark Xpress (but not a word processor like Word), you can manipulate text with great precision and create exactly the look you want. You can choose the size of the type in **points** and the space between each line of text (known as **leading**). A common choice for a book would be 10 point type with 2 points of leading, known as '10 on 12'. Type size does matter – if you make it too large, your product may suggest that its readership is young children. If it is very small, it might be difficult for older people to read (your eyes start to weaken in your forties!). Type can be squeezed up

---

fonts were originally 'founts' – from the foundry, where they were cast in metal type. Germany and America were the main producers of metal type – e.g. Afga, Monotype, Linotype etc.

'Times' is a **serif** typeface

Times

serif

Helvetica is a **sans-serif** typeface

DESDEMONA is a **display** typeface

Zapf Chancery is a **script** face

The credit sequence of the film *Gattaca* (US 1997) makes clever use of typography to distinguish the letters **A**, **T**, **C** and **G**, which are always shown in a different font. The name 'Gattaca' is derived from the four 'letters' of the DNA code; they stand for the chemicals **A**denine, **T**hymine, **G**uanine and **C**ytosine.

The same idea is observable in *Brassed Off* (UK/US 1996), which features a brass band contest. In the credit sequence all the letters *f* and *p*, the musical symbols for 'loud' and 'soft', are shown in bold italic and a different colour.

Look at the information at the front of the book, opposite the Contents page to see how the typesetting on this page has been organised.

or strung out along a line, either by selecting a specially designed
'extended' or 'compressed' typeface or by manipulating the space between
characters (sometimes known as *tracking*).

The look of a column of text is also affected by the use of alignment or
justification (also referred to as 'ranging'). If you justify the text to both
the left and right side (sometimes known as 'flush') the result will be a
smooth edge, but on each line the space between words will be adjusted,
and between some lines it will be noticeably different. The alternative is
standard spacing between words, but a ragged right edge to the column
of text. This choice is said to be personal, but be careful of using
justification with narrow columns.

Grids and white space Before you start designing a page or a poster, it is
worth thinking about a grid – a basic structure of columns and rows.
This will determine the shape and feel of the page, with the body of text
sharing space with drawings, photographs etc. and balanced with open
spaces – so-called *white space*.

Again there are some basic conventions. If a column is too wide, it can
be tiring to read to the end of a line. A single column across an A4 page
is not advisable. On the other hand a very narrow column might not
work if you only get two or three words per line. Horizontal grid
divisions will produce a page with a series of boxes which can be used for
text and illustrations. Three columns and three horizontal grid divisions
on an A4 page probably gives the best range of options and most
flexibility.

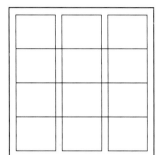

Figure 5.1   A simple layout grid

ACTIVITY 5.2

Grids

Devise a selection of grids on a desktop publishing program. Create or find some
text and **clipart** and try laying out a page using different grids. Which do you find
easiest to work with? Which gives the most attractive result? Compare your own
efforts with the layouts in the publications you selected for Activity 5.1.

---

clipart is commercially produced
artwork – drawings of a wide
range of objects and people,
available copyright-free on
CD-ROM.

Refer to Figure 5.2 as an example of a page layout. The space between
columns is the **gutter**. Note the different margins at top and bottom –
this particular design uses a wide margin at the top. The margins on left
and right are relatively wide. If you are designing a magazine with
narrow margins, it is worth noting that, whichever form of binding you
use, the 'inside margin' will need to be a little wider than the outside

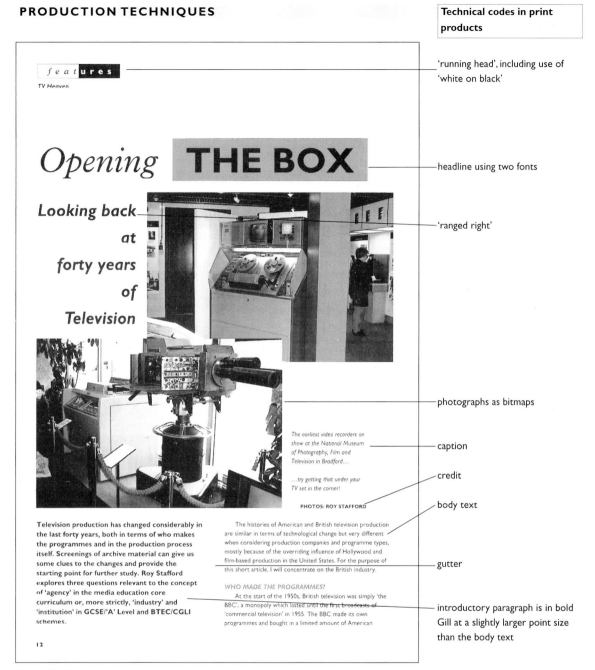

features
TV Heaven

Opening THE BOX

Looking back
at
forty years
of
Television

'running head', including use of 'white on black'

headline using two fonts

'ranged right'

photographs as bitmaps

The earliest video recorders on show at the National Museum of Photography, Film and Television in Bradford...

...try getting that under your TV set in the corner!

PHOTOS: ROY STAFFORD

caption

credit

body text

Television production has changed considerably in the last forty years, both in terms of who makes the programmes and in the production process itself. Screenings of archive material can give us some clues to the changes and provide the starting point for further study. Roy Stafford explores three questions relevant to the concept of 'agency' in the media education core curriculum or, more strictly, 'industry' and 'institution' in GCSE/'A' Level and BTEC/CGLI schemes.

The histories of American and British television production are similar in terms of technological change but very different when considering production companies and programme types, mostly because of the overriding influence of Hollywood and film-based production in the United States. For the purpose of this short article, I will concentrate on the British industry.

WHO MADE THE PROGRAMMES?

At the start of the 1950s, British television was simply 'the BBC', a monopoly which lasted until the first broadcasts of 'commercial television' in 1955. The BBC made its own programmes and bought in a limited amount of American

gutter

introductory paragraph is in bold Gill at a slightly larger point size than the body text

12

Figure 5.2   Page layout

margin to compensate for the part of the page we can't see easily as it disappears into the fold. This means that you will need two layouts – one for the right-hand or **recto** page and one for the left-hand or **verso** page. You will also be able to think about a *double-page spread* for the two centre pages if you are single stapling or just folding a small magazine. On these pages you can run text or images across the fold in the centre. The example in Figure 5.2 is a verso page – how can you tell? The example comes from a magazine for media teachers and the design dates from the early 1990s. Note that there is a two-column grid, but that, to allow for images of sufficient size, the two photographs 'break out' of the columns and overlap. The designer has 'balanced' this effect by using a sub-heading on one side and a caption on the other. Another 'broken rule' is the use of a sans-serif face (Gill) for body text. This became quite common at this time and is used in this book for case studies.

Images There are two kinds of images which you can use in a DTP program. The first is called a **bitmap**. This is an image which is made up of an arrangement of pixels of different colours – a 'map' of 'bits' of information. Bitmaps usually start life as photographs which are scanned in to the computer, but you can create them yourself using a 'paint' package. The quality of the bitmap as a printed image depends on two factors – the number of colours and the size of the individual pixels. A very high-quality image in a fashion magazine will have 'millions of colours' and a massive bitmap of very small pixels. The result is that you cannot see the individual pixels in the image on the page, and the vast range of colours means that the reproduction will be as close as possible to the original colours of the photograph. This is a *high-resolution* image. At the other end of the scale is an image with a limited number of colours and a relatively small bitmap. When a bitmap is enlarged or reduced (scaled up or down) the individual pixels are each enlarged or reduced, so that, if the printed image is larger than the original, it is possible to see the individual pixels in a very 'blocky' presentation. This is a **low-resolution** image, which you will sometimes see in newspapers when the content is so important that the picture editor is prepared to accept the low quality.

Figure 5.3 A **low-resolution bitmap** showing the pixels

Scanning and printing photographs is a tricky business, and there is not enough space here to go into detail. As a producer, you will usually want to get the best-quality image into your publication. Unfortunately, high resolution files are very large (over 1 megabyte) and your equipment may not be able to handle them. Go for the best quality you can handle and scale down, never up.

The second type of image is known as a **vector** drawing or 'structured' or 'outline' drawing. Instead of the fixed bitmap, a vector drawing is made up of a set of points which are joined by curves. These are stored in the computer file as a formula. When the vector drawing is used in a DTP program, it can be scaled up or down and the computer re-calculates the formula for the curve. This way, the image will always be high-quality. This is the basis for much of the clipart you will find on your computer. The image is high-quality but often has few colours and does not attempt to replicate a photograph. You can draw such images yourself, but you need great skill and knowledge of the drawing software. The industry standard drawing programs are Illustrator and Freehand.

There is another form of 'image' which you may wish to use, called an **EPS** or 'encapsulated postscript' file. This isn't an image file as such, but rather a text file describing an image in great detail for a print program – on a similar principle to the vector drawing. **Postscript** is a print description language used extensively in publishing (largely on Macintosh computers). The files are very good for printing, but are sometimes difficult to load into DTP programs.

EPS clipart, like this Illustrator drawing, will retain its detail when scaled up or down.

Clipart is useful in relatively informal documents but can look out of place in formal publications.

Text as image Fonts for DTP should always be 'outline' fonts which can be scaled like the vector drawings or Postscript files described above. Beware bitmap fonts which work only at a set size – if you enlarge them they become blocky. You can use certain fonts in a drawing program and then manipulate characters or whole words as if they were images.

Manipulation of images One of the great benefits of computerised page layout is the range of possibilities for manipulating text and images – changing colour, shape, texture etc. in a seemingly unlimited number of ways. This boon is also a curse if you let it run away with you. Just as in video production (which includes many of the same effects), it is important to have a purpose rather than just to create an effect for the sake of it. Why might you want to manipulate or distort images and/or text?

Firstly, you may simply want to 'enhance' or improve the image. There are many tools available to do this, including colour controls, balance of light and dark in an image ('equalisation'). Often enhancements may not be obvious at all and so may not act as a code (except in coding 'perfection' or 'high standard of finish'). You may wish to use effects to emphasise text, such as shadow or outline, or a 'fill' pattern instead of solid black or colour.

You may also wish to distort the shape of images or construct new images by putting together a collage of some kind. Many of these effects are already programmed for the industry standard image manipulation package, Adobe Photoshop. New effects are known as 'plug-ins' for the program. These effects will be noticeable, and you might need to be careful not to just follow trends because there is a new plug-in. You can see these trends developing in the magazines – such as the use of soft grey shadows for headline text a little while ago. Ideally, you want to appear contemporary – clearly up with trends – but also distinctive.

Figure 5.4 A wave distort digital effect has been applied to this photographic image

Technical codes in video production

A video image is actually made up of a matrix – a set of rows and columns of pixels – which can be individually charged to show a particular colour. Your computer screen offers a video image of a specific resolution – in effect a bitmap (which is why you can 'grab' your computer screen as an image and use it in a print product, as we have done in this book). 'Full motion video' changes the image twenty-five times per second to give the impression of continuous movement. Each full frame of video corresponds to a single frame on a strip of film, which passes through a projector at the slightly slower speed of twenty-four frames per second.

The two main differences between analogue video and film are that the video image is relatively low-resolution (i.e. a small bitmap – see print image section above) and exists only when a timing signal can stabilise the image (i.e. it is difficult to distinguish the single frames easily). Film is high-resolution and stable. Digital video is beginning to close the gap in many ways, so for our purposes we can for most of the time treat film and video together. (Much of this section will also be relevant for still photography.)

The single most important element in the film or video image is light, or more specifically, light captured by a lens. Technical codes can therefore be classified as follows:

- light
  - sources (positions)
  - type of lamp (colour of light, area covered)
  - brightness, intensity
- lens or aperture
  - focal length
  - size
- sensitivity of film or light sensor
- shutter speed
- special effects

These are all codes relating to the contrast between light and shade and the effect of light in 'modelling' or shaping figures in an environment. There are some basic rules for a lighting set-up as shown in Figure 5.5. Traditionally, film and television uses a **set-up** with three kinds of **lamps**. The **key light** is a bright, powerful light which illuminates a person or object and throws a deep shadow. It is usually above and at an angle to the subject. Smaller **fill lights** are used from complementary angles to fill the shadows with a softer light. Finally a **back light**, above and behind the figure, helps to bring it forward from the background and create some depth in the image.

PAL Video standards, as used for UK television, have a bitmap of 720 x 576 pixels.

Many computer screens offer higher resolutions.

The term **lamp** describes the physical device which provides the 'light' and is used to avoid confusion.

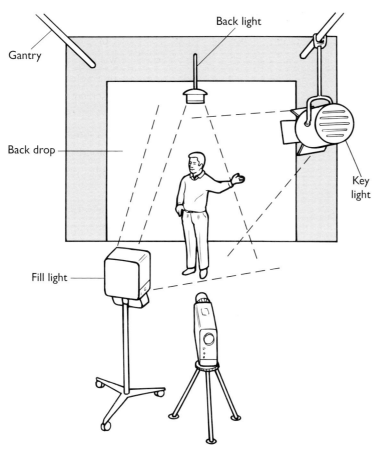

Figure 5.5   Three-point lighting set-up

In mainstream film and television, most comedies, musicals, talk shows and light entertainment are presented in **high-key** lighting. This means that the ratio of fill to key is high – most of the shadows are filled in. Light has a texture which is either 'hard' – producing deep and sharp shadows – or 'soft', creating only slight shadows. The texture depends both on the intensity of the lighting element (brightness) and the extent to which the light is 'direct' or diffused in some way with a 'scrim' (a fine mesh) or gauze. Light is brighter when it is concentrated on a 'spot'. This can be achieved with lenses in the lamp or 'barn doors' (metal hinged flaps). Softer light can be achieved by 'bouncing' or reflecting light off the ceiling or a white sheet.

Light is angled on to its subject and the texture can be controlled. A third factor is 'colour' – depending on the power of the lamp, light has a **colour temperature**. The most powerful light is bright daylight, which is 'hot' and produces a blue sky. Artificial lights are by comparison 'cold' and tend towards reddish yellow. If you shoot in colour, you must ensure that

Figure 5.6   This crowded shoot on location shows a white reflector and a 2,500-watt key light with 'barn doors'. The umbrella is for the rain, but white umbrellas can be used as reflectors

The origins of *film noir* lighting are argued to be in German cinema of the 1920s and 1930s – the practice spread to Hollywood and other European cinemas with the emigration of talent following Hitler's seizure of power in 1933 and became prevalent in drama and horror.

Figure 5.7   Out of the Past (US 1947) is a classic *film noir*. In this shot, a table lamp is offscreen to the right, throwing a bright light up on to Robert Mitchum

Figure 5.8   A modern colour film which used *film noir* techniques was *Blade Runner* (US 1982). Here lighting is used to create metaphorical prison bars across the lovers

either the film stock or the video camera is adjusted for indoor or outdoor lighting. The video camera adjustment is known as **white balance**. If these adjustments are not made, the image will have a blue or yellow cast.

Fine gradations of light are difficult to distinguish on a video screen, but are revealed in all their glory in the classic black and white cinematography of 1940s cinema. It is worth trying to see re-issued 1940s films on a large cinema screen to get the full effect. *Film noir* lighting was '**low key**' – often dispensing with fill and back lights to produce stark images with single, hard key lights. Thus 'low' fill to key ratio.

Many different kinds of lamps were used in classical cinema and you may find references to some exotic names, such as 'pups' or 'babies', 'inkies', 'scoops', 'juniors' and 'seniors'. These refer to lights of different power and purpose. During your course, if you do get access to lighting equipment it is likely to be a kit of 'redheads', so named because of the warmish colour at relatively low power. You will see these in use by some news crews in an interview set-up on location. The more powerful portable light is a 'blonde' (again because of the colour of the brighter light).

Natural light also varies in power and texture and film-makers will often select to shoot at only certain times of day to capture a particular lighting effect. Natural light can be used indoors (i.e. through windows, doorways) and can be manipulated via reflectors (and suitable adjustment for colour temperature).

ACTIVITY 5.3

Experiment with lighting

The best way to learn about lighting and lenses is to experiment. Unfortunately, many inexpensive video cameras are designed to prevent you doing just that. Equipment for 'home' use has automatic controls which try to standardise the image. Look for a video camera with 'manual' iris or aperture control, or at least some means of altering the aperture setting.

- Try to create a *film noir* image, applying some of the lighting techniques described above. Start with a set as dark as possible – a studio or a room with blackout – gradually adding 'lamps' to achieve effects of light and shadow typical of the *noir* image.

Any video camera will be worth using for the next task:

- Try to manipulate natural light by shooting in a room where you can control sunlight through a window to act as a key light. Use a reflector to act as a fill source.

PRODUCTION TECHNIQUES

- What happens to the lighting on your subject if you are pointing the camera towards the window or at a white wall? You should be able to work out what is happening (and learn to avoid it – unless you want to create an effect).

Lens and aperture

Light is captured by the camera via the lens and passes through the aperture to reach the film or video light sensor. The lens and aperture function just like your eye in focusing on the subject and controlling the amount of light. When you are faced with a bright light your iris contracts. In the same way the camera aperture can be made smaller. The smaller the aperture, the longer the focal length achieved by the lens. A longer focal length means a greater depth of focus in the image. Conversely, a shorter focal length means only a limited field of focus.

It's easy to be confused by the terms photographers use. 'Depth of field' is also a function of the type of lens. A 'standard' lens for a 35 mm film or still camera is given as 50 mm focal length – the distance between the lens and the film on which a sharp image is focused. This lens will produce an image with roughly the same perspective as your own view of a scene. A shorter or **wide-angle** lens of 25 mm will produce a scene which seems further away, but which 'crams more in'. A long lens, often called a **telephoto** lens, of 80 mm or more will compress the distance between you and the scene. The confusion comes when you realise that the long lens means a shallow field of focus while a short lens means very deep focus. You don't need to know all the details about lenses (unless you want to be a director of photography), but you should be able to distinguish between the use of a widescreen and telephoto lens as shown in the examples here.

You can check out some of these ideas about lenses with a video camera. Modern video cameras use a **zoom** lens to simulate shorter and longer lenses, so a typical small video camcorder will have a zoom lens offering 'lengths' from, say, 10 mm to 120 mm (these are the equivalent of 20 mm to 240 mm on a 35 mm camera), with controls often marked 'W' and 'T' for wide angle and telephoto. If you want to create great depth of field in a scene, use a relatively short lens with characters relatively close to the camera and plenty of action in the background.

One of the disadvantages of a wide-angle lens is that objects very close to the camera can become distorted, even when still in focus. This can work well in a horror film or *film noir* where the face looming into the camera with bulging eyes etc. can be quite shocking. Other distorting

You will recognise the long lens used by the sports photographer to take close-ups of the action. Some are so long that they need a separate support or the camera would be impossible to hold.

Figure 5.9   Wide-angle distortion in *La Haine* (France 1995)

In the *film noir, Crossfire* (US 1947), the 'villain' is photographed with different lenses as the film progresses. Each time, the lens is slightly shorter, so at the climax of the film his appearance is very disturbing.

Figure 5.10   *The Good, the Bad and
the Ugly* (Italy 1966)

lenses can be used to create more obvious effects, such as the circular or
'goldfish bowl' effect.

Our striking still from *The Good, the Bad and the Ugly* (Figure 5.10)
shows the dramatic effects of a wide-angle lens and a small aperture. The
foreground and the deep background are both in sharp focus. This is an
extraordinary shot and was achievable only with the bright desert
sunlight and a particular widescreen film format called Techniscope (see
Salt 1992) which was both cheaper than and avoided the lighting
problems of CinemaScope.

The widescreen formats introduced in the 1950s all required more
light through the lens to capture and project a bigger image. At first in
1953/4 it was thought that 'epic' pictures would all be set outdoors or on
sets with very shallow fields of focus. The lens manufacturers improved
their products dramatically, and improvements in the other parts of the
system meant that, eventually, everything that studio cinematographers
of the 1940s had achieved could be replicated in widescreen and
Technicolor.

You should note from this that the history of technical codes in cinema
and television has been largely concerned, in terms of the image, with the
problem of light. There are three aspects of the problem:

- getting enough light, of the correct intensity, tone and texture on to
  the scene, where it is required
- developing a lens to capture the light
- developing the 'light sensing' device in the camera.

'Film' is a photochemical technology. An emulsion of chemicals on a
celluloid base reacts to exposure to light and changes colour. Throughout
the history of the cinema, the basic technology has remained the same,
but improvements have been made to the emulsion to make it more
sensitive and to respond to a wider range of lighting possibilities. Video
cameras have light-sensitive chips which transmit information to be
stored on tape or disk. Again their development involves increasing the
data flow – the lighting information to be recorded. Film or video
sensing devices can be ranged from 'fast' to 'slow' in terms of how quickly
they can capture light. A fast film can operate in relatively poor lighting
conditions, but the resulting image will be quite 'grainy' – a feature you
might notice in newsreel footage from the 1940s or 1950s. Slow film
needs plenty of light to produce very smooth and glossy images.

Colour film depends on chemical processes which can produce different
palettes. If you read what successful cinematographers and directors say
about their films, you will sometimes find references to a choice of
Eastmancolor or Fujicolor because they favour one group of colours rather
than another. It is also possible to alter the way the colour will be

Figure 5.11   *The Battle of Algiers*
(Algeria 1965) was a famous
example of a feature film with a
'feel' of actuality, achieved partly
through documentary camera
techniques and a grainy fast-film
appearance

recorded, by use of filters on the camera or lamps, or the way it will be 'printed' on the final film, by adjusting the developing time or temperature.

Shutter speed

The sensitivity of the light-sensing device is affected also by the length of exposure of each 'frame' to light. A film camera has a shutter which closes the aperture and allows the film to be fed through the gate at a rate of twenty-four frames per second. This speed is matched by the cinema projector. But speeds can be manipulated in a number of ways to speed up and slow down the action. 'Speeded-up' action is sometimes featured in comedy films, while slow motion was used to great effect by action director Sam Peckinpah for scenes of violence, such as the climax of *The Wild Bunch* (1969) (Figure 5.12).

Video cameras do not have a physical shutter, but they can simulate a very fast shutter, like those used in still cameras. A shutter operating at 1/500th of a second can capture a video still image of a rapidly moving subject, which on film would be simply a blur. This function is sometimes used to record sporting action or industrial processes for instructional purposes. A fast shutter requires much more light and is not suitable for standard use (be careful you don't set such a switch by accident when using a video camera).

Figure 5.12   The Wild Bunch (US 1969)

Special effects

Some of the digital effects used in photographic images for print are also relevant for video and film and as edit suites move from analogue to digital nonlinear, more and more effects become available. Entire films can now be made using computer-generated animated sequences such as those in *Toy Story* (US 1996), and others can include spectacular digital sequences such as the **morphing** liquid metal in *Terminator 2* (US 1991). It is worth remembering, however, that special effects using double exposures, glass matte screens and front or back projection have been common in cinema since 1896.

Digital video editing techniques allow slow motion to be achieved during editing, and if necessary the computer can calculate and draw the 'in between' frames which would be caught by a high-speed shutter.

There isn't space here to analyse animation techniques, but it is worth distinguishing between using a computer to edit traditionally drawn images and **CGI** or computer-generated images like the dinosaurs in *Jurassic Park* (US 1993).

ACTIVITY 5.4

Lenses, shutters and film stock

It is difficult to experiment with these codes (although some of you might be lucky and have access to video cameras with a range of controls). It is also quite difficult to recognise some of the subtleties of film stock and colour palettes when watching films on video. But you can learn something by watching a variety of films from different periods.

Watch the openings of three or four films from the history of cinema, ideally one from silent cinema, one from the 1940s, one from the 1970s and one from the 1990s. Note the differences in

- depth of field
- use of wide-angle or telephoto lenses
- quality of the image – colour, grain etc.
- use of special effects.

What conclusions do you draw about changing techniques?

Technical codes in audio production

Ray Dolby (born 1933) An American working in the UK in the 1960s, Dolby pioneered work on noise reduction and revolutionised the quality of sound from cassette recorders and, later, cinema projection.

It is possible to think about sound in much the same way as light. The cinematographer 'models with light', the sound designer models with sound. It isn't very likely that you will have access to full **Dolby** Stereo sound recording for your productions, but it is important that you should know something about the principles of sound design in film and television and the work of the recording engineer in the music or radio studio.

It might be helpful to begin by thinking of a radio broadcast or a film soundtrack as representing a 'soundscape' (like a visual landscape) or a sound stage (like a theatrical stage). On this stage will be a number of performers, a distance apart, with background sounds such as traffic, birdsong etc. How can this be represented to an audience? The secrets are in the capture of particular sounds via microphones and then the mixing and editing process.

Recording sounds

The nature of recorded sound is a function of the microphone, the acoustic qualities of the location and the sensitivity of the recording medium.

There are several different kinds of microphones, categorised by different mechanisms for capturing sound and by different pick-up or **response** patterns (see Figure 5.13). A directional microphone with a very tightly defined response will capture dialogue without background sound. The same effect could be achieved with a microphone positioned close to the speaker's lips like a 'tie-clip' microphone. By contrast, an omni-directional microphone will pick up dialogue plus all the background noise. Some microphones can be 'switched' between different responses.

PRODUCTION TECHNIQUES

The sound that is 'picked up' will have various qualities determined by the frequency range of the microphone – its capacity to pick up high and low frequency sounds such as a whistle and a bass drum. Other qualities are more difficult to describe, but sound engineers will refer to the texture of sound – 'hard' or 'soft', 'fat' or 'thin', or the 'colour' of sound – 'warm', 'bright', 'round' etc. Some of these qualities will be emphasised by particular types of microphone. For example, the large microphones which you might see in newsreels from the 1940s are renowned for giving a rich fruity sound. If you are interested in developing audio production ideas, you should investigate the different kinds of microphone available for your practical work, but note that professional microphones are expensive and you may find only a limited choice.

More controllable, and equally important in terms of the quality of sound, are the acoustic qualities of the recording location. Sound is carried in waves created by pressing air. When the sound waves meet a soft absorbent surface they are effectively 'soaked up'. You've probably been at a party where, as more and more people arrive, the music has to be turned up louder – almost as if the bodies soak up the music. Conversely, when sound waves meet hard, shiny surfaces, they bounce back and in some cases produce echoes. If you set out to record a conversation in a student canteen, with vinyl floors, formica tables and large glass windows, you will probably get a terrible clattering noise, even with a reasonable-quality microphone. But the same conversation in a room with carpeting and curtains may be perfectably acceptable. Just as a television or film-maker may elect to shoot in a studio, where the lighting can be set up very precisely, sound recordists may use a studio space which is designed to be acoustically 'dead' – i.e. there is no background '**noise**' or atmosphere. Suitable sounds can then be added to create the finished product.

The recording format is important because it too has a frequency response and may alter the quality of the sound. You may have several options on your course including traditional formats such as cassette or open reel tape, digital audiotape (**DAT**), **MiniDisc** or hard disk recording on the computer. Formats tend to be chosen for specific purposes and the current situation is very flexible. You will find professionals who favour one format over another.

Editing and mixing

Until very recently it was standard practice for all radio interviews and features to be physically edited by 'cutting and splicing'. Increasingly, there is a move to disk-based editing and you might get involved with

---

Technical codes in audio production

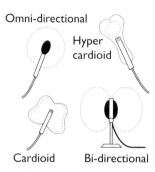

Figure 5.13 Microphone response patterns (cardioid = 'heart-shaped')

microphone types 'omni-directional' for vox pops – interviews in the street. Directional 'shotgun' style microphone on a 'boom' (pole) or with a pistol-grip, being pointed at the action in a drama or interview. Tie-clip used in a studio. Radio mike used by a performer on stage.

Noise in sound recording is a term used to describe any unwanted sound.

both. But, as well as assembling the audio material you want, the editing stage allows you also to 'process' the sound and to add sound effects.

We've noted that one practice used to achieve the effect of a 'location' is to record the dialogue in a studio and add the atmosphere as a sound effect. This involves using an audio mixer, which allows different sound sources on separate 'tracks' to be mixed together. The 'level' and frequency ranges of sounds can also be manipulated to produce a fluid 'soundscape', analagous to an edited visual sequence.

Audio mixers range from simple 4 track machines to much larger 8, 16 or 32 track machines.

ACTIVITY 5.5

Compiling a radio sequence

Again, your opportunities to experiment will depend on the equipment available. In order to develop audio skills, tape two or three short interviews (a couple of questions only) with a range of people. If possible, conduct one interview in a location with 'atmosphere' and one in a 'dead' acoustic space.

- Try to add some atmosphere to the 'studio' interview
- Edit the interviews together and add an introduction and a link.
- Listen to your edit. Are the 'levels' (the loudness) consistent throughout?
- Are the joins noticeable – how could you make them less obvious? (This will depend on your equipment.)

Stereo and the sound stage

Stereo means 'solid' – i.e. that sound has width and depth.

All of the comments above apply to 'mono' recordings, where the sound has been recorded at a single point via the microphone. It is also possible to use a stereo microphone to record sound 'in depth' – not only to record the sounds but to place them in position on the sound stage. It is also possible to take a mono recording and to place it within a stereo sound stage set-up using an audio mixer. The creation of the stereo sound stage is at the creative heart of modern stereo radio, television and cinema sound. The sound designer will attempt to create a 'sound image' which will mean that every person who speaks and every significant sound (a footstep, a phone ringing etc.) is heard clearly, but also in the context of a believable background – a city street, a busy office etc. This is all possible with modern technology, which has allowed a greater frequency range and less noise through the use of noise reduction systems like Dolby.

Modern film sound is highly sophisticated and will usually be carefully re-recorded after shooting using 'looping studios', where

actors repeat under studio conditions their lines spoken on location.
Foley technology is then used to add the sound effects (Figure 5.14).
Typical effects produced by Foley artists are footsteps and the rustle of
clothing etc., which is difficult to 'close mike'.

In terms of 'technical audio codes', it is useful to have a set of terms to
describe sounds used in a mix, based on a combination of the technology
used to create or capture them and their narrative function (see 'Realisms'
and 'Narratives', Chapters 16 and 3). In a mix for narratives (in drama or
advertising?) in radio, film or television, we can distinguish:

- dialogue spoken by the important characters in a scene
- sound effects – the specific sounds which carry narrative information,
  such as a knock on the door
- background or ambient sound which gives the scene atmosphere – the
  general hubbub in a bar
- 'non-**diegetic**' sound – sound which doesn't come from the fictional
  world of the narrative. The clearest example is theme music. Music
  playing on a jukebox in the scene is diegetic.

ACTIVITY 5.6

Types of sound

Can you distinguish between these different types of sound? Record a short
sequence (a few minutes) of a popular film on television. Replay it a few times and
study the sound mix to distinguish the four types above.

Sound is one of the areas of film studies which has received less
attention than it deserves. Since the success of *Star Wars* and Dolby
Stereo in 1977, film producers and cinema managers have recognised
its importance (see Murch 1995). The recent introduction of digital
sound systems has enhanced its importance, and over the next few
years the quality of sound from the domestic television set will also
improve dramatically. Next time you go to the cinema, especially to
see a Hollywood blockbuster, try to listen carefully to the soundtrack,
along the lines suggested in Activity 5.6. You will notice how the
opening music tries both to wake you up – pay attention, back there! –
and to pin you to your seat with sheer volume. But in the main
narrative it is the range of sound frequencies which is important.
Watch out for moments when the movement of the narrative hangs on
a sound. Walter Murch describes his work on the opening of *Apocalypse
Now* (US 1979):

Technical codes in audio production

Jack Foley was a Universal
Studios sound engineer who
developed techniques for
recording sound effects.

Figure 5.14   Preparing to lay down
sound effects in a Foley studio at
Lucasfilms

The classic 'sound recording' film
is *The Conversation* (US 1974) with
Gene Hackman as the surveillance
agent who becomes obsessed with
a recording.

Living in Oblivion (US 1996) is a
recent 'independent' film, about a
low-budget film producer, with
interesting sequences about sound
recording.

Technical codes in audio production

Traditional dialogue recording in film or television allows each character to talk in turn. More 'realistic' is the technique which 'overlaps' lines by different characters. This can be achieved by miking each character in a scene and allowing each a track on a mixing desk. An appropriate balance can be achieved later. This multitrack technique was pioneered by director Robert Altman.

You are looking at Saigon, you are in a hotel room, but you begin to hear the sounds of the jungle. One by one the elements of the street turn into jungle sounds: a policeman's whistle turns into a bird, the two-stroke motorcycles turn into insects, and item by item each thread of one reality is pulled out of the tapestry and replaced by another one. You are looking at something very improbable which is a man sitting in an hotel room … Although his body is in Saigon, his mind is somewhere else.

(Murch 1996, p. 161)

ACTIVITY 5.7

Sound and vision

Take a short sequence (two or three minutes) of video, either something you have shot yourself or a sequence copied from a film or television programme.

- Play the sequence without sound and concentrate on the meaning suggested by the images alone.
- Take two or three very different music tracks (or sound effects) and play them in conjunction with the visuals.
- How much difference does the sound make?

We've discussed sound and mentioned music only in the last few sentences. We just don't have space to cover every aspect of production techniques. You should explore as many different production techniques as you can. This is an area of study where the widest possible range of experience is definitely a good thing.

References and further reading

Chion, Michel (1994) *Audio-vision: Sound on Screen*, Chichester: Columbia University Press.

Hedgecoe, John (1979) *Introductory Photography Course*, London: Mitchell Beazley.

Malkiewicz, Kris (1989) *Cinematography*, London: Columbus Books.

Miles, John (1987) *Design for Desktop Publishing*, Hatfield: John Taylor Book Ventures.

Salt, Barry (1992) *Film Style & Technology: History & Analysis*, London: Starword.

Books by practitioners or interviews with them are sometimes useful in revealing how they work. The *Projections* Series edited by John Boorman and Walter Donohue for Faber & Faber carries excellent materials on film production techniques, e.g.:

Projections 4 (1995): Walter Murch 'Sound Design: The Dancing Shadow'.

Projections 6 (1996) has a section of interviews with cinematographers such as Vittorio Storaro and Freddie Young as well as Walter Murch on sound in *Apocalypse Now*.

The film *Visions of Light: The Art of Cinematography* (US/Japan 1992) is available on video and demonstrates techniques from the history of Hollywood cinema.

See also references for Chapter 6.

6 Production organisation

In this chapter we deal with the organisation and management of media production tasks. Along with 'Production techniques' (Chapter 5), the information and advice here will enable you to understand the production process and to approach your own productions with confidence.

The production process in outline

If you discuss the concept of the production process with professionals who work in different media (i.e. magazine publishing, television etc.), they will probably stress the differences – the specificities – of their particular work practices. In 'Industries' (Chapter 22), we outline a five-stage production process which, while primarily concerned with film and television, will serve equally well for other types of media production, even if the professionals concerned would not necessarily recognise the terms used:

negotiating a brief

pre-production

production

post-production

distribution and exhibition

These stages represent the production process for a single, coherent product. An established, daily, media product won't need to involve endless negotiation and pre-production (although the inclusion of some material will still need to be negotiated), but when the product was first devised the production team will have gone through these stages. A television or radio series will be commissioned in blocks and can be treated as a single production.

Setting out

Whatever the production task, there are several important questions which need to be asked at the outset.

Purpose

Why are you producing a media text? Most likely it will be to 'educate, inform or entertain'. If it isn't one of these, then it is probably intended to persuade. All production must be entertaining to a certain extent or else readers won't persevere with the text. Your production will be assessed according to the extent to which it 'fits its purpose', and you should bear this in mind throughout each stage of the process.

Target audience

The meaning produced by a text depends to a large extent on the intended reader, and it's futile to try to construct a text if you don't know who that reader is. The audience profile will include the standard age, gender and class information as well as more culturally based distinctions which might include religion, sexual orientation, marital or family status etc., and environmental factors such as geographical location (see 'Audiences' (Chapter 32) for further discussion of the descriptions used by media industries).

Budget and funding

Media production requires money – large amounts in many cases. Where does it come from?

Direct sales Not many producers can be self-funding – generating enough income from sales to fund the next production. In most cases, the preparation costs and the delay in receiving income mean that the outlay is too big for a small company to cover. There are then a limited number of options available. Borrowing the money from a bank will mean high interest payments, putting more pressure on the 'need to succeed'. Selling an interest in your production to a backer is perhaps a less risky venture, but of course it means that, if you do well, a share of the profits goes to your backers.

Pre-sales Continuing production can be guaranteed if you can 'pre-sell' your products at a fixed price. This way you might cover the whole of your budget with a guaranteed sale. The disadvantage is that, if your product is very successful and could command a higher price, you will have forgone potential profits.

Selling rights to a distributor This saves you the trouble and the risk of selling your product in territories (or to other media) which you don't

'Now that farmers are being paid for *not* growing crops ... might I suggest that this is a policy the Arts Council could adopt ... they could pay writers *not* to produce books, (adapted from a letter by David M. Bennie to *The Literary Review*).The same view might be applied to a wide range of media products which don't have a clear purpose and a recognised audience.

know much about. A distributor pays you a fixed sum. Once again, you lose profits if the product is successful.

Selling ideas If you can sell your production idea, you can save yourself the bother of producing at all. You can also negotiate to make your product as a commission for a major producer, leaving someone else to worry about budgets while you just take a fee.

Sponsorship or advertising You may get someone else to pay for the production (or part of it) as part of a sponsorship deal. Companies may be interested in being associated with a quality product, especially if it addresses a specific target audience. A specialised form of sponsorship involves **product placement**. Print products and possibly radio broadcasts may be funded by the direct sale of advertising space. The danger of sponsorship is that the sponsors' views on the production may compromise your own aims.

Grant-aid If you have no money and little experience, you may actually be better placed to get started on a project than if you have a track record. Many arts agencies offer grants to new producers. These may be quite small – a few hundred pounds up to a few thousand – but enough to get started. Look in the reference section for details of the British Film Institute, Arts Council and regional arts boards etc. Be warned, grant applications have strict schedules tied to annual budgets and quite detailed application forms. Make sure you have enough time to get advice and fill in the forms properly. You will also need to evaluate your work – you will probably find that your Media Studies work is useful in explaining what you want to do. Many grants are aimed at giving help to particular groups of new producers or new forms of production.

For many producers, 'independence' from control or 'interference' by funders is a big issue. On the other hand some funders can be helpful in budgeting for you (and also giving you 'backing' which will allow you entry into other negotiations with potential buyers etc.).

Style

What style or genre will you use? No matter how 'original' you attempt to be, you will be making references to media conventions – if you don't make these references your readers may have difficulty following the text. You will perhaps be warned not to imitate professional work slavishly, but, at least when you first start out, it is difficult not to draw on work you enjoy or admire. The best advice is to make open your intention to

Product placement This refers to the prominent position of consumer items in the decor of films and television programmes and crucially the use of such products by stars – Coca-Cola and Pepsi are reputed to have spent millions getting their products used by stars in Hollywood features (see 'Advertising and marketing', Chapter 30).

Grant aid has enabled many currently successful film-makers to make a start. See 'Independents and alternatives', Chapter 28, for more on grant aid and the role of funders generally.

Lottery funding is a relatively new source of support, mainly for organisations, but also for smaller ventures – check with your local arts board.

Working in a familiar genre can mean greater 'freedom' because the conventions are so well known that audiences can be introduced to new ideas on the back of familiar ones.

work 'in the style of' an existing producer and to begin by trying to understand all the conventions of a particular genre or style. If you want to go on and break with convention, it is useful to know which 'rules' need to be broken.

If you are clear in the aesthetic or the formal approach which you wish to adopt, you will find it much easier to explain what you want to do, both to the commissioner of the work and to the rest of your production team.

Schedule

How long have you got to complete the production process? Planning and preparation are going to be essential for a successful production, but even the best plans will come to nothing if the overall task is impossible. Calculate the time each part of the process will take and ensure that you know everything about the schedule from the outset. For instance, you may be required to show the unfinished work to your commissioner in order to confirm the inclusion of contentious material, but will that person be available when you reach the crucial decision-making stage? Can your **schedule** be adapted to cope with these problems?

Your schedule will distinguish different parts of the process and you will be able to plan when and where each can take place. Be careful, because some aspects of production are more time-dependent than others, e.g. video post-production always takes longer than you imagine. Some parts of the production process are dependent on other parts having been completed first, so, for instance, if you want titles on your video production which 'overlay' the images in the opening sequence, you must prepare them before you start editing – you can't add them afterwards. 'Managing the schedule' is one of the most important aspects of production and perhaps the least appreciated by beginners. Check that you know, at the outset, all the stages your production needs to go through and include sufficient 'recovery time' for each stage in case things go wrong.

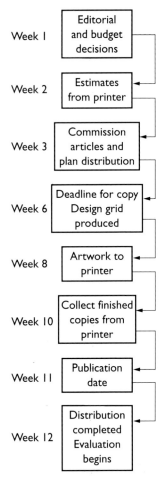

Week 1	Editorial and budget decisions
Week 2	Estimates from printer
Week 3	Commission articles and plan distribution
Week 6	Deadline for copy Design grid produced
Week 8	Artwork to printer
Week 10	Collect finished copies from printer
Week 11	Publication date
Week 12	Distribution completed Evaluation begins

Figure 6.1 Magazine production schedule

A schedule for magazine production

Imagine you are setting out to produce a fanzine or a small specialist magazine, say a sixteen-page, 'single colour' (the cheapest form of printing in which you choose just one ink colour) A4-size magazine. You have a number of friends who are going to contribute articles and you hope to distribute five hundred copies. All the DTP will be done by you and you will then take hard copy or a computer file to a printing company. How do you organise the schedule?

The first decision will be the date of publication. This is the date when you want readers to have the magazine in their hands – you need to set a date well before the first date for any events or 'forthcoming attractions' you might list. You can then work backwards to set deadlines for each stage of the production process. You might come up with something like the schedule in Figure 6.1.

This might seem like a long production schedule for a small magazine and you might well be able to shorten some stages – but even so, it will take you a couple of months to complete the process (in the professional magazine industry, each monthly magazine can take up to three months to produce so that staff are working on two or three magazines at any one time, with issues being planned while one is being copy-edited and another is being printed). Notice the constraints. You can't be sure about commissioning pieces if you don't know the editorial policy or how much space you will have to fill given the budget. If you want to sell advertising you must first give the advertiser a sense of what the publication will look like. Once the artwork (i.e. your designed pages) has gone to the printer, there isn't a lot you can do to affect the timing so Week 8, 'going to print' day, is very important.

If you publish a magazine during your course it will need a schedule like this and you will probably need a whole term to do the job properly.

Constraints

Time and money are both constraints, but there are several others. Availability of appropriate technology is an obvious constraint and so is the availability of **talent** (actors or presenters in an audiovisual production) or creative people on the production team. There may be constraints on the availability of inanimate resources as well – locations, props or archive materials.

Less obvious, but equally important, are constraints on **permissions** – the rights to use a piece of music, a photograph, a poem etc. – and restraints created by law: slander, libel, obscenity, the Official Secrets Act etc.

Your ability to develop a production in relation to the imposed constraints is a major factor in demonstrating creativity in a vocational context. 'Problem-solving' or 'working within constraints' is what defines the effective media producer. Sometimes, working within constraints produces the most interesting work.

Constraints and creativity in film production

In the early days of the Soviet Union, when the new state was being blockaded by the West, a shortage of film stock prompted experiments by Kuleshov in which he spliced together 'offcuts' of exposed film and discovered novel effects of juxtaposing images. This was later developed by Eisenstein, amongst others, into the celebrated Soviet 'montage' style. A modern echo of this 'discovery' were the early 1980s 'scratch videos' produced by young and poorly funded video editors who 'stole' clips from broadcast television in order to produce satirical comments on contemporary society (see 'Realisms', Chapter 16, on Eisenstein).

More recently, the director and cinematographer of *Se7en* (US 1995), David Fincher and Darius Khondji, produced an original 'look' for their film, partly as a result of various constraints. 'The reason it rains all of the time is that we only had Brad Pitt for 55 days, with no contingency. So we did it to stay on schedule, because we knew that if it ever really rained we would have been fucked … We decided we wouldn't build any flyaway walls. If the kitchen is only 12 feet, then hem him in. We live in an age when anything is possible, so it's always important to limit yourself. It's important the blinders you put on, what you won't say. I wanted to take an adult approach – not, "Oh wow, a Luma crane".' (David Fincher interviewed in *Sight and Sound*, January 1996, p. 24).

Figure 6.2 Morgan Freeman and Brad Pitt in a tight space in *Se7en*

Important health and safety issues

You may not think of media production work as being particularly dangerous, but *it can be* in certain circumstances and, like every other 'public' activity, it is covered by a legal obligation on you to protect both yourself and others from injury.

The best way to learn about specific media production hazards is to address them 'on the job'. Your lecturer should always make clear the fire exits from any accommodation you use and should outline the particular safety requirements when dealing with equipment. These include electrical connections, trailing cables, very hot and fragile lights, noxious chemicals in photography etc. If you aren't told about these things – *ask*. Remember that the legal obligation can fall on you – you have a right to be told. A good source of advice and information is often the appropriate union (e.g. BECTU for video), who may well have health and safety advisers. The technicians in your college should be well aware of potential hazards.

As a producer, you should be aware of some of the less obvious health and safety issues:

- *Stress* is a potential hazard for production personnel who are often under pressure to make decisions or to operate equipment quickly and efficiently. You will notice this in 'live' television or radio productions. Stress can build up and affect performance (which in turn could lead to 'unsafe' decisions).
- *Public liability* requires you to be very careful when out on location, where you might cause an obstruction with cameras, cables, lights etc. As well as seeking permission, you need to warn passers-by of the hazards.
- *Special effects* and *stunts* can add a great deal to video productions, but there is a danger that in the excitement of creating an effect, you forget about the dangers, especially in driving or attempting falls etc.
- *Lifting and moving*   In the frenzy of getting equipment to *where* you want it and then *how* you want it arranged, it is all too easy to strain your muscles with heavy or awkward objects (and sometimes to damage expensive equipment). Learn how to handle equipment properly and find the crew and the time to move it safely.

Negotiating a brief

Once you have prepared your ideas by considering the issues above, you are ready to try them out and 'pitch' them to a potential funder or a commissioner for a publisher (e.g. a broadcast television or radio company or a print publisher), perhaps in response to a 'tender document' such as the one in Figure 6.3. To do this effectively you will need to encapsulate the main points of want you want to do into an **outline**, preferably no more than a couple of sides of A4 paper.

An alternative, when you have an idea but there is no specific tender document, is to send in a **proposal** 'on spec'. A proposal will include an outline and an argument as to why it would be successful with a specific target audience or readership. You should address the proposal to the relevant commissioner or editor and it is sensible to study carefully which market a particular publisher targets. A proposal may also include a 'sample' of writing or script and will therefore be more substantial than a simple outline.

Many **proposals** to write articles or stories are rejected by magazines because they are clearly unsuited to the readership in terms of either content or style.

For more ideas about proposals for television see Holland (1997).

COMMISSIONING BRIEF – Ref No CI/F24

CHANNEL
BBC ONE

CLASSIFICATION
Observational Documentaries

DAY
Midweek/Weekend

SLOT
Pre- and post-watershed

EDITORIAL GUIDE
Overcrowding is the danger of this highly competitive and successful sector. New subjects and original treatments which extend and refresh the format are particularly sought. It is important to suit the treatment to the slot with a clear differentiation between pre- and post-watershed.

AUDIENCE
Available Audience   Minimum Audience Target:
Range: **20m – 25m**   **40% share: 9m – 11m+**

DURATION
30'

EPS PER STRAND
6 upwards

TOTAL SLOTS
80 – 100 slots

PROGRAMME EXAMPLES
Children's Hospital, Airport, Vets in Practice, Hotel, Holiday Reps, The Cruise, Neighbours at War

PRICE/COST INFORMATION – See also Introduction section 1.4

– Target price, net of BBC Worldwide or other third party investment, would be in the range of £65K – £80K per episode depending on subject matter but lower for runs of more than six.

– Filming on tape is assumed as the norm and a reduced price expected on longer runs. The editorial/production imperatives that require greater funding expenditure in the range would have to be clearly demonstrated.

– Investment could be in the range of £5K – £15K per episode depending on subject and domestic bias.

– Factual programmes in this classification would be considered low to medium cost. **Ideas fulfilling the Commissioning Brief but which require less than the target range due to innovative production techniques or use of resources will be given preferential consideration.**

COMMISSIONING BRIEF REF. NO: CI/F24

Figure 6.3   An example of a 1998 BBC tender document from 'BBC One Factual'

A term often used in television is **treatment**. The meaning of this term does vary. Sometimes it refers to the style or approach which will be taken to a particular programme idea and sometimes it is a full working through of ideas or a 'filling in' of the outline, describing what will happen. The production process may require an outline, which is developed into a treatment and finally into a production script.

The process of 'negotiating a brief' will lead to a point where you will be offered a deal with a set of conditions on cost, schedule etc. Be careful not to accept unrealistic deadlines – it always takes longer than you think. Note also that the commissioner will probably specify points at which you will need to report progress and allow the commissioner to suggest changes. You have a deal and a brief, but remember that, unless you are publishing the work yourself, the commissioner can always decide to shelve your work rather than publish it, so you will need to argue your case carefully throughout production.

Pre-production

Research

Sometimes a proposal will have come out of research – perhaps for another purpose. In this sense, research comes before the brief is agreed. Usually, research is a major component of 'pre-production'. There are two main types of research: primary and secondary. **Primary research** implies that the researcher is the first agent to collect and collate material. An interview is the clearest possible example of primary research – asking questions and obtaining responses which are 'original'. Interviews may be used to form the background material from which a script or an article could be written. Alternatively, the interviews may appear in the finished text, as in the traditional Sunday magazine profile of a prominent figure. A genre of film documentary has also developed where eye-witnesses describe what happened at the time. Such interviews are usually re-recorded for the production itself.

Other primary sources might be government records such as the register of births and deaths or the correspondence and personal papers of individuals or organisations. These are sometimes formally organised into 'archives' (see below).

'Deep' research, rather like the ethnographic studies carried out by academics, might begin by the researcher living in a community for some time and simply recording daily life. This is the kind of research novelists might undertake to 'get the feel' of a location.

In film and television research it is worth distinguishing between *content research* (understanding the background) and *production research* (finding things to use directly in the production, such as costumes, props, locations etc.).

ACTIVITY 6.1

Research sources

Next time there is a broadcast of a documentary series covering an historical period, check the credits for details of the research sources (if you have satellite or cable, try the Discovery Channel).

- How many different film archives have been used?
- Are there individuals who have contributed material?
- How many researchers are named?

Secondary research implies that someone else other than the researcher has collected and organised material and made it available for research. Secondary research takes place in a library or archive and/or uses compiled records such as reference books. Media production relies heavily on specialist archives, not just as a source of information but also as material to be used directly in a media product:

Picture libraries Many newspapers and magazines as well as television companies have an in-house picture library where they keep carefully filed copies of images they own (or where they have acquired reproduction rights), covering topics like famous personalities, important buildings, locations etc. These are then instantaneously available if a news story breaks. All photographs taken by staff reporters on a newspaper will be automatically filed for possible future use. These libraries represent important assets for the media corporations and can be sold or leased for considerable sums. In some cases such libraries have survived the deaths of the publications which created them and have become profit-earners in their own right.

The market for images is such that photographers have built up their own archives of standard shots (sunsets, cute babies etc.) which they offer as commercial library pictures. With the growth of CD technology and on-line services via the Internet, there are now many ways in which media producers can acquire high-quality images for advertising or promotion at a relatively low cost. At the moment the competition in the market place is still fairly cut-throat, but it is worth noticing that the 'international image market' is such that companies like Microsoft are carefully buying up the rights to an enormous range of images, all of which will eventually be available on CD – credit card account permitting. In all these cases, users of images will pay for different services (see the section on copyright, later in this chapter).

The distinction between **primary** and **secondary research** is not always clear-cut. Is a photograph in a newspaper archive secondary or primary? Once it has been 'collected' with other similar photographs in a book, it definitely becomes secondary. The distinction is really about whose interpretation of the material comes first.

Hulton-Deutsch Picture Library, one of the biggest photographic archives in the world, grows daily by receiving all the photographs taken by the Reuters International News Service. It reached its current size by acquiring other libraries such as those of the celebrated *Picture Post* magazine of the 1930s to 1950s and also the *Daily Herald* library of the same period.

Sound libraries 'Library sounds' – collections of mood music and sound effects at relatively low cost – are available on CD to be used by corporate producers via various licence agreements. Other audio recordings are owned by the broadcasters or the large recording companies. There is also the National Sound Archive which holds a collection of historic and representative recordings.

Regional film archives Your region may have established a film archive, possibly associated with a university or a library. Films made in the region by professionals and amateurs may be held, along with stills and production materials. Some material is being issued by archives (e.g. Scottish and North West Film Archives).

Film and video libraries Up until the 1940s film companies often threw their products away once their initial release was completed. Early television recordings often went the same way. Now they have recognised the value of their products and have begun to archive them carefully and in some cases have bought other collections as well.

Film archives have the advantage over video in that the basic technology has not changed over a hundred years and, provided that the film has survived physically, it is usually possible to make a viewing copy of any footage. Video formats change frequently and it is already proving difficult to replay some of the older formats because the players are no longer in working order.

The National Film and Television Archive provides a service for film students and researchers and other national and regional organisations have now begun to market their materials for educational and commercial use. Film research is a highly specialised business and the British Universities Film and Video Council publishes a guide for researchers.

ACTIVITY 6.2

Research project

Set yourself a research project aimed at collecting material for a magazine article. Choose something general like 'National Lottery winners' or 'medical stories'.

- Compile a cuttings library over a couple of weeks, looking through newspapers and magazines for text and photographs (look at a good spread of papers).
- Tape television or radio programmes or use a notebook to jot down programme details. Make sure you always record your source reference, including the names of photographers or the rights holders for images.
- At the end of your allotted time, review your material. Do you have enough material to help you generate ideas for an article?
- Have you found good images or quotes?
- Have you got all the references?

This is a good practice exercise for all media students – at some stage in your course you will probably have to do this as an assignment.

Recce

Good preparation is essential for effective media production, and before any audio or video or photography work takes place on location a production company will undertake a series of 'recces' (reconnaissance). These will include checks on electrical power sources (often broadcasters' needs are so great that they will bring their own generators), on access for people and equipment and on health and safety generally. Facilities such as changing rooms, refreshments and possibly press and public relations spaces are important too. These are the producer's main concerns. The director, camera and sound crews will also want to select locations for aesthetic reasons and to begin to build the constraints created by the location into the production schedule.

Film commissions Many UK cities and regions have recognised the economic benefits film and television productions can bring to the local economy and have set up offices to help producers find locations, crews and facilities and to sort out permissions. Liverpool and Yorkshire have been particularly successful – look in the *BFI Handbook* for a full list.

Figure 6.4 A studio production like this will require a crew of at least five – camera operator, floor manager, sound mixer, vision mixer and director to keep them in order. Prior to recording the lights will have had to be arranged and the 'talent' briefed

(Solihull College-Media Course) © Simon Derry

ACTIVITY 6.3

Locations

Take a close look at any film or television series (tape it so you can study it in detail) and carry out an analysis of the locations used.

- How much of it is shot in a studio, how much on location?
- List all the separate locations. Could you find substitute locations in your locality?
- Now consider the task of the producer. Think of your substitute locations: how would you organise the shooting so that you cut down travelling between locations?
- What kind of permissions do you think you would need for the locations you have chosen?

Design

Saul and Elaine Bass are famous as designers of title sequences for Hollywood, in particular for Alfred Hitchcock (including *Psycho*) and recently for Martin Scorsese. See Pat Kirkham, 'Looking for the Simple Idea', *Sight & Sound*, vol. 4, no. 2 (February 1994).

Every media product is 'designed'. Think of a couple of very different products – a magazine and a feature film. In both cases, an important member of the production team will be the Art Editor or Art Director. They are responsible for the obvious art and design elements in the products – the dramatic layout of pages and the use of illustrations, especially on the cover of a newsstand magazine, the stupendous sets of a Hollywood musical and the credit sequence of the film. But they also contribute to a much broader concept of design – the overall fitness of purpose and coherence of the media product. The opening credit sequence of a film, the choice of typeface in a magazine, are not just attractive and appropriate in themselves. They are designed to announce and complement the other features of the product.

You might want to think about a media product in the same way as one of those exquisitely crafted Japanese lacquered boxes or an Armani suit – whichever way you look at them as you turn them over, they present a beautifully finished surface. And when you use them for their intended purpose, they do the job effortlessly. Good design doesn't have to cost a fortune, though. A zippo lighter or a box of matches can be designed well and so can the supposedly insignificant media products, such as the continuity announcements and **idents** on television or the local football fanzine. And it isn't just in visual terms that we can detect design features. Radio programmes are designed as well and it will be quite apparent if the sound text is not coherent in its style and 'feel'. Good design means that products work well with users and that must be the first priority for media production.

See 'Production techniques' (Chapter 5) for more on design ideas. Note here that design issues need to be addressed at the preparation stage. Design will need to inform other aspects of production and to develop from the initial ideas about the product.

Production

This is the stage when the main work is done on the material which will appear in the finished product – see 'Production techniques' (Chapter 5) for details. It is useful at this point to discuss who does what and how the roles are defined and integrated as a part of a production team.

The production unit and production roles

The units which you form to undertake production tasks in education or training are not that different from their industrial counterparts. Even in very large media corporations, creative staff work in relatively small teams and in some sectors a production company might be just a couple of people, who hire in freelances to work on specific jobs. In every case we can identify a close-knit production team, who work together over a period of time and who are augmented at particular stages in production by larger groups of people who perform relatively routine tasks in an industrial process.

Let's take our previous example of a small specialist magazine and look at its production in more detail. Perhaps this is one of many titles produced by a large international publishing group such as IPC or perhaps it is a private venture. Either way, the 'production team' may comprise only a few full-time people such as the editor and an assistant, a couple of 'staff writers' and perhaps an art editor. Outside this circle will be others who, while committed to the magazine, may also be involved in other titles. The same commitment (i.e. to the individual title) will not be found in the printers and distributors who deal with many different titles over the year. Each production unit is likely to include the following job roles:

Producer Somebody must take charge of the production as the 'organiser of scarce resources' and the financial controller. This role will also usually require an overview of the purpose of the production and the creative intent. The term is used in both film and television and radio and sound recording, but there are differences. In film production, the producer is very much the provider of budget and the organiser of resources – in most cases the creative control of the project lies with the director, although

A good example of the creative power of the producer in television is the rise of Phil Redmond, who gained a profile first as the writer who developed *Grange Hill* in the 1970s, but consolidated his position by forming Mersey Television and producing *Brookside* for Channel 4.

'Each picture has some sort of rhythm which only the director can give it. He has to be like the captain of a ship' (Fritz Lang from *Halliwell's Filmgoer's Book of Quotes* (1978)).

Time-based media a term used mainly by practitioners with art and design backgrounds to distinguish television, film and radio from still photography. *Lens-based media* brings together film, television and photography, but, with the convergence of digital production, *imaging media* may be the new term.

Refer back to Activity 6.1 and compare a low-budget and prestige documentary in terms of the amount of research required to mount the programme successfully.

there are some very 'hands-on' producers (including well-known directors who retain the producer role themselves – delegating some tasks to assistants). In radio and television, the producer is also usually the creative force behind a series. In sound recording too, the producer might be seen as a creative force. In publishing, the same role is likely to be shared by an editor and a production manager.

Director or editor This role is about *creative* control – making decisions during the course of the production and maintaining a clear idea of the form and style of the product. In **time-based media** such as film, television or radio, the director is the co-ordinator of the creative process, literally directing the crew and the talent. In broadcasting, the creative controller tends to be termed an editor when the programme material is news or current affairs. The editor of a newspaper or magazine tends to oversee creative and production manager roles. The role of the director raises interesting questions about the managerial style of the decision taker. The director or editor has to take decisions – 'the buck stops here'.

Researcher (See the Research section above.) Every production needs some research, but not always a separate researcher. Most research is 'background' – the checking of information or the compilation of information and ideas on a specific topic. Some production research requires special skills and knowledge, firstly in the general academic skills of using and checking sources, secondly in relation to a specialist subject (such as military history).

Archives can be very specialised, and film, picture or sound researchers may be seen as specialised roles, perhaps undertaken by freelances or small research companies.

Finding contestants for *Blind Date* or guests for a talk show would also be seen as 'research', but here the skills are rather different. They may involve developing a 'feel' for what will be televisual, what will be popular, what will be a ratings winner. They may also include the ability to charm or cajole reluctant performers into appearing (for the smallest fee). This aspect of research may be performed by a production assistant – someone much closer to the producer role than the autonomous researcher.

Investigative newspaper reporters might also be seen as researchers. They might also write up their own reports – something denied to most broadcast researchers.

Creative personnel This is a loose term and might include everybody involved in the production, but here we are referring to those members of the team who are charged with making specific contributions based on specialist skills such as writing, camerawork, design etc. The task for creative personnel is to carry out the wishes of the producer or director in a professional manner, contributing to the overall production as effectively as possible. Conflicts are possible if the individual contributors wish to 'do their own thing'. There are interesting questions about authorship here – once a scriptwriter has completed work on a film, does she or he have the right to be consulted if the producer or director then decides to cut from, add to or alter the finished script?

The director or producer will work hard to maintain a good working relationship with all the creative staff, consulting them (which means explaining *and* listening) on particular aspects of their work and perhaps incorporating their suggestions into the overall production. The director's role requires her or him to maintain the coherence of the whole media text, so if a particular contribution is threatening to upset the balance it needs to be corrected, even if, on its own, it represents a very effective and entertaining piece of work. Here are the seeds of conflict, especially in the supercharged atmosphere of most production processes.

The success of a creative team will depend on good working relationships. This doesn't necessarily mean that everyone in the team likes each other, but they must respect each other's work and be prepared to submit to the 'general will' of the team and the ultimate decision of the acknowledged leader. The most successful producers tend to be those who have built up and maintained a creative team which has lasted several years (see 'Producing in the studio system', Case study 7).

Technical personnel Somebody must be responsible for the operation of equipment and for its efficient performance (i.e. they must maintain and set up equipment so that it performs to manufacturers' specifications). Variously described as 'technicians' or 'engineers', these people ensure that creative ideas can be realised within the constraints which the technology demands. Some technical operations such as maintenance and servicing may be required even when no productions are scheduled.

It is a fine line which separates the 'creative' from the 'technical', and many media practitioners combine both roles. For example, a *director of photography* (DP) on a feature film is very much part of the creative team, responsible for the overall 'look' of the film and the supervision of camera and lighting operations. Operation of the equipment will be handled by the **camera crew**, but the DP, who will have begun a career as part of the technical crew, will select lenses and perhaps even override equipment specifications and solve technical problems, based on long experience. Some media practitioners are seen as possessing 'craft' rather

Camera crew on a film set will normally comprise an operator and assistants to look after loading, focus pulling and camera movements (the job of the *grip*) etc. An electrical crew led by a *gaffer* with a *best boy* will set up lighting under the DP's supervision. See the diagram of the film production process in 'Industries' (Chapter 22).

than technical skills – implying a more personal, 'creative' skill with technology, beyond that of 'operation'.

In an ideal situation, creative staff will have sufficient knowledge of technical operations to be able to communicate effectively with the technical team. In turn, technical staff will be able to recognise the creative opportunities which their equipment makes possible and to advise accordingly. In the production unit, an integrated creative and technical team will generally produce the best results. Often, however, the technical team may be made up of freelances or in-house staff who are allocated to production units on a rota basis. The ability to communicate effectively and to develop working relationships quickly then becomes even more important.

The need for close communication between creative and technical teams raises two issues about media production training which are important for all media students:

- It helps if all production staff know something about each aspect of production – too much specialisation means that effective communication becomes more difficult.
- It isn't necessarily those with the most creative ideas or the best technical prowess who make the best production team members – good working relationships are also important and training should be geared towards development of the appropriate personal and organisational skills.

Freelance The term goes back to the period when medieval knights returning from the Crusades would roam Europe offering their services to different rulers.

Freelances The **freelance** is a long-standing figure in many parts of the media industries. At one time the term referred to relatively well-known figures such as high-profile writers or journalists who were in such demand that they could afford to offer their services to whoever would pay, rather than relying on the security of permanent employment. This usage continues and now includes television personalities as well as film directors. However, the big growth is in the number of rather less well-known media workers who would probably prefer to be 'employed' as they were in the past by broadcast television companies or daily newspapers, but who now find themselves made redundant and perhaps offered work on a short-term contract basis – often for a series of articles or work on a television series. Whether this should be called 'freelance work' in the strict sense is debatable (they may in some cases be little better off than the notoriously badly treated 'homeworkers'), but in the film, video and broadcast industry freelances now constitute more than half the total workforce.

Freelances pose problems for the continuity of the production team and they are less likely to be followers of a 'house style'. On the other hand, they may bring new ideas and ways of working to a team. In practice, freelances might end up working for a particular production unit on a fairly regular basis so this might not be a great change. What is likely, however, is a gradual breakdown of the 'institutional' ethos of some of the large media corporations like the BBC and a reliance on more generic output (i.e. an industry 'standard') from the host of smaller independent companies (see 'Institutions' and 'Independents and alternatives', Chapters 26 and 28).

As a media student you should note that in your own productions it is often possible to 'buy in' some freelance help from students on another course who may have specific expertise (especially in areas like design). Also, if you are looking for employment in the media industries, you should prepare yourself for possible freelance status. A good start is to begin preparing your portfolio of completed production work as soon as possible, keeping a CV up-to-date and looking for opportunities to gain experience and to acquire a wide range of skills. Freelances have to manage their own financial affairs and actively seek work – it is a very different life from that of a paid employee who has to worry only about doing what she or he is told and then waiting for the salary cheque to appear in a bank account. Many higher education courses now include units on business studies, personal finance, portfolio management and CV-writing which are designed to help the potential freelance to survive.

Administrative personnel Media students are often told about the difficulty of obtaining employment in 'the industry' and the example of starting 'at the bottom'. Making the tea or being a 'runner' are quoted as the lowest entry point. At the other end of the scale, the accountant is sometimes seen as the villain, not only for curtailing creativity through budgetary control but for being 'boring' as well. Making tea and doing the books are of course essential elements in any enterprise, and media production is no exception.

A large-scale production like a feature film will involve hundreds of personnel with an enormous variety of skills and qualifications (see Figure 22.1 in 'Industries', Chapter 22). Even a small production will need an 'office'. For convenience we have termed these 'administrative' in that they are primarily concerned with making sure that production can go ahead with all the needs of the creative and technical teams catered for. Again, we can distinguish between administrative personnel who are integral to the production team – very often in roles as the extra arms and legs of producers – and those who are brought in as needed, either as freelances or from some central, in-house, agency.

Some roles may be termed 'organisational' rather than administrative in that they are directly concerned with the operation of the production process. The floor manager in a television studio or the continuity role in feature film production are good examples of such important roles where an understanding of the production process is central. It is also worth pointing out that while the skills necessary for the other administrative roles are generalised rather than specific, the roles do allow new personnel to pick up a great deal of knowledge about the production process.

Figure 6.5 Be prepared for your stint before the microphone!

(Solihull College) © Simon Derry

Presenters One aspect of production work that many of us fear is presenting – speaking on radio or television (especially direct to camera) or introducing events at screenings or exhibitions. No matter how embarrassed you feel, you should try it a couple of times for the experience and so that you have some idea about what presenters feel in the situations which you might create for them as writer or director. If you are going to become a presenter, then you will need to seek out specialist advice on how to train your voice, how to breathe, how to use a microphone and how to read a script. You will also want to study a range of professionals (not just one, or you might end up a mimic).

If you are a writer, the most important thing to remember is to provide the presenter with 'spoken language'. A speech may look great on paper, but it may sound laboured when read out. If you can't find a presenter amongst the other media students, look elsewhere, just as you would for actors. Because you study the media it doesn't necessarily mean you want to appear as the 'talent'.

Production roles in education and training So what should you take from these role descriptions in terms of your own education and training? First, wide experience of different production contexts will help to develop your theoretical understanding, and your preparation for 'post-entry' training in any specific production role. Try as many roles as possible. You may have thought that being a writer was your dream, only to discover that you have a real flair for sound recording and that the radio studio gives you a buzz.

Copyright and permissions

Media products are often referential or intertextual, making use of previously recorded material. In a highly commercial industry, almost anything that has any kind of commercial potential – i.e. it could be used in another publication – will be 'owned' in terms of the rights for reproduction.

If the reproduction rights on a work have lapsed (which in Europe means seventy years after the author's death) and have not been renewed, the work passes into the **public domain** and anyone can reproduce it without charge. There is a difference, however, between the work of art and the physical media product. For instance, most nineteenth-century novels are now in the public domain, and this means that any publisher can sell a new edition of Dickens etc. But the 'Penguin edition' will remain in copyright as a printed text – you cannot simply photocopy it. If you want to use an image in a magazine article, you will need to do three things: get a copy of the original photograph (you may need to pay a fee for a 10 x 8 inch print, the preferred size); obtain permission from the rights holder; and probably pay a further reproduction fee based on the nature of your publication, the size of the image on the page and the position of that page in the publication (you pay most for the front cover).

Audiovisual recordings can involve you in several different sets of 'permissions' and rights issues. Say you want to use a recording of a popular song in a video programme. There are three potential rights holders here. First the person who wrote the song will want a 'reproduction fee'; next, the singer needs payment for reproduction of the performance and finally the record label wants a fee for reproduction of their specific recording. In practice two of these may be dealt with by the same agency.

A conversation about permissions for material in this book: 'I'm trying to get permission to use a few stills from the Creek ad for Levi's jeans … $5,000 each for the last educational publisher in the US? We need to ask everyone involved in the ad? Does that include the horse? He has an agent?' (This last bit is a joke – but only just.)

The industry has developed specific paperwork for media producers to use to request permissions – usually producers don't buy a whole song but only a few seconds. One solution for small producers is to use 'library music', specifically written and recorded for audiovisual productions and catalogued on CDs according to themes. A producer buys the CD and then pays a set fee for a track. This is usually cheaper and less administratively complex than using well-known pieces. Use it carefully, though, as overfamiliar library music can sound bland.

Post-production

Once the main material has been produced, or 'found' and collated, it must be shaped into the final product. This involves several different activities.

Public domain and digital technology   Digital versions of images and text (and software) are easy to distribute and copy. Public domain (PD) material is distributed free of charge as long as the distributor does not attempt to make a profit. 'Shareware' allows products to be used free, but business users are expected to pay a small fee.

Music rights   Performers' rights are handled by the Performing Rights Society (PRS). Recordings are handled by the Mechanical Copyright Protection Society (MCPS). PPL handles Phonographic Performance Licences for use by broadcasters etc.

Authors' rights are negotiated by the Society of Authors and the Publishers' Association, and copying fees are collected by the Author Licensing and Collecting Society.

Figure 6.6   The edit suite is where a video production is shaped and structured. This is a nonlinear suite using Media 100 hardware and software

Rewriting and editing

It's very unlikely that you will get your production right first time. Sections in this book have gone through several versions – sometimes altering radically, sometimes just a tweak. During your academic career you have probably suffered from constant pressure from teachers to check your work and, even when you think you've finished, to go back and rewrite parts or even the whole of your work. If you took that advice and got into good habits, you are now going to reap your reward.

Rewriting shouldn't be seen as simply a process of spotting mistakes and correcting them. It should also be a creative process – material is 'shaped' during production. Both the original writer and the editor will be involved in trying to work on the script or text. It is worth reminding yourself here that editing is a constructive process, not just a 'cutting out' of the bad bits. It is also time-consuming, and a sensible schedule will take rewrites into account. Do be careful about labelling each version of your text, especially when working on a computer means that you could create several versions of the same picture or text extract in a few minutes – there is nothing more frustrating than finding that, when you want to go back to a previous version, you can't easily distinguish which is which.

Editing is usually carried out by someone else, other than the writer or director. This means that it is important to establish good communication within the team. There has been a tendency to think of print editing and audiovisual editing as rather different activities. The

A good slogan for you: 'Writing is rewriting'.

move to digital production, using a computer interface, means that such differences are disappearing and all forms of editing now involve structuring the text and selecting the most appropriate material to be juxtaposed (Figure 6.6).

Copy-editing is a specialist editing role in print production. It ensures that the raw text is checked for spelling mistakes, inaccurate information and adherence to house style. A similar aspect of video editing might be a check to ensure that colour grading was matched on separate video sources. **Sub-editing** is a specific newspaper production activity in which experienced staff cut stories to fit the space available and write headlines and captions.

Special effects and graphics are prepared and added to programmes at the editing stage. In print production, the typesetter will attempt to combine text and graphics according to the laid-down design grid.

Proofing

When you get very wrapped up in a production project it is sometimes difficult to be objective about your own work. Sometimes it is even difficult to see what is there at all and this is where a 'proof reader' comes in. Their job is simply to spot unintentional errors. Ideally, someone who proofs not only has a sharp eye (or ear) but knows something about the subject as well. Authors are usually supplied with proof copies of their work to check.

Now, Voyager is a famous Hollywood melodrama, starring Betty Davis. In a recent American film magazine, an advertisement for film soundtracks listed two separate films, *'Now'* and *'Voyager'* under a 'classics' heading.

'Proofs' also refers to draft copies of print documents required to check the correct colours to be printed.

Test marketing or previewing

If you are unsure about your product in some way (perhaps the design features are not quite right or you simply panic about your great idea), it may be possible to test a draft version of the product on a small selected group of readers and see what kind of a response you get. This isn't foolproof, and you could select the wrong test group. Some might argue as well that you shouldn't be frightened of making mistakes and that the previewing policy leads to very bland products.

Sunset Boulevard (US 1950) is narrated by a corpse floating in a swimming pool. Director Billy Wilder originally opened with two corpses discussing the story in a morgue, but the Illinois preview audience thought that was too much (according to Otto Friedrich in *City of Nets*).

Finishing

The most successful media products offer the audience a special pleasure which derives from a quality 'finish'. This means that presentation is as good as it can be within the constraints of the format and the medium. Good finish means that your video begins from black with music and titles fading up smoothly in sync. Titles are accurate and carefully designed to complement the visuals. If you have a great set of photographic prints, it does matter how you present them. A good display with thought given to lighting and carefully printed captions or catalogue will enhance the experience for your audience. This should be the final production stage before the product is distributed for the eager public.

Distribution and exhibition

If you don't present your product to your audience directly, you will need some form of distribution. Other chapters stress that in the media industries this can be the most important part of the production process. You don't want to produce a magazine only to discover that nobody gets to read it or to broadcast a radio programme which nobody hears. Student productions can get a wide audience if distribution is organised in good time. Check back on the magazine schedule at the start of the chapter, which suggests organising the distribution at an early stage – perhaps finding shops, pubs, cinemas etc. who would be willing to distribute copies (you can afford this if you sell advertising to cover your costs). Several schools and colleges have taken the opportunity under the radio broadcasting legislation to apply for a Restricted Service Licence (RSL), allowing them to broadcast for a couple of days in a local area. Video productions can be timed to be ready for the various festivals of student work. If you have any ambitions to become a media producer, here is your starting point to get your work recognised.

Exhibition

This stage is relevant only for film and video or photography, but it is very important to present your work to an audience in the best possible conditions – it is the equivalent of 'finishing' in print production. For a video screening you will want to make sure your audience are comfortable and have good 'sight-lines' to see the screen. The sound and picture quality must be as good as possible with the monitor or video projector set properly and sound levels appropriate for the acoustics in the room. You will want the tape to start at exactly the right place, so set it up carefully beforehand. Would the audience benefit from some screening notes?

Think about your own experience of going to the cinema. What do you expect in terms of the best viewing environment?

Audience feedback

At the beginning of this chapter we made the point that media production is meaningful only if you know the audience to whom you hope to present your work. It follows that your production isn't finished until it has reached the intended audience and you have gained some feedback. Only then will you be able to evaluate the production decisions you have made. You will also be able to use the feedback material to inform your next production – audience feedback supplies the link which helps to make production a cyclical process.

There are numerous ways in which you can gauge audience reactions to your work. Sitting in with an audience can be useful – when do they go quiet and concentrate? When do they fidget and yawn? What kind of comments do they make to each other? You can formalise this by organising some form of discussion after a screening, or when everyone has read through your magazine. Get someone else to chair the session and be prepared to be open with your audience about what you were trying to do. If all of this sounds a little daunting, you can always devise a simple audience feedback questionnaire which can be given to everyone when they first come into contact with the product. Audiences will be happy to fill in questionnaires if the questions are appropriate and if the spaces for answers are inviting. If you are lucky, the questionnaire will produce a greater number of responses and perhaps a wider range of respondents than the face-to-face discussion.

What will you expect from your audience feedback? We all like praise and to know that what we have produced has given people pleasure, but more important we want confirmation of what has worked and what has caused confusion or even misunderstanding. You should not be dismayed if audiences have read your work in very different ways (in 'Narratives', (Chapter 3) we have emphasised that this is a function of the reading process). Every response is useful and will make you more aware of the range of possibilities.

After studying the audience feedback, the final task is to undertake your own evaluation of your production experience. In order to help you do this, your tutor will probably want to organise a formal 'debriefing'.

Debriefing

Most media production courses operate a procedure whereby you are briefed before an activity on what you are required to do and what constraints you face. You are then debriefed at the end of the activity. This is an important part of the process – perhaps the most important part, because it is here that you work out what you have learned and identify your strengths and weaknesses. Most debriefings are group discussions – either everyone has worked individually on the same activity or work has been organised in groups.

Debriefings work best when everyone is committed to the activity and is supportive of each other. This means accepting criticism from the other group members and in turn making positive, constructive comments about their performance. This isn't easy. If the production has not gone well you might be sorely tempted to 'get your blame in first' or to defend your own actions. If it has gone well you might be tempted simply to tell each other 'you were great'. Neither of these approaches is particularly helpful. If it worked well, why was that? If it didn't, can you work out why, without apportioning blame? The likelihood is that you will have to follow-up the debriefing with an evaluation, so you need answers to these questions.

Learning from production

We hope these notes will be helpful, but there is no substitute for production work itself. Get involved as much as you can. Make things with a view to finding out about the production process as well as reaching an audience. Listen and learn from other producers. Above all, reflect on what you have done and try to do better next time. And have fun.

References and further reading

Dimbleby, Nick, Dimbleby, Richard and Whittington, Ken (1994) *Practical Media*, London: Hodder & Stoughton.
NCVQ (1996) *Working in Print*, London: NCVQ.
(See also the various textbooks published to cover Intermediate and Advanced GNVQ courses, and in particular the production units.)

An accessible book with plenty of good ideas on relatively low-budget video production is:
Harding, Thomas (1997) *The Video Activist Handbook*, London: Pluto Press.

Rather more mainstream and industry-based is:
Jarvis, Peter (1996) *The Essential Television Handbook*, Oxford: Focal Press.

Job roles in film and television are well covered in:
Langham, Josephine (1996, 2nd edition) *Lights Camera Action!: Careers in Film, Television and Radio*, London: BFI.

For background on production organisation in different media sectors see the Routledge Handbook Series:

Brierley, Sean (1995) *The Advertising Handbook*.

Holland, Patricia (1997) *The Television Handbook*.

Keeble, Richard (1998, 2nd edition) *The Newspapers Handbook*.

Wilby, Peter and Conroy, Andy (1994) *The Radio Handbook*.

Useful reference sources, published annually:

BFI Film and Television Handbook.

The Guardian Media Guide.

The Writers' and Artists' Year Book, A.C. Black.

The Writer's Handbook, Macmillan.

Technical manuals, dealing with different aspects of production and different technologies are published by:

BBC Enterprises

The full range of material can be seen in the BBC shop opposite Broadcasting House on Portland Place, London W1. Publications include guides to scriptwriting and Training Manuals which are listed in a catalogue obtainable from BBC Television Training, BBC Elstree Centre, Clarendon Road, Borehamwood, Herts WD6 1TF.

Focal Press

This imprint specialises in media technical handbooks and manuals, in particular the Media Manuals series. A catalogue can be obtained from: Focal Press, Linacre House, Jordan Hill, Oxford OX2 8DP. (Most of these manuals are written for professional or semi-professional media users.)

Useful addresses

BECTU, 111 Wardour Street, London W1V 4AY.

Community Media Association, 5 Paternoster Square, Sheffield S1 2BX.

Mechanical Copyright Protection Service, Elgar House, 41 Streatham High Road, London SW16 1ER – information and advice available on request.

Performing Rights Society, 29–33 Berners Street, London W1P 4AA – information available from the Public Affairs Department.

7 / Case study: Producing in the studio system

The Hollywood studio system offers an example of a fully mature media production system which has been documented in detail. It therefore provides a useful model against which to measure other forms of production practice.

Defining the system

The terms 'Hollywood' and 'studio system' tend to be used glibly and it is important to try to be more rigorous in definition. The studio system in its full form lasted for no more than twenty years. It had its origins in the 1920s but did not reach maturity until the early 1930s. The full system operated until the beginning of the 1950s and then gradually broke up over the next decade. The 'golden age' of the studio was 1930–50. Historians are now likely to refer to this period as 'classical Hollywood' (see Neale and Smith 1998).

During this time 'Hollywood' (a term applied to both the outer suburb of Los Angeles and the **mainstream** American film industry) was dominated by five studios:

- Paramount
- MGM
- Twentieth Century Fox
- Warner Bros
- RKO.

These were known as the **majors** or the 'big five'. Universal and Columbia were the 'minors'. An eighth 'studio' of note was United Artists, but UA owned no facilities and was effectively a financier and distributor. With Universal and Columbia, UA formed the 'little three'. There were a number of other smaller studios and distributors (Disney, Republic and Monogram are the best known), but the industry recognised the eight majors and minors as dominant because they alone could guarantee access to 'first-run' cinemas (i.e. those which took new films only) for all their product.

The relative market positions of the studios is shown in Table 7.1.

Table 7.1 Gross domestic film rentals from distribution within the United States of ten motion picture companies, 1939

Studio	$ million	%
Loew's (MGM)	43.2	21.5
Twentieth Century Fox	33.2	16.5
Warner Bros	28.9	14.4
Paramount	28.2	14.0
RKO	18.2	9.1
Universal	14.2	7.0
United Artists	13.5	6.7
Columbia	13.2	6.5
Republic	6.2	3.1
Monogram	2.5	1.2
Total	201.3	100.0

Source: Mae D. Huettig, 'The Motion Picture Industry Today', in Balio (1985)

The features of the system

The studio system was a **mature oligopoly** of **vertically integrated** companies (see 'Industries',

98

Chapter 22, for definition of these terms). The majors made their money from exhibiting their own films in their own cinemas. To this extent, the great cinema chains of Loew's and Paramount were as much part of the system as the studios in Hollywood. The cinemas demanded a product to show, and the job of the studios was to produce it efficiently and punctually. The distributor arms of the majors promoted the films and the stars to the public (see 'Making stars', Case study 25). We will concentrate on the studio production end.

Division of labour

The system was based on a strict **division of labour** – the dominant mode of capitalist manufacture at the time, often associated with the production line of Henry Ford. The theory was that organising workers so that they concentrated on one or two skilled or semi-skilled tasks would mean that they would contribute more (and more efficiently) to the production process than if they performed a wide range of less specialised tasks. This might mean that their work was more repetitive and that they had less 'control' over their role in production (clearly an important consideration in a 'creative industry').

Unit-based production

The studio owned land on which were based the **sound stages**, administrative offices, preview theatres and writers' accommodation. Directors, crews and stars were all contracted to the studio and production was organised by salaried producers. In some studios there were **units** set up within the system so that a producer got to work with the same director and crew over several films. Integration meant that the studio had to provide its distribution arm and its cinema chain with a constant flow of A and B pictures, serials, newsreels and cartoons, fifty-two weeks a year. The distinction between an **A picture** (90 minutes or more run time, a budget of $500,000) and a B (under 90 minutes, budget $200,000) was very clearly defined and offers us a useful guide to the overall approach.

Figure 7.1   Shooting *Becky Sharp* in 1935. This was the first Technicolor feature (note the enormous camera) and was made by an independent company with the support of RKO Radio Pictures

The task of the studio boss was to utilise capital equipment and contracted staff to the full. If work could not be found inside the studio, facilities and stars would be hired out to another studio or to one of the independent producers such as Samuel Goldwyn or David Selznick. During the 1930s, they might also be sent over to England, where several of the studios opened a British operation to make cheap films as part of their quota of 'British' productions (necessary to satisfy UK government regulations).

Specialist product

This constant **production cycle** necessitated the development of particular methods of organisation and specialisation in particular products. The most obvious development was that of **genre**-based production and a concomitant studio style or 'look'. In modern Hollywood it is not possible to distinguish a film made by an individual studio. Audiences in the 1940s and film historians in the 1990s, however, would have no difficulty in distinguishing a Warners picture from an MGM feature of the same period during the studio era. They would recognise:

- *the genre* – downbeat and gritty for Warners, glamorous and glossy for MGM

- *the style* that went with the genre: low-key lighting for Warners, high-key for MGM
- *the contract stars* – Gable and Garbo for MGM, Cagney and Davis for Warners. The directors and other creative personnel would also be recognisable; Michael Curtiz or William Wellman at Warners, George Cukor or King Vidor at MGM.

Unit production at Warner Bros

Warner Bros operation in the late 1930s is a good example of tightly organised production, and it is well documented in two books, Thomas Schatz's *The Genius of the System* (1989 and 1998) and Nick Roddick's *A New Deal in Entertainment: Warner Brothers in the 1930s* (1983). Schatz places the producer at the centre of the system and identifies a 'production unit' system at Warners.

Half the fifty-plus features per year which the studio produced were classed as A features and were divided up between different genre-star production units. One unit concentrated on '**biopics**' of important historical figures such as Louis Pasteur who 'discovered' inoculation, or the controversial nineteenth-century novelist Emile Zola – both characters fighting authority and in many ways in line with heroes from other genres in this 'socially conscious' studio. Little remembered now, these films were both very popular and critically well-received with Paul Muni playing the lead, William Dieterle directing, Tony Gaudio in charge of cinematography and Henry Blanke as producer.

The biopic team had great success with *The Story of Louis Pasteur* in 1936, with Muni winning the Best Actor Oscar. He was then loaned to RKO while the production team made *The White Angel* – another biopic, this time about Florence Nightingale. The team would also be used by other units, and in 1936–7 Dieterle directed a total of eight pictures. In the meantime, work began on the script for *The Life of Emile Zola*, which went into production as soon as Muni and the crew were free. Shooting was scheduled for forty-two days but in the event ran over by ten. However, post-production was completed very quickly and the film premiered just three months later.

> Now, I could refuse to do it. All Warners directors could refuse three scripts. But here is how it worked: you get a story you don't like – out it goes; you get one you like even less – so there's your second refusal; then you get one that's even worse, and you begin to think that the first one isn't so bad. That's how it worked. They were so clever at Warners. They knew there were many ways to skin a cat.
>
> (Director William Dieterle, interviewed in *Velvet Light Trap*, no. 15, 1975)

Dieterle went on to make three more biopics with the same unit before leaving Warner Brothers for RKO in 1941.

William Dieterle

A look at Dieterle's career tells us a great deal about how the studio system worked in the 1930s. He began as an actor in the Berlin theatre of the 1920s, working with the great theatre director Max Reinhardt before moving into film, first as an actor and later as a director. He did some work for Warners' German operation and in 1930 he was called to Hollywood to produce 'synchronisations' – foreign-language versions of new productions designed to maintain Hollywood's position in the world market after the coming of sound.

Learning to reshoot whole features in around ten days, using the same sets and costumes, was good experience and he was contracted to work on English language pictures very quickly. Dieterle's subsequent work is interesting evidence for the industrial production versus creativity argument. He was popular with the studio bosses because he was efficient and kept to budget and this meant that he was perhaps forced to take on poor material and produce work with little apparent value. But also it meant that he worked consistently, that he brought his theoretical knowledge and his understanding of lighting and set design into a fruitful partnership with director of photography Tony Gaudio and art directors such as Anton Grot. The studio invested in these creative teams over a long period and the end result was arguably a more consistent quality product than is now possible.

A day in the studio during the making of *Anthony Adverse*, a prestige costume drama released in 1936. (Taken from material presented by Nick Roddick.)

- Day begins with the arrival on the backlot (eighteenth-century street scene) of the prop men at 7.00 a.m. followed by the camera crew and the wardrobe, hair and make-up staff at 7.30. The rest of the crew, including the director, have arrived by 8.15.
- The principal cast members arrive and begin rehearsing at 8.20 and the first shot is completed by 8.35.
- Shooting then carries on until lunchtime (12.45) and restarts an hour later (although the crew take only half an hour for lunch) finishing for 'supper' at 3.40. The cast do not return for the evening, but the crew go on to complete a number of night street scenes between 6.30 and 11.00 p.m. when the day officially ends.

All of these details were meticulously recorded on the 'Daily Production and Progress Report'. Everyone was timed on and off the set. A note at the foot of the report states that any delays caused by late arrival of artists must be recorded and an explanation given. Sheets like this are still in use on the set.

Around four minutes of acceptable footage was achieved on a typical day. The 136-minute picture (excessively long for the period) was completed in seventy-two days.

The continuity system

An important feature of the studio system was the development of particular narrative styles and techniques which Bordwell and Thompson (1994) define as **continuity editing** or the *continuity system*. In 'Narratives', 'Ideologies' and 'Realisms' (Chapters 3, 12 and 16) we look at the importance of this system in setting up audience readings of narratives which became 'transparent' in that they disguised the means of their own construction. Techniques were developed for relating *cause and effect* and moving the narrative along economically without drawing attention to themselves. They also had an industrial production line function in laying down continuity rules such as 'not **crossing the line**' or **shot**/reverse shot for showing a dialogue exchange (see 'Narratives', Chapter 3, for explanation of these terms).

These 'rules' were first introduced in the 1910s and 1920s but finally developed into a definable system during the 1930s (many had to be re-cast or introduced for the first time after the coming of sound and the problems with early sound-recording equipment). If ruthlessly enforced they could speed up the production process. There was no need to agonise over each shot and think about all the various options for camera angles, framings and movement – there was an accepted way to make a Hollywood feature.

There is also some evidence that studios imposed rules in order to emphasise what they believed to be selling points for the picture, such as close-ups of stars. Studio heads were also conscious that some techniques, e.g. using cranes or long tracking shots, were more expensive and more difficult to get right. Consequently they tried to curtail their use.

The best source for material on the continuity system is Bordwell, Staiger and Thompson (1985). What appears to be clear is that there was a general understanding of a system which operated at every studio. There were, however, different interpretations of and attitudes towards it. Some studio bosses demanded that the same scene should be shot from several angles so that they

Figure 7.2 John Ford and crew at work on *How Green Was My Valley* for Twentieth Century Fox. This 1941 film was feted for its re-creation of a 1900 Welsh mining village on the studio lot

could select the most appropriate take at the post-production stage. Others allowed the more respected directors to shoot only one way (i.e. the way the director wanted to see the edited scene). John Ford is perhaps the best-known example of a director who 'edited in the camera' in this way.

(See Williams (1994) and Salt (1992) for a sustained critique of the importance attached by Bordwell, Thompson and others to continuity 'rules'.)

Institutional developments

The majors recognised themselves as 'the industry' and formed the the MPPDA (the Motion Pictures Producers and Distributors of America), the forerunner of today's **MPAA**. They set up their own censorship system (the Hays Code) and lobbied Washington to prevent legislation against their oligopoly power. This was a closed system, and Douglas Gomery described the majors in this period as being 'like a chronically quarrelsome, but closely-knit, family' (Gomery 1986).

Analysing the value of the system

We have identified several common features of production in the studio era and we can add a few more

to make a useful summary:

- vertically integrated companies undertook production, distribution and exhibition
- ownership and control of studios rested with companies whose main business was movies (although it is important to note that exhibition contributed more profits than production)
- continuous production of a range of cinema product – A and B features, newsreels, cartoons etc.
- physical studio assets and equipment in constant use
- a division of salaried or contracted staff into highly specialised departments
- the contracted star system
- a producer-unit system and a definition of genres
- a continuity system governing narrative construction
- a specific studio 'look' or style applied to A features
- a system of self-censorship and mutual protection against attacks by government
- an international market for studio product.

The major issue which often arises from consideration of the system is the potential conflict of 'industry' versus 'art', or the mechanised and organised process of production versus the creative team. It is clear that, although the system exerted pressure on all those involved to 'maintain production' and in many ways creative personnel were constrained by budget or genre definition or star vehicle, the discipline so engendered enabled creative teams to produce work of high craftsmanship and powerful narrative appeal. Dore Schary, an executive producer at both RKO and MGM, noted that:

Efficiency experts trained in other industries are usually baffled when they try to fit the making of a movie to their standard rules. The fact is, a movie is essentially a hand-craft operation ... but it must be made on a factory-line basis, with production-line economics, if we're to hold the price down within reach of most of the people. The job is to do this without losing the picture's individuality.

One of the lost things you can look back on in that era and say was good was the system of patronage that enabled us to keep together a group of highly talented people and let them function rather freely and profitably.

(Dore Schary quoted in Bordwell, Staiger and Thompson (1985))

The quality of the best pictures produced during the studio era is evident for any viewer of BBC2 or Channel 4, channels that continue to show 'classic Hollywood'. But, it should be remembered that these are perhaps the cream of a very large crop and that the majority may not bear as much scrutiny.

The other major question might be 'Who got to choose which pictures were made?' The studios in this period were still run by the (white) men who had set them up, the so-called 'movie moguls', characters like Jack Warner or Louis B. Mayer. These studio bosses had very strong views on what should be made and they exerted their authority. They were effectively producers not directors, but, unlike the executives who gained control of the studios in the 1970s, they were creative movie people who wanted to make movies which would fill theatres.

The legacy of the studio system

The death of the studio system was a prolonged and complex process – too complex to describe here. Many factors led to the break-up, but the major event which precipitated the decline was 'the Paramount decision' in 1948, when the federal government finally took action against the majors as oligopolists and forced them to sell their cinema chains over the next few years, thereby ending the integration which was the basis of the system.

The 1950s saw the rise of independent producers who effectively replaced the in-house production units (there had always been a small number of independents – now they were to become the norm). The studios would still distribute a set number of major films each year, but instead of making them all themselves, they would 'pick up' or finance product from an independent. (See 'Industries' and 'Independents and alternatives' (Chapters 22 and 28) for definitions of 'independent'.)

In the 1990s the studio system is in one sense long gone. For a period in the 1960s and 1970s British television broadcasters tended to organise production on a unit production system with studio complexes turning out dramas, light entertainment etc. and specialist units for sport and natural history. But this system too has been broken up and replaced by independents and in-house producers using 'facilities' rather than a 'factory production line'. Modern technology and an environment of de-regulation and 'free market' competition has seen off the controlled production environment. Some theorists see this as part of the 'post-**Fordist**' industrial environment (see 'Postmodernisms', Chapter 18).

The real legacy of the studio system is now revealed to have been the enormous body of work, now growing in value as libraries of material, the extraordinary longevity of copyright images such as the cartoon characters of Disney and Warners and the trademark of a logo recognised all over the world. Warners, Paramount and Fox, along with Disney, are still on top of the media pile, although now their position is even more dependent on what they distribute and exhibit than on what they actually make.

ACTIVITY 7.1

The studio image

Most of the examples in this case study have been drawn from Warner Bros or MGM. Take either Paramount or Twentieth Century Fox, the other survivors of the big five, and research the image presented by the studio. Who were the contracted stars or directors? What kinds of genres were popular at these studios? What were the most important events in the history of the studio? How did they promote the studio and its films (has the logo remained marketable)?

References and further reading

Balio, Tino (1985, revised edition) *The American Film Industry*, London: University of Wisconsin Press.

Behlmer, Rudy (ed.) (1986) *Inside Warner Bros*, London: Weidenfeld & Nicolson.

Bogle, Donald (1994) *Toms, Coons, Mulattoes, Mammies and Bucks*, New York: Continuum.

Bordwell, David and Carroll, Noël (eds) (1996) *Post-Theory: Reconstructing Film Studies*, Madison and London: University of Wisconsin Press.

Bordwell, David, Staiger, Janet and Thompson, Kristin (1985) *The Classical Hollywood Cinema: Film Style & Mode of Production to 1960*, London: Routledge.

Bordwell, David and Thompson, Kristin (1997, 5th edition) *Film Art: An Introduction*, New York: McGraw-Hill.

Gomery, Douglas (1986) *The Hollywood Studio System*, London: BFI/Macmillan.

Gomery, Douglas (1992) *Shared Pleasures*, London: BFI.

Gomery, Douglas (1996) 'Towards a New Media Economics', in Bordwell and Carroll, *Post-Theory*.

Gomery, Douglas (1998) 'Hollywood as Industry', in John Hill and Pamela Church Gibson (eds) *The Oxford Guide to Film Studies*, Oxford: Oxford University Press.

Kerr, Paul (ed.) (1986) *The Hollywood Film Industry*, London: Routledge & Kegan Paul.

Maltby, Richard and Craven, Ian (1995) *Hollywood Cinema*, Oxford: Blackwell.

Neale, Steve and Smith, Murray (1998) *Contemporary Hollywood Cinema*, London: Routledge.

Roddick, Nick (1983) *A New Deal in Entertainment: Warner Brothers in the 1930s*, London: BFI.

Salt, Barry (1992) *Film Style & Technology: History & Analysis*, London: Starword.

Schatz, Thomas (1989 and 1998) *The Genius of the System: Hollywood Filmmaking in the Studio Era*, London: Faber & Faber.

Williams, Christopher (1994) 'After the Classic, the Classical and Ideology: The Differences of Realism', *Screen*, vol. 35, no. 3.

8 Genres

The term 'genre' is a French word for 'type' or 'kind', as in biological classifications of plants and animals. In study of the media, it involves some long-standing debates about the categorisation of mass produced popular forms, and audiences' pleasure in them.

Q How many students does it take to change a lightbulb?
A Eight. One to hold the bulb and seven to drink until the room spins.

A lightbulb joke depends on the same kinds of knowledge and expectations as any genre product. Unless you've never heard one before, as soon as you hear the question you are likely to begin thinking in certain directions rather than others for the answer.

Q How many LA cops does it take to change a lightbulb?
A Six. One to change the bulb and five to smash the old bulb to
   smithereens.

In other words, the question will be *framed* or *categorised* for you in a certain way; it announces itself as a joke, a fiction, *not* a mathematical or electrical puzzle, or a serious comment on all students.

Q How many Real Men does it take to change a lightbulb?
A Real Men aren't afraid of the dark.

If you enjoy lightbulb jokes, you will both know and not quite know what to expect from it. In other words, a *system of expectation* is set up around it, one which involves both **repetition and difference**.

Q How many psychoanalysts does it take to change a lightbulb?
A Only one: but the lightbulb has to really want to change.

The repetition is of the bare framework of elements: a lightbulb, a group of people about which certain stereotypes exist, and a number which relates the two in an amusing way.

A very Media Student's lightbulb joke: 'How many Microsoft executives does it take to change a lightbulb? None – Bill Gates will just redefine darkness as the industry standard.'

'Articulation' term developed by Ernesto Laclau to think how elements of social orders (or media messages) are connected. The image is not of a direct or inevitable connection, but of a process working like a complicated joint (or as in 'articulated lorries'). Something may have an original, historical meaning (e.g. the Bible) but we need to look at its full, working contexts to understand how it means in each of them (e.g. Rastafarians' use of Biblical images).

The difference lies in *how* the particular connections between those elements will be made *this* time. It's the particular **articulation** or combination of the three, rather than something called 'difference' alone, which makes the new joke enjoyable. As the genre becomes established, play can be made with its conventions (see the 'Real Men' and 'psychoanalysts' jokes). Part of their pleasure is their satirical reference to well-known stereotypes, and thus to your feelings about real world groups of which you may or may not have some personal knowledge.

The economics of genre production

Media products are divided into genres or types. As a way of organising the costly and volatile business of making films and television this helps to minimise risk and predict expenditure. **Economies of scale** require **standardisation of production** (see 'Producing in the studio system', Case study 7, for definitions) though this is in order to reach *different* audiences, through *different* genres. So it is not adequate to see genre production as simply about sameness. Television companies, for example, depend on predictable annual income from the licence fee (BBC) or advertising (ITV and cable companies) and divide up budgets according to departments such as Light Entertainment, Drama, News and Current Affairs. Soap operas are a particularly useful genre in this effort at standardised schedules, building audiences in the early evening. It makes it worth investing in a whole close of modern houses for Brookside Productions Ltd, or for Granada to build a permanent set and even employ a serial historian to avoid embarrassing mistakes in the long-running *Coronation Street*. Commercial television in particular needs to be able to promise advertisers the attention of different audiences at predictable times of day and night, for which regularly scheduled genre slots are invaluable.

So in terms of economics, audiences for television genres (and increasingly for film genres too) are often created as targets for advertising. In an attempt to target ever more specialised, small segments or **niches** of the potential audience, media forms have become more and more cross-generic, as different kinds of music, television and film clash and mix genres which were previously held apart: comedy-horror, cyberpunk, docu-soaps. Nevertheless, media products are still marketed according to such generic categories, even if mixed. And audiences are not rendered the helpless mass, duped into consumption, as some theories suggest, but often have sophisticated expectations of the genres they enjoy.

'Niche' originally meant a little nest or recess in a wall; **niche marketing** now refers to attempts to reach specialised but highly profitable groups of potential consumers with particular media products or aspects of products.

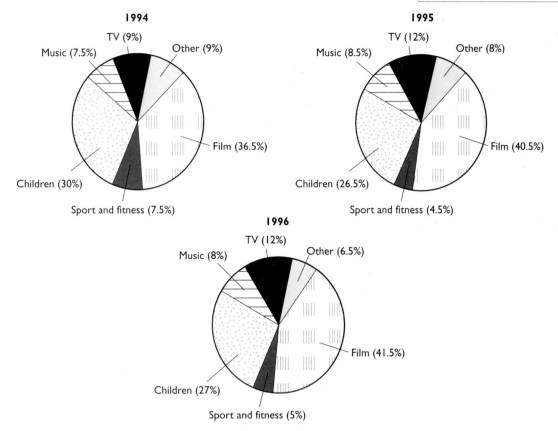

Figure 8.1   Volume of video retail sales by genre (number of tapes sold). Source: British Video Association

---

ACTIVITY 8.1

Next time you are in the book or music section of a major book retailer (e.g. W. H. Smiths or Waterstones) note the different genres announced by album or CD covers and book categories: romance, gardening, thriller, country and western and so on.

● What seem to be the signifiers of particular genres? Do any of them seem to be mixed together?

Zap through the channels on your television or radio. Look at title sequences.

● How quickly are you able to tell what kind of programme or music is on offer?

● *How* were you able to tell? What kinds of differences are signalled through: music, colours, kinds of dialogue, voices, pace of editing, costume, lighting etc.?

Try turning down the sound on the title sequence of a television genre and substituting another kind of music.

● What difference does this make?

● Can you tell gardening or cookery programmes from motor racing coverage just by the title music for example? Or by the kinds of voices used?

The status of genre, 'the real' and verisimilitude

Though most of us, as audience members for different genres, are able to operate *genre awareness* quite speedily, media theorists have been interested in genre because of:

- its importance in understanding the *low status* of mass-produced media products in relation to *higher-status* art forms
- its capacity to help us understand the nature of genre categorisation and the role of *repetition* and *difference* in this
- its focus on how *entertainment* or **escapist** forms might work to organise and either narrow or expand the expectations and identities through which we understand and imagine the world and its possibilities.

Mass-produced movies, pop music, television etc. have long been seen as being a lower kind of cultural production to 'true art' simply because they involved industrial production and were aimed at non-elite audiences. Hollywood's products, for example, were initially intended to entertain working-class audiences for an evening between one day's work and the next, rather than to be pondered over or sampled at elite gatherings (as with opera performances). Because of this, Hollywood has been assumed incapable of producing anything worthy of serious attention, let alone anything 'artistic' or 'realistic'. A low estimate of the audience has always been inseparable from contempt for genre forms.

Such suspicion still surfaces in the (highly classed and gendered) metaphors used to dismiss genre products. It's a suspicion based not in objections to the ways profit-led industries tend to treat the people who work for them or try to rig markets for their products. Instead it is based in nineteenth-century images of a Real Artist or Author as someone working alone, often against the grain and in a pre-industrial way (see 'Independents and alternatives', Chapter 28). It draws heavily on the simplest kinds of suspicions of the capitalist cultural industries.

Added to such hostility, Hollywood had the disadvantage, for British and European critics, of being American. In the late nineteenth century

'Repetition and difference' is a key way of rethinking the supposed 'sameness' of mass media products. It also relates to the (over-) high estimate of 'difference' within structuralist and post-structuralist theory. If your course demands knowledge of these approaches, look again at 'Languages of media', Chapter 1.

Escapist, meaning 'one who seeks escape, especially from reality', is a term used disparagingly of mass cultural forms, seen as encouraging their audiences simply to escape from, and not to face up to the stern demands of 'the real'. Often used as synonymous with 'entertainment'. (Origin: es-cape: literally, taking off one's cloak and thus 'throwing off restraint'.)

Terms like 'fodder', 'run of the mill', 'familiar recipe', 'served up', 'staple diet', 'junk food culture', 'pap', 'pulp' (referring to books made from poor quality wood pulp), 'the Dream Factory' all emphasise repetition and inferior quality, as though films were just like the output of any other factory – or kitchen.

ACTIVITY 8.2

Take a press account of a recent debate on an American media product seen as 'trashy'.

- Note which points are hostile to the product simply because it is American.
- What kinds of stereotypes or connotations of 'American-ness' are circulating in its language?

the US was an increasingly successful competitor for world markets; a nation, therefore, often represented as composed of upstarts and emigrants from Europe who couldn't quite speak proper English. This snobbery persists even today.

In a move that gave status to a connection to 'the real', entertainment forms have also been described as, contradictorily, *both*:

- the carriers of capitalist **propaganda** or ideology (i.e. related to 'the real') *and yet*
- pernicious because they encouraged audiences to escape from 'real' questions via fantasy.

Clearly, though all stories and entertainments are imaginary, not 'real life' in one sense, they are a material part of most of our real lives in several others. We pay money to experience them, directly or indirectly (e.g. through advertising-funded television); we spend time and imaginative energy in their worlds; and genre forms such as soap operas, appearing several times a week, often find themselves entwined with news debates: think of the 1998 campaign to free Deirdre in *Coronation Street*. Of course, when such debates enter the news agenda, they are reported in terms which make their audience look stupid or gullible. Newspapers love to focus on the relatively few people who seem to believe in the soap's events as though they were real (even if, on the next page, they may be writing of an actor as though really the character she or he performs). Yet, arguably, being asked, night after night, to imagine, through your identification with a particular character, what it is like to be a single parent, or be wrongly charged with fraud, is a crucial part of thoughtful public debate on the key issues within news.

ACTIVITY 8.3

Make a note of the different kinds of fiction you enter into this week.

- How much time do you spend in each fictional world?
- Which is your favourite genre? Why?

There is another position which tries to link even less 'realistic' aspects of genre forms to the real. Richard Dyer (1977) argued that entertainment or genre forms are pleasurable (the hostile term would be 'escapist' or even 'fantasist') precisely because they allow a kind of fantasy escape from a reality often experienced as full of scarcity, exhaustion and alienation, into a fictional world coded as abundant, energetic, transparent, intense and with moments of community. Following the

Ernst Bloch (1885–1977) German Marxist cultural theorist of utopian impulses in art. *The Principle of Hope* (1954–9) was written during exile in the US.

Mikhail Bakhtin (1895–1975), the Russian cultural theorist, wrote on sixteenth-century carnival as an expression of desires to 'turn the world upside down' in a moment of utopian celebration (published 1984).

Russian literary theorists **Bloch** and **Bakhtin**, he called them **utopian** pleasures, not in the sense that they literally represent or speak about political utopias, but in that key moments and qualities give sensuous expression to such feelings that 'things could be better'. His work was originally with musical forms, but has been applied to less obviously escapist forms. For example in the Western genre these would include: chases, pounding music and fights exemplifying *energy*; expansive landscape as *abundance*; 'face out' and confrontational dialogue as *intensity*, while the morally unambiguous hero of 'classic' Westerns might embody *transparency*. Finally, the townships and the cowboy camaraderie might make up the Utopian category *community*.

ACTIVITY 8.3

Look at the chart below, adapted from Dyer (1977). Using these categories:

- Can you find any or all of these kinds of utopian qualities in a contemporary genre product?
- You might explore the National Lottery Show, morning DJs on radio, pop videos, romances, comic books or less obviously 'escapist' forms such as hospital drama series or soap opera.

'"Utopia" is derived from the Greek meaning, ambiguously, 'no place' (*ou topos*) and 'good place' (*eu topos*). It has been used from Sir Thomas Moore's book *Utopia* (1516) onwards of ideal social orders.' p.221 Brooker.

Social tension/inadequacy	*Utopian feeling or fantasy, and its coding in entertainment forms*
Scarcity e.g. actual poverty and shortages; unequal distribution of wealth	**Abundance** elimination of poverty and inequalities *coded in* lavish sets, costumes, colours, FX, sweeping camera movements etc.
Exhaustion e.g. work as a grind, alienated labour, pressures of work and home	**Energy** work and play the same thing *coded in* energetic song and dance forms; fast, sassy dialogue; swift editing; bold lines of comic strips etc.
Dreariness e.g. predictable routines of work and home; work experienced as meaningless	**Intensity** excitement, drama *coded in* action sequences (often involving violence); exciting love scenes; testing in serious or dangerous situations; dramatic news stories

Manipulation e.g. of work routines; awareness of advertising ploys, of 'spin doctoring', of roles played in social life

Transparency open, spontaneous, human communication
coded in declarations of love in romance; of protest in political and realist forms

Fragmentation e.g. breakdown of neighbourhoods; short-term contract insecurity; spatial dislocation of commuting

Community all together, emotionally and physically, in one place
coded in 'all pulling together' moments; 'everyone getting involved' in war films, action adventures, musicals etc.

Jackie Stacey (1993) has argued that Dyer's categories need to be thought through more specifically, in relation to gender, class, ethnicity and different historical periods, as well as to the places where entertainment happens, such as the luxurious escape into cinemas for women in the 1930s and 1940s.

Others would argue they are more about fantasies of wholeness than the political impulses needed for the complications of modernity.

But they are still a valuable way to begin to understand the pleasures/fantasies of genre forms – and of politics and even news.

The real and 'verisimilitude'

Finally there is the useful concept of '**verisimilitude**'. All genres, from television news to heavy metal music, are constructed, working with codes and conventions: there is no neat division to be made between 'the real' and 'the imagined'. Yet some genres are perceived as having more verisimilitude, or connection to the 'real', than others, which makes a key difference to assumptions as to what their ideological work might be. For example, the first step taken by many media campaigners on excessive violence on television is to *mistake* how far cartoons are connected to reality for their audiences.

This 'real-seemingness', the ways that media forms will combine systems of what seems 'real', 'likely' or 'probable' in texts, involves two areas:

- *generic verisimilitude*: sets of expectations which are internal to the genre, such as how a 'proper' or 'real' vampire film or science fiction film should proceed (respectively: with garlic as magical, not a cooking ingredient; and with scientists as probably mad, not sane). These can,

Verisimilitude from the Latin for 'truth' (*veritas*) and *similis* = 'like', 'similar'.

'only through the imagination, which is always subjective, is "objective reality" assimilated: a life without imagination does not exist' (Ien Ang, *Watching Dallas: Soap Opera and the Melodramatic Imagination* (1985), p. 83).

in some cases, produce a degree of fantasy and play with identities and situations which are otherwise unimaginable.

- *cultural verisimilitude*: the genre's relationship to expectations about the world outside the genre.

For example, the gangster film or the 'courtroom drama' has always had higher status than, say, the musical, because it makes more explicit reference to public or political events in the historical world outside the film (using newspaper headlines, naming real-life politicians or criminals, and so on). In its style of filming, this genre has traditionally worked in black and white (often seen as closer to the realist codes of documentary and history), and until relatively recently (it is part of how the *Godfather* films reworked the genre) made little use of the flamboyant colour, camera angles and movements enjoyed by fans of the musical (and felt to be 'unrealistic' by non-fans). Similarly the happy ending (so 'proper' for a musical) is not considered realistic in a gangster movie, even though many real-life gangsters are alive and well and living in expectation of a comfortable death. (*Goodfellas* (US 1990) was seen as groundbreaking partly by representing this situation.)

What complicates things even more is that in a media-image saturated culture, the conventions of fictional genres are often used not just in advertising, but also to make news stories more vivid. The serial killer Frederick West's home was called 'The House of Horror' in tabloid headlines, triggering the horror genre's resonances. News and documentary stories of the struggles against the Mafia regularly use music from and even shots that resembled the *Godfather* gangster films, in order to add glamour to the story in a ratings-conscious television system. Such images often feed back into the 'reality effect' of the next gangster movie or television series, and so on, in that process called intertextuality.

Intertextuality the variety of ways in which media and other texts interact with each other, rather than being unique or distinct. It is different to 'allusion', which is a more conscious referencing by one text of another.

Repetition and difference: repertoires of elements

The Ancient Greek philosopher Aristotle first used the term *genre* in the context of art, rather like scientists trying to classify plants and animals. He tried to divide literary output (which then consisted mostly of performances) into groups or types (tragedy, comedy, drama, epic and lyric), and then to rank them.

Unlike modern writers, he did not rank according to *difference* (as we might, praising a movie for being 'a bit different from your average action adventure/romance/horror …'). He was much more interested in valuing a performance for how well the genre's rules had been *obeyed* or acted out. This remained a major standard of classical value in European art for many centuries, though, by the late eighteenth century, ideas of novelty and originality were becoming bound up with higher artistic valuations: in literature the *novel* takes its name from this higher valuation of the 'new' or 'novel'.

One of the most widespread ways of dismissing genre, entertainment or **popular** forms is the charge that 'They're all the same' or 'If you've seen one, you've seen them all'. Of course for the owners of media industries these profitably **standardised** practices are an attractive part of genres. But this emphasis on 'sameness', 'repetition' or 'standardisation' does not work when we come to audiences' enjoyment of genres. Not only are there different genres to appeal to different audiences. But even separate genres are not the same as other industrial products. You may be happy to stick to your favourite brand of toothpaste, and indeed *hope* that each tube will be very similar, but you do not want similar absolute repetition in cultural products.

Standardisation has a double meaning: it can signify 'sameness'; but can also denote the maintenance of standards, in the sense of quality. Another point to bear in mind in the huge debates around 'sameness' and 'difference' in Media and Cultural Studies.

ACTIVITY 8.4

Take your favourite soap and record an episode without watching it live. Play it back and stop the recording at a key moment of enigma or drama for the plot. Now try to predict what follows next on screen before looking at your tape for the rest of the sequence, and then of the storyline.

● How easy was it to do this?

● Were you right in your prediction? In exactly how it was done?

● What does this suggest about repetitiveness and genre products?

You may have been broadly right in your plot prediction (perhaps because you had knowledge of a plot development from newspaper or magazine gossip about the serial). But it is the actual phrasing, setting, pacing of this (the *articulation of elements*) which is key to audience pleasure – and hard to achieve.

The most important recent development in thinking about familiar entertainment genres has been to put them into the context of audiences' understandings and activities. Genres are no longer seen as sets of fixed elements, constantly repeated, but as working with '**repertoires of elements**' or fluid systems of conventions and expectations. These are shared by makers and audiences, who are *both* active on *both* sides of meaning-making, though often in ways that go unvoiced, until they are studied and thought about.

The point is often made that it's almost impossible to find a pure genre Hollywood film. Most of them, for example, combine, in a *hybrid* or mixed form, a romance story with their other main genre elements. Can you think of a pure genre film or television fiction?

Iconography comes from art history, where it refers to books of the fifteenth and sixteenth century guiding artists as to the correct colours, gestures, facial expressions etc. with which to encode Christian doctrine. Since cinema and television work with moving, audiovisual images, the term **signification** (see 'Languages of media', Chapter 1) is probably more useful.

These conventions and expectations include the areas of:

- narrative
- audio-visual codes of signification (for which the term **iconography** or **mise en scène** is still sometimes used)
- ideological themes.

The term '**convention**' is usually understood very conservatively, as a form which is only able to reinforce and repeat normative values – as in verdicts like 'He's a very conventional singer'. But in fact conventions, precisely in order to survive, need to be able to adapt and shift in more dynamic ways than this. Critics of popular forms for example, often imply that they would prefer each product to be utterly different. But if any story, or video game, or melody were utterly different to all others, we would have no means by which to understand it. (see 'Languages of media', Chapter 1).

For example, *Reservoir Dogs* (US 1992) was praised for its 'difference' and 'originality' when it came out. But these were to some extent dependent on generic conventions. It was in many ways an arthouse movie which played with and against the expectations of the male-centred action adventure film: a crime; intense relationships exclusively between men; violence. Within this 'sameness' or familiarity, the pacing and arrangement of the plot, the importance given to a quirky kind of dialogue, the handling of violence, the use of pop music and so on could be experienced as comprehensible 'difference'.

Examples: gender and genre

Photoplay story told like a strip cartoon but using photos instead of drawings.

The **romance** genre (such as the so-called 'woman's film') whether in novel, **photoplay**, television or film form, will work with narratives whose starting point will often be the arrival into the life of the female hero of a male who, shall we say, interests her romantically.

This sets in play issues such as the nature of intimate relations between men and women, and expectations about the family, work and marriage. The narrative will often proceed by means of intimate conversations and encounters, coincidences, mistakes and so on, delaying and thus intensifying the audience's desire for the couple(s) to 'get it together', and usually ending happily in terms of the central, romantic relationship. *Casablanca* (US 1942) plays with the elements in combination with those of a political thriller, and a male central character, while *Titanic* (US 1997) is an example of a lavish blockbuster using romance, rather than the more usual blockbuster action-adventure narrative (Figure 8.2).

At the level of the audiovisual, romance has particular traditions: lavish clothes and domestic settings; much greater use of close-ups,

Figure 8.2 Blockbuster special FX romance: *Titanic* (US 1997)

especially focused on the eyes, for male and female actors; less use of
fetishised shots of women's bodies; certain styles of intimate acting and
dialogue; use of female stars in strong roles; all amplified by a particular
kind of music: sweeping chords, piano and string sections of the orchestra.

Male genres have traditionally had higher status, in terms of budgets
and critical esteem, and, as outlined above, have apparently been less
emotional (or deal with different kinds of emotion?) and more concerned
with public issues, situations, references.

Figure 8.3 Death tableau from *The Roaring Twenties* (US 1939)

A famous moment from a *gangster* movie (Figure 8.3) illustrates the crystallisation of generic elements from the gangster repertoire. Some of these are the result of the pressure of censorship bodies on Hollywood to 'punish the gangster' (a very popular figure in Depression America's cinema) by public death (usually on the street); some accumulate as a genre developed (along with technological possibilities such as sound, colour etc.); all of them allow efficient and economic signification through the details of well-known conventions being *re*-played, but always with *difference.*

The policeman represents a public calling to account, or punishment for the gangster, while the woman, often cradling the gangster's head, perhaps embodies audience affection for him. The church steps have, for experienced gangster film fans, resonances of repentance (from the early years of the genre), as well as providing a sumptuous setting for a tableau or frozen expressive moment, which Hollywood inherited and reworked from stage **melodrama.**

The bulk of this chapter has tried to argue that cultural forms require and indeed produce a certain amount of *innovation*, not simply repetition. Yet key questions remain:

- What kinds of innovation are unacceptable in commercial genres?
- Unacceptable to whom? Why?
- How true is it to argue that 'the audience wants a happy ending' or 'you can't have a political film ending like that'?

Censorship exists, for example, not only in the HUAC (House UnAmerican Activities Committee) investigations of leftist work in Hollywood during the 1940s and 1950s, or in television's controllers banning programmes. It is part of a spectrum of *institutional* assumptions about unacceptable activities within particular genres, which can be invoked to suppress or dismiss difference. During the years of struggle against apartheid and its effects on sport in South Africa, it 'just wasn't done', within the genre of cricket commentary, to bring such politics into coverage. Censorship can take place in 'the nicest possible way', by forms being called a 'mishmash' or 'inappropriate mix' (of generic conventions). Certain genres have been taken as the place where some but not other closely related kinds of activity are appropriately fictionalised and handled. In television, for example, recent events in the real world are categorised as part of the *news genre.* After a certain time, though, such events are classified as the *history genre* and come under quite different rules, notably involving less need for impartiality.

A cultural or ideological approach to genres is interested in these questions. It asks whether some of the repetitions within genres, such as the sense of what constitutes a ' happy ending', excludes some identities

Melodrama (from Latin *melos* = 'music' and French *drame* = 'middle-class drama'): term for a kind of theatre which emerged from censored seventeenth-century drama which was not allowed to use words. It evolved an elaborate language of gesture and spectacle, much of it inherited by early cinema. Normally a term used derogatorily. See Gledhill 1987.

Censorship is used of decisive acts of forbidding or preventing publication or distribution of media products, or parts of those products, by those with the power, either economic or legislative, to do so.

'We loved the vampire because he had great dress sense, lots of money and wasn't going to expect you to do the washing up' (female vampire movie fan).

and imaginings, and might be reinforcing dominant and sometimes oppressive sets of values.

References

Bourdieu, Pierre (1980) 'The Aristocracy of Culture', reprinted in R. Collins, J. Curran, N. Garnham, P. Scannell, P. Schlesinger and C. Sparks (eds) *Media, Culture & Society: A Critical Reader*, London and Beverly Hills: Sage.

Dyer, Richard (1977) 'Entertainment and Utopia', reprinted in *Only Entertainment* (1992), London: Routledge.

Gledhill, Christine (ed.) (1987) *Home Is Where the Heart Is*, London: BFI.

O'Sullivan, Tim and Jewkes, Yvonne (eds) (1997) *The Media Studies Reader*, London and New York: Arnold.

Further reading

Barker, Martin (1989) *Comics: Ideology, Power and the Critics,* Manchester: Manchester University Press.

Buscombe, Ed (ed.) (1988) *The BFI Companion to the Western,* London: Andre Deutsch/BFI.

Gledhill, Christine (1997) 'Genre and Gender: The Case of Soap Opera' in Stuart Hall (ed.) *Representation: Cultural Representations and Signifying Practices*, London: Thousand Oaks, New Delhi: Sage (to which this chapter is indebted).

Goodwin, Andrew and Whannel, Gary (1990) *Understanding Television*, London: Routledge.

Lusted, David (1998) 'The Popular Culture Debate and Light Entertainment', in Christine Geraghty and David Lusted (eds) *The Television Studies Book*, London and New York: Arnold.

Neale, Steve (1990) 'Questions of Genre', *Screen*, vol. 31, no. 1.

Ryall, Tom (1998) 'Genre and Hollywood', in John Hill and Pamela Church Gibson (eds) *The Oxford Guide to Film Studies*, Oxford: Oxford University Press.

Stacey, Jackie (1993) *Star Gazing: Hollywood Cinema and Female Spectatorship*, London: Routledge.

Applying 'repertoires of
elements' to SF
Sameness and difference
Changes in the SF genre
SF in different media
References
Further reading

9 / Case study: Science fiction

Science fiction (hereafter SF) is and has been an
important genre across several media. In literature it
stretches from Mary Shelley's novel *Frankenstein* (1818)
to the work of Ursula Le Guin, Doris Lessing, J. G.
Ballard and many others. But it has also been produced
in cinema, television, computer games, comic books or
'graphic novels' and even radio (*The HitchHiker's Guide
to the Galaxy*). Though film SF still sometimes gets
dismissed as: 'all about little green men and bug-eyed
monsters', it offers for its fans several possible
pleasures:

- the playing out of 'what if' speculations about future
  social or scientific developments
- in ways in which these often relate to contemporary
  social or scientific hopes and fears
- the display of expensive cutting-edge special effects
  (hereafter SFX) in cinema and television (though
  computer games and even graphic novels (Figure 9.1)
  can also be spectacular).

Applying 'repertoires of elements' to SF

The label 'SF' conjures up broad expectations in the
areas of:

- ideological and cultural themes
- audiovisual signifiers (settings, costume, FX, objects,
  kinds of music, editing, framing etc.)
- narrative patterns.

  In its cultural and **ideological** themes, the story will
tend to pose 'what if' questions like:

- What if it were impossible to tell the difference
  between a human being and a cyborg or other

Figure 9.1   Howlett, *Tank Girl*

alien life form? (*Blade Runner* (US 1982); *The Stepford
Wives* (US 1974)).

- What if time travel were possible (the *Terminator*
  series)?
- What if science or capitalism or patriarchy were to
  get 'out of control'? (*The Handmaid's Tale* (US 1990);
  Godzilla (US 1998)).

- What if other planetary life forms were utterly alien and hostile to humankind?

This speculative play with scientific and, often, related political themes may involve highly technological and class-stratified futures, or global disasters evident in the post-apocalyptic landscape of *Tank Girl* comics, *Blade Runner* or the *Mad Max* films (US 1979, 1981, 1985).

Questions of good and bad leadership (also important in action films and Westerns) have a special weight in these SF stories exploring future social orders (e.g. *Star Trek*'s Captain Picard's 'Make it so', or the pleasure of, and limits to, Sarah/Linda Hamilton's decisiveness in the *Terminator* films (US 1984, 1991)).

As in all genres, certain fondly greeted lines such as 'Take me to your leader' can resonate with previous such moments. They can also be the **signifiers** of scientific-ness (techno-babble?) in a sentence like: 'If we were to match warp factor 26 then we reverse the negativity and put the ship in overdrive to escape the force field.'

Interestingly, the playing out of these 'what if?' questions is often recognisably related to current scientific or political knowledge and debates. Those opening words 'Sometime in the not too distant future' signal that current knowledge is to be evoked and deployed, even if the story is set in a galaxy a million light years away. Though the genre's escapist elements are often implied to lie in its audiovisual qualities, with FX and lavish costumes and sets evoking exotic future cityscapes, it could more plausibly be said to reside in the satisfactions of a genre where powerful, incomprehensible enemies and technologies are sometimes, though not always, understood and efficiently dispatched.

SF will tend to work through **narratives** whose starting point, or initial disruption, may often be broadly similar to that of action adventure or Westerns (e.g. 'someone has been mysteriously or violently injured by an enemy') and will offer plenty of violent chases, puzzles, spectacles and cliffhangers along the way to the final efficient dispatch of the enemy (who/which is often associated with advanced technology). The **stars** of this genre, so important in the ways they connect narrative with the 'look' of films, will often be those of action adventure or thriller: Harrison Ford, Arnold Schwarzenegger.

ACTIVITY 9.1

Try applying the ideas of Propp about the narrative elements at play to a recent SF text, e.g.

1 The hero reports destruction caused by aliens, which is confirmed.
2 Conferences between the military and scientists take place.
3 The aliens commit further atrocities.
4 After more conferences, ingenious attempts to discover the vulnerability of the aliens etc., they are repulsed.
5 But the question remains: 'Have we seen the last of them?'

Q Do such elements occur in all SF? If not, what are the story's enigmas?

ACTIVITY 9.2

List the last three fictions you have encountered, in any medium, which you would classify as SF.

- Why would you categorise them thus?
- Which elements of the outline above apply to them?
- What was the initial 'enigma' of the narrative?
- Did they relate to any contemporary fears or debates?

Give examples of such debates.

Sameness and difference

All genres, including SF, will use difference as well as similarities, depending on:

- the different combination of generic elements from our three main areas

- changes to the genre and the culture it is embedded in, over time
- which medium (print, film, radio, CD-ROM) is being used.

Genre films always involve some kind of 'hybridity' and are never 'pure' Westerns or horror films etc. Hollywood, and earlier nineteenth-century cultural forms, have always tried to attract as many audience segments as possible, and, for example, one way of guaranteeing some female audience for 'male' genres, like action adventures and SF, was assumed to be a romance strand in the plot. SF, perhaps more than other genres, is neither one thing, nor always the same. But there are of course provisional boundaries – which, however, can mutate.

Examples

- The 'what if?' cannot involve magic (which codes the fantasy genre as in *Edward Scissorhands* (US 1990) or *The Nutty Professor* (US 1997).
- The villains in the James Bond stories are usually connected to high technology, but this does not make them part of SF since the Bond series is so heavily coded as thriller/spy genre.
- *The Birds* (UK 1963), though arguably dealing with ecological change, is set in 'the present' and coded as thriller, in which there is no motive for the birds' malevolent behaviour, and also as 'Hitchcock': if it wasn't it might exist on the supernatural/SF boundary.

Even the most obvious 'rules' of a genre can shift. Until the massive success of *Men in Black* (US 1997) (Figure 9.3) it would have seemed obvious that the titles of SF films had to signal their subject matter: *Star Wars* (US 1977); *Stargate* (US 1994); *Star Trek* (films and TV series) etc.

Men in Black (US 1997) is a comedy/SF hybrid, but also refers to the phenomenally successful television SF series *The X-Files* and the 'men in black' said to visit and intimidate recipients of extra-terrestrial visitors.

Figure 9.2   Men in Black (US 1997)

Let's look at the generic repertoire of 'stock elements' and how they can be combined and re-combined.

- The *chase or adventure narrative* is well established, partly because it allows such luscious display of cutting-edge FX. But there are many SF films which don't work with such narrative shaping. *2001*, for example, though full of the audiovisual signifiers of SF, refused the chase, and became known for the languid movement of the spacecraft in time with the *Blue Danube* waltz: a play of difference within repetitions
- Though futuristic machines, cityscapes, laboratories and so on are often thought of as a 'staple' 'stock element' of the genre, almost as soon as you've thought of such sets of **audiovisual signifiers** you will see a piece of SF which ignores or plays with them. *The Abyss* (US 1989) was set under water; *Gattaca* (US 1997) is mostly set in offices and corridors.

But its theme is clearly SF: about a character, biologically conceived in the usual way, who is 'trying to pass' in a future society where elite human beings are genetically designed. Its most unfamiliar 'landscape' is the magnified one of the tiny bodily traces which can 'give you away' in this genetically policed world. Fingernail clippings in huge close-up land with the thudding sound of forest trees in the title sequence.

Figure 9.3   Romance/comedy/SF in *Mars Attacks!* (US 1996)

Even if we cite ideological and cultural themes as identifying the SF genre, we find the situation is richer than might be imagined. SF seems a particularly 'shape shifting' genre, overlapping with and dissolving into such related genres as horror, and shifting its gender roles as its audiences change. How would you classify *Jaws* (US 1975) for example? Action adventure or chase, yes. But also horror (the monster-shark; the menacing music) with strong SF elements (a threat to a social order, the town Amity, which needs science to defeat it).

SF, horror and gender: Frankenstein *and* the Alien *series*

Frankenstein, originally a novel by Mary Shelley (1818), introduces the central themes of SF: the limits of science in the gap between what Victor Frankenstein, the scientist, thinks he is doing (assembling the perfect man from different bodies in the graveyard) and the horrific result of his labours.

Later SF often refers visually to the image in the 1931 film of *Frankenstein* when the bolt of electricity flashes at the moment of 'creation' (in a kind of parody of Michelangelo's painting of God's creating Adam, see Figure 28.1). It has been used in the 'birthing' scene in *Alien* and in both *Terminator* films at the moment when the cyborgs land on Earth: as part of the spectacle, and a resonance from this key SF moment. This is one of the strengths of popular or genre forms: the power and ease with which they can communicate to their audiences, often by the smallest generically charged intertextual details (like a spot of Ripley's blood sizzling on the floor in *Alien 4*).

Verbally 'Frankenstein' is usually misremembered as the 'monster' rather than the scientist. Horror often results from the failure of science: the idealist-rationalist Victor leads to the 'mad scientist' figure in much SF and horror. Genetically modified food is called 'Frankenstein food' by some tabloids. It has traditionally been in the horror film that anxieties about, and on the scale of, the body have been imagined, and the appropriate special FX developed to make that an exciting genre. But both genres embody deep anxieties about science and technology, called **technophobia.**

You may well ask: is there any genre in which we can imagine scientific futures with optimism? Does it pose the same problems for SF as 'good news' does for news genres?

The *Alien* series is particularly interesting in the ways it has played with the visual and narrative links to technology and horror (the scary monster is 'inside the house' or space craft). The long time between each of the films also partly accounts for the ways it has re-articulated gender and other political positions in pace with its changing historical contexts.

Narratively and audiovisually it moved from an SF/horror *hybrid* in *Alien* (1979, slogan: 'In space no one can hear you scream') through a reliance on the war-movie genre in *Aliens* (1986, slogan: 'This time it's war') to the strange, almost medieval mise en scène and horror narrative of *Alien 3* (1993) and then the extreme genetic-body horror of *Alien 4: Resurrection* (1997).

In these different generic contexts the *gender* relations of SF mutate through the decision to cast Sigourney Weaver in the role of Ripley (originally designed for a male actor), the capable astronaut given maternal *narrative* motivations from the second film onwards (with the child Newt, and in her monstrous pregnancies). Precisely because the genre had previously tended to have men in leadership and hero roles, the charge of this strong, cool, intelligent female character was immensely refreshing, a good example of how even the most conservative *conventions* of a genre can be productive.

In terms of the broader *cultural-ideological* debates which were the contexts for the various films in the series, with the long gaps between them, Amy Taubin (see Polihronis) has argued that *Alien* plays on 'anxieties set loose by a decade of feminist and gay activism'; *Aliens* works as 'a Pentagon-inspired family values picture for the Reagan 80s' which pits the good mother against the bad; and *Alien 3* is an allegory of AIDS. Michael Eaton has suggested about *Alien 4* that the 'gruesome climax … cannot but recall a Right to Life campaign [except] that here, abortion is seen as deliverance not for Ripley but for the whole human race' (Eaton 1998).

- If you know the series, jot down your responses to these suggestions.

Changes in the SF genre

There is not space to go into all the changes in cinema SF since its low-budget, low-status stage in the 1950s, when it was often used as part of US 'Red scare' campaigns, imagining communists as an alien threat. But a few more examples of its elasticity as a genre may be helpful in understanding the rich possibilities of genre capacities, and the ways they relate to 'the real'.

- *E.T.: The Extra-Terrestrial* (US 1982) turned the alien into a lovable, benevolent figure, and followed *Star Wars* (US 1977) in opening up the SF genre to the 'family adventure film', a key move in Hollywood's desire for multi-generic blockbusters. The release dates, often coinciding with family holidays, meant that

parents as well as children might be attracted to nostalgic pleasures (a sense of wonder and spectacle) and an identification with the incomplete family units on screen. But more than this, films like *Terminator-2: Judgement Day* (US 1991: usually *T-2*) and the *Back to the Future* series are fascinated by the problems of the single parent (and thus potentially attractive to women audiences) and the limited solutions on offer: even the cyborg father figure in *T-2* is lost to the boy at the end (see Krämer 1998).

- On the other hand the television series *The X-Files* (Figure 9.4) has been enormously influential in other directions. Not only does it reverse, or play with, the female-irrational/male-rational opposition through Mulder and Scully, but it has for monster 'that father of all conspiracy theories, – the killer of Kennedy … the constant concealer of UFOs and monsters – the Big Bad US Government itself' (Pirie 1996, pp. 22–3).

Figure 9.4

- In recent SF, critics have argued that the key question is often: is it human or not, and if it isn't, does it matter? This, embodied in the fascination with **morphing** and with android or cyborg characters, is said to mirror **postmodernism**'s blurring of the boundaries between the real and the simulated and thus make SF a key genre (see Kuhn 1990).

SF in different media

Because cinematic SF has tended to use SFX for visceral action adventure (thrill a minute; sound systems to make your chair vibrate), many fans have argued that film SF simply uses the future as a spectacular setting for what are basically action adventures in costume. Comic strip SF and novels are said to have been much better at exploring the scientific and political questions raised by possible futures.

- A television series like *Star Trek*, with its often comparatively static, dialogue intensive narratives, could be argued to be made into something quite different when it becomes a cinematic, big-screen, big-budget movie.
- The drive of blockbuster budgets to 'put the money on screen' in huge explosions etc. drives against *T-2*'s anti-nuclear, almost pacifist message (just as the pacifist discourses of a Western like *Shane* (US 1953) are narratively obliterated by the generic drive of the Western: to end up in a morally and aesthetically satisfying shoot-out).
- *Gattaca*, for all the hostility of its narrative to a society run by a eugenic elite is, as a film, bound up in the contradictions of the star system. It shows little interest in its older actors (Ernest Borgnine, Alan Arkin and Gore Vidal) when Uma Thurman is on screen.

Against this, we could argue that cinema, being an audiovisual medium, has often been able to make comments not so much in its dialogue but in sets, casting etc., and that the visceral horror of the nuclear blast in *T-2* more than justifies the ambiguities of the use of mega-SFX. Although *Blade Runner*, another example, spends a

lot more time on its *film noir* love story, and not as much on political imaginings of a **dystopia** as the original novel (Philip K. Dick's wonderful *Do Androids Dream of Electric Sheep?*), its spectacular sets do embody some unforgettably striking implications about that future.

Whereas '**Utopia**' refers to a perfect, if impossible future society, **dystopia** is its opposite, and is often associated with *technophobia* or fear of technology or machines.

ACTIVITY 9.3

Q If you can, look at the first scene of *Blade Runner*, and take notes on what kinds of political or scientific developments are implied by the settings.

A Earth in 2019 is bathed in constant polluted rain, making the air so hellishly murky that the neon handles of umbrellas are a rare source of light. The buildings (echoing the sets of the 1926 German SF classic *Metropolis*) clearly embody a highly class-stratified social order, with the headquarters of the Tyrell corporation at the top of pyramid-like skyscrapers. Though the flying cabs of the elite and the police speed through the skies, the streets are dark, dirty and confusing (unfortunately it is all too easy to read a distaste at the racial mix on the street as part of these scenes). One of the most striking things for audiences when it first came out was the use of contemporary advertising slogans and brands (Coca-Cola) on the sides of the buildings, which economically suggested that this future dystopia was an extension of contemporary global capitalism.

ACTIVITY 9.4

Think of your own 'what if?' question and try to devise a simple story around it.

- Which medium would it best work in? Why?
- What would be the advantages of that medium, especially for your setting (radio's low budget and ease of fantasy effects; cinema's capacity for spectacle and dynamism; literature's ability to argue, debate and accumulate effects)?
- What would be the disadvantages of that medium for your particular theme?
- Take your own favourite SF novel or graphic novel and suggest what would be (or perhaps already has been) gained, and what lost by a transition to film, or television.

References

BFI Library Information Services (1994) *Blade Runner*, Information Source pack.

Bukatman, Scott (1998) *Blade Runner*, London: BFI Modern Classics.

Eaton, Michael (1998) 'Born Again', *Sight and Sound*, December 1997.

French, Sean (1996) *The Terminator*, London: BFI Modern Classics.

Krämer, Peter (1998) 'Would You Take Your Child to See this Film? The Cultural and Social Work of the Family-Adventure Movie' in Steve Neale and Murray Smith (eds), *Contemporary Hollywood Cinema*, London and New York: Routledge.

Kuhn, Annette (ed.) (1990) *Alien Zone*, London: Verso.

Pirie, David (1996) 'In the Cold', *Sight and Sound*, April 1996.

Polihronis, Andreas (1996) 'Constructing Ripley' in Roy Stafford (ed.), *ITP Film Studies Reader*, Keighley: ITP.

Stafford, Roy (ed.) (1996) *ITP Film Studies Reader*, Keighley: ITP.

Stafford, Roy (1997) *ITP Science Fiction Project*, Keighley: ITP.

Further reading

Hardy, Phil (ed.) (1995) *The Aurum Film Encyclopaedia: Science Fiction*, London: Aurum Press.

Internet Movie database on *http://uk.imbd.com*

Kellner, Douglas, Liebowitc, Flo and Ryan, Michael (1984) '*Bladerunner*: A Diagnostic Critique', *Jump Cut*, no. 29.

Neale, Steve (1990a) 'Questions of Genre', *Screen*, vol. 31, no. 1.

Neale, Steve (1990b) 'You've Got to be Fuckin' Kidding', in Kuhn, *Alien Zone*.

SFX Magazine: useful monthly magazine.

Sight and Sound Supplement, *Cloning the Future* (November 1996) comparing major chronologies in 'science fact' and 'science fiction'.

10 Representations

One of the key concepts of Media Studies is 'representation', a rich term with several related meanings.

- It can signal the way some media re-present certain events, stories etc. over and over again.
- Yet, however realistic or plausible media images seem, they never simply present the world direct. They are always a construction, a *re-presentation*, not a transparent window on to the real.
- 'Representation' also prompts the question: how have groups, or possible identities, that exist outside the media been represented in the media? This has broadly political implications, related to the world of (broadly) political representatives: people who 'stand in ' for us – as union reps, or our representatives in Parliament etc.

The media give us ways of imagining particular identities and groups which can have material effects on how people experience the world, and how they get understood, or legislated for or perhaps beaten up in the street by others. To come full circle, this is partly because the mass media have the power to re-present, over and over, some identities, some imaginings, and to exclude others, and thereby make them unfamiliar or even threatening.

Stereotyping in this context has been a key issue (see Case study 11). It raises such questions as:

- Do the media, in the identities and understandings they so powerfully circulate, suggest to large audiences that x or y character is typical of that group, and therefore that the whole group should be viewed in certain ways?
- Are these ways best described as negative?
- How does the relationship between media images and particular groups or identities get changed?

Stereotype comes from Greek *stereo* = 'solid'. It was a printer's term for a solid block of type which could be used to represent something which would otherwise need lots of work with individual pieces of type to show fine detail. Some would argue that, just as electronic publishing has replaced 'solid' print, so this concept of stereotyping groups needs to be rethought.

Representations and gender

One of the richest areas of discussion of representation and media forms exists around gender identities. Though there exist confusing differences

'Lesbian and gay studies does for *sex* and *sexuality* approximately what Women's Studies does for gender.' (Henry Abelove *et al.* (eds) quoted in Medhurst and Lunt, 1997, p. 68.

To put it another way, sex says 'It's a boy'; gender says 'Oh, good' and gets out the blue baby clothes, the train set and guns, and a whole set of assumptions (adapted from Branston 1984).

in the ways the terms are used, the distinction between *sex* and *gender* is very useful. Sex in this context is not the same as sexuality (which refers to people's sexual orientation, their object choice, sexual activities and imaginings). *Sex difference* refers here to the division of people into male and female, depending on physical characteristics: sex organs, hormonal make-up and so on.

Gender differences are culturally formed. They exist on the basis of the biological, but build a huge system of differentiation over and above it. So whereas your sex will determine broadly whether or not you can bear a child, for example (though even this is not a universal truth), gender-based arguments have insisted that because women bear children, therefore they should be the ones to stay at home and bring them up. 'It's only natural' says a whole social system of laws, tax arrangements, childcare and so on.

Figure 10.1

ACTIVITY 10.1
- How can you tell which of the very simply drawn characters in Figure 10.1 is male and which female?
- Which lines on the drawing told you?
- Try to find other, similar examples in birthday cards, or children's comics and cartoon characters.
- What does this suggest about the ease with which assumptions of gender difference circulate in our culture?

Some of these assumptions are circulated through the media, and **feminist** positions keen to challenge them have developed key approaches to representation. **Content analysis** is a valuable starting point. It assumes that there is a relationship between the frequency with which a certain item (say 'women in the kitchen', 'black people as criminals') appears in media texts and the responses of its audiences to the group or activity involved in it.

Studies of gender roles in magazines and advertising show that women are still represented according to long-standing cultural stereotypes. Some elements have changed since the late 1970s and early 1980s when, for example:

- only 13 per cent of central characters in UK ads were women, while they made up 41 per cent of UK employees
- women were repeatedly shown 'as housewives, mothers, homemakers'
- men were often represented 'in situations of authority and dominance over women' aided by the use of male *voice-overs* (usually signifying authority on the soundtrack) or roles where only men are scientists or knowledgeable experts about the product which women 'just' consume.

Ten years later, in 1990, Guy Cumberbatch found that there were still twice as many men as women in television ads; the male voice-over was still predominantly used, even in ads for women's products; and the women in ads were usually younger and more conventionally attractive than the men, who were twice as likely to be shown in paid employment as women – and so on (see Strinati 1995).

'Two weeks ago, the National Association for the Advancement of Coloured People announced that it was going to wage "economic warfare" on the main four networks (CBS, NBC, ABC and Fox) for producing an entire autumn schedule with no major black characters in 26 new series or dramas.' (Duncan Campbell, *The Guardian*, August 2nd 1999).

ACTIVITY 10.2

Conduct your own random survey across one to three hours of television ads. Take a category such as age, ethnicity or gender (as in the examples above) and try to discover how that group or identity is now represented according to:

- The numbers of characters in ads who visibly belong to the group.
- How are they represented – as narrative heroes? As consumers or as experts? With or without dialogue? In what kinds of genres: comic? Serious? For cheap or expensive products?
- Do the voice-overs seem to belong to the group being represented?
- Are they repeatedly shown in some situations but not others, e.g. at work or in the home; as people preoccupied with their appearance?

'Gay characters and references to the existence of homosexuality were routinely laundered off the screen for … half a century' (Russo, in Medhurst and Lunt 1997, p. 63).

Such quantitative evidence is striking and demands careful thought, though objections have been made to content analysis and simple forms of stereotyping analysis. In the case of gender and representation you should think about their basic assumption: that what is needed is more realistic portrayals of women since the media are said to reflect society, and such reflections should always be accurate. What about questions such as:

I'll
be a
post
feminist
in
post
patriarchy

Figure 10.2a

Figure 10.2b Lara Croft, Tomb
Raider – and post-feminist?

- Might the relative neglect of wider structures of economic and political power make it arguably 'realistic' to show more women than men active in the home, for example?
- How do *different* genres affect these imaginings?
- Is it only irrational or ignorant prejudice that accounts for stereotyping?
- Is it true that the media have huge powers all on their own to socialise people into beliefs, roles and behaviour? There is plenty of evidence that people are not always successfully socialised in this way.

The term '**post-feminism**' suggests that we are now 'beyond' the need to struggle for gender equality: 'postmodern' playfulness or irony is the proper response to oppression. Young women are now argued to take for granted the respect, equality etc. struggled for by earlier feminists.

'It's OK to enjoy shopping and wear lipstick' points to the pleasure of 'trying on' identities, as well as to the need to re-read a woman's sexualised appearance as not necessarily subordinating her to men.

Q How far do you think that 'girl power' (as enacted by the Spice Girls or All Saints or the computer game character Lara Croft, Figure 10.2b) represents feminist achievement?

- How far does it fit with what's sketched here as 'post-feminist'?

Representations and the real

Calls for 'realism' or positive images of disadvantaged groups can ignore the ways that media texts belong to genres and forms that don't have a straightforward relationship to the rest of the real. To say that a media text is 'distorted' or 'unrepresentative' may ignore the following points:

- It is a representation in the other sense of the word: a construction with its own formal rules and fascinations. It will work with particular materials: time-based film and television, with their ability to stage action forms, or radio relying on spoken words etc.
- Its images may belong to a genre (radio comedy or horror film) which is not experienced by audiences in the same way as, say, the news. Audiences' degree of familiarity with its conventions is important for its 'reality effect': in action adventure genres, violence, for example, may be taken for granted as 'staged', as needed to dramatise the story. In news or children's fictions it may, however, be deeply disturbing because seen as more closely related to the real world. ·
- The idea of reflection is far too straightforward and mirror-like, especially for fantasy forms (e.g. horror or romance). It suggests there is a fairly simple thing called 'reality' to be 'reflected' in a one-to-one,

undistorted way, whereas some forms, such as comedy, have been argued to *depend on* exaggerations, sometimes involving stereotypes.

Example

When Les Dawson said the line: 'I knew it was the mother-in-law 'cause when they heard her coming, the mice started throwing themselves on the traps', there were several pleasures on offer: his delivery, voice and timing; the verbal surprise; comic exaggeration; and the economic elegance of a good joke. This economy is able to work only because a quickly recognisable stereotype is in play. The stereotype (here of the mother-in-law) could be said to offer the pleasure of community, of feeling a 'we' and a 'them'-ness for a moment.

Questions that then need asking include:

- From whose point of view is it being told? Whose point of view is excluded; who is the 'them' outside this cosy community?
- How is the audience positioned, not only by the joke but by the context in which it is told: all-male club; television show; radio documentary?
- How does the group on the receiving end of the joke seem to be treated in the rest of the media? Does that change how we might experience the joke?

To make this last point clearer: in the case of mothers-in-law, we may feel OK to laugh, since this is rather an outmoded target. Changes in family structures have eroded the considerable power of the mother-in-law of the working-class couple who had to live in her home for the first few years of married life. We may even feel that the degree of exaggeration itself is signalling the joke's distance from reality. To put it in *semiotic* language: pleasure is more from the play of the signifiers than from agreement with the way the *sign* represents its *referent*.

However, you might feel differently if you were an older woman, and the object of a great number of contemptuous jokes and comedy sketches. (Or you might not, if this were only a relatively unimportant one of your several identities.) And when jokes centre, say, on a group that is being abused on the streets or in the home, for whom there are fewer 'communities of feeling' to enter, it becomes a much less easy thing to laugh along with them.

The comedy series *Goodness, Gracious Me* (Radio 4 and BBC 2) plays with stereotypes from within the British Asian community and with 'role reversals' – as in the now famous sketch where a group of middle-class Indians go out for an 'English'.

Some women have felt that the (hegemonic?) balance has recently tilted back towards sexist images and language, for example in the 'laddishness' of breakfast television, or magazines like *Loaded* or *FHM*; or the use of women in traditionally 'sex object' casting poses, in Wonderbra ads etc. (see *post-feminist* above). Points raised include:

- How far can such imagery be always read ironically, as 'postmodern play'? After all, it does involve real jobs, advertising budgets, space taken up, and other images excluded.
- If you object to such imagery you may be called 'humourless' and 'repressive' or even 'PC' (**politically correct**). This is itself a very powerful stereotype of 'unthinking political conformity', deployed against a variety of attempts to change oppressive imagery and behaviour.

Questions of positive and negative images

'I don't want my cultural representations to be respectable. I want the most powerful, vivid images for me and other gays' (Alan Sinfield, conference paper, Staffordshire University, 1994).

History suggests that, once an oppressed group, such as women or 'black' people, perceives its political and social oppression, it begins to try to change that oppression at the level of representation, often trying to replace 'negative' with 'positive' images. This, however, is a complex process, involving the following areas:

- debates around how to define the 'community' being represented
- questions of what is to count as 'positive' representations
- the effect of employment practices in the media on such images
- the differences that the understandings of different audiences will make to the meanings of certain kinds of images, including genre competence, religious beliefs etc.

Groups that are heavily stereotyped (as 'problems') are likely to have less **access** to influential positions in the media, or to other kinds of power. This can set up a vicious circle of unemployment. It may also mean there may be few images or stories that centre on them sympathetically (as opposed to ones where they feature as villainous or untrustworthy: see long histories of the stereotyping of gays; of ethnic 'others' such as Mexicans and Indigenous Americans in Westerns, or Irish people in British cinema). This may be the result of violent historical processes, including wars or colonialism, which have left a long legacy of trivialising or insulting images.

When images of the group do begin to be produced, they have to bear what has been called the **burden of representation**. This involves:

'There is a sense of urgency to say it all, or at least to signal as much as we could in one film. Sometimes we couldn't afford to hold anything back for another time, another conversation or another film. There is the reality of our experience – sometimes we only get the one chance to make ourselves heard' (Pines 1992, p. 101).

- What is taken to be the object of representation? It is always crucial to ask: what is the 'reality' being represented? For huge groups such as women, or British Asians, which members of the group are doing the defining of 'the community'? Or of what is positive and what negative about an image? To imply that 'Asian British' is a homogeneous group, all sharing the same experiences of age, class, gender, sexuality and so on, is clearly foolish.

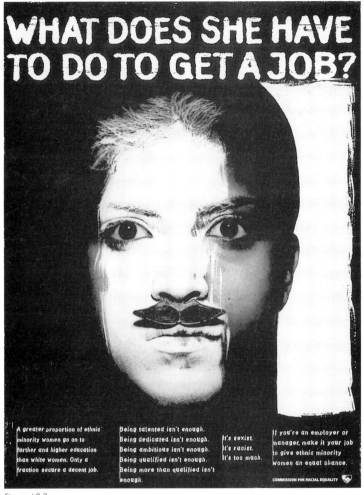

Figure 10.3

Racism   the 'stigmatising of
difference in order to justify
advantage or the abuse of power,
whether that advantage or abuse
be economic, political, cultural or
psychological' (Shohat and Stam
1994). The black activist Du Bois
emphasised the obsession with
'colour, hair and bone' used to
construct absolute (binary)
difference between 'black' and
'white' (see Hall 1996).

- There is also the question of how to construct characters belonging to the group (which is particularly visible in the case of skin colour) if they have been relatively absent from media images previously, and may therefore be read as 'representing' the whole community.

For many years there were so few images of black British on television, and those images which did exist were of blacks as 'problems' or (more sympathetic, if patronising), as 'victims'. When black characters *did* appear, they were often felt to 'stand in for' or represent the whole of their particular 'community'. These 'positive' images sometimes produced characterisations of strict parents, near-noble teachers and so on. But this was still a narrowing of the range of representation compared to the roles available to white characters. As a result, some members of such groups felt that being represented in various and ordinary, even 'negative' ways would be a positive step.

'Meera Syal (script writer of *Bhaji
on the Beach* (UK 1993)) described
'how an Asian man, bloody angry,
rang me up to abuse me for
showing our community in such a
negative light. How dare you show
women doing such things? Talking
about sex, and, what's worse, doing
it before marriage … Painting our
men as violent, when the real
violence is against us by the white
people' (Dunant 1994, p. 13).

'I longed to be an actress.
Unfortunately the only role
models I had, the only visible Asian
women in the media, were a barely
literate woman in a sari in [a]
sitcom … and a young beautiful
presenter on a kids' show' (Meera
Syal quoted in Dunant 1994).

ACTIVITY 10.3

Asian and Afro-Caribbean British have, after many generations' residence, begun to be imaged differently. Other ethnic groups are nevertheless often represented in very thin, or negative terms.

● Take a week's news coverage, across as many media forms as possible (radio, television, press) of Eastern European refugees or 'gypsies' (e.g. from Bosnia) in Britain. How do racists (e.g. in British National Party propaganda) construct their 'otherness'?

● Are there any students in your school or college whom you could interview about their experiences of such representations?

'Pictures of perfection make me sick and wicked' (Jane Austen).

EastEnders' variety of black characters – some involved in petty crime, some parents coping with family difficulties, some in love and so on – was argued as a kind of advance. Others, in the mid-1980s, picketed the film *My Beautiful Laundrette* (UK 1985) because of its images of gay and drug-dealing Asian British characters. 'Negative' images are not always best opposed by (someone's idea of) 'positive', but by the availability of a range of fuller ways of being imagined. This is arguably easier in a soap opera than a feature film, and is certainly easier when plenty of the group in question are employed in the meaning-making industries.

There is another, quite different attitude towards 'positive' and 'negative'. Supposing a group with good grounds for surliness, and for

Figure 10.4   Cotton picking in the American pre-Civil War South
Q 'seen' from whose point of view?

lack of co-operation with a social system or situation (slaves in plantation conditions, as imaged in *Gone With the Wind*) are represented as always smiling and whistling contentedly at their lot? They may well wonder if this image is 'positive' only for those who want to be reassured that all is well with an unjust set-up.

Sometimes groups heavily stereotyped by comedians, cartoonists and so on have responded by taking on the denigrated identity that the stereotype or abusive nickname gives them. Examples would be black groups calling themselves 'niggers' or gays calling themselves 'queens' or 'queers'. In fact, there is no such thing as the '100% right-on text' or 'positive image' which will guarantee to change audiences in progressive ways all on its own. Texts have always to be understood in the context of audiences, power structures and production practices. Fictional entertainment texts have an extremely complex relationship to audiences' sense of the real.

'Taking on the previously denigrated identity is a way of wrong-footing bigoted opponents' (Andy Medhurst).

'I like the sissy [stereotype of gay men]. Is it used in "negative" ways? Yeah. But my view has always been: visibility at any cost. Negative is better than nothing' (Harvey Feirstein in *The Celluloid Closet* (1996)).

Other ways of changing representations

It is important that debates over representations should not keep simply to the level of textual analysis. Other activities are also crucial in shifting taken-for-granted assumptions. These include:

- political change and the ways it can widen (or narrow) imaginings and the range of images possible (such as 1960s and 1970s feminist movements, or black Civil Rights struggles in 1950s and 1960s US)
- employment patterns and production achievements in media industries. These can be 'positive' in a usefully limited sense, helping to produce expectations and role models rather than the unspoken conviction that 'women/blacks/gays can't do that work because I've never seen one doing it'.
- access to dissenting mechanisms like the **right of reply**
- audiences' ability to come across, and feel comfortable with a wide range of media forms and imaginings, from the 'different' films of art cinema to low-status comic forms.

'*Premiere* magazine's 1997 100 Most Powerful people in Hollywood had twelve women, none in the top 10, the first (Sherry Lansing, co-head of Paramount) at no. 13, then nothing until Jodie Foster at 57' (*Time Out*, February 1998).

It may seem odd to suggest that dominant **discourses** (see 'Ideologies', Chapter 12) can be shifted at the level of production, simply by having women or blacks making certain kinds of films, television or music. But the assumption that a woman would be too frail or scatty to get together a big-budget action film is dispelled by Kathryn Bigelow's work, or Gale Anne Hurd's key role in the *Terminator* films. Similarly, racist assumptions about African-Americans' organisational and creative abilities may be countered by Spike Lee's success in getting big projects together.

Affirmative action or *equal opportunities* policies usually apply to less high-profile positions, and simply mean that, wherever possible, people

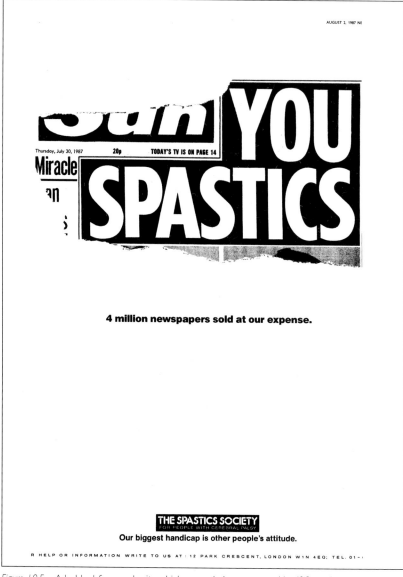

AUGUST 2, 1987 NI

Thursday, July 30, 1987   20p   TODAY'S TV IS ON PAGE 14

Miracle

Sun YOU SPASTICS

4 million newspapers sold at our expense.

THE SPASTICS SOCIETY
FOR PEOPLE WITH CEREBRAL PALSY

Our biggest handicap is other people's attitude.

R HELP OR INFORMATION WRITE TO US AT : 12 PARK CRESCENT, LONDON W1N 4EQ; TEL. 01-

Figure 10.5   A bold ad. from a charity which, nevertheless, re-named itself 'Scope'

'Disabled people are the largest "minority" group in the UK (estimated at 10–12%). Most of us will at some point in our lives be disabled – whether congenitally, or through old age, illness, or accident and so on … Craib argues … that our culture is dangerously close to denying the inevitability and necessity of … messy or "negative" feelings, as part of normal life' (Jessica Evans in Briggs and Cobley 1998).

from particular groups (such as women, or those with disabilities) will be appointed to jobs if their suitability is more or less equivalent to that of other candidates. For groups so far marginalised in paid media work this can open up the following possibilities:

- Crude stereotypes can be countered by the presence of members of such groups in the workforce. If you have people with disabilities working on a newspaper, it makes it much harder to resort to the stereotype that 'disabled people are always helpless victims'. Several black journalists have commented that racist headlines by **tabloid** papers would be harder to justify in the newsroom if there were more non-white British journalists employed there.

- Such media workers may well (though not inevitably) be more alert to, or simply know about 'angles' on news stories, or have ideas for credible storylines about members of that group. *Cagney and Lacey* and *French and Saunders* resulted partly from such inputs from women in media.

A different group and approach: there's a lovely moment at the end of the film *Sleep With Me* (US 1995) involving a character who throughout the film has been a keen card player, always impatient at delays to the card sessions. Only in the very last shot do we see him away from the card table, and suddenly realise he is in a wheelchair. Without any reference to disability, he has been constructed for most of the film as 'just the same as the other characters'.

'Right of reply' policies are also important. Newspapers like the *Sun* during Margaret Thatcher's years in power were large institutions with

---

Other ways of changing representations

'The presence of six black journalists in the *Sun* newsrooms would do more good than any number of disciplinary actions against them for racist reporting' (Lionel Morrison, one of the first black journalists to work in Fleet Street, *New Society*, 2 October 1987).

STATEMENT ON RACE REPORTING

1 The NUJ believes that the development of racist attitudes and the growth of fascist parties pose a threat to democracy, the rights of trade union organisations, a free press and the development of social harmony and well-being.

2 The NUJ believes that its members cannot avoid a measure of responsibility in fighting the evil of racism as expressed through the mass media.

3 The NUJ reaffirms its total opposition to censorship but equally reaffirms the belief that press freedom must be conditioned by responsibility and an acknowledgement by all media workers of the need not to allow press freedom to be abused to slander a section of the community or to promote the evil of racism.

4 The NUJ believes that the methods and the lies of the racists should be publicly and vigorously exposed.

5 The NUJ believes that newspapers and magazines should not originate material which encourages discrimination on grounds of race or colour as expressed in the NUJ's Rule Book and Code of Conduct.

6 The NUJ recognises the right of members to withhold their labour on grounds of conscience where employers are providing a platform for racist propaganda.

7 The NUJ believes that editors should ensure that coverage of race stories be placed in a balanced context.

8 The NUJ will continue to monitor the development of media coverage in this area and give support to members seeking to enforce the above aims.

Guidelines on Race reporting

● Race Reporting

Only mention someone's race if it is strictly relevant. Check to make sure you have it right. Would you mention race if the person was white?

Do not sensationalise race relations issues, it harms Black people and it could harm you.

Think carefully about the words you use. Words which were once in common usage are now considered offensive, e.g. half-caste and coloured. Use mixed-race and Black instead. Black can cover people of Arab, Asian, Chinese and African origin. Ask people how they define themselves.

Immigrant is often used as a term of abuse. Do not use it unless the person really is an immigrant. Most Black people in Britain were born here and most immigrants are white.

Do not make assumptions about a person's cultural background – whether it is their name or religious detail. Ask them, or where this is not possible check with the local race equality council.

Investigate the treatment of Black people in education, health, employment and housing. Do not forget travellers and gypsies. Cover their lives and concerns. Seek the views of their representatives.

Remember that Black communities are culturally diverse. Get a full and correct view from representative organisations.

Press for equal opportunities for employment of Black staff.

Be wary of disinformation. Just because a source is traditional does not mean it is accurate.

● Reporting Racist Organisations

When interviewing representatives of racist organisations or reporting meetings or statements or claims, journalists should carefully check all reports for accuracy and seek rebutting or opposing comments. The anti-social nature of such views should be exposed.

Do not sensationalise by reports, photographs, film or presentation the activities of racist organisations.

Seek to publish or broadcast material exposing the myths and lies of racist organisations and their anti-social behaviour.

Do not allow the letters column or 'phone-in' programmes to be used to spread racial hatred in whatever guise.

GUIDELINES ON TRAVELLERS

✗ Only mention the word gypsy or traveller if strictly relevant or accurate.

✗ Give balanced reports seeking travellers' views as well as those of others, consulting the local travellers where possible.

✗ Resist the temptation to sensationalise issues involving travellers, especially in their relations with settled communities over issues such as housing and settlement programmes and schooling.

✗ Try to give wider coverage to travellers' lives and the problems they face.

✗ Strive to promote the realisation that the travellers' community is comprised of full citizens of Great Britain and Ireland whose civil rights are seldom adequately vindicated, who often suffer much hurt and damage through misuse by the media and who have a right to have their special contributions to Irish and British life, especially in music and craftwork and other cultural activities, properly acknowledged and reported.

Figure 10.6 National Union of Journalists codes on race reporting. See how far they apply to the last newspaper you read

massive power to circulate headlines, employ cartoonists, angle photos which maintained hostile images of groups such as Irish people, or the GLC leader Ken Livingstone. Those targeted had far less power to circulate their positions and were often discredited by unfounded allegations which were later quietly retracted in an obscure part of the newspaper. The right of reply lobby asks for the reply to such stories to be given equal prominence to the original story. Thus an untrue front-page headline would have to be corrected on a later front page.

References

BFI Education Department (1982) *Selling Pictures*, London: BFI.

Bogle, Donald (1994, 2nd edition) *Toms, Coons, Mulattoes, Mammies and Bucks: An Interpretative History of Blacks in American Films*, New York: Continuum.

Briggs, Adam and Cobley, Paul (eds) (1998) *The Media: An Introduction*, Harlow: Longman.

Dunant, Sarah (ed.) (1994) *The War of the Words: The Political Correctness Debate*, London: Virago.

Durkin, Kevin (1985) *Television, Sex Roles and Children*, Milton Keynes: Open University Press.

Hall, Stuart (1996) 'The problem of ideology: marxism (sic) without guarantees' in D. Morley and Kuan-Hsing (eds) *Critical Dialogues in Cultural Studies*, London and New York: Routledge.

Lewis, J. (1991) *The Ideological Octopus*, New York and London: Routledge (esp. ch. 7).

Medhurst, Andy and Lunt, Sally R. (eds) (1997) *Lesbian and Gay Studies: A Critical Introduction*, London: Cassell.

Pines, Jim (ed.) (1992) *Black and White in Colour: Black People in British Television since 1936*, London: BFI.

Shohat, Elaine and Stam, Robert (1994) *Unthinking EuroCentrism: Multiculturalism and the Media*, London and New York: Routledge.

Further reading

Baehr, Helen and Dyer, Gillian (eds) (1987) *Boxed In: Women and Television*, London: Pandora.

Brunsdon, Charlotte (1997) 'Post-feminism and Shopping Films' in *Screen Tastes: Soap Opera to Satellite Dishes*, London and New York: Routledge.

MacDonald, Myra (1995) *Representing Women: Myths of Femininity in the Popular Media*, London and New York: Arnold.

11 / Case study: Stereotyping

Stereotyping has been part of key debates over representation in Media Studies such as:

- Do the media, in circulating images that involve particular kinds of people, suggest to large audiences that *x* or *y* character is typical of certain groups, and therefore that the whole group should be viewed in certain ways?
- Are these ways usually inadequate?
- Are 'negative' and 'positive' useful terms for such discussion?
- Is there a difference between information and entertainment or fiction forms in such debates?

What are stereotypes?

Stereotypes are not actual people, but widely circulated ideas or assumptions about particular groups. They are often assumed to be 'lies', and to need to be 'done away with' so we can all 'get rid of our prejudices' and meet as equals. The term tends to be much more derogatory than 'type' (which means very similar things).

It is more useful to think of stereotyping as a process of categorisation necessary to make sense of the world, and the flood of information and impressions we receive minute by minute. We all have to be 'prejudiced', in its root sense of 'pre-judging', in order to carve our way through any situation. We make mental maps of our worlds to navigate our way through them, and maps represent only parts of the real world, and in particular ways.

- We all employ typifications in certain situations.
- We all belong to groups that can be typified, and stereotyped.

For example, if you were being interviewed by a man wearing a pin-striped suit and waistcoat, with an English upper-class accent, you would probably, quite fast, make certain deductions about him, and maybe modify your behaviour accordingly. After ten minutes, you might have changed your attitude towards him, because of his behaviour, but you would still be interpreting him through stereotypes or categories on the basis of certain signs. This would be a perfectly reasonable procedure on your part. We all make sense of people on the basis of gestures, dress, voice and so on, very much as we construct a sense of characters in the media. In other situations you might make certain deductions on first meeting someone dressed in a particular way which are equally a categorisation, but a *sympathetic* rather than a negative one (depending on your taste in clothes). Stereotypes are not always negative.

> Such accents of course signify differently in different contexts: 'we've all known for ages that baddies, aliens and vampires in Hollywood movies have to come from Surrey … if the baddie isn't actually English … an eyebrow-swivelling Englishman is shipped in to play a villain from a nearby European country: Jeremy Irons and Alan Rickman in the *Die Hard* series, for instance' (Harry Thompson, *The Guardian*, 13 January 1998).

Though a dominant assumption in our culture is that we are all unique individuals (which is in some ways true), it is equally true that we share certain broad structures of social experience: around age and gender for example. These make it possible to understand many of the experiences we have as being typical. Indeed, it's arguable that our differences are due not to 'unique essences' but to the particular ways that very typical forces (such as class, gender and ethnicity) have intersected in our unique instance. This broadens the opportunities both for understanding other people's experiences, and perhaps for changing the social structures that produce them.

The usual trap in thinking about stereotyping is to feel that all typing is bad, and that all characterisations that present themselves as being complex are good. But complex characterisations, to be recognisable at all, need to relate in some way to the 'typical' (see Smith 1995).

Stereotypes and media

It is often argued that stereotypes are an unavoidable part of mass media representations. Hollywood cinema, for example, grew out of an early film industry aimed at illiterate, multi-ethnic American audiences. It soon learnt how to communicate via quickly established visual stereotypes (often adopted from theatre melodrama, with its silent frozen tableaux and polarised virtue/vice characterisations). Costumes and sets condensed various stereotypical meanings: the vamp (slinky low-cut gowns); 'poor but honest' settings (gingham tablecloth); good cowboy (white hat); shady Mexican (moustache, unshaven); 'homosexual' (limp-wristed gestures) and so on. The recourse to stereotypes is useful for such widely circulated entertainment products.

Such examples are often used to suggest that all stereotypes are very simple, and open only to fixed interpretations. As Gillian Swanson (1991) has suggested though, even such an apparently simple stereotype as that of the dumb blonde turns out, on closer examination, to be quite a complex cluster of characteristics. We might produce a list such as: strange logic, innocence, manipulativeness, humour, blondeness and other characteristics emphasising the body, childlike nature and adult knowingness. As Swanson points out:

Mask-like make-up, for instance, can simultaneously suggest vacancy and cluelessness, glamour and attractiveness, as well as a certain class position through connotations of brashness and overt sexuality. It may equally suggest a deliberate refusal to be accessible, as in more recent stars such as Annie Lennox and Madonna.

(Swanson 1991, pp. 133–4)

ACTIVITY 11.1

Take some media 'dumb blondes' (e.g. Marilyn Monroe, Barbara Windsor, Phoebe (Lisa Kudrow in *Friends*) and see whether the list applies to them.

- How many of the elements are contradictory?
- Which elements are repeated, which are combined differently in particular actresses?
- Is the stereotype still as widespread as previously?

She goes on to argue that it is not so much that some images of women 'escape' the stereotypes, but that, in the ways they combine typical and atypical elements, they change the terms in which particular stereotypes can be understood. This is rather like the way in which repetition and difference work in genres (see 'Genres', Chapter 8).

In addition, the processes of watching apparently stereotyped fictional situations may turn out to involve shifting patterns of identification. Swanson cites the example of a rape scene shown through the eyes of the male perpetrator:

Girls and boys may not identify with him in quite the same way, however. If the only way to participate in the suspense of the narrative is to adopt the male point of view, female spectators may be able to do so by their familiarity with the conventions of this kind of story. But the clash between the social formation of our identity (here, female) and the position we are asked to occupy to get pleasure (here, male) may produce anxiety in our viewing and response.

(Swanson 1991, p. 125)

Stereotyping and the real

So stereotypes, like genres, can be said to exist, even if their elements shift over time as well as within and across particular media, and even though audiences understand them in often ambiguous ways. They have been argued to have the following characteristics:

- They involve both a categorising and an evaluation of the group being stereotyped.
- The evaluation is often, though not always, a negative one.
- Stereotypes often try to insist on absolute differences where in fact the idea of a *spectrum* of difference is more appropriate, whether thinking of the colours of human beings, or sexualities, or degrees of 'masculine' and 'feminine' attributes.
- The group being stereotyped often has few means of affecting, of having a say in these representations.
- Stereotypes change over time. O'Sullivan *et al.* (1994: 127) give an example of 'working class-ness' which has shifted from the 'cloth-cap worker' of the 1950s to the 1980s 'consumerist home-owner who holidays in Spain'.

Stereotypes work by taking some easily grasped features presumed to belong to a group, putting them at the centre of the description, and implying that all members of the group always have those features. They also suggest that these characteristics, which are often the result of a historical process, are themselves the cause of the group's position.

One of the strengths of stereotypes is that they can point to features that appear to have 'a grain of truth', which we could indeed say are, or have been typical of particular groups. But even if such apparent evidence exists, the stereotype then repeats, across a whole range of media and informal exchanges, that this characteristic is *always* the *central* truth about that group. Let's take an example. Women are still often powerfully stereotyped as erratic and dangerous drivers. This stereotype can be seen as relating to historical and social factors:

- In order to drive well, a relatively expensive investment needs to be made in a car; in time, petrol

and training to drive it; and in experience of using it. These are all more easily available to people in reasonably paid jobs, which have traditionally been occupied by men rather than women.

- Part of this historical disadvantaging of women is **discourses** around technology and gender which have constructed 'the truly feminine woman' as unable to cope with technology – or driving.
- Since there are many poor drivers on the road, there's a fair chance that women actually will compose a number of them, and can thus be pointed to as examples of the truth of the stereotype. But it is the stereotype that makes the perception of such a connection likely in the first place.
- There is a kind of formal pleasure in the jokes to be made, even by women, about women drivers. They can be made in such a way as to distance the teller from the 'truth content' of the joke. This relates to the capacity of some fictional genres, with their repetition of certain entertaining elements (such as the 'scatty woman driver' in comedies) to keep negative stereotypes going and to appear simply 'harmless'. Anyone objecting to these repetitions can easily seem 'humourless' or 'PC' meaning **politically correct** (see p. 130).

How do stereotypes change?

If this sounds like a 'no-win' situation for women, it's interesting to note that this stereotype seems to have diminished over the last few decades.

- Active lobbying for less demeaning images of women have had some effects across the cultural industries which represent them.
- Relatedly, more women have entered the workforce and gained experience in driving. In fact 42 per cent of drivers were women in 1994, though they still started driving later in life than men, and drove fewer work-related miles.
- If you have access to minority publications, such as insurance companies' journals, or even some business pages of newspapers, you will see that some insurers

charge women lower premiums, considering them a lower risk than men.

- The stereotype has shifted partly because women have been more targeted recently as potential car buyers. The ecology lobby may also have had an effect, making the display of machismo through gas-guzzling power play in big cars less acceptable. (For one thing, advertising agency workers are highly media-literate metropolitans, used to tuning in to trends and new ideas. They do not want to appear to hold 'Jurassic' prejudices.)

As a result of these processes, images of competent women drivers are produced and widely circulated (even though they are rarely imaged as in charge of the big, authoritative saloon cars advertised on Sunday night television).

A **pluralist** position (see 'Ideologies and discourses', Chapter 12) might argue that this shows that there are no such things as powerful stereotypes. But it is important to remember that major institutions such as advertising and the tabloid press have much more power to circulate inadequate, as well as new or challenging, stereotypes and assumptions. So the mere existence of counter-stereotyped images has to be judged in relation to where, and how often, they are likely to be seen and accepted.

are an inextricable part of the real world, never just an add-on extra.

Cause and effect in stereotypes

Another key point about stereotypes is that they can take something that is an effect of a group's situation and encourage audiences to feel it is the cause of that group's low status. For example, for a long time in Hollywood cinema and other discourses, black slaves working on cotton plantations before the American Civil War of 1861–5 were often stereotyped through such signs, among others, as:

- a shuffling walk
- musical rhythm, and a tendency to burst into song and dance readily
- (in characterisations of female house slaves) overweight bodies, uneducated foolishness and childlike qualities (*Gone With the Wind* (US 1939) contains two notorious examples in 'Mammy' and Prissy)

To say that these demeaning stereotypes embody a grain of truth may seem in itself insulting, but consider the following facts:

- Slaves on the Southern plantations in the nineteenth century would have had their calf muscles cut if they

ACTIVITY 11.2

Collect and study ads and news stories involving women drivers. Test the above suggestions. Look at health and safety ads on the dangers of drunk driving.

- How do they gender drunk drivers?
- Is/would it be a shock to see a woman represented as one? Why?

Figure 11.1 Scarlett and Mammy in *Gone With the Wind* (US 1939)

Even though you may feel it is only 'changes in the real world' which will shift stereotypes, struggles around representations are always also needed. Representations, discourses, stereotypes of the real,

tried to run away from slavery (the shuffling gait of the stereotype).

- Slaves were given hardly any educational or cultural opportunities. (Hostile use of the stereotype demeans efforts to make music and dance out of very simple resources to hand. It attributes 'rhythm' to primitive, animal qualities, thus justifying slaveowners' positions like 'they couldn't benefit from education anyway'.)

- The women were often treated simply as breeding stock by the slave owners. When this function was over, once they had given birth to numbers of new slaves and their bodies were perhaps enlarged by repeated pregnancies, they were often moved into the main house and used as nursemaids to the white children. Again, hostile use of the stereotype invites us to account for the Mammy's size in terms of physical laziness or ignorance rather than her exploitation at the hands of the slave system.

ACTIVITY 11.3

If you have the chance, try to compare *Gone With the Wind* with the recent Steven Spielberg film *Amistad* (US 1997) in terms of the construction of the slave characters, the lines they are given, their role compared to those of the white characters.

- What has changed, what remains constant in such representations and narratives?

A final note: though you may feel that large, historically oppressed groups such as black American slaves, or Irish people have been heavily stereotyped, this usually happens through more than one stereotype, and it is possible to imagine them being used sympathetically, as in black reformist propaganda, or the broadly sympathetic if sentimental use of Irishness in recent Hollywood films such as *Titanic* (US 1997). More usually, though, even if there is often a grain of truth in particular stereotypes at some moments in history, they keep being circulated long after the end of the situations that

Figure 11.2

gave rise to them. *Gone With the Wind* was released in 1939, not 1839.

This may partly be due to the pressures from tourist and heritage industries for marketable, nostalgic imagery, often coming out of successful media products. *Gone With the Wind*, for example, is a huge source of souvenirs, theme parks, tourist attractions in Georgia. These offer pleasures that are analogous to escapist fascinations of entertainment forms: updatings of the South's history, ingenious spectacle, fun, lighthearted engagement with the otherwise heavy and heartbreaking tales of slavery. It becomes difficult but necessary for black groups, as for any group trying to align political issues of representation to the entertaining pastimes of the media, to object that the nostalgia is for an order founded on slavery, mostly perceived from the white plantation owners' point of view (see Figure 10.4 again).

References

Bogle, Donald (1994, 2nd edition) *Toms, Coons, Mulattoes, Mammies and Bucks,* New York: Continuum.

Briggs, Adam and Cobley, Paul (eds) (1998) *The Media: An Introduction,* Harlow: Longman (part three).

Dunant, Sarah (ed.) (1994) *The War of the Words: The Political Correctness Debate,* London: Virago.

Geraghty, Christine (1991) *Women and Soap Opera,* London: Polity.

Medhurst, Andy and Lunt, Sally R. (eds) (1997) *Lesbian and Gay Studies: A Critical Introduction,* London: Cassell.

O'Sullivan, Tim, Dutton, Brian and Rayner, Philip (eds) (1994, 2nd edition) *Studying the Media:. An Introduction,* London, New York, Melbourne and Auckland: Edward Arnold.

Perkins, Tessa (1979) 'Rethinking Stereotypes', in M. Barrett, P. Corrigan, A. Kuhn and V. Wolff (eds) *Ideology and Cultural Production,* London: Croom Helm.

Pines, Jim (ed.) (1992) *Black and White in Colour: Black People in British Television since 1936,* London: BFI.

Smith, M (1995) *Engaging Characters: Fiction, Emotion and the Cinema,* Oxford: Oxford University Press.

Strinati, Dominic (1995) *An Introduction to Theories of Popular Culture,* London: Routledge.

Swanson, Gillian (1991) 'Representation', in David Lusted (ed.) *The Media Studies Book,* London: Routledge.

Taylor, Helen (1989) *Scarlett's Women: Gone With the Wind and its Female Fans,* London: Virago (esp. pp. 174–80).

12 Ideologies and discourses

The concept of **ideology** has been a key one for Media Studies. The term refers to:

- sets of ideas which give some account of the social world, usually a partial and selective one
- the relationship of these ideas or values to the ways in which power is distributed socially
- the way that such values are usually posed as 'natural' and 'obvious' rather than socially aligned.

For instance, **sociobiology** provides 'taken for granted' ideological assumptions coming from the study of genetics or the natural world, that all human beings are 'naturally' acquisitive, competitive and selfish. A counter view would be interested in:

- examples from the natural world that provide other metaphors, of a non-competitive kind
- tracing whether sociobiology's particular emphasis seems to accompany the rise of positions celebrating (or stating as natural) a ruthless 'survival of the fittest' version of capitalism in the 1980s and 1990s
- emphasising that people are formed by their capacity to change their culture as well as by 'natural' limits and boundaries.

Some ideas, though they form a system and are quite rigid, will not be classified as 'ideological'. Someone may have obsessive *ideas* about personal cleanliness, and relate them *systematically* to the fullness of the moon, but these would not necessarily be called *ideological* since they cannot be shown to relate to the distribution of social power.

'Greed ... is good. Greed is right. Greed ... captures the essence of the evolutionary spirit ... Greed has marked the upward surge of mankind' (Gekko/Michael Douglas, a character and speech based on that of an actual US stockbroker, from Oliver Stone's *Wall Street* (US 1987)).

Marxist approaches

The first time it was argued that ideas are not free-floating but instead systematically linked to social power was in France, in the period leading up to the 1789 Revolution. Most discussion of ideology in Media and Cultural Studies comes out of the work of Marx, who later, in the nineteenth century, questioned another, supposedly 'natural' but unequal order of things. He analysed the new profit- and market-dominated system – **capitalism** – and the power of two classes within it, the rising industrial manufacturers or capitalists, and the working class (or proletariat).

A key European world view before then was that the earth was made by God, with the sun revolving round it, and that everything on earth had its natural place in a divinely designed order which could not be questioned. This was eventually challenged by scientists such as Galileo (1564–1642).

apitalism a competitive social system, emerging in the late feudal period in Europe, based on **commodification** and the drive of the owners of the means of production to maximise the profits of their companies.

Class Marxism defines class in terms of the antagonistic social formations created and perpetuated in the process of production (i.e. owners of and workers within various industries).

A Marxist objection to adverts is that they make products appear as if by magic, obliterating the central importance of people's labour in production processes. Key ideological questions would be: Who produces these goods? Under what conditions? In what relationships to the profits and policies of the company? See Ross (1997), ch. 9, on garment workers and also Williamson (1978).

Antonio Gramsci (1891–1937) Italian Marxist activist who took part in complex political struggles in Italy, involving church and state, North and South, peasants and modern industrial workers. As a result his theories showed a keen awareness of the need for complex struggles and negotiations.

Marx emphasised the importance of **class** difference, or people's different relationships to the means of production, as key to the kinds of values and political ideas they will have. Do they *own* factories, banks, country estates, or do they have to earn their living by *working for* the owners of factories, banks and so on? He was especially interested in capitalists' relationship to their employees, the working classes who, he argued, had the power to change history by their united action.

He used the concept of ideology to account for how the capitalist class protected and preserved its economic interests, even during years of unrest and attempted revolutions. Three of his emphases have been particularly important for Media Studies:

- The **dominant** ideas (which become the '**common sense**') of any society are those which work in the interests of the ruling class, to secure its rule or dominance. Those who own the means of production thereby, also, control the means of producing and circulating the most important ideas in any social order. This is the key to why the meaning-making bodies (which now include the modern media) in any society represent political issues as they do. It implies that the working class needs to develop its own ideas and struggle for the means of circulating them if it is successfully to oppose the capitalist class.

- Related to this, he argued a **base–superstructure** model of the social role of institutions such as the media. The ways in which the basic needs of a social order are met (industrial capitalist, or feudal–rural relations, for example) determine its superstructure, i.e. its 'secondary', less basic, ideological and political institutions, like religion and cultural life. Such a model is also often called **economic determinist**, since the economic 'base' is argued crucially to determine, not just influence, cultural and political activity.

- A final important step is the argument that, through these sets of power, the dominant class is able to make workers believe that existing relations of exploitation and oppression are natural and inevitable. This power 'mystifies' the real conditions of existence, and how they might be changed, and conceals the interest it has in preventing change.

Gramsci's term **hegemony** was a development of this model and became a key way of thinking how dominant value systems change through struggle. Instead of an emphasis on the imposed dominance of a ruling class, and the determining power of the economic base, Gramsci argued that particular social groups in modern democracies struggle for ascendancy using persuasion and consent as well as occasional brute force. Because of this, power is never secured once and for all but has to be constantly negotiated in a to-and-fro tussle.

The key point for Media Studies is that people are not forced, or duped into a false consciousness of the world, but have their consent actively fought for all the time, nowadays almost exclusively through the media.

Example: defining 'the global'

The processes of **globalisation** are handled in highly ideological ways. The *hegemonic* version emphasises globalisation as being:

- such an enormous process as to be irresistible
- associated with instantaneous, global technologies which are simply baffling and therefore beyond most people's control
- related to **chaos theory**, that the world cannot be in any way rationally and morally accounted for (perhaps most vividly phrased as: 'the butterfly flapping its wings in Brazil causes a cyclone in the Bay of Bengal').

Such emphases encourage the (admittedly complex) processes of globalisation to be seen as utterly chaotic, autonomous, and beyond the wit, design and regulation of human beings. It becomes a mysterious destiny, rather like the inscrutable God of some religions, in the face of which we are relatively powerless and cannot be held personally accountable. Very little close scrutiny takes place of the role of multinational conglomerates and how they might be directed, or regulated differently.

Counter-hegemonic views include:

- those of the ecology movement, arguing that there *is* some provable cause-effect relationship between 'local' actions (such as the US refusal to sign the 1997 Kyoto agreement on pollution control) and global results (the widespread fogs and floods of a polluted planet).
- attempts to cancel the 'debt' of the world's poorer nations to the World Bank so as to allow their economies to develop and trade on a more equal footing
- publicising how the multinational conglomerates and richest nations operate. The **MAI** (Multilateral Agreement on Investment) for example, involving the twenty-nine richest countries, will stop any country from protecting or boosting its own domestic businesses (including tourism) over those of big foreign companies
- an emphasis on the preferability of 'small' technologies for certain purposes, for example the importance of bicycles and their many uses across the world (Figure 12.1).
- related to this, questions of gender, and how global change impacts differently on men and women.

Counter-hegemonic positions see globalisation not as inscrutable and irresistible but as open to *some* kinds of regulation and direction.

Children's mobile library

Figure 12.1   Schoolchildren's mobile library, Sri Lanka, an example of sustainable technology

Exploring this example

ACTIVITY 12.1

Collect quotes from television or press news which use the word 'globalisation' or 'global trends' etc. and see how far they support either of the above positions.

- Where did you find the dominant, and where the opposing views?

ACTIVITY 12.2

Collect adverts which seem to be evoking a sense of the global (perhaps by a globe, as in British Airways, or BT or Coca-Cola ads).

- How is this 'globe' or 'world' or 'planet' represented? Does this relate to any of the debates above? (See Figure 12.2.)

Propaganda indicates direct manipulation of information for political purposes, usually by governments or political parties. It can more generally be understood as a kind of **discourse**, one which openly presents itself as wanting to persuade its audience of something. Though it usually urges political positions ('Vote for *x* or *y* party'), propaganda may also be used for apolitical messages (e.g. not to drink and drive).

The two activities of **propaganda** and **censorship** can be seen to reveal moments and areas where this struggle for willing consent has come under intense pressure, and a resort is made to more conscious manipulation of ideological positions (often accompanied by physical force). Government propaganda is used at moments which it has the power to define as 'national emergency' (e.g. wars; important strikes),

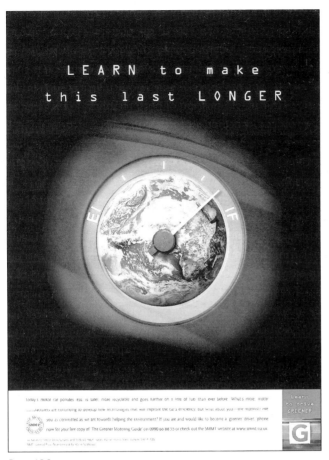

Figure 12.2

when it will try to control and shape public perceptions in particularly coercive ways such as:

- direct censorship of reports, especially of casualties or enemy successes
- allowing only a certain 'pool' of approved journalists into a war zone (as in the 1982 Falklands and 1991 Gulf War)
- banning fiction and entertainment material which it perceives as related to the war (e.g. *Carry On Up the Khyber* was pulled from the schedules during the Gulf War).

Such examples of state (and conglomerate) control could be argued as simply the taking to an extreme of a quite routine process, such as

- MI5 vetting of staff in the BBC until very recently
- the occasional direct government pressure on news and current affairs (as in government objections to critical *Panorama* and *Newsnight* programmes and interview styles)

Huge conglomerates like News Corporation, whose incomes can be the size of many nation states, also wield powers of censorship, as in Rupert Murdoch's intervention in 1998 to prevent publication of Chris Patten's memoirs, critical of the Chinese regime at a time when Murdoch was developing business links with them. And powerful figures may deploy government-scale propaganda offensives to shift public perceptions, as Mohamed Al Fayed seems to have done around the reasons for the deaths of his son, Dodi, and Diana, Princess of Wales, in 1997.

- the key everyday processes of news shaping by 'official sources', the lobby system, self-censorship as a 'good professional' etc.

The other name you will come across in this Marxist tradition is that of **Althusser**, who argued that economic determinism works only in 'the last instance'; that parts of the superstructure are 'relatively autonomous'. Class rule is sustained by two kinds of organised and related power, the *Repressive State Apparatus (RSA)*, which includes the army, police, prisons and law courts, which wins and maintains state power by force and the *Ideological State Apparatus (ISA)*, which includes education, the church, party politics, the family and the media, and maintains power at the ideological level, in people's minds, by producing imaginary relations to real structures of power. It does this partly by naturalising assumptions and ideas which are ideological in that they manufacture and maintain consent to the existing social order.

Althusser's approach differs from classic Marxist emphasis on cultural forms as expressions of, or forces determined by, the economic base. But it is much more rigidly inescapable than the Gramscian idea of hegemony. It implies there can be 'no way out' of ideology ('common sense' is always to be distrusted) and this, of course, fails to account for his own work, since in theory he must be outside its grip to write about it at all.

More recently, **political economy** approaches, such as those of Peter Golding and Graham Murdock, have revived Marx's emphasis on the determining role of ownership, as against media theory's overemphasis on textual or cultural elements. They argue that those who own and control huge proportions of the media (such as Rupert Murdoch or Bill Gates) share in the privilege of the dominant class. This group as a whole will ensure that the social imagery and knowledge which is circulated through the media is broadly in its interests, and reproduces the system of class inequalities from which it benefits.

This does not necessarily deny that **oppositional** ideas (such as those of socialist **feminists**) don't struggle for **access** to the media, often with

Louis Althusser (1918–90) French philosopher who developed a structuralist version of Marxism. His ideas are most clearly laid out in *Ideology and Ideological State Apparatuses* in *Lenin and Philosophy and Other Essays* (1971).

Figure 12.3 'Green' and anti-consumerist ideas often circulate in the small-scale medium of the postcard

some success. But the increasing concentration of power in the hands of a very few media conglomerates inevitably leads to:

- a decline in the range of material available, e.g. in satellite and cable television programming, as global conglomerates exclude or swallow up all but the most commercially successful operators
- an exclusion of the voices of those lacking economic power or resources, both in the media and as consumers of the expensive new technologies

- the prevalence of 'easily understood, popular, formulated, undisturbing, assimilable fictional material' (see 'Genres', Chapter 5).

Critics of these positions have asked:

- how far such economic determinist accounts of the media can choose to argue for the mere *interplay* of economic and cultural
- why popular cultural products such as films, television and music are popular (unless we write off the audience as dupes) (see 'Pleasures' below).

Challenges to Marxist approaches

Several recent changes in the world have affected the power of 'classic' Marxist theories:

- the collapse of Eastern bloc state socialism (seen by many as the same as 'Marxism')
- accompanying this, the renewed power of consumer capitalist 'free market' emphases, including their media theory equivalents: celebration of audiences' power in relation to the media
- the influence of some **postmodern** positions, which have abandoned any kind of attempt at a rationally accountable or improvable world
- a growing scepticism about the claims of science to absolute truth. (This matters, since Marxism had often claimed scientific status for its theories.)
- the challenge of newer politics (based on gender, ethnicity, sexuality, often seen as crucially 'affecting life chances' rather than being absolute determinants). These have replaced the class-focused analysis of Marxism with a focus on other ways of analysing inequality, and are sometimes called **identity politics**. Feminists have pointed out that inequality also derives from the realm of *reproduction*, with men exploiting women's household work for them and their children (see Andermahr *et al.*). Black theorists have explored the ways in which inequalities between races have been constructed and maintained, and have often cut across class difference.

Since we still live in deeply unequal societies, driven by the classic capitalist logic of profit and competition, now on a global scale, Marxist interest in economic power and its relationship to social transformation has continued to be relevant for radical politics.

But several qualifications need now to be made:

- To talk of one dominant ideology implies an improbably coherent, argument-free ruling class, smoothly making the rest of us go along with its interests. Such analysis often makes very patronising assumptions about anyone other than the person doing the analysing. If the wheels of ideology roll so perfectly smoothly to produce

Some argue that class is now invisible in serious analysis of inequality. 'Whereas the old left tried to help people who were humiliated by poverty and unemployment ... the post-sixties left tried to help people ... humiliated for reasons other than economic class. Nobody is setting up a programme in unemployed studies, homeless studies or trailer-park studies because the unemployed, the homeless ... are not "other" in the relevant sense' (Richard Rorty, *New Statesman*, 8 May 1998).

Identity politics the practice of basing one's politics on a sense of personal identity – as female, Black, gay etc. as opposed to membership of larger 'party' politics.

Figure 12.4   Cartoon by Posy Simmonds published in the *Guardian* in the 1970s. Stereotypes of groups of women work within larger discourses about 'what women are like'

conformity, how has the person analysing their workings come to have their 'outsider' perceptions?

- A renewed exploration of the role of ownership and political-economic structures in general is needed in Media Studies. But a Marxist analysis argues the *determining* power of the economic base. Yet, if ideas and culture can affect that base (as in religious fundamentalism, struggles over free speech, environmentalism etc.), how can this degree of emphasis be retained?

- Even within the still very influential Gramscian emphases, the weighting given to '*dominant ideology*' was challenged by writers (Abercrombie, Hill and Turner 1980) insisting that, though dominant ideologies do exist, they are not the most important means for making social orders hang together. The fact that huge state bodies for surveillance and armed control exist suggests we do not inhabit unified social orders, running contentedly along. They suggest that it is *'dull compulsion of the economic'* (and, feminists might argue, of domestic labour) as well as the power of state force which leaves us little room, time or power to challenge systems of values which most people disagree with, or feel to be personally irrelevant.

Discourses

Michel Foucault (1926–84) post-structuralist philosopher, sociologist and historian of knowledge. Best known for his work on the relationship of power and knowledge, involving the power of **discourses**, especially in the areas of madness and sexuality.

Examples: Some of Foucault's writing argues that discourses actually create 'regimes of truth' and therefore our perceptions. The term 'child' has not always been used of 'young adults' and is notoriously hard to define in years, and between different cultures. But the *power to define* someone as a 'child' has enormous legal, financial and other implications. See Holland (1992). Another example might be the power to define actions as criminal.

The argument that there are dominant ideologies and identities (connected to gender, ethnicity, disability etc.) rather than one dominant set of ideas simply dependent on economic struggle has been associated in Media Studies with an interest in the work of **Foucault** and his writings on **discourse**. This involves another emphasis in thinking about power and the media, one which takes the rather abstract work of semiotics into a study of how *socially situated* languages shape our worlds. 'Discourse' is a term from linguistics, meaning any regulated system of statements or language use which has rules, conventions and therefore assumptions and exclusions. Foucault explores how these rules and the material practices, which support and enforce them, come to organise or regulate knowledge and serve (or even produce) particular kinds of power relationships. 'Thus, it may or may not be true that single parenting inevitably leads to delinquency and crime. But if everyone believes so, and punishes single parents accordingly, this will have real consequences for both parents and children and will beome "true" in terms of its real effects' (Hall 1997, p. 49).

ACTIVITY 12.3

Think of the different discourses you operate in language (for example in relation to teachers, to parents, or a police officer or close friends).

- Write short letters to a range of them asking for some kind of help.
- How differently would you phrase and arrange these; what would you avoid mentioning in each; would you consider handwriting some but not others?
- How do these different discourses relate to your power in relation to each of them?

Discourse analysis is interested in exploring what values and identities are contained, prevented, or perhaps encouraged by the practices and (often unspoken) rules of a particular discourse, which for media can include visual as well as verbal codes. If you have studied science you may have used 'scientific discourse' to describe experiments. 'The bunsen burner was lit', for example, is one of a number of ways in which 'scientific impersonality' will be signified in writing up an experiment. The account will ideally seem to come from nowhere (no mention of the person who lit the burner), and therefore to conceal its human fallibility in favour of a kind of remote authority. British television news often operates in a similar way (see next Case study).

Examples

The word 'famine' for food crises in the 'Third World' has been argued to obscure financial–political relations, and their colonial histories. It does this by introducing part of a Biblical, pre-industrial discourse, in which mysterious scourges come from God. This works to obscure processes such as:

- western 'food mountains'
- price fixing of harvests in the interests of the West
- the policies of the IMF (International Monetary Fund) and other big banks
- the 'futures' speculation on commodities (i.e. crops) on western stock exchanges.

Images of the victims of such shortages often work with a particular visual discourse: the camera usually above the pitiful victim, preferably a child, who is given no name, or access to the soundtrack or translation facilities (if seen on television). This invites western audiences to think of them as existing in a victim's dependency relationship to the West (whereas it is the West that is dependent on raw materials, at a certain price, from the 'Third World'). Such images are also argued to perpetuate the situation by excluding a sense of such people as active in their own fates.

The purely visual discourse of the family photo album has been argued to exclude certain kinds of imagery. Family arguments, the sharing of work in the home, child labour in the paper-round etc. are not part of the discourse. Other poses and arrangements *are*, e.g. those which emphasise 'the family' as a harmonious, happy unit; certain 'dependencies' e.g. of male on female, young on old, by height, gesture, positioning etc.

'Far from being in debt to rich countries, the world's poorest nations are owed billions of dollars by them for the disproportionate amount of environmental damage they inflict on the planet says a [Christian Aid] report.' (*The Guardian*, September 20th 1999).

Jot down some key phrases of financial reporting, e.g. 'the pound had a bad day/was buoyant'; 'the Footsie bounced back'.
- What do they mean?
- What kinds of knowledge, information do they exclude?
- How do they image Stock Exchange activities?
- How is this ideological? Discursive?

ACTIVITY 12.4

See whether you can find examples of discourses around childhood in your family photo albums. Try to devise photos which would challenge them. How do these images relate to the ways 'children' are defined, sexualised etc. in the discourses of advertising photography? (See Spence (1986), Holland (1992).)

Thanks to the debt
one industry is now thriving in Zambia

Is there any sight more sad than a child-sized coffin? In just one four week period since March, in a single cemetery in Zambia, some 200 young children have been committed to tiny graves.

The effects of war? Corruption? A natural disaster? No. The cause is a man-made disaster: debt. The repayments bring already poor countries to the brink, robbing families of food and medicine.

The United Nations has estimated that 21 million children will die in Africa alone before the end of the century unless action is taken.

At Christian Aid we're taking that action, with a campaign to end the debt crisis by 2000. We'll be there at the G8 summit, lobbying for change as part of Jubilee 2000. We need you to help us, starting right now by taking at least one simple action - add your name, wear your chain or join the human chain in Birmingham. If you need any further impetus, look again at that child-sized coffin. And imagine how it feels to be the mother of the child.

ACT NOW. Send the coupon or call 0345 000 300

Please send me a copy of the Jubilee 2000 petition ☐ Christian Aid Debt Action Sheet ☐

Name _____

Address _____

_____ Postcode _____

Christian Aid, Freepost MR8192, Manchester M1 9AZ.
Please visit our web site www.christian-aid.org.uk

Christian ♟ Aid
We believe in life before death

Registered Charity No. 258003

Figure 12.5 A charity ad. which tries to avoid the charitable 'look' (of pity towards a passive victim) and to raise campaigning issues instead

'The pop industry is throwing its weight behind the Jubilee 2000 campaign to write off Third World debt ... Jubilee 2000 aims to present the biggest petition of 22 million signatures to world leaders at the G8 summit' (*The Guardian*, 12 February, 1999).

Think about the suggestion that, if there is a dominant ideology at the turn of this century, it is this: 'Everything is relative. There are no big power structures. We all have lots of freedoms. There is no such thing as a dominant ideology.'

Critical pluralism

Pluralist models see the media as floating free of power, emphasise the diversity and choice in media forms and argue that, if certain values are dominant, it is because they are 'genuinely popular' and have won out in the 'free market of ideas'.

Golding and Murdock's political economy approaches (described above) angle this emphasis, acknowledging that alternative, even radical ideas and identities circulate in the media, but emphasising the importance of economic power in allowing some ideas and imaginings to circulate much more freely than others. Such **critical pluralism** acknowledges that there may be struggle between competing discourses, but insists that it is not an amicable free-for-all (as in pluralist theories and the 'free market' values they so closely relate to). Some discourses are part of powerful institutions and have easier access to material resources and publicity. Examples include:

- 'the commercial speech of the consumer system' (i.e. **marketing** and advertising)'and the identities and desires it repeats
- the conservative political positions of right-wing ideologues such as Rupert Murdoch, or the US politician Newt Gingrich. Their positions (urging legislative changes in media ownership and **deregulation**, or encouraging right-wing 'shock-jocks' in circulating certain 'limit' political positions, like outright racism, sexism and **homophobia**) have much more visibility than those of opponents.

Routine news practices also encourage some kinds of speedy assumptions and discourage others.

Homophobia fear of homosexuality, expressed in a spectrum of activities from hostile or demeaning vocabulary to legislation.

Example

In 1995 a federal US government building in Oklahoma City was bombed, involving nearly two hundred dead, and harrowing scenes on television news. For days there was speculation about who the bombers were. But only hours after the bombing a tiny agency, Inter Press, pointed the finger at the American far-right militia movement. They worked not on inside information, but on simple deduction, involving

- the date (the anniversary of the ending of the Waco siege, highly significant for the militias)
- the fact that a government building was bombed (given the militias' hatred of central government)
- the proximity of Oklahoma to Waco.

Given the long historical involvement of the US in oil-rich states, and the recent turns that history has taken, the assumption that Middle Eastern terrorists might be to blame for Oklahoma City is not totally unreasonable or unlikely. But it seems that another ideological position had very little immediate access to the minds of journalists: one which would have connected the bombing to the rise of extreme right-wing armed movements inside the US, to the easy availability of weapons as promoted by the National Rifle Association (NRA) and so on.

(a)

(b)

Figure 12.6 One radical journalist seeks to make some connections between the effects of terrorism and the effects of unemployment: (a) is of the result of bombing;, (b) is of the result of 'downsizing' a car factory

(From Michael Moore *Downsize This!* (1977) New York: Crown Publishers Inc.)

An example of the debates around pluralism: the Co-operative Bank in 1994 began to advertise its product (banking) with various promises that it would change its relationships to oppressive, exploitative and polluting regimes or companies (see Figure 12.7). It was fronting a critical, 'alternative' position on the capitalist regime in which it is involved, but also, in classic capitalist fashion, seeking to signal a crucial market difference between itself and its competitors.

Figure 12.7

ACTIVITY 12.5

Taking the Co-operative Bank advertisement outlined above (Figure 12.7):

- How far does this break the rules of advertising and of Marxist expectations of the media?
- Is this ad an example of how discourses that were previously considered ideologically alternative, or 'outside' the mainstream can enter and change it?
- Or is this an example, on the other hand, of *incorporation*, a term first used by the **Frankfurt School** to describe the capacity of capitalist media industries (such as advertising) endlessly to absorb and circulate images of oppositional movements and positions?

How does this relate to questions of ideology raised in this chapter?

Pleasures

Just as the Marxist emphasis on class relations alone has been replaced by an interest in other kinds of inequality, so Media Studies' early focus on '**bias**'-centred ideological studies of ('public') news processes has been replaced by an exploration of ('private'?) fiction, entertainment and fantasy forms. These try to avoid seeing the pleasures of entertainment forms as simply the 'sugar on the pill' which helps the 'medicine' (ideology) go down. They also try to respect audiences' capacity to compare media with non-media experience. Some have even stressed the importance of exploring audience's disappointments in their favourite entertainment media.

'Pleasure' is not just one thing, nor are pleasures value free or equally available to all. Though often seen as 'feminine' pastimes, miles away from 'men's business', the pleasure of entertainment forms turns out to be several things, not just one, and to include thrills, for men and women, which directly relate to the world of information and 'the public'. Media offer formal pleasures (the elegance of costumes, or script or performance), erotic ones (the turn of a face or the sound of a voice), but also cognitive pleasures (to do with knowledge): of finding out, or being offered recognitions of long ignored experiences. There is the thrill of hearing a marginalised position given stirring expression, or of being offered an image which suddenly seems to help us understand complex phenomena. 'Utopian' pleasures (see 'Genres', Chapter 8) suggest the linkage between fiction forms and a sense of 'how life might be'.

Dahlgren (1985) and Stam (1983), focusing on 'pleasure' in relation to news programmes, suggested that, far from audiences absorbing the 'bias' or 'dominant ideologies' in television news, they often slip in and out of

Bias originally meant 'oblique line', and by the end of the sixteenth century was applied to the game of bowls. It is now a term for ideological 'slant' in debates around factual reporting, though its origins suggest a reliance on a very 'binary' view of the, in fact, plural values and pleasures which may be struggling for dominance in any news story.

See 'Audiences', Chapter 32, on **cultural competences**.

attentiveness to its messages. They take pleasure in its form and the sense it gives them of 'being up to the minute' in its reassuring tendency, however horrendous the stories, to flatter viewers into a sense of being privileged witnesses, of having the world scanned and under control. The newscasters chatting together at the end of the bulletin, for example, is perhaps a reassurance that 'we' can all return to the 'normal' world of the domestic – and the ads (Figure 12.8). This takes us a long way from 'ideology', and opens very different possibilities for media study.

'What exactly is it that makes enjoying popular literature, a tabloid [paper] … so bad for democracy? And how can anyone guarantee that "serious" news media are not secretly consumed as if they were the equivalent of a sports match?' (Hermes 1998).

References

Abercrombie, Nicholas, Hill, Stephen and Turner, Bryan S. (1980) *The Dominant Ideology Thesis*, London: Allen & Unwin.

Althusser, Louis (1971) 'Ideology and Ideological State Apparatuses', in *Lenin and Philosophy and Other Essays*, London: New Left Books.

Andermahr, Sonya, Lovell, Terry and Wolkowitz, Carol (1997) *A Concise Glossary of Feminist Theory*, London and New York: Arnold.

Dahlgren, Peter (1985) 'The Modes of Reception: For a Hermeneutics of TV News', in P. Drummond and R. Paterson (eds) *Television in Transition*, London: BFI.

Golding, Peter and Murdock, Graham (1991) 'Culture, Communications and Political Economy', in James Curran and Michael Gurevitch (eds) *Mass Media and Society*, London: Edward Arnold.

Figure 12.8   The pleasures of reassurance?

Hermes, Joke (1998) 'Gender and Media Studies: No Woman, No Cry', in John Corner, Philip Schlesinger and Roger Silverstone (eds) *International Media Research: A Critical Survey*, London and New York: Routledge.

Holland, Patricia *What is a Child? Popular Images of Childhood*, London: Virago.

Ross, Andrew (ed.) (1997) *No Sweat: Fashion, Free Trade and the Rights of Garment Workers*, London and New York: Verso.

Spence, Jo (1986) *Putting Myself in the Picture*, London: Camden Press.

Thompson, John B. (1990) 'Ideology and Modern Culture: Critical Theory', in *The Age of Mass Communications*, Stanford, Ca.: Stanford University Press, p. 7.

Williamson, Judith (1978) *Decoding Advertisements: Ideology and Meaning in Advertising*, London: Marion Boyars.

Further reading

Eagleton, Terry (1998) 'Ideology' (1994), in Stephen Regan (ed.) *The Eagleton Reader*, Oxford: Blackwell.

Foucault, Michel (1988) *Politics, Philosophy, Culture: Interviews and other Writings 1977–1984*, London: Routledge.

Gramsci, Antonio (1994) *Selected Writings from the Prison Notebooks*, London: Lawrence & Wishart.

Hall, Stuart (ed.) (1997) *Representation: Cultural Representations and Signifying Practices*, London: Thousand Oaks, New Delhi: Sage.

Intermediate Technology campaigns to enable poor people in the South to develop and use technologies which give them more control over their lives and contribute to sustainable development.
Tel.: 01788 560631; `e-mail:itdg@itdg.org.uk`.

Marx, Karl and Engels, Friedrich (1965: first published 1888) *The German Ideology*, London: Lawrence & Wishart.

Strinati, Dominic (1995) *An Introduction to Theories of Popular Culture*, London: Routledge (esp. chs 2 and 4).

Tolson, Andrew (1996) *Mediations: Text and Discourse in Media Studies*, London and New York: Arnold.

13 / Case study: Selecting and constructing news

News is a globally important media form. This section explores:

- its relationship to **dominant discourses** and **ideologies**
- how these are negotiated as parts of news media **institutions**.

News discourses

Two points are often made about news within Media Studies:

- It is not transparent, not the 'window on the world' it often sets itself up to be.
- Its constructed versions of events are not unbiased and usually serve dominant interests. This matters particularly with television news, from which most

The audience for the main British television news bulletins each night is consistently seven to eight million, twelve million on days of real political significance (e.g. the release of Nelson Mandela). Slightly more people read the *Sun* (roughly ten million) though according to the ITC 62 per cent of people say television is their preferred source of news; only 17 per cent say this for newspapers (from Gaber 1998). The BBC Radio 4 *Today* programme claims an audience of 1.84 million or 16 per cent share at that time of day (last quarter of 1997) and is influential in setting the day's news and often domestic political agenda.

people get their sense of the world's happenings.

In the 1970s, when the Glasgow University Media Group (GUMG) was among the first to explore the ideological influence of the ways in which news is constructed, the BBC and ITN news programmes claimed enormous authority for themselves, and were unchallenged by cable, Channel 5 and Channel 4 styles of news, or by 'rolling' twenty-four-hour news programmes. The strikes and war stories they investigated were more polarised than now seems the case, in a post-Cold-War, 'de-regulated' world, where Media Studies' claims for the influence of news are made more cautiously (see 'Ideologies and discourses', Chapter 12).

Nevertheless, though news programmes may not have power of *direct effect* on behaviour and belief, many would argue that they can *influence* audiences by their selection of items for news. They are able to set the **agenda** of issues which we find ourselves thinking about, selecting some information for consideration and leaving some unannounced.

News is also often able to set the agenda for current affairs and investigative documentaries teams.

An **agenda** is a list of items to be discussed at a meeting, usually drawn up by the person chairing the meeting, who has the power to arrange them in order of importance. Terms such as 'hidden agenda' or 'agenda-setting' in relation to news suggests that such powers are being exercised covertly by those in control of it.

ACTIVITY 13.1

Make a note of a day's major news headlines. Think whether they affect what you and your friends talk about. Then note the headlines a few weeks later.

- Do you wonder what happened to stories which, in the first set of headlines, seemed urgent and important?
- When and how did they recede into less important status?
- Does this mean that you and your friends forgot about them to some extent – that they went 'off the **agenda**'?

This is a huge power. It may, for example, encourage those already confident of sharing majority opinion to voice their opinions, while those who do not conform fall silent. When Diana, Princess of Wales, was killed in a drink-driving accident in 1997, for example, it was very difficult to use those words for what had happened, or to say that you were not particularly moved, or were even annoyed by the scale of this news event. The term 'spiral of silence' was coined to describe such processes.

ACTIVITY 13.2

Watch the title sequences of late evening BBC and ITV news bulletins. How do they announce the nature (or genre) of the programme to follow? Note:

- the kinds of imagery and music used (science fiction? the hi-tech studio? an emphasis on futuristic, speedy news-gathering technology?)
- the dress, demeanour, accent, tones, positioning of the presenter
- the degree to which the signs of the hustle and bustle of news processes are visible.

Q Are such arrangements trying to claim authority for the news?

Compare them to Channel 5 television news or any other 'different' television news format you can access.

- How do these different news programmes relate to power centres such as Westminster and Washington?
- How far do they share the agenda and presentation of BBC and ITV news? Which rules do they break, and which ones keep to?

'News professionals'

The argument that news does not exist, free-floating, waiting to be discovered in the world outside the newsroom, has accompanied the development of theories of **news values**. These are argued to *construct* rather than simply *accompany* the gathering of news. They are not consciously held values. Indeed, many journalists would say their main professional ideal is the achievement of objectivity.

This theory sees news as the end product of a complex process which begins with a systematic sorting and selecting of events and topics according to professionalised news values: 'the professional codes used in the selection, construction and presentation of news stories in corporately produced press and broadcasting' (O'Sullivan et al. 1994). They are professionalised in the sense that they have to be acquired in order

- to become a journalist, through training on the job, or achieving qualifications
- to function effectively as a journalist (which may involve less formal learning contexts, such as canteen gossip about who's in and who's out, and why); what is now the 'house style' of your paper or radio station; whether, like the *Sun*, it employs no foreign correspondents, or, like the *Independent*, tries to avoid 'royal' stories; which qualities are being valued by professional awards, and promotions, and so on (see Hood and Tabary-Peterssen 1997).

It is often argued (Schlesinger 1987) that, like most television professionals, journalists make programmes for other television professionals, partly because their sense

These are often referred to as **gatekeeping** processes, 'named after the way a farmer stands at the door of a pen and, by moving a gate from side to side as the cattle or sheep pass through, separates them for dipping, for the market or the slaughterhouse' (Hood and Tabary-Peterssen, 1997, p. 12).

of the rest of their audience is very flimsy. 'They won't understand it', 'We'd love to run the story but the public just don't want to hear about it' are statements often made on the basis of very little systematic attempt to find out exactly what audiences might want (even if simple overnight ratings figures are now quickly available).

Schlesinger (1987) also pointed out that news teams quickly develop a sense of 'who to rely on' for 'hard stories' i.e. stories full of facts, statistics and quotes from official sources which don't risk libel action. These tend to come from 'accredited sources' such as a big world news agency: Reuters, Press Association, Associated Press and United Press International, which send stories directly into the computer systems of bodies like News International, or, increasingly, one of the big PR (Public Relations) companies. Controversy has raged in recent years over the degree to which government **spin doctors** or highly skilled press officers should intervene to construct news.

All these, and the press office of a corporation or government department rather than, say, a campaigning leaflet, are the preferred sources of news for its primary definers. They are sorted so that 'copy tasters' can select items to be used. Most newsrooms scan the morning newspapers and listen to the radio from early in the day. This is now more of a two-way street than it once was, as up-to-the-minute television news, and even television news pictures, let alone Internet items, often constitute newspapers' headlines the next day. But whatever the direction of the flow, such news structures will tend to favour those who already have enough power to employ press officers, to distribute press releases and publicity and to hire

Reuters to make up a VNR (Video News Release) (Figure 13.1). Far fewer foreign correspondents are now permanently employed to develop expert, intimate knowledge of a particular country. Covering 'sudden' foreign stories (the 'fireman' approach), 'packs' or 'pools' of journalists are often parachuted into an area together, stay in the same hotels, share information and stories rather than investigate for themselves, while also competing for 'the big story'.

This tendency may be intensified by the ability of news agencies to arrange speedy satellite transmission of such instant judgements – itself a good example of the priorities of much modern television journalism. It is also, of course, intensified by the sheer danger of certain assignments. This in turn has always produced a

QUESTIONS AND ANSWERS VIDEO NEWS RELEASES

WHAT IS A VIDEO NEWS RELEASE?

A VNR is just the same as a written press release, except that it is produced on video. It means that broadcasters can be supplied with news pictures without the need to send out their own film crew or correspondents. A VNR is paid for by the corporate client - broadcasters get it free of charge.

WHAT IS THE REUTERS TELEVISION VNR SERVICE?

We use the unique global resources of Reuters to deliver VNR's to broadcasters in the most cost-effective way possible. No other VNR supplier has resources to match.

We provide VNR's to broadcasters in the same way that we provide any news story, except that we identify the item as a VNR and say who the client is. VNR's are normally between four and ten minutes long, often with a short voiced version called an 'A' roll.

WHY SHOULD REUTERS TELEVISION HANDLE MY VNR?

Because our service works. We are already known and trusted by broadcasters everywhere, so that when news editors receive an offer of free pictures from us, they give the story proper consideration. We already have the delivery system running smoothly, so we can keep costs down.

HOW MUCH DOES IT COST?

That depends on what we are asked to do. We always prepare a detailed price estimate, but as a guide, an average cost of production, distribution and monitoring in a single European country is between £6,000 and £10,000. A Europe-wide service concentrating on national broadcasters costs £10,000 to £15,000, and world-wide distribution costs about £20,000

WHO USES REUTERS FOR VNR WORK?

Recent clients include the European Space Agency, Smirnoff, SmithKline Beecham, the Corporation of London, Glaxo, Johnnie Walker whisky, Chemical Bank, BT, the London Docklands Development Corporation, McDonalds, Beefeater gin, the Diamond Information Centre, P&O and Du Pont.

Figure 13.1

CNN came within seconds of announcing George Bush's death when he publicly collapsed at a banquet in Japan. They were nearly the victim of a hoaxer who rang in pretending to be Bush's doctor – as well as of the institutional drive to be first with the news rather than sure of it (described in Rosenblum 1993).

highly gendered aspect to foreign reporting, seen as a 'hard' form unsuited to women, despite the distinguished careers of women from Martha Gelhorn in the 1930s to Kate Adie.

> 'In the 1950s, women reporters interviewing people on the streets were assumed to be soliciting. More recently Associated Press reporter and Vietnam correspondent Edie Lederer had to get an "I am not a prostitute" certificate from the authorities before she could travel in Saudi Arabia to report the Gulf War.'
>
> (Sebba 1994)

Correspondents may also learn a professional, authoritative (very masculine?) language with which, for example, to sanitise wars (see any number of accounts of the 'smart bombs', 'usherettes', 'carpet bombing' and so on in the Gulf War). Financial news, on the other hand, will be 'professionally' described through obscure phrases like 'the pound had a bad day' or 'getting the economy back on the rails' which re-mystify the already mysterious workings of stock exchanges.

Frenzied circulation and ratings wars between organisations have tended to accelerate the professionals' emphasis on being 'first with the big story' rather than 'the one that got the story right'. This trend is accentuated by new technology, such as digital cameras, portable computers and satellite phones. These mean a reporter can input a story with photos into a newsdesk terminal almost as soon as it is written. Again, the Internet has become a volatile (and only partly reliable) source of news stories taken up very quickly by mainstream media.

News values

There have been many different definitions of news values since Galtung and Ruge laid out a now famous pioneering list in 1965 (Galtung and Ruge 1981). The most important, adapted from their list, are:

- *Frequency* Those events which become news stories will be of about the same frequency as the news bulletins, i.e. of about a daily span. An oil spillage will be perceived as a news story; the slow work over time of legislation which makes it less (or more) likely to occur will not feature as news.

- *Proximity* Since news is circulated on the whole by national broadcasting organisations, news will consist of items that relate to that nation. Many people may be involved in a boat capsizing in Thailand, but, until the number reaches hundreds, it is not likely to compete for British headline space with a boat capsizing in the English Channel. Since these 'First World' stories often constitute much of the material of the big news agencies, which get sold to 'Third World' broadcasting stations, the circle can be a rather vicious one. Broader processes of language in news (and outside) carry the same kinds of skew: why are military commanders called 'warlords' in the 'Third World' (or Bosnia) but 'Chiefs of Staff' in the West? 'Continuous' or 'out-of-hours' news can often set a rather different agenda, and handle foreign items differently from the big 'flagship' news programmes.

ACTIVITY 13.3
Listen to the BBC World Service (and/or watch CNN or Euronews or BBC 24 Hours) to see how different is the sense of a news agenda and coverage of 'non-domestic' items.

- *Threshold* The 'size' of an event that's needed to be considered 'newsworthy'.

- *Negativity* 'If it's news, it's bad news' sums up the feeling that long-term, constructive events are much less likely to feature as news than a catastrophe. It is also suggested that news takes the normal for granted, and so is driven to make stories out of the deviant: crime, dissidence, disaster. In turn, news processes will add to stereotyping and scapegoating of 'out' groups, because of the ways it feeds on the thrill of their deviancy. It may also shape news coverage of 'Third World' issues in terms of 'coups, crises and famine' since they fit more dramatically into existing understandings of those areas than do items about small initiatives (such as adapting bicycle technology to help a village).

- *Predictability* If the media expect a kind of event to happen, it will be reported as having occurred. Examples include the large anti-Vietnam-War demonstration in October 1968. This was peaceful, but had been expected to be violent. The few skirmishes that occurred were heavily focused upon, so the event was reported, as predicted, as being 'violent'. The same used to be true for the Notting Hill Carnival, and is sometimes true of World Cup football matches etc.

  Another meaning for 'predictable' is that events termed 'news' are often known about years in advance, such as conferences, anniversaries, annual reports, book or film launches and so on. (Though, of course, predictable famines are not part of the diary for coverage.) 'The news should really be called the olds' as someone once put it.

- *Unexpectedness* Oddly enough, news is *thought* to consist of the unexpected, even though this can occur only within broad patterns of what is expected, even predicted. As a consequence, where there are big issues, such as unemployment, and homelessness, there's a feeling that, though they go on happening, the journalist cannot keep on writing the same story, and so looks for a 'twist', perhaps a way of personalising or even sensationalising it, or simply leaves it as 'not news'. Hence news items suddenly focus on homelessness at Christmas, while treating it as 'not newsworthy' the rest of the year. 'By the time the pictures are horrific enough to move people, it is almost too late', as one journalist put it.

- *Continuity* If an event is big enough it will be covered for some time, and often even 'non-events' which are part of that story will be covered. 'The driver of the car in which Diana, Princess of Wales, was killed has still not regained consciousness.'

- *Unambiguity* 'News' is constructed as something clear, not needing subtle interpretation even if it fits into a complex situation, like a war. (Though often listed as a news value, this can be argued to be a feature of the way a story gets told rather than of the event itself.)

- *Composition* The 'story' will be selected and arranged according to the editor's sense of the balance of the whole bulletin, or page. If many foreign stories have been used, even a fairly unimportant 'home' story may be included.

ACTIVITY 13.4

Regarding the predictability of news events:

- Note from current news how many items are of this kind.
- Why do you think journalists favour them?
- Jot down other events (e.g. famines) which seem to have been predictable but have not been focused on.

ACTIVITY 13.5

Look at the balance of items in a bulletin. Again, using broadsheet papers as your source of a fuller news agenda, see whether you feel the composition has been adjusted as suggested above.

- Within the bulletin, do certain items seem ordered so as to be grouped together, either for contrast, or to suggest connections?
- List the items in an order that would invite different connections.

- *Personalisation* Wherever possible, events are seen as the actions of people as *individuals*. Thus hospital waiting lists may be put on the agenda by 'Baby X' not getting the operation s/he needs. This links closely to two areas not part of the classic area of news values, but of larger drives: narrativisation and visual imperatives.

- *Narrativisation* of news. Items are from the start called 'stories' (see 'Narratives', Chapter 3) and they are shaped into narrative form as soon as is possible. When they become long-running 'sagas', the individuals on whom the spotlight has been focused often become characters, as happens with shifting coverage of the royal family's 'heroes and villains', and with war coverage. Often war news stories inherit, and re-jig, other story shapes. The Falklands War coverage drew on an existing repertoire from Second World War fictions, with themes such as 'War is Hell but it makes Heroes', 'The Women Wait while the Men Fight', and with the Argentinian leader, Galtieri, called a 'little Hitler', a 'tinpot dictator'.

- *Visual imperatives* are said to be especially important in television news (and unimportant in radio, where

'On the day of her death Diana became, unproblematically, a news story … the news agenda was very quickly established and the … blame for the accident placed on the activities of the paparazzi and the tabloid press … the discussions of that day were a classic example of the way in which news stories take hypotheses as fact and preclude alternative explanation. Monday's announcement of the results of blood tests on the driver were shocking; not just for what it revealed, but for the way … it threatened the neatness of the news story … established the previous day' (Geraghty 1998).

Figure 13.2   One story that was deemed worth visualising (*UK Press Gazette*, 27 March 1995)

sound codes are key). They drive towards stories that have strong pictures, whether of celebrities or of 'Biblical'-looking famines. Increasingly, if wars are heavily censored or inaccessible to picture technology, computer-aided graphics will be used to give a sense of what might be happening (Figure 13.2). The debate on visual imperatives needs critical consideration.

- First, radio's agenda is very similar to television's, despite the absence of pictures.
- Television or press stories deemed important will have computer-aided graphics to assist visualisation, so pictures do not always 'lead'.
- 'Less newsworthy' controversial or speculative stories, or ones involved with long-term processes, are rarely helped in this way, even though they could be. Again, the visual imperatives tend to follow, not lead existing news priorities.
- 'Soundbites', or vivid short phrases used over and over in coverage of some stories, could be argued as equally important, and as deriving from verbal, radio-related forms. Yet they do not get celebrated in media study in the same way as visual determinants. Why?

ACTIVITY 13.6

Watch a few television news bulletins.

- How have 'visuals' been used? What do they contribute to stories?
- Do you agree with the suggestions on 'visual imperatives'?
- List the stories featured on BBC, ITN and radio news during a day. Then list the spread of stories in two of the broadsheet papers.
- Are there any overlaps in the choice of television and radio stories? Do these follow the priorities of news values?
- Why was the story of Diana's death such a huge one? How can you relate it to the main news values?

Impartiality in news

Broadcast media in Britain are legally required to be politically impartial: i.e. broadcasters cannot express a point of view on 'major matters' but, in a linked phrase, have to make balanced reports. But a balance is always between certain forces, and these tend to be those points of view that are assumed to reflect existing public opinion. Thirty years ago, this was defended as reflecting the Labour–Conservative axis of parliamentary politics, with a stopwatch eye to how much time each party was given on television. Now, the political spectrum stretches further (though opinion that falls outside 'parliamentary democracy' is still deemed unacceptable by BBC and ITV).

The Glasgow University Media Group has since the 1970s employed **content analysis** involving hundreds of hours of recorded news broadcasts, focused initially on industrial items such as strikes. They argued that the news consistently favours the interpretations of the already powerful because journalists share assumptions about the real world which are rarely seriously questioned, such as the view that strikes are harmful and disruptive. Furthermore, journalists rely on official sources to an extent that systematically outlaws different accounts of events. For the 1984–5 coal strike, for example, there was hardly any discussion of the Conservative 'Ridley plan' from years before to defeat the miners as a way of closing the pits and weakening trade union power generally. Suggestions that the police provoked strikers during the strike were very marginalised. (These latter were given thirteen times less coverage than violence attributed to pickets (see Philo (1995) in 'Audiences', Chapter 32).)

It is crucial that such critical positions on news continue to be tested out, but you should bear in mind that objectivity or impartiality is an impossible goal for any statement or story because:

- To decide to select an item for the news is to make a decision about other items that cannot be told, because of time or space restrictions, and therefore to prioritise, or set a value on it.

- Since there are always several positions from which to tell a story (see 'Narratives', Chapter 3), and it is impossible to produce an account from completely 'outside', a position on it will inevitably have been chosen.

- To say that objectivity is possible is to imply that an unarguable interpretation of an event exists prior to the report or story.

Nevertheless, if we adopt the position that news can and should be *as adequate and informative as possible for particular purposes*, then, when a national audience needs to be informed about the justification for and conduct of, say, a war or major government spending decisions, it is right to object to unnecessary censorship or 'spin' on such stories.

ACTIVITY 13.7

Think about how you would like to see news organised.

- Would it work better within an openly argumentative or 'biased' current affairs system, with each programme having a stated position (green/feminist/free-market/socialist etc.) which they argued in publicly accountable ways? This would need a built-in 'right of reply' mechanism, and proper regulation to ensure there was no gross imbalance towards one tendency or another, across television channels.

- How would news then function?

News now

'News' exists now not just as BBC or ITV news. However limited their agenda, new forms are driven to offer somewhat different accounts of events. CNN (Cable News Network in the US) has posed interesting problems for news managers, given its ability to deliver twenty-four-hour-a-day news during, for example, the Gulf War. The many radio stations offer more sources of news, as well as news-related forms such as phone-ins. The Internet, said to be unpoliceable and unregulatable, is a growing source of news stories and ways of

organising around them, as Internet opposition to the 1990s Gulf War, or the cascade of stories about President Clinton's sexual behaviour in 1997–8, showed. Investigative documentaries, though under real funding pressure, give audiences another source of information on which to judge the news.

Newspapers, far from cultivating a transparent, 'unconstructed' style, do not have words like 'impartiality' in their charters, and often try to entertain and galvanise their readers as much as (some would say less than) to inform them. This sometimes makes them appear like an arm of the PR industry, at other times it produces an attractive irreverence. Colin Sparks (1991) argues that fewer and fewer journalists are what we have always thought of as journalists – the reporter of political and social information necessary for democracy to function – but are more and more working in entertainment or specialised information provision in what used to be the magazine section.

ACTIVITY 13.8

Make notes across a week's reading and viewing to support a debate on the following positions about general trends within British news forms:

- 'In the 1960s a third of Fleet Street journalists were based outside London, either in the regions or on foreign postings. Now 90% of national newspaper staff work in London' (Nick Cohen, writing on the current growth of lifestyle, opinion and 'light' columns as compared to investigative or first-hand reporting, *New Statesman*, 22 May 1998).

- The media are now used as a 'weapon of mass distraction' (Schechter 1998).

- There is a gender snobbery in the ways that 'hard news' is defended against 'softer' forms such as chat shows, lifestyle and opinion journalism. *Oprah*, for example, was a crucial opening out of news agendas to ordinary, often disadvantaged voices (see 'Audiences', Chapter 32, for more discussion).

THE Sun 23p

Thursday, April 27, 1995   23p   Audited daily sale for March 4,134,571

SEX CONFESSIONS OF TAKE THAT
See Pages 12 & 13

FREE
2 Tickets to Alton Towers
Token 4 on Page 19

Sun EXCLUSIVE

PAM v SAM
See Page 15

£100m FORGED NOTES RACKET BUSTED BY COPS

By DAVID WOODING and MIKE SULLIVAN

£100million international forgery racket was smashed yesterday when cops seized a record haul of fake bank notes from a lock-up garage.

Bundles of perfect £50 and US $100 counterfeits with a total face value of £18million were stashed under a pile of baby booties.

The swoop was a triumph for officers who spent two years tracking a ring that has flooded the world with forgeries of many currencies.

Five detectives of the South East Regional Crime Squad raided the £15-a-week garage in Bow, East London — and were astonished at the size of the cache.

Eight large boxes were stuffed with £10million in £50 notes, the biggest-ever seizure of fake sterling.

Another three cartons contained £8million in $100 bills, the second biggest haul of forged US currency in Britain.

The forgeries were in bundles of 500 tied with elastic bands. Police

Continued on Page Seven

WINSTANTS CHURCHILL

Fury as MP scoops Lottery cash for Winnie's wartime papers

TORY MP Winston Churchill faced outrage last night after the Government used £13.25million of National Lottery cash to buy his grandfather's wartime papers.

Mr Churchill, 54, will personally make several millions after negotiating the sale of 1.5 million documents held by his family.

He exploited a loophole in Sir Winston's will to clinch the deal.

The MP's payout is like winning the Lottery's Instants jackpot dozens of times over.

But last night the sale was branded "a shabby trick." Oxford University history professor Norman Stone said: "It's like

By TREVOR KAVANAGH and PASCOE WATSON

selling the great wartime leader in a raffle.

"This is another sign of the sheer bloody tackiness of this country.

"The Government should have rushed an Act through Parliament to make them available

Continued on Page Four

Under fire . . . Winston Churchill

Figure 13.3

ACTIVITY 13.9

Look at the front page illustrated in Figure 13.3.

- How are 'information' and 'entertainment' values in play here? What are the signifiers of each?
- How does this whole front page address its readers? As what kind of people?

The argument that television news is constructed, not transparent, is no longer surprising. Even the 'rule' that music is never to be used as accompaniment to stories is occasionally broken. Television programmes such as *It'll Be Alright on the Night* take for granted, and add to, audience knowledge of news codes and constructions. Do they, however, help audiences to understand the broader processes of news construction?

The analysis of news for dominant values and assumptions is important, and far more telling than a few funny 'out takes'. But it is clear that

- 'dominant values' now go further than stories of strikes and wars, and need to include discourses around powerful identities such as age, ethnicity, gender and sexuality
- the effect of news on audiences needs to be understood in relation to the ways they *use* news, as well as striking examples of their rejection of certain stories. Boycotts, such as that of the *Sun* on Merseyside for libelling Liverpool soccer fans after Hillsborough, or examples of resistant understandings like the following, need to be further explored.

'the survey demonstrates that most viewers believed oil supply was a main reason for the hostilities, while television's favourite explanation was "to liberate Kuwait", followed by "to uphold international law". Oil featured in 4% of BBC's reports, 3% of BBC2's and 5% of Channel 4's'

(Georgina Henry, in *The Guardian*, 20 January 1992, reviewing David Morrison's *Television and the Gulf War*, London: John Libbey & Co.)

References

Eldridge, John (ed.) (1995) *The Glasgow University Media Reader*, vol. 1, London: Routledge.

Gaber, Ivor (1998) 'Television and Political Coverage', in Christine Geraghty and David Lusted (eds) *The Television Studies Book*, London and New York: Arnold.

Galtung, J. and Ruge, M. (1981) *The Structure of Foreign News: The Presentation of the Congo, Cuba and Cyprus Crises in Four Foreign Newspapers*, extract in S. Cohen and J. Young (eds) *The Manufacture of News*, London: Constable.

Geraghty, Christine (1998) 'Story', in 'Flowers and Tears: The Death of Diana, Princess of Wales', *Screen*, vol. 39, spring.

Hood, Stuart and Tabary-Peterssen, Thalia (1997, 4th edition) *On Television*, London: Pluto Press.

Philo, Greg (ed.) (1995) *The Glasgow Media Group Reader*, vol. 2, London and New York: Routledge.

Schechter, Danny (1998) *The More You Watch, The Less You Know*, New York: Seven Stories Press.

Schlesinger, Philip (1987) *Putting 'Reality' Together*, London: Methuen.

Sebba, A. (1994) *Battling for News*, London: Sceptre.

Sparks, Colin (1991) 'Goodbye Hildy Johnson: The Vanishing Serious Press', in Peter Dalgren and Colin Sparks (eds) *Communication and Citizenship*, London and New York: Routledge.

Further reading

Carter, Cynthia, Branston, Gill and Allan, Stuart (eds) (1998) *News, Gender and Power*, London and New York: Routledge.

Cohen, Phil and Gardner, Carl (1982) *It Ain't Half Racist, Mum: Fighting Racism in the Media*, London: Comedia.

Curran, James and Seaton, Jean (1997) *Power Without Responsibility: The Press and Broadcasting in Britain*, London and New York: Routledge.

Goodwin, Andrew (1990) 'TV News: Striking the Right Balance?', in A. Goodwin and P. Whannel (eds) *Understanding Television*, London: Routledge.

Harris, R. (1983) *Gotcha! The Media and the Falklands War*, London: Faber.

Hartley, John (1982) *Understanding News*, London: Routledge.

Philips, D. (1992) *Evaluating Press Coverage*, London: Kogan Page.

Philo, Greg (1990) *Seeing and Believing … The Influence of Television*, London and New York: Routledge.

Rose, Chris (1998) *The Turning of the 'Spar*, London: Greenpeace.

Schudson, Michael (1991) 'The Sociology of News Production Revisited', in James Curran and Michael Gurevitch (eds) *Mass Media and Society*, London: Edward Arnold.

14 Technologies

Science fiction **dystopias** (see
'Science fiction', Case study 9)
offer a discourse on 'technology
out of control' – a good example
is *The Terminator* (US 1984).

Debates about technology are perhaps the least systemised within the Media Studies syllabuses. They appear in relation to a range of issues and key concepts, both in terms of how media texts are produced and how they are read. In this chapter we want to address ideas about technology directly and develop an understanding which will inform your studies elsewhere in the book.

Some of these ideas are being developed in a wider discussion about contemporary society:

- Technology is developing too quickly, that it is affecting all of us (and particularly children) to an unknown extent – that it is 'out of control'.
- Technology is gendered and not universally available and accessible.
- Technology might be liberating in allowing us to participate more and learn more.
- The 'user-friendliness' of computer technology is deskilling workers.
- 'New technologies' are viewed as a threat to established employment patterns, on the reasonable assumption that technology usually replaces human labour eventually. Thus the jibe about 'new **Luddites**' to describe critics of computer technologies.

Other ideas are concerned more specifically with media work:

- Artists and producers must change their methods and patterns of work and perhaps their whole approach to 'creativity'.
- Technology threatens the link between 'reality' and media representations.

Luddites textile workers in the
early nineteenth century who,
fearing their jobs would be taken
by machines in the new factories,
organised themselves and
destroyed the new machines if
they were used in this way. Ned
Ludd was a fictitious name used to
protect the leaders of the struggle.
'Luddite' is generally a term of
abuse, but the workers were
correct in their analysis – the
machines *were* used to replace
their skilled labour.

'Art' has an original meaning which
includes the application of
practical skills: at one time 'artist'
and 'technician' may have had a
similar meaning.

Defining 'media technology'

Technology isn't just about machines or equipment – the **hardware** aspect which puts off those of us for whom the insides of a computer or a washing machine represent examples of life's great mysteries. Technology is also about *methods*, *means* and *skill* – essentially about how we can make use of our knowledge in order to produce something useful. This forms the **software** in modern systems.

'**Technology**: the practice of any or all of the applied sciences that have practical value; technical methods in a particular field of industry or art; technical nomenclature; technical means and skill characteristic of a particular civilisation, group or period (from the Greek, *techne* = art)'

(*Chambers 20th Century Dictionary*)

Take a junior reporter attending the local Magistrates Court. He or she uses simple but effective technology – a pencil and a notepad – to record what is said. Of course, these may seem simple, even primitive, technologies, but the modern pencil and paper are the result of hundreds of years of technological development in the application of chemical knowledge about graphite and wood pulp and techniques for manufacture and good design, to allow them to be 'operated' effectively.

The technological input does not stop there. A special system of writing, Shorthand, with its own set of characters, was developed to enable the reporter to record material more quickly. In this example we have a marriage between hardware (the equipment – pencil and paper) and software (the systemised applications knowledge – Shorthand), which we can recognise in all forms of media production. Finally, we can note that the reporter works within the **institution** of journalism, with its developed techniques for constructing news stories – a further extension of the idea of news technology.

In fact, there is a book devoted to the pencil and its history: Henry Petroski's *The Pencil: A History of Design and Circumstance* (London and New York: Faber & Faber and Knopf, 1990).

See 'Institutions', Chapter 26.

ACTIVITY 14.1

- Can you list the different technologies used in a local radio studio?
- Can you divide them into software and hardware?

Technology: focus of conflict

The 'methods, means and skill' definition of technology is not always appreciated. This is the result of a mix of factors which tend to obscure the real issues and to promote cruder, more simplistic ideas.

- *Class* undoubtedly plays a role in this. In Britain, class positions depend largely on education and occupation. Technologists have traditionally had lower status than professionals like doctors or lawyers. The Colleges of Advanced Technology, founded in the 1960s, were quick to rename themselves as 'Universities' when they realised they were perceived as inferior. This is perhaps a uniquely British problem in that, despite their importance during Victorian times, 'engineers' have never gained the

Scientists and technicians In *The Man in the White Suit* (UK 1951) Alec Guinness plays an inventor of a cloth that never gets dirty and won't wear out. He is bewildered when laundry workers and textile workers attack him as anti-social. He is saved in this social comedy when the cloth disintegrates after only a few days – but not before his invention has created further social and economic upheavals.

There are several common stereotypes of scientists and technicians, many of which present them as a 'threat' to society. Are they balanced by the scientist heroes who find cures for diseases etc.?

status they have achieved elsewhere in Europe. You will also be aware that 'vocational' courses, which imply a closer attention to technology, have less status in education than 'academic' courses.

- These class differences perhaps lead on to distinctions between '*doers*' and '*thinkers*' in media production and media education. Sometimes it is the commercial producer, who sees 'new' technology as either cost-cutting or possessing a 'wow' factor, versus the creative artist, who wants to retain 'ideas' and traditional skills. (Be careful here, though, **avant-garde** artists often embrace new technologies first – see 'Independents and alternatives', Chapter 28). Sometimes it is the pragmatic broadcaster versus the academic theorist. Much of the time it boils down to a difference between those who actually use the technology on a daily basis and those who don't.

- Media technology is *gendered* so that in many cases girls will have been put off media production work because of its association with 'boys' toys' and a macho culture of bigger, faster, louder etc.: some boys will have suffered from taunts about their excessive interest in equipment rather than people, 'the trainspotter syndrome' or the '**anorak**'. These gender differences are not all clear cut. In the film industry, it is not unusual to find women film editors and there are now a handful of successful women directors, but women cinematographers (i.e. the persons in charge of lighting and camerawork) are very rare. There is evidence to suggest that this wasn't always so and that in the early years of cinema women were very active. Indeed the first director of a narrative film may well have been a woman, Alice Guy Blaché, who directed a short feature in 1896. In 1911 she wrote: 'There is nothing connected with the staging of a motion picture that a woman cannot do as easily as a man, and there is no reason why she cannot completely master every technicality of the art' (quoted in Acker 1991).

But these early roles for women were not maintained. Women (the stereotyped view says) have traditionally 'worked well with people' (director) or 'at a bench on a production process' (editor), but not in a role which requires application of both technical knowledge and artistic vision. The prejudice against women artists and composers has perhaps passed across to cinema. A more obvious reason is that camera operators have traditionally needed knowledge of optics and women have suffered from lack of access to the necessary school physics.

Technology is a potential stumbling block in the path of good working relationships. If you know about technology, you will think it is important and want to consider its implications. If you don't feel happy with it you will perhaps try to ignore those implications. This will be a real issue for you when you begin to produce your own media texts. Many

Anorak What does this term of abuse say about general attitudes towards detailed knowledge of specific technologies? Is it a recognition that an obsession about technology is anti-social and unhealthy or does it suggest that those who use it as abuse are fearful of technology?

Women in Hollywood 'Guy power dominated the business, as it still does: to this day it is rare to have women running studios or directing films, and unknown – for here lies the voyeur's magic – to let them photograph a movie' (critic David Thomson on contemporary Hollywood, *Independent on Sunday*, 8 January 1995).

Reel Women by Ally Acker (1991) provides a directory of prominent women in all sections of the film industry since the 1890s. There is plenty of evidence to show that women were very active in the early period of cinema (even to the extent of three camerawomen in the sound cinema).

ACTIVITY 14.2

Technical roles for women

Is this criticism of the film industry also applicable to television? Have a look at the credit lists of a range of television programmes and films.

- How many women are listed as camera operators/directors of photography?
- How many women write the music for films and television (as distinct from performing it)?
- Which jobs are most likely to be filled by women?

The first woman member of the BSC (British Society of Cinematographers) is Sue Gibson, who worked for director Marleen Gorris on the Virginia Woolf adaptation *Mrs Dalloway* (UK/US 1997).

---

media producers and critics would agree that technology *in itself* is not very interesting, what is important is *what is produced as a media text*. A pamphlet which has changed history, a photograph which will always be remembered, a sound recording which moves a listener to tears, may all have been produced on primitive equipment with basic techniques – the lack of sophisticated technology did not stop them communicating. On the other hand, would you choose to ignore the most modern technology if it was available to you (even if it meant tackling something you didn't totally understand)? We won't solve this dilemma, but we should be sensitive to the issue. The best we might hope for is for everyone to agree to select the most appropriate technology for the job, rather than allowing the technology to do the selecting for us.

Technological change

Technology interests us most when it changes. From the first cave painting to the latest hi-tech feature film, media producers have striven to develop both hardware and software in order to achieve a better product. In media education we want to ask: 'What does "better" mean? – cheaper, more realistic, more beautiful, more easy to understand, more exciting, more uplifting, more easily available (and who decides the standards against which these are to be judged)?'

At the turn of the century, the 'technological imperative' – the general feeling that we are being driven forward by the increasing pace of technological change – is perhaps more evident in relation to media and communications than any other area. In past decades attention has centred on the 'space race', weapons technology, new cars or medical breakthroughs. Now the biggest industry in the world produces 'information' and 'entertainment' and more people are employed in it than in any of the traditional industries.

Computer design Early computer graphics showed their origins clearly (suggesting a 'technology-driven' product). The software could not produce 'realistic' colours and textures, but looking 'futuristic' was then fashionable, so the product was acceptable. Now, design philosophies and computer power allow more 'naturalistic' images (i.e. as if painted with an analogue paintbrush).

Microsoft, founded by Bill Gates, has grown rich by selling the basic PC operating systems, MS-DOS (Microsoft Disk Operating System) and Windows. It has replaced the hardware manufacturer IBM as the world's richest company.

The biggest companies in the media industries are now the manufacturers and distributors of software, rather than the manufacturers of hardware. Companies like **Microsoft**, which makes the world's leading business computer software, and the cable television companies which are beginning to provide the vast new range of information services, are the rising stars of the media industries. They are at the forefront because they are initiating and exploiting the process of technological change.

Analogue to digital

Digital television offers many extra channels provided by a **multiplex** system: 'In the analogue era, we called them repeats, in the digital age, it's multiplexing' (Adam Singer of Flextech, quoted in the *Economist*, March 1998, and proving that 'new' technology does not necessarily mean 'new' products).

You won't have failed to notice that **digital** is a key word in all the new technologies. Media producers talk about 'going digital', musicians argue about 'digital sound'. Few stop to think that what we are experiencing is possibly the biggest technological revolution since the introduction of mechanical devices such as the printing press over four centuries ago. In every aspect of media production there has been a shift from analogue to digital and understanding what this shift means will help us to recognise the interrelationship of many of the debates about technology.

> **analogue**: that which is analogous to something else (bearing some correspondence or resemblance), from the Greek *analogia* = 'according to' and *logos* = 'ratio'
>
> **digital**: represented by numbers (digits = fingers)

An analogue device works by recording and storing or displaying information in a suitable form, after first converting measurements from their original form. In this way, what is mediated by the device is an 'analogy' of the real thing in another physical form.

The oldest such devices are measuring instruments like the sun dial or the hourglass. The 'chronometer' in all its guises is a good guide to developing technology. The ability to measure time accurately changed the way we live dramatically (timed hours of work were a major feature of

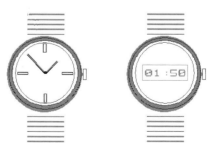

Figure 14.1 Analogue and digital watches

the factories built in the Industrial Revolution). Devices developed from reliance on the sun, to mechanical springs of great precision and finally to the digital accuracy of microchips.

At one time, all media technologies were based on analogue processes. Photography relies on light-sensitive chemicals reacting differentially to the reflected light from a subject captured by the lens. Microphones capture sound by measuring vibrations caused by sound waves and then converting them, first to electrical impulses and then to magnetic charges which can be stored on tape. In each case, the information stored is a physical representation of the original 'image'.

Digital technology is concerned only with numbers – everything which is captured must be converted to numerical data. The microphone and the camera lens are still used, but a sensing device 'reads' the information about sound waves or patterns of light and converts it to numerical form. From then on all processing is done by means of computation – the device contains a computer.

The CD revolution

The first digital media technology to catch the attention of the general public was probably the compact disc. Vinyl records had already started to display the words 'Digital Recording' in the early 1980s, with record buyers being offered a format which promised digital playback and greatly improved sound quality.

In a digital recording, the sound captured by microphones is converted to numerical data and stored on a computer device such as a hard disk or digital tape rather than a conventional audiotape. This recorded information is then mixed and a 'master copy' produced which is in turn transferred to an analogue tape, a vinyl disc or a consumer digital format such as a **CD** or **DVD** for sale to the public. Gradually the digital formats are taking over for consumer use.

CDs were accepted by the public quite quickly, but other formats such as **DAT** and **Mini-Disc** have succeeded with professionals only. An attempt to build on the popularity of the audio cassette – the DCC (Digital Compact Cassette) – failed completely. At the time of writing, the **DVD** (Digital Video Disc) is being promoted, as a replacement for both the videocassette and the CD-ROM, used for computer data.

Is 'digital' better?

Why did the CD succeed in revolutionising the consumer music market? The manufacturers claim that CDs give a clearer, more 'authentic' sound because nothing is lost or added to the original performance. This claim is worth investigating. If a sound has been produced in a studio, it will have been captured by a microphone and then recorded – in this sense there is no difference between analogue and digital recording. Some musical instruments are digital themselves – a digital keyboard can be programmed to sound like other instruments, because the 'sound' it

Samples are analogue sounds, captured and stored on a computer disk as digital data. They can be manipulated, edited together and turned into new music productions. Use of samples not only provides the means for the 'bedroom recording star' to make music – it also raises interesting questions about the copyright on sounds.

produces is initially in the form of digital information rather than soundwaves. It comes from the on-board computer's memory rather than, say, a vibrating piano wire, and the digital information can be recorded directly. In this latter case, the recorded data is certainly a replica of what the musician 'played'. (Another way to think of this is that you can 'make music' without musical instruments at all – simply by 'playing' the sounds already stored as digital 'samples' in the computer memory.) A microphone can however produce only a representation of a sound image (just as a camera can produce only a representation of a visual image).

There are some philosophical arguments here – can any natural sound be recorded 'authentically'? Leaving this aside (see 'Realisms', Chapter 16), the major difference comes during the next two stages of the process.

An analogue recording requires a physical transfer of data during the editing and mixing stage and then again during the duplication stage. Every time this physical exchange takes place some data is lost and some extra noise is added. The tape, the recording heads, the cables, the electrical wiring and earthing – all of these can be the source of 'noise' (noise is any unwanted sound). The digital process may use similar media – tape, cables etc. – but since it is numerical data which is being transferred, the computer can monitor the data exchange, constantly checking that the data 'adds up' (computer data has 'check numbers' inserted in the data stream which allow number checking and correction). In this way the digital recording process can guarantee that degradation of data and the presence of noise are kept to an absolute minimum.

This isn't quite the end of the story, however. Digital processes share one feature of analogue processes – the more detail you want in the recorded 'image', the more storage space you need. In analogue terms this means that the area of tape needed to record music is so great that the tape must be passed at high speeds across the recording heads. In digital terms it means that, in order to fit all the necessary data on to a suitable disc (or disk), it may be necessary to leave out some of the very high or very low frequencies of a sound recording or to 'compress' the data so that it takes up less space.

Both these actions will alter the original recording and this means that it is still possible that the analogue equipment with the highest specification (and the highest price) can produce a more 'authentic' sound than many digital systems.

Disc or **disk**. For convenience, we have used the British English spelling 'disc' to refer to conventional vinyl records or music Compact Discs. The American English spelling 'disk' is used to refer to computer disks (floppy, hard, optical etc.).

Consumer demand – the market for new technologies

So CDs do not necessarily have a 'better' sound – apart from anything else, sound quality is always a matter of personal taste, and a significant minority of audiophiles continue to play vinyl records. The clue to the popularity of CDs is consumer use. Vinyl records were easily scratched or warped by heat and dust in the grooves clogged up the stylus. In fact, the whole process of playing a record now seems like a medieval ritual. Most consumers responded to ease of use, the reduced storage space and the extra functions of the CD player (programming the order of tracks etc.). Further proof of the importance of 'use' over 'sound quality' is the survival of the analogue audiocassette and the failure of attempts to produce a digital version. Cassettes offer the lowest quality of reproduction, but they are recordable and easily portable.

CDs did cost more and they did require the purchase of a new machine. The social and economic factors which helped their success were varied.

- They appeared at a time when the consumer market was waiting for a new product (this was before the 'home computer' boom and after colour television).
- The record companies targeted older, more affluent consumers with re-releases of successful 'back-catalogue' material on the new format. Like many technological innovations, the switch to CD was built on the availability of the right content.

The case of VHS

Perhaps the clearest example of the importance of consumer demand arises in the famous case of the VHS videocassette. When this first appeared in the late 1970s, there were three completely different cassette systems. Of the three, Sony's Betamax was generally considered to have the best technical specification – effectively the best sound and picture. Matsushita, promoters of VHS, had the marketing clout and also the links with other companies in America and Britain which meant that most of the VCRs for sale or rent used VHS. This in turn meant that the video rental market for films – the major vehicle for promoting use of VCRs – was quickly dominated by VHS as well. Sony withdrew (but managed to use the technology in the development of Betacam – eventually the broadcast standard for videocassettes). Philips was the other, unsuccessful, competitor.

The importance of consumer demand in relation to technological change is crucial to our understanding. It is very easy to be seduced by the 'wow' factor of any technological 'advance'. This can lead to the assumption that anything new which is obviously 'better' in terms of technical quality will automatically be adopted by media producers or accepted by media audiences. What can follow is an underestimation of the judgement of audiences in particular. There are plenty of examples of 'failed' media technologies.

ACTIVITY 14.3

Technological failures

Do some research on the history of media technology (magazines or books from the 1970s or 1980s are interesting). Can you find examples of 'failures'? Consider these two examples in particular:

- Widescreen cinema was invented and briefly introduced in the late 1920s, only to be withdrawn and not re-introduced until 1953. Why?
- Laserdiscs promised much better-quality films on home television sets, but have had only limited success, in America. Why do you think they failed in the UK?

Quality

Quality is also a matter of the expertise needed by the user and the technical specifications of equipment. Media technology has for many years been categorised by manufacturers as suitable for 'domestic', 'semi-professional' or 'professional' use. These distinctions have been important for many years in terms of radio and television, with BBC and ITV technical officers decreeing what is suitable for broadcast use. (Recently, with new broadcasters from satellites and 'narrowcasters' on cable considering material for screening, the BBC/ITV regulations are becoming less important.)

The distinctions are based on a number of factors, the most important being the quality of the audio or video signal that can be recorded and input to an edit suite. In simple terms, the professional technology provides more information from larger **format** media.

Formats Professional analogue formats are usually physically larger to increase definition. The 'large format camera' used by a professional photographer produces a 2.5-inch-square negative compared to the 35 mm frame of the hobbyist. Digital formats will not have the same requirement of physical recording area.

The domestic equipment designed for the home user will often have fixed or automatic controls which limit the possibilities of creating certain types of images (audio or visual). Conversely, the professional equipment, which allows great control over the recording process, also requires considerable skill on behalf of the operator. Perhaps the major distinguishing feature, however, is cost – £600 for a domestic camcorder, £10,000 or more for a broadcast machine.

Digital technology threatens all these distinctions. The format is no longer relevant because all data is digital, the controls on the equipment are likely to be more flexible, more user-friendly and possibly more 'intelligent' (see below) and the price differential between domestic and professional is likely to narrow dramatically. Soon an amateur media producer will be able to produce broadcast quality (in the technical sense at least) material without buying professional equipment. Already there

Figure 14.2   Media 100 is one of the leading 'nonlinear editing' systems which have brought digital editing to audio, video and multimedia applications

Nonlinear editing   Video and audio material can now be stored on a computer hard disk as digital data and sequenced and manipulated endlessly for viewing before 'printing' to tape or broadcast. Analogue editing was always **linear** – images and sounds would have to be physically 'joined' in a linear sequence to be viewed as such.

Two or three companies dominate the new digital editing market. AVID is the major broadcast system, Lightworks is used in film production and Media 100 in medium-budget production.

are bedrooms across the country packed with equipment which is more powerful and better specified than similar professional equipment in broadcast studios of ten years earlier. Here is one source of the argument that says that new technology can provide greater **access** to media production, and it has been most vigorously championed in relation to music technology with 'bedroom composers' achieving hit records.

But can the professionals 'allow' this gap to be closed? Almost certainly not. The broadcasting industry seeks to maintain its lead in 'quality' sounds and images by developing new delivery systems such as stereo broadcasts and 'high definition' images on widescreen television sets.

Intelligent machines?

If the stored data is digital it can be accessed and used in many other ways. Digital devices can provide information about what they are doing and can perform automatic operations – in effect they can be programmed to perform, just like any other computer. At the simplest level, a CD player can play the tracks on a disc in any order. At the most complex level, a digital video edit suite can read an edit decision list and put together an entire programme while you go off for a cup of tea ('auto-conforming'). All of this makes digital technologies potentially more creative in the sense that they can make possible new ways of doing things and even suggest new things to do with spin-offs from the extra information they provide. Again, this is most evident with music technology because digital production has been established longer in that field. New forms of video production are now appearing and many of you will use digital video and audio technology during your course.

Miniaturisation and transmission

Photography is considered to be no longer a useful term by many critics and has been replaced by 'electronic imaging or digital imaging'. Traditional photography is a medium of photochemistry. In the new 'digital darkroom' images from different sources (video, computer, chemical photography) are combined.

Digital storage, via compression, can lead to smaller devices and as we have noted, consumers moved from CDs to vinyl discs because they were more convenient to handle (which augurs well for DVD). Digital processing is handled by microchips which get smaller and more powerful by the day. The process of miniaturisation goes on non-stop. This means that new consumer products and especially new portable products will appear. The same advantages also aid the transmission of data which will be generally cheaper, quicker and more reliable than analogue methods (and can also utilise existing technologies like telephone lines).

Multimedia was the buzz-word of the early 1990s, and multimedia texts like CD-ROMs and Internet websites are fast becoming a commonplace. These texts combining computer text and graphics, moving images and sounds, and which are controllable by a reader or viewer, have been made possible by digital devices which can use the same hardware to store, manipulate and output sound and images, both still and moving. This is the final stage of the analogue to digital transition. The 'essence' of each separate medium has disappeared and with it many of the institutional aspects of media production in that area.

Figure 14.3 Early video equipment was large and bulky, like this reel tape recorder. Similar quality is now possible with equipment which could be carried in a briefcase

Sound editing technology now looks the same as video editing or photographic retouching technology: all data appear on a computer screen and are manipulated via mouse and keyboard (as in Figure 14.2). Multimedia programmes are 'authored' by someone who writes a script comprising a set of instructions which in effect command the software to play a video sequence or a sound sequence or to display text or still images, all of which are just datafiles to be 'called up'.

> '... just as cut-and-splice methods in sound recording suggested an intriguing link with film in the sixties, the exact equivalence of digital "composing" programmes like Cubase and video editing programmes like AVID placed the two disciplines within morphologically similar techno-grids. In both cases the praxis is the same – bunch of folks in an airless city room staring at a screen.'
>
> (Sinker 1995)

Culture and technology

We have already noted that attitudes towards technology vary enormously. Some of us are 'anti' (technophobes), others are 'pro' (technophiles). It is worthwhile then to look at some of the critiques of technological change which have come from outside the media industries.

Pam Linn, an educationist writing in the mid-1980s, points to several disturbing aspects of the introduction of personal computers and computerised household goods. One is what she terms *technological immanence* – the way in which technology pervades our lives and changes the way we do things, without our really noticing it. She refers to her experience of buying an automatic washing machine, which led her to change her habits; washing at different times, looking at the labels on clothes, changing the washing powder etc. Then the machine broke down and she realised that she had changed her practices so much that she had no fall-back position. Writers who have changed all their habits to become computer-users are often terrified at the prospect of losing all their work when a hard drive crashes. Technological change has brought 'liberation' and new creative opportunities, but also anxiety and insecurity.

A second issue which she raises is that of *user-friendliness* and effective *deskilling*.

- Modern machines have several automatic functions and 'default settings', which allow anyone to use them without having to learn how to operate them fully or to understand how they work.
- Computer displays are designed to be user-friendly by presenting the user with a screen which effectively mimics the environment which it

Transferable skills are highly valued by governments and employers who want workers to be able to move easily between different jobs. Computer skills are potentially 'transferable', but most training emphasises understanding of specific software like Microsoft Word, rather than how the technology works. So, is the understanding transferable to other packages and other computer platforms? Are keyboard operators more or less 'skilled' than the typists of previous generations?

It is worth noting that 'professional' media technology has fewer 'automatic' settings and allows greater control over actions. This is good for the designer or editor, but 'dangerous' for the keyboard operator in the office, who is expected to follow routines – software as 'control'?

has replaced. A desktop publishing program mimics the designer's desk and the software is designed to be 'intuitive' so that the user can move objects about the screen without having to understand what the computer is doing. This feature has been a major factor in the success of the new technologies but Linn argues that it is based on a 'deficiency model' of the user's competence: 'In practice "user friendliness" makes a program easier to use at the cost of understanding how the program actually achieves its effects. Ease of use is related to powerlessness, rather than to control' (Linn 1985).

The issue here is 'skill transfer'. If you learn to use one software package, can you transfer your skill to another package on another machine? And do you know what to do if the computer does not perform as you expect? You cannot transfer your skills if you do not 'own' them, and skill ownership is another important issue. Linn might argue that the skills are 'owned' by the software.

ACTIVITY 14.4

Skill ownership

Think about the media technology you use on your course.

- How much do you know about how it works?
- Can you distinguish between decisions you make about how to use the equipment (altering sound levels, changing camera lens settings) and settings given to you automatically?
- How much do you need to know before you can feel in control of the technology you use?
- Try to think of one production you worked on. Could you describe how you could have achieved a similar result using different technology?

You may well have already come to this conclusion if you learned how to use one computer in lower school and then found that the computers in sixth form or college did not use the same software. Or perhaps you have a machine at home, but find that other computers won't read your disks? The computer manufacturers and software writers could make your life easier, but often it suits them to frustrate you into buying their product and then sticking with it. Your ability to transfer skills is a potential loss to them because you could easily transfer your allegiance. These questions of skill ownership and operator's 'control' over the technology are important in all areas of media production.

Deskilling

These questions of skill ownership and 'empowerment' lead to a general discussion about 'deskilling'. This implies that jobs are becoming less reliant on specialist craft skill and more on a range of lower-level general skills. Another term for this is 'multiskilling', which has special resonance in the media industries where one or two 'generalists' can now manage the work previously carried out by several specialists. For example, the traditional crafts of typesetting and picture retouching required highly skilled staff with years of training. These have now been replaced by computer software. With the two 'industry standard' software packages, Adobe **Photoshop** and **QuarkXpress**, any reasonably computer-literate person can learn the basics of how to lay out a page and how to manipulate an image after only a few days tuition – the software has effectively given us a concentrated version of all the skills and knowledge which the craft operatives have learned over many years.

But does this make us 'typesetters'? Are we really capable of 'desktop publishing'? Well, sort of. What we don't know is what makes a good page layout, why some typefaces are not appropriate for particular uses – in short we are not trained designers (see 'Production techniques', Chapter 5). The 'best' software will actually try to do this for us as well, suggesting standard layouts. Unfortunately, most software has bland standard settings which mean that there are now many examples of badly designed leaflets and posters, immediately recognisable as 'DTP' publications. The same is now beginning to happen with images, thousands of which are already available on CD-ROMs. This use of **clipart** means that many people without developed drawing skills are able to produce illustrated work (as we have done with two drawings in this chapter). We could see this as increased access to opportunities for a wider range of people to engage in production, but some employers may see an opportunity to pay less for skills and reduce staffing levels. Introduction of new technology inevitably leads to redundancy and redeployment – investment in capital equipment displaces labour.

The introduction of new technology has led to the disappearance of traditional roles. The clearest example of this was the war waged by Rupert Murdoch on the Fleet Street print unions. As newspapers moved away from '**hot metal**', the print unions managed to maintain staffing levels even when the range of job tasks was reduced. Murdoch broke them by computerising the whole process, which also meant that journalists found themselves increasingly responsible for the initial preparation of their copy.

QuarkXpress This is the software used by nearly all magazine publishers for sophisticated page layout. The only serious rival has been **Adobe PageMaker** (now being superceded by a new Adobe product, **InDesign**). Image manipulation is dominated by **Photoshop**. Although the Macintosh is the usual computer for publishing, all three programs are available on 'Wintel' PCs as well.

Hot metal Blocks of type moulded in molten metal were 'set' on trays for printing and afterwards melted down and re-used. The term is now used to characterise the newspaper industry before computerisation.

Videojournalists were employed by a local cable company, Channel 1, in London. They worked on their own as a combined reporter, camera operator and sound recordist. See Griffiths 1998.

In some local newspapers, the picture editor has gone and the news editor now selects the images. In broadcasting, the television four-person film news crew (two on camera plus a sound operator and a reporter) has been reduced to a video team of two – and sometimes the reporters might find themselves on their own as '**videojournalists**'. What were once specialist 'graded posts', fought for by craft unions, are being replaced by 'multiskilling'. The ultimate situation is complete automation.

> TV-AM, which held the franchise for Breakfast Television on ITV during the 1980s, used to operate a series of remote studios in various provincial cities. These studios had make-up rooms, reception areas for guests and a single set with a lighting rig and a camera 'remotely controlled' from London. *One* full-time employee operated the studio.

'Things don't take less time. Instead you get people doing things in more detail, more accurately and better than they did before. These days most stations are pretty slim, and on air you're using the same number of people' (Paul Fairburn, Programme Controller of Heartland FM interviewed in *Broadcast*, 21 April 1995).

In America some radio stations are completely automatic, broadcasting from banks of tapes with pre-recorded continuity announcements and not a DJ in sight. In the better radio stations the computer has not replaced staff, but has instead enabled them to work more quickly and therefore to spend more time 'getting it right'. Technology in itself is not a threat to labour – it is always a case of how management attempts to use it.

Communication: instant and accurate – but fragile?

The scale and scope of technological change means that our perceptions of the world have altered significantly. For example, in 'Globalisation', Chapter 20, we discuss a global market which is constructed by a network of data exchange matching developments in transport facilities. The media themselves are bigger, brighter, faster etc. It is worth remembering, however, that the new systems go wrong as spectacularly as they go right. Early in 1998, a mistake by an employee at one of the major Internet service providers meant that millions of business users lost all chance of communication with the outside world for half a day. When digital systems 'crash', everything goes down. When American cinema owners began to install digital sound systems in the 1990s, they often included a 'failsafe' analogue system alongside the new digital one (see Allen 1998).

Rights and royalties

A rather different consequence of the move to digital media is of concern to 'creative' rather than 'technical' personnel. Digital product is easily and accurately copied – indeed the copy is indistinguishable from the original. In practical terms it is difficult to stop piracy. Technology can, however, be used to protect itself, with built-in codes which will corrupt the file if unauthorised copying is attempted. There are many legal problems – how do you prove that your version is the original? What happens when, in the case of the Internet, material is copied (downloaded) in a country with laws different from those in the originating country?

The ease of digital piracy has encouraged many relatively poor people to steal material from rich and powerful media corporations. There is clearly some mileage in viewing this as a form of 'underground resistance', but it hurts the upcoming performer as well, who may lose out on royalty payments.

Computers are also very good at logging digital files as they are used – have you ever thought about how anyone calculates the royalties due to a musician whose recording is played on radio stations and in shops or bars?

The record company behind the band Oasis was one of the first to take action against Internet sites set up by fans which carried copyright material.

ACTIVITY 14.5

Copying

How much copying have you benefited from? Have you ever copied CDs, computer games, videotapes? Think through these issues on copying:

● Do you think copying is theft?
● What are the issues raised by sampling in relation to popular music?
● Why do you think the media corporations put so much material on their own Internet sites if they are so afraid of copying?

Censorship and regulated content

Allied to fears about greater piracy with digital technology are a range of concerns about censorship and regulated content. Much of this debate is centred on the Internet and is dealt with in the case study which follows, but some general points can be raised here.

First, we should note that the first group of producers to embrace new technologies tend to be the pornographers. There are good reasons for this:

● Pornography is concerned with sensation, and anything which improves the quality of sound and image, relatively inexpensively, will be used as soon as it is available.
● Pornography is sold on the promise of excitement, and 'new technology' promises to add to excitement.
● New delivery systems like satellite and the Internet enter the home directly, enabling the user to avoid the mails or visits to cinemas etc.

(this 'invasion' of the home has perhaps increased the controversy surrounding the issue, with access by children an obvious concern).

- New technology is initially unregulated and in the interim, before the authorities can act coherently, pornographers will rush to make profits. During the early years of videocassette technology, satellite and then CD-ROM, pornography was probably (accurate figures being hard to verify) the single biggest sector in the industry. This has been the case also with the Internet.

Two other factors are important in the swift take-up of digital technology by pornography. Several of the new distribution systems (satellite, Internet) are difficult to control within national boundaries, so that material freely available in other European countries where censorship is less severe can be transmitted to the UK without difficulty, requiring UK authorities to take action against individual users rather than the supplier. The quality and ease of digital copying means that a single cassette or CD can be brought into the country and 'duped' many times.

Some of the same arguments would also apply to material which was politically 'unacceptable', although the demand and the incentive to produce it may be less. Whatever the form of 'unregulated' media activity, it is in the interests of the major media corporations to regulate themselves and ensure that at least the 'legal' part of the media industries is seen to regulate itself. The growth of the Internet is beginning to see moves to censor controversial materials in which the companies who provide the computer connections 'pull the plug' on some producers and individuals. Again, this can be seen to be following the process set by earlier media producers and distributors. In the 1930s the Hollywood studios adopted the **Hays Code** to protect themselves against charges of corrupting the audience. Later the video rental industry in the UK agreed to a similar move. We could suggest a tentative rule about the development of a new medium:

Hays Code Production code named after Will Hays, President of the Hollywood Producers Trade Association. Effective from 1933, it controlled screen sex and violence (e.g. a man in bed with a woman had to keep one foot on the floor). Its power waned with the end of the studio system.

> As a new medium broadens its appeal beyond the adventurous few looking for new excitements, it is more and more likely that providers of products on the new medium will begin to censor their own products.

So far in this chapter we have discussed some of the possible effects of technological change in relation to *industrial* or *institutional* issues (see also 'Industries' and 'Institutions', Chapters 22 and 26). The issues can be summarised as:

- 'gendered work' and access to employment and consumption for women

- distinctions between 'amateur' and 'professional' production threatened
- convergence of different media sectors now using the same technology base
- deskilling and multiskilling, which have altered the structure of employment
- new technology underpining globalisation
- copyright and censorship.

Some further issues about distribution technologies and access are taken up in the case study on the Internet. There is still a crucial aspect of technological change to consider here – the impact on the nature of media language and the 'difference' of the digital image.

Digital imaging

> The drive behind much of the technical development in cinema since 1950 has been towards both a greater or heightened sense of 'realism' and a bigger, more breathtaking realisation of spectacle … towards reducing the spectators' sense of their 'real' world, and replacing it with a fully believable artificial one.
>
> (Allen 1998, p. 127)

> The reduction of the photographic image to numbers implies the possibility of its reversal, in other words the creation of fictional, but photographically 'real', imagery (and spaces).
>
> (Henning 1995, p. 218)

These two quotes neatly represent major concerns within what might now be termed 'image technologies'. They both play with the idea of the photorealistic – the achievement of an iconic image which attempts to represent the 'real' world. We explore the issue of 'realisms' and their importance within Media Studies in the next chapter, but what interests us here is the impact of technological change and the difference between the attitudes developed within photography and cinema.

The drive for greater realism has propelled technological development in cinema throughout its history. It is not just a question of a bigger, brighter, more sharply focused image with more 'natural' colours, but also a depth and clarity of sound. Somehow Hollywood has managed to contain the contradiction of a more 'realistic' image associated with an extraordinary spectacle – culminating in the massive investment in special effects technology to create the spectacle of *Titanic* (US 1997). Allen goes on to point out that, although we recognise that the spectacle is created by new technologies, we still insist that the effects are seamlessly melded into the fictional world of the film – we know that

Morphing is a technique ideally suited to computer operation. It refers to the process of changing the shape of an object in a smooth, continuous process. The computer is given the original image and the 'changed' image and then calculates the frames in between, each of which shows a slight alteration.

Henri Cartier-Bresson (born 1908)   French documentarist with an enormous impact on photography practice. His first collection of photographs was published in America in 1952 under the title *The Decisive Moment*.

Manipulation   In July 1995 Russian President Boris Yeltsin returned to public duty after treatment for heart disease. A photograph was released as proof of his recovery. Much discussion followed, in which some observers claimed that they remembered the photograph from an earlier period – only the shirt he was wearing had been changed.

'morphing' isn't possible, but if it was it would look as 'real' as it does in *Terminator 2* (US 1991). By contrast, when the material of a film *is* actuality, one of the dominant conventions is to foreground the construction of the image by emphasising the hand-held camera and the use of the interviewer's microphone.

Photography starts from a different position. The 'dominant' mode of photography for most of the history of the medium has been the documentary strand which upholds the photographic image as 'evidence' of something which has happened. Perhaps because the photographic print is a 'fixed' permanent record (unlike the 'time-based' status of film, which exists only as a flickering and temporary image on a screen), it is seen as 'capturing' reality in a 'decisive moment' (the phrase made famous by **Henri Cartier-Bresson**).

There are other modes of photography, and several photographic artists have embraced new technologies and used them to develop a wide range of techniques in order to produce innovative work for exhibitions and commercial (advertising, fashion etc.) work. But though these works attract interest and debate, they do not represent the challenge which the latest digital imaging has brought to the status of the photograph as evidence. The quote from Henning refers to an anxiety about a 'post-photographic world' in which there is no certainty. What appears 'real' may be a fiction. Of course, it has long been possible to 'doctor' a photograph, but before digital **manipulation** the procedure was quite difficult and the results often less than satisfactory. In Figure 14.4 a simple manipulation has been carried out – the lampposts have been 'rubbed out'. This casual editing is now a commonplace. If you check the newspapers when a big story breaks, you will sometimes see the same agency photograph used in different newspapers with different 'digital enhancements'. These are often designed to clarify the meaning of an image with some background details removed. How do you feel about this? Have we finally reached the dreadful world of

Figure 14.4   It is a simple task to 'rub out' the lampposts in the image – and to remove individuals from the march if necessary

Orwell's *1984* – or perhaps we have been freed from the tyranny of 'real images'? Some critics recognise this as another feature of a 'postmodern' condition (see 'Postmodernisms', Chapter 18) – a world of surfaces with no fixed meanings.

Conclusion

We've tried to deal in this chapter with a wide range of issues to do with technological change. In doing so we've tried to avoid some of the glib determinist statements in which the impact of technology has easily recognised effects (usually bad). We've presented a series of sometimes contradictory analyses which are relevant to many media debates and we recognise that the pace of change is so great that you will need to be on the look-out for news stories in order to keep up-to-date. Try to use this chapter to develop a starting point for your own analysis.

References

Acker, Ally (1991) *Reel Women*, London: Batsford.

Allen, Michael (1998) 'From *Bwana Devil* to *Batman Forever*: Technology in Contemporary Hollywood Cinema', in Steve Neale and Murray Smith (eds) *Contemporary Hollywood Cinema*, London: Routledge.

Griffiths, Richard (1998) *Videojournalism*, London: Focal Press.

Hayward, Philip (ed.) (1991) *Culture, Technology & Creativity*, London: John Libbey.

Henning, Michelle (1995) 'Digital Encounters: Mythical Pasts and Electronic Presence', in Lister (ed.) *The Photographic Image in Digital Culture*.

Linn, Pam (1985) 'Microcomputers in Education: Dead and Living Labour', in Tony Solomonides and Les Levidow (eds) *Compulsive Technology: Computers as Culture*, London: Free Association Books.

Lister, Martin (ed.) (1995) *The Photographic Image in Digital Culture*, London: Routledge.

Neale, Steve (1985) *Cinema and Technology: Image, Sound, Colour*, London: BFI/Macmillan.

Sinker, Mark (1995) 'Music as Film', in Jonathan Romney and Adrian Wootton (eds) *Celluloid Jukebox*, London: BFI.

Further reading

There are very few books which address new media technologies in an accessible form for students – and many that do soon become out of date.

Articles in newspapers (i.e. the broadsheet dailies and Sundays) and magazines (both 'hobbyist' and professional) are sometimes more useful, but beware exaggerated claims about the possibilities of change. The following have some historical material and some background on the issues. (See also Case study 15 references.)

Convergence: The Journal of Research into New Media Technologies from the University of Luton Press is a useful source.

'Digital Dialogues' (1991) Special Issue of *Ten 8*, vol. 2, no. 2.

Wollen, Tana and Hayward, Philip (eds) (1993) *Future Visions: New Technologies of the Screen*, London: BFI.

15 / Case study: Digital publishing and the Internet

The term 'new media technologies' has been around for twenty years or so and tends now to refer to the shift from analogue to digital devices described in 'Technologies', Chapter 14. In your study of the media you will be expected to know about the 'effects' or impact of these changes on:

- employment patterns and organisational structures
- media products and their uses.

Most discussion of these effects has focused on the newspaper and magazine industry, where computerised page layout and typesetting saw the redundancy of traditional typesetting workers, the multi-skilling of journalists and also the rise of new magazine titles (because launching a new title is now not such an expensive proposition).

Although this process is still going on (the daily evening paper in Bradford went over fully to digital production only in 1997), the major impact was in the late 1980s. So this is hardly a 'new' technology at the end of the 1990s. Most change has so far occurred at the *production* stage – what is still 'new' is the development of digital *distribution*. It seems appropriate therefore to focus this case study on digital publishing.

The term 'publishing' conjures up images of print material – books or magazines. It means 'to make available to the public', so it could be used to refer to cinema, radio and television as well. Until now, though, these have all been separate industries, with their own technologies and institutional customs and practices (see 'Institutions', Chapter 26). (The secondary meaning of publisher – someone who distributes work on behalf of an author – has already made the move

to television with Channel 4 being the first UK 'broadcaster publisher'.)

Now that these industries are coming together and **converging** – because:

- the digital technologies used in each industry use similar computer software
- the same media conglomerates own companies in each industry

Figure 15.1 The CNN website

– it is possible to reconsider the idea of publishing and to talk about electronic or digital publishing. A good current example of what is happening is the development of 'continuously updated' **Internet** sites, such as those of CNN (Figure 15.1) and the *Daily Telegraph* newspaper group. Here, a television channel and a traditional newspaper are offering the same service – news pages which are close to being 'live broadcasts' direct to your computer screen. Other sites offer the chance to hear radio broadcasts via the computer (but at the moment these require more than the average computing power and software).

All media products go through a production cycle. Material is researched, 'captured' or 'produced', post-produced or edited, distributed and exhibited. All parts of the cycle will eventually be subject to the change from analogue to digital.

ACTIVITY 15.1

Electronic newspapers

Try to access some of the electronic newspaper sites such as the *Guardian*, *Times*, *Daily Telegraph* etc.
- Is it obvious that the website is linked to the print title?
- How much advertising is there on the site?
- Is the target audience the same for the website and for the paper?
- What do you think is the main purpose of the website?

In the 1970s the first big change in distribution came with the development of new types of communications cable – using fibre optics (thin filaments of glass fibre) rather than copper wire – which could carry many more channels of television, radio and telecommunications. Around the same time, the Internet began to develop as a closed system, linking large computers in military and university institutions. When the Internet became more widely available in the 1990s, it suddenly opened up the

possibility of new forms of communication for a very large group of users.

What follows is an analysis of the new forms of digital distribution in terms of products and uses and some discussion of employment and organisational structure.

Digital distribution media

Cable

When you sign up for connection to a cable system, you are joining a 'closed' system (i.e. a network in which there are connections between a central supplier and a known group of users and no chance to 'escape' into the wider world), albeit one with at least the potential for two-way communication. Most cable service providers are publishers in the traditional sense – they distribute programme material produced by other companies. One difference, however, is that they can easily target distinct communities for particular programmes – for example it is possible to send down the cable an advertisement for a supermarket, targeted at only those subscribers in the same postcode district as the store. Cable providers also have a residual obligation to distribute some 'community-based'

Have you ever wondered what all those supermarket reward cards are all about? One aim is to persuade you to keep shopping at the store, and to spend more when you shop. As part of this, but also producing valuable extra market research information, is the collection and collation of details about your spending habits. When that smart card is swiped through the Sainsbury's till, it means that a complete record of all your brand preferences can be logged against your personal details, so later you can be direct-mailed with special offers. Eventually, perhaps, the supermarkets will suggest what customers want in their weekly shop and will deliver it automatically – the ultimate in 'push technologies' (see below).

> Tesco has found that men who shop for white wine on a Thursday or Friday also buy condoms. Men who buy nappies also often buy six-packs of beer.
>
> (*Guardian*, 14 April 1998)

programming, where the 'content' is locally produced. The interactivity of cable has so far been restricted to a response from the viewer expressed as a willingness to pay for special programmes on an individual basis – so-called Pay Per View (**PPV**), an important factor in current television and film markets. The profusion of channels, especially with digital television, promises new ways of watching television in which viewers can select other kinds of services such as banking and shopping. These are being widely discussed, but there is still no guarantee that there will be a swift take-up. Most of these services will mirror the way in which Internet services have developed.

Digital television

Digital television transmission promises hundreds of extra channels. At the time of writing, different delivery mechanisms for digital television are planned. Launch dates have already been missed, but the services should be available by the time you read this. Satellite will come first and cable companies may carry these services. Later will come **multiplex** broadcasts – several new channels on a single wavelength. The UK will have six of these.

The digital service providers claim that the numerical data in the 'digital' television signal can be compressed without losing quality (although there are doubters who say quality will suffer), so more data can be carried by each cable or broadcast channel. This means that picture resolution can be increased as well as more channels offered. The UK television standard for analogue television is 625 lines. Digital television could double this (but the lack of a standard for Europe and North America still makes the industry nervous). More lines mean more data and this means a sharper picture (and probably a **widescreen** format – the 16:9 **aspect ratio**). Higher resolutions, known as High Definition

Television (**HDTV**), will require a new television set, as well as a digital decoder. The extra expense means that it could take ten years before all viewers convert. (The government has suggested that there will be a definite 'cut-off' date for analogue broadcasts, but when this will be is not clear.)

Many of the new channels will be PPV – perhaps the same film on offer at different starting times on different channels – or shopping services. Such a service, 'Front Row', began offering PPV movies on cable in March 1998.

Digital television will be matched by digital radio services. These too will require new equipment and take-up may be slow (the BBC has had great difficulty in persuading many listeners to switch to FM reception on analogue radios). Digital broadcasting will develop, but it will take longer than expected and the companies who develop it will need deep pockets.

Internet

When you 'log on' to the network in your college, you are joining a 'closed network' – you have access only to the other machines physically linked to the college system. Many college networks now offer Internet access and this allows you so much more. The Internet is simply a 'network of networks', so a link can be made from your college network to thousands of other networks around the world. The Internet itself is thus theoretically completely 'open'.

Once connected, there are a whole range of different ways in which you can use the Internet. Visiting sites on the **World Wide Web** is only one possibility:

- The 'Web' isn't the complete Internet – it is the network of sites with 'browsable' pages of **hypertext**, images and sounds which you can select and view by clicking on links.
- **e-mail** allows messages between any two Internet addresses (every registered Internet user has a unique 'user name' and every access point has a unique address).
- **ftp** (file transfer protocol) lets you 'upload' or 'download' files from your computer to a special kind

of Internet address. You can use this to acquire free 'public domain' software or animations or music modules. It also allows individuals to set up and maintain their own website or 'home page'.

- **IRC** (Internet relay chat) lets you 'chat' in a 'conference room' with other Internet users.
- **telnet** is a protocol which allows you literally to use another computer thousands of miles away, without leaving your desk (telnetting was used to check the bibliographies in this book by searching through the library catalogues of different universities).

`http://www.routledge.com`
is the website address for our publisher.
`http://www.brad.ac.uk`
is the website for Bradford University. '**http**' stands for 'hypertext transfer protocol'. '**com**' is a company and '**ac**' is an academic institution. Unless you are an international company, '**uk**' is necessary to designate a site outside America ('**org**' designates a non-profit organisation like a charity or public body, e.g. '**bfi.org**' for the British Film Institute).

`info.media@routledge.co.uk`
is the e-mail address for queries about Routledge's media books in Britain. '**info.media**' is a user name (a separate mailbox). One important point to note is that electronic addresses must be accurate. Send an ordinary letter ('snail mail') to A. S. Smyth instead of 'A. S. Smythe' and the letter will probably get to the right person, but send an e-mail to 'infomedia' rather than 'info.media' and it will be returned as 'undeliverable'. This is progress? (Well, it is, but it does point out that technological change means altering some of our ways of working.)

Some of these uses are 'interactive' in that they involve two-way communication, and even 'surfing' the web (jumping from one site to the next, following 'links') is about choice. But the future of the Internet may be very different.

Changing uses: 'push technologies' and 'easy access'

A major concern for some users is the development of so-called 'push technologies'. Surfing is based on the idea of 'pulling' images and text on to your computer screen, because you want to see them. To do this you need a basic understanding of desktop computer operations. To do it efficiently and effectively, and to know what to do if things go wrong, you need more advanced skills. This is one reason why, at present, the number of *regular* Internet users is still relatively small (despite all the claims to the contrary).

Why is it called 'surfing'? One possibility is that 'browsing' websites is analogous to 'riding a wave' as you move from one site to another. The image of surfing calls up ideas of Californian chic: this was important in selling the idea to the young and affluent, but will it help to promote the Internet to a mass market ?

There are concerns that current access protocols and the 'culture' of the Internet may favour some users rather than others. Gender is an issue if the UK experience of 'information technology' education continues to see relatively low take-up by young women. The Internet can be seen to promote a laddish culture, which builds on the stereotype of computer technologies as 'boys' toys'. There are, however, plenty of examples of women who have used the Internet to promote a very wide range of issues and concerns. What do you think of what you find? You might want to consider how the films *The Net* (US 1996) and *Copycat* (US 1996) represent both the Internet and the women who use it (and perhaps contrast them with *Mission Impossible* (US 1997)).

The language of the Internet is primarily English. Other European languages tend not to have too many problems, but, because of the ways computer keyboards and operating systems work, languages with different alphabets have problems, especially those like Arabic which also differ in reading from right to left. Arabic is a major world language, yet the relatively few websites in the Arab world have to use English because of the software problems involved in using Arabic with web browsers.

A rather different problem affects visually impaired people. If more and more information is available only via the net, this could exclude the visually impaired. But the solution – software which turns links into sound codes – could make for much better access to information than is possible with traditional media.

Another reason why many people are excluded from Internet access is because it is relatively expensive for the personal user (the most frequent users are academics with free access). In our current economic system, the growth of the Internet can be seen to be dependent on companies investing in the technology in order to make future profits. They must find ways to generate income through control of information or access to information.

It is worth thinking for a moment about who benefits in economic terms from the expansion of the Internet. First there are the computer manufacturers – of modems and cables and of bigger, faster computers. Next come the software developers who write the browsers and **protocols** (the software which makes possible the connection of computers for different purposes), the telephone or cable companies which carry the data, the server companies – the **Internet service providers** (**ISP**s), whose computers make possible all the links between networks – and finally the **content providers**, very often media companies who want to market films, music etc. (or to sell them by 'e-mail order'). The most talked about companies are the providers of 'search engines' such as Yahoo! – 'gateways to the Internet' which carry advertising. There will also be small design companies and freelances who will design pages and build the sites.

You should recognise that there are companies involved here who are active in several of these different technologies. A good example is Microsoft. Microsoft market one of the two main Internet software packages, Explorer. Microsoft founder Bill Gates is actively pursuing

Figure 15.2 Microsoft Network doesn't know national boundaries – here is the French version

partnerships and mergers with telephone and cable companies, and MSN (Microsoft Network) is a major service provider.

Microsoft software is 'bundled' with most new PCs – i.e. it is already loaded on to the hard drive of the machine when you buy it, with Internet software now part of Windows 98. 'Bundling' means that you have to have it, even if you don't want it – and it can be difficult to remove. This has led to the US government attempting to force Microsoft to 'play fair' and allow rivals like Netscape the chance to sell their products to new users.

Microsoft is one of the success stories of recent years. From humble beginnings as creator of the operating system MS-DOS and its successor Windows, the company has come to dominate the computer world with 90 per cent of all computers using its operating system. This kind of market domination would not be tolerated in most other industries, and it is not surprising that Bill Gates is revered by many and attacked ferociously by others.

'Automatic' connection to Microsoft Network is often the easiest option for a new user, and Gates hopes to create more and more Microsoft disciples. Microsoft is attractive to new users because the name is well-known and so much is automatic or 'built-in' that the computer novice will feel safer than with a lesser-known service provider. However, Microsoft wants to *sell* services, rather than allow users simply to gain access to the 'free Internet'. New users are less likely to be prepared to look for what is freely available and so may be prepared to take up the offer to pay for services.

Once you are linked to the Internet, your address becomes known to any other computer you contact. Conventions at the moment mean that reputable users don't make use of this knowledge. Any messages you send can also be intercepted by more unscrupulous users, unless they are made secure by encryption – a service offered by the companies who sell products and services across the Internet and ask for your credit card details. Commercial sites which you visit may ask you to accept a 'cookie' in order to register as a user – a tiny file which sits on your computer and gives the commercial company all your details as soon as you log on. This means that what you see has been 'personalised', just for you. It is the first stage in 'pushing' services to you. The technology to make this possible is computer-based, but traditional computers with keyboards and mouse are still off-putting to many people. What if using a computer was as easy as changing channels on a television set with a remote control? This is where the set-top box comes in.

Set-top box

The future lies in a computer which sits on top of the family television set (or at least that is what the experts tell us – be prepared for them to be wrong sometimes). In one sense this computer already exists in the form of a decoder for satellite or cable, but the new version will include Internet access as well. All the services will be available on an on-screen menu and web pages will be displayed on the television screen. The possibilities are endless, and the service providers will hope that 'ordinary television viewers' will be attracted to a broad range of services. You won't be surprised to learn that Microsoft bought one of the pioneer American companies in the field, Web TV, in 1995. The largest UK cable provider, Cable and Wireless, announced a deal in March 1998 with Microsoft's Internet rivals, Netscape

and Oracle, to use their set-top box technology for Internet access via digital television.

Some analysts see the introduction of a wide range of services entering the home via the television set as another example of 'dumbing down' or 'couch potato' activity (see 'Audiences', Chapter 32). If an audience for this type of 'push' service exists (and there is evidence from trials conducted in Britain and America to suggest that it isn't *necessarily* there), it will certainly be more 'passive' in the sense of 'zapping' from one channel to the next, rather than 'searching' for a specific website. The content of these new services will be 'pushed' to the 'consumer' rather than 'pulled' by a 'user'. This will be a form of publishing which could be argued to appeal to the passiveness of the reader rather than his or her discernment in seeking out a particular book or magazine.

Language is important in these debates. Video on Demand (VOD) is one of the proposed services. Consumers 'demanding' to see a particular film is an interesting concept. In reality, the choice is likely to be limited by the deal between the service provider and particular film distributors.

Conversely, we might view the idea of a 'user-friendly' form of Internet access as a democratic move, offering many more people the chance to communicate. This will depend, of course, on whether or not the set-top box allows other modes of access such as e-mail, inter-relay 'chat' (IRC), or the use of **search engines**, such as Yahoo! The last is very likely, because the search engines which help users to find websites on selected subjects, are important sites for advertising on the net.

The possible benefits or otherwise of the expansion of 'digital publishing' will depend on who controls the Internet. We suggested at the beginning of this chapter that the Internet was 'open', and indeed, compared to most other forms of communication, it is. Because the Internet is not bound by the laws of any particular country, it is theoretically possible to publish anything or to find anything that has been published on the net.

Using a search engine

The Internet is a valuable source of material for research exercises – much of the information in this book has been discovered on or checked against a wide range of Internet sites.

If you are going to find useful material on the web, you need to learn to search. There are several freely available search engines to help you. They are often available simply by clicking on a menu from within your browser. The most popular engine is Yahoo!, which has a UK site at `http://www.Yahoo.co.uk`. This site helps you to restrict the search to UK sites if that is useful (don't forget that most users are in America, so most search results will be American too). Searches need to be planned with 'filters'. We'll try AltaVista, a good general purpose engine. Type *Hollywood Cinema* in the box provided and you will be presented with over 800,000 sites. The engine looks for any site with 'Hollywood' or 'Cinema' as words used in the text on that site. You can filter out most of the dross by using double quotes around both words, i.e. *"hollywood cinema"* or by using a plus sign, i.e. *hollywood+cinema*. This looks for the exact phrase. A lower case entry is best as it will find both lower-case and upper-case words. The result should now be a more useful thousand sites, ten of which will appear on screen immediately. The engine will always try to present the ten 'best' sites first – those which it thinks conform best to your search criteria (this might mean the number of times the keywords are used on the site, or their presence in headings etc.). In each case you can select a site just by clicking on the address. You will always get a brief description of the site (assuming it has been properly put together) to help you choose.

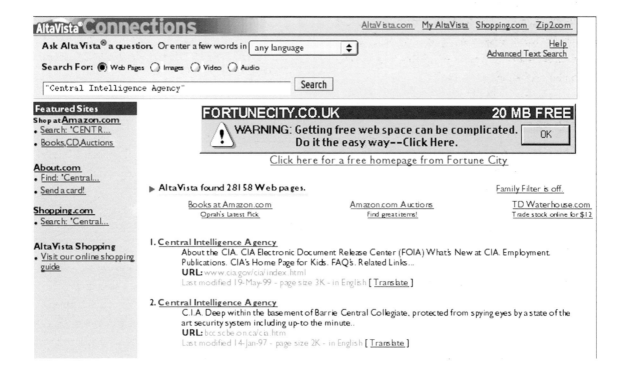

Figure 15.3 An Internet search engine from AltaVista. Note the advertising display and the entry searching for sites dealing with the CIA (Reproduced with the permission of Compaq Computer Corporation. AltaVista, the AltaVista logo and the Compaq logo are trademarks of Compaq Computer Corporation)

AltaVista lets you search for sites by language and also has 'advanced' features, explained in a help menu. Other search engines might have slightly different criteria, but all work on the same basic principles. Yahoo! lets you access several other different engines.

- You can test out a search by looking for "*Media Student's Book*". We haven't bothered to give you an address as it might have changed before the book comes out. If you want to e-mail us with your comments on the book, you should search for "*Gill Branston*" or "*Roy Stafford*" and look for a site with a 'mail to:' feature against our names. You can click on this and send a message.
- Try some other searches and decide on the quality and variety of material you find. Does it suggest an open Internet with easy access?

When you find something, remember to 'bookmark' the page, or print out or save the page. When you do, you may be breaking *copyright*. The larger corporations will have detailed legal statements asserting their rights, although the precise force of current legislation and the way in which it applies to the Internet is not yet clear. Certainly it is easy to 'copy' the material on the net and to put it into another product. What do you think the law should be?

The digital frontier

At first, people were happy to wander round, exploring the new frontier, surfing the internet. Now, they are putting down roots, building their own home pages. Soon there could be 50 million of them … the phenomenon of electronic homesteading.

(*Guardian online*, cover story 'How the Web was Won', 19 March 1998)

The emphasis on publishing as an industrial activity has perhaps underplayed the pleasures of creativity that characterise many users' times spent on the Internet.

There is as much enthusiasm as pessimism about 'virtual life'. Many exciting interactions take place, not least the fun people have playing games together (or against each other) and the passions roused in newsgroups and chat rooms by a myriad of topics.

The quote at the head of this section develops a well-used, but none the less illuminating, metaphor for Internet exploration. There are two kinds of 'home pages' – those built on the free space granted by a service provider when you agree to pay for a year's access and those provided by specialist servers like GeoCities in the US, who allow individuals to build inside specific 'lifestyle communities'.

The minimum 'free' home page allowance is 5 megabytes of space on the server's site. If you are careful with images, 5 megs is a lot of space – enough for a full-length novel if you were so inclined, or a couple of songs you have recorded at home. In practice most users support a page about their favourite movie star or musician. GeoCities had over 1.5 million 'homesteaders' in 1998. Even if 90 per cent of those are the equivalent of the photos on the fridge door, that still leaves 150,000 potentially interesting and useful sites. Someone out there may know all about that obscure musician you are desperate to study or about that rare disease someone you know has just contracted.

ACTIVITY 15.2

Build your own home page

You may be in a school or college where you can add a page to a website. If you are not, you can still design a page and keep it on a floppy disk to view on any computer with a web browser. There are numerous software packages available to help you create a page and you should be able to get some support to help you. Here are some planning issues to think about:

- What topic would you choose?
- How would you appeal to a casual 'surfer' who came across your site by accident? How would you address viewers or readers?

- Would you want to say something very personal or would you opt for something that was just 'fun' or 'straight and serious'?
- How would you feel about your site being seen by unknown groups of people anywhere in the world? (They could find your site if you register with a search engine.)

So, in one sense at least, the Internet is the greatest opportunity for 'free', personal publishing we have seen so far. Governments have tried to censor what some people put up there, but so far with only limited success. At the time of writing, the UK government is trying to stop access to images of child pornography, posted in unregulated newsgroups. This is censorship which would gather wide support, but it would also set a precedent which might threaten all the other 'freedoms' to publish less offensive material.

Censorship on the Internet

For a British Internet user, the range of material available on American and other European websites can be quite surprising. British government has always been secretive in comparison with Washington (although this is being addressed by civil servants – at least on a promotional level – and Whitehall sites often appear under the heading of 'open.govt.').

British films and television are heavily censored compared to many other countries and there is no doubt that just as with satellite television, the Internet allows access to far more sexually explicit and violent material than could be found legally in UK print magazines, film or television. Whether you think this is a good or bad thing, it is clearly happening and presents national governments with problems of regulation.

Gatekeepers of the Internet

The crucial agencies for the functioning of the Internet are the service providers. These organisations provide the links between the networks which make access possible to the full range of addresses. The service provider has suites of computers which receive your telephone calls and switch them to other networks to allow you to make connections.

Occasionally, you may attempt to look up a website only to get a message from your service provider saying that an address is 'not available on this server'. The most likely explanation for this is that the link is down – it is a technical fault. But it might be a case of self-censorship, with the server deciding not to allow a link to be made. This emphasises the potential **gatekeeping** function of the server. The idea of a gatekeeper who restricts entry to debates or participation has been recognised in media studies for many years (see 'Selecting and constructing news', Case study 13). So far, most ISPs have resisted attempts to censor, but Germany has seen pressure on ISPs from the government, which has been successful in banning certain newsgroups.

Rate of change

These developments are taking place at an incredibly fast pace. When we began to write the first edition of this book in 1994, the Internet was something we had heard about, but not experienced. When the book was being completed eighteen months later we were starting to see media companies using the net to reach potential customers. For the second edition, we both used the Internet regularly – much of the book has been discussed via e-mail and much of the research material has been downloaded from websites.

But this may be a brief golden age – information now free may cost in the future. The pace of change is not going to slow down. We can't predict how things will be in two or three years' time. Much will depend on the pricing policies for telephone calls. Eventually, local calls in Europe may be free as they are in America. This will encourage wider Internet use. But then, the Internet itself may be replaced by more organised services offered by Microsoft and its competitors. (Microsoft and BT announced a deal in March 1998.)

Access and value for money

This pace of change is something you should be very aware of – and the hype which surrounds it. There are some well-known 'street guides' to developments in computing power, including the cost of data storage and the speed of processors. If you had bought a personal computer in 1994, the hard drive which would have come with the machine might have been as big as 160 megabytes. By 1998, for the same price, you could have bought a 1.6 gigabyte drive – ten times larger. Processors are similarly much much faster. So, computers should be faster and cheaper? But they aren't.

Programmes have got bigger as well, and most of the extra speed and storage has been swallowed up by coding which is far less efficient than when storage space was scarce. Apart from games, which use the extra technological power to achieve greater 'realism', most of the things we use computers for – writing letters, e-mailing friends etc. – don't require all this new storage and speed, but we have to have it, because that's what sells computers. 'It's bigger, it's faster!'

Some pundits have described a future where we will access the net through tiny devices, no bigger than a wristwatch. The pace of innovation in chip manufacture – all the necessary software in ROM (read-only memory) to download data – means that this would be feasible in a few years' time. But will we see such a thing? You are probably familiar with the old saying about the everlasting lightbulb. Such a product could perhaps be made, but no manufacturer would make it, because the market would eventually dry up.

Digital technology is rapidly becoming a mass industry, built on the idea of obsolescence, like the motor vehicle industry. The manufacturers will encourage

> Computers are becoming status symbols like cars – modern PCs are 'gas guzzlers' by comparison with the original Model T Ford. Using a computer to send a simple letter has been described as 'taking Concorde to do your local shopping'.

us to throw away perfectly usable equipment, in order to make way for something bigger and faster we don't really need (but may well enjoy).

This production-led drive to sell digital power has serious consequences for access. If computers were smaller and cheaper, everyone who wanted access to the Internet could get it at low cost. The 'net computer' already exists. It works by simply downloading software when it is needed and doesn't need a big hard drive for storage – the set-top box could be developed to provide just such access at low cost. The iMac, an 'Internet-friendly all-in-one computer', was acclaimed on its release in autumn 1998. The lack of a hard disk drive and reliance on the Internet for data exchange was seen as a signal of a new kind of personal computer.

Public service broadcasting (see Case study 29) is based on the idea of a 'universal service', rather like the provision of free public libraries. The Internet could be shaped as a public service, with every local library offering free access, rather like the 'cybercafés' (Figure 15.4) which have sprung up in various parts of the country (and which charge by the hour). This is an idea which has not slipped by the politicians, in either the US or the UK. However, rather than see the development in the public sector, they have in both countries invited the media and communications corporations to lead the projects. Will BT and Microsoft be as concerned about public access as the broadcasters were in the 1960s and 1970s? Will UK-based service providers be regulated? Is there any point in regulation when the Internet does not recognise national boundaries?

Figure 15.4 The cybercafé in the Kirklees Media Centre

Publishing and controlling communication

Throughout history powerful people have always tried to control the means of communication. Each new media technology has at various times been seen as threatening the balance of power, by providing new means of communication for those with less power. Political pamphlets from secret printing presses, 'pirate' radio and television, video campaign material (see Harding 1997) and the early DTP fanzines are all examples of this resistance through counter-publishing and the Internet is the latest site of struggle.

Digital publishing and employment

Digitalisation has generally led to a reduction in skilled workers in specialised production roles. So, what will happen with digital distribution?

There certainly won't be a massive increase in 'content production' or employment in production for all the new forms of distribution. Many of the two hundred channels broadcast by digital satellite will be showing material already made for analogue transmission.

There will be employment for web page designers and staff to maintain pages. But these may not be quite what we expect. The experience of digitalisation in the newspaper office saw journalists keying in their own copy. Will future journalists be updating their own stories on the web page as well as inputting copy for a print version – the difference may be only a few mouse clicks?

One aspect of future employment does seem a fairly safe prediction. Digital information travels easily at low cost and therefore it doesn't matter where digital workers are located. The global economy (see 'Globalisation', Chapter 20) has already produced examples of work being contracted out around the world. Imagine that you have an office in New York. Your staff work from 8 until 6 (it's hard work in New York) and to get more staff in during the night-time you would have to pay higher rates. Why not contract it out to the other side of the world – in India perhaps where it is daytime and rates are cheaper anyway?

Your work could be done on a computer link between the two offices.

India is a good example of a country with unemployed graduates who can be trained for programming work. Software development takes place all round the world, and the development staff tend to congregate wherever they fancy – California is a safe bet. The UK is a centre for games development.

The employment structure of the future appears to be throwing up a number of contradictions. Digital communication has had a major impact on financial services and the 1990s have seen a shake-up in banking. Many people have stopped using a high-street bank and have postal or telephone accounts. They might be expected to move to Internet banking, but there is some lack of trust of the impersonality of the computer, as well as the security worry. The result is that telephone services are increasing, with real people at the ends of phones. The telephone service room is becoming the factory of the future. As if to emphasise the need for a human touch, many of these 'call centres' are situated in Scotland or the North of England, because research shows that local accents and dialects from these areas convey reassurance and trust.

Conclusion

The switch to digital distribution is the last stage in the process of moving from analogue to digital technologies. It promises to change the way we access media texts in a fundamental way (we will also see digital distribution of films to cinemas in the near future) and to offer us the chance to publish our own texts.

Unlike the earlier digitalisation of production, which did not change the media product as such, we may begin to enjoy and use new products as a result of the new distribution technologies, but this is not yet proven on a wide scale.

The opportunities to use the new technologies for personal or community purposes are real and attainable. We all have a chance (given the necessary funds and computer skills) to engage with a wider range of communication technologies and to enjoy new and exciting experiences. But it is also true that technological developments in this area are largely controlled by powerful oligopolies which are likely to make bigger profits if they can sell us packaged services, rather than grant us the access to use the new technologies as we wish. The 'digital domain' will increasingly become a site of struggle over the future of personal access and use of media technology.

References and further reading

Understand how a website is constructed:

Holyer, Andy (1997) *HTML in Easy Steps*, Coventry: Computer Steps.

And what all those Internet terms mean:

Pfaffenberger, Bryan (1996) *Internet in Plain English*, New York: MIS Press.

Information on the technologies:

Lax, Stephen (1997) *Beyond the Horizon – Communications Technologies, Past, Present and Future*, Luton: University of Luton Press/John Libbey.

Access issues:

Harding, Thomas (1997) *The Video Activist Handbook*, London: Pluto Press.

A useful history of technology which attempts to deal with some of the myths about the 'technological revolution':

Winston, Brian (1998) *Media Technology and Society*, London: Routledge.

Websites:

Media students are likely to find these two UK university sites at Aberystwyth and Glasgow particularly interesting:

`http://www.aber.ac.uk/~dgc/media.html`
`http://www.arts.gla.ac.uk/tfts/FTVrescon ts.html`

16 Realisms

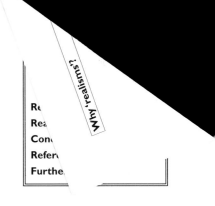
Why 'realisms'?

Realism is a concept which writers and producers fight over – a politically charged term with an apparently obvious meaning, but also a long and varied history, which needs to be understood if it is going to be useful.

What is in dispute? Look at any historical drama on television. A programme which depicted life at the court of Elizabeth I would be ridiculed if someone was wearing a wristwatch, but we accept that all the characters speak a recognisable English, even though we know that the people of the time spoke something we would find hard to follow. The wristwatch breaks the rules of historical detail, but the dialogue translation is an acceptable realist convention, which has been rendered 'invisible':

- Realism is something we have learned to decode.

A similar point arises with the selection of colour or black and white filmstock in an image. For older readers of texts, black and white photography often denotes realism. They are familiar with events from wartime in which they have a personal emotional investment, being documented in monochrome in family snapshots or **newsreels**, whereas colour images of the same events seem like a fiction. Younger readers are likely to reverse this meaning and to take colour as real and monochrome as a style feature.

- Realism as a term draws attention to a desire to connect with the rest of the real world especially around broad social questions such as unemployment, war, homelessness etc.

However, you can't simply point a camera at such events and expect to produce realism:

- Realism is an **aesthetic** construct which is produced by means of recognisable codes and conventions which change over time.
- There is no single 'realism'; different cultures and different contexts produce different 'realisms'.

The controversy around realism is explained by its connection to social issues – which themselves are often the basis for conflict – and by the

Newsreels during the 1930s and 1940s were all presented in monochrome and remained as 'evidence' of the period until the 1970s and 1980s, when researchers discovered 'amateur' film footage of the war years, shot in colour.

Aesthetics refers originally to the 'principles of taste and art' or the 'philosophy of the fine arts'. It has come to be used to refer to an interest in visual style or 'the look' of something. A **realist aesthetic** is an approach to media production which consciously attempts to use a visual style which will help to produce a realist effect.

contradiction inherent in its use as an approach to media production, i.e. that a **realism effect** requires careful preparation and perhaps considerable artistry on behalf of the producer: it is never just a case of 'simply capturing reality'.

Actualities was the name given to the first short films of 'real events'. The term *documentary* appeared during the 1920s and has tended to be reserved for films over a certain length (perhaps twenty minutes).

- In the 1994 film *Forrest Gump* Tom Hanks shakes the hand of President John Kennedy, thirty years after Kennedy's death. We can now produce **photorealistic** images of events that never happened – not even as an acted-out scene, never mind as documented **actuality**. This technique was applied in an entertainment film and audiences were amused rather than threatened, but it does raise the question: If we break the link between concrete reality and its representation, where does this leave our trust in **documentary** evidence? (see 'Technologies', Chapter 14, for more on this issue).

Documentary 'The use of the film medium to interpret creatively and in social terms the life of the people as it exists in reality' (from the title page of *Documentary Film* by Paul Rotha (London: Faber & Faber, 1939)).

- Most viewers react to depictions of violence on the cinema or television screen, but some argue that 'realistic' violence is acceptable because it enables us to understand what the effects of violence really are, whereas 'cartoon violence' is simply gratuitous and likely to corrupt because it asks us to enjoy someone else's pain through a fantasy. Others argue the opposite – that, because we know that some violent acts we see are a fantasy, they do no real damage; but realistic violence appeals to our prurient, voyeuristic nature.

  Whether or not children can distinguish between the 'real' and the 'fantastic' in this context is an important consideration, but this point tends to be lost if the two sides of the argument don't understand how realism works. (See 'Genres' and 'Audiences', Chapters 8 and 32, and comments on this issue and **verisimilitude**.)

Historical background

Realism as an artistic movement is associated with the rise of capitalism and the industrial revolution of the 1840s in western Europe. As a movement in painting it is seen as predominantly French, covering the period 1840–80 (Nochlin 1971). Some of the techniques used in realist painting (e.g. perspective and accurate scale) had been known since the Renaissance, but their application now coincided with the birth of photography – the first technology to offer a direct representation of 'reality'. Novels such as those by **Charles Dickens** and **Elizabeth Gaskell** were notable for attention to detail in the descriptions of the characters' lives and an interest in the social conditions of contemporary society at a time when two new classes, the industrial poor and the urban bourgeoisie, were becoming established. Earlier novelists had tended to use characters to explore either emotions or moral values, whereas the

Charles Dickens (1812–70) wrote about the experience of 'ordinary' people in London.
Elizabeth Gaskell (1810–65) wrote about the cotton workers of Manchester.

realists described their lives (which isn't to say that realist novels were
lacking discussion of values).

We can trace many of the contemporary debates around realism back
to these two forms – the photograph and the 'bourgeois novel'. The two
central issues might be the use of technology to get us closer to 'reality'
and the debate about an aesthetic which constructs narrative time and
space so that it seems to represent the 'real world' *transparently* to us as
readers, inviting us to identify with an individual hero (rather than the
exemplary 'everyman' of earlier stories).

Realisms and technology

Photography is a process involving drawing ('graph') with light ('photo'),
and the first photographic technology was used to help artists to draw
more realistic pictures. The concept of a '**camera obscura**' (literally a
dark room) into which light can be introduced through a tiny aperture to
create an inverted image on a white background was first suggested by
the Arab scientist Alhazen in the ninth century and 're-discovered'
during the Renaissance. In the late eighteenth century, portable 'light-
boxes' with a focusing lens (known as 'camera lucida') were introduced,
and eventually the image was captured on light-sensitive materials –
photography was born.

A photograph is a two-dimensional image of a three-dimensional reality,
and this requires an understanding of certain 'ways of looking' in order to
understand how to 'read' the image as if it were 3D. We could argue that
this is what visual realist conventions allow us to do. The optical devices of
the eighteenth century introduced artists to new ways of producing images
cast on paper, which could then be sketched or traced to make a permanent
record. They were particularly useful in making possible accurate
reproduction of *monocular perspective*. Perspective describes the angle of view
which changes as lines are drawn towards a point on the horizon. Monocular
perspective implies a single point from which these lines are drawn – i.e. the
representation is constructed such that a single viewpoint is allowed. The
viewer is 'in control' of the world he or she surveys. In earlier painting styles,
perspective was treated quite differently. If you go to an art gallery and look
at pre-Renaissance paintings or those from non-European cultures (see
Figure 16.1), you will find the size and placement of figures in a landscape
presented in various ways. We are so used to the constructed sense of 'depth'
in a photographic image that we find it difficult to 'read' these earlier
images. Yet they serve to remind us that what we see in any representation is
an artificial construction. The realist image is a 'learned' image – it is not
something 'natural' (see Neale 1985 for more on perspective).

transparency the idea that the
reader or viewer treats the
constructing devices in a text as
invisible and sees only the 'reality'
which is represented. It is opposed
by the idea of foregrounding the
construction (as when we see a
microphone boom in shot).

Camera obscura are included in
some museums or specially
constructed towers and are worth
visiting for the insight they provide
into the pre-electronic 'world-
view'. Try Edinburgh or Dumfries
among others.

A Matter of Life and Death (UK
1946) is a famous fantasy film by
Michael Powell and Emeric
Pressburger. It includes a striking
scene in which a country doctor
uses a camera obscura to spy on
his neighbours. Powell was an 'anti-
realist' fascinated by the camera as
controlling eye.

Figure 16.1   A fourteenth-century representation of samurai warriors from *Kitabakate monogatari*

Sound recording and realism

Much of the argument about realist aesthetics is taken up with visual codes, but we must not neglect 'aural realism'. The later nineteenth century saw the development of sound recording technology, and with it a similar development of arguments about 'realist sound'. We can talk of the 'sound image' in much the same way as the visual image (see 'The Languages of media', Chapter 1, and 'Analysing images', Case study 2). Our problem is that the terminology for discussion of sound images is not so well developed as for that of visual images, and as a consequence we are far less confident about discussing the realism of sound reproduction. A simple test will demonstrate the strangeness of discussing realist sound.

The sound of your own voice

Look at a recent photograph of yourself. Is it a good likeness? Most of us recognise ourselves in photographs. We might not like what we see, but we can accept it as a resemblance. Now listen to yourself recorded on tape. This is much harder to accept. Is that strange voice really you? Why are we so surprised to hear ourselves? Possibly, because our ears are less *trained to listen* to voices than our eyes are to look at pictures. There is also a physiological reason. When we speak we push out or pull in air which in turn creates sound waves. As a consequence we *feel* the vibrations from the act of speaking. When we hear our voice coming from speakers we don't feel anything (unless the speaker is so large and powerful that it makes the floor quake).

Perhaps this is what makes our own voice sound so alien – because it isn't accompanied by the familiar sensations of speaking. What would be even more strange would be to play a recording of ourselves backwards. This would be unintelligible. Yet, the visual equivalent would be simply to look in a mirror – a perfectly ordinary thing to do, but in fact an inverted representation of how we look, which we have learned to 'read'.

Tuning in to sound effects

Andrew Crisell (1994) makes the point that a particular sound on the radio works quite differently on television. The radio sound is more appropriately called a **sound effect**. Galloping horses being simulated by the production assistant banging together two halves of a coconut shell is a good example. On radio we accept this sound as a realistic representation. If we were offered an authentic recording of 'real' horses galloping along 'real' highways, we might not even recognise the sound, without its accompanying visual signifier. So, as well as the 'quality' of sound reproduction, we must consider the realist codes necessary to convey meaning.

For the visual image, realism would normally imply that most of the component signs were **iconic**, i.e. they physically resemble real world objects they represent. A realist visual account of horse-riding would show real horses and would use the iconography of 'horse culture' – bridles, saddles, stables etc. In the sound image, icons are much more problematic. All the associated sounds of horse riding, such as the heavy breathing of the horse, the squeak of the leather saddle, the clomping of hooves etc., are 'mixed' within the sound image and we may be unable to distinguish one from another. Their resemblance to real sounds becomes a problem. We are more likely to respond to an identifiable sound (perhaps a single whinny followed by a snort of breath) which signifies the presence of a horse, than a realistic *mélange* of sounds. In this case the sound image is more **indexical** than iconic, an index being a sign that works by establishing a relationship between itself and reality rather than simply offering a resemblance. The horse sound tells us about the *presence* of a horse. This whole exercise serves to remind us that we also use abstract signs – a character could use the word 'horse', the sound of which has neither resemblance nor indexical relationship to the real animal.

The history of media technology during the twentieth century has been dominated by the drive for 'greater realism'. In one sense this is a technical challenge to the innovator, in another it is an aesthetic challenge to the producer, but it is also always a social and cultural issue about representing events and ideas.

Realism and social issues

Major technological advances in sound recording have concentrated on clarity and the establishment of a realistic stereo 'soundscape' – see 'Production techniques', Chapter 5.

The nineteenth century not only saw technological developments which allowed the detail of 'reality' to be represented to an extent never before contemplated, it also saw new industrial and social conditions which changed so quickly and so profoundly that they in turn prompted a demand for new ways of classifying and communicating the extent of that change. Journalistic writing and photography were developing alongside social investigations and industrial warfare. Two good examples would be the coverage of the American Civil War – documented in great detail by contemporary photographers and journalists whose work was used in the television series *The Civil War* (broadcast on Channel 4 in 1994) – and the work of Dr Barnado's in creating a photographic archive of the street urchins 'rescued' in Victorian London (exhibited in 1995).

The realist movement in painting and literature was over by the end of the century, but the use of photography and film to represent social issues has persisted and has produced fierce debates over 'realist aesthetics' during the twentieth century (see 'Postmodernisms', Chapter 18, for more on this history). We will concentrate here on film and video, which will encompass sound and visual realism. Similar arguments can be explored in relation to still photography and sound-only recording.

Realisms in film and video

Cinema has developed over a hundred years with a constant tension between its twin roots of 'photorealistic' image technology, capable of documenting reality, and a fairground mentality of fantasy and magic. For every **Lumière** 'actuality' there is a **Méliès** fantasy with special effects and trick photography. This might suggest that the history of cinema is of documentary *or* fantasy, and of course it isn't. Instead, film-makers moved between the two and combined elements of both to present a remarkable range of different kinds of film texts (including documentaries with the appearance of fantasy and vice versa), in which the distinction between 'fiction' and 'fact' is blurred. This diversity is something to celebrate. We are discussing 'realisms' as part of a range of different approaches to the medium.

We've suggested that one distinguishing factor of realist film-making might be a concern with representing social issues. This would push out of the frame most **mainstream** films, which, although they reproduce aspects of the real world accurately enough to signify a familiar location, are not interested in making use of the real events which might happen there every day. Instead, they pursue familiar story structures (providing the pleasures of genre) or special stories with 'larger than life' characters and unusual events. The level of realistic detail in a Hollywood film may be very high and the original story idea may have come from a newspaper or magazine. A film like *Working Girl* (US 1988) might tell us something about New York office life and will certainly enable us as students to enter a discourse about 'women and work', but for our purposes here it isn't realism.

One of two other elements must be present in a realist film:

- The film-makers are concerned to capture something about the experience of real events, to represent them as faithfully as possible for the audience and to **mediate** them as little as possible; *or*
- The film-makers have something specific to say about the real world *and* have developed a specific style, using realist conventions.

The first of these is a pragmatic approach which tries to get as close as possible to an event in a physical sense and tends towards a documentary

Lumière brothers Auguste and Louis, French brothers often credited with the first cinema screenings in 1895. *Workers Leaving the Factory* and *A Train Arriving in the Station* were two of the 'actualities' of a few minutes' length which comprised the opening programme.

George Méliès was the first 'showman' of cinema. His short films in the first years of cinema included *A Trip to the Moon* (France 1902).

Dramadoc and *docudrama* are terms used to describe the mix of fact and fiction in modern television productions. Often a play will be written based on the transcripts of a 'real' courtroom drama or the memoirs or diaries of politicians etc. and using the visual techniques of documentary. Some critics get very agitated about the confusion between the documented fact and the written fiction – others see it as quite acceptable.

approach. The second is a more obviously 'political' position and is as likely to encompass 'realist fiction' as well as documentary. Again, we might see the former as developing from photography and journalism and the latter from literature – but it isn't quite as simple as that. We will investigate four celebrated historical examples, selecting from a wide range of possibles. We think you need this detail in order to explore ideas about realism. All the examples have resonances in contemporary media production which we hope you will pick up, but please be careful not to take any of them as representing 'fixed' positions about realistic aesthetics – this is one of the dangers of superficial studies which look for easy categorisations. You will find contradictions between the approaches, but also similarities.

Direct Cinema

Similar work (but with a different underpinning philosophy) was also carried out in France and an alternative title is *cinéma vérité* (cinema truth).

The high point of the 'direct approach to recording reality' came in the early 1960s and was known in America as Direct Cinema. The modern term is 'fly on the wall' to describe standard television documentary techniques which enable viewers to eavesdrop on what appear to be 'real events' (i.e. not specially staged for the camera).

The simple premise of this approach is that a camera and microphone are as close to events as possible and that the film or tape is running continuously. Everything that happens is recorded. The pioneers of this work had three main problems:

- finding camera and microphone technology which was lightweight and sensitive
- avoiding becoming part of the events and causing subjects to 'play to the cameras'
- deciding how to reduce the hours of footage to a reasonable length for audiences while avoiding a particular editorial position.

The early 1960s was the period when lightweight 16 mm film cameras could for the first time be combined with good-quality lightweight audio recorders for synchronised sound. With film stocks sensitive enough to provide reasonable monochrome picture quality under most lighting conditions, including small hand-held lights, the documentary crew were ready to go almost anywhere – and they did.

The new approach began with *Primary* (US 1960), in which a crew followed presidential candidates John F. Kennedy and Hubert Humphrey on the campaign trail. The film was made by an independent television producer Robert Drew, working with three documentary film-makers who would become the core of Direct Cinema – D. A. Pennebaker, Richard Leacock and Albert Maysles. As Monaco (1980) points out, the aim of Direct Cinema was a sense of 'objectivity' – the events and people who were the subjects of films were able to speak for themselves, avoiding voice-over narration (the conventional accompaniment to many documentaries up to that point).

Conventions can soon develop and become 'naturalised' as part of the medium. In the sophisticated 1990s we have become used to the presence of the camera in all kinds of unlikely places and we have also grown sceptical about the 'objectivity' of documentary approaches. In 1960 not only was the technology new but the eavesdropping on ordinary lives was also novel. In many ways, Direct Cinema was less an *aesthetic* and more a *practice*, by which we mean it was less important that the films had a particular look or style and more important that the production was completed in a particular way.

The problem of subjects who 'played to the camera' and therefore behaved 'unnaturally' was partly avoided by selecting subjects for whom 'playing to an audience' was simply part of their usual behaviour. Politicians were followed by performers of various kinds, including Bob Dylan in probably the best-known and commercially most successful Direct Cinema feature, D. A. Pennebaker's *Don't Look Back* (US 1966) and the Rolling Stones in the Maysles Brothers' *Gimme Shelter* (US 1971).

Problems were faced by Frederick Wiseman, who began a series of 'institutional' documentaries in the late 1960s. Wiseman tackled a police force, a high school and various other welfare agencies. His aim was to spend long enough with his subjects, filming all the while, for them to begin to feel that he and his crew were 'part of the furniture'. When he eventually came to the editing stage he had miles of film to sift through and the question of mediation became crucial. The initial approach of Pennebaker and Leacock was to try to subordinate editing decisions to the flow of events – i.e. not to develop a particular viewpoint through selection of shots but simply to show whatever the camera 'captured'. (Monaco makes a good point here when he emphasises this notion of 'capturing' rather than 'creating' images.) Wiseman couldn't do this with his hours of film – he was forced to make decisions and effectively to enter into the relationship between the camera and the subject, in other words to mediate.

Wiseman's films were controversial and it is worth considering the links between his approach and other media forms. The 'closeness to the subject' and the revelations which might ensue were associated with photojournalism – as were many of the technological developments in cameras, lenses and film stocks. A parallel 'movement' to Direct Cinema was '*New Journalism*', a development in newspaper and magazine journalism in which feature writers began to adopt some of the strategies

Shooting ratios for verité documentaries are very high – 20:1, twenty or thirty hours of film for a one-hour programme. The programme is really 'scripted' in the edit suite.

of realist novelists in order to present stories. This meant detailed descriptive writing and also the possibility that the journalist could become part of the story, recording how he or she felt. In a sense this was in conflict with the 'objectivity' of Direct Cinema. Yet, in another way it shared what we might see as an immersion in the issue, especially following the Wiseman approach. Some of the better-known New Journalism pieces by **Hunter S. Thompson** and **Joe Eszterhas** belong to a 'counter-culture' view of America in the late 1960s and early 1970s (i.e. writing opposed to the values of the establishment). They display the first signs of a coming together of television, cinema, rock music and magazine writing which is now commonplace in 'style' magazines like *The Face* and a range of 'lifestyle' television programming. A marker of this synthesis is *In Cold Blood* (US 1967), a Hollywood feature based on a New Journalism 'documentary novel' about a pair of murderers, by Truman Capote.

Joe Eszterhas is now well known as the Hollywood scriptwriter of *Basic Instinct* etc. A film of **Hunter S. Thompson**'s best-known work, *Fear and Loathing in Las Vegas*, was released in 1998.

'Many of them seem to be in love with realism for its own sake … They seem to be saying: "Hey! Come here! This is the way people are living now – just the way I'm going to show you! It may astound you, disgust you, delight you or arouse your contempt or make you laugh … Nevertheless, this is what it's like! It's *all* right here! You won't be bored! Take a look!" '

Tom Wolfe on the 'New Journalists' (Wolfe and Johnson 1975)

The 'excitement of the real' has been recognised by Hollywood film-makers who can use Direct Cinema techniques in features to add to the controversy of stories based on real events. Oliver Stone's films such as *JFK* (1991) and *Natural Born Killers* (1994) provide good examples.

In the early 1970s, the leading 'fly on the wall' documentarist working in the UK, Roger Graef, found the BBC to be institutionally opposed to the Direct Cinema approach: 'The BBC published the Green Book on how to make documentaries: do a few days research and then restage what was "typical". Such a process involved the invasion by a crew of technicians, moving the furniture and turning each location into a film studio' (Graef 1995).

The other important feature of Direct Cinema was that it was conceived in terms of television screening. The Drew Associates films were destined for television, and Wiseman was commissioned by National Educational Television. Crucial features of television in the 1960s were:

- poor picture quality – fuzzy black and white
- the importance of the soundtrack: many theorists believed it carried more weight with audiences than the image track.

These two factors meshed with the approach to camera framings and editing – a direct style was suitable, as any complex compositions and framings would be lost on the small television screen while the jerky hand-held camera was acceptable – and the innovation of live 'direct' sound. The films were also assured a relatively large audience and one used to the 'live' feel of television.

This distinction between television and cinema in terms of audience involvement is important for the direct approach. A cinema audience, sitting in the dark in a secluded environment, can become immersed in the film, a feeling of 'being there'. But where is 'there'? The cinema also suggests that the whole experience is 'magical' and 'special' and that the events we experience are somehow happening out of time. By contrast, the television broadcast suggests that we are able to eavesdrop on an event which is happening *now* in a place which we could visit.

By the early 1970s the Direct Cinema pioneers were already looking to video and the first portable 'rover' packs. Leacock in particular has continued to argue for more access to production for more people. The contemporary heirs of Direct Cinema are not too difficult to find. The early techniques quickly passed over into the current affairs documentary (e.g. *World in Action* in the UK) and then into both the 'safe' and the controversial **institutional documentary** series. In recent years we have seen *Video Diaries* and other similar camcorder documents which are in a direct line of descent.

The changes to UK broadcasting in the early 1990s were at one stage seen as a threat to documentary forms, but documentary series, with a much stronger 'entertainment' objective proved to be so popular with audiences that by 1998 arguments were being presented that there were too many series in what was becoming known as the '**docusoap**' format. A new form of 'unmediated' video production is now available via the Internet in the form of the 'jennicam' website on which two cameras record and broadcast live every moment in the study and bedroom of a web designer. This in turn refers to the appearance of entertainment programmes based on footage taken from surveillance cameras and other forms of 'evidence' recorders, raising questions about privacy and possible voyeurism on the part of of the audience.

Institutional documentaries following the Wiseman lead have been popular on UK television. Mostly the exposure of institutions at work is informative or amusing, but those looking into the police and education have created great controversy – which probably says more about those institutions than about the documentary technique.

docusoap is a term applied to a documentary series (e.g. six programmes) recording the lives of people in a particular situation (e.g. *Driving School*, *Hotel* (both 1997) and *Clampers* (1998)). Each of these particular programmes produced a 'star' performer and the accusation that 'entertainment' rather than 'information' was the aim of the programme.

ACTIVITY 16.1

The fly on the wall

Where would you like to be a fly on the wall? Select a subject which you think would interest an audience and which you could visit with a camcorder. Ask yourself the questions posed by the Direct Cinema approach.

- Where would you place yourself to capture sound and image effectively? Could you capture all the material you would need to represent your subject to your satisfaction?

- What strategies would you use to ensure that your subjects did not 'perform' for the camera?
- Do you think your subject would automatically produce a story, or would you have to re-structure the events during the editing process?

In this first example of cinematic (and televisual) realism, we have emphasised a number of factors:

- the role of technology
- the importance of a practice – how to do it in practical terms
- the importance of institutional links to other media forms (which in turn suggests something about how audiences will engage with the material).

Formulating a realist aesthetic

Less pragmatic film-makers than the Direct Cinema group have at various times attempted to develop approaches which would combine an exploration of social issues using the full range of the possibilities of cinema. This is a less 'pure' and more sophisticated position than that of Direct Cinema in recognising that 'Realism in art can only be achieved in one way – through artifice' (**André Bazin**). This emphasises that realism is about a set of conventions. We shall discover that very different conventions can be made to serve similar ends.

The central issue is about how to involve an audience, not in terms of identifying with the individual hero of a conventional narrative but in social issues, albeit played out in the lives of ordinary people. A realist film-maker is making a contract with the audience which implies a joint project to explore the real world through the medium of film. We've chosen to look at two influential historical figures and a controversial contemporary realist.

André Bazin (1919–58) An influential critic whose essays are collected in two volumes published in English in the late 1960s under the title *What is Cinema?* They are still in print (see Bazin 1967, 1971).

Roberto Rossellini

Roberto Rossellini (1906–77) a film-maker for forty years, constantly changing his approach to realism. Also an important teacher and lecturer on film and a major influence on younger film-makers such as Jean-Luc Godard.

Rossellini is best known as one of the founders of **Italian neo-realism** – an approach to film-making which flourished in the immediate aftermath of the Second World War and which was characterised by very low budgets, location shooting, non-professional actors and 'real' stories.

The subject of the neo-realism film is the world; not story or narrative. It contains no preconceived thesis, because ideas are born in the film from the subject. It has no affinity with the superfluous and the merely spectacular, which it refuses, but is attracted to the concrete … It refuses recipes and formulas … neo-realism poses problems for us and for itself in an attempt to make people think.

(Roberto Rossellini in *Retrospective*, April 1953, reprinted in Overby 1978)

This argues for cinematic realism as a **progressive aesthetic** opposed to 'entertainment cinema' and in favour of 'education'. (Rossellini was taken up by Marxist critics in the 1970s, but he remained a Catholic humanist intellectual throughout his life.)

Neo-realism represents a mix between the pragmatic (in 1945 the Italian film industry was, like the rest of the country, in ruins with abandoned studios and a lack of basic film-making materials) and the idealistic. The aesthetic had been developed first in France during the 1930s and later under the fascist regime in Italy, for which Rossellini began his career with documentary-style stories about the armed forces. The stylistic feature we want to highlight is the use of the long shot and the long take.

The **long shot** is the ideal framing device to show crowds and the movements of soldiers in battle. Its use in Hollywood tends to be restricted to **establishing shots** and genres like the Western where 'figures in a landscape' are important. Usually, however, stories are told in mid-shot and medium close-up with attention paid to individual characters. Long shots are also difficult to organise on studio sets, where framing is often required to disguise the fact that a set is just a collection of 'flat' walls without a ceiling. Allied to the long shot is the use of **deep-focus**, which allows the film-maker to compose a shot in depth with objects in the foreground and the background, both in sharp focus. Different actions can take place within the frame and the audience can select to look at the foreground or background. Deep-focus works well on location and, like the long shot, was common in silent cinema before bulky sound equipment began to restrict camerawork.

A **long take** is any shot lasting longer than about twenty seconds. For the film-maker, the long take poses problems because all the actions must be carefully worked out in advance. Long shots and staging in depth help because they give greater possibilities of movement in the frame. Alternatively, moving the camera by panning or tracking allows greater freedom. The panning and tracking camera, shooting in long takes, is a feature of Rossellini's films at various times.

Paisà was made in Italy in 1946 (the title refers to a colloquial Italian word for 'countryman' or simply 'friend') and represents the best example of Rossellini's approach to realism in this period. It is concerned with the story of the Allied advance through Italy at the end of the war. Different characters appear in each of six separate episodes – there is no possibility

Rossellini's first postwar film, *Rome Open City* (Italy 1945), shot under difficult circumstances on the streets of the newly liberated city, caused a sensation in France and the US.

Deep-focus is covered in 'Production techniques', Chapter 5.

Shot length Various film scholars, including Bordwell, Staiger and Thompson (1985), have undertaken surveys of shot lengths from a range of films and production periods. The Hollywood average in the studio period was around twelve seconds, but is currently much less.

of us identifying with an American hero who 'makes it through'. The story derives, in Rossellini's terms, from the concrete reality of the situation and the approach he takes to the production supports this aim. The six episodes are intercut with actual newsreel footage, titles and voice-over in such a way that it is difficult to distinguish 'real' from staged footage. The Americans in the film are professional actors (but not 'stars'), but many of the Italians are played by local people in the 'real' locations which Rossellini uses whenever possible. In the final episode, the incidents are very much based on events recounted by the 'real' partisans.

At the end of the final episode, which features Italian partisans and American and British agents fighting the Germans in the Po delta, the partisans are captured and shot and the protesting American leader is executed. The film ends with a partisan's body floating out to sea and a title explaining that the war ended a few weeks later. This bleak ending would not be possible in a Hollywood film, but for Rossellini it is not the end of the 'story'. As Bondanella (1993) points out, for Rossellini the 'reality' is the triumph of the human spirit over adversity as understood in Christian philosophy.

The argument in favour of the long take and the long shot is clearly demonstrated in Figure 16.2. We are presented with a series of long takes

Figure 16.2 A typical shot from the last sequence of *Paisà*. Note the camera angle which effectively mimics the partisans' view of their world and the long shot which encompasses the mixed band of partisans and British and American special forces – privileging no single character

in which the action unfolds, often in relatively long shot. The scenes are carefully orchestrated to flow almost seamlessly. Although there is clearly a 'leader' (the American officer), we are not invited to adopt his viewpoint. When mid-shots or medium close-ups are used, they pick out particular narrative incidents rather than develop individual characters. Most of all, the camera is used to create for us the viewpoint of the partisans who live in this unique environment. As Bazin writes:

> the horizon is always at the same height. Maintaining the same proportions between water and sky in every shot brings out one of the basic characteristics of this landscape. It is the exact equivalent, under conditions exposed by the screen, of the inner feeling men experience who are living between the sky and the water and whose lives are at the mercy of an infinitesimal shift of angle in relation to the horizon.

(1971, p. 37)

There are two important features about Rossellini's visual style in *Paisà*:

- The style attempts to 'reveal' the reality in the story, it doesn't draw attention to itself. It does, of course, 'construct' a representation of reality, but in doing so it fits Bazin's maxim that the representation of reality requires artifice.
- The relationship between film-maker and audience is such that the audience is invited to select where to look in the long-shot composition and is allowed to follow the action in the long take. The director, by avoiding close-ups and fast cutting, is not shouting 'look here!', 'look at that!'.

Fiction from fact

The basis of the neo-realism approach was neatly encapsulated by one of the main scriptwriters of the period, Cesare Zavattini. He referred to a typical starting point for a neo-realist film:

> A woman goes into a shop to buy a pair of shoes. The shoes cost 7,000 lire. The woman tries to bargain. The scene lasts perhaps two minutes, but I must make a two-hour film. What do I do? I analyse the fact in all its constituent elements, in its 'before', in its 'after', in its contemporaneity. The fact creates its own fiction.

(Quoted in Williams 1980)

Zavattini did this to great effect in the celebrated *Bicycle Thieves* (Italy 1947), in which an unemployed man can't look for work unless he finds his stolen bicycle. Jim Allen used a similar starting point for the Ken Loach film *Raining Stones* (UK 1993), which was based on an unemployed man who wants to buy a communion dress for his daughter. *Bicycle Thieves* was also a model for the first African feature film Ousmane Sembene's *Borom Sarret* (Senegal 1963).

If you are interested in scriptwriting, trying out Zavattini's method is excellent practice. Take a simple action like the above and work backwards and forwards from it to create a story.

Rossellini went on in the 1950s and 1960s to explore ideas about realism in many different ways, but let's turn to another film-maker who had similar concerns, but very different and equally influential methods.

Sergei Eisenstein

Soviet cinema in the 1920s was dedicated to celebrating and promoting the revolution of 1917, and this produced a potentially contradictory set of impulses. Films were at once experimental – part of the revolutionary artistic work of a new society – but were also required to document and represent the successes of the revolution, providing 'evidence'. Later, in the 1930s, this contradiction would be resolved in terms of a state-approved 'socialist realism' with a didactic narrative and heroic characters, but in the 1920s much more variety was possible.

Sergei Eisenstein formulated a theory of '**dialectical montage**'. *Dialectics* is the Marxist term for a process of analysis in which change is identified as a struggle between opposites which in turn produces a new synthesis (expressed as thesis – antithesis – synthesis). *Montage* is the process of putting images together so that new meaning is created through a particular juxtaposition. If images are chosen carefully, montage can 'represent' ideas quickly and dramatically. The shock of a juxtaposition can be concerned with the *content* of the image – a starving child juxtaposed with a gluttonous financier – or with *formal* differences of size of shot or framing – a long shot of a crowd and an extreme close-up of a face. Montage might result in a rapid succession of briefly held shots in a sequence, whereby a 'real' process is speeded up, or a sequence of shots which extends time by repeating images.

Eisenstein argues that montage is the best way to engage the audience in a learning process. Through montage the film-maker exposes his or her thought processes and this enables the viewer to participate in the process of 'creation' of meaning which takes place through the juxtaposition. This is both the opposite of Direct Cinema (*creating* images not *capturing* them) and a refutation of the Bazin/Rossellini method. Eisenstein says to his audience: 'Here is A, here is B, what do you make of putting them

---

Sergei Eisenstein (1898–1948) was the leading experimental director of the Soviet Union in the 1920s as well as a writer and teacher of film theory. He gained considerable recognition in the West and was lured to Hollywood (not a successful move).

Eisenstein quotes a 'miniature story' by the American writer Ambrose Bierce. In *The Inconsolable Widow*, a woman is weeping by an open grave. A stranger approaches and comforts her saying that 'there is another man somewhere, besides your husband, with whom you can still be happy'. 'There was,' she sobbed, 'but this is his grave.' The juxtaposition of weeping woman and grave and our conventional reading are all that is needed to make the story (Eisenstein 1968, p. 5).

Figure 16.3   The baby at peril from the famous 'Odessa Steps' montage sequence from *Battleship Potemkin* (USSR 1925) – subsequently copied in *The Untouchables* (US 1987)

together? Yes, it's C isn't it?' Watching the film becomes a dynamic process of making the links and understanding the synthesis.

Eisenstein is best known for the films which tell the story of the revolution and the struggles which went before, such as the 1905 mutiny on *Battleship Potemkin* (USSR 1925). *October* (USSR 1928), which he co-scripted and co-directed with Gregori Alexandrov, was a tenth anniversary film about the revolution itself. Photographed almost entirely in Leningrad (St Petersburg or Petrograd in 1917) the actors are largely local people – one similarity with the neo-realist approach. There is also the occasional use of long shot and 'very long shot' to show the mass of workers and soldiers. There the similarity ends. The montage film uses relatively short takes throughout and framings are designed not to 'reveal' actions but to present shapes and symbols which create new meanings.

Often framings show us just faces – selected as being particularly suggestive of cruelty, jollity etc. – or just hands, arms etc. The strutting officers of the Tsar's guards are intercut with a mechanical peacock strutting and preening itself. As the mass of workers rush across the wide streets of Petrograd in very long shot like ants, they are intercut with two images of machine guns with a leering gunner gleefully firing away. These two images are of guns pointing in opposite directions and when they are shown in sequence for just a few frames each they appear to be flashing – a purely visual suggestion of the gunfire which is dispersing the workers and also an emphasis on the class betrayal by the soldier. Note here that *October* is a 'silent' film, which would usually have been viewed with some kind of musical accompaniment, and possibly sound effects.

At the start of the film the workers' initial success is signified by a statue of Tsar Alexander III which literally falls apart – the head rolling off, the arms dropping off etc. Later in the film, when the workers appear to be losing, Eisenstein and Alexandrov simply play the same sequence backwards and the statue is restored to power. Do these kinds of tricks negate the 'realism' of *October*? Certainly some critics have taken montage to represent **anti-realism** or '**expressionism**' because of these exaggerated filmic devices. A debate about montage cannot divert us from the central point, however, which is that Eisenstein's aim is to explore a real historical event and to ask the audience to learn from it.

Ken Loach (born 1936) began as a young television director at the BBC, working with Tony Garnett. They produced a series of powerful contemporary filmed television dramas about working-class life. *Cathy Come Home* (UK 1966) remains one of the most controversial moments in UK television history – a shocking indictment of the treatment of the homeless which caused a public outcry.

Ken Loach: contemporary realist

The best-known 'realist' in contemporary world cinema is probably Ken Loach, who shares with the early neo-realists a passion for everyday life and its problems, understood in a political context.

Loach's left politics are leavened by a sense of fun, and he quotes the Czech New Wave cinema of the late 1960s as an influence on his work. This cinema of social realism used comedy to deflate the authoritarianism of Soviet communism, and its echoes are found in such Loach triumphs as *Kes* (UK 1969). In recent years Loach has sometimes found it difficult to get a wide release for his films in the UK, yet elsewhere in Europe they have had great critical and commercial success.

Many of the characteristics of a Loach film refer back to neo-realism:

Stock company   a theatrical term for a group of actors, each of whom plays a similar role in a number of productions at the same theatre.

- use of actors who are not stars. Some may be members of a stock company (e.g. Ricky Tomlinson, once Bobby Grant of *Brookside*), others may be performers (e.g. Chrissie Rock, the nightclub comedian who plays the mother in *Ladybird, Ladybird* (UK 1994)) but not necessarily actors.
- naturalistic acting style, built up by encouraging actors to become involved with the issues instead of worrying about the script
- shooting scenes in narrative sequence and not revealing the script beforehand so actors' responses to events are more 'natural'

During the shooting of *Carla's Song* (UK 1996) Loach told Robert Carlyle that 'something' would happen in the next scene when he was sleeping in a hammock. The explosion which followed threw Carlyle out of the hammock and he gave a believable response.

- location shooting
- regular director of photography Barry Ackroyd 'covers the action' using documentary techniques, rather than using contrived set-ups
- characters walk in and out of frame, dialogue overlaps.

ACTIVITY 16.2

Try to look at two or three of Loach's later films (*Raining Stones* (1993), *Ladybird, Ladybird* (1994), *Land and Freedom* (1995), *Carla's Song* (1996) are all widely available on videotape).

- All the films include at least some scenes set in contemporary Britain. Do they represent a Britain you recognise?
- If they do, which particular aspects of the films carry the connotations of 'realism'? Is it:
  - the casting?
  - the dialogue?
  - the locations?
  - the camera style?
  - reference to particular 'real world' political issues?
- Are the references to neo-realism helpful in understanding the films? Or are there other distinctive features which distinguish them from 'mainstream' contemporary films?

Figure 16.4   The volunteers to fight fascism in *Land and Freedom* (UK/Spain/Germany 1995)

Realism and politics

Most realist film-makers are 'left of centre' to some extent – their desire to represent 'the real' very often derives from a wish to expose something and thereby to help to get the situation changed.

Some of the critics who support 'the realist aesthetic' are to the 'right of centre', especially in the UK. They tend to be keen on authentic detail, especially if a film celebrates their view of British history. There have been some very odd controversies over the 'political' films made by Loach and others, where, in order to to undermine the potential exposure of 'real issues', critics have dismissed the authenticity of the films on the grounds that soldiers are 'wearing the wrong buttons'.

Realist approaches have also been criticised by left critics who object to the **transparency** of the representation of the real world (i.e. that audiences become too easily involved in the story and don't understand the processes of representation). This anti-realist position was most evident in the *counter-cinema* movement of the 1970s (see 'Independents and alternatives', Chapter 28) which in turn referred back to some of the ideas of Soviet cinema of the 1920s.

Ken Loach remains a committed political film-maker who rather unfashionably believes that it is possible for ordinary people to take control of their lives to achieve things. He works with a group of colleagues who have been able to find sufficient backing outside the Hollywood system to keep on making films which have something politically worthwhile to say, utilising a clearly defined approach. In this sense he is a realist film-maker.

Conclusion

Realist media texts are predicated on the assumption that they say something about the real world. In the case study which follows we look at what happens when some of the aesthetics of realism are adopted for primarily entertainment forms, and in 'Postmodernisms', Chapter 18, and *Pulp Fiction*, Case study 19, we explore a contemporary view that seems to deny the possibility of saying anything meaningful about the world at all.

References

Bazin, André (1967 and 1971) *What is Cinema?*, vols I and II, London: University of California Press.

Bondanella, Peter (1993) *The Films of Roberto Rossellini*, Cambridge: Cambridge University Press.

Bordwell, David, Staiger, Janet and Thompson, Kirstin (1985) *The Classic Hollywood Cinema: Film Style and Mode of Production to 1960*, London: Routledge.

Corner, John (1996) *The Art of Record*: *A Critical Introduction to Documentary*, Manchester: Manchester University Press.

Crisell, Andrew (1994, 2nd edition) *Understanding Radio*, London: Routledge.

Eisenstein, Sergei (1968) *The Film Sense*, London: Faber.

Graef, Roger (1995) 'Flying off the Wall', *Guardian*, 6 October 1995.

Monaco, James (1980) 'American Documentary since 1960', in Richard Roud (ed.) *Cinema: A Critical Dictionary*, vol. 1, London: Martin Secker & Warburg.

Neale, Steve (1985) *Cinema and Technology*: *Image, Sound, Colour,* London: BFI/Macmillan.

Nochlin, Linda (1971) *Realism*, London: Penguin.

Overby, David (1978) *Springtime in Italy: A Reader on Neo-realism*, London: Talisman.

Williams, Christopher (ed.) (1980) *Realism and the Cinema*, London: Routledge & Kegan Paul/BFI.

Wolfe, Tom and Johnson, E.W. (eds) (1975) *The New Journalism*, London: Picador.

Further reading

Barnouw, Erik (1993) *Documentary: A History of the Non-fiction Film*, New York: Oxford University Press.

Barsam, Richard M. (1992) *Non-fiction Film*, Bloomington: Indiana University Press.

MacDonald, Kevin and Cousins, Mark (1998) *Imagining Reality: The Faber Book of Documentary*, London: Faber.

McKnight, George (ed.) (1997) *Agent of Challenge and Defiance: The Films of Ken Loach*, Trowbridge: Flicks Books.

Winston, Brian (1995) *Claiming the Real*, London: BFI.

17 / Case study: Realism and the television police series

The British experience

The previous chapter refers to an argument which sees television as, in some ways, a more 'realist' medium than cinema. Television largely took over the role of documentary film exhibition in the 1960s and exploited the immediacy of 'live' reports in current affairs and news programming. At the same time, television drama began to concern itself with realism in the two ways set out in the chapter – by concentrating on contemporary social issues and by using new lightweight 16 mm film equipment on location. *Cathy Come Home* (1966), one of the BBC *Wednesday Play* series, dealing with homelessness is a good example (see Corner 1996).

The two television genres which have been most concerned with realism on British television have been soap operas and police series. In 1960 Granada introduced *Coronation Street*, which immediately attracted attention because of its depiction of northern working-class characters, seen as 'realistic' in much the same way as similar characters in the 'British New Wave' cinema films of the period such as *Saturday Night and Sunday Morning* (UK 1960). The appeal of *Coronation Street* was in the stories and the characters – the studio sets could not invoke the world outside in Salford.

In 1962 the BBC launched *Z Cars*, a serial as important as *Coronation Street* in altering perceptions of television drama. This programme was developed by the BBC Documentary Drama Group and featured the two-man crews of police cars operating in a thinly disguised fictional version of Merseyside. These were not the 'friendly bobbies' or pipe-smoking detectives previously seen in British television series (and it is important to note that the 'police series' is also known as the 'police procedural' – distinct from the 'detective series' where the concentration is on solving a specific crime). The police brought their private lives into their work and the work was often routine and small-scale (e.g. dealing with domestic violence and juvenile delinquency). Again audiences responded to the characters and the stories as 'realistic'. The urgency of the programme was achieved first by the linking of scenes using the radio calls to the cars from the women in the control room. Later location shooting was added.

Like *Coronation Street*, *Z Cars* was drawing on realist traditions from British cinema of the 1940s and especially the conventions of the war film with individuals in the group 'typed' by regional accents etc., so the crews included Scots, Northern Irish, Scousers etc. No matter how 'constructed' this image of police might have been, however, the programme gained a strong following and a good deal of criticism for portraying the police and crime in a realistic way. So much so that the Chief Constable of Lancashire withdrew his support for the programme (see McQueen 1998). *Z Cars* spawned a separate series, *Softly, Softly* (1966–76) based on a regional crime squad, and continued to run in different formats up to 1978.

Z Cars established a set of 'realist' conventions for British police series which are still recognisable in the construction of contemporary productions (i.e. they are followed or actively opposed):
- urban, not glamorous locations
- a range of characters, including beat officers as well as senior staff

- 'realistic' dialogue
- a mix of 'domestic' stories (i.e. 'social issues') and big crimes
- interest in the private lives of the police

This mixture has also helped to set up 'popular debates' which have continued to run:

- worries about the realism of representations of violence – the fear of 'copycat' crimes
- questions about the 'truth' of the police behaviour depicted – are the police like this?
- fears that police officers will emulate their fictional counterparts

We can trace these debates through the discussion around any number of police series. Good examples would be *The Sweeney* (1975–8) and, more recently, *The Bill* (which became a serial in 1988). These two programmes can be seen to have pushed the *Z Cars* formula in opposite directions while holding on to the central premise. *The Sweeney* made use of advances in film technology and shooting styles to convey the feel of the street and the excitement of the chase, while *The Bill*

Figure 17.1 Eli Wallach, police officer, shoots a villain in 'Death of Princes' in a *Naked City* teleplay

developed the 'institutional' aspects of the station house soap opera.

If you wish to follow up these ideas, there are many series to investigate, including those re-running on cable and satellite. Interesting questions in terms of realism were raised by series like *Juliet Bravo*, which placed a female senior officer at the centre of a similar mix of stories (see comments on *Cagney and Lacey*, below). The formula does not always work and the failures might be interesting to analyse. Phil Redmond, of Mersey TV and *Brookside* fame, introduced *Waterfront Beat* on BBC1 in 1990 without much success and at the time of writing in 1998 *City Central*, based on a Manchester police station, is struggling to capture the Saturday night audience.

The American experience

So far, we have established a link between soap opera and the police series in the UK, but we haven't acknowledged the crucial role of American films and television in developing a sense of realism.

Hollywood experimented in the late 1940s with the 'social problem', police and crime movies filmed on the streets of cities like New York and Los Angeles, partly influenced by **Italian neo-realism** (see 'Realisms', Chapter 16). One of the most notable of these was *The Naked City* (US 1948) directed by French exile Jules Dassin. Ten years later a police series of the same name appeared and quickly gained a huge reputation for the same mix of domestic and crime stories we noted above in *Z Cars*, each investigated by a pair of police officers. Each show ended with the immortal tag-line, 'There are eight million stories in the Naked City … and this has been one of them.'

The original film had been inspired by the photographs taken by Weegee (Arthur Fellig), published in the book *Naked City* in 1945. Weegee was a famous crime photographer, who always appeared at the scene of the crime to get the most striking images. The television series was concerned to promote not only the acting abilities of the host of young hopefuls who appeared on the show (Dustin Hoffman, Robert Redford etc.) but also the variety of locations throughout New York City. The show ran for only four seasons and is not available on tape, but its influence was undeniable.

There were other significant influences on the police procedural:

- Another early filmed television series was *Dragnet* (1951–8) with its 'casebook' approach to police work, informed by the work of consultant police officer Jack Webb (referenced in the character played by Kevin Spacey in *LA Confidential* (US 1997)).
- There were also popular police procedural crime novels such as the '87th Precinct' series written by Ed McBain.

Nevertheless, the dominant mode of American police and crime series in the 1960s and 1970s was more concerned with action and the adventures of maverick or unusual police officers in the mould of *Kojak*, *Starsky and Hutch* etc. These shows related to debates outlined above, not so much because of their realism but because of fears of the 'effects' on audiences, and the police, of the more spectacular stunts and unusual behaviour. Francis Wheen quotes a British chief constable as saying: 'when the *Starsky and Hutch* series was showing, police on patrol duty were adopting sunglasses and wearing their gloves with the cuffs turned down. They also started driving like bloody maniacs' (Wheen 1985). Thus the same kind of complaint about the behaviour of police officers was made about an action show as about the 'realist' *Z Cars* in in an earlier period.

The visual spectacle of the American police series reached a high point in *Miami Vice* (1985–90). This was about as far from the realist police procedural as it is possible to get. The two police 'buddies' were at times indistinguishable from the villains and were as interested in clothes and cars as in crime and criminals. Dubbed 'MTV cops' by some critics, *Miami Vice* was quoted as the first **postmodern** cop show, because of its reliance on style. David Buxton (1990), quoted in McQueen (1998), points out that the series made use of 'neurophysiological research …[which] has shown that viewers tend to become impatient with overly elaborate stories or characterisations'.

Miami Vice was a major project for film director Michael Mann, best known recently for *Heat* (US 1995). The strong connection between film and television police narratives means that Hollywood often takes risks with police heroes, such as Clint Eastwood in *Dirty Harry* (US 1971), and then television develops similar ideas in a watered-down form. As we have noted in 'Realisms', Chapter 16, Hollywood films, although stuffed with realistic details, are essentially *not* realist because of their single narratives involving unusual or 'special' circumstances. Television series, by definition, have narratives which although 'closed' in one sense (the 'episode' will usually see a resolution) must still develop an interest in the continuing characters and the institutional base – the precinct house. Thus, although television was very action-orientated in the 1980s, there was still the possibility for realist drama.

One of the most successful and most talked-about series of the 1980s was in effect a 'female buddy series', *Cagney and Lacey* (1982–8). Tyne Daly had appeared as the (dispensable) partner in the third 'Dirty Harry' film, *The Enforcer* (US 1976). Now she teamed up with Sharon Gless in a series which stimulated a passionate audience response – look at the Internet 'Episode Guide' for examples of the kinds of articles which appeared in the American press (see also Baehr and Dyer 1987).

ACTIVITY 17.1

The story mix

Most police series feature male duos. It was argued that the great strength of *Cagney and Lacey* was that not only was the show rooted in the 'reality of the street', but that the same scripts could have been used for a male duo show. Yet, as the show developed, more stories picked up on the private lives of the two actresses and raised issues which male shows could not.

- What kinds of different stories do you think might develop in a long-running show about two police detectives (Lacey was married, Cagney wasn't)?

● Take any male duo (or male and female) police procedural storyline from a current series and re-write it for two women. Are there any differences?

Figure 17.2 Cagney and Lacey – a different kind of 'buddy' series

Police and soaps

1980 saw the first series of *Hill Street Blues*, created by Steve Bochco. An immediate critical success, it gained a niche in the American network and, like many similar American shows, became a Channel 4 programme in the UK in 1985. The innovation of *Hill Street Blues* was the mixing of a multi-thread soap opera narrative with occasional *ciné-vérité* style camerawork and 'realist **mise en scène**'. In one sense, this was a similar strategy to *Miami Vice* – distinguishing a police series from the host of competitors through a different visual style. But in this case the appeal was not to the MTV audience but to a more sophisticated group, for whom the visual trait of the hand-held camera signified 'documentary', 'art film' or

simply 'realism' and for whom the complex interweaving of different stories was a puzzle and a challenge. This was a return to the idea of 'real' equals 'quality'. Indeed the production company behind the programme, MTM, was open in its desire to promote 'quality television' (see Maltby 1989 and Feuer et al. 1984).

Hill Street Blues and other MTM shows such as *Lou Grant* and *St Elsewhere* were relatively expensive to make and held their network slot only because they appealed to upmarket viewers who were attractive to advertisers. In this way, a form of quality 'cult' television was born. This concept of quality and indeed the general critical reception of *Hill Street Blues* was carefully examined by Susan Boyd-Bowman (1985), who cast doubts upon the consistency of visual style being claimed. She argues against the claim that the series borrowed heavily from contemporary Hollywood cinema: 'slow motion, hand-held camera, syncopated shots [an unconventional rhythm to the cutting], long travelling shots'. Instead she supports the minority view of Steve Jenkins, who downplays the visual style and claims that the difference is its two main generic components: the crowded street realism of the police series and the languid melodrama of the home life (Jenkins in Feuer et al. 1984).

Whatever we wish to make of the real differences achieved by *Hill Street Blues*, the changes within American television are clear in contemporary programming. The soap opera (melodrama) cross with the police or hospital series has continued to gain a prestige/cult status at least and in the case of *ER* a ratings smash. Cinema aesthetics have transferred to television, not just in the spectacle of the car chase but also in the sense of the realist codes discussed above. Where once these codes signified political or social comment and commitment, especially in a European context, they now tend to signal 'quality American television programming'. There is a sense in which these programmes are 'equal opportunities' employers in terms of the ethnic and gender range of the casting, but it is some time since a series like *Lou Grant* (which starred Ed Asner as a campaigning newspaper editor) was pulled because it was too critical of American ideals for the advertisers.

Homicide and *Blue*

In the late 1990s the two flagships for this style of American television are *Homicide – Life on the Street* and *NYPD Blue*, both screened late night on UK television by Channel 4. These two programmes have much in common. *Homicide* is based in a Baltimore police station, *NYPD* in New York. Both have teams of paired detectives investigating crime on the streets, and in both the gender and ethnic mix is an important ingredient in representing the communities of the respective cities. The domestic lives of the characters are important in the development of stories, in the way pioneered by *Cagney and Lacey*.

NYPD Blue is a modern equivalent of *Naked City* – emphasised by the credit sequence and the staging of scenes in the dramatic cityscapes of skyscrapers and waterfronts. This isn't just a case of location shooting – *NYPD* achieves the sense of action amongst the everyday hustle and bustle of the streets which characterised some of the earlier neo-realist films.

Homicide is at the same time more downbeat and less spectacular, but also more cinematic (it is produced by Hollywood director Barry Levinson, director of *Rain Man* (US 1988) etc.). Its principal creator is Paul Attanasio, screenwriter of the 1997 gangster film *Donnie Brasco*.

The opening credits of the two series are similar visually, with staccato credit sequences offering a **montage** of city scenes and police procedural signifiers. Both series use a trademark 'whip pan' instead of a conventional **shot/reverse shot** to show two characters in conversation. This results in an urgent, somewhat frenzied style (because the panning camera emphasises movement and the change of shot which classical editing renders seamless). In *NYPD Blue* this device often seems simply that – a device to signal urgency. In *Homicide*, however, the approach is more subtle, with the moving camera often becoming part of an elaborately conceived single take in which several characters, often with different stories to pursue, are gradually revealed in the station house. This decidedly European visual style (dating back to the 1930s) is, however, sometimes

Figure 17.3 The 'ensemble' casting for *NYPD Blue*

interrupted by shots that appear to have little or no definite narrative purpose.

NYPD and *Homicide* are the clearest examples of this particular modern practice, but it is evident in other series. The distinctive shot in *ER*, as in many hospital dramas, is the rapid tracking shot in which the camera retreats before the Emergency Room team and the stretcher, as they rush down the corridors of the hospital, clattering through doors and eventually arriving in ER. This can be a smooth 'ride' because of the **Steadicam**, and the effect is literally to sweep us along in the exciting events of the drama, but again the camerawork is exaggerated and self-conscious. We recognise these shots from the earliest *ciné-vérité* documentaries and news reports. We know that the reporter and camera crew only have the one camera, so by necessity they must film conversations with pans and follow subjects down corridors and through doors.

So, do the modern series use these devices to add a veneer of 'realism' to their fictional stories? If that is the intention, why exaggerate the camera techniques? Why adopt such conventional framings (medium close-ups and close-ups) at other times? Sometimes it appears that these techniques are selected purely for effect – as if there is a knowingness about the visual style which says. 'Hey guys, look at these cool camera movements!' It's also noticeable that 'realist sound' is not such a priority and we get fewer experiments in the use of overlapping dialogue or the stumbling speech of 'real people' – the characters in these dramas have well-written lines.

Postmodernists might argue that these visual quirks are simply an expression of the breakdown of distinctions between realist and non-realist conventions. Television programme-makers are free to 'play' with visual style without worrying about realism. They merely have to make programmes distinctive enough to gain attention and to give pleasure to audiences media-literate enough to enjoy the play of relatively meaningless signifiers. Some critics have pointed out that this self-consciousness is evident in the script – in *Homicide*, for instance, in one of the many snippets of inconsequential chat, one detective says to another, 'it's television Stan, it's not supposed to be real'.

'Real-life' drama?

Police series are mainstream dramas which have absorbed many of the innovations of the earlier realist film-makers, such as location shooting and the hand-held *ciné-vérité* camera. They are the most common and longest-lived form of drama on television. Most series are far more conventional than those described here, and overall the police series is a conservative rather than radical form.

What some critics now argue is that realism·on television is now a matter of sensational *content* – the 'real-life' crime drama, whether it is the so-called 'tabloid news' programmes or the soap opera that developed around the O. J. Simpson trial. These are all stories which begin with actual crimes, but are highly stylised and 'narrativised' for audiences (a tradition which goes back to *True Crime Magazine* and the other 'pulp' magazines of the 1940s and 1950s). Added to

these forms are the reconstructions of crimes for programmes like *Crimewatch* in the UK and the 'docusoaps' and compilations of police footage of driving offences etc. In all these cases 'real events' have been turned into entertainment for a mass audience, while fictions with elements of a realist visual style like *Homicide – Life on the Street* have become art for discerning audiences.

Conclusion

An analysis of the depiction of 'police procedures' in both fictions and 'actualities' on television reveals an ongoing debate about realism and realist effects. In some cases realist devices have been employed in a genuine attempt to help us understand 'life on the street' and a range of experiences. Largely, though, the realist aesthetic could be argued to have become just another style feature, another ingredient in the postmodern media environment, and it is to such questions that we turn in the next chapter.

ACTIVITY 17.2
Select two American television police series (ideally *NYPD Blue* and a more conventional series).
Test out our comments on visual style.
- Can you 'justify' the camera movements and framings – do they help to push the story along or develop the characters – or are they more self-conscious?
Listen carefully to the soundtrack.
- Is it in any way unconventional, does it act as a complement to the visual style?
- Overall, do these realist devices succeed in making you interested in watching – or is your interest taken primarily by the content of the programmes?
- Are they markedly different in visual style to UK series?
- Is the use of realist style features matched by an interest in the social issues covered in the stories?

References and further reading

Baehr, Helen and Dyer, Gillian (eds) (1987) *Boxed In*, London: Pandora.

Boyd-Bowman, Susan (1985) 'The MTM Phenomenon', *Screen*, vol. 26, no. 6.

Brunsdon, Charlotte (1998) 'Structure of Anxiety: Recent British Television Crime Fiction', *Screen*, vol. 39. no. 3 (autumn).

Buxton, David (1990) *From The Avengers to Miami Vice: Form and Ideology in Television Series*, Manchester: Manchester University Press.

Corner, John (1996) *The Art of Record: A Critical Introduction to Documentary*, Manchester: Manchester University Press.

Feuer, Jane, Kerr, Paul and Vahimagi, Tise (eds) (1984) *MTM: Quality Television*, London: BFI.

Hill, Val and Tasker, Yvonne (1990) 'Tonight I Made No Difference', *Over Here, Reviews in American Studies*, vol. 10, no. 2 (winter) (for review of Buxton, *From The Avengers to Miami Vice*).

McQueen, David (1998) *Television: A Media Student's Guide*, London: Arnold (esp. ch. 8).

Maltby, Richard (1989) *Dreams for Sale: Popular Culture in the 20th Century*, New York: Equinox.

O'Reilly, John (1995) 'The Real Macabre', *Guardian*, 3 July 1995.

Wheen, Francis (1985) *Television*, London: Century.

Postmodernisms

As soon as you enter current debates in media theory, you will come across the fashionable term **postmodernism** (and other terms, often used very loosely and interchangeably, such as postmodernity; postmodern). It is argued that we are living in postmodernity, recognisable in the media, architecture, food, fashion – in fact our whole sense of ourselves. Unfortunately 'postmodernism' is not only a puzzling word in itself (if the modern is 'now', how can we be living in the 'postmodern'?) but has been used to mean at least *four* different things, which David Morley usefully outlines as:

- a period of social life
- a form of cultural sensibility
- an aesthetic style (e.g. in media forms)
- a mode of thought useful for analysing the period.

We will focus on the first three of these, though they involve the fourth.

Key theorists of postmodernism are: **Jean-François Lyotard** (1925–98) (*The Postmodern Condition: A Report on Knowledge* 1979) and **Jean Baudrillard** (see *Selected Writings*, ed. Poster, 1988). The term itself was coined in the late nineteenth century but really 'boomed' in the late 1980s. 'The *Books in Print* index shows no book titles ... on postmodernism between 1978–1981, but 14 ... in 1988, 22 in 1989 and 29 in 1990 ... 241 [articles] appear[ed] between 1987 and 1991' (Strinati 1995, p. 222).

A period of social life – postmodernity?

The prefix 'post-' clearly implies a break, a relation to a period which has gone before. In the case of 'postmodernism' the previous period is clearly 'the modern' or '**modernity**', whose definition again has involved heated debates. One major emphasis is that computer technology and cybernetics have replaced the early twentieth-century factory production line of standardised goods, made by (usually male) workers who were each devoted to a specialised part of the whole labour of production. **Fordism** is one name for this, after Henry Ford and his factory production line methods of car-making.

We are now said to be living in **post-Fordist** times. The most adequate descriptive term for our world is still 'capitalist' but it is one where mass standardised production lines are obsolete, whether for cars or films (as in studio Hollywood's output). Production is now centred on smaller, more versatile units, closely integrated to the information technologies needed to respond flexibly to a highly developed set of

Other terms which imply some kind of a radical break in the period we are living through include: the information society; late capitalism; post-industrial society; post-Fordist society; the society of the spectacle; late modernity.

Fordism   A method of mass industrial production, established by Henry Ford in the USA by the 1920s, using concentrated production on the assembly line in one enormous factory complex, and a specific division of labour by the workforce (called 'Taylorism'). 'You can have any colour as long as it's black' (a saying attributed to Henry Ford about his newly mass-produced model T Ford car).

Post-Fordism method of commodity production which subcontracts parts of the production process to a number of firms, and uses new technology to make production more responsive to consumer demand. 'You can have any colour – and would you like a personalised number plate, a CD player, sunroof …?' ('Post-Fordist' car dealer's pitch).

The power to distribute is *still* the key to power in the film industry, and *still* rests with the handful of majors, where you will *still* find names such as Paramount, Fox and Warners in association with huge conglomerates: Sony, News Corporation, Seagram, Time Warner.

Zapping 'the technique of rapidly cutting between television channels using a remote control device … can lay claim to being one of the most characteristically postmodern acts. The channels themselves are treated like some kind of continuous narrative which can be connected together in any order at all, according to the whims of the … viewer' (Sim 1998).

consumer demands, as in the 'package unit' rather than studio system for making contemporary movies. In a further step, *consumption* is often emphasised as an active process, indeed as both the equivalent of citizenship and as the major way we construct our identities. In this sense it has taken over the key role of *production* and our identities as workers or owners in Marxist accounts, and it relates to a celebration of audiences' activities in Media Studies.

More sceptical voices have insisted that:

- The term *postmodernism* over-dramatises these breaks from earlier periods. 'Heavy' capitalist industries and mass production lines have not disappeared, but have often simply been re-located into low-wage areas such as those of the 'Asian tiger economies' (currently in crisis) and Eastern bloc countries – or sometimes into the low-wage economy of home-workers (usually female) in the West.

- The emphasis on small-scale flexible capitalism blurs perceptions of long-established huge power structures which are still alive and well. Contemporary Hollywood for example is not run by small groups of equal individuals getting film 'packages' together (see Case Study).

- And, though the attention to the activities of consumers and audiences for popular media is a welcome move, we need to remember that the ability to consume certain goods is highly dependent on income, education and location – and this is true for media goods too. Not everyone is able to 'shut up and shop'; issues of who controls production and how it might be transformed are still key for many kinds of politics – and media.

A form of cultural sensibility characteristic of this period?

Writers on postmodernism (such as Lyotard, Baudrillard and Jameson) oddly enough often use a traditional Marxist base/superstructure model (see 'Ideologies', Chapter 11) to argue that these socio-economic changes produce particular 'structures of feeling' or a 'cultural logic'.

Typical assertions include claims that, mostly thanks to television, we now live in a 'three-minute culture' (the length of most people's attention spans, it is said, shaped by advertising); or that we are part of an over-visual society, a 'society of the spectacle' – again, owing to the preponderance of television. This has implications for realist forms of all kinds, since our sense of reality is now said to be utterly dominated by popular media images; cultural forms can no longer 'hold up the mirror to reality', since reality itself is full of advertising, film, video games, and television images. Advertising no longer tries seriously to convince us of

VANISHING CREAM.

Figure 18.1a

BODDINGTONS. THE CREAM OF MANCHESTER.

Figure 18.1b

BODDINGTONS. THE CREAM OF MANCHESTER.

Figure 18.1c

THE CREAM OF MANCHESTER.

Figure 18.1d

its products' real quality but, for example, just shows us a cool joke about the product (Figure 18.1).

The important perception that our sense of reality is *always* partly formed by language and the media is here taken to an absolute extreme. The self is imaged as nothing more than a hall of mirrors. This echoes positions from the **Frankfurt School** onwards, deeply distrustful of popular cultural forms, and the people who enjoy them. It is a much more pessimistic position than the argument that it is because of

Confusingly **modernity** is sometimes used to refer to the ideas and intellectual inheritance of eighteenth-century Enlightenment thinkers (think of the French Revolution's slogan 'Liberty, Equality, Fraternity'), and sometimes of a period of time which is clearly still going on. **Modernism** in the arts is used to refer to experimental moves in the early years of the twentieth century. McGuigan (1999), Morley (1995) and Strinati are helpful on these distinctions.

bombardment by a multitude of media signs that the work of making meaning is often rejected – as a kind of defence against 'overload'.

Such theorists have also written of the 'death of the grand narratives' or the death of 'the Enlightenment project'. Very broadly, this refers to those movements in political thought and other ideas from about the eighteenth century onwards which proclaimed the importance of Reason, and the knowability of the world through it. The next step was to argue that, if the world could be known, it could be changed – still a key component of realist media forms and, indeed, of any politics or education. Postmodernist critiques, however, describe Marxism, feminism, belief in scientific progress and so on as nothing more than *grand-narratives* or *master-narratives*: stories about history, naively structured with happy endings. Instead it offers *micro-narratives* which do not necessarily add up, but which may be woven together (see Andermahr et al.).

There is some truth in the perception that large claims to political truth are often shaped towards a goal, such as Marxism's claim that working people acting together will eventually bring about socialism. And feminist, black and gay theorists have pointed out the gaps and blindnesses of white, male western power to define what is 'Reason' (and 'reasonable behaviour'). But, however conscious and critical we now are of narratives shapes in scientific and political rhetoric, it seems we cannot easily do without them and the meaning they give to experience. What else is postmodern theory but another such story or image, though a very cynical one, which in some versions sees the whole of global culture as 'partying at the end of history', with politics now pointless in the aftermath of the triumph of global capitalism?

An aesthetic style?

Another (confusing) usage of *postmodernism* is as a term which points to a distinction between itself and modernism in the arts. The modernist movement is usually dated from the period around the First World War, part of a huge set of social and economic changes (though some postmodern writers use it to refer to much earlier art work). These prompted new ways of expressing new ideas and sensibilities.

- In literature, for example, writers like Virginia Woolf and T. S. Eliot ruptured existing traditions of 'good' taste and 'proper' rhyme schemes, and established new ways of writing novels. Such breaks often took the form of a kind of **avant-gardist** or experimental play with different media (often high-status media such as painting or classical music or literature). Examples would be experimentation with verbal form (playing with extreme puns and allusions, the words, or signifiers, coming close to separating from their usual meanings), or visual form (the montage breaks of Eisenstein's editing in early Soviet cinema).

Tarantino is linked to the modernist period by his often-quoted reverence for Jean-Luc Godard, the 1950s 'New Wave' film director, though what attracts Tarantino is not the political, post-1968 Godard but the early Godard who 'played' with Hollywood conventions. Other directors, such as Scorsese, De Palma, Coppola, make references to 'modernist' New Wave films, though generally within a traditional Hollywood aesthetic and narrative shaping. Indeed, it might be argued that Hollywood has effectively swallowed some of the stylistic features of modernism without having gone through the pain of experimentation.

- Part of *political artistic modernism* was often a **self-reflexivity**: a text makes open reference to its constructedness as a text and does not try to conceal it. Sometimes, as in the work of Brecht or later Godard, this was politically motivated, trying to de-mystify the production of art, showing it as a kind of work and trying to connect it to the rest of the real world.

Postmodern forms now routinely play with this, as in the discussion on how to end *Wayne's World*; *Tank Girl*'s occasional address to the artists drawing the comic strip; adverts; or television programmes like *It'll Be Alright on the Night*.

- *Crossover* or **hybrid** forms which *level hierarchies of taste* are suggested as proof that all distinctions between 'high art' and popular culture have gone, or become blurred. Andy Warhol's multi-prints of Leonardo's *Mona Lisa*, Talking Heads' eclectic mix of levels of reference, the use of classical melodies in pop music, the collage mixes of rap, house and hip hop, or advertising's extensive play with images from all over culture and history – all these contribute to the feeling that there are now no distinctions between the 'high' and the 'popular' culture, and that genre boundaries have become blurred. Postmodern texts 'raid the image bank' so richly available through video and computer technologies, the recycling of old movies and shows on television, the Internet etc. Music videos often provide good examples of such processes, also called **intertextuality** and **bricolage**.

Bricolage: a French word ('jumble') used by structuralists to refer to the process of adaptation or improvisation where aspects of one style are given quite different meanings when juxtaposed with stylistic features from another. The original meaning or signification is changed by the new, and the term implies a kind of creativity on the part of the 'bricoleur'.

Watch the next Oscars ceremony to see whether Billy Crystal (or equivalent) is still introducing this 'serious' event with a comic turn, and offering his tape editing together the award-nominated films in a deliberately comic and deflating way, as he did in 1997 and 1998. In what way could this be called 'postmodern'?

Intertextuality 'describes the variety of ways in which texts interact with other texts, and in particular the interdependence between texts rather than their ... uniqueness' (Andermahr et al. 1997, p. 113). See 'Genres', Chapter 8.

Q In what ways do the *Scream* films illustrate both intertextuality and self-referentiality?

Q But how many *different* ways are there of texts interacting with other texts? Parody, homage, re-working ...

For Dick Hebdige (in *Subculture: The Meaning of Style*, 1979) youth subcultural groups such as punks with their bondage gear are bricoleurs when they take clothes associated with different class positions or work functions and convert them into fashion statements 'empty' of their original meanings. In a very postmodern way, this emphasised *consumption* as key to processes of subversion and adaptation, rather than *production* (as in Marxist models of social change). A more recent, feminised example would be the combination of Doc Martens and summer dresses often worn by young women and girls.

Q Can you think of any others, from fashion or other contemporary styles?

- *Disjointed narrative structures* said to mimic the uncertainties and extreme relativism of postmodernity. *Pulp Fiction* is sometimes said to operate in this way (see Case Study). Or else it is said that film, television and literary narratives often can't guarantee identifications with characters, or the 'happy ending' in areas such as love, the future, the defeat of the enemy, which have traditionally been achieved at closure. They can only manage 'micro-narratives' or there will be a play with multiple or ambiguous endings.

'It is plausible to imagine that, over the next few years, the inflation of hyper-real illusion will result in audiences so jaded that there will be a massive backlash against digital fantasy; viewers will want guarantees that they are seeing reality itself' (Romney 1997, pp. 222–3).

- In recent science fiction, critics have pointed to the frequency with which the key question will be: is it human or not, and if it isn't, does it matter? This, along with the fascination with morphing, android or cyborg characters etc., is said to mirror postmodernism's blurring of the boundaries between the real and the *simulated* or *hyperreal* (see 'Science fiction', Case study 9).

- Along with the claim that art can no longer be realist (because how would audiences know the real anyway?) is the assertion that there is a *waning of a sense of history*, for example in the 'no-where, no-time' settings of *Blue Velvet* (US 1986) or *Forrest Gump* (US 1994) where signifiers of a number of different eras are jumbled. This is argued, again, to work to de-politicise audiences.

- Fredric Jameson, an influential postmodern theorist, has argued that there is no position 'outside' contemporary culture from which to critique it, which results in the prevalence of *pastiche* (simply imitating past forms) rather than *parody or satire* (imitating in order to critique with a view to change).

The limits of these arguments

- *Realisms*: many postmodern emphases seem uninterested in the extent to which spectacle, special effects, remakes, generic mixing, have

always been a part of Hollywood and popular genres, and have always
been understood as such by audiences. It is assumed that audiences and
the popular forms they enjoy are always to be distrusted and
bemoaned. The extent to which special effects and spectacle are part of
contemporary Hollywood and advertising may indeed be
unprecedented. But do these changes render any kind of realist media
work impossible?

- *Blurring of boundaries*: it's easy to see how many boundaries between
  'high' and 'low' cultural reference have been eroded, and such emphases
  are attractive because of their democratic implications: there's no such
  thing as bad taste; you can enjoy (shop for?) what you like; class
  hierarchies are said to have disappeared here, as everywhere else.

But paradoxically, for there to be any thrill in transgressing
boundaries, like those between 'high' and 'low' forms in Baz Luhrman's
William Shakespeare's Romeo and Juliet (US 1997) or *Shakespeare in Love*
(US 1998), those boundaries need still to have some meaning – and
indeed they do, if you think of the industry still associated with the
status and name of Shakespeare, the cultural importance of being able
to influence what appears on school and college syllabuses, and so on.

> **Digital imaging technology** has
> blurred these boundaries. Anything
> is now representable, from the
> feather in the title sequence of
> *Forrest Gump* to the convincing
> dinosaurs of *Jurassic Park*. Hyper-
> *real* is loosely used of these
> effects, but it ignores questions of
> genres, of publicity around them,
> and therefore exactly how
> audiences are engaging with their
> apparent reality in a kind of
> 'double' response or attention.

ACTIVITY 18.1

Make a diary of your own use of media products during the day in similar terms.

- Are these best understood as 'postmodern' or as parts of a
  global/local/regional capitalist economy?

Other writers have pointed to the similarity between postmodern
approaches and **camp**, understood not as cross-dressing but as a particular
sensibility. They share:

- a delight in surface, style
- a delight in trivial rather than dominant forms: conversations about
  burgers in *Pulp Fiction* or hairstyles in John Waters's camp film
  Hairspray (US 1988)
- an off-centring, giddying tone involving a scepticism about serious
  value, a refusal of depth.

Andy Medhurst (1997) has argued, however, that there are important
differences, which are to do with where the two approaches emerge from.
Where 'pomo' will collapse and relativise value, camp laughs *at* certain
values, especially those of straight society. As he points out, no camp man
can claim the pompous authority of many white males, so he may as well
laugh at things that are taken seriously.

Camp, as almost every commentator ... has ... noted ... eludes a
single, crisp definition ... It is a configuration of taste codes and a
declaration of effeminate interest ... It revels in exaggeration,
theatricality, parody and bitching ...

... [in 1990] I [argued that] 'postmodernism is only heterosexuals
catching up with camp' ... But ... I was wrong: postmodern aesthetics
can easily be confused with camp, but while camp grows from a
specific cultural identity, postmodern discourses peddle the arrogant
fiction that specific cultural identities have ceased to exist.

(Medhurst, p. 290)

References

Andermahr, Sonya, Lovell, Terry and Wolkowitz, Carol (1997) *A Concise
Glossary of Feminist Theory*, London and New York: Arnold.

Baudrillard, Jean (1988) *Baudrillard: Selected Writings*, ed. Mark Poster,
Cambridge: Polity.

Hebdige, Dick (1979) *Subculture: The Meaning of Style*, London: Methuen.

Hebdige, Dick (1988) *Hiding in the Light*, London: Comedia/Routledge.

Jameson, Fredric (1991) *Postmodernism, or, The Cultural Logic of Late
Capitalism*, Durham, NC: Duke University Press.

Lyotard, Jean-François (1979) *The Postmodern Condition: A Report on
Knowledge*, Manchester: Manchester University Press.

McGuigan, Jim (1999) *Modernity and Postmodern Culture*, London: Open
University Press.

Medhurst, Andy (1997) 'Camp', in A. Medhurst and S. Lunt (eds) *Lesbian
and Gay Studies: A Critical Introduction*, London: Cassell.

Morley, David (1996) 'Postmodernism: the Rough Guide', in J. Curran,
D. Morley and V. Walkerdine (eds) *Cultural Studies and Communications*,
London and New York: Arnold.

Romney, Jonathan (1997) 'Million-dollar Graffiti: Notes from the Digital
Domain', in *Short Cuts: Film Writing*, London: Serpent's Tail.

Strinati, Dominic (1995) *An Introduction to Theories of Popular Culture*,
London: Routledge (esp. ch. 6).

Further reading

Brooker, Peter and Brooker, Will (eds) (1997) *Postmodern After-images*,
London and New York: Arnold.

Hayward, Phil and Kerr, Paul (1987) Introduction to *Screen* Special Issue
on Postmodernism, vol. 28, no. 2, provides a useful history of the rise
of the term.

Huyssen, Andreas (1993) 'Mapping the Postmodern', in Joseph Natoli and Linda Hutcheon (eds) *A Postmodern Reader*, Albany: SUNY Press.

Smart, Barry (1993) *Postmodernity*, London and New York: Routledge.

19 / Case study: *Pulp Fiction*

Pulp Fiction (US 1994) has been called 'the cult film of the 1990s', and it made a 'star' of its director-scriptwriter Quentin Tarantino. Many critics have called it a typically **postmodern** movie, so it seems worth testing it against some of the questions outlined in Chapter 18.

- In what sense can it be called postmodern?
- Which characteristics does this term describe?
- Through what other theoretical approaches can it be discussed?

As you'll have gathered, the term 'postmodernism' is a slippery one, and has been applied to very different movies.

ACTIVITY 19.1

List some recent films, ads or television programmes which you would call 'postmodern'.

- Say why you think they deserve this label.
- In what other ways have they been understood or received? (For example, a lot of the emphasis when *Pulp Fiction* came out was on its violent imagery and language.)

Applying postmodern textual criteria to *Pulp Fiction*

Intertextuality is evidently in play. The film makes references to gangster, blaxploitation, boxing, war, musical, romance and even arthouse genres (in its homage to the French (modernist) director Jean-Luc Godard). The references include possible ones across to other

Tarantino films (is Vince the cousin or brother to Vic, 'Mr Blonde' Vega in *Reservoir Dogs* (US 1992)? Or related to Suzanne Vega, the singer, as he says at one point?). They include the stars' other performances: Harvey Keitel as 'cleaner-up of murders' in *The Assassin* (US 1993); Travolta as playing someone with the possible future of the character he played in *Saturday Night Fever* … the potential references are almost infinite, and certainly partly intended by Tarantino.

The name of the production company for the film, 'A Band Apart', is the title of a film by Godard; Vincent and Mia's dance in Jack Rabbit Slim's is a homage to a similar scene in the Godard film, and Mia/Thurman's hairstyle and 'look' deliberately echoes that of Anna Karina, an actress closely associated with Godard's life and work.

Figure 19.1   The scene in the trendy diner Jack Rabbit Slim's is full of references to 1950s stars and movies

- *Modernist techniques* Though *Pulp Fiction* makes fairly traditional use of editing for continuity and cinematography for 'legibility' of meaning, conventional lighting etc. of stars, the film also represents some variation on these. There is some use of disruptions to the 'Hollywood style' (though compare the *Naked Gun* spoofs or *Wayne's World* films): the film occasionally works with some odd angles (such as the shots of the backs of Jules's and Vincent's heads); some unusually long takes, and moments such as the one where Mia/Thurman mimes drawing a 'square' which unexpectedly appears on screen.
- *Absence of history* The film has no specific location or setting in time or history. The present or early 1990s seem to be referenced in the McDonald's chat, Jules's cellular phone, the talk of body-piercing, but a lot of the retro-cultural references (music of the 1960s and 1970s; Vince's 1974 Chevy car and the style of some of the dialogue) are in an ambiguous area of 'no-time'.
- *Hybridity* The tone of the film is disorienting in the way it clashes and mixes different kinds and levels of feeling. Vincent is killed, absurdly, while on the toilet, reading a piece of pulp fiction, just as Butch's toaster alarm goes off – in fact, *because* it goes off.

> 'Butch doesn't move, except to point the M61 in Vincent's direction.
> Neither man opens his mouth.
> Then ... the toaster loudly kicks up the PopTarts
> That's all the situation needed.'
>
> (From the screenplay of *Pulp Fiction*)

Several scenes feature off-hand shootings (deliberate and accidental) where the killer does not even look at the victim in a shocking juxtaposition.
- *Narrative structure* It's argued that the film's narrative is fragmented and disorienting in terms of time and space (working with *micro-narratives*? giving a fragmented sense of location and history?) – and therefore postmodern.

The relationship of plot and story

One of the favourite parts of the narrative for Tarantino fans is the way that huge stretches of it are devoted to 'trivial' conversations – about foot massage, burgers, pot bellies or tummies etc. This is not like the time given in *Psycho* to the apparently trivial action of Norman cleaning up the bathroom, which serves the narrative (giving audiences relief after shock, swerving suspicion away from Norman etc.).

Instead, in *Pulp Fiction* real screen/**syuzhet** time is given to mundane discussions – interestingly often about verbal definition, and the difficulty of making it (what <u>is</u> the status of a foot massage? the difference between a tummy and a pot belly?). These conversations about trivial meanings seem to relate both to a kind of realism (most of us spend quite a bit of time in trivial conversations) and to postmodernism's sense of the slipperiness of the signified, of words – like Jules's puzzling over the meanings of the Bible, or the opening title's double dictionary definition of 'pulp'.

Plot/syuzhet order

- 'Prologue' (Honey Bunny and Pumpkin in diner, up to the start of the robbery)
- 'Vincent Vega and Marcellus Wallace's Wife'
- 'The Gold Watch' (including death of Vincent)
- The Bonnie Situation
- Epilogue (in the diner, during the robbery and its aftermath, taking us to a few minutes after the end of the Prologue).

Story/fabula order

- (Early section of 'The Gold Watch' with Butch's father's friend giving him the watch when Butch was a child)
- Vincent and Marcellus's wife
- The Bonnie Situation
- Prologue
- Epilogue

- The ending of 'The Gold Watch' and the escape of Butch and Fabien

Q Which is the last event of the fabula (story)?

A Fabienne and Butch making their getaway on the chopper, at the end of 'The Gold Watch'.

Q Which is the last event in the syuzhet (plot)?

A Vincent and Jules walking out of the diner (well before Vincent is killed during 'The Gold Watch').

Q Is this complex narrative structure unprecedentedly random?

Does it have any sympathies, key characters?

What genre does it belong to?

A No, several other Hollywood (and independent) films, have been comparably complex, including *The Killing* (US 1956), which Tarantino acknowledged as one of many influences. It clearly plays with traditionally male genres focused on honour: 'you don't leave a guy you've shared hell with' as we're invited to feel when Butch goes back to save Marcellus, an act which echoes that of his father's friend (however off-centre or comic is the scene describing how the gold watch came to him). The context is male bonding, (missing) father–son relationships, male professionalism (Mr Wolf/Keitel making a brutal parody of a housewifely 'clearing up'), coping with violence in this small-time killers' underworld.

So how to interpret the decision to end the *syuzhet* (and film) where it does, with Jules having turned his back (perhaps temporarily) on violence, and Vince jauntily walking out of the diner (to be shot on the toilet a little later)? The Brookers (1996) argue that the narrative is arranged so as to emphasise transformation and 'new lives':

- Butch's decision to act honourably, save Marcellus and begin a new life free of boxing with Fabienne (at the end of the fabula)
- Mia's resurrection (brought back from the dead) from the overdose, in a scene whose tone shifts the film's generic base almost to that of a vampire or horror movie
- Vincent and Jules's gaining of new purpose as they stride out of the diner at the end of the syuzhet

(instead of the film ending close to the time when Vince is slumped dead in the toilet).

Q What do you think of this way of understanding the narrative's shape?

Does it suggest a 'random postmodernity' 'about nothing but style'?

What might the popularity of this two-hour thirty-four-minute film say about the position that we all inhabit a 'three-minute attention span culture'?

ACTIVITY 19.2

To explore its points of identification you could try literally, or in summary form, re-editing the film's events (summarised above) in chronological order.

Pulp Fiction: the production and promotion history

One of the problems of postmodernism as a theory is that it tends to be uninterested in histories of production, preferring to imply that a successful film somehow mysteriously expresses the 'spirit of the age'.

The production history of this film suggests another way of understanding it: as a post-studio independent movie – remembering the complexity of that term 'independent' now.

It was assembled as a package deal: after the success of *Reservoir Dogs* (US 1992) Jersey Films (with Danny de Vito a key player), owned by TriStar, paid Tarantino $900,000 in advance. This enabled him to go to Amsterdam to work on a screenplay. However, when Tri-Star saw the script, they were anxious about the film's length, and the scene where Vincent injects himself with heroin. They sold it to Miramax who had bought *Reservoir Dogs* and knew the foreign earnings potential of its successor. Pre-sold foreign sales in fact covered the $8m production costs of *Pulp Fiction*.

However the success of the film was also determined partly by the fact that just before its US release (May

1993) Miramax was bought by Disney. This meant that Disney's huge conglomerate clout (through its distribution company Buena Vista) allowed the expensive gamble of releasing what was basically an art house movie into 1,300 US cinemas. The gamble paid off; the film opened with $9.3m receipts, top of the US charts, which allowed further publicity and marketing possibilities. Disney exploited these with a promotional budget eventually as big as the production costs, and Tarantino proved a talented salesman for the film, especially on the festival circuit after it won the Palme d'Or at the Cannes Film festival. (A further historical determinant: some sceptics pointed out that the jury at Cannes was headed by Clint Eastwood and ignored the claims of more obvious contenders. Others suggested that the Cannes award was a French effort to sweeten the Americans after rumours that they would in future boycott the festival in retaliation for the GATT controversy.)

Thus the film was able to appeal to several different potential audiences. In addition, Disney launched it with a US television ad campaign promoting its humorous aspect, with posters featuring Travolta dancing. They coped with the fear of controversy about its violent content with the slogan 'YOU WON'T KNOW THE FACTS UNTIL YOU SEE THE FICTION'.

The successful British release can be read as partly ensuing from Tarantino's previous notoriety: the release of *Reservoir Dogs* in 1992 had overlapped with the Jamie Bulger trial (when two young boys were convicted of brutally murdering a two-year-old child) and an accompanying moral panic over the effects of violent film material. This ensured high media coverage and cult status (as 'forbidden texts') for both films. In addition, *Reservoir Dogs* had still been refused a certificate when *Pulp Fiction* was released on video (though with one well-publicised alteration: a change of the angle of shot when Vincent plunges the heroin needle into his arm).

Tarantino, authorship, postmodernism

Oddly enough, for a figure so often called 'postmodern', Tarantino has been marketed as, and

'Yeah. Keep it in the shot. Movie geeks like me'll be analysing this scene for years to come.'
(Tarantino on the accidental inclusion of an orange balloon in a shot from *Reservoir Dogs* quoted in Clarkson 1995, p. 161)

talks of himself as being very much an 'auteur-star-director', like others in post-studio Hollywood (Scorsese, Coppola, Spielberg). Certainly his use of music, of albums including key dialogue sections, and of casting decisions can be argued as innovative (though you might like to debate how far they are 'postmodern'). Like Hitchcock and others he often makes appearances in his films (in *Pulp Fiction* as a polite, domesticated coffee geek).

It is possible to read the adulation of him in a number of ways:

- as generational: a familiar delight by the young in anti-authority figures, and also in someone who's 'made it' in ways many (young men?) could hope to emulate. The idea of a smart kid from a single-parent family, a one-time videoshop salesman, 'the slacker as auteur' (Brooker 1996) is one which understandably appeals, and is a refreshing change from terms like 'genius' and more pompous celebrations of authorship. This career description is also interesting in that it does not start with his time in elite film schools or privileged access to the industry. It works with that postmodern sense of the world as risky, as full of nooks and crannies, not the old established certainties – a point of identification for many would-be film-makers. (Though see the role of Disney in his career above.)
- as a search for stable meanings by some fans ('what is in the suitcase? Tarantino can tell us') among the sliding signifiers and relativism of *Pulp Fiction*
- as expressing a sense of the individual as the source of meanings, authenticity, intention, which, contradictorily, postmodern theorists have suggested has vanished from the world.

Figure 19.2 Quentin Tarantino

Tarantino himself takes a postmodern stance on meaning, audience and authorship, at least in some of his statements: of Oliver Stone's more political films (*Platoon, JFK, Wall Street, Nixon*) he has said: 'He wants every single one of you to walk out thinking like he does. I don't. I made *Pulp Fiction* to be entertaining. I always hope that if one million people see my movie, they saw a million different movies' (quoted in Brooker, 1996, p. 142).

ACTIVITY 19.3

If you have access to the Net, look up some Tarantino websites (at last count there were nearly 13,000 of them!) and take notes on how his author-director-star image is constructed there.

- How is he being understood/celebrated?
- What are the words that most often occur? Which anecdotes, quotes?
- One of the main websites is called '*godamongdirectors*': how might this relate to 'postmodern' theories of the individual and authorship?

Questions of representation

Postmodern approaches, while claiming to delight in the breakdown of old hierarchies, are not much interested in questions of representation, since they do not believe either in 'the real' or in the ability of language, or media, to represent it.

In contrast to this ('it's all ironic', 'it's all postmodern play') are such questions as:

- Though young women often enjoy the film, and its lack of simple sexism, some have seen it as yet another male-centred story revelling in violent action and talk, in a cinema dominated by such films. It broadly constructs its female characters mostly as either *femmes fatales* (like Mia) or the child-woman Fabienne, and even the vivid 'Honey Bunny' of the first scene is reduced to hysterical screeching in the last one, as though the film doesn't know quite what to do with her.

  They also point to the phenomenon of 'laddishness', and suggest there are problems in the kinds of jokes which particular films (and DJs, writers, singers etc.) circulate, however the films situate them. This raises one of the central riddles of postmodern textuality: is the 'ironic' reading of a 'reactionary' character or text or joke necessarily a progressive thing?

- Opponents of this position have suggested that both men and women enjoy the film, and the key status of the bulk of its fans is as *students* rather than male or female. They'd also say you have to take each film on its merits, and *Pulp Fiction* is not sexist or racist in its totality.

Q Explore this issue with friends, or in class if you can.

- Tarantino's repeated scripting of *racist language* in the mouths of his black characters caused most controversy in relation to *Jackie Brown* (1998). He has argued:

a) The black actors involved do not object, therefore why should anyone else?

b) Such language is natural for his characters, and does not mean the same in the mouth of a black American as it does for others.

c) Critics such as Spike Lee are jealous of his standing in the Afro-American community (interview with Barry Norman, BBC, March 1998).

'If you're writing a black dialect, there are certain words you need to make it musical and "nigger" is one of them … Sam Jackson uses "nigger" all the time in his speech, that's just who he is and where he comes from … Also I'm a white guy who's not afraid of that word. I just don't feel the whole white guilt and pussy-footing around race issues. I'm completely above all that.'

(Tarantino, *Sight and Sound*, March 1998)

His critics argue:

a) The characters are constructed, not described, by Tarantino: to argue 'that's just how they are' is thus a cop-out.

b) Spike Lee has said that if he had put anti-semitic words (like 'kike') into the mouths of his black characters in *Mo' Better Blues* to the extent that Tarantino does in his films, he would have been in deep trouble.

c) Tarantino seems to be fascinated by, deeply desirous of having, 'black cool' – but this is defined in very stereotyped, some would say negative, ways: as meaning coping with violence, being street smart, 'dealing' with women.

● Gay viewers have felt his films to be unsympathetic, if not threatening, in their unproblematic sympathy for violently macho characters and, here, in the location of 'the heart of darkness' in the grotesque male rape scene, which could also be said to re-circulate the oldest prejudices about the 'redneck' South of the US.

(A very ambitious) ACTIVITY 19.4
Debate these issues in class, with arguments for and against this position, in relation to issues raised by it for 'the politics of representation', and by postmodernism.

References and further reading

Brooker, Peter and Brooker, Will (1996) 'Pulpmodernism: Tarantino's Affirmative Action', in Deborah Cartmell, I.Q. Hunter, Heidi Kaye and Imelda Whelehan (eds) (1996) *Pulping Fictions Consuming Culture Across the Literary/Media Divide*, London and Chicago: Pluto.

Clarkson, Wensley (1995) *Quentin Tarantino: Shooting from the Hip*, London: Judy Piatkus.

Sight and Sound, May, November 1994; February 1995.

Tarantino, Quentin (1994) *Pulp Fiction*, London: Faber & Faber.

Search the Web!

20 Globalisation

This chapter explores:

- what is meant by **globalisation** and the emphasis on global–local relations in Media Studies
- theories which try to understand the history, structures and consequences of globalisation
- attempts to theorise the peculiarity of this modern 'global–local' world.

Globalisation

Power structures and activities on a larger than national scale have existed for many centuries (e.g. the Chinese, Persian and Roman Empires, and then the Roman Catholic Church across medieval Europe and beyond). Globalisation is something rather different, and distinctively modern. It grew from the expansion of trade in the late Middle Ages which itself was accompanied and followed by the growth of western imperialist and then colonialist power over the rest of the world.

Globalisation has been said to occur when:

- activities take place in a global (not national or regional) arena
- they are deliberately organised on a global scale
- they involve some interdependency, so local activities in different parts of the world are shaped by each other
- they are often instantaneous, as opposed to previous forms of speedy communication.

Examples of the speed of global processes

- The instantaneously registered demands of 'western' food shoppers at supermarket checkouts have abolished dependence on local annual growth and harvesting cycles – for some. For others 'agribusiness' means constant labour and water dependency. Salads picked and washed in Kenya, on estates using huge amounts of precious water, are airfreighted in forty-eight hours to 'save the time' of British consumers.

Figure 20.1 Islamic tribute to Diana outside Harrods: globalisation?

- News items, instantaneously and globally broadcast, can now have direct, material effects on jobs and sometimes governments, e.g. news of the 1997 stock market collapse of the 'tiger economies' of south-east Asia led to speculation on prices around the world, collapse of more currencies, jobs etc.
- 'Diana dies everywhere and instantly – on the Internet, CNN … the radio, in every newspaper, … the first … to fully live and die in the global village' (Bryan Appleyard, *Sunday Times*, 7 September 1997).

ACTIVITY 20.1

Some accounts of globalisation characterise it as a homogenising process, leading to '**McWorld**'. Others suggest that 'local' characteristics do flourish, sometimes as fierce ethnic loyalties, more usually in local foods, customs and versions of history, but that these are often cultivated for the tourist trade, and therefore shaped in some ways and not others.

- Explore your nearest local tourist industry. What is 'local' and what 'global' about its images?

McWorld (and associated terms such as *McJob*, for associated low-wage, non-unionised repetitive work): coined from the worldwide spread of the US McDonald's food chain. Because of the standardisation of a narrow range of product in the twenty-thousand worldwide McDonald's outlets, and its identification with US capitalism, the term often signifies a completely standardised, Americanised world, despite slight 'local' variations to McDonald's products, pricing and image.

Figure 20.2 'McWorld': the global/local economy

ACTIVITY 20.2

Look at a tape or photos of the opening ceremony of the current or 1996 Olympic Games (or any other world sports event).

- Research the ratings figures for the ceremony.

'in the sunshine of this California afternoon, ancient Greek rites, Hollywood fantasy and the reality of life in 1984 will find common ground' (David Coleman, 1984 Los Angeles Olympic opening ceremony).

- How are 'Third World' nations represented or orchestrated in the ceremony?
- How is the 'local' place of the ceremony represented?
- To what extent are differences, disputes between nations represented?
- What are the 'production values' of the event?
- Which countries do these represent?
- How is the spectacle 'gendered'?

If you have the chance, record coverage of the Para-Olympics (for athletes with disabilities) and note the main differences in the ways this event is constructed.

Figure 20.3   Atlanta Olympics 1996

Communications media have been crucial to the development of the global economy, beginning with the invention of paper and printing in China, spreading through trade to Europe, allowing books and pamphlets to circulate well beyond the places where they were produced. Crucial for later expansion were the development of underwater cable systems by the European imperial powers and companies such as Cable and Wireless, now the UK's biggest cable company, and the establishment of international news agencies (see Thompson 1997, pp. 152–9). (It may come as a surprise to learn that underwater cables were so important, yet until the 1850s telegraph systems were land-based and thus quite restricted. By the 1870s submarine cables had been laid throughout south-east Asia, along the coast of Africa. Europe was soon linked to China, Australia and South America. It was the first global system of comunication which separated the sending of messages from the need to transport them physically.)

News agencies likewise gathered and disseminated news over huge areas, and eventually, in 1869, agreed to divide up the world into mutually exclusive spheres of operation which more or less corresponded, like the reach of the underwater cable systems, to the spheres of influence of the major European imperial powers.

'In 1924, at the British Empire Exhibition, King George V sent himself a telegram which circled the globe on all British lines in 80 seconds' (Thompson 1997, p. 154).

The cultural imperialism thesis and its critics

Thus from the outset the global spread of media corporations has been intimately linked with imperialist histories. In addition there is ample evidence of a highly profitable, mostly one-way flow of news, information and entertainment from the major western countries, led by the US, to the rest of the world. (Importantly, more 'regional' flows also exist, often dependent on the global spread of imperial languages like Spanish, English, French; see the importance of Mexico and Brazil as producers and exporters of 'telenovelas' or soap operas to the rest of Latin America and parts of Europe.)

In the light of such inequalities, and the desire of much early Media Studies to theorise the media in fully political ways, Marxists such as Noam Chomsky, Armand and Michele Mattelart and especially Herbert Schiller have argued that the globalisation of communication has been driven, particularly since the Second World War, by the commercial interests of the large US-based corporations. These often act in collaboration with American political and military interests, which have replaced the British, French, Dutch and other older empires as a new form of imperialism. It is not a giant leap, then, to argue that US media power is a form of **cultural imperialism**. Traditional, local cultures are

'The sun never sets on the British Empire.' 'Because God doesn't trust the British in the dark' (joke circulating in Hong Kong, 1997).

'The USA … still excels in producing missiles, and selling entertainment commodities' (Wasko 1994). Media products are often said to be America's second largest export area, though see Gomery 1996.

In many countries skin creams are on sale to lighten black skins; plastic surgery is available to widen 'oriental' eyes. How could this be argued to relate to such global media and advertising?

Some have pointed to US concerns that their national identity is being diluted by television being increasingly scripted with an eye to foreign audiences, or dominated by Australian output, or by the casting of European stars like Sean Connery as a Hollywood lead. See Miller in Hill and Church Gibson.

Visual images often give a misleading sense of these complex relations. For example, a photo of a woman with a mobile phone in Bangladesh might suggest huge ('yuppie') privilege in the midst of poverty. Yet though as many as 80 per cent of the world's population have no access to a phone, it can save enormous amounts of time and energy by avoiding wasted journeys.

Figure 20.4   Remember this, from Chapter 12?

argued to be destroyed in this process, and new forms of cultural dependency shaped which mirror older imperialist relations of power.

Schiller is probably the best known of these critics, arguing also that the dominance of US advert-driven commercial media not only forces this US model of broadcasting, print etc. on the rest of the world, including indigenous, non-commercial cultures, but also inculcates the desire for American-style consumerism in societies which can ill afford it.

Several criticisms have been made of this approach:

- Schiller was developing his argument in the 1950s and 1960s when US economic dominance in the global system seemed secure and unchallengeable, the very 'heart of the beast' that was also fighting a brutal imperialist war in Vietnam. Later theorists have argued that it does not adequately describe the shifts of the post-1945 period, nor the significance and persistence of other systems of belief, such as nationalisms and religions.

- It is even more difficult, as Schiller has recognised, to apply the theory to the 1990s. Global restructuring has now to *some* extent eroded the economic pre-eminence of the US (though see below). Some major US media have been bought by foreign companies – Sony for example buying Columbia and TriStar pictures in 1989, to add to CBS records, Bertelsmann buying RCA and Random House publishers, and the Canadian Seagram buying Universal Studios.

Schiller now argues that the idea of American cultural imperialism should be replaced by the (unwieldy) term 'transnational corporate cultural domination'. Critics of the cultural imperialism theory argue that even this is an inadequate term for the complex flows, networks and uses of media products in the contemporary world.

- The cultural imperialism thesis also implies that, before the arrival of US media, Third World countries were enjoying a cosy golden age of indigenous, authentic traditions and cultural heritage, untainted by values imposed from outside.

Choice of terminology is important in all this.

- Who defines 'development', or what is to count as 'progress'? Why do we assume that one form of 'development' (i.e. a highly industrialised consumer-capitalist economy) is best for all countries?

- What terms are to be used – the 'Third World'? the 'Global South' ? the 'Developing World'? the 'poorer countries'?

- One riposte has been to call 'the Third World' *under-developed*, i.e. deliberately starved of investment and exploited for raw materials (food, vegetables, minerals, oil) needed by western powers in the interests of the *over-developed* world (Californian drivers currently pay less for petrol than they do for bottled water).

Media Studies on its own cannot alter these inequalities – but it can point out the images and words which help sustain them.

Later theorists have argued that this perspective risks being patronising to what are seen as 'weaker' nations, and of romanticising as 'indigenous' those cultures whose traditions and 'heritages' have been shaped by very long and brutal processes of cultural conflict, often involving the imposition of external values from centuries back, not just by the modern US, and resulting in rich **hybridities**.

Interestingly, bodily adornment and cover is called 'fashion' (and linked to modernity) in the West, but 'tradition' (and linked to the past) in the 'developing world'.

Hybridity   term used to describe any product which is formed by a combination of two different technologies or cultural forms.

'Traditional British' customs such as Christmas celebrations result from similar histories of incorporation and adaptation. They are in fact a **hybrid**, or mixture, emerging partly from

- ancient Latin celebrations, called Saturnalia, which fell towards the end of December, when agricultural labours were over and there was a need to brighten the darkest point of the year (the winter solstice)
- Christian religious imagery, imposed on these pagan festivities during the Roman conquest of Britain
- the nineteenth-century Germanic custom of the decorated indoor Christmas tree, introduced by Queen Charlotte and later the German Prince Albert
- commercial pressures since the 1950s to celebrate via spectacular gifts, street lights in the shopping districts, over-eating and lots of television watching

In some parts of Britain the 'Christmas' lights are now preceded by those for Diwali (a Hindi festival) in a further hybrid refreshing of traditions.

- Another problem with the classic cultural imperialism thesis is that it implies that US television programmes will unavoidably express consumerist values, both in the programmes themselves and in the advertising which finances them. This ignores the huge diversity of images, themes and information which can appear on commercially funded television (including occasional material which is critical, up to a point, of corporate interests).
- It also implies that audiences inevitably become, or want to become, consumers *simply as a result of watching such programmes*. Research suggests a more complex situation. Liebes and Katz (1993) for example explored how US, Japanese and Israeli audiences watched and understood the US television soap opera *Dallas* (a 1980s soap opera

which is still being shown on the world's cable television). This process of reception involved not a one-way brainwashing of audiences with hardly any brains to wash but an encounter between the soap opera and individuals belonging to social groups and with particular histories who brought to bear a range of assumptions and resources to the images on screen (see 'Audiences', Chapter 29). When Israeli Arabs and Moroccan Jews recounted the programmes they'd seen, for example, they emphasised kinship relations, whereas Russian émigrés were more likely to see the characters as manipulated by the writers and producers.

- John B. Thompson (1997) has argued that images of other ways of life constitute a resource for individuals to think critically about their own lives and life conditions. Citing James Lull's research into the viewing of Chinese state-controlled television programmes in the 1980s, he points out that, even though the Chinese broadcasting system was strictly controlled, it provided viewers with ample material to engage in 'symbolic distancing' from their own culture, to compare it with other cultures, to form views of their life conditions which often varied from official government views, and fuel resistance to them.

'In our daily lives we just go to work and come home, so we want to see something that is different from our own life. Television gives us a model of the rest of the world'. Fifty-eight-year-old accountant from Shanghai, quoted in Lull 1991, p. 171.

ACTIVITY 20.3

'When people watch international news … they pay as much attention to street scenes, housing and clothing as to the commentary which accompanies the pictures from foreign lands' (Thompson 1997, p. 176).

- Does this apply to your viewing? Make notes when you next watch international news coverage.
- Ask your friends and relatives about their news viewing in this context.
- If you know anyone who has come to Britain from another country, ask them whether they ever made this use of news before they came here.

Indeed, Thompson argues that such viewing may have triggered some of the more dramatic conflicts of recent years. Lull suggests that the stream of television programmes transmitted through China in the 1980s created a cultural reservoir of alternative visions which produced political questionings. Whatever role that may have played in the Tiananmen Square uprising of students and workers, those events, and their brutal suppression, would not have been witnessed by a huge global audience, leading to enduring protest, without television.

Other recent work (see Ross 1997) has looked at global campaigns in the fashion industry to improve the rights of garment (often sports shoe)

workers, usually located in the 'developing world' though sometimes in
the homes of 'outworkers' in British cities. Global sporting spectacles
such as the Olympic Games and prominent ad campaigns from Nike and
others mean the possibility of a 'high news profile' to stories of child
labour in Indonesia, Pakistan etc. These rely crucially on the global
media's appetite for stories around such spectacular events and huge
corporations – and the ingenuity and commitment of design workers and
trade unionists in publicising such struggles (see Nike example in
'Advertising and marketing', Chapter 30).

Rigging the 'free market'?

We don't need to adopt the full-blown media imperialism model to argue
that conglomerates like News Corporation or Time Warner do not foster
a truly 'free market' (or 'level playing field', as it's sometimes called).

Media conglomerates operate as **oligopolies** – a few large organisations
dominating the market. They also often work together (like **cartels**) to cooperate on perpetuating 'free trade' treaties which will further their
interests – see the **GATT** struggles with European media in 1997. The
media corporations that control the market are mostly owned by
American, European and Japanese capital, though they are usually based
in the US and use US imagery. (Even the Australian Rupert Murdoch has
had to take on US citizenship in order to acquire more large US interests.)

Key phrases in this debate come
loaded with connotations. 'The
free market' evokes images of a
friendly place resembling a rural
market on a sunny day. 'The level
playing field' likewise is an image
many miles away from the clamour
of the Stock Exchanges and private
meetings of powerful cartels.

'we took an opportunity – anybody
could have set up Sky Television,
anybody, and we started it and
people are still free to start against
us, but they'd rather write articles,
bitch and moan, lay around and say,
no we'd rather just keep our lazy
way of life' (Rupert Murdoch,
Guardian interview, May 1995).

> Time Warner is the largest media corporation in the world. Formed from the
> merger between Time Inc. and Warner Communications Inc. in 1989, it
> acquired Turner Broadcasting (CNN etc.) in 1996. Its 1997 sales were $25
> billion, that is, a tenth of the GNP (Gross National Product) of India.

These corporations divide the world into a series of regional markets or
'territories': in descending order of 'market importance':
1 North America (US and Canada)
2 Western Europe, Japan and Australia
3 developing economies and regional producers (including India, China
   and Brazil, and Eastern Europe)
4 the rest of the world.
(These categories are based mainly on film and television distribution,
but are useful indicators for all media markets.)

There are many media producers, located in groups 2 and 3, who are
able to operate in different regional markets such as Latin America – very
effectively in many cases. However, they have little chance of penetrating

READER'S DIGEST IS READ BY MORE AFFLUENT ASIANS THAN ANY OTHER PUBLICATION (21%), MORE LUXURY WATCH OWNERS, CAR BUYERS, FREQUENT FLYERS AND SCOTCH WHISKY DRINKERS THAN TIME, FEER, NEWSWEEK, ASIAWEEK AND YZ! IF YOU REALLY WANT TO COMMUNICATE WITH YOUR MARKET TALK TO THEM IN THEIR OWN LANGUAGE! ONLY 20% OF ASIA'S ELITE USE ENGLISH AT HOME. READER'S DIGEST PUBLISHES 17 ASIAN EDITIONS IN 4 LANGUAGES - CHINESE, THAI, KOREAN AND ENGLISH. FOR DIRECT ACCESS TO THE LATEST ATMS CALL PENNY MORTIMER OR KAREN FAIRBROTHER (44) 171 715 8170

ASIA'S BIGGEST SELLING MAGAZINE

Figure 20.5   The global/local faces of a 'big one'

'If *Kojak* endangers your culture, you've got problems with your culture' (Colin Davis, MCA TV).

See O.U. TV programme: *James Bond: Global Culture?* For Understanding Modern Societies course.

the major market in North America. US-based corporations, in contrast, can market effectively in all the markets, including the poorest.

Why is this? US television entertainment heads often talk as though US programmes themselves simply and effortlessly win global assent and popularity, that they have 'universal appeal'. It *is* important to realise the huge experience which the US entertainment giants have accumulated in making successful product. In cinema, for example, the early 'American' makers and exhibitors in the 1890s were often first or second generation immigrants to the US, and thus in very close contact with European popular taste to which they were exporting.

But what is key to understanding their global penetration is the role of commercial strategies of distribution, such as **differential pricing**, as well as of adaptations to product (titles, casting, plots chosen to appeal to as broad a market as possible). Once a US television series, for example, has been distributed in the North American continent (which usually allows it to recoup its production costs), it will be offered to every broadcaster in the world, but at different(ial) rates. The money made thus is often clear profit. In the 'developed' countries these charges are based on audience size (e.g. on the relatively affluent and concentrated audiences who can be contacted by media in big cities). But in Africa the rates may be lowered dramatically so programmes can be virtually given away for relatively little cost.

Such low charges are not inspired by charitable motives. The process both ensures *overall* profitability and consolidates habits of enjoying US-style entertainment forms. It seems to help develop an appetite for the products placed in them, by audiences whose lifestyles are usually remote from those targeted in US advertising-funded programmes. Rates are so low that they impact on local production, since African or West Indian broadcasters, for example, cannot hope to produce programming of a similar technical quality at a lower price, and their station managers cannot afford *not* to buy in.

> Often strange results can come from tussles over such inequalities of trade through the imposition of **quotas** or limits to the amount of foreign material which a country will allow to be imported. '*Baywatch*, ITV's American made drama about the lives and loves of the Californian coast guards, is officially classified as a British production … because ITV pays 25% of the costs and commissions the programme for its Saturday night schedule [counting] as part of the British broadcasters' 25% independent production quota' (*Guardian*, 13 July 1995).

In addition, in many African countries, for instance, film distribution is almost entirely in the hands of overseas companies which are unwilling to distribute African films, even though local producers are not lacking in creative ideas or production skills. Several theorists argue that this distribution imbalance could be tackled, especially with government support. (This is currently also being argued in the context of the British film and television industries.) Activists in poorer countries urge alliances to build satellite and video transmission and distribution systems. Others urge western educationalists, in Media Studies for example, to teach about other cinemas than Hollywood entertainment forms so as to develop an understanding and appetite for films which are trying not to copy that model but to do something different.

Local producers have two other main problems: training and equipment. Training needs to be 'on the job' for at least part of the time on (expensive) broadcast quality equipment. Most readers of this book will take for granted access to videotapes, batteries, cables etc. But broadcasters in some parts of the world may be hundreds of miles from mains electricity and water, let alone such equipment. And cameras etc. designed for broadcast use in North America, Western Europe and Japan

'In Dominica and St Lucia, for example, both of which suffer from high unemployment and illiteracy, ordinary people happily discuss how President Reagan looks or the latest American politics, fashion, or crime without knowing what is going on in the Caribbean … the "local input" [to one of the two television channels on St Lucia] is just a 30 minute news and feature programme each night, including about 10 minutes foreign coverage from CNN' (Tanya Hutchinson, *Observer*, 12 July 1987).

Actitivity 'ZTV [Zimbabwe television] can only afford to produce about twelve hours of indigenous drama a year, albeit incredibly cheaply, with the actors also doing day jobs and providing their own costumes. [Such] drama series are very popular with the majority black audience but … ' (Tony Dowmunt 1993, p. 6).

Q How do you think this sentence might end?

will not necessarily perform efficiently in tropical conditions. The upshot is that trainees are sent to North America or Europe or the training is offered by the equipment manufacturers on their terms.

Myths of globalisation?

At the other end of the spectrum to Marxist theorists of media imperialism are those who argue that 'we' are now living in a 'global village' (the influential phrase of the 1960s Canadian theorist Marshall McLuhan), all of us sharing the same imagery and products in a kind of electronic, instantaneous democratic community. Talk of the 'freedoms' of the Internet are now part of this kind of rhetoric. However, such talk often works at the expense of understanding the real inequalities in media power relations, including who is the 'we' that has access to telephones, let alone the computers and modems needed to 'surf the global Net'. Evidence of universally globalised and concentrated media have seemed like myths used to support the idea that existing patterns (or 'the market') are irresistible. There are also risks in the celebrations of active audiences across the world, argued to be able to construct resistant meanings no matter what is on their screens. It is one thing to point out what Chinese audiences seemed able to do with the most unexpected nooks and crannies of news images in the turbulent 1980s, and quite another to argue that therefore there is no need for national investigative journalisms or publicly supported and regulated media, that 'the global market' will do it all for us.

Some critics, while agreeing about the importance of instantaneous global media communication, such as the Internet, ask whether evidence of such changes have been exaggerated. Clearly 'local' or national boundaries, laws, television, press and radio institutions, taxation structures still exist, and have huge economic and ideological power. It seems that national identities are transformed, not obliterated by globalisation, as with the attempt to promote 'cool Britannia' through globally recognisable entertainment figures.

For some the world economy is best thought of not as global but as centred round regions, which can be defined:

- as areas of advanced consumer-capitalist power (North America, Europe, and east Asia before the recent collapse of the 'tiger economies')
- by language use (regions often inherited the languages of the imperialist powers, such as the Hispanic or Spanish-speaking areas of 'Latin' America, or the increasingly marginalised French-speaking or Francophone parts of Africa)
- by religions and cultures (the Islamic 'Middle' East; state socialist China)

The Lone Ranger and his trusty sidekick Tonto face an overwhelmingly large posse of hostile Apache. 'We're in real trouble Tonto' says the Ranger. Asks Tonto: 'Who's this "we", Paleface?'

'... the distribution of television is very uneven world-wide; in countries like Britain, it is close to saturation, while in the non-Arab countries of Africa, there are only 13 sets per thousand people' (Abercrombie 1996, p. 95).

'Air travel might enable businessmen to buzz across the ocean, but the concurrent decline in shipping has only increased the isolation of many island communities ... Pitcairn, like many other Pacific islands, has never felt so far from its neighbours' (D. Birkett, New Statesman and Society, 15 March 1991, p. 38).

This can work to marginalise French-speaking media industries in some parts of Africa. British, Australian and Canadian cinemas are generally Anglophone (English-speaking), with the advantages and disadvantages of being in the same first-language market as US cinema.

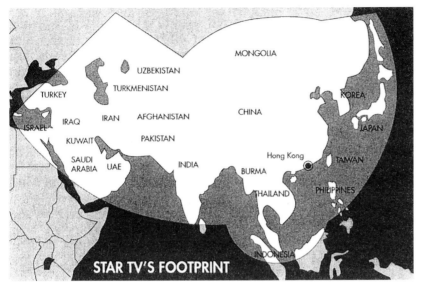

Figure 20.6 Footprint of the Star satellite

- by technological factors such as the 'footprint' of a satellite (MTV Europe or Star TV in Asia – or television signals in parts of the UK) (Figure 20.6).

ACTIVITY 20.3

List the number of ways in which your experiences over the last week have been affected by:

- living in a global media economy
- living in a national media economy
- living with media which mix global and national characteristics.

ACTIVITY 20.4

'Analysis of the mass media industry through time tells us that we ought to seek to understand corporate oligopolists and then find a way, through governmental action, to prod them to optimal performance' (Gomery 1996)

- What kinds of 'optimal performance' would you like to 'prod' a big oligopolist like News Corporation or Fox Searchlight to perform in Britain?
- Devise a list of demands and suggestions which you would make to them given the opportunity. Would it consist of different kinds of films? Different forms of distribution? Different distribution of profits?

'it is a question of steering between the dangers of an improper romanticising of "consumer freedom" on the one hand, and a paranoiac fantasy of "global control" on the other … of finding ways of combining interpretative studies of people's "lifeworlds" with attempts to map the contours of the wider formations that envelop and organise them' (David Morley, 'Where the Global Meets the Local', *Screen*, vol. 32, no. 1 (1991)).

Like some theories of **postmodernity**, the term 'globalisation' can *over*emphasise historical breaks and differences. Nevertheless it can be argued these mixes are now occurring to an unprecedented degree, and need to be seen as half of the double, contradictory nature of contemporary global mass culture:

- it remains firmly centred in the West (via the concentration of capital, of patterns of ownership, distribution, technology, advanced training and labour as well as of stories and imagery), *but*
- it does not (to use Stuart Hall's metaphor) 'speak the Queen's English any longer ... It speaks a variety of broken forms of English.' The most explosive modern musics, for example, are crossovers, operating the aesthetic of the hybrid and the **diaspora**.

Diaspora   dispersal across the globe of peoples who originated in a single geographical location, such as the dispersed community formed from the black diaspora of the Afro-American slave trade.

Hybridity originally referred to the cross breeding of plants but is now used to describe media products that mix different sets of cultural values and formal properties, such as Bhangra 'crossover hits' in pop music; the mix of comedy and horror-sci-fi in *Men in Black* (US 1997) or of comedy, social drama and Indian popular film in the British movie *Bhaji on the Beach* (1993).

References

Abercrombie, Nicholas (1996) *Television and Society*, Cambridge: Polity.

Gomery, Douglas (1996) 'Towards a New Media Economics', in *Post-theory: Reconstructing Film Studies*, Madison and London: University of Wisconsin Press.

Hall, Stuart (1991) 'The Local and the Global: Globalisation and Ethnicity', in A. King (ed.) *Culture, Globalisation and the World System*, London: Macmillan.

Hill, John and Church Gibson, Pamela (eds) (1998) *The Oxford Guide to Film Studies*, Oxford and New York: Oxford University Press (esp. section on world cinema, and Toby Miller: 'Hollywood and the World').

Liebes, Tamar and Katz, Elihu (1993 edn) *The Export of Meaning: Cross Cultural Readings of 'Dallas'*, Cambridge: Polity.

Lull, James (1991) *China Turned On: Television, Reforms and Resistance*, London: Routledge.

Lull, James (1995) *Media, Communication, Culture: A Global Approach*, Cambridge: Polity.

Ross, Andrew (ed.) (1997) *No Sweat: Fashion, Free Trade and the Rights of Garment Workers*, New York and London: Verso.

Schiller, Herbert I. (1996) *Information Inequality*, London and New York: Routledge.

Sreberny-Mohammadi, Annabel, Winseck, Dwayne, McKenna, Jill and Boyd-Barrett, Oliver (eds) (1997) *Media in Global Context*, London and New York: Arnold.

Thompson, John B. (1997) *The Media and Modernity: A Social Theory of the Media*, Cambridge: Polity.

Tomlinson, Alan (1996) 'Olympic Spectacle: Opening Ceremonies and Some Paradoxes of Globalisation', in *Media, Culture and Society*, London, Thousand Oaks and New Delhi: Sage.

Wasko, Janet (1994) *Hollywood in the Information Age*, Cambridge: Polity.

Further reading

Castells, Manuel (1996) *The Rise of the Network Society*, Malden, Mass. and Oxford: Basil Blackwell.

Dowmunt, T. (ed.) (1993) *Channels of Resistance*, London: BFI/Channel 4.

O'Sullivan, Tim and Jewkes, Yvonne (eds) (1997) *The Media Studies Reader*, London and New York: Arnold (esp. section 5).

21 / Case study: Making and enjoying global music

The music industry has long been associated with other media industries, and is now becoming even more closely linked through the process of **convergence**. Yet there are significant differences between music and television and film, and many of these differences become evident in relation to 'globalisation'. This case study presents recorded popular music as simultaneously 'global', 'regional' and 'local', in terms of both its production and its consumption.

Recorded music as global product

The gramophone was invented at roughly the same time as film projection, and together the new technologies spread around the world at the turn of the century.

> 'Film shows' using the Lumière brothers' equipment were being seen in every part of the world within two years of their 1895 Paris launch.
>
> (George Sadoul, *Louis Lumière*, Paris: Seghers, 1964)

The Gramophone Company of India (better known in India as HMV) is synonymous with Indian music. It is the repository of India's rich and diverse musical heritage. The company was incorporated in Calcutta as 'The Gramophone and Typewriter Company Ltd.' in 1901. The following year, Fred Ginsburg, the assistant to the inventor of the phonograph record, Emil Berliner, came to India on a mission to capture the music of India. The first Indian artiste to be recorded was the famous Calcutta dancing star, Gauhar Jan, on 5 November 1902. The first record

factory outside of the UK, was started at Dum Dum in Calcutta in 1907, just two years after record production began in England.

> (from the Internet site of HMV India)

The European colonisers and entrepreneurs, with their wealth and desire to maintain links with 'home', certainly helped to establish distribution channels for both the hardware and software of cinema and recorded music and in this way encouraged a local industry. In territories like Latin America and south-east Asia, a parallel music industry developed with the importation of European and North American recorded music alongside indigenous music, which also developed in recorded form.

With the arrival of the 'talkies' in 1927, film distributors around the world were faced with the problem of dubbing or subtitling prints into and from a wide range of languages. The music industry escaped this problem. The appeal of popular music crosses language barriers. (Record buyers will always prefer song lyrics to be in their own language, but, if a recording has a strong appeal, language will not be a barrier – for a brief period in the 1960s British performers did attempt to record their UK hits in other European languages, but this was not particularly successful.)

At the same time, local or indigenous producers of music could enter the marketplace far more easily than local film-makers: the technology for making master recordings and subsequently pressing records was, and still is, less expensive and simpler to manage than film technology. It is also possible to promote and 'exhibit' local music through a local radio station. The Jamaican film *The Harder They Come* (1973) shows this very well with its story of a 'rude boy' singer, played by real life reggae star Jimmy Cliff.

The structure of the industry

The same handful of large media conglomerates discussed in 'Industries', Chapter 22, are the 'majors' in the music industry worldwide:

- Time Warner as Warner Bros
- Sony as Sony/Columbia
- Bertelsmann as RCA/BMG
- Seagram/Universal as MCA.

At the time of writing, Seagram has just bought the fifth major, Polygram, from Philips, and the repercussions of the deal are not yet clear. There is also a sixth 'major' in the form of EMI, the British company which 'de-merged' in 1996 from its electrical/electronics partner Thorn. EMI claims to be able to do everything the other majors can do, even without other media interests.

Two 'major' Hollywood-based groups, Disney and Viacom/Paramount, are classed as 'independents' in the music industry (see 'Independents and alternatives' and 'Industries', Chapters 28 and 22). News Corporation is the only media conglomerate without a significant music industry interest.

The music industry is not 'integrated' in quite the same way as cinema. The 'majors' are indeed primarily distributors and producers, but not so much 'exhibitors' – in the case of the music industry, the exhibitors are effectively the radio and television stations and the retail outlets. Note here that Disney (owner of American broadcaster ABC) and Viacom (owner of MTV, VH-1 and Blockbuster Video) have a major presence as exhibitors.

It is in global markets that the music majors differ from the usual approach of the multinational conglomerates. The Hollywood studios rarely attempt to make films directly (i.e. to finance a local operation) in overseas territories (apart from the UK). Infrequently, they pick up local films for possible international distribution, but mostly they deal in American films. By contrast, the music companies tend to buy local record labels and to acquire a *roster* of local artistes in addition to their marketing of global acts. The reasons for this must lie in the different nature of the media product.

The music market is organised regionally. The two pie charts (Figures 21.1 and 21.2) show the share of the market in terms of the value of sales and the volume of sales. Note the stark difference in the charts in relation to Asia. This is explained by the low price of cassettes in India – a massive market – and the high price in Japan.

India is very much a *local* market – 98 per cent of music sold in India is recorded there. Indian film music is also important regionally across much of South Asia and the Middle East. By contrast, the UK is relatively *open* with only 50 per cent of local product and a large American proportion plus significant imports from other parts of the world. Because some UK acts have made the leap to international status, the UK has a strong *global* presence.

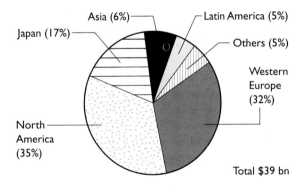

Figure 21.1   Value of global music sales by region, 1995

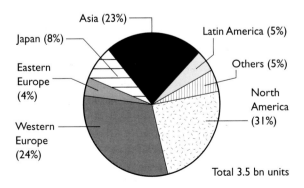

Figure 21.2   Volume of global album sales by region, 1995

What does globalisation mean in this context? It clearly isn't about selling the same product everywhere in the world:

> Globalisation is the organisation of production and distribution across national boundaries … it has very little to do with music. We compete (with the other majors) in **A&R** [Artists and Repertoire], sales and marketing, we compete for the artists, manufacturing records is not a significant area of competition. Globalisation of the supply chain has nothing to do with globalisation of music.
>
> (Alan McElroy, senior director EMI UK, addressing A Level students in Bradford, 1997)

The five majors have their own areas of dominance outside Europe and North America. You can research what they do by visiting the companies' Internet sites. Here are two edited extracts from the archives of press releases stored on websites:

BMG Asia

Since its inception in 1987, BMG Entertainment International's Asia Pacific region has increased revenues by more than 450%.

Headquartered in Hong Kong, the region spans three continents and includes offices in Australia, India, Japan, Malaysia, New Zealand, the Philippines, Singapore, South Africa, South Korea, Taiwan and Thailand.

BMG Entertainment International, Asia Pacific has bolstered its regional infrastructure both by developing its local rosters and by seeking partnerships with companies that not only understand local tastes but have strong relationships with international artists who appeal to wide-ranging, multicultural audiences. In 1996, joint ventures with Fun House Co. Ltd in Japan, Music Impact in Hong Kong and Elite Music in Taiwan significantly extended the company's regional influence. Artists include E-Kin Cheng, Masaharu Fukuyama and Andy Lau.

PolyGram Latin America

October 11, 1995: PolyGram Boosts Presence In Latin America With Purchase Of Rodven, The Region's Leading Independent Record Business

The acquisition will increase PolyGram's share of the $2 billion music market in Latin America from approximately 13.5% to 16% while doubling its share of the Hispanic music market in the US and significantly increasing its business in Colombia. The new agreement will also facilitate the establishment of a seventh Latin American subsidiary for PolyGram, in Venezuela.

Based in Caracas, Rodven Records is Venezuela's leading record company with subsidiaries in Colombia, Mexico and the USA. Its strength in the region and the US is derived from its large catalog of Latin and tropical music and its broad roster of recording artists.

Manolo Diaz, PolyGram Latin America's president, said: 'The strategic benefits of this acquisition are substantial, especially in Venezuela where we will start our new operations as leaders of the market and in the US where the Latin music market is growing rapidly. The strength of Rodven's catalogue and artist roster in the tropical music segment combined with the power of PolyGram as a distributor of international repertoire in Latin America will considerably enhance our business in the region.'

PolyGram has become Latin America's market leader in international repertoire and has been consistently gaining share in local repertoire, an effort which will be substantially enhanced by the acquisition of Rodven.

PolyGram, the global music and film group, is one of the largest record companies in the world. Its famous popular and classical record labels include A&M, Decca, Def Jam, Deutsche Grammophon, Island, London, Mercury, Motown, Philips Classics, Polydor and Verve. PolyGram is quoted on the Amsterdam and New York stock exchanges.

Aside from its music division which is being sold to PolyGram, Rodven also owns a record pressing plant in Venezuela and the country's largest record store chain, Discocenter. Through its affiliate, Big Show Productions, it promotes artist tours throughout Latin America. It also sells home videos in Venezuela where it is the market leader. Rodven is part of the Cisneros Group of companies which features one of Latin America's largest media and telecommunications companies amongst its diverse range of businesses.

These extracts demonstrate many of the significant features of the music industry. Convergence is clearly an issue for both BMG and Polygram. BMG Asia includes on its roster artists like Andy Lau, a Hong Kong star with a major movie career, poised for exposure worldwide (Figure 21.3). Polygram refer to the need for both international and local repertoire, and both companies are organised regionally. There is also a reference in the Polygram statement to the importance of the Hispanic market in the US. This is especially important in Florida, Texas, California and

New York, but remains barely visible to English audiences, apart from the crossover of major artists like Gloria Estefan (from the Florida Cuban exile community) into the pop mainstream. Like the spread of Indian film music, this is a good example of the strength of music production in languages other than English.

Repertoire

The music industry is organised around the development of A&R – artists and repertoire. This means that the companies want to find 'talent', develop it in terms of performance and recording, controlling recording and music publishing rights. It is in their interest to develop specific repertoire for each territory in which they operate. They know that attempting to sell just a handful of American stars across the globe will not work. This is something that the music video satellite providers have also recognised with the development of programming with significant local content, whether it is for different parts of Europe or Asia.

Figure 21.3   Andy Lau, a star in Hong Kong, Singapore, Malaysia and anywhere with a Cantonese community

ACTIVITY 21.1

Classifying the international music markets

Arm yourself with a good atlas and a reference book giving details of the population structure in different countries.

● How would you divide up the world into regions in which to sell music recordings? What criteria would you use – size of population, language group?

● Find out from the music companies' websites and, if you can find them, the trade magazines, *Billboard* and *Music Week*, which regions are targeted by the companies themselves.

● What do you think are the major differences between the regions? Where would you select to develop a market?

The music

'Popular music' is defined here, very crudely, as all music which isn't (western) classical music. (There is a global market for classical music and there are important performers from all over the world, but the repertoire is relatively fixed.) Popular music bears a direct relationship to local culture – indeed some popular music is termed 'roots' music, emphasising that it comes from a specific community.

American culture, in the form of Hollywood, dominates world cinema and to a certain extent we could argue that, despite the strengths of local and regional music outlined above, American popular music forms dominate the world music market. The difference is that, while American cinema draws heavily upon European literature, art and theatre, American popular music is the product of a long engagement between African and European forms (and in which African forms might be seen to dominate). Further to this, much popular music derives from 'oral traditions' – songs sung by travellers who were able to carry new ideas from place to place far more easily than they might have carried 'finished' works like art, sculpture or paintings.

> The 1996 novel by E. Annie Proulx, *Accordion Crimes*, links stories about the different musicians who play a button accordion originally taken by a Sicilian peasant to America in the 1890s. Each of the characters represents a different immigrant community (Italian, German, African, Mexican etc.), each of which has contributed to 'American popular music'.

The result of these different beginnings is a much greater possibility for 'two-way' traffic between America and other cultures in terms of music.

Music is a unifying force for **diaspora** communities and this has both provided a foundation for smaller 'ethnic' music markets within America and Europe and also provided support for the importation of music from the 'home' countries.

In the UK the clearest example of this effect is the importance of Jamaican music during the 1960s, 1970s and 1980s. During this period, various musical styles such as ska, rock steady and reggae were introduced into the UK by Jamaican promoters who set up record labels and brought over artists from the Caribbean. The records were bought first by the West Indian community, which had arrived in the UK in the 1950s, and later by the UK record-buying public in general. This success then allowed the music to enter markets in Canada and America as well as sustaining the small-scale industry in Jamaica. A similar story could be told about the immigrant communities in other European countries such as France (especially North African and West African) and, to a lesser extent, Germany.

Although the structure of the music industry, and therefore the range of recorded music in circulation, has been developing for nearly a century, it is probably true to say that the range of musical styles on offer has been extended significantly since the 1960s. Musicians have always 'borrowed' ideas and developed compositions from other forms of music (composers of 'classical' music worked on what were then called 'folk tunes' in the nineteenth century), and contemporary musicians have the opportunity to hear and respond to an enormous variety of recorded music.

Internet technology is still relatively exclusive because of its cost and availability in different countries, but it is beginning to make possible exchanges of music between countries, without the input of a music industry distributor.

Hybridity in popular music

The influence of cultural studies within Media Studies and the development of postmodernism (see 'Postmodernisms', Chapter 18) has created interest in the concept of **hybridity**, which can be seen being developed in relation to popular music. Peoples of different cultures have been seen to mix and produce new cultural forms. The extent to which this is distinctly different from the traditional 'borrowings' of musicians is explored below.

There are various possible reasons why such hybrid forms might come about as a result of the movement of people around the world. An obvious example is the idea of America as a 'melting pot' culture – immigrants from many different cultures arriving in the Americas and bringing with them musical traditions. This is true for Central and South America (which gave the world sexy dance music such as the tango, samba, rumba and bossa nova) as well as North America. The diaspora cultures of more recent times have brought a more developed musical tradition into a 'host' country.

There has also been a much more long-standing 'hybridisation' which has resulted from the movement of travellers across Africa and Asia and the displacement of people as a result of wars and expulsions. Where there is a similarity in rhythms, melodies and 'tones' across western (i.e. African-European) music, there is also some similarity between music in Arab, Indian and Chinese cultures. This is evident, for instance, in the Middle East. Here, traditions of Arabic music, both sacred and secular, mix with sacred music from other Islamic cultures and also commercial film music from India. At the same time African-American and European music penetrate the region through satellite television and the records and tapes brought into the country by those who have travelled in the West.

The results of this mixing can be dramatic. Here is an extract from a review of a book celebrating the fiftieth anniversary of the state of Israel:

> a synthesis will emerge like the hip-hop chazanut (rabbinic singing) or the Hebrew ballads sung to Arabic melodies played on electric guitars by blond, blue-eyed 'Jews' from Odessa who have decided on the basis of their own hybrid experience that it is better to live by messy compromise than to die for neat dogma.
>
> (David Cesarani, *Guardian*, 12 February 1998)

Israel is, of course, a very unusual state in which Jews from very different cultures in Russia, America and Africa have migrated to an area which already supports Jewish and Arab cultures. This quote suggests that music has become a form of expression of 'identity', albeit a new and surprising identity (it may also be a sign of conflict as much as integration). Some Arab youth in Palestine will

listen to Israeli radio and enjoy Israeli and American performers. In many countries the people who return from working or studying abroad are often the ones with money and newly acquired tastes which they will use to prompt the local radio stations.

The hybridity evident in the Middle East is also starting to appear in Western Europe. In Britain, France and Germany there are significant populations of Arab and south Asian peoples who both want to hear the popular music of their own culture and are prepared to experiment in developing new forms which combine Arab and south Asian music with American and European forms.

Two rather different approaches to the idea of a more 'global' music are explored below:

Natacha Atlas

Once, during a stressful and exhilarating trip to Israel, Natacha Atlas described herself as 'a human Gaza strip'. She was referring to the complex *mélange* of influences – both genetic and environmental – that have shaped her both as an individual and as a performer.

Although her father was a Sephardic Jew, Natacha grew up in the Moroccan suburbs of Brussels, becoming fluent in French, Spanish, Arabic and English, immersing herself in Arabic culture, and learning from childhood the *raq sharki* – belly dance – techniques that she uses to devastating effect on stage today. Even more striking than Natacha's dance moves, though, is her voice, which swoops and soars, blending unfettered talent and the complexities of Arabic musical theory into a burst of sound that is thrilling, immediate and evocative.

It's a melodic weapon which has seen service in a variety of musical projects since she moved to England as a teenager and became Northampton's first Arabic rock singer. Later, dividing her time between the UK and Brussels, she sang in a variety of Arabic and Turkish nightclubs, and spent a brief

stint in a Belgian salsa band. As she shuttled between Northampton and Brussels, however, she began to attract the attention of musicians in the UK, including the Balearic beat crew Loca!, and Jah Wobble, then assembling his Invaders Of The Heart.
(edited extract from the biography of Natacha Atlas, posted on her website in 1996)

Figure 21.5   Ben Ayres and Tjinder Singh of Cornershop

Natacha Atlas (Figure 21.4) is a good example of a musician who has embraced hybridity consciously and positively (her 1995 CD was called *Diaspora*). Her recordings and live performances are not in the mainstream – they inhabit a new territory which encompasses the UK dance market but also the so-called 'world music' sector. Her approach to music is to seek out and perform with established musicians from Egypt and the Maghreb, singing mainly in Arabic, taking on her 'roots' directly, while still using a dance beat. Her 1997 CD, *Halim*, was a tribute to a popular Egyptian singer, who like Natacha herself, was half Jewish, half Muslim. The world music label seems to fit, because there is no definable 'national' label to fix to the music.

Natacha Atlas is firmly placed in the UK, in the independent market, appearing on Nation Records, a label of Beggars' Banquet, the long-established 'indie' music company. Just to emphasise the reach of the majors, all Natacha Atlas's compositions are published by Warner Chappell (a Time Warner company).

Cornershop topped the singles chart in the UK in 1998 with 'Brimful of Asha', a song about a 'playback singer'– the voice on the soundtrack of Indian popular films. The song is a tribute to perhaps the greatest playback singer of Hindi cinema, Asha Bhosle, now in her sixties but still capable of attracting enormous audiences to live performances. The writer-singer-producer of Cornershop is Tjinder Singh, a British-born Sikh, whose 'take' on music appears to be both eclectic and angry.

Whereas Natacha Atlas referred directly to the idea of 'Diaspora', Tjinder Singh called his band 'Cornershop' as an angry response to the stereotype of the Asian shopkeeping dream. He has reacted negatively to attempts to define Cornershop as fitting a 'world music' label, and it does seem that a wider range of western cultural influences are evident on the third Cornershop CD, *When I Was Born For the 7th Time*. A country duet, guitars reminiscent of the Velvet Underground, an accordion intro, Allen Ginsberg reciting beat poetry and trip-hop beats make for a wide-ranging sound. The decision to end the album with a version of the Beatles' 'Norwegian Wood', sung in Punjabi, comes across as making a subtle comment on musical influences generally – *Rubber-Soul*-period Beatles music saw the

Figure 21.4   Natacha Atlas on the cover of her CD *Diaspora*

use of sitar music following the visit to the Maraheshi Yogi in India in 1966.

'I think the term "world" sucks,' he spits. 'World music is something that was brought over from different countries basically to the West. For it to do that, there has to be an element that links it to the West. That's why a lot of the stuff, like African music or Asian bhangra music, has bass slapped on it or other elements like electronic drums – it just doesn't work for me. A lot of world music just rubs off the wrong way on people because they're not seeing it in its more pure form as it would have been, say, twenty years ago.' At first glance, such a statement seems surprising, especially given the fact that Singh himself plays bass and utilizes a drum machine on 'Woman's Gotta Have It', a disc that's as likely to shimmer with the metallic drone of a tamboura as it is to kick with guitar licks worthy of your neighbor's garage. But unlike the music of Sheila Chandra and others whose hybridizations do small justice to the traditions they plunder, Cornership digs deeper and throws more into the pot.

(Extract from a 'New Times' website 1996.
Interview by Amy Kiser)

Cornershop were an 'indie act' in 1998, yet were able to score a number one single. This followed a period when the band opened for Oasis on their 1996 tour. They also came to the attention of world music 'guru' David Byrne, who took American rights for their records and signed them to his Luaka Bop label. So, while they remained on the independent label Wiiija in the UK, in America they appeared under the Warner Bros banner, home of David Byrne, guaranteeing much wider exposure.

ACTIVITY 21.2

Hybridisation and 'world music'

It is quite possible that by the time you read this, neither of the performers we have featured here will be working in the same way. But the issue of 'hybridisation' and 'world music' won't go away.

- Survey the current commercial and indie music scene. What evidence can you find for either of these concepts?
- Can you find examples of music which directly address a particular cultural heritage like Natacha Atlas? Or of more eclectic 'borrowings' like Cornershop?
- Many people are passionate about their tastes in music. Organise a debate or discussion around the idea of 'global music', taking Tjinder Singh's comments as a starting point. Is it a worthwhile aim or does it lack authenticity for popular audiences?

Reference

Chanan, Michael (1996) *The Dream that Kicks*, London: Routledge.

Further reading

Burnett, Robert (1995) *The Global Jukebox*, London: Routledge.

Hutnyk, J., Sharma, A. and Sharma, S. (1996) *Dis-Orienting Rhythms: The Politics of the New Asian Dance Music*, London: Zed Books.

Longhurst, Brian (1995) *Popular Music and Society*, Oxford: Polity.

Marre, J. and Charlton, H. (1985) *Beats of the Heart: Popular Music of the World*, London: Pluto.

Negus, Keith (1992) *Producing Pop: Culture and Conflict in the Popular Music Industry*, London: Edward Arnold.

Negus, Keith (1996) *Popular Music in Theory: An Introduction*, Oxford: Polity.

Shuker, Roy (1994) *Understanding Popular Music*, London: Routledge.

The common view of 'the media' equates their activities with glamour
and excitement, creativity and controversy. There are such moments, of
course – more perhaps than in other types of work. The defining feature
of media activity, however, is its status as an industrial process, and in
this chapter we explore the activities in the media industries, using the
tools of economic analysis and concentrating on the major media
corporations and their business practices. In a separate chapter
('Independents and alternatives', Chapter 28) we explore the organisation
of media production outside the **mainstream**.

Media production and the manufacturing process

Media production is a manufacturing process much like many others. Let's
take a particular form of media production, a daily newspaper, and compare
it with a production line for a familiar manufactured product – tinned
baked beans. Surprisingly, perhaps, there are several common features:
- initial investment in plant and machinery – fixed assets
- continuous demand for the product, necessitating continuous
  production and a constant supply of raw materials
- distribution of the product to all parts of the economy
- market research to ensure up-to-date information about performance of
  the product and the satisfaction of customers
- advertising of the product to keep it in the public eye and to attract
  new buyers.

These common features are important – media industries usually make
decisions based on standard business principles. Even so, media industries
are different from most other forms of manufacture in a number of ways
and it is these differences (or 'specificities') which we want to explore in
more detail. Let's stay with the production of print-based news:
- The 'raw material' is not homogeneous – skill and cultural, aesthetic
  and political judgements are necessary in selection of events which will
  be marketed as 'news'.

- The price of news varies – some is free, some might be very expensive to purchase or access.
- The product is not always a necessity and demand could fall dramatically if consumers' tastes change.
- Production and distribution patterns are not fixed – the product can be transmitted electronically and reproduced locally.
- Staff costs will generally be greater than in other forms of manufacture because a greater variety of skills are required in the process.
- This particular product has a shelf life of only one day (really, only half a day).
- Revenue from sale of the product is only part of the business – a large proportion comes from the sale of advertising space. Advertisers therefore have influence on the fortunes of the product.

These points suggest that managing a media production process is a particularly complex (and risky) business. The two most important considerations for the newspaper producer are the collection and processing of suitable news material and the distribution of the finished product.

The actual production (i.e. page make-up and printing) of the newspaper is perhaps not as crucial as you might think in determining the success of the product. Certainly, the quality of the feature material and the 'look' of the paper will contribute greatly to its long-term reputation, but they won't necessarily boost the circulation dramatically like a sensational story, nor immediately impress the advertisers, and, if poor distribution means that the product doesn't get to the customer in time, all the production effort will be wasted (see 'News Corporation' and 'Local newspapers and advertising', Case studies 24 and 31).

Long-life media – a different process?

In film or music production there is a rather different production process, or at least a different emphasis, from that of the daily newspaper, or even the daily or weekly television programme. Purchase of a ticket for the cinema or a concert has to be a more calculated decision. The 'product' is not 'consumed' completely – we may return to experience it again at a later date or we may purchase a recording on tape or CD. With a shelf-life longer than the single day of the newspaper, there is the possibility of building an audience over several weeks and developing a number of associated products.

It is even possible that as a collector's item the product will increase in value over time. Since the product is also reproducible from a 'master copy', it can be 're-launched' again in the future at minimum cost and attract a new set of buyers. Walt Disney was the first to recognise this

Gone With the Wind (US 1939) is still the most successful film ever made (adjusting box office for inflation) and has been re-released many times. In 1998 it was released by New Line, the 'independent' arm of Warner Bros. Time Warner acquired the rights when they merged with Ted Turner's company. Turner had bought *Gone With the Wind* as part of the MGM film library and it was the most valuable asset in his portfolio. The new release added twelve minutes of new footage in a digitally re-mastered version. Two hundred prints were released (*Screen International*, 12 June 1998).

Merchandising   The marketing of a wide range of consumer goods bearing images from a specific media product has a very long history, but the sheer scale of current merchandising dates from the release of *Star Wars* in 1977.

Retro design is popular in Japan where sports cars have been produced with a 1950s 'look'. Some critics would see this as part of 'postmodern style' (see 'Postmodernisms', Chapter 18).

phenomenon and in doing so saved his studio. He saw that animated films did not date as quickly as live action features and that, since a large part of his audience was made up of young children, he could re-release classic films such as *Snow White and the Seven Dwarfs* (US 1937) and *Pinocchio* (US 1939) every seven years. This strategy has been altered by the advent of video, but it is still relevant and has been applied to other classic films such as *Gone With the Wind* and *Star Wars* (US 1977). A recyclable product is also a recyclable brand name, and the modern Disney company has benefited further from **merchandising** spin-offs. Like Warner Bros, Disney has recognised the value of its brand names and has opened retail outlets to maximise profits.

The distributors of CDs also recognised that there was an enormous potential market in the re-release of popular music albums on the new format in the 1980s. Here we are dealing with something very different from other products (although certain design elements of products like cars and furniture can be recycled – the so-called 'retro' look).

To explore these unique features of the film and record business, we need to look more closely at the production process.

Although newspapers have a brief life as consumer products, they have always had a long-term value as **archive** material. In the past, this tended to be limited by the demands of storage space to one or two titles in major libraries. Now major newspapers are available on CD-ROM and, with the advent of global computer networks, almost any material will be available to the researcher (with an automatic debit from a credit card account, of course). What does your library hold on CD-ROM?

The production process: feature films

Every media production process has its specificities. We have the space to study only one in detail – that of the modern Hollywood feature film, based on the 'package' system of individual films (see Case study 7 for a view of Hollywood under the studio system).

Background to contemporary Hollywood

The Hollywood majors studios capable of distributing twenty big budget films every year, in North America and internationally. The current six majors (Warners, Paramount, Universal, Columbia, Disney and Fox) have survived seventy years of Hollywood history. Newcomers tend to last a few years before disappearing.

Films are conceived as individual products which are put together by a producer as a 'package' of a story, stars and a director and crew. There are a number of ways in which the package can be financed, but for big-budget films the 'deal' will nearly always involve one of the **major studios**. The idea for a new film could come from many sources, but in the relatively 'conservative' atmosphere of Hollywood it will probably require some evidence of previous success to interest the studios. Sources might be:

- a sequel to a recent box office hit (e.g. *The Lost World: Jurassic Park* (US 1997)
- a remake of a European box office hit (e.g. *Three Men and a Cradle* (France 1985) remade as *Three Men and a Baby* (US 1987))
- an adaptation of a best-selling book (e.g. *The Firm* (US 1993) from the John Grisham novel)
- an original story by a proven scriptwriter
- an original idea from a successful director/star team
- a new twist on a story from a currently popular genre cycle

– or any combination of the above. *Godzilla* (US 1998) must have seemed the perfect blend – an effects-driven aliens/disaster movie from the current cycle, by a hit producer/director team, based on a Japanese original. Nobody is perfect, and at the time of writing *Godzilla* is a relative flop. But it will easily pay for itself through the mountains of merchandising sold in its wake.

The movie business displays a seeming contradiction in that a conservative financial sector can take enormous risks in terms of production budget, when the chances of success at the cinema box office are actually quite small – most films lose money on theatrical release. (The combined total of *expenditure* on new films by Hollywood studios is often not much less than the total box-office *receipts* in the same period.) There are, however, good reasons why Hollywood continues to make profit.

Each of the major Hollywood studios will finance a **slate** of seven or eight big films every year at a budget of around $50 million or more each, aiming for a smash hit during the two critical seasons which run in North America from May to August and Thanksgiving (late November) to Christmas. Some critics refer to these as 'ultra-high-budget films' (see Maltby 1998). The studio will also probably release another dozen or so 'medium budget' films. The budget for each film will include half as much again to spend on **P&A** (prints and advertising), giving a 1997 average of $75 million per film for the big-budget pictures. With an outlay of over $600 million on the slate, at least one film must be a big hit (grossing $100 million or more) for the studio to cover its costs. If a studio is very lucky and has a record-breaking blockbuster (e.g. *Titanic* with $1.3 billion in 1998), then profits can be substantial (*Titanic* was so expensive to make and market that it took two studios to distribute it). However, many films flop completely at the cinema box office (losing $40 or $50 million on a single picture is not unknown – Kevin Costner managed it with *The Postman* (US 1997)).

'Tentpole movie' is another term for the 'ultra-high-budget' film, presumably on the grounds that one big blockbuster supports the rest of the slate in the way the tentpole holds up the tent – this is the kind of term you find in the famous entertainment newspaper, *Variety*.

United Artists The sorry tale
of the decline of United Artists is
told in *Final Cut* by Bach (1985).

For Hollywood, 'domestic'
describes the US and Canada;
everything else is 'international'.

Video and the majors See
Gomery (1992) on the growth of
the video rental and retail in the
US and the attitudes of the
studios towards it. Jack Valenti of
the MPAA once denounced the
VCR, claiming it would kill movie-
going. By 1986 revenue from video
rental and sell-through exceeded
the cinema box office, which was
itself buoyant. The majors rapidly
moved in to control the video
market themselves.

The Player The 'pitch' process is
brilliantly satirised in Robert
Altman's film (US 1992). One of
the best explanations of 'the deal'
is in Pirie (1981).

The most dramatic example of box-office failure was the epic Western
Heaven's Gate in 1980. So much was lost that the studio, **United Artists**,
collapsed completely and is now little more than a name. That was at a
time when the majors were relatively vulnerable (Hollywood is notorious
for declaring crises – some of which are real). The relative stability of the
majors' more recent operations is explained by two developments over the
last ten years:

- the increase in the importance of the international theatrical (cinema)
  market, which in 1994 surpassed North America for the first time
- the development of ancillary markets in video, pay television,
  computer games and merchandising, which are also now more
  important than the traditional test of success at the North American
  box office.

(The situation in the UK mirrors the American experience. UK audiences
pay most to watch films on satellite and cable. Video retail comes next,
then video rental and, finally, the smallest market is in cinemas. See the
BFI Handbook for figures.)

The result of these changes in markets means that a higher
proportion of ultra-high-budget features are likely to go into profit
eventually. Richard Maltby (1998) suggests that as many as half the
blockbusters will turn a profit, compared to the one in ten in the pre-
video days. What we should note is that, in economic terms, the majors
can expect very long 'streams' of income from a successful film, so that
in any single financial year they are guaranteed some income even if all
the current releases are relative flops. It is this guarantee that keeps
them in business and allows them to price out competitors by pushing
up budgets. The guarantee is valid only for what have been termed
'high concept' movies. Justin Wyatt (1994) sums up what is needed as
'the look, the hook and the book'. Maltby (1998) describes them as
having a 'straightforward, easily pitched and easily comprehended
story'. The six bullet points at the beginning of this section refer to this
process and, if you add big stars and spectacle to the mix, you should be
able to 'pitch':

ACTIVITY 22.1

The pitch

What ideas have you got for a new film – one which would definitely interest a
Hollywood studio?

- Look back through the section above and develop your idea along the
  suggested lines. Try to limit your outline to a single page.

- Think carefully about whom you would cast and, most important, try to sum up the idea in a single line.
- Test out your outline on a friend. How well does it stand up?

This strange business, in which producers feel more secure with a large budget, has other effects. Investors become nervous about 'low-budget' pictures. The budget may be artificially forced up towards the average (a form of 'institutional constraint'?) and star names added at large fees, even when the story doesn't necessarily need stars. What might be a 'big-budget' production in Europe – $10–20 million – is automatically seen as a 'small film' in North America and thereby marginalised for North American distributors.

There are some small independent producers and distributors who succeed outside the orbit of the majors. Sometimes they can spot new markets ahead of the majors, or they are prepared to take on controversial issues or even controversial audiences. It is still possible to make low-budget films on strict production schedules and to sell them to specialist markets without the massive P&A spends of the majors. But it is becoming much more difficult. In the late 1990s nearly all the successful independent distributors had been 'acquired' by the majors, who continued to run them as separate businesses to maintain their image of 'independence' and, arguably, as their 'Research and Development' arm (see Wyatt 1998 on Miramax and New Line). Independent film-making is discussed in 'Independents and alternatives', Chapter 28 and 'Making films outside the mainstream', Case study 29.

The Full Monty (UK/US 1997) is a film 'without stars' in an American sense. The budget was low, allowing a very big international spend on promotion by distributor Fox Searchlight (an 'independent' operated by a major).

French producer/director Luc Besson made The Fifth Element (France 1997) in English on an $80 million budget. A relatively modest hit in North America, the film did Hollywood blockbuster-style business around the world. More big-budget European films are expected to follow this lead.

Setting up the package

Given this background, it is not surprising that the setting-up period can be lengthy and scripts may pass through the hands of many studio executives before they are 'greenlighted'. The gestation period for some films might be ten years or more. During this time a good deal of development money might have been spent by a studio on an **option** on the rights to the idea (known as the **property**) without a foot of film ever having been shot. What the owner of the property fears most is it being put into **turn-around** – a limbo-land for script ideas which languish with one studio until another comes along which is prepared to pick up the option (i.e. to pay enough to cover the development money paid out by the first studio). It's a wonder films get made at all.

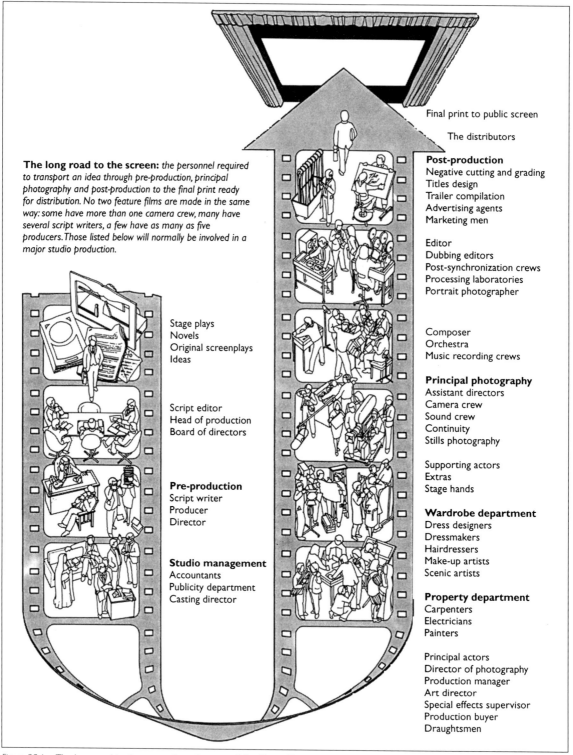

Final print to public screen

The distributors

The long road to the screen: *the personnel required to transport an idea through pre-production, principal photography and post-production to the final print ready for distribution. No two feature films are made in the same way: some have more than one camera crew, many have several script writers, a few have as many as five producers. Those listed below will normally be involved in a major studio production.*

Post-production
Negative cutting and grading
Titles design
Trailer compilation
Advertising agents
Marketing men

Editor
Dubbing editors
Post-synchronization crews
Processing laboratories
Portrait photographer

Composer
Orchestra
Music recording crews

Stage plays
Novels
Original screenplays
Ideas

Principal photography
Assistant directors
Camera crew
Sound crew
Continuity
Stills photography

Script editor
Head of production
Board of directors

Supporting actors
Extras
Stage hands

Pre-production
Script writer
Producer
Director

Wardrobe department
Dress designers
Dressmakers
Hairdressers
Make-up artists
Scenic artists

Studio management
Accountants
Publicity department
Casting director

Property department
Carpenters
Electricians
Painters

Principal actors
Director of photography
Production manager
Art director
Special effects supervisor
Production buyer
Draughtsmen

Figure 22.1 The long road to the screen, from *Anatomy of the Movies* (Pirie 1981). This is still the same complex process twenty years later, although the post-production stage has now 'gone digital'

INDUSTRIES

Pre-production

Once the go-ahead has been given, the production team has a great deal to do before shooting begins. Parts must be cast (the lead players were probably decided as part of the original deal), locations chosen, costumes researched, dialogue coaches and wranglers (animal handlers) hired, hotel rooms booked etc. All this might take several months, during which time the script may be reworked and the direction of the project altered. A starting date will be announced and reported in the trade press (*Hollywood Reporter*, *Variety* etc.) and eventually the cameras will roll (although it is not unknown for the plug to be pulled on the whole enterprise at this stage).

Since a trade announcement is part of the process of drumming up interest in a production project, many more films are 'announced' than are actually made.

Production

This stage is often called **principal photography**, and it is likely to be the shortest period of all. Modern films usually **wrap** in around fifty days of shooting – an average of two to three minutes a day – depending on the demands of the script. The low-budget producer will aim to halve that time by clever use of **set-ups** and tight scripting. Efficient directors are those who can come in 'on' or even 'under' budget. Keeping a whole crew on location a day longer than the planned schedule can add considerably to the overall cost, and directors and crews who can stick to schedules will be rehired.

Special effects which require shooting with actors can be a major problem and mean some productions coming back to studio lots or specialist facilities (including those in Britain), where others will go to locations offering cheaper labour or good deals on **permissions** (using famous buildings or locations), taxation etc. In recent years, many Hollywood films have been shot in the south-eastern United States (Florida, Georgia, Alabama) or Canada.

New York is often impersonated in American films by Toronto. Liverpool and Manchester have represented European cities in several films.

Film production services

The film production process depends on access to a wide range of specialist services and it is the provision of these which is another factor in preserving the dominance of Hollywood in the industry. Technology for filming (cameras, lenses, lighting, mounts etc.) and for post-production (editing and film-processing) is a specialised industry which requires high levels of investment and close co-operation between film-makers and technologists. The major studios have sought to maintain these relationships – even to the extent of buying into the companies involved.

Film equipment American companies dominate equipment supply, although French and German companies have also been important. UK-produced equipment has often copied American designs.

Other services such as financial, legal and promotional are perhaps more mobile and more flexible, but their concentration in Los Angeles remains an important factor in maintaining the 'Hollywood community'.

Post-production

The longest stage in the process may well be post-production. Here the film is edited – some might say this is where the film narrative is actually created. The relationship between the director and the editor (or 'cutter') may be relatively distant or it may be very close, as in the case of Martin Scorsese and Thelma Schoonmaker, who will work together for many months to complete a picture.

The increase in the importance of film sound during the last ten years has added to the work in post-production with more time spent on tidying up dialogue through 'looping' or Automatic Dialogue Replacement (**ADR**) (actors record their lines again while watching themselves on a loop of film, played through until they can lip-sync perfectly) and adding sound effects using the **Foley Studio**. Special visual effects will also be added at this stage. The completed film will then go to the laboratories for **colour grading** and other adjustments required to produce suitable screening prints.

See 'Production techniques', Chapter 5, for more on **Foley**.

Distribution

Every part of the process is important. The success of a film can depend at least as much on how it is handled by the distributor as on the film itself. Distributors promote and market films in particular **territories** and negotiate **release patterns** with exhibitors. The distribution of most big-budget Hollywood films is directly controlled by the majors themselves. In North America each major studio usually distributes its own pictures. In the UK, two of the majors have formed a joint distribution company (Paramount and Universal, with MGM-UA, are joint owners of **UIP**). In the other important cinema markets around the world they may have an agreement with a local distributor, but as the international market grows they are increasingly opening their own offices in every territory.

In 1997 the six 'major studios', through their own distribution companies or in partnership, took over 80 per cent of the North American (US and Canada) or 'domestic' market. A majority share for American films is evident in most territories in the world with rare exceptions such as India and China (although Hollywood distribution is

UIP (United International Pictures) also now distributes films from the new Spielberg studio, DreamWorks SKG. Its strength in European markets is such that in 1998 the European Union threatened to investigate its dominant position.

Internet The majors now invest in elaborate websites for individual films offering trailers, sound clips, games etc. Studio homepages give information on new releases. If you have Net access this is a good way to get advance news on films you may wish to study.

growing here). The recent growth of exhibition sites, especially in Europe and South America, has seen the international box office take precedence over the domestic market.

The distribution process begins early. Announcing a project in the trade press is the beginning of a promotional campaign designed to build a 'profile' for the film, first with other potential distributors in different territories or on other formats and later with exhibitors.

Each major film is a separate marketing project, and the advertising and promotional budget, on top of the production cost, represents a terrifying investment, placing even more burden on the producer to 'get it right'. The consequence sometimes is the use of previews, where selected audiences get to comment on a film before it is released (and before the most expensive part of the advertising campaign gets under way). Depending on audience reactions, producers will change endings, cut sequences etc., or even decide to **shelve** the film and not release it at all.

At the preview stage, the producers will have at least some idea of whether or not they have a hit. The next major dilemma is how many prints to make. This is becoming increasingly important as a consequence of the large advertising spend. If a great deal of money is being spent on television advertising and promotional tie-ins on review programmes etc., spreading the message to every part of the country, there is little point urging everyone to go and see the new film if it is showing only in Los Angeles and New York or in London or Paris. What is needed is a print for screening in every major town. In America that means over two thousand prints (in the UK, three hundred), and each one costs around $1,500 to $2,000 to duplicate (70 mm prints for the biggest city-centre screens cost more). To gain the benefit from a big advertising campaign, a distributor needs to spend another $2–3 million on prints. Everything then depends on the opening weekend.

Media interest in the US in big new films is intense and to be pronounced a 'hit' a film needs to pull in a screen average of around $5,000 and a three-day total of over $10 million. A poor opening is very hard to shake off and, without the news of 'good box office', advertising will not really take off.

Blitzing every screen in the country is not the only way, of course. For an 'art film' or one with a clearly defined audience, a distributor can select a handful of screens, aim advertising locally, and then build on **word of mouth** and advertising and promotion in specialist magazines. Table 22.1 shows the opening figures for selected new releases at the start of the summer 1998 season. There are two clear hits here, *Deep Impact* and *The Truman Show*. *Godzilla* gained a massive opening, but this was only after a similarly massive marketing push, and the industry thought the

Shelved films   Video has saved many films from total extinction, but it is still an admission of marketing fear when a film with a major star goes 'straight to video'. In 1995 *Blue Sky*, starring Jessica Lange and made in 1991, got a limited release in the US and Lange won the Best Actress Oscar.

Film Education   Sponsored by the UK film industry, Film Education publishes education material for new films, including information on marketing. Colleges should be able to get on the mailing list.

results disappointing. *The Horse Whisperer*, *A Perfect Murder* and *Six Days, Seven Nights* were all 'solid' openers and were expected to have 'legs' as they would benefit from word of mouth. The two flops were Warner Bros' animation, *Quest for Camelot* and Universal's thriller, *Black Dog*.

Film data Many daily newspapers now carry the top ten films in the UK and the US each week. The monthly film magazine *Empire* gives slightly more information, but for the most detailed analysis you must turn to the weekly trade paper *Screen International*. The *Annual Handbook* produced by the BFI is an excellent source of information on production and distribution of all films in the UK.

Table 22.1   Selected film openings, summer 1998

Date	Title	Distributor	Screens	3-day total ($)	Screen average ($)
1–3 May	*Black Dog*	Universal	2,025	4,809,375	2,375
8–10 May	*Deep Impact*	Paramount	3,156	41,152,375	13,039
15–17 May	*The Horse Whisperer*	Buena Vista	2,039	13,685,488	6,712
15–17 May	*Quest for Camelot*	Warner Bros	3,107	6,041,602	1,945
22–25 May	*Godzilla*	Sony Pictures	3,310	35,726,951	16,836
5–7 June	*The Truman Show*	Paramount	2,315	31,542,121	13,625
5–7 June	*A Perfect Murder*	Warner Bros	2,845	16,615,704	5,840
12–14 June	*Six Days, Seven Nights*	Buena Vista	2,550	16,485,276	6,465

Source: Screen International

Note that this selection includes several of the 'preferred options' – a remake (*A Perfect Murder*, based on Hitchcock's *Dial M for Murder*), a hit novel (*The Horse Whisperer*), a producer formula (*Godzilla*) and star vehicles (*The Truman Show* and *Six Days, Seven Nights*). By contrast, *The Full Monty* (UK/US 1997) was released as an 'art house' picture in North America. Starting on only a handful of screens as a **platform release**, *The Full Monty* gained very high screen averages before widening to a maximum of 850 screens. It stayed on the American box office chart for a staggering thirty-five weeks and grossed over $45 million.

Platform release   a distribution strategy which puts a film on at selected major cinema sites and then uses the good results to bolster a wider distribution at a later date. See the *Trainspotting* case study in Finney 1996.

Exhibition

In the US the major studios were barred from ownership of significant cinema chains (following the **anti-trust legislation** at the end of the 1940s which signalled the decline of the studio system), until very recently. Overseas there were no such restrictions and in the last few years Warner Bros and UCI (owned by Paramount and Universal) have built multiplexes in many cinema markets, including the UK where other American chains like Showcase (also owned by Viacom/Paramount) are also receptive to Hollywood films.

Ownership or control of every stage of production is known as **vertical integration,** and it has obvious advantages for the majors in ensuring that they will have a cinema available to take a film when it is ready for release. This isn't always the case for independent distributors who are trying to find outlets for their films. Coupled with the cost of advertising and prints, this lack of access to cinemas is one of the main ways in which new entrants to the film business are kept out. In 1997 six major exhibitors in the UK (Odeon, ABC, Virgin, Showcase, UCI and Warner) dominated the market and sold 70 per cent of the tickets.

The lack of cinema screens on which to release new films became a problem in the UK in the mid-1980s and was a factor in the building boom within British exhibition. The producers and distributors of art films tried to respond to the majors by copying them and becoming integrated distributors themselves (e.g. Artificial Eye and Curzon, with screens in London available for openings).

The distribution pattern of films and the exhibition practices in the UK have changed significantly since the American exhibitors moved in and now much more resemble what happens elsewhere in Europe and North America. Attendance habits have changed as a result. Although there are more screens, there are fewer cinemas (older cinemas have continued to close as multiplexes open) and virtually none in suburbs or small towns. Even in larger towns there might be only a single cinema. People will travel further to the cinema and, as well as the long-standing ABC and Odeon chains, most of us now have a multiplex run by Warner, Virgin, UCI or Showcase with ten or more screens within half an hour's drive.

ACTIVITY 22.2

The local cinema audience

How well served is your local area for cinemas? Get a map showing the largest centre of population and a twenty-mile radius around it. This is the target area for the multiplex. A ten-screen multiplex needs something like a million admissions each year to be profitable. On average the UK population goes to the cinema just over twice per year so a population of nearly half a million is needed to support a multiplex.

- You will need to calculate the population in your area and then plot the location of the cinemas.
- Do you have a multiplex? Does the population warrant one? Does the exercise suggest you have too few or too many cinemas in the area?

Either way, you might have some interesting material to discuss with cinema managers or local planning officials.

UK cinema audience   The class base of the audience has been a factor in the changing nature of film exhibition in the UK since the earliest days. The location of the multiplexes favours cinemagoers with transport and the extra spending power to pay higher admission prices. Research released by CAVIAR (Cinema and Video Industry Audience Research) in 1995 clearly shows that, even though more people were recognised as belonging to C2DE socio-economic groupings, the cinema audience was skewed in favour of ABC1s, who were much more likely to be 'frequent cinemagoers' (see also 'Advertising', Chapter 30).

The building boom is expected to end in 2000, but in 1998 the predictions being made were that building 'citiplexes' (town centre, smaller multi-screen cinemas) and 'artplexes' (specialist multi-screen art cinemas) would be the next trend. Despite the new building, the UK still has fewer screens per head of population than the US – but do we have the same cinemagoing habits? The new building means that the number of screens has risen to over 2,300 – still only about half the number of screens operating in the 1940s. However, the regular cinema attendance is only 10 per cent of what it was then, so there are more screens per person than ever before – surely that must mean more choice? Unfortunately not. The end of the old Odeon/ABC **duopoly** has not meant greater flexibility, in fact the opposite to some extent.

Exhibition duopoly The dominance of UK exhibition by two chains, Odeon and ABC, from the 1940s until the 1980s has been criticised as a major factor in the decline of the industry, especially when 'barring' practices stopped independent cinemas getting big films if they might threaten a 'big two' cinema nearby.

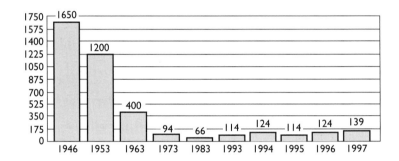

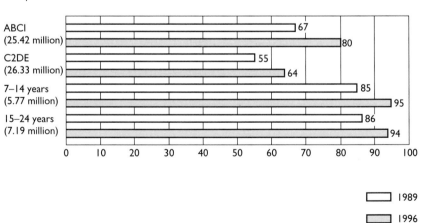

Group size 1996

1989

1996

Figure 22.2 UK cinemagoing. *Above:* annual admissions to UK cinemas, 1946–97 (millions). These are approximate figures, taken from various sources and rounded – they should be taken only as indicative of trends. *Below:* The rise in the population (aged seven and over) who 'ever go to the cinema'. The upper part shows the difference between social classes. The lower part shows the two age groups which are the most frequence attenders. Sources: primarily *Screen Finance*, CAA, CAVIAR, *Screen International* and *BFI Yearbook 1998*

Films now stay at the same cinema, sometimes for several weeks (perhaps changing to a smaller auditorium as the audience falls) and, where there are two or more multiplexes in the same city region, they often show the same selection of films from the major distributors. The effect of all this is to increase still further the domination of Hollywood product on British screens and to make it virtually impossible to place an independent film on the screen. Even if an independent does make it, without the massive advertising and promotion spend available to the majors it is unlikely that a sufficiently large audience will be attracted to justify the venture, making it more difficult to persuade exhibitors next time round.

The film production process as a model

Because 'film studies' came before 'media studies' and because 'film-making' was one of the first media practical activities in schools and colleges, the production process outlined above has been widely applied in media education. We can find equivalents for five production stages in every media industry (distribution and exhibition have been merged for general use):

- negotiating/setting up production
- pre-production
- production
- post-production
- distribution/exhibition.

ACTIVITY 22.3

The production process model

To test out your understanding of this five-stage model, jot down some notes on what would happen in each stage of the production process for

- a new magazine for dance enthusiasts
- the first recordings by a new band.

You might have difficulty in deciding into which stage to put a particular activity – don't worry about this: using the model is not necessarily about getting 'right answers' but more about helping you to study and understand the process. This exercise should help in both your industry studies and your production work.

Organisation of production

Once we have been able to develop a model to describe the production process, what kinds of issues do we wish to explore? Here are some of the questions an 'industry study' has traditionally explored:

Structure

How does the production process relate to the ownership and control of different companies or organisations in the industry? How significant is the structure in determining how media products are produced and what kinds of products appear? Two important questions centre on integration and regulation.

Integration refers to the growth of organisations by means of acquisition of other organisations in the same industry. Vertical integration refers to an organisation established in one part of the production chain, gaining control of the other parts of the production process, e.g. a Hollywood studio being bought by a cinema chain. A fully integrated media organisation would control every aspect of the production process. In the past, this has meant newspapers being produced by companies who owned the trees from which the paper was made.

Horizontal integration refers to media organisations acquiring control of their competitors within that segment of the production process (it is theoretically possible for an organisation to be both vertically and horizontally integrated, but that would mean that one organisation was effectively the whole industry). Ultimately, one organisation might control a majority share of the market – a **monopoly** position. More usually, there will be at least one other competitor – creating a **duopoly**, as in UK cinema exhibition for many years, or UK television – or a small number of competitors of roughly equal status: an **oligopoly**. Most media industries – indeed most large-scale industries of any kind – are oligopolies.

Economists refer to the relationships between organisations in an oligopoly situation as **imperfect competition**. There are likely to be unwritten agreements between the oligopolists as to standards, pricing policies, labour relations etc. Because governments are likely to be concerned at the political implications of media monopolies, action is likely to be taken against 'too much' integration. This concern has increased as traditionally separate industries such as publishing, broadcasting and film have moved closer together.

Cross-media ownership is a sensitive issue in the UK, which is unique in having a history of a strong national press with large circulations and a public service broadcasting environment. Fears grew of monopoly power in the mid-1990s. Tight controls have relaxed a little in the late 1990s, allowing 'consolidation' of ownership in independent television, but it remains an issue (see 'News corporation', Case study 24).

ACTIVITY 22.4

Researching ownership

Use the newspaper archives in your library and/or the Internet to trace the changes in ownership and control of UK media activities in the last few years involving any one of these groups: Carlton, Granada, EMAP. This should give you some idea of the complexity of UK media business.

Control of acquisitions in the media industries and subsequent oligopoly practices can be exercised in two ways:

● Public sector media organisations, financed and controlled by the public purse and public accountability, can be set up. Nearly all countries have some form of public broadcasting (radio and television) and many have set up government agencies which play an important role in financing and distributing films and other media products.

● The activities of media organisations can be regulated by government or public sector 'watchdogs'. Regulations often cover not only monopoly ownership or control and financial dealings but also the range and 'quality' of products (including technical quality) and sometimes the sensitive content of products.

Some media industries (like cinema and popular music) have always been international in outlook, but technological change means that national boundaries are ceasing to be barriers to a wider range of media products. Controlling multinational media corporations from a national perspective is becoming increasingly difficult.

Attitudes towards regulation have also changed. The drive towards **privatisation** in the UK, instituted by the Thatcher government in the 1980s, has been mirrored in other countries, and has been fuelled by a belief that the growth of media industries should be encouraged if it will increase employment. **Light-touch regulation**, involving a simple 'quality' test, is one innovation. International regulation is another possibility. Multinational corporations might be required to deal directly with the European Union for instance. The dispute between member states in 1995 (France being in the minority) over how to support indigenous film industries in the face of American imports is indicative of how difficult this may be to put into practice.

Overall, the process of deregulation has been the central issue in most media industries during the 1980s and 1990s. On the other hand, more conservative attitudes towards media images have led to an increase in some areas of censorship of the content of media products (see 'Institutions', Chapter 26).

MPAA The Motion Pictures Association of America is an effective body lobbying against 'protectionism' by the EU to allow American media corporations access to European markets.

Quality threshold The UK Broadcasting Act of 1990 set up the much-criticised process of bidding for ITV franchises. In theory, the highest bid would be accepted if the bidding group convinced the ITC (Independent Television Commission) that it could pass the 'quality threshold' in terms of promised programming. Assessment of bids in relation to quality was seen by many observers as inconsistent.

Location and local–global relations

The location of media industries is important for two main reasons.

● As a major employment sector (possibly the largest in some parts of Europe), the location of media production facilities is a contentious issue in many countries.

- If the media producers are all located in one area, then their media products are likely to be influenced by the culture of that area, which may or may not align with that of media consumers elsewhere.

The Hollywood studios have always prided themselves on the international appeal of their products. Yet, within the US, studios have traditionally been careful to censor material in order not to offend audiences in more conservative areas. Once, of course, this meant pandering to a form of apartheid in the South. Getting the balance right (between culturally conservative and liberal parts of the country) is difficult. Films and television programmes are usually financed in New York and made in Los Angeles and this twin axis has traditionally controlled the American media. The location of Ted Turner's operation (CNN especially) – a new competitor based in Atlanta – was therefore of some significance. The South is both the area of economic expansion and the home of even more conservative political views. The phenomenon of bigoted talk radio 'shock jocks' (another southern strength) is also a symptom of a shift in the geography of the American media.

In the UK the concentration of media production in London and the south-east has led to many complaints about **metropolitan bias**. The growth and spread of a new speech pattern – so-called 'estuary English' – has been blamed on the London base of media commentators, and the restructuring of both ITV and the BBC has been scrutinised for the guarantee of **regional production**. Similar arguments could be made about national newspapers, which once had major regional editorial offices – Manchester, for instance was the base for several dailies (including the *Manchester Guardian*, which moved to London).

Perhaps the major concern over location is the fear that media production in one country may be completely controlled from another country. This fear extends to both the news media and those seen to be important agents in building a cultural identity. It can be argued that the spread of 'international news services' like CNN has had a beneficial effect in those parts of the world where repressive governments can muzzle their own media but cannot stop the inflow of satellite images (or indeed BBC World Service radio broadcasts). On the other hand, most western countries have expressed concern about the ownership of media companies operating within their national boundaries being held by non-nationals (Rupert Murdoch had to take out US citizenship in order to acquire his US television holdings). This fear relates to general anxiety over the 'unregulated' international media market outlined in the previous section (see also 'Globalisation', Chapter 20).

The economic benefits of attracting media business into an area can be considerable. With a weak sterling/dollar exchange rate, the choice of the

Regional production The sensitivity of the BBC to charges of **metropolitan bias** has produced some strange practices. In an attempt to be seen to be operating 'in the regions' BBC Television transferred departments like religious programming to centres like Manchester. When the successful Radio 4 series *The Moral Maze* was tried on television in 1994 it became a Manchester production, even though the presenter and guests had to be flown up from London by shuttle, housed in a hotel overnight and the programme made in studio space rented from Granada because none was available at BBC North (as reported in *Guardian*, 12 June 1995).

UK and Ireland as the base for Hollywood feature film production in the early 1990s generated a great deal of local business in some of the more remote parts of Wales, Scotland and especially Ireland (where government policy has been to invite production companies in directly and to offer a range of incentives) (see 'Production organisation', Chapter 6). In the late 1990s the strength of the pound raised fears that American producers would move to cheaper locations.

Work patterns and employment

Work in the media is often perceived as glamorous and highly paid. In reality, this description fits only a small percentage of the workforce. We can recognise different groups of workers:

- technical (production, transmission etc.)
- creative (writers, performers, designers etc.)
- production organisation and management
- professional services (finance, legal etc.)
- auxiliary support services (clerical, administrative, catering etc.)

Technical staff represent a problem for employers in terms of both initial training and reskilling and the associated costs. The move to new technologies has produced conflicts in all sectors. Introduction of computerised processes has in some instances led to 'deskilling' of tasks (see 'Technologies', Chapter 14). Elsewhere it has opened up new production opportunities and led to skill shortages where existing technical staff need retraining (e.g. in broadcast television). Media corporations in some sectors (film especially) have a poor record on training, expecting staff to 'work up from the bottom' or simply recruiting staff trained by somebody else (the BBC used to train the majority of broadcast technicians before deregulation). This 'short-termism' (i.e. not worrying about the future) is now being addressed, but overall it remains a problem.

Lower labour costs for technical staff led to shifting locations for media work. Much colour printing is now undertaken in the 'Pacific rim' countries, which have access to both high technology and lower wage costs (and digital material can easily be transmitted from editorial offices in Europe and North America). Hollywood productions are periodically attracted abroad because of lower staff costs. UK studios offer very highly skilled technicians, especially for big-budget productions with special effects (the *Star Wars* series is a good example). Eastern Europe has become an attractive location with basic studio facilities at very low cost.

ACTIVITY 20.5

Media industries in the local economy

Investigate your local authority (at a county or city level) and its attitude to media development.

- Does it operate a film office?
- Does it have a media policy? Or does it refer to 'cultural industries'?
- What kind of economic benefits are expected?

NVQs Like every other industry in the UK, film, video and broadcasting has been required to develop 'standards' and recognised qualifications for various job functions. These National Vocational Qualifications (SVQs in Scotland) have taken several years to develop and are still being resisted by some sectors of an industry unaccustomed to formal training.

In 1999, Fox Studios opened a new facility in Australia and announced future *Star Wars* films would be made there.

Creative personnel have usually been considered by media theorists in terms of how personal expression survives within an industrial system (see 'Producing in the studio system', Case study 7). Other issues relate to the ownership of creative ideas and the rights which ensue. Media corporations attempt to control these as much as possible through contracts. Most of the high-profile cases of disputes over rights have come from the music industry (e.g. George Michael's battle with Sony).

Production management staff are those who make sure that the project is completed and that it gets distributed. The most significant development in production management, as in the other sectors, has been the move towards freelancing or subcontracting to smaller independent production teams. The trend is perhaps most marked in film and broadcasting, with 50 per cent or more of staff in the UK freelance, but is common also in newspapers and magazines. Media corporations tend to concentrate on ownership of properties and rights rather than direct control over employment. They do of course control what freelance staff and independent production groups do through contracts and financial support. Supporters of the system maintain that the arrangement means that production groups are 'lean and mean' and highly competitive, that they are not hampered by institutional inertia. One disadvantage is that training and retraining and other initiatives which require industry-wide action become much more difficult to organise.

The professional services sector in the media industries requires a high degree of specialisation, especially in legal and financial fields, and again tends to favour location in metropolitan centres (where specialist agencies will find sufficient work to support a practice). More general support services are not so location-conscious (further discussion of employment issues can be found in 'Institutions', Chapter 26).

Technological development

'Technologies', Chapter 14, and 'Digital publishing and the Internet', Case study 15, provide both background and analysis of technological change in the media industries. Technological change affects every part of the production process and not just the 'production' stage. As an example, the development of **broadband cable** and the transmission of digital media products at high speed around the world is primarily about distribution, but there is equal interest in the exhibition of the product in the home or in the presentation theatre. The development of the 'set-top box' – the computer interface which controls the display of new services on the television set – will be the focus for a battle between the various cable, telephone and computer companies. The 'deal', especially the international deal, will perhaps be aided by video-conferencing and access to Internet sites enabling dissemination of specialist information and research material. Post-production may also benefit – digital video can be edited 'on location' and beamed back to the studio.

Conclusion

The future of the media industries sector is tied up with the application of new technologies and the collapsing of old sector boundaries. New technologies throw up new companies with only a few staff which grow very quickly and can soon become 'players' – Bill Gates and Microsoft is the classic example. Yet the Hollywood studios which were formed in the 1920s remain key to the future structure of media industries. We explore the issue of 'who owns the media' in the case study which follows.

References and further reading

Most of these references are also suitable for further reading:

Bach, Steven (1985) *Final Cut*, London: Jonathan Cape.

Balio, Tino (ed.) (1976) (rev. 1985) *The American Film Industry*, London: University of Wisconsin Press.

Balio, Tino (1998) '"A Major Presence in All of the World's Important Markets": The Globalisation of Hollywood in the 1990s', in Neale and Smith, *Contemporary Hollywood Cinema*.

Finney, Angus (1996) *The State of European Cinema*, London: Cassell.

Gomery, Douglas (1986) *The Hollywood Studio System*, London: BFI/Macmillan.

Gomery, Douglas (1992) *Shared Pleasures*, London: BFI.

Gomery, Douglas (1996) 'Toward a New Media Economics', in David Bordwell and Noel Carroll (eds) *Post-theory: Reconstructing Film Studies*, Madison and London: University of Wisconsin Press.

Harvey, Sylvia and Robins, Kevin (eds) (1993) *The Regions, the Nations and the BBC*, London: BFI.

Izod, John (1988) *Hollywood and the Box Office 1895–1986*, London: Macmillan.

Maltby, Richard (1998) '"Nobody Knows Everything": Post-classical Historiographies and Consolidated Entertainment', in Neale and Smith, *Contemporary Hollywood Cinema*.

Maltby, Richard and Craven, Ian (1995) *Hollywood Cinema*, Oxford: Blackwell.

Miller, Toby (1998) 'Hollywood and the World', in John Hill and Pamela Church Gibson (eds) *The Oxford Guide to Film Studies*, Oxford: Oxford University Press.

Neale, Steve and Smith, Murray (eds) (1998) *Contemporary Hollywood Cinema*, London: Routledge.

Pirie, David (ed.) (1981) *Anatomy of the Movies*, London: Windward.

Wasko, Janet (1994) *Hollywood in the Information Age: Beyond the Silver Screen*, London: Polity.

Williams, Granville (1996) *Britain's Media: How They Are Related*, London: Campaign For Press and Broadcasting Freedom.

Conglomerates
Libraries, brands,
    distribution and synergy
Independents and
    oligopolies
Conclusion
References and further
    reading

23 / Case study: Who owns the media?

Conglomerates

The ownership and control of media companies is an issue in Media Studies because of a belief that the nature of the product, and in particular the content of news and factual material or the ideological limits of a whole range of products, may be influenced by business considerations or the 'proprietorial' whims of chief executives. Conversely, the lack of production opportunities for smaller and non-commercial producers means a narrow range of media products are available.

Recognising the possibility of proprietorial control was relatively straightforward when newspapers were run by 'press barons' and Hollywood studios by autocratic moguls. Or at least that is the stereotypical view of these entrepreneurs (see 'Producing in the studio system', Case study 7). In 'News Corporation', Case study 24, we try to explore one specific example of individual proprietorial power.

Modern media companies are most likely to be part of a **conglomerate** – a division within a much larger company, 'organised on the principle of multiple profit centres which reinforce each other … designed not only to generate revenue and profits, but to keep such monies within the corporation' (Robert Gustafson on conglomerates (in Balio 1985 and quoted in Izod 1988)). The parent company is likely to be engaged in several different media sectors and probably related sectors such as the manufacture of technology or the provision of telecommunications. We have borne this in mind in constructing the world map of corporate media activity shown in Figure 23.1. We haven't tried to show all the

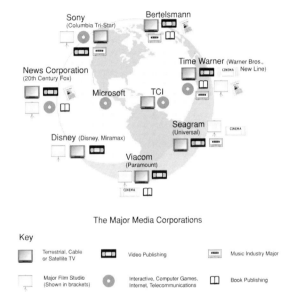

Figure 23.1 Multinational media corporations

top media corporations, nor have we tried to rank them, since it is difficult to agree criteria for ranking (or, indeed, for defining what is a 'media corporation'). The range of activities encompassed by the widest definitions of media is vast and includes some of the fastest-growing industrial sectors. It is inevitable that our representation will need updating by the time you read this, but it should still give you a good grasp of the international market. Note these features:

● The Hollywood majors are well represented, even though they are all part of larger groups.

- The major media corporations span North America, Europe and Japan.
- Microsoft and TCI (Tele-communications Inc.), companies which are not primarily media producers, are included because we believe they will have an enormous influence in the next few years, possibly merged with other companies.

Financial control

Modern media corporations are effectively owned by shareholders. The 'cross-holding' of shares of one media corporation by another is widespread (especially in Europe). The major shareholders are often 'institutional' – insurance companies or pension funds far removed from the production which generates the profit. Thousands of small shareholders are represented by 'fund managers' and have little chance to influence corporate affairs. The future of the corporation lies very much in the hands of accountants and financial advisers who look at the balance sheets rather than the product as an indicator of the health of the company.

This observation, which is relevant for all modern corporations, shouldn't be seen as 'proof' that all industrial media production is devoid of creative work or that because it is industrial it will all be the same. It does, however, suggest the kinds of influences which are present when media corporations make decisions to buy or sell subsidiary companies or to cease production (i.e. close down a newspaper title or shelve a feature film). There are a few media industry figures with a personal fortune big enough to enable them to become significant 'players' in the media market and there are a handful of executives whose reputation is such that their activity (or even their presence) can dramatically affect the financial status of a company, but even so the accountants set the 'bottom line' on most projects.

Media production takes place in what can sometimes seem a quite contradictory business environment. Financial security matters more than individual creativity, yet in the mid-1990s a financially secure company like Sony made a mess of operating two Hollywood studios,

Columbia and TriStar, while good creative management turned round a company in difficulty like Disney (a few years later Sony had bested Disney). We might argue that some management strategies are more effective in allowing the development of an environment in which creative decisions can be made. We might also note that the attitude of financial markets towards media industries is important. In the US there is a positive attitude towards investment in the media industries, especially Hollywood, despite the disasters. For good or ill, American investors are attracted by the glamour and will risk their money. Contrast this with the UK, where it has proved very difficult to persuade financial institutions to finance British films or new media generally.

Time Warner: media conglomerate

The Hollywood majors have been through many ups and downs. After they lost their exhibition chains in the 1950s, they were not large companies by American standards. In the last forty years they have been bought and sold many times – Columbia was once owned by Coca-Cola, Paramount was part of an industrial conglomerate Gulf and Western, United Artists belonged to an insurance group and MGM, in a sad tale for the one-time industry leader, was bought by a hotel chain.

Our example studio, Warner Bros, eventually fell into the hands of Kinney National Services in the 1970s. Kinney's main interests were car parks, car rentals, building and funeral services. Warner Communications, as the company came to be known, was a conglomerate offering a range of services, with film product as only a minor factor. New ventures included video games (Warner owned Atari and made big profits before the bubble burst on the arcade games market) and cable television. But it was not until the explosion of video (the ever-expanding market for filmed entertainment delivered to the home really took off in the 1980s) that the true potential of the Warners 'brand name' was properly developed. Warner Communications then merged with Time Inc., a major publisher and another early entrant to the cable market, to produce the world's then biggest media corporation, Time Warner. In 1996 Time Warner took over Turner Broadcasting, the producer of CNN. This widely reported move, which followed the Disney acquisition of the American television network ABC, signalled a new 'consolidation' of power in the media industries.

European media corporations

The list below identifies a number of UK, French, German and Italian media corporations which have sufficient turnover to count as 'major players' in European and international markets:

Bertelsmann	German music and printing giant, moving into video and television
ARD	German public service broadcaster (see 'Public service broadcasting', Case study 27)
Havas	French book and newspaper publisher and advertising company, moving into 'interactive' publishing
Fininvest	Italian television group, now making links with others across Europe. Owns Inter Milan football club. The main interest of Silvio Berlusconi – recently involved in Italian politics
BBC	UK public service broadcaster, moving into interactive publishing and subscription services
Reed Elsevier	UK/Dutch publisher which concentrates on business information
Matra-Hachette	French publisher, now part of a conglomerate including high-tech engineering
RAI	Italian public service broadcaster
Carlton	UK ITV broadcaster, film and video
Pearson	UK publishing, television, theme parks etc.
Kirch	German film and television group (a private company with a high profile proprietor – Leo Kirch)

Note that News International is not included in this list because the parent company, News Corporation, is American.

Only one of these corporations is included on our world map, and European media corporations differ from their American counterparts in the following ways:

- Public sector broadcasters have had a central role in European media. ARD, BBC and RAI up to now have been more secure within their home markets than the private-sector American broadcasters CBS, NBC, ABC and Fox (ABC and CBS were both taken over in 1995). The Japanese public sector broadcaster, NHK, is another major player, but the future for public service broadcasters is doubtful (see 'Public service broadcasting', Case study 27).

- Broadcasting and publishing are much more important for European media corporations (i.e. than 'filmed entertainment'). This is partly a matter of 'own language/culture' markets, less easily penetrated by American producers, and some of these companies have a very long history in industries like printing and publishing. National barriers are starting to come down with digital media processes.

- European corporations (especially German groups) have tended to expand within Europe rather than to look more widely for opportunities. There is a complex web of cross-ownership of shares in different European media corporations. The high start-up costs of new technologies such as satellite and the long-established practices of film and television co-productions have led to various partnerships. UK media groups, sharing a common language with the Americans and with a history of overseas investment, have been more international in outlook. Once again, this situation is changing. The Americans are looking towards new European television markets in cable and satellite and the German corporations (especially Bertelsmann) are looking to North America.

- The European Union has recognised the vital importance of 'media industries' and has developed policies and funding arrangements to assist future growth. European co-operation is seen as the only realistic response to the power of American corporations represented by trade associations like **MPAA**. Generally, Europe is thought to be 'tightly regulated'. The US government, though concerned about monopoly power at home, is generally supportive of US media corporations trading abroad.

Libraries, brands, distribution and synergy

The contemporary media business environment is in a constant state of turmoil as conglomerates buy and sell companies in an attempt to keep on board the bandwagon – a wagon which is surely rolling, but no one is sure in exactly which direction. There are extravagant claims about the business potential of new technologies and new media products, but most of these are yet to be realised. We have picked out four trends which do seem to be important and which we think you should study: libraries, brands, distribution and synergy.

Libraries

The major growth in media activity is in distribution systems or 'new media' such as satellite television or CD-ROMs. These are proliferating faster than the output of new product. Anyone who controls a library or 'back catalogue' of recognisable media products is now in a good position to exploit these resources. Hollywood film libraries, the rights to well-known popular songs, photographic archives – all these are being snapped up by the large media corporations. The computer software company Microsoft has set up a subsidiary specifically to buy important photographic images from around the world. These are catalogued and presented on CD-ROM in different collections, generating revenue as immediate product and then again as they are reproduced by their media users.

Libraries are also a form of security for the major studios in the precarious business of film distribution. DreamWorks SKG, the new studio set up by Steven Spielberg, Jeffrey Katzenberg and David Geffen, was already

beginning to have problems in 1998 because, when its new releases failed at the box office, it did not have revenue from library material coming in at a steady trickle – the lifeblood which sustains the established majors.

Brands

As the international media market grows and companies attempt to operate in several different countries, the **marketing** of new products becomes more problematic. If a company wants to build its presence in Poland, Thailand and South Africa, will it need different logos, a different company image to appeal in different cultural contexts? **Brands** are expensive to develop. The power of the international brand, instantly recognisable everywhere, goes some way to explaining the longevity of the Hollywood studios. There cannot be many parts of the world where Warner's shield, Paramount's mountain and MGM's lion are not familiar to a mass audience. (Many of MGM's famous films are now owned by Time Warner, but the lion stays on them.) The move to merchandising, utilising the studio logo to the full, is evidence of the new importance of the logo.

The UK premiere of *Batman Forever* in summer 1995 took place in Leicester, where a new Warner cinema opened this Warner picture. The launch was accompanied by Warner Radio broadcasting (on a restricted service licence) from the cinema. Music on Warner record labels, merchandise in the Warner shops, computer games, DC comics (another Time Warner company), tie-in deals with McDonald's – the potential is endless.

Conglomerates think carefully about brands and company names. When Canadian drinks company Seagram bought MCA, it changed the film operation back to 'Universal Pictures' – the traditional studio name. But when Disney bought Miramax, it kept the name alive because it was a strong 'brand' in the 'independent film' market.

Distribution

'Technologies', Chapter 14, analyses the move to digital media products, all of which (sounds, pictures and text) will move down **broadband cable**. The companies which control the cable systems will be in a powerful position. Once again, the world market is very much dominated and influenced by the major North American companies which have prospered in the largest telecommunications market. Instead of the Hollywood studios this story is about Ma Bell and the **Baby Bells.**

The American Trust Laws forced the break-up of the giant Bell telephone company in 1982. This produced A,T&T as a separate long-distance service provider and a host of regional telephone companies – the 'Baby Bell' companies. The telephone business generated large amounts of spare cash, and in the late 1980s some of the larger Baby Bells were attracted to the new British cable television franchises.

The Thatcher government, desperate to force a competitive environment in this new industry, allowed the development of the least regulated cable market in Europe. It was a perfect opportunity for the American telephone and cable companies (and their equally experienced Canadian counterparts) to move in and experiment with their spare cash. Their interest was not in making television programmes but in developing delivery systems for telecommunications, television and sound broadcasts. The result is a UK market dominated by American interests. This is an extraordinarily volatile market, and in 1998 a spate of mergers suggested that control would eventually be in the hands of three or four groups. The biggest of these is the new style Cable & Wireless Communications which has formed a company with Nynex (the New York Baby Bell). Two other major players in 1998 were Telewest (controlled by TCI and two more Baby Bells) and NTL, a group formed partly around the television transmitter network used for Channel 3 and 4, privatised after the 1990 Broadcasting Act.

These new companies are in battle with the major traditional telephone companies like British Telecom and Deutsche Telecom, who are themselves attempting to carve out a market share in television and Internet services.

Tele-Communications, Inc.

TCI
The Company

TCI in
Your Area

Questions?

For specific cable services, type in your zip code here and click "ENTER"

[ENTER]

Figure 23.2 TCI claims to be one of the world's biggest cable television operators – a relatively invisible presence for a major player

There are big corporate battles ahead in Europe, but it is the American telecommunications market which still holds the key, with the prospect of mergers between the cable companies and telephone companies on the one hand and mergers or at least close co-operation between the owners of digital networks and the 'software' providers like Microsoft and the Hollywood studios on the other.

The other noticeable feature of the television industry is the takeover of small specialist film and video equipment suppliers by larger companies with more broadly based business telecommunications or information-handling concerns. A good example is the takeover of Lightworks, a supplier of computer editing equipment for broadcasters and Hollywood, by Tektronix, a major video and networking company and a leader in distribution technology.

ACTIVITY 23.1

Cable television in the UK

Investigate the cable market in your area. Unless you live in one of the more remote parts of the country (in which case you may want to look at the telecommunications market more generally), there will have been a cable franchise offered.

● Has it been bid for?
● Has a bid been accepted?
● Who has won the franchise?

- Are they connected to the Baby Bells (or to any other supplier of telecommunications or similar services)?
- What kind of services are they offering?

You can try finding out locally or look at the Internet site: `http://www.inside-cable.co.uk`

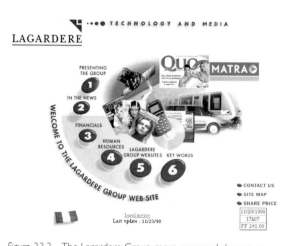

Figure 23.3   The Lagardere Group, more commonly known as Matra-Hachette, has a website emphasising the marriage of 'Media' and 'Technology'

Synergy

Synergy is media industry jargon for integration of different but complementary business interests. It implies that, by putting two companies together, the resulting conglomerate will be more valuable than its separate parts, producing new products or creating new markets. The marriage of cable television and telephone supply is one example, but the famous attempt at synergy, which so far has had very mixed results, was the takeover by the Japanese equipment manufacturers Sony and Matsushita of the Hollywood studios Columbia and TriStar (Sony) and MCA-Universal (Matsushita). It seemed like a good idea – guaranteed supply of product for the new technologies in video and computer games being developed by the Japanese parent.

But both ventures ran into trouble. The pundits have argued that it was the clash of cultures, that the Japanese managers did not understand Hollywood and made poor decisions on appointments. Both companies lost millions of dollars on a string of unsuccessful pictures and Matsushita finally got out, selling well below the buying price in 1995.

Almost as if to prove the difficulty of managing a 'software' business from a 'hardware' base, the Dutch electronics company Philips sold its controlling interest in Polygram Music and Films in 1998. This history is, however, unlikely to put off Microsoft and possibly the telecommunications companies who think they can see commercial advantages in synergy with media producers.

There are several references to **convergence** in this book, and it is noticeable that the move towards synergy can come from different directions as digital technology

brings separate industries together. We have noted that European media conglomerates often come from publishing. Hachette claims to be the world's number one magazine publisher – *Paris Match*, *Elle* and *Premiere* are titles you might recognise. It also publishes newspapers and rivals Havas as a leading book publisher. Like the German groups it has big printing presses and also a chain of newsstands – a vertically integrated empire. Through its experience with the Grolier encyclopedia group, Hachette has entered CD-ROM and interactive publishing. This, in turn, has led to its place in a larger group which includes the electronics and engineering group Matra, producer of weapons technology, racing cars etc. Matra-Hachette now has telecomms links with the Canadian company Northern Telecomm and some access to North America. Meanwhile in Europe the group is expanding into radio, television and film production.

Independents and oligopolies

'Independent' means several quite different things in the media industries, and in 'Independents and alternatives', Chapter 28, we explore the concept in some detail. Here, as a footnote to our study of the majors, we are dealing with companies which are 'independent' only in the sense that they are relatively new in the field or have consciously positioned themselves (or have been positioned) 'outside' the established **oligopolies** in their sector.

We have argued and demonstrated that media industries are dominated by a small number of large media conglomerates, operating in the context of oligopolistic competition. In practice this means that the major players in the industry work in similar ways to keep out other competitors. The Hollywood studios have maintained an effective control over the film industry for sixty years or more. There have been attempts to set up new studios (like DreamWorks SKG) and these have had varying success for limited periods, being recognised as 'independents'. They tend to last for a few years and are then often 'absorbed' into the majors. In the late 1990s a glance at *Screen International*'s box office chart for independents reveals that all the distribution companies with listed films are in fact owned by the majors – New Line (Warner Bros), Fox Searchlight, Sony Classics etc. These are brand distinctions rather than differences of ownership.

We've noted that convergence can introduce new competitors into different media sectors. This means that the Hollywood studios could be faced with a corporation of similar wealth and experience, but not specialist film industry knowledge. In 1997 Polygram Filmed Entertainment, a UK-based division of the largely Dutch-owned parent, attempted to join the majors. It set up a US distribution company and bought an existing independent, Gramercy Pictures. It had successes such as the comedy *Bean* (US/UK 1997), but struggled to make a major impact. Then in 1998 the major shareholder, Philips, sold its stake in Polygram to Seagram, which wanted the Polygram Music division. At the time of writing, Seagram has decided to keep PFE as a separate company with a European base, but its long-term future is still not secure. The point to note here is that Polygram was a music industry major but a film 'independent' (see 'Making and enjoying global music', Case study 21).

The computer industry in the 1980s saw the emergence of new companies which grew from very modest beginnings – e.g. Apple and Microsoft.

These companies created a new sector in an industry in which the traditional leader, IBM, was very slow off the mark. When the same thing happened with Netscape in the 1990s, Microsoft, now a major, retaliated swiftly (see 'Digital publishing and the Internet', Case study 15).

Convergence is under way, and new media industry sectors like satellite and cable are already seeing 'consolidation' – the gradual reduction of competitors through mergers and takeovers. The chances for independents are not good. The majors gradually squeeze out competition. They are quite capable of sharing costs and revenues where it is mutually beneficial – *Titanic* was distributed by Twentieth Century Fox and Paramount – and also exchanging subsidiaries or rights to operate in specific territories.

ACTIVITY 23.2

Industry profile

One of the major corporations is covered in detail in 'News Corporation', Case study 24. Take any of the other 'major players', American or European, and research the following:

- How did the company start and what are the significant moments in its history? (Does anything explain why it grew so big?)
- What are its main activities and how does it organise them (e.g. in separate divisions)?
- What kind of results did it achieve in the last financial year?
- What is the latest news story featuring the company?

You can often find all this information on the Internet. Otherwise newspaper archives are useful. You could try writing to the companies and asking for an annual statement, but be prepared for a long wait in some cases.

Conclusion

There is a seemingly inevitable move towards an increased domination of media activity by a group of 'major players'. Convergence and the attractions of synergy point to a future where conglomerates straddling print, music, film and broadcasting will predominate. The shift of focus from 'production' to distribution and the exploitation of archives of existing product suggests that 'delivery' companies in telecommunications and digital systems will become important partners for media conglomerates. Against this inevitability, we should also recognise that the media environment is volatile, new technologies do not automatically succeed and there is always the possibility of new companies which innovate successfully coming along.

In the next case study we consider one media corporation in more detail.

References and further reading

The business operations of the media corporations are best followed in the trade publications for each industry. *Screen International*, *Variety* and *Billboard* are particularly useful in that they cover a wide range of 'entertainment media'. For a more defined UK perspective look at *Broadcast*, *Media Week*, *UK Press Gazette* etc.

Many of these publications will operate a website – it will probably require a subscription to get at detailed information, but there will be 'free' headline news stories as well. All the corporations mentioned in the case study have websites giving useful information (sites that may be listed as French or German often have links to English versions on the index page, or you can use the rough translation services offered by some of the search engines).

Balio, Tino (1998) 'The Art Film Market in the New Hollywood', in Geoffrey Nowell-Smith and Stephen Ricci (eds) *Hollywood in Europe*, London: BFI.

Finney, Angus (1996) *The State of European Cinema*, London: Cassell.

Gomery, Douglas (1997) 'Toward a New Media Economics', in David Bordwell and Noël Carroll (eds) *Post-theory: Reconstructing Film Studies*, Madison and London: University of Wisconsin Press.

Izod, John (1988) *Hollywood and the Box Office 1895–1986*, London: Macmillan.

Murphy, Brian (1983) *The World Wired Up*, London: Comedia (for background on Baby Bells).

Pilati, Antonio (ed.) (1993) *Media Industry in Europe*, London: John Libbey.

Wasko, Janet (1994) *Hollywood in the Information Age: Beyond the Silver Screen*, Cambridge: Polity.

24 / Case study: News Corporation

No company in the world can match News Corporation in its ability to maximize its own product across multiple distribution platforms around the world.

(Chairman's statement 1997 from the News Corporation website)

This statement sums up a corporate strategy which neatly covers the two major elements of media activity recognised by all the global media conglomerates – the ownership and exploitation of 'software' or 'content' and the control of distribution channels. News Corporation is one of a handful of corporations able to produce and distribute media texts in a global environment.

In this case study we look at the way one media corporation has become the focus for a series of debates about ownership and control across the world and especially within Europe with its tradition of **public service broadcasting** (see Case study 27). The major 'player' in the British media environment is News International, which, despite the 'international' tag, represents the UK operation of News Corporation. Unusually, for such a large company, it is the undeniably charismatic founder and 'hands-on' proprietor, Rupert Murdoch, who is the focus for interest. Over the last twenty-five years Murdoch has become a demonic figure, not only in his native Australia, the UK and Europe but also to some extent in the United States, Latin America and Asia. By focusing on Murdoch and News Corporation we can look both at the *industrial* questions raised by the operations of a global media corporation and at the impact Murdoch's personal philosophy has had on media institutions.

Figure 24.1   Rupert Murdoch – 'demon' or innovator?

Rupert Murdoch

Rupert Murdoch was born in 1931 in Australia. On his return from Oxford University he inherited a stake in News Ltd, publishers of the *Adelaide News* and, in what sounds at times like the narrative of a **biopic**:

'After forty-two years of relentless struggle, in which he has run the gamut of nationality laws, regulators, politicians and bankers and even – for a brief time in 1990 – the threat of bankruptcy, [he] has all but arrived where he always wanted to be: at the top of the global media pile.'

(Alex Brummer and Victor Keegan, *Guardian*, 13 May 1995)

'I did not come all this way not to interfere' – Rupert Murdoch's words to the departing editor of the *News of the World*, Stafford Somerfield, in 1970, quoted by Bailey and Williams (1997)

In 1985 Murdoch took out American citizenship in order to meet federal requirements on ownership of American companies. In the late 1990s, as he comes to the end of his active career (handing over to his daughter?), he can look back on a turbulent period in which News Corporation has seldom been out of the media limelight:

- In the UK News International has been the subject of several campaigns by other media conglomerates attempting to prevent Murdoch getting access to a terrestrial television channel, as in the bidding for Channel 5.
- UK government and European Union policy on 'cross-media ownership' has been widely perceived to be designed to prevent News Corporation gaining a bigger share of national media markets. In 1998 Murdoch lectured European industry heads on the need for a more open market.
- Through his 40 per cent stake in BSkyB, Murdoch has been largely responsible for the recent changes in major sports in the UK including Premier League Football and Super League Rugby League. Further exclusive television deals with professionalised rugby union and cricket involved links with Australian broadcasting.
- BSkyB emerged as the frontrunner in launching digital television services in the UK from satellite, promising News Corporation a central role in the next television age.
- In the US, News Corporation used its ownership of Hollywood studio major Twentieth Century Fox to develop a fourth television network. Fox Television now rivals ABC, NBC and CBS and produces hit shows like *The X-Files*, *The Simpsons* and *NYPD Blue*.
- News Corporation is involved with various telecommunications companies in the US as part of a strategy to secure delivery systems for its film and video 'content'.
- In Asia, Murdoch has done deals with the Chinese government over news broadcasts and the expulsion of the BBC News service from Star TV, which he acquired the year before.
- In the UK, News International, as owner of Times Newspapers, waged a price war in the broadsheet press market, losing £150 million but dramatically increasing sales of *The Times* and threatening the long-term future of the *Independent*.
- Murdoch has been invited to make industry speeches in the UK and continues to be widely interviewed and profiled with attention focused on his increasing domination of UK media production.
- Tony Blair, while still opposition leader, travelled to meet News Corporation executives in Australia. Controversy surrounded this visit, but later News International titles shifted support to Labour. In 1992 the *Sun* declared that it had helped the Tories win the election. In 1997 it helped Labour. In 1998 Labour Chancellor Gordon Brown flew to Ohio to address editors of News Corporation papers.

News International

Murdoch began his collection of British media products with the purchase of the *News of the World* and the *Sun* in 1969 (ironically, the *Sun*, formerly the *Daily Herald*, had been the newspaper owned by the trade union movement). Initially, Murdoch simply copied the best-selling paper of the period, the *Daily Mirror*, and then added extra sex and sensation (see Holland 1998). Expansion came in the 1980s with the purchase of *The Times* and *Sunday Times*, and the launch of Sky Television.

In moving the newspaper offices from Fleet Street to Wapping, Murdoch successfully took on the print unions (with the help of the Thatcher government's anti-trade-union legislation). It was the long-established work practices of these unions which had previously prevented a rapid conversion to 'new technology' in newspaper production and the consequent forced redundancies of printing workers.

As part of the war against the unions, Murdoch also ensured his newspaper distribution by making a deal with TNT (in which he bought a 12 per cent share), the road transport carrier company. With his own carrier he could avoid potential problems with rail unions. (His action, copied by other newspapers, had a major impact on railfreight business, accelerating its decline.) At the other end of the process, he could ensure a good supply of 'news' and skilled journalists because of his widespread interests elsewhere.

With the purchase of *Today* (founded in the mid-1980s as the first newspaper to be produced using new technology by Eddie Shah – himself a Murdoch figure of lesser stature), Murdoch achieved a 'full house' of **tabloid**, **mid-market** and **broadsheet** daily papers as well as the best-selling tabloid and broadsheet Sunday papers. Add to this his newspaper interests in Australia, the US and elsewhere, plus his television interests in the UK and the US – not to mention the book publishing and specialist magazine titles. It is not too difficult to see that Murdoch can fill his papers with stories derived from his film studio or that he can find the talent he needs within his existing staff or pay to entice it from elsewhere.

This last point, the purchasing power in the market place, is crucial to the News International operation. The high risk factor in media production can be covered if 'cross-subsidy' is possible. One successful newspaper title can subsidise another which is losing money. In the Murdoch empire the 'milch cows' – the sources of fat profit – are the *Sun* and the *News of the World*, which make enough money to support the losses on *The Times* (and on some of Murdoch's American papers).

In return *The Times* gives News International status and greater access to AB readers. (One problem for Murdoch in the early days of Sky was that it was seen to be 'downmarket'. Listings for Sky programmes and sympathetic coverage of the output in *The Times* and *Sunday Times* helped to correct this view.) The newspapers originally helped to pay for losses on Sky TV, and once

Sky became profitable (after its merger with BSB) the returns from that could be used to subsidise other areas of operation.

In competitive markets the major battle is over the entry of new firms or new products into the market place. Economists refer to the theoretical 'perfect market' as one in which new sellers are free to enter the market and compete on equal terms with existing sellers for the attention of perfectly rational consumers. In the new market-speak this is known as 'a level playing field' scenario, but in reality, even if the field is flat and open, the biggest players can usually manipulate the rules and are always likely to win the game.

During 1994 and 1995 Murdoch used his considerable reserves to fight a price war, in both the tabloid and broadsheet markets. The object of the war was simply to destroy one of the current opposition titles and seriously to damage the others, while enhancing the market position of the Murdoch titles. The chosen broadsheet victim was the *Independent*, one of only two new daily newspapers in the last forty years. At the time of writing the *Independent* is still in business, but looking shaky.

Murdoch can afford to lose millions on *The Times* in order to lure readers away from the *Independent* and

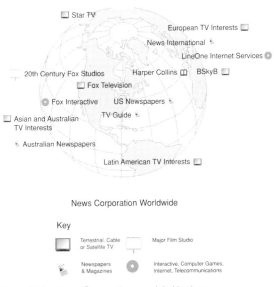

News Corporation Worldwide

Key

Terrestrial. Cable or Satellite TV

Major Film Studio

Newspapers & Magazines

Interactive. Computer Games. Internet, Telecommunications

Figure 24.2   News Corporation – a global business

the *Daily Telegraph*. The *Guardian* is relatively safe from Murdoch, not just because of the political stance of its readers, who are the least likely to defect to a right-wing paper, but also because it is supported by the revenue from other companies in the Guardian Media Group. The GMG purchase of the *Observer* in 1993, however, was a risky venture and is more vulnerable to an aggressive *Sunday Times*.

The *Independent* has been forced to lose its 'independence' in order to fight off the Murdoch attack and became part-owned by The Mirror Group and various European newspaper interests before the Irish Independent Group took control.

The other aspect of this 'entry to the market' is the possibility of access to the crucial distribution channels. Most publications which appear on the newsstands are handled at wholesale by the main distributor W. H. Smith, which also directly owns many of the newsstands. If W. H. Smith won't take a publication – and it can be very choosy if it doesn't like the content or if it has no faith in the appeal to readers – it will be impossible for the new entrant to compete with Murdoch because no one will get to see the product. The power of the distributors is evident when new types of publication do break through, gain acceptance on to the newsstands and immediately become very successful – the obvious example is *Viz* in the late 1980s and, to a lesser extent, fanzines such as *When Saturday Comes*.

Internationally, News Corporation cannot afford to stand still or one of the other major players will take market share away. In 1995, Murdoch's intervention in the future of rugby league had an enormous impact in northern England. To many diehard fans who had supported a small-town team for decades it was almost incomprehensible that their game (one of the last to be rooted in local communities) could be taken away from them in order to allow Murdoch to compete with another media corporation in Australia (led by another 'mogul' figure, Kerry Packer) and to provide coverage of a top-class sport at low cost for the new Murdoch satellite empire in Eastern Asia. Murdoch's intervention effectively barred the smaller British clubs from joining

the Premier League and severely disrupted the Australian League and the prospects for international matches. But this is just one example of how the 'national' or 'sectional' interest is swiftly superseded by that of the multinational corporation.

Murdoch the demon

Rupert Murdoch attracts a great deal of media attention and a high level of criticism. He has been called 'the most powerful man in the world' and also the most dangerous.

- To some Murdoch is 'the dirty digger' (an ironic form of stereotypical abuse in keeping with the style of the *Sun*?), to others 'the Citizen Kane of the global village' (*Guardian*, 13 May 1995) or the 'prince of darkness' (*New Statesman and Society*, 10 September 1993).
- The celebrated television writer Dennis Potter was a vitriolic opponent of all the changes in UK broadcasting during the Thatcher era and he named the final cancer which led to his death in 1994 'Rupert'.
- In 1997 Murdoch was the most likely basis for a new 'Bond villain', played by Jonathan Pryce in *Tomorrow Never Dies* (US/UK 1997) – a media mogul who attempts to provoke a war in order to promote his satellite news programme.
- Murdoch is one of the few media industry leaders to have a 'public face'. His squabble with the only other media figure in a similar position, Ted Turner, founder of CNN, was news for several months in 1996.

He is the demon of British media producers and consumers alike. There is evidence to suggest that he has had a considerable effect upon the media environment, but to blame him for everything is a crude response to a complex situation. News Corporation is a major player in the international media market and acts accordingly.

'Industries', Chapter 22, demonstrates that large media corporations are just like large businesses in other fields. They cannot survive as the playthings of rich 'barons'. Instead, they will be constantly looking for better ways to increase their wealth-earning potential. Sometimes this will mean buying new companies or even running businesses at a loss in order to win market share. Sometimes it will mean selling businesses in order to raise cash or to move to more profitable markets. Murdoch is skilled in these operations. Despite its seeming strength, News Corporation has more than once become 'over-extended' – carrying more debt than its assets justified – causing new acquisitions to be sold or proposed deals to lapse. Unlike the cautious corporate strategy adopted by some other media giants, Murdoch could be seen to take bigger risks. The establishment of Fox Television and the profitability of BSkyB are undoubted achievements in the face of doubters. This puts a burden on Murdoch's leadership and position (which at the time of writing is threatened by a divorce action, with severe financial implications).

One of Murdoch's strengths in maintaining the position of News Corporation in the market place is a conviction about where the industry is going and a resolution to act on that conviction. His success in predicting the future is chilling for critics concerned about his expanding empire. Here is his view of the future, expanding on the statement at the beginning of this case study:

'we cannot just confine ourselves to being newspaper publishers, or just to television, or terrestrial television, or to pay-television or whatever it is. We are a software company, we believe that what is important and what will always have value are databases, knowledge and books, a copyright if you will – whether it be copyright film, books or news. We have to make sure that we have access to all the different delivery systems that are emerging …'

(from a BBC2 *Money Programme* interview, reported in *Guardian* 22 May 1995)

The borderless world opened up to us by the digital information age will afford huge challenges and limitless opportunities in the years ahead. It will continue to be a period of turmoil in terms of changes in technology and challenges posed by regulatory authorities around the world. The winners will be those who capitalize quickly on changing

opportunities. The challenge is to move early and innovate often. This is not always a comfortable path, but it is the only one which will lead News Corporation to success in the global market of the 21st century.

(from News Corporation, Chairman's statement 1997)

It is worth noting that, despite the criticism of Murdoch as a media mogul and the overall charge that News Corporation has 'lowered standards', the *Sunday Times* and the *Sun* are skilfully produced newspapers which lead their respective markets as much because of professional expertise as sensational stories or low price. In a famous defence of his staff, the then editor of the *Sun*, Kelvin Mackenzie, once claimed that although his staff were quite capable of producing the *Guardian*, he didn't think it was true the other way round. *Guardian* staff were not quick to refute his claim.

What is at stake here (and in similar debates about television and radio) are concepts of 'quality', 'integrity', 'diversity' and 'choice'. These are complicated, ideologically loaded ideas, which you should consider in relation to 'Ideologies and discourses' (Chapter 12), 'Industries' (Chapter 22) and 'Institutions' (Chapter 26). Let's consider them here in relation to the charges made against Murdoch.

Quality and integrity

Broadsheet newspapers in the UK, at least at national or regional level, are referred to as the 'quality press'. The debate over the future of the BBC and the regulatory climate for independent television revolves around ideas about 'quality television' (see 'Institutions', Chapter 26 for definitions of tabloid, quality press etc.). In a wider context, most UK organisations (including your college) have issued 'quality statements' in the last few years. There are two, possibly opposing, ideas about quality in broadcasting (see also Brunsdon 1990):

- The quality document, now found in most organisations, refers to some form of accounting or auditing procedure which looks for evidence that services are meeting pre-ordained targets. To a certain extent this meaning carries over to broadcasting, where 'requirements' are set for the UK public service broadcasters, BBC and Channel 4.

- 'Quality' television is a much more vague term. All other broadcasters in the UK (i.e. the non-PSB providers) are only lightly regulated. Their programming must cross the 'quality threshold', but it is not clear what criteria the ITC uses in evaluating this. For the viewer, 'quality' might refer to high production values or 'prestigious' programmes like costume drama.

On the newspaper front 'quality' refers not only to the writing style found in the broadsheets but also to the integrity with which journalists pursue stories and present findings.

The charge against Murdoch is that he has undermined the quality ideal in the UK national press and that he threatens to do so with terrestrial television as well. Dropping the price and introducing upmarket bingo in *The Times*, sensational stories in the *Sunday Times* (e.g. the Hitler diaries fiasco, when large sums were paid for documents which turned out to be fakes) as well as the wholesale corruption of the tabloid market (in the mid-1960s the *Daily Mirror* was widely seen as a 'quality' tabloid) have all contributed to this view. The battle over the move to Wapping was fought out with journalists as well as printing workers. Many distinguished journalists left News International titles, which were in turn boycotted by readers (e.g. the *Times Educational Supplement*, which also lost advertising to the *Guardian*).

Murdoch's defence against these charges is that without his intervention the quality press would have succumbed to television. It was hidebound by tradition, poorly designed, expensively produced and losing readers. The Murdoch 'victory' over the print unions benefited all the papers in that they too could move out of Fleet Street into greenfield sites with new technologies. The shake-up in the market made possible the launch of the first new quality broadsheet daily of the twentieth century in the *Independent*, and prompted major re-designs of the *Guardian* and the *Daily Telegraph*,

as well as *The Times*. The broadsheets went on to introduce colour, Saturday supplements and two-part daily papers. They did lose some readers, but not significantly large numbers.

The new sections of the 'qualities' do not necessarily contain high-quality journalism, and the charge that quality newspapers have become more interested in traditionally tabloid material may have some foundation.

For a more objective view of the quality press it is worth making a comparison with other national markets. The UK is unique in the number and range of *national* newspapers available to readers across the country. In the US, for instance, the only national newspapers in a British sense are the tabloid *USA Today* and the gossip sheet *The National Enquirer*. The qualities like the *New York Times* and the *Washington Post* are city newspapers which because they emanate from the financial and political capitals of the country have some form of national circulation. Newspapers of all types are declining in the US and in most cities there is no competition for readers. In only thirty-six cities can you find more than one newspaper available.

'It is no coincidence that the great American broadsheets all look as if they were laid out in the fifties; no impudent challenger like the *Independent* has ever forced them into a facelift.'

(Ian Katz, *Guardian*, July 1995)

US newspapers have proportionately fewer readers than in the UK and the qualities are more ghettoised. Their dull style would not attract the broader range of readers expected by UK qualities.

Sky News and Sky Sports have been innovative television channels in the last few years. Sky News provides a rolling news service from a UK base (i.e. in competition with CNN) and carries a full range of news stories. Sky Sports has expanded to three channels and has certainly introduced new ideas into coverage of traditional sports like football and cricket. Even if these are not available to large numbers of viewers, the innovations they bring are diffused through influences on BBC and ITV coverage. (Sky Sports viewers found the 1998 World Cup coverage by French television to be very 'old-fashioned'.)

Murdoch's main concern has been to bulldoze the 'level playing field' which enables News Corporation to operate unilaterally. After the merger with competitor BSB (in which Sky was the dominant party), Murdoch holds only 40 per cent of the new company. This still makes him a powerful influence in the company, but we should remember that there are other corporations with a stake in BSkyB as well, including Pearson and Granada.

Diversity and choice

The major claim of the free market supporters is that deregulation allows competition which in turn will lead to greater diversity of material available in response to consumer demand. In the debates in the late 1980s which resulted in the lessening of regulations in radio and television in the UK and elsewhere, Murdoch was a vociferous supporter of 'consumer-led' television programming.

Since News International began to stir up the UK media market in the 1980s, there has been an undoubted increase in the number of media products and distribution systems available. Besides the *Independent*, there have been several failed national newspaper launches such as *News on Sunday*, *The Sunday Correspondent* and *The Post*. (*Today*'s closure was a strategic decision by News International – not a direct failure in the marketplace.) Murdoch's price war has damaged other titles – the *Daily Express* and *Sunday Express* have managed to survive despite predictions of their demise, although it is noticeable that they are now part of the United News and Media Group and supported to some extent by other media interests.

The 'red-top' tabloid market, still dominated by the *Sun*, is shrinking while the broadsheet market remains reasonably healthy. The UK tradition will probably help to maintain a selection of titles longer than in most other countries, but Murdoch himself has little faith in the future of newspapers in the face of television and electronic media generally.

The big growth has been in cable and satellite television. Although only a minority of viewers has chosen to access the new channels, there has been enough of a take-up to register on the television ratings: BSkyB is at the forefront of digital television

> In June 1998 the total share of the viewing audience claimed by all the non-terrestrial channels (i.e. not BBC1 and 2, ITV, Channel 4 or 5) was between 12 and 13 per cent. This now exceeds Channel 4 and threatens BBC2 and represents significant progress over the previous three years. In homes with satellite or cable, the audience share for non-terrestrial channels was 35 per cent (and, according to News Corporation's Annual Statement, has exceeded 50 per cent on occasions).
>
> (*Broadcast*, 26 June 1998)

developments in the UK and has formed a partnership with Matsushita (Panasonic and JVC), BT and Midland Bank to create BIB (British Interactive Broadcasting), which is scheduled to launch the first services via satellite. BSkyB will also be carried on the two other delivery systems, digital terrestrial and digital cable, broadening the possible audience for Sky channels.

But do more channels mean more diversity and more choice? The standard cable package with an extra subscription to take the full range of BSkyB and other encrypted channels offers viewers over thirty new channels including films, news, children's television, sport, lifestyle, shopping, cult, adult etc.

ACTIVITY 24.1

Programming diversity

Get hold of a satellite listings magazine (the newspapers and the normal television listings guides don't give that much information) and check the range of programmes available on satellite and cable.

- What is 'new' or 'extra' – not available on the five terrestrial channels?
- What is missing in these channels which you would find on the terrestrial channels?
- What do you think of the choice on offer? Is there now greater diversity or simply 'more of the same'?

Oligopoly power

The central charge against Murdoch is that too much of the UK media market is dominated by News International activities and that this domination will adversely affect other media producers. Despite the **convergence** of media industries, there are few figures available which accurately reflect the strength of News International and News Corporation across all the sectors of the UK media map. However, we can list some indications of market share in different sectors:

- *National newspapers.* News International has the best-selling daily and Sunday tabloids plus important broadsheets, giving a market share of 26 per cent of daily and 33 per cent of Sunday readership (NRS 1998).
- *Television.* BSkyB has approximately 4 per cent of all television viewers. In addition, terrestrial channels carry Fox TV programmes such as *The X-Files* and *NYPD Blue.*
- *Cinema.* Twentieth Century Fox had 20.5 per cent of the UK film distribution market in 1997 (*Screen International*).
- *Video.* Fox Guild had 14 per cent of the video rental market and 6.2 per cent of video retail in 1996 (BVA/CIN, *BFI Handbook* 1998).
- News Corporation also has a share of the UK book publishing market through Harper Collins, of the specialist education press with *The Times Educational Supplement*, *Times Higher Education Supplement* and *Times Literary Supplement*, and of Internet services through LineOne.

Diversity and choice are subjective matters (which is why you should try the activity above and not rely on what commentators tell you). What is clear, though, is that the new channels have not offered much so far in the way of new UK-made programmes, unless they are relatively low-budget productions. Much of the new series programming on Sky1 or other channels owned by Disney, Paramount etc. is imported North American or Australian material. Here is where 'quality' meets 'choice'. The imported programmes belong to similar genres and tend to represent 'more' rather than 'different'. It is worth noting that the amount of American 'series' material shown on ITV and BBC1 has fallen in the 1990s. While occasional series like *The X-Files* may be popular, UK drama series like *Ballykissangel* and *Heartbeat* are the genuine ratings winners. Sky may use *The Simpsons* as a 'come on' to entice new subscribers, but many of the other series are 'fillers'.

Murdoch's critics are going to have a case as long as BSkyB fails to fund new 'quality' programmes, i.e. drama series or documentaries to complement sports coverage. More seriously, BSkyB is in danger of contravening the quota requirements for European origin programming set down by the European Union. This partly explains Murdoch's aggression towards the EU. BSkyB argues that its sports coverage is 'programming of European origin'. Note that the argument here is about direct News Corporation support for European production. BSkyB offers a package of channels from other providers such as Discovery with its documentary series made by European and American production companies.

The major concern which underpins the cross-media ownership debate is that News Corporation could buy an existing broadcaster or acquire a new terrestrial franchise and build up television interests to match those in the national press. There is now in place a complex web of rules to prevent any group gaining such control directly. However, there are several other features of media ownership in the UK which the concentration on Murdoch tends to obscure:

- The merger of any two from several other UK media groups could produce a market share greater than that of News Corporation companies in particular sectors (e.g. there has been some discussion about the three major ITV groups eventually becoming a single organisation).
- Although the major players in the UK market are openly competitive they also have stakes in each other's businesses (e.g. BSkyB and Granada are joint owners of Granada's satellite channels).
- Other large global corporations are gaining a strong position in UK media markets (e.g. Time Warner in cinemas, TCI in cable, various groups in publishing etc.).

Actual market share figures are perhaps not what the argument is about (although they are important in terms of legally enforceable monopoly rulings). More important, perhaps, is the perception that Rupert Murdoch is deliberately attempting to raise a particular profile for News Corporation in a media environment which he has described in particularly disparaging terms. A sworn enemy of any form of regulation, he relishes a challenge to the established ideas about the UK media. A good example of this was the alacrity with which Murdoch was able to respond to BBC attempts to argue the value of the services it provides for the cost of the licence fee. Murdoch was able to claim that BSkyB offered 'better value for money' for the package of channels on its Astra satellite. Despite its small UK market share, BSkyB is discussed as a 'major broadcaster' (by the *BFI Handbook*, for instance). This perception is crucial. If viewers can be persuaded that they have a simple choice between the cost of the BBC service and the cost of BSkyB, Murdoch will have swept away the importance of the residual idea of public service and replaced it with a straight commercial transaction.

Conclusion

Because of its cross-media interests, News Corporation, through News International, is the biggest local player in the UK, but not the biggest global player (News Corporation has an annual turnover approximately half that of Time Warner). The UK marketplace is becoming deregulated and the strength of public service media is declining (see 'Public service broadcasting', Case study 27). An open market will mean domination by the shrinking number of powerful oligopolists. The entry of small independents into the marketplace will become more and more difficult, unless they are sponsored by a major. In Chapter 28 we consider the role of the independents.

References and further reading

Bailey, Sally and Williams, Granville (1997) 'Journalists' Memoirs in the UK 1945–95', in Michael Bromley and Tom O'Malley (eds) *A Journalism Reader*, London: Routledge.

Brunsdon, Charlotte (1990) 'The Problem of Quality', *Screen*, vol. 31, no. 1 (spring).

Curran, James and Seaton, Jean (1997, 5th edition) *Power Without Responsibility*, London: Routledge.

Holland, Patricia (1998) 'The Politics of the Smile: Soft News and the Sexualization of the Popular Press', in Cynthia Carter, Gill Branston and Stuart Allan (eds) *News, Gender and Power*, London: Routledge.

Williams, Granville (1996) *Britain's Media: How They Are Related*, London: Campaign for Press and Broadcasting Freedom.

Most publications in this area date very quickly. The only way to keep abreast of changes in ownership is via the news and financial pages of the quality papers and trade journals such as *Broadcast*.

The News Corporation website is very detailed and a useful source for research.

25 / Case study: Making stars

In this case study we look at the use of stars within the Hollywood studio period and at the way stardom has developed as an institution in contemporary media.

Richard Dyer (1979 and 1998), coming out of sociology, was interested in the role of stardom in society generally. Breaking with earlier writing, which often celebrated stars as 'magic', he emphasised stars as:

- economic factors in the Hollywood studio system (and in other studio systems such as Bombay cinema)
- constructed phenomena, rather than 'gifted' or 'authentic' or 'magical' individuals. This construction of image, or **persona** (originally meaning the mask which players in Roman dramas wore) is significant because it may help to account for the popularity, and therefore economic power, of stars. Their images were constructed largely, but not exclusively, by the studios.

This then leads to exploration of why certain stars should be popular at certain times, and to questions of **ideologies**, **dominant discourses** and representation.

Stars and the studio system

Although 'stars' as such were a feature of nineteenth-century theatre and music hall, it was not until the popularity of cinema was extended and supported by 'secondary' media, such as radio and illustrated magazines in the 1920s, that the star system was fully formed.

In the early years of cinema, actors' names were not featured in publicity. It was the subject matter or the visual spectacle which was promoted – one argument

has been that the producers didn't want to name actors because it might lead them to demand higher fees. It was not until around 1910 that information about the players appeared in trade journals and 'lobby cards' appeared in cinemas. (Cards featuring photographs of the stars were distributed with films and were displayed in the lobby – the foyer in British cinemas – in special holders before and during a run.)

Producers who did name 'featured players' were rewarded with increased rentals of their films – a sure sign that audiences were interested in selecting films to watch on the basis of favourite players. Once this precedent was set, it spread quickly and during the period 1915–20, as films lengthened and became more expensive to produce, the importance of stars was widely recognised. One of the first companies to recognise this called itself 'Famous Players' and went on to form the basis for Paramount – the first of the Hollywood majors. Very quickly it became apparent that this was something more significant as a phenomenon than the fame of 'live' stage performers. A clear indication of this was the formation in 1919 of United Artists, a company founded by three actor 'stars', Charles Chaplin, Mary Pickford and Douglas Fairbanks and a 'star director', D. W. Griffith. One of the executives at another studio referred to this as 'the lunatics taking over the asylum' and for the next thirty years the studios would battle to keep control over their contracted stars.

When the studio system ended in the 1950s, the stars emerged in a stronger position and many were able to become producers or directors and to negotiate a privileged status (and a similarly privileged salary). Clint

CASE STUDY: MAKING STARS

Eastwood is a good example of a star who has made a successful transition to producer/director, but others like Kevin Costner have had problems. 'You're only as good as your last picture' is a well-known saying in contemporary Hollywood. In the studio system, another star vehicle would be along very quickly to help recover from a flop, but when you have to raise the money yourself it gets more difficult.

The 'system' explained

The star was an integral part of the **unit production system** (See 'Producing in the studio system', Case study 7). Each studio had a contracted 'roster' of stars, chosen and then groomed to fit the genres and styles of that studio. When first contracted (perhaps from the stage), most young actors would serve an apprenticeship in B features (where they might be leads) or lower billing in A features. The system operated quite rigidly, and weekly salary and the position of a name on the billing (i.e. the 'credits') of a film would be clearly related and renegotiated as status was increased.

Bette Davis was contracted to Warner Bros, which was notorious for its treatment of stars. Davis fought hard to gain control over her own image, attempting to have the services of her favourite lighting cameramen built into her contract as well as fighting for stronger roles. She was able to wring concessions out of Jack Warner, which brought her the serious and challenging roles she sought in order to complement the routine vehicles she was required to take. By 1942, after ten years and forty-two features, but also two Best Actress Oscars, Davis was an icon for women in the industry as well as in the audience. She was a major female star in a predominantly male system who had managed somehow 'to reshape her screen image into a star persona that was as powerful and provocative – and

distinctly feminine – as any in the industry' (see Schatz 1989, pp. 218–20).

If Bette Davis was associated with her roles and her strength in presenting herself as an actress, **Rita Hayworth** was a star on the basis of her glamour and her talent – as well as acting in a range of genres, she could sing and dance exceptionally well. Contracted to the 'mini-major' Columbia, Hayworth was that studio's biggest single asset, proving a major box-office draw. But while her films were popular, Hayworth's star image was also built on a high-profile social life and her five marriages, most famously to Orson Welles (1943–8) and the super rich playboy of the period, Aly Khan (1948–52).

Figure 25.1 Rita Hayworth, like many other stars during the Second World War, helped to support the war effort. Hollywood knew that stars must be kept in the public eye, and this US government promotional photograph enhanced Hayworth's reputation into the bargain.

Contracts usually lasted seven years and were written in the studios' favour, a major source of concern to the successful stars. The legal battles of stars like Bette Davis to gain freedom from her contract at Warners were an important feature of the arguments which led to the decline of the system. (You might want to link this to modern football stars contracted to clubs and arguing about 'constraints of trade'.)

In respect of the importance of stars to the economics of cinema, Dyer suggests four ways in which stars could be seen as important economic factors in the studio system:

- Stars were *capital*, just like plant and equipment, to be exploited. The major studios could preserve their position of dominance in the industry by gaining control over the production of stars and keeping control of those already formed. MGM claimed to have 'more stars than there are in the heavens' – and by default everyone else had fewer.

    > Your studio could trade you around like ball players. I was traded once to Universal for the use of their back lot for three weeks.
    >
    > (Jimmy Stewart quoted in Bordwell, Staiger and Thompson 1985)

- Stars were an *investment*, a security against potential loss. 'Added value' comes in here – a studio which had a cheap story (perhaps a remake) could add stars and offer it for sale as something more special.

- Stars were an *accounting outlay*, an important part of the budget. The hierarchy of stardom enabled the studios to devise ways of costing actors' time and to control payments. It was a way of negating the power of acting unions and of costing elements of the production process which would otherwise be nebulous (i.e. 'talent', 'expertise' etc.).

- Stars represented a way of organising *the market*. The star name offers an alternative to genre recognition as the basis for presenting a film to the public e.g. John Wayne in …, and a readily identifiable image. In the most extreme cases this could be an 'iconised' image where only a part of the star's photographic image was necessary to summon up the whole – the silhouette of Chaplin as tramp, Marilyn Monroe with skirts billowing over an air vent, Groucho Marx as a pair of spectacles and a cigar.

The star system could be an organising principle for **marketing**, even when a film had no stars. Today you wouldn't see a poster advertising 'a film about ordinary people featuring nobody you have ever heard of', but you may be attracted to a film offering 'a cast of fresh young talent, burning to be tomorrow's stars' or 'destined to become the next Tom Cruise, we present …' The 'narrative of stardom' was part of the system and used as the basis for **biopics** and musicals especially as well as in the numerous magazines. The classic narrative is laid out in *A Star Is Born*, which features a star couple – one on the way up, the other on the way down. Made first in the 1930s, again in 1954 with James Mason and Judy Garland, the 1976 version made the characters into rock stars played by Barbra Streisand and Kris Kristofferson.

Since stars functioned economically, as commodities, for the studios, the star performance needed to be recognisable and saleable (sometimes via tie-in products such as costumes, make-up, hair styles; see 'Advertising and marketing', Chapter 30). Stacey (1994) interviewed a sample of British female cinema fans who spoke not only of their enthusiasm for particular 1940s and 1950s female stars as identification figures but of the pleasures of trying to copy the dress, hairstyles, make-up they wore in films. In wartime Britain, for example, the sight of abundant materials and beautifully made costumes might certainly be argued as one of the Utopian pleasures of Hollywood, as well as the Utopian 'community' pleasures of going to comfortable cinemas with others.

In the modern era of digital production, when it is possible to use a computer to 'create' a realistic image of a recognisable star, it is worth noting that 'economically, stardom is a patent on a unique set of human characteristics … [which] include purely physical aspects' (Wyatt 1994).

What is a star?

So far we have taken for granted that we share some understanding of what 'a star' was in the studio system (and still is to a large extent today). But it is not as obvious as it seems. Dyer argues that 'stars' are different to their images or personae, which deserve to be considered separately.

> 'Everyone wanted to be Cary Grant. Even I wanted to be Cary Grant.'
>
> (Cary Grant, born Archibald Leach)

Dyer suggests that there were four elements which contributed to the star persona:

- *Promotion*: what the studio let be known about a star, especially in the period when he or she was being 'groomed' for possible stardom. (One problem with Dyer's account is that this is often called 'publicity' both by the studios and by other histories.)
- *Publicity* or public material about the star which was often, though not always, outside studio control, such as newspaper speculation.
- *Films*: including the 'star vehicle', specially built around the star image, involving roles, for example, which allowed Katherine Hepburn's lips to tremble, or Garland to do a wistful solo number.
- *Criticism and commentary*: including that written after the death of the star. In the case of Marilyn Monroe or James Dean, this already exceeds what was written about them during their lives. (It also helps to feed the reputations of modern stars marketed as being 'the second James Dean' and so on.)

John Ellis offers another interesting definition: 'a star is … a performer in a particular medium whose figure enters into subsidiary forms of circulation, and then feeds back into future performances' (Ellis 1982, p. 91). This relates to 'subsidiary circulation' in newspapers and magazines in the studio era, and to television appearances and tabloid publicity today.

The present/absent effect of the star

Ellis, drawing partly on psychoanalytic theory, argues that, during the studio period, cinema offered an image which depended on being at once both 'present' and 'absent' – offering fulfilment and then denying it. The film we see is obviously a recording of events – we are far removed from the actuality displayed on the screen. Yet the technology of cinema strives to make us feel 'present'. We sit in the dark knowing that what we see on the screen is a recording, but we enjoy becoming wrapped up in the 'now' of the events. This effect (which Ellis (1982) argues is much less strong with broadcast television which presents itself as 'live') works with stars in two interconnected ways:

- The **secondary image** of the star in a magazine was both 'present' and 'absent'. Only part of the full image was available in the posed photograph or the voice on the radio (i.e. in the studio era before television), and this acted as an invitation to seek the full **star-image** in the cinema. Ellis defines the magazine image as incomplete, requiring a visit to the cinema to gain completeness.
- The major stars all straddled the divide between 'ordinary' and 'extraordinary'. They had to be at once unattainable and god-like on the screen and yet believable as the boy or girl next door, if audiences were to engage in the dream that perhaps they could meet or even *be* a James Dean or an Elizabeth Taylor. The tension between the screen image and the secondary image in circulation must be there to perpetuate interest in the star – it is the delicious sense of striving for the unattainable which propelled audiences into the cinema.

Stars in circulation

If we take this more sophisticated idea of a star-image on board, it suggests that there was much more to 'stardom' in the studio system than simply the physical qualities of the actor, and we need to consider the role of stars not only in the production and consumption of film texts but also in 'secondary circulation'. We should look at ideas about performance (which includes acting) and the perceived relationship between the actors themselves, their star-images and the roles they played.

There is a real debate around whether the studio stars could act. They were at the height of one branch of the acting profession, and yet it is often argued, usually of the biggest stars like Wayne or Monroe, that the bigger the star the worse the acting. Do you think this is true? Might it be a way of devaluing popular cultural forms such as Hollywood? Or indeed of downplaying key qualities for cinema such as physical presence or beauty (an area of huge contemporary debate, especially in terms of dominant discourses around ethnicity). It is certainly true that some very competent actors, beautiful by conventional standards, have never become stars.

Another way to approach this is to think of the skill with which star-image can be used in a film. In the famous Western *The Searchers* (US 1956) much of the power of the film derives from the performance of the 'heroic' John Wayne in the role of the embittered and racist Ethan Edwards. Similarly, Henry Fonda, well known as the portrayer of liberal heroes, is shocking as the cold killer in *Once Upon a Time in the West* (US/Italy 1968), in which his famously warm eyes were transformed by startling blue contact lenses.

Dyer puts less emphasis on performance than on the ways that stars always have a systematic relationship to dominant discourses or ideologies. For example Monroe's star-image, of the 'innocently sexy dumb blonde' formed a focus for audiences in the 1950s partly because of the way it related to an emerging feminist emphasis on women's capacity for sexual, as well as other kinds of independence and assertiveness. In such a context Monroe may have functioned as a kind of reassurance to men. (It is said that she never, in films or quoted statements, expressed desire for anyone, but seemed to be innocently the object of others' desire.)

Sometimes, the star-image was so important to the studio that it required suppression of any aspects of the star's 'real life' which might damage the constructed image. The most notorious examples of this concerned gay actors like Rock Hudson, who had to appear as 'sexually available' to female audiences. Sometimes the star-image crossed over into real life:

> Rita Hayworth once turned to her best friend, the screenwriter Virginia Van Upp, when one of her marriages was breaking up and said, 'It's your fault!' 'Why?' 'Because you wrote *Gilda*. And every man I've known has fallen in love with Gilda and wakened with me.'

The studio system demanded stars as part of the production system and although many stars received considerable reward for their work, they were on the whole treated like commodities. Modern stars face at least the potential for more control over their lives, both professionally and in private. So what has changed?

Stars in contemporary media

The end of the studio system didn't see the end of stars, but it did see a change in the way they were used. Three factors became important in the 1950s:

- 'Big' films were now promoted much more as single commodities, not as a continuous flow of studio product.
- Stars were breaking free from long contracts – they could select work more widely *but* they were not guaranteed work on the next 'studio picture'.
- The rise of television and later 'pop' or 'rock' music established competition for cinema as the premier 'star-making' industry.

As a result, we can see a number of consequences for the place of stars within the media industries.

- The 'star-machinery' is now controlled by agents and managers, rather than by studios. Does this give the star more freedom? Or are they still commodities?
- Stars probably make fewer films (or records or television shows) than they would have done under the studio system.
- There are perhaps more minor stars and fewer major stars – and 'making a star' is perhaps more difficult in the kind of media market which now operates.

Whether or not modern stars have such powerful star-images as those of the studio era is doubtful. You can

Figure 25.2   Jodie Foster, the scientist hero of *Contact* (US 1997)

How would you relate these to the writing around Hollywood stars of the studio era?

ACTIVITY 25.1

A modern star-image

How would you go about discussing the star-image of contemporary Hollywood stars? Two of the most important are John Travolta and Jodie Foster.

- Can you describe the star-image of these two stars? What kind of man or woman is suggested by 'Travolta' and 'Foster'? The composite star-image will be made up of ideas drawn from the parts they have played, aspects of the actors' 'real lives' and the kinds of narratives which are constructed around them in the media.

do your own research by looking at the photo-books and posters available in your local shop or library. There are still an enormous number devoted to long-gone stars such as James Dean and Marilyn Monroe, to name the most obvious.

As cinema (or, more correctly, *film*) audiences increased in the 1980s, movie stars seemed to regain some eminence, but Ellis's present/absent tension does not seem as powerful. Modern stars make fewer films but more 'secondary' appearances, especially on television, where the 'complete image' has less resonance. Does the appearance of Demi Moore in just one or two films each year make each appearance more or less powerful if she is also seen on television talk shows in between? 'Live' appearances now tend to be more powerful, e.g. the attraction of Hollywood stars like Nicole Kidman on the West End stage – is this because television is such a mundane medium?

Ellis was writing in the early 1980s, at a time of declining cinema audiences, when it was often argued that the new 'stars' were to be found in pop or rock music rather than cinema. Recently critics have noted that the music industry has not successfully produced a new major star since Madonna or Michael Jackson. Might this be because it has been too preoccupied re-releasing old material, and younger audiences are attracted to styles like dance music which don't produce stars in a traditional way? What of sports stars or supermodels?

Figure 25.3   Jodie Foster, glamorous Hollywood star

- More specifically, what do you think would be the main difference between the star-image of John Travolta as a young man in *Saturday Night Fever* and *Grease* and that after his 'return' in *Pulp Fiction*?
- How important do you think are the roles that Jodie Foster had as a 'child star'?
- How do you think Foster's star-image compares with that of Bette Davis in the studio era?
- Check out the fan sites for these stars on the Internet. Jodie Foster has around twice as many mentions as John Travolta – why do you think this might be?

Stars and global appeal

You're not a star until they can spell your name in Karachi.

(Humphrey Bogart quoted by Paul Kerr in Pirie 1981)

The power of movie stars is tied to the worldwide marketing and distribution power of the Hollywood studios. Up until the recent spread of satellite television, cinema was perhaps the only truly international medium. American television series are also seen across the world, but the 'secondary circulation' of television stars is not co-ordinated (series may be five, ten or even twenty years old before they reach some markets) except on rare occasions like the high point of *Dallas* transmissions.

Because stars are commercial assets, the film industry wants to know who is 'hot' at any particular time. In the past, this was often done by asking cinema managers and other industry professionals to rank stars on the basis of their ability to attract audiences. This tended to favour established stars who could ride poor results on individual films. In 1996 *Screen International* adopted a new strategy and ranked stars according to the box office returns on the last three films on which their name was 'on the marquee'.

In the 'international' (i.e. non-North-American) market, number one in 1997 was Will Smith with *Bad Boys*, *Independence Day* and *Men in Black* giving an average of $220 million per film. The next four slots were filled by Tom Hanks, Tom Cruise, Brad Pitt and Pierce Brosnan. This method can produce rankings distorted by a single film's takings (so Whitney Houston still ranks on the back of the monster success of *The Bodyguard* in 1992). Nevertheless, the dispassionate box office placed three African-Americans in the top ten (Morgan Freeman is tenth), which didn't happen with the voting method. The top fifty include twelve women, but only Glenn Close and Jodie Foster appear in the top twenty with Whitney Houston.

The current academic interest in the box office might help to prevent future historians being misled as to the popularity of stars. During the 1940s, the annual top ten of box office stars, as selected by cinema owners, was dominated by Bing Crosby and included comedians like Abbott and Costello and 'singing cowboys' like Roy Rogers and Gene Autry. The studio histories, by contrast, tend to concentrate on the stars of the classic films like Humphrey Bogart.

(Rankings in Steinberg 1981)

Action stars are privileged because their star-image loses least when their voices are dubbed into another language. (Non-American action stars benefit as well, e.g. Bruce Lee in the 1970s, Jean-Claude Van Damme recently.) Pop and rock musicians are equally privileged because 'the song remains the same' in different territories. Also, the relatively greater success of black performers in music has encouraged the spread of the star phenomenon in parts of the world where cinema and television are less important. The whole question of the impact of modern black Hollywood stars in the international market has yet to be properly researched. Bogle (1992) provides both a fascinating account of the struggles of black stars in the studio system and a coda on current cinema – but only from an American perspective.

ACTIVITY 25.2

Sports stars

It could be argued that the most universal media activity is that which shows pure action – the coverage of sports on television for instance. Take four sports: football, tennis, boxing and athletics.

- Which of these is most likely to produce a universal star – someone recognised all over the world?
- You should think carefully about the popularity of different sports in different countries and with different target audiences.
- Has there been, or could there be, a sports star with as much appeal as the stars of the studio system?

Conclusion

We have concentrated on the mechanics of the star system and the theories about how stardom works as a focus for our interest. What you should note is that stars are both structuring devices in texts (refer to 'Narratives' and 'Representations', Chapters 3 and 10) and a focus for audiences (see 'Audiences', Chapter 32) as well as commodities to be marketed. Here is a final activity to test your understanding:

ACTIVITY 25.3

Commutation test

Test out your understanding of a particular star-image using the commutation test (Thompson 1978). This involves trying to imagine replacing one star by another

in a particular role. It is a good party game and starting point for thinking about stars. Consider John Travolta as Vincent Vega in *Pulp Fiction*. Now try a different, but plausible, male star in the same role – Nicholas Cage or Kurt Russell perhaps.

- Does the film still work in the same way? If it doesn't what has changed?

You should be coming up with aspects of the star-image of both stars which don't match and therefore change the meaning. Try the exercise with your own pairings in other film examples. If nothing happens and your 'stars' are interchangeable, then they aren't stars at all. If they have a recognisable, distinct, star-image it will cause a difference.

References and further reading

All these titles are reasonably accessible.

Bogle, Donald (1994, 2nd edition) *Toms, Coons, Mulattoes, Mammies and Bucks: An Interpretative History of Blacks in American Films*, New York: Continuum.

Dyer, Richard (1987) *Heavenly Bodies*, London: Macmillan/BFI.

Dyer, Richard (1990) *Now You See It*, London: Routledge.

Dyer, Richard (1998, 2nd edition) *Stars*, London: BFI.

Ellis, John (1982 and 1992) *Visible Fictions*, London: Routledge.

Gledhill, Christine (ed.) (1991) *Stardom: Industry of Desire*, London: Routledge.

Schatz, Thomas (1989) *The Genius of the System: Hollywood Filmmaking in the Studio Era*, London: Simon & Schuster.

Stacey, Jackie (1994) *Star Gazing: Hollywood Cinema and Female Spectatorship*, London: Routledge.

Steinberg, Cobbett (1981) *Reel Facts*, London: Penguin.

Thompson, John O. (1978) 'Screen Acting and the Commutation Test', *Screen*, vol. 19, no. 2.

Wyatt, Justin (1994) *High Concept: Movies and Marketing in Hollywood*, Austin: University of Texas Press.

26 Institutions

The concept of a media institution is difficult to grasp because it refers to a set of processes and relationships rather than a 'thing' itself. This chapter attempts to define what we mean by 'institutional' in Media Studies by working through an example of a specific media institution and then applying the ideas raised to a series of key debates which can in turn be picked up in several of the other chapters and case studies, allowing you to integrate 'institutional analysis' with such key concepts for our chosen institutions as 'objectivity', 'quality' and 'regulation'.

An institutional analysis of photography

Rather than try to define a media institution at the outset, let's consider 'photography' as an example of a media *practice* – an organised media activity which has developed over a long period and is easily accessible as a means of creating a media text. It's an interesting example because, although a photograph can exist as a media text itself, most of the time we come across photographs as collections in an album or an exhibition or as photographic images which are used in other media texts such as magazines, newspapers, posters, CD-ROMs etc.

This dual role of the photographic image sets up a number of broadly 'institutional' questions, involving both the production and the reading of photographs:

- Is the photograph on its own the same as the photographic image reproduced in a magazine or newspaper?
- Can the meaning of a photographic image change, depending on the type of media text in which it appears?
- Do photographs have a different value or status, depending on the context within which we see them?

An analysis of a specific image will enable us to explore these issues. Figure 26.1 shows a young woman kneeling by a flowerbed. She is in focus in the foreground, looking not at the camera but to her left. Slightly out of focus, in the background, other people are sat on benches

Figure 26.1

– some of them might be looking at the young woman. This is a description at the **denotative** level. By analysing the image carefully at the **connotative** level, we can interpret the image. The young woman's clothes (especially the hat) and make-up suggest the 1950s. The formal flower bed, wide path and benches suggest a public park. Foliage on the trees and the display of tulips suggests late spring or early summer (further supported by the deep shadow thrown by the woman in the strong sunlight). The framing draws attention to the woman and this is emphasised by the use of depth of field which blurs into the distance. The woman's posture suggests a 'pose' in that it looks quite uncomfortable (although this might be because of her outfit) and arranged for the camera. She is kneeling on the cut grass, on the 'wrong side' of a wire in a very formal garden, suggesting that a rule has been broken and that her behaviour is in some way 'naughty'. So far, so good. But this is a photographic image, taken out of context.

See 'The languages of media', Chapter 1, and 'Analysing images', Case study 2.

- Where and when might the image have first appeared?
- What is the purpose of the image in that context?
- What type of photography is this?

These are interrelated 'institutional' questions, and we can draw up a list of possible answers in terms of recognisable types of photography.

- A *snapshot*. Could this be a snapshot taken for a family album? It seems unlikely, partly because the woman doesn't look at the camera. Also we might expect a rather closer shot with less background. It could, however, be a 'staged' shot for the album – perhaps with some kind of story behind it?
- A *still from a film*. Could this be a photograph taken on a film location? Is it a film made in the 1950s, or a 1990s film set in the 1950s?
- A *paparazzi photograph*. Is the young woman famous and has the photographer caught her playing in the park?
- A *promotional photograph*. Perhaps she is famous and has posed for publicity photos?
- A *fashion photograph*. Although this is possible, the clothes are not given sufficient prominence for this to be very likely.
- An *advertising photograph*. Perhaps this is an intriguing image which is anchored by an advertising tag-line (supply your own!).
- A *feature photograph*. Newspapers and magazines often use photographs to improve the look of a page and this may be simply meant to represent the picture editor's idea of a 'welcome to spring' image.
- A *documentary photograph*. Is this an attempt to 'document reality' – to record a moment in a park on a sunny day?
- An *art photograph*. Might this be part of a collection in a book or for a gallery exhibition, organised around a theme or a particular technique?

All of these are just about possible, although some seem much more likely than others. These types of photography might be seen as **genres**, but we should note that as genres they are distinguished only by sometimes quite subtle differences in framings. We've shown that the same image could belong in several different genres and we won't be able to pin it down unless we know more about who the photographer was and the context of its publication. (We should also note that there are other types of photography which might have different subject matter or very different framings – portraiture, landscape, medical, industrial, news, wildlife etc.)

The original photograph was taken by **Bert Hardy** and appeared in *Picture Post* magazine in May 1950. It features a young Audrey Hepburn, who a few years later would become an international star in films like *Breakfast at Tiffany's* (US 1961) and *My Fair Lady* (US 1964). *Picture Post* was an extremely popular weekly illustrated magazine, which

See 'Genres', Chapter 8, on 'hybrid' forms – similar images being utilised in a range of **genres**.

Bert Hardy (1913–95) was a self-educated photographer, who began work as a messenger boy and developed his expertise with the German Leica camera.

Picture Post   The archive of photographs from the magazine is now administered by Hulton-Deutsch, and several individual images have become widely used on postcards and posters.

was published between 1938 and 1957. It specialised in news and current affairs and 'human interest' stories and carried many of the black and white images which have now become associated with the social history of the period. Bert Hardy was a 'staff photographer' on the magazine, who gained a high reputation with a recognisable style derived from his innovative use of a small 35 mm camera. He pioneered documentary-style shooting, making use of available light, especially in a series of features depicting life in working-class communities. Many of his best photographs capture the humanity and vitality of 'ordinary people'. When *Picture Post* closed in 1957, Hardy became a sought-after advertising photographer. He was one of the earliest photographers to have his work collected and exhibited when, during the 1970s, photography began to gain more recognition as an 'art form'.

What does this knowledge about photographer and publication context do to limit the range of possible types of photography which might describe the Audrey Hepburn photograph? It clearly rules out some categories and erects barriers between others. The context suggests that this was a 'light feature' item, a 'pretty girl greets the spring' story (Gardiner 1993). There is a hint of the promotional tie-in, with the magazine giving a helping hand to Hepburn's career and, despite the nature of the job, Hardy's style and interest in documentary come through – this is also a study of Kew Gardens, a popular place for Londoners to visit. In the 1990s the image appeared in a collection of *Picture Post Women* (Gardiner 1993) and could conceivably appear in an exhibition of Hardy's work. Thus as the context changes, so does the category, and this image is now primarily an 'art' image or an historical document. What do these changes tell us?

The categories of photography are based on *purpose* rather than *content* and the purpose also affects the practice – how the photograph is taken – and its status, both with other photographers and with audiences. There are clear distinctions between an 'amateur' snapshot and a 'professional' feature photograph – not least that the latter is a commercial operation. There are also differences between 'commercial' photography and 'art' or 'documentary' photography. In the former, images may be cropped or manipulated by a designer or picture editor – the photographer gives up 'ownership' in return for a fee or salary. In the latter, images are likely to be published 'as is' or after processing by the photographer alone. Of course, 'amateur' photographs are sometimes published and commercial photographs do appear in galleries, but the original status is maintained and the 'crossing over' into a different category is noticeable. The definitions of categories change over time and it is worth noting that a photograph will normally be accompanied by 'anchoring text' which

When amateur prints are used, a publication may announce them as such. A similar policy on television news will add the title 'amateur video' to any footage which has been accepted for broadcast. This signals that the poor quality is not the fault of the broadcaster. The force of this distinction is gradually receding as more 'non-standard' video material is shown.

makes the category explicit (even if it is only 'Majorca 1996' scribbled on the back of a snapshot).

Who makes the decisions about which category is appropriate for which kinds of photography? Who decides which category has higher or lower status? Can anyone become a photographer and contribute work in these particular categories? These too are institutional questions. Photography is an *organised* activity. No matter that anyone can point a camera and press a button, we all recognise a more formal media institution called 'photography' exists with its rules and regulations. At its simplest level, the distinction between amateur and professional is based on the organisation of professionals. You can't become a 'professional' simply by selling a photograph. The definition of professional is based on:

- status as an employed or self-employed person with a reputation for good work
- training and qualifications
- membership of a professional association
- competitions, awards and recognition
- access to 'industry standard' equipment and the skills to use it

These criteria are important in excluding some people from becoming professional photographers and in 'standardising' expectations about what constitutes a 'professional photograph' or even a 'good photograph'. They are 'institutional constraints' within which photography practice develops.

- *Employment status* is important in that it will influence decisions about what will sell or what will meet a set brief. Most professionals are dependent on the work they produce having currency in the contemporary market. Some photographers might be 'grant-aided' enabling them to undertake 'avant garde' work (see 'Independents and alternatives', Chapter 28), but they too will be constrained by the funding criteria.

- *Training and qualifications* are important in photography which, like journalism, but unlike the film industry, has had a long history of 'scientific' and 'technical' training provision, as well as more art- and design-orientated education. There is a limited number of specialist courses at certain colleges which have become associated with certain types of photography, such as the documentary tradition at Newport (Gwent College of Higher Education). Students are influenced by their tutors and the traditions of the department and carry these into their future practice. Assessment in the form of National Vocational Qualifications is a way of 'proving' professional competence.

professional is an example of a term with two rather different meanings in everyday speech. It can refer to adherence to a code of conduct and a high level of skill – 'she is highly professional in her work', or a rather automatic performance of the expected role – 'don't worry about him, he's a cynical old pro'. See '**Standards**' in 'Genres', Chapter 8, for a related 'double' term.

Like many other activities which began in Victorian Britain, photography has a 'Royal Society' which welcomes amateur and professional members. Compare this with the Royal Television Society which is professional only. Film and radio don't appear to warrant royal patronage.

- *Professional associations* support members and help to 'maintain standards'. They may operate a code of ethics (see below) which modifies behaviour and puts pressure on members to conform. They preserve the status of members by lobbying government in their interest and negotiating better deals and conditions with buyers of photographic services and equipment suppliers. They also publish journals which act as a forum for discussion as well as the circulation of new ideas.

The Code of Ethics of the BIPP (British Institute of Professional Photographers)

- A member shall present himself, his work, his services and his premises in such a manner as will uphold and dignify his professional status and the reputation of the Institute.
- A member shall exercise all reasonable skill, care and diligence in the discharge of his duties, and, in so far as any of his duties are discretionary, shall act fairly and in good faith.
- Any confidential information acquired by a member in the course of his professional duties shall not be divulged by him to any third party.
- No member shall corruptly offer or accept any gift or inducement.
- A member may use in conjunction only with his own name the Institute designatory letters to which he is entitled; and he shall not use any other designatory letters or other description to which he is not entitled.
- A member shall at all times and in all respects conduct his professional and business operations within the law, both criminal and civil.
- A member knowingly condoning a breach of this Code shall be responsible as if he himself had committed the breach.
- A member shall cooperate fully with any investigations into an alleged breach of this Code.

- *Awards and prizes* are important in confirming which groups of photographers are recognised as being at the forefront of contemporary practice. They will receive publicity which will strengthen moves to change practice.
- *Industry standard equipment* is another barrier to new entrants to the profession, not just because of cost but also because of the training needed to use it – often, the necessary support to learn new techniques is available only through professional associations.

Awards are often given by the professional bodies and sponsored by major manufacturers – reinforcing the sense of an organised and institutionalised practice.

An institutional analysis of photography

Photography is very much associated with ideas of 'identity' and the politics of who controls the images which contribute to those ideas. You will find plenty of examples of photographers working against 'institutional' influences on identity.

'"Amateur photography" can also feel like an institution, especially if it excludes "outsiders": there is little in amateur or popular photography magazines to help us map our course. There, the concept of photography is limited, being addressed mainly to white heterosexual males. Not much is offered to women and the existence of working-class, black, or lesbian experience is barely acknowledged. It is orientated, primarily, to "know-how" and assumes an interest in tourism, the landscape and glamour.'

(Spence and Solomon 1995)

'Disability imagery' is one example where the 'subjects' of institutional image-making have fought back: 'My personal journey of private crisis, of the slow gaining of understanding of disability as an external oppression, and on into the disability movement, vitally informs my photographs ... Charity photography is a form which is at once stubborn and fragile. A photography which ... is based on a medical view (or model) of disability cannot lead to the empowerment and liberation of disabled people (Hevey 1992).

Sit-coms and **soap operas** on television and radio are often based on daily happenings within 'institutions' such as hospitals, prisons, schools etc. as well as social institutions such as marriage. The rules and regulations and the social interaction give plenty of scope for drama.

This quote from Spence and Solomon recognises the force of institutional factors in photography. It also emphasises how much they can be perceived as discriminatory. Various groups of photographers have recognised this and set up organisations or campaigns to promote their own interests, which would otherwise be seen as marginal.

Defining 'institution'

This investigation of photography enables us to move towards some tentative definitions of 'institution' based on **social**, **cultural** and **political** relations. Institutional analysis is derived largely from sociology and is concerned with the social structure of organisation. Tim O'Sullivan defined institutions thus:

> enduring regulatory and organising structures of any society, which constrain and control individuals and individuality ... the underlying principles and values according to which many social and cultural practices are organised and co-ordinated ... the major social sources of codes, rules and relations.

(O'Sullivan et al. 1994)

O'Sullivan here is referring to institutions generally, and it is helpful to think about the different kinds of institutions you already find familiar.

The great 'institutions of state' such as the monarchy, the church, the law etc. are concerned with organising and constraining authority and power, whereas the 'welfare' institutions – education, the health service, social security, etc. – are concerned more with the provision of services. A rather different form of institution is 'marriage' – a social institution, a formalised relationship between two people, recognised by society as serving a particular function. Media institutions like photography are as varied in nature as these very different examples and may share several of their features:

- Institutions are *enduring* – they are recognised as having been established for some time. They have a history that informs (and perhaps constrains) the present and the future work undertaken by them. There are no 'overnight' institutions and inertia can act as a restraint. In the 1990s photography is struggling to come to terms with digital imaging and the challenge to very long-held views about photographs as evidence.

- Institutions *regulate and structure* activities: they make rules and they suggest specific ways of working. In broad terms, institutions provide stability and preserve the status quo (although they can, of course, 'organise change'). The professional associations are important in regulating the behaviour of their members.

- Institutions are, in one sense, *collectivist*. They constrain individuals and individuality in order to achieve a common goal. (This goal may be that chosen by a small group or even an individual at the top of the hierarchy – institutions are not necessarily democratic.) This is particularly important in media institutions in which individual creative ideas are prized, but may have to be sacrificed for the good of the group (often the financial security of the organisation).

- Institutions develop *working practices* that have an underpinning set of assumptions about the aims of the institution and its ethos.

- All the people associated with the institution – directors, managers, employees – will be expected to share the *values* associated with the ethos and to behave accordingly in their relations with others, both inside and outside the institution. It must be staffed by recognised professionals, whose education and training will effectively exclude casual intruders as new staff.

- The wider public will be aware of the *status* of the institution and of their own expected relationship to it. Again this is particularly important for media institutions, because the audiences for media texts are 'organised' as part of the network of relationships.

At this point, you should be able to go back and check the discussion of photography to see if it conforms to this model.

'Leadership in the competitive universal field of entertainment takes the dedicated talents of a diverse, highly motivated team. It also takes a deep respect for each team member, without whom success is unattainable. With this at the heart of Paramount's corporate philosophy, the resulting career environment is interactive and supportive' (extract from the Career Opportunities Page of Paramount's website).

The reference to the BBC as 'Auntie' during the 1970s and 1980s is a good example of the audience view of a broadcasting institution. It suggested that the corporation was 'one of the family', but, worryingly for BBC executives, an older and perhaps more conservative relative than they might wish.

'Audiences', Chapter 32, discusses the role of audiences, especially in terms of 'passive' and 'active' responses to texts.

ACTIVITY 26.1

Take any two contrasting types of photography (e.g. portraiture and sports photojournalism) – check out books and magazines dealing with photography and look at how the two types of work are presented. Try and list the differences between the two types in terms of:

- relationship with a client – who pays the photographer's fee?
- relationship with the subject of the photograph

- the environment in which they work – how much control do they have?
- the equipment they might use
- a description of a typical working day
- what they might consider as a 'good photograph'
- the different markets in which publications carrying the photographs might be sold.

How important are these *institutional* differences in thinking about the photographs themselves?

Media institutions and society

Photography is a useful way of introducing ideas about institutions, and, especially through the social practice of the snapshot and the formal documenting of 'reality', the role of the media in developing ideas about who we are, what we have done and where we might be going.

Human society has always had the means to express ideas and emotions through forms such as storytelling, dance, music and art. Modern media have extended those capacities, in terms of realism, reproduction and distribution to mass audiences. The institutional questions which arise are not necessarily 'new', but they arouse concern and interest because their potential impact is so great. Consider the following issues about the role of the media and the nature of media texts:

- the 'truth' of claims to represent 'reality'
- the hurt and damage to individuals caused by offensive media texts
- the potential damage to society inflicted by stories celebrating corruption and depravity
- the potential loss of national, regional and cultural identity through submission to dominant culture.

See 'Representations' Chapter 10), 'Ideologies and discourses' (Chapter 12), 'Realisms' (Chapter 16) and 'Industries' (Chapter 22).

These issues are raised in other chapters and case studies as well, and in some cases they are linked with questions of economics – what kinds of media activity can we afford, what are the implications for employment or balance of trade? Here we are more concerned with society's attempts to *regulate* media activities (i.e. in production, distribution and consumption) in the interests of the individual and the society as a whole.

O'Sullivan's definition points us to regulation in terms of 'constrain and control', 'organise and co-ordinate', 'codes, rules and regulations'. There are several ways for such regulation to work:

- Authoritarian regimes can themselves control media activity directly.
- Democratic governments can appoint 'independent' regulatory bodies to monitor the behaviour of specific media industries.
- Media producers can 'self-regulate', constraining themselves.

- The general legal framework can act as a restraint on activity.
- The 'market' can be seen to regulate, with audiences using their own judgement.
- Audiences can form pressure groups which lobby producers and legislators.

All countries have a media environment which is governed by a mix of the above. Some countries are still openly controlled by regimes which intervene directly (Burma, Iraq etc.). It isn't so long ago that the UK government prevented the voices of IRA spokespersons being heard on radio or television or issued 'D' notices warning that news stories were covered by the Official Secrets Act and should not be published. In this respect the UK has a relatively 'closed' form of government, which is often revealed as such in comparison with the 'open' American system.

British and American models of regulation

The development of the media in the UK has been closely linked with similar events in the US and the two media environments are often compared. The differences are interesting, as are the fears, mainly from a British perspective, that the two may be becoming more similar.

All American media industries and markets are bigger and more effectively financed. American producers are unlikely to be too concerned about 'foreign competition' and, because of the strength of a large market, and a tradition of valuing 'competition', most producers favour 'the market' as the main base for regulation. This in turn has led to 'self-regulation' – protecting producers against opposition from

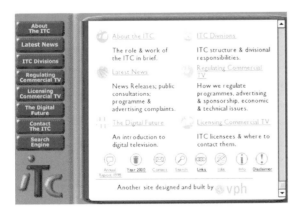

Figure 26.2   These are the websites of the ITC and FCC. Note the difference in emphasis and the range of industries addressed by the FCC. The ITC site at `http://www.itc.org.uk` is well worth a visit and carries a comprehensive overview of the requirements for independent television in the UK

consumers. Self-regulation is a real issue in a society with a long tradition of pressure groups formed by religious and culturally conservative organisations. By contrast, the American constitution gives rights of free speech to the individual artist. The history of business regulation in the US has also seen attempts to preserve the possibility of market share for smaller producers in the form of government actions against 'monopoly' arrangements (e.g. the Paramount Decrees 1948 and the more recent actions against Microsoft). 'Professional' media practitioners are expected to be trained and qualified in America, where the 'meritocracy' of college education is seen to be important in conferring status – this is noticeable in the number of journalism courses in print and broadcasting.

We could very broadly represent the differences between the US and the UK as a set of oppositions:

US	UK
• 'free' media market	• some government intervention in markets
• large domestic market	• smaller domestic market
• strong domestic media industries	• weaker domestic industries – more imports
• 'loose' regulation of broadcasting	• stronger broadcasting regulation
• self-regulation of non-broadcast	• self-regulation of non-broadcast
• powerful audience lobby groups	• less powerful lobby groups
• constitutional 'free speech'	• no statutory right as such
• widespread training experience	• less formalised training (but developing)

'Free' markets are in practice likely to be dominated by the large media corporations. In Europe public money often supports specific media such as film and 'new media'.

A similar exercise could be to compare the UK and the US with other European countries, or with Australia (which has strong media links with both the US and the UK). The growing power of the European Union, especially in terms of market intervention and regulation, would then become more apparent. A different exercise would compare any of these environments with those for media institutions in Africa, Asia or Latin America (see 'Globalisation', Chapter 20).

Broadcasting is at the centre of these debates, primarily because of its direct entrance into the home, its immediacy and its importance as an information source. As such, we have devoted the case study which follows this chapter to public service broadcasting – the dominant model of organising and regulating provision of radio and television services in Europe. Here, we will consider three more broadly based issues:

• 'truth' and partiality
• 'quality' in media texts
• the role of the audience.

'Truth' and partiality: the case of journalism

Journalism is the practice of reporting and commenting on events. We can think of it as a set of working practices and an institution like photography, though one which is even more bound up with that hotly contested concept of 'truth'.

The cub reporter at the gardening club show, the columnist on a national paper, the sub-editor who writes the captions on pin-ups, and the foreign correspondent reporting for the BBC in a war zone are all journalists. They share certain values and are subject to similar institutional constraints, but there are also important differences.

Journalism is one sector of the UK media industries with a history of clearly defined training routes for entry and progression through the profession. The NCTJ (National Council for the Training of Journalists) and the large regional newspaper groups have organised training schemes which allow journalists to start 'at the bottom' and learn their trade 'on the job'. To some extent these schemes are now in competition with degree and postgraduate level courses which produce highly qualified entrants with less experience (an innovation not warmly welcomed in some parts of the industry). Nevertheless, most journalists receive an introduction to acceptable working practices with a strong institutional sense of what it means to be a journalist. This introduction is not value-free, and discrimination based on gender or race has been identified and challenged by journalists who established new codes of conduct within the profession. Campaigns against racist reporting have been developed alongside pressure groups designed to promote opportunities for black media workers (see Cohen and Gardner 1982). More subtle forms of 'gendered' training expectations prepare women to work on 'human interest' stories rather than, for example, on sports reporting.

A beginning on a local newspaper is often the first stage on a progression through different media institutions, including local radio, regional television and then national newspapers, radio or television. The maintenance of journalism as a professional practice across the three media has been strengthened by the decision of the BBC to introduce '**bi-media journalism**' (i.e. merging radio and television journalism training). It is also noticeable that BBC Radio 5 and other talk-based radio and television programmes are making increased use of print journalists as commentators and reporters.

Journalists in any medium are expected to share skills, knowledge and understanding about what makes a 'good story' and how to produce accurate and interesting material to deadlines. However, the different media have different institutional constraints. Broadcast journalism has

The expansion of local radio in the 1990s has provided opportunities for women such as Sybil Ruscoe and Jane Garvey, both of whom have gained a national profile through Radio 5.

'Women leapt in to fill these [radio] vacancies and they were largely university-educated women who were not there because they had financed their own trip abroad, or because their husbands, fathers or brothers had played any role in their career' (Sebba 1998).

The NUJ (National Union of Journalists) operates a 'Code of Conduct' which can be viewed on its website.

traditionally operated 'impartially', drawing on a sense of 'balanced reporting' as required by the charter of the BBC or by the Independent Television Commission (ITC) and Radio Authority in the case of other broadcasters. By contrast, print journalists work in a more politically charged environment where stories clearly have **angles** and columnists in particular are expected to represent the editorial **line**. This isn't expressed as partiality, of course, but as 'comment'.

See 'Narratives', Chapter 3, on 'story construction'.

A tabloid might list 'ten things you never knew about salmonella' – another **angle**.

An **angle** on a story refers to the direction from which the journalist approaches the material. A news item on the agency wires might refer to an outbreak of food poisoning. One journalist might decide to follow up the story by concentrating on the issue of public health: which shop, factory etc. might be responsible, how are the local authorities handling the outbreak of infection? Another journalist might approach the same material by linking it to other recent outbreaks and asking questions about central government food policy. These are two angles on the same story.

A **line** is a policy set down by the editor (perhaps at the behest of a proprietor like Rupert Murdoch) stating what the paper believes in and therefore how stories will be presented. The idea that such a line exists will be denied by many editors and journalists, but it becomes apparent whenever the paper decides to go against its usual line. The most obvious example of a line is the general support for one particular party at election time. In 1997 the *Sun* surprised most readers by switching allegiance from Conservative to Labour.

ACTIVITY 26.2

Editorial policy

Over a couple of weeks try to follow the same few big news stories in the *Sun, Mirror, Daily Mail, Guardian* and *Daily Telegraph*.

- Can you identify an editorial line in any of the papers on a particular story?
- Can you find examples of reporting or comment which appear to contradict the editorial stance of the paper?

A famous fictional **editorial policy** was set out as a front page manifesto by Orson Welles as Charles Foster Kane in the film *Citizen Kane* (US 1941).

Beginning with a campaign against the British release of the film *Crash* in 1997, the *Daily Mail* began a campaign to champion certain kinds of films and to rail against others. This was clearly an editorial policy as in the 'critics charts' each week the *Daily Mail* stood out in attacking films generally supported by the *Independent, Guardian* etc.

Before the changes in the national press which followed Rupert Murdoch's acquisition of the *Sun* in 1969, it was possible for popular newspapers to follow a particular editorial line and yet to employ journalists known to hold opposing views. Although it is still possible to find writers with opposing political views on broadsheets (especially in the *Guardian* and the *Independent*), it is increasingly the case that the press is seen to be 'partisan'. This emphasises the difference between print and broadcast journalism, but also puts pressure on the broadcasters. Newspapers can 'set an agenda' on a particular story which is picked up by radio and television. Viewers and listeners then expect impartiality from broadcasters, but, with the context of the story already set, it is difficult to 're-set' it. And, with the increased competition in news presentation, ignoring the story may not be possible. The result is that broadcasters can be sucked in to a style of coverage they may not be trained or professionally inclined to handle.

The broadcasters' aim of impartiality is put to the strongest test when news stories involve issues of 'national interest' or 'national security'. In these circumstances there is a temptation to slide into an 'us against them' style of reporting. During the Cold War there was some (but not total) agreement as to who the 'bad guys' were, and this allowed a certain amount of positioning of the journalist without breaching the impartiality code. In recent struggles, such as the civil war in Bosnia, the position of journalists has become more difficult. There is no meaningful balance between superpowers and no immediate bad guy. Surely this means that impartiality is a given – the journalist reports what he or she sees? In reality this is (*a*) difficult and (*b*) not necessarily 'good television'.

Journalists in Bosnia found themselves involved in the war – used as hostages, shot at and generally not able to 'stand back'. The war itself was seen as so confusing that to grab attention news editors were looking for angles on stories which increasingly attempted to determine who the bad guys were. In 1996, at an international conference on news reporting in Berlin, the BBC journalist Martin Bell made a protest about what he termed 'bystander journalism' – the reduction of the 'objectivity' of the reporter to an onlooker's role. Bell went on to leave the BBC and to get elected to Parliament as an 'anti-sleaze' candidate, but his comments ignited a debate about the 'journalism of attachment'. 'In the news business it isn't involvement, but indifference that makes for bad practice. Good journalism is the journalism of attachment' (Martin Bell, from *In Harm's Way*, 1997).

This debate is important in terms of the state of contemporary journalism, but it is not a clear-cut issue. Bell was supported and attacked with equal force by distinguished journalists. He maintained that he was not arguing against objectivity or hard factual reporting. It emerged that one of his targets was the concept of rolling news (BBC 24 Hour News was then being developed), which critics argue is reliant on ill-prepared, 'instant' reports, rather than the deep coverage provided by the traditional professional foreign correspondent.

ITN explained to a Parliamentary Defence Committee on the reporting of the Falklands War that it tried to give 'a nightly offering of interesting, positive and heart-warming stories of achievement and collaboration born out of a sense of national purpose'. The BBC stated that an impartial approach was felt to be 'an unnecessary irritation'.

'a UN unit was despatched by an officer from another nation to deal with a protesting crowd of hungry civilians … The UN unit, the "Blue Berets" happily beat them to a pulp. Asked why, they said "This is how we do it at home." Are they the "good guys"? … War zones are deceptive, and eye-witness reports sometimes need to be verified even when it is your eyes' (Adie 1998).

Figure 26.3 Welcome to Sarajevo (UK 1997) deals with many of the issues surrounding contemporary broadcast journalism

Rolling news is a response to a competitive international news market driven by better communications technology, but also by changes in definitions of news and editorial policies. It is tempting to polarise the debate surrounding Bell's remarks as traditional factual reporting versus attached, committed journalism. But this would be misleading. Perhaps the most celebrated foreign correspondent of the last fifty years was **James Cameron**, who saw 'this famous "objectivity" as not only virtually impossible, but maybe even undesirable' (Cameron 1980). On the other hand 'commentators' who are given the space to step outside 'reporting on events' to write or broadcast about issues more generally may have few worthwhile opinions about important issues and therefore tend to support the status quo by default.

One of the features of contemporary newspapers is the rise of the 'columnist', which to a certain extent has matched the decline of the 'reporter' and the general move to more 'entertainment' (or 'infotainment') forms. Newspapers have responded to what their proprietors have seen as the market trends by shifting resources away from large numbers of relatively poorly paid reporters 'on the ground' to a smaller number of highly paid commentators based in London (most national daily papers are now entirely London operations, whereas they once operated out of large bases in Manchester, Birmingham and other cities). This change has had an impact on, and has in turn been influenced by, changes in journalism training and the consequent 'institutionalisation' of the new forms. To a certain extent the same process is evident in local newspapers where 'features' have grown at the expense of 'news'.

James Cameron (1911–85) was a journalist with a high reputation for integrity, commitment and courage. An annual award for foreign correspondents is named after him.

'The changes initiated by the *Sun* in the 1970s pushed the meaning of popular in a new direction. The *Sun* was no longer feminised, but *sexualised*. Central to its appeal was the provocative image of a woman's body' (Holland 1998).

We've used three terms for different sectors of 'the press' so far:

- *Broadsheet newspapers* are so called because of their large size – the largest size commonly available for print products. In the UK the national broadsheets (*The Times, Daily Telegraph, Guardian* etc.) are all treated as 'serious news' papers, with a reading age commensurate with further education. This leads to the alternative term **quality press** (i.e. the high quality of journalistic writing).
- *Tabloid newspapers* are smaller in page size, roughly half as big as broadsheets. The term 'tabloid' has generated a second meaning which refers to sensational stories and striking page layouts with large images and headlines, exploiting the shape of the page. This second meaning tends to push tabloids 'downmarket' and has also been carried over to television where it again implies sensation and screaming headlines. The tabloids have also been termed the *popular press*. But beware. In Europe it is

commonplace to find a 'tabloid-sized' paper which is 'serious', and the mid-market papers in the UK such as the *Daily Mail* and *Daily Express* decided that the gain from the 'manageability' and layout features of the tabloids outweighed the pejorative image when they moved from broadsheet to tabloid size in the 1980s. In order to distinguish this middle market from the *Sun*, *Mirror* and *Star*, the latter group are now being referred to as the 'red-top' tabloids. Notice too that the *Independent* has followed the *Guardian* in producing a tabloid second section. 'Tabloid' and 'broadsheet' are also misleading when considering the regional press.

- The *regional press* describes most UK newspapers apart from the twenty or so national titles based in London (or Scotland). These may be different sizes and morning or evening dailies or weeklies, but institutionally they all differ from what used to be called the 'Fleet Street nationals' because of their recognition of a specific 'local' audience and, most importantly, a local advertising market (see 'Local newspapers and advertising', Case study 31).

We've argued that 'journalism' is recognisable as a set of work practices and ethics which runs across different media. The process of **convergence** of technologies and ownership has been matched by a similar convergence of attitudes towards previously distinct forms of journalism in press and broadcasting. A useful summary of where journalism is heading is provided by Michael Bromley (1997):

Debate over the state of journalism in the late twentieth century and its likely future in the early part of the twenty-first century involves four inter-related areas:

- technological change
- new business structures
- the functions of news
- the coherence of journalism as an occupation.

ACTIVITY 26.3

The state of journalism

Taking Bromley's four points above, check through the preceding section and the relevant sections of other chapters and case studies in this book to put together a coherent view of the 'state of journalism'. You should look in particular at 'Selecting and constructing news' (Case study 13), 'Industries' (Chapter 22) and 'Technologies' (Chapter 14).

'Quality'

'Quality' is another term perhaps best left in quotes. It is an important concept in relation to the cultural policies of powerful media institutions and has been used by opponents in debates about the future of broadcasting, print, cinema etc., often in contradictory ways. A definition of 'quality' used as an adjective refers to 'a high grade of excellence' (*Chambers 20th Century Dictionary*). It isn't difficult to argue that any society should aim to produce, circulate and consume media texts of quality. But who decides what is 'high grade', and does use of the term imply that there will be other texts which are of different grades? How do these grading decisions become institutionalised?

The 'who decides?' question can easily slide into an issue of class, education and social standing, where 'quality' becomes associated with 'elite'. There is also a distinct possibility that 'quality' will become seen as the opposite of 'popular', as in the long tradition of debates about 'high' (quality) culture and popular culture in the UK. Note the distinction between 'quality press' and 'popular press' outlined above.

These distinctions matter because they can help to influence our ideas about what kinds of texts we want or we think should be provided, and they can form the basis of important economic decisions about which forms of media activity should be supported (i.e. financed). 'Quality' tends to suggest a high budget to produce the 'excellence' expected in the text. But will it be 'popular', will it appeal to a relatively small audience, which will need to pay

Who pays for 'quality'?

One of the most expensive art forms is opera. To maintain a traditional opera house requires high maintenance charges plus salaries and fees for performers who must rehearse for long periods in order to give only a few public performances. In the UK the Royal Opera House, Covent Garden, receives large public grants to maintain this level of excellence, yet admission tickets still cost a great deal. Opera is a minority interest with a largely (but not completely) 'elite' audience.

Popular music receives little if any public support, the argument being that it is supported by a commercial industry. Yet it is well known that in the UK many aspiring musicians have been unofficially supported on the dole, while they have attempted to get experience writing and performing.

Government plans to force unemployed musicians on to 'welfare-to-work' schemes coincided with the decision to award a large Lottery grant to Covent Garden in 1998.

a high price – thereby restricting access? At the time of writing, this issue is being played out in terms of UK government support for the arts.

'Quality' has also been used as a concept in debates about UK television. Here the concept has been changed to refer not to one particular type of television as 'excellent' but to the variety of programmes available on UK television generally. This is not just a debating term but is built into the licensing agreements for Channel 3 and Channel 5 franchise holders – the so-called 'quality threshold' which must be exceeded in terms of proposed programming by any applicant. In the 1992 franchise bidding, and again with Channel 5, there was considerable unease about the way this requirement was seen to be applied.

The 'quality television' concept was developed during the 1960s in the UK in an environment of competition between the BBC and an ITV network which was relatively tightly regulated by the Independent Broadcasting Authority (IBA) – the predecessor of the current ITC. Relatively secure from outside competition, the two networks enjoyed a stable income. Programming could afford to be broad in terms of variety, and occasionally progressive in terms of trying new ideas, which could afford to fail or could be given relatively long runs to 'build audiences'. The term 'Golden Age' has been applied to UK broadcasting in the 1960s and 1970s in recognition of what was seen to be a vibrant and exciting period. You should always be suspicious of nostalgic references to 'better days in the past', but there is certainly an argument to be made that some forms of television, especially drama and current affairs, produced many memorable programmes in this period and that equivalent programmes are unlikely to be made in the current environment. What has changed?

A good example of this 'Golden Age' approach is found in *Talk of Drama* (1998) in which critic Sean Day-Lewis interviews television scriptwriters of the period and promotes an argument in favour of 'writer-led' television drama.

The Thatcher government of the 1980s was opposed to the culture of regulation which operated within UK television, preferring the American idea of a 'free market' philosophy. A debate was started which was intended to make the BBC more 'businesslike' and to open up commercial television. A long struggle ensued, with the BBC fighting to retain its full public service role (see O'Malley and Treharne 1993), and the eventual outcome was marked by the *Broadcasting Act of 1990*. Amongst other things this released ITV from most of its public service obligations and introduced the **25 per cent production quota** which required 25 per cent of all broadcast material to be commissioned from independents (this affected the BBC as well). Opening up the broadcast market was welcomed by many small and not-so-small 'independents' (see Chapter 27), but its main consequence for the broadcasters was to bring pressure on production units which would now perhaps not be fully employed. The result was the 'headcount reduction' policy (i.e. making redundant large numbers of staff, who might be invited back on a freelance basis).

' of the ITV
ree main groups
employment
ell over half of all
ITV network ... urs are provided
by Granada Group companies
(including LWT, Yorkshire and
Tyne-Tees) (source: ITC).

Ratings are crucial to ITV
companies selling advertising
space; they are equally important
to the BBC, which must justify the
licence fee by reference to the
popularity of its programming –
see 'Public service broadcasting',
Case study 27.

Reports in the UK media in 1999
about 'fake guests' on talk shows
and 'fake documentaries' raised
doubts about the quality of
programme research.

The BBC then went one step further, as if to meet the free-marketeers head-on, with the introduction of **producer choice**. This allowed producers to use outside production facilities, if these could be shown to be less costly than remaining '*in-house*' This idea of an *internal market* has been introduced also in the health service and education. The introduction of the quota and producer choice has had a number of direct consequences:

- The production base of the BBC and the major ITV companies has shrunk.
- British broadcasters can no longer make some types of programmes without co-production deals, often with overseas broadcasters.
- There are more small independent companies with broadcast production experience.
- Broadcast staff are now more likely to be freelance or employed on fixed-term contracts. This is sometimes described as *casualisation* of the workforce.

The overall effect of these changes is that the 'culture' of television production has changed – producers are more concerned about future employment contracts, and the range of programming is less varied and more influenced by ratings. Television has become 'advertising-led', responding to perceptions about what the market will bear rather than what programme-makers think would be interesting and challenging.

The broadcasting unions and work practices

Staff in television production before the 1990s were often regarded as craft workers with strict demarcation of graded posts according to job function. The broadcast unions were able to negotiate very tight regulations for what constituted a recognised 'crew' on a broadcast shoot. The result was the development of a workforce with high levels of specialist skill. Broadcast (and film industry) work was virtually a '*closed shop*', with all recognised technicians requiring a union card specifying a job grade. The overall effect of this was to create a unique production environment in which work of very high technical quality could be guaranteed and with it a degree of creative freedom for writers and directors who could rely on efficient production practices. In protecting their members' jobs and working conditions, however, the unions (including the actors' union Equity) could also be seen as putting a brake on any rapid change in the nature of broadcasting production (and programming).

The film and broadcast union **BECTU** was formed in 1991 after a merger of two smaller unions. This strengthened bargaining power through co-ordination of negotiations, but the environment had changed

BECTU   The Broadcasting, Entertainment, Cinematograph and Theatre Union has a useful website detailing its activities.

dramatically with the shift to independent production and the gradual move to *multiskilling* within the BBC and ITV companies, which has broken down much of the specialisation. BECTU has become much more concerned about the training of freelances and has slowly come to accept that the changes in work patterns brought about by deregulation and the adaptation of new technologies have to be negotiated. Broadcasting now looks much more like a competitive industry. Becoming 'leaner and meaner' has not, however, prevented the gradual erosion of overall market share held by the terrestrial broadcasters in the face of increased activity by satellite and cable operators. Enough of the public are voting with their remote controls for other forms of television to make further changes to the idea of broadcasting institutions inevitable.

Involving the audience

The irony of the changes in broadcasting is that, while critics accuse the broadcasters of thinking about audiences only in terms of 'numbers' for 'delivery' to advertisers, the broadcasters themselves are increasingly turning to audiences as part of the programming. One of the main growth areas in radio has been the 'phone-in' talk show and on television the talk show featuring 'ordinary people' in extraordinary situations such as *Jerry Springer* or *Oprah*. These shows are popular with broadcasters because they can attract high ratings on the basis of relatively low production costs. They are despised by some critics pursuing that definition of quality associated with 'excellence', because of the relatively 'low level of debate'. Yet they meet the other quality criterion of a variety of programming. The problems may arise if this form of programming 'drives out' more expensive productions, eventually reducing the range.

See 'Audiences', Chapter 32, and in particular Activity 32.9.

The terms of this debate are steeped in class and gender divisions. Talk shows like *Oprah* are perceived as appealing not only to the 'lowest common denominator' audiences but also primarily to women rather than men. The two extreme positions – 'the market will decide' and 'the programme-makers should make what they think is important' – are unlikely to find much favour with audiences generally. What is the alternative? Are we likely to see more attempts to run 'focus groups', to organise 'open days' and to encourage more audience response programmes?

One observation seems clear. The number of 'national broadcasting events' with an assumed large-scale audience is diminishing all the time – the coverage of the Football World Cup in 1998 stands out. Successful network television programmes now average ten million viewers – five million fewer than at the start of the 1990s. Audiences are gradually beginning to see themselves not as an automatic part of a national audience but more a part of a particular audience for a particular type of programme. The possible consequence of this is that viewers and listeners will begin to think about paying for a particular programme rather than for a general radio or television programme. Such a change would be revolutionary in terms of the institution of broadcast television and is covered in more detail in the case study which follows.

Censorship and audience responses

Much of the discussion in this section on broadcasting has been based on the move to more 'market-led' programming, but there are other market ideas which are also important. We might want to consider the idea of a 'social market', i.e. a competitive market in which social policies or constraints play a role (a key aspect of the Blair government's 'Third Way'). In media markets this is quite noticeable in respect of ideas about 'acceptable media products' and the need for 'self-censorship' by media institutions. This goes beyond broadcasting to include print media and cinema.

See 'Technologies', Chapter 14, on pornography on the Internet and the institutional moves to 'self-regulate'.

In a 'free market' we might expect to see a thriving trade in pornographic material, as is the case in many European countries, if that is what people wish to buy. However, the very advocates of the free market are often amongst those who wish to control access to the marketplace for certain kinds of products. The result is that in terms of 'sex and violence' we expect to see the development of some form of *self-censorship* in all media, whereby the distribution companies in that medium agree to set standards for acceptable products. This has happened with film, magazines and more recently video and computer games. It is also largely what happens in broadcasting, where producers are not usually censored as such but attempt to second-guess the regulators in terms of what might be considered acceptable.

In this respect broadcasting has again been treated differently from the press. The newspaper industry still regulates itself through the industry-based Press Complaints Commission which investigates and pronounces on the actions of individual newspapers. The 1996 Broadcasting Act created the Broadcasting Standards Commission from two existing bodies. This is independent of broadcasters and investigates both personal complaints about invasion of privacy and general audience complaints about offensive material, but has no punitive powers. Both the PCC and BSC are relatively toothless, but the broadcasters are more sensitive about possible complaints because their environment is governed by legislation to a greater extent than print publishing.

The oddity of the debate about sex and violence in broadcasting (or in print or on film) is that the issue is rarely put to the market test. We don't know what would happen if 'hard' material were freely available – if it is unacceptable to a large number of media consumers, perhaps 'the market' would drop it from general release when it didn't sell? There are many pressure groups arguing for censorship but few actively campaigning against. One argument might be that the current attitude to self-censorship is patronising towards the audience. If someone is capable of making a decision about whether a media product represents 'value for money', why can't they also decide whether or not it is offensive and 'liable to corrupt'? And if they can't decide, what makes a programme-maker better qualified to decide? This is the argument as presented by the libertarian right and is a complete refutation of public service broadcasting, without the qualifications of the social market position 'if I like it, it's erotic, if I don't, it's pornographic'.

In some respects this libertarian position looks very attractive (assuming that children are protected from 'offensive' material). However, 'freedom to choose' is also the freedom to be assailed by fierce marketing and the possibility that the acceptability of more explicit sex or violence will lead to more of such programming and less overall variety of material.

During 1998 various research activities suggested that audiences were less concerned about sex on television than was generally believed. Channel 5 turned to regular late-night programming of material which had previously been considered as 'soft porn'. At the same time, ITV and Channel 4 screened drama series featuring nudity, which some critics saw as a return to 1970s 'broadcast standards'.

ACTIVITY 26.4

Censorship of offensive material

How do you think censorship of offensive material should be handled in the media? How would you define 'offensive material'?

- What would be the consequences of a media environment without any censorship of offensive material? What do you think would happen in a free market?
- What are the arguments for and against such material only being available through licensed outlets at premium prices (could it be taxed like cigarettes and alcohol)?
- What are the arguments for banning such material altogether?
- Why is self-censorship preferred to an 'official censor' in UK media industries?

This topic is a good one to choose if you want to try producing a video or audio 'debate'-style programme. You should quite easily find people prepared to adopt specific positions. But first you will have to decide whether it is going to be a 'balanced' programme, or whether as producer you want to slant it in any particular way – in other words, you need to think about the institutional factors.

The development of **spin doctoring** and the effective control of ministers to keep them 'on message' by the Downing Street Press Office, introduced by the Blair administration, is part of the same process.

Censorship in relation to political issues is handled rather differently by UK media institutions. Once again the main burden falls on the broadcasters, who are expected to uphold access to the media for a range of viewpoints and to present them within a broadly balanced programme schedule. Broadcasters are always attacked by politicians in power, by either of the main parties. One strategy employed by government to undermine broadcasters is to introduce subtle changes to the funding environment. A second is to conduct a public campaign of criticism in an attempt to move public opinion against broadcasters. Newspapers can be important in this action – being used to support government or acting as a forum for defence of broadcasters. In the face of sustained criticism, broadcasting chiefs are made to feel defensive and may be persuaded to cut controversial programming.

This 'bad-mouthing' can be accompanied by occasional destructive physical actions. In 1987 a BBC programme about British spy satellites was not broadcast because the tapes were seized under the Official Secrets Act. Usually, the UK authorities avoid being seen to censor. The stark evidence of censorship – a blank page in a newspaper – is often self-defeating, drawing attention to what cannot be said. We noted above the denying of a 'voice' for the IRA on television or radio (withdrawing the 'oxygen of publicity' in Margaret Thatcher's words) as an example of government intervention. It is a good example of a misunderstanding of audiences and their role in the broadcasting institution on the part of government advisers. Allowing an IRA represenative to be shown while an actor spoke his words irritated IRA supporters, angered Loyalists who wanted the IRA banned altogether and struck the bulk of the audience as plain silly.

References

Adie, Kate (1998) 'Dispatches from the Front: Reporting War', in Mike Ungersma, *Reporters and the Reported*.

Bell, Martin (1997) *In Harm's Way*, London: Hamish Hamilton.

Bromley, Michael (1997) 'The End of Journalism? Changes in Workplace Practices in the Press and Broadcasting in the 1990s', in Michael Bromley and Tom O'Malley (eds) *A Journalism Reader*, London: Routledge.

Cameron, James (1980) *Point of Departure*, London: Granada.

Carter, Cynthia, Branston, Gill and Allan, Stuart (eds) (1998) *News, Gender and Power*, London: Routledge.

Cohen, Phil and Gardner, Carl (eds) (1982) *It Ain't Half Racist, Mum: Fighting Racism in the Media*. London: Comedia.

Gardiner, Juliet (1993) *Picture Post Women*, London: Collins & Brown.

Hevey, David (1992) *The Creatures That Time Forgot: Photography and Disability Imagery*, London: Routledge.

Holland, Patricia (1998) 'The Politics of the Soft Smile: Soft News and the Sexualization of the Popular Press', in Cynthia Carter, Gill Branston and Stuart Allan (eds), *News, Gender and Power*, London: Routledge.

O'Malley, Tom and Treharne, Jo (1993) *Selling the Beeb*, London: Campaign for Press and Broadcasting Freedom.

O'Sullivan, Tim, Hartley, John, Saunders, Danny, Montgomery, Martin and Fisk, John (1994, 2nd edition) *Key Concepts in Cultural and Communication Studies*, London: Routledge.

Sebba, Anne M. (1998) 'Women and the Fourth Estate', in Ungersma, *Reporters and the Reported*.

Spence, Jo and Solomon, Joan (eds) (1995) *What Can a Woman Do With a Camera?*, London: Routledge.

Ungersma, Mike (ed.) (1998) *Reporters and the Reported: The 1998 Vauxhall Lectures on Contemporary Issues in British Journalism*, Cardiff: Centre for Journalism Studies, Cardiff University (also available on the Internet at `http://www.cardiff.ac.uk`).

Further reading

An accessible collection of short essays which addresses many of the issues relating to broadcasting:

Ralph, Sue, Langham Brown, Jo and Lees, Tim (1998) *What Price Creativity?*, Luton: University of Luton Press/John Libbey Media.

The Media Handbook series from Routledge provides useful material on institutional issues, especially:

Holland, Pat (1997) *The Television Handbook*, London: Routledge.

Free Press, the Newsletter of the Campaign for Press and Broadcasting Freedom, is a good source of information on stories concerning industrial relations, regulation and other institutional issues. Visit the CPBF website for updates on Campaign policies.

As well as the Michael Bromley article cited above, there are several other useful articles in *A Journalism Reader*.

27 / Case study: Public service broadcasting

In 1997 the BBC celebrated 75 years of broadcasting. Although it began life as a private (i.e. 'profit-driven') company, within five years the BBC had been taken into the *public sector* (i.e. resourced from public funds like the licence fee) and has ever since been an integral part of the concept of **public service broadcasting** (PSB) in the UK. The concept of radio and television broadcasting which 'serves the public interest' has developed and changed considerably over those seventy-five years and now faces real challenges. The concept of PSB is examined in detail in this case study, which begins by identifying the current PSB institutions.

A brief outline history of PSB institutions

The expansion of UK broadcasting which followed the introduction of what was then called 'commercial television' in 1955, 'commercial radio' in 1973 and Channel 4 in 1982, was in each case shaped by the context of the existing public service broadcasting environment. This was perhaps less the case with the rather low-key introduction of Channel 5 in 1997, but the discussion surrounding the launch of digital television services in 1998 drew heavily on ideas of PSB.

In the late 1990s the PSB sector in the UK comprises:
- BBC Television and Radio
- Channel 4 and S4C

Most viewers recognise the PSB responsibilities of the BBC, but C4 is often assumed to be a private company, probably because it carries advertising.

The BBC was established by Royal Charter, which has been renewed on a ten-yearly basis (2006 is the next renewal date), in order to provide radio and television services in the UK plus the World Service. Governors are appointed by the Crown and they in turn appoint the executives. The Corporation is, in theory, 'independent' of the government. In practice, pressure can be exerted on BBC management in two ways:
- Governors may be appointed because of their sympathies for government policies.
- Parliament decides the size of the licence fee and there is no guarantee it will rise with inflation to meet perceived costs.

The BBC is *self-regulating*. Responsibility for all broadcasts lies with the senior management. There are relatively few external restraints on BBC operations, and the Corporation has recently established BBC Worldwide, a separate organisation in financial terms, which exploits BBC programme material, selling to subscription channels in the UK and abroad and direct to the public in magazines and videos. Profits from this venture are fed back into programme-making, supplementing the licence fee.

Channel 4 has a remit first established by Parliament in 1981 and then revised in the Broadcasting Acts of 1990 and 1996. Initially a subsidiary of the Independent Broadcasting Authority (the forerunner to the Independent Television Commission), Channel 4 became a public corporation in 1993 with a ten-year licence from the ITC. The non-executive directors who make up the majority of the Board of Directors are appointed by the ITC, which is also the regulator for Channel 4. Channel 4 is funded by sale of advertising time. Originally this was organised via the Channel 3

companies, which took some of the income, but Channel 4 is now able to sell time on its own behalf and to keep all the income.

S4C is a statutory authority set up in Wales to provide a service using programme material from the BBC and Channel 4, as well as commissioned work. It is like the BBC in being a self-regulating broadcaster (even though it must follow ITC rules on advertising). S4C must broadcast some programmes in the Welsh language.

Regulation bodies

The ITC also regulates the operation of the privately owned companies which broadcast via the Channel 3 network (ITV), Channel 5 and cable and satellite. This regulation is 'light-touch' and requires only a general

C4 INFO

Channel 4 is a public service for information, education and entertainment. The Broadcasting Act 1990 requires that Channel 4 programmes shall: appeal to tastes and interests not generally catered for by ITV, encourage innovation and experiment, be distinctive, maintain a high general standard and a wide range, include a proportion which are educational, provide high quality news and current affairs, include proportions which are European and are supplied by independent producers.

The channel has steadfastly maintained its commitment to this remit since the start of its transmissions in 1982 and through many subsequent changes in the United Kingdom broadcasting industry.

Figure 27.1 Channel 4's policy statement on its website, reflecting the licence conditions

adherence to 'quality programming' rather than the specific public service requirements which existed before 1992. The ITV network is no longer a PSB provider (it had been between 1955 and 1992). The PSB ethos is still discernible in individual Channel 3 programmes, but is slowly disappearing from scheduling.

There are two other public sector authorities with regulatory duties. The *Radio Authority* regulates independent (private sector) radio stations and is therefore not directly concerned with PSB (although it does also grant Restricted Service Licences (RSLs) to community groups, including schools and colleges). The *Broadcasting Standards Commission* publishes decisions on complaints made by the public about both PSB and private sector broadcasting.

Defining PSB in the 1980s and 1990s

PSB is a term which is freely used, but not always with a clear sense of understanding. This checklist of features is based on work by an independent agency, the *Broadcasting Research Unit*, during the 1980s (see O'Malley and Treharne 1993). PSB should:

- provide a full range of programming to meet audience needs for education, entertainment and information
- be universally available (i.e. throughout the UK)
- cater for all interests and tastes
- cater for minorities
- have a concern for 'national identity' and community
- be detached from vested interests and government
- be one broadcasting body financed directly by the body of users
- promote competition in good programming rather than in numbers of viewers
- be run on guidelines which liberate and do not restrict programme-makers.

This is a more useful set of criteria than traditional definitions which simply quote the relevant sections of broadcasting legislation or the BBC's Charter. It refers to many of the debates about the institution of broadcasting which have developed since the mid-1980s, when 'free market philosophy' was first brought to bear on all aspects of public provision by the Thatcher government. It also helps us think about changes in technology and global issues of media production and distribution as they affect the UK.

Specified programming aims

The BBC and Channel 4 are both required to carry educational programming and significant news and current affairs. This is written into the BBC charter and Channel 4 licence. The removal of education programming from the ITV network after the 1990 Broadcasting Act was both a symbolic move away from an ITV PSB role and an opportunity to develop morning and afternoon programming.

Universal access

A universal service is one provided according to need rather than profit and is based on 'equality of access'. The same argument applies to most of the privatised utilities, implying that every consumer is entitled to the same service, despite the difference in cost of supply – the low-cost services effectively subsidise the high-cost ones. A good example is the Post Office. We all expect to send and receive letters with the same charge for a stamp and the same guarantees on delivery whether we live in a London suburb or on a remote Scottish island.

The 'capture' of exclusive screenings of popular sporting events by BSkyB is a good example of the 'equal access' to a service being replaced by the willingness to pay for an encrypted service. It has therefore become a matter for parliamentary debate as to which sporting events are of special national interest and should be reserved for 'free access' terrestrial television. This has proved to be a difficult debate. In 1998 the cricket authorities argued that, without the extra money that BSkyB was willing to pay for exclusive coverage, the game might not be able to maintain the standard of test cricket in the UK (i.e. not enough money comes in via the gate receipts and sponsorship).

Equal access arguments have also been recognised as powerful levers on opinion by the BBC in promoting its services. A major row broke out in 1998 with the launch of '24 Hour News'. This was made freely available to all cable companies, as well as being broadcast on terrestrial television during the night-time gap between daily transmissions. Many cable companies then dropped Sky News from their packages because BSkyB charged them a fee. BSkyB used this case to argue that the BBC was acting unfairly.

However, the BBC has itself entered into various agreements and deals which see it participating in delivery of programming on cable and satellite which is restricted in some way. 1998 saw the introduction of a package of cable channels (UK Horizons, Style and Arena), largely filled with BBC programmes and delivered in partnership with the American company Flextech.

Access also relates to physical location. The postal analogy is useful here. A broadcast signal (as distinct from satellite or cable) is notoriously difficult (and expensive) to deliver in parts of the country where hills prevent reception. Should broadcasters receive extra public funds to enable transmission to these areas? Channel 5's launch suffered from real or imagined difficulties in delivering a worthwhile signal to around 30 per cent of the population. Channel 5 is a private sector organisation, but should government have done more to enable potential viewers to receive the signal (some areas cannot be covered because a broadcasting frequency is not available)?

Catering for all interests and tastes (and minorities)

Equality of access also extends to consumer tastes – does the public service provider broadcast 'something for everyone', including some programmes which will have limited appeal? There is a limit to the range of specialist interests which can be included (and some may be deemed offensive to other groups) but there is a clear duty for both BBC and Channel 4 to act in such a way to guarantee a range of programming, from *EastEnders* to *The Late Review*, *Countdown* to *World Cinema*.

The BBC aims to provide a broad spread of popular programming on BBC1 and to supplement this with more varied material on BBC2. Channel 4 has the licence requirement to cater for interests beyond those targeted by Channel 3 (ITV network), in terms of both programme content and 'experimental and innovative approaches to broadcasting'.

One of the ironies of the 'competitive market conditions' which have developed in recent years is that this requirement to cater for more specialised tastes has not, at first sight, been the weak point of PSB provision. The commonly held view that 'dumbing-down' in the face of commercial competition from satellite and cable was inevitable, can be challenged. The figures show that it is ITV which is losing audiences while BBC and Channel 4 are keeping roughly their share (see Table 27.1).

Table 27.1 Audience share for UK broadcasters 1995–8

	BBC1	BBC2	ITV	C4	C5	Others
1998 (1st qtr)	30.8	10.8	32.1	10.3	3.4	12.7
1997 (year)	31.8	11.4	35.2	10.3	n.a.	11.2
1995 (year)	31.4	10.4	38.6	10.9	-	8.7

('Others' includes all non-terrestrial satellite and cable and cable viewing)

In line with the general policy towards public services during the Conservative administrations of 1979–97, the transmission of programmes was taken away from the broadcasters in the 1990 and 1996 Broadcasting Acts and vested in separate organisations. 'Broadcasters' is therefore perhaps an inappropriate term for all the terrestrial channels in the UK – they are really 'publishers' (see 'Digital publishing and the Internet', Case study 15).

ACTIVITY 27.1

Audience share

Look at Table 27.1 carefully.

- What has been the main impact of the arrival of Channel 5 on the audience shares of the other broadcasters?
- Has broadcasting funded by advertising increased its share since 1995?
- Has the PSB share changed significantly?
- Try to check the current figures in *Broadcast* – what has happened since 1998?

You may be surprised by your answers to the Activity questions. (What the figures don't tell you is that the relatively small increase in viewing of satellite and cable represents a large increase in revenue for the subscription channels.)

There is an argument that suggests that the relative success of Channel 4 and BBC2 is indeed because they have gone for more popular programming. However, advertisers are pleased to see that in relative terms (i.e. as a proportion of any audience) Channel 4 attracts more ABC1s than other channels, considerably more sixteen- to twenty-four-year-olds and nearly 25 per cent more of the hard-to-capture 'light viewers' (Channel 4 *Annual Report* 1997). This is an issue about '**niche**' or specialised markets. As long as these markets are supported by ABC1 consumers, there is going to be a demand for programming to target them (and by extension, a case for BBC2 to offer a service). The problem comes when the 'minority taste' is shared only by relatively poor consumers who are not of interest to advertisers.

The **segmenting** of audiences by ethnic or language grouping is interesting in that providing programming for all so-called 'minority communities' was a main aim of Channel 4 programming in the 1980s but has arguably been less noticeable in the 1990s. In the meantime, two satellite and cable channels have developed to serve

South Asian communities in the UK, with a third, the much glossier Sony channel, in 1998. It is difficult to obtain viewing figures for these channels (they are not published regularly by BARB), but there is a large potential market, partially served by video rental and the resurgence of cinemas showing Bollywood films. Looked at a different way, there are over a million Muslims in the UK – a sizeable market with a common interest.

ACTIVITY 27.2

Minority audiences

A newspaper report in 1997 revealed that opera was one of the least well-supported forms of programming on UK television. The figures showed audiences of less than 180,000. This represents many more people than ever get to see productions at Covent Garden, but it is said to be unacceptably low for broadcasting. Try the following in discussion with other students:

- Bearing in mind the comments about 'minority tastes' above, draw up a list of types of programming which might appeal to specific minority tastes.
- Draw up a second list of criteria to use in deciding which programmes should be broadcast on a public service channel. What would be your cut-off point for audience numbers?

Concern for 'national identity' and community

This issue has already been broached in relation to the 'reserve' list of television events, especially sporting events. Its long history and its active role in supporting morale during the Second World War has helped to create a sense of the BBC as a national 'institution', which has great resonance for older viewers and listeners. Much of this has been passed on to younger audiences (not least because the BBC is able to use its archives to support commemorations such as those for D-Day in 1994 and thereby to re-establish its reputation).

Figure 27.2 The BBC has developed an extensive website which attempts to present a view of the corporation as accessible

Diana, Princess of Wales, suggest that 'reading the public mood' may be difficult.

The main point here is that the PSB dimension does give an advantage to the BBC, and perhaps, to a lesser extent, to Channel 4. Private sector companies like BSkyB would find it difficult to present a case for their own programming to be seen as representing national identity, especially when the major interest in the channel is held by Australian-American Rupert Murdoch (although it has to be said that the *Sun* newspaper has often been successful in waving the Union Jack). Similarly, the separate companies which make up Channel 3 have rarely managed to compete effectively with the BBC over coverage of national events via the operations of ITN and ITV Sport. This was demonstrated again by the audience responses to World Cup football coverage on the two channels, with the BBC once again gaining higher ratings.

The BBC helps to sustain a uniquely British, immensely varied national identity, across every part of the United Kingdom. We try to stretch audiences and to stretch talent. We are the bridge between the two.

(John Birt, Director-General of the BBC,
75th Anniversary Lecture, January 1998)

But this sense of national leadership can also provoke resistance to a sense of stuffiness or superiority (particularly a sense of metropolitan condescension for audiences outside London). As if to counter this perception, the ITC licence has now been amended to require Channel 4 to originate more than 30 per cent of UK production from outside London by 2002.

Channel 4 has a PSB role to 'innovate', not an assumed leadership role – indeed, it could be argued that its role is to counter the BBC's appeal and offer a different sense of national identity, which it has done at Christmas with an alternative 'Queen's Speech'. Do you see this as a bit of fun, mildly offensive or as making a serious point? Certainly, there is an obvious question about what is the 'national identity' for audiences in the UK (see 'Globalisation', Chapter 20). The more difficult aspects of the question arise with the coverage of the death of members of the royal family. The reactions to the coverage of the funeral of

---

ACTIVITY 27.3

Idents

Refer back to 'The languages of media' (Chapter 1) and discussion of logos. Consider the **idents** or channel logos for the main broadcasters (and cable stations if possible).

● What do the idents signify about the ethos of the programming on the channel?

● In particular compare idents for the PSB and private sector channels – is there an obvious difference?

● Do any of the idents pick up on ideas of national identity?

Detachment from vested interests and government

At the centre of the PSB argument is the idea of an independent and impartial broadcaster, serving the interests of the whole population of the UK, not just the government of the day or private shareholders.

The system works by vesting the legal authority for the operation of the PSBs in legislation or Royal Charter. This in turn sets up management structures independent of government and a reasonable period of guaranteed 'licence' in which to operate. It is worth remembering, however, that a government minister, in 1998 the Secretary of State for Culture, Media and Sport, effectively appoints the Chair of BBC Governors and of Channel 4. The government is also able to determine the BBC licence fee and to change the rules governing Channel 4's finances.

One broadcasting body financed directly by users

This criterion perhaps best reveals the 1980s arguments which underpin the list. In relation to the increasingly global media production and distribution environment and the similarly 'open' financial environment (i.e. the absence of protective legislation against multinational corporations moving into national markets), it is difficult to predict the future of PSB.

The principle at stake is clear. 'One body' states a case for a dedicated PSB provider, unencumbered with distracting and possibly conflicting aims in other sectors or territories or with partners of any kind. Both the BBC and Channel 4 have found it necessary to seek partners in order to finance productions. Often this is with other PSB providers in North America or Europe, but the BBC sees itself as a major 'player' and has made deals with a number of private sector organisations including Discovery Channel and Flextech.

The BBC is indeed a major broadcaster – ranked sixteenth in the list of global media corporations for 1996 with an audiovisual turnover of $3.275 billion. This is behind other PSB broadcasters, the German ARD (seventh) and Japanese NHK (eighth) and a long way short of the giants Time Warner, Disney, Sony and Viacom.

(*Screen International*, 13 December 1996)

The licence fee does see the BBC funded directly by its 'users', whereas Channel 4 relies on sale of advertising. The BBC also raises revenue from the sales of programmes and related material. Subscription income has come from encrypted programming and the Flextech package takes advertising.

If the principle is clear and the danger identified – a broadcasting environment dominated by multinational media corporations unlikely to conform to PSB strictures – the direction of future policy is not so clear. The cultural importance of a securely financed 'British broadcaster' is such that any UK government is likely to feel that it is in the public interest to allow the BBC to make its deals and to retain a place in the international market. This might also explain why governments have been amenable to the 'consolidation' of the ITV network companies into three main groups – rather domination by Granada, Carlton and UNM than possible entry by larger American players. (Cable is already an American-owned sector.)

Competition in programming rather than numbers of viewers

UK television moved during the Thatcher years from programme-led production to advertising-led production. This was the inevitable result of the promotion of the market as determining factor. It is difficult to assess exactly how the 'ethos' of an organisation changes, but in 'Institutions' (Chapter 26) there is an analysis of the changing 'culture' of production. If the late 1990s are compared to the so-called 'Golden Age' of the 1970s, there is little doubt that current producers are much less likely to be supported by management if risky ventures don't show immediate returns in terms of audience numbers. The future of PSB is in doubt if 'ratings' become the only basis for judging the success of programmes.

In defence of BBC and Channel 4 schedulers, it must be said that during 1996–8 they have played the numbers game pretty well. It remains to be seen whether or not this can be translated into greater future security for PSB aims.

Liberation not restriction for programme-makers

This criterion follows on from the last one. Again, it suggests harking back to a Golden Age when programme-makers were supported and nurtured. The impact of the 25 per cent production quota has been to:

- create a group of small independent production companies with loose ties to broadcasters
- assist in the breaking-up of the long-established production units in the BBC.

While it will still be possible to maintain short-term relationships with creative partnerships of writers, directors and producers, there is no going back, and, as the BBC continues to become more 'efficient' it risks alienating many of its previous supporters.

A feature of the late 1990s has been the movement of production executives between the BBC and the main ITV groups such as Granada. This has been a two-way process, suggesting that there is perhaps now less difference in the ethos operating in the two organisations. The move of Michael Jackson, hailed as the successful head of BBC2, to the top job at Channel 4 was also significant. It is not always the individual personalities who are so important as the teams of people they bring with them and the messages which such moves send out to the industry as a whole.

The movement of senior staff between organisations is also a function of competition and, now that we have established the basis for the PSB tradition, it is time to look more closely at the contemporary broadcasting environment.

Digital broadcasting and global media

The ideas about PSB discussed above were all developed at a time when broadcasting remained largely a concern of nationally defined organisations. (One feature of the earlier period was the limited number of broadcast frequencies allocated by international agreement and then internally by national governments – 'spectrum scarcity'.) The loosening of regulatory controls, government policies fostering competition and the development of new technologies for programme delivery (i.e. satellite, cable and digital broadcasting) mean that all territories are opening up to penetration by global rather than solely national broadcasters.

In this context the BBC seems, at first glance, in a stronger position than Channel 4. The BBC is a 'global broadcaster' and has been so for longer than any other body. The radio World Service has been for many critics the epitome of a PSB ideal, offering a degree of impartial news and comment on events in all parts of the world, delivered in many languages. But it has become increasingly short of resources, as well as being marginalised by the expansion of television services such as CNN. In order to fund BBC World Television, the corporation has had to divert resources from other areas or raise extra money (UK licence payers funding a World Service is an issue).

A different challenge comes in the home market, where PSB faces a difficult future. In order to get some perspective on this debate it is helpful to compare the UK situation with other countries. Television Studies has often tended to compare the UK and the US, partly because of the familiarity of some of the programme material, partly because the difference in status for PSB in the two systems is so great.

In the US broadcasting is dominated by four commercial networks: ABC (owned by Disney), CBS, NBC and Fox Television (owned by News Corporation). These networks have local 'affiliates' who take their programming and they also compete with independents, cable and satellite in terms of entertainment and news services. The Public Broadcasting System (PBS) is an affiliation of small television and radio stations in the major cities, with limited budgets and small (but elite) audiences. They have limited capacity to make programmes and buy in material like *Absolutely Fabulous* from the BBC and other larger producers. (They also co-produce with the BBC.)

> It is one of the ironies of the trade in television programming that American audiences see popular British shows on the minority PBS network, while UK audiences get top-rated American shows like *Friends* and *er* on Channel 4 or BBC2.

The PSB situation in the US is so 'bad' (i.e. so limited by lack of resources) that in the UK it is assumed that 'it could never happen here', or the situation is used as a dire warning about what might happen if competition gets out of control.

PSB in Germany

More useful as a comparison is the German situation. German broadcasting, with its history of domination by the Nazi Party in the 1930s and during the Second World War, was restructured on the British model after 1945. There are two PSB organisations, ARD (a very long German title roughly translated as Federation of Broadcasting Organisations), which offers general programming, and ZDF (Zweites Deutsche Fernsehen – 'Second German Television'), which has a more 'cultural' focus. Each operates several different channels.

Because of Germany's federal system, ARD and ZDF are regulated and managed by structures set up by the *Länder* (the regional governments) rather than by the federal government. They are financed through a licence fee system and face competition from private sector broadcasters. In 1996 the combined audience for PSB in Germany was 39 per cent, similar to the BBC, but less than BBC plus Channel 4.

Figure 27.3 The combined website of ARD and ZDF shows the range of PSB radio and television channels, including Kinderkanal (Children's), ARTE (Joint Arts channel with a French partner) and the regional stations

There are two notable differences between Germany and the UK in terms of PSB. German law gives PSB a constitutional right to 'extend the scope of its broadcasting provision', but the same organisations are restricted from engaging in commercial partnerships. By contrast, the BBC has less recourse to law, but more freedom (within certain limits) to explore partnerships.

Up until the late 1980s there was no real private sector television in Germany. Now more than 80 per cent of homes are connected to satellite or cable and the two main private channels, SAT-1 and RTL, now take the largest audience share. Penetration of satellite and cable is closer to 30 per cent in the UK. How much is this a factor in explaining the difference in audience share?

ARD and ZDF programming has tended to be 'worthy' and politically very 'balanced', and some commentators have suggested that, just as the arrival of ITV in 1955 provoked the BBC to change, the German PSB channels have also become more adventurous.

An important similarity between the German and British broadcasting environment is the role of the powerful press corporations, Springer and Bertelsmann, with stakes in the private sector television channels. Springer owns *Bild*, a *Sun*-like German tabloid. News Corporation, so far unable to break into UK terrestrial television, has also been involved in German developments.

The PSB funding dilemma

German and British PSB (excluding Channel 4) rely on a licence fee paid by all viewers, irrespective of whether they use the service. The major advantage of this system to the broadcaster is a guaranteed income. The disadvantage is potential interference from the legislators in terms of setting fee levels. In return for the fee, PSB must be universal and accountable to the general audience.

The private sector competition has for long been dependent on advertising income. This can rise or fall with the strength of the economy and is always vulnerable to competition from other media selling space. Some of the newer private services are funded by direct fee for each programme watched (Pay Per View – **PPV**) or subscription to a channel (BSkyB now gets an annual income from movie subscription channels which is greater than the annual UK cinema box office). These new methods mean that viewers are now more closely tied to 'products purchased' than to a PSB ideal.

The dilemma for PSB is clear. Stick with the licence fee and watch production values fall and audiences with them (the rise in the licence fee has failed to match inflation in production costs for several years now) or go for more popular programming ('dumbing down'?) and face criticism from important political supporters? The BBC move to find new partners and increase commercial revenue is similarly fraught with dangers. Seeing the BBC logo associated with a commercial venture might make some audiences think about 'selling-out', while others will wonder why they pay a licence fee if the corporation can make money through charging for its services.

ACTIVITY 27.4

Paying for television

There are several ways to pay for television services:

- advertising – e.g. current ITV, Channel 4 etc.
- licence fee – e.g. BBC
- PPV – e.g. 'one-off' sports events, concerts
- subscription – e.g. Sky Movie Channels.

Think about your own viewing habits. Imagine that you could have only one form of television service, paid for by only one of these methods. Which would you choose? Now think about two other groups of viewers: a family with young teenagers, an older person living alone. What would be best for them?

- What does this exercise tell you about the dilemma for PSB?

The German comparison also reminds us that in the global/regional media market the future of UK broadcasting is to a large extent tied up with Europe and the EU.

European requirements of Channel 4 licence

In 1997 Channel 4 sourced 63 per cent of programmes from Europe (against a quota requirement of 50 per cent), of which 46 per cent met EU definitions of 'independent production' (against a 10 per cent minimum).

(Channel 4 *Annual Report* 1997)

Policies relating to PSB are discussed at EU level and are to a certain extent 'built in' to regulatory duties expected of appropriate agencies in all EU member countries (similar PSB and private sector issues are found in most parts of Europe). It was no surprise then, that Rupert Murdoch was a key speaker at the 1998 European Audio-Visual Conference, where he sought to counter the views of the BBC and to woo EU commissioners.

Jeannette Steemers (1998) is a useful source on the European dimension of this issue as well as the future of PSB in the brave new digital world of more than two hundred channels. This is a very complex debate and we can only pick out a few main points here, but they will act as a summary of this case study and should be considered in relation to other parts of the book (including 'Digital publishing and the Internet', Case study 15):

- The digital 'revolution' in which the PSB providers will participate with the private sector, will take some time to make a big impact – five years or longer from 1999.
- The BBC is taking steps to become a major digital player. Channel 4 is more circumspect, with only a film channel and an education service as 'extras' planned in 1998.
- The future of the licence fee is still doubtful; subscription is becoming an important revenue source for broadcasters.
- The principle of PSB still has mileage in the twenty-first century, *but* the PSB institutions of the last twenty

years may not be the most appropriate organisations for the future.

- The convergence of media technologies means that other forms of public access to media may be appropriate as well as, or instead of, PSB (e.g. guaranteed Internet access for all households).

References

O'Malley, Tom and Treharne, Jo (1993) *Selling the Beeb*, London: Campaign for Press and Broadcasting Freedom.

Steemers, Jeannette (1998) 'On the Threshold of the "Digital Age": Prospects for Public Broadcasting', in Jeannette Steemers (ed.) *Changing Channels*, Luton: University of Luton Press/John Libbey Media.

Further reading

Abercrombie, Nicholas (1996) *Television and Society*, Cambridge: Polity.

Ardagh, John (1995) *Germany and the Germans*, London: Penguin.

Crisell, Andrew (1997) *An Introductory History of British Broadcasting*, London: Routledge.

Geraghty, Christine and Lusted, David (eds) (1998) *The Television Studies Book*, London and New York: Arnold.

Hood, Stuart and Tabary-Peterssen, Thalia (1997, 4th revised edition) *On Television*, London: Pluto.

O'Sullivan, Tim, Dutton, Brian and Reyner, Philip (1998, 2nd edition) *Studying the Media: An Introduction*, London, New York, Melbourne and Auckland: Arnold.

Robillard, Serge (1995) *Television in Europe: Regulatory Bodies*, London: John Libbey Media.

Scannell, Paddy (1990) 'Public Service Broadcasting: The History of a Concept', in Andrew Goodwin and Gary Whannel (eds) *Understanding Television*, London: Routledge.

Thompson, John B. (1995) *The Media and Modernity: A Social Theory of the Media*, Cambridge: Polity.

The websites for Channel 4 and the BBC are excellent with massive amounts of useful information. The Channel 4 *Annual Report* and similar BBC documents are also extremely useful.

28 Independents and alternatives

Most discussion of media production and consumption involves the **mainstream**: large-scale activity, with a clear commercial purpose, driven primarily by a profit motive. 'Independence' is often presented as an attractive, rebellious place completely outside the commercial compromises of that mainstream. It may seem odd, then, to ask you to think of this 'mainstream' as in some ways a minority part of total media production. All of us produce media texts on a regular basis, even if we don't recognise them as such, and many media producers prefer to work to different priorities and to challenge many of the drives of the 'mainstream'. This chapter looks at some of these **independent** producers, mostly in the area of film and video, although our emphases and approaches apply equally to radio, photography and music.

Non-**mainstream** media might include educational and training material, parish newsletters, fanzines and 'amateur' and hobbyist material which might range from a few 'snaps' to sophisticated film narratives.

Myths of independence and authorship

Two of UK television's best-known programmes, *The Bill* and *Neighbours*, are produced by an 'independent'. **Pearson plc** is a media corporation with global operations, yet when its major UK television arm, Thames Television, lost the franchise to broadcast in London it became an independent supplier to ITV network – i.e. providing programming to the network as part of the 25 per cent independent production quota. If this is a surprising definition of 'independent', it is partly because the word still has strong romantic connotations of being completely 'free', 'creative' and 'outside'. These come in the end from powerful myths of authorship and independence which often get in the way of thinking about the actual problems and possibilities of independent production today. So we'll first look briefly at the history of this powerful emphasis.

Pearson plc is one of the largest European media corporations, with substantial television interests. It claims to be the world's biggest television production company, specialising in serial drama and entertainment and making programmes worldwide. Its subsidiaries include Thames, Grundy and Alomo. Pearson has an extensive network of websites – look for 'pearsontv' or simply 'pearson.com'.

Authorship

The idea that 'the author' is the source of meaning and value in artistic texts has been a persistent one. We talk of Shakespeare's plays or Austen's novels in ways that suggest that William Shakespeare and Jane Austen are uniquely gifted and independent individuals, solely responsible for everything in their work. This view of art credits the author with power through having genius, and/or special experience, and emphasises the individual and 'special' over the social and the shared. This individualism is part of the world view that accompanied the rise of capitalism in Europe in the mid-sixteenth century (Murdock 1986). Until then, the idea of creation was reserved for God's act of creating the world. Cultural producers such as painters thought of themselves and were treated as merely skilled craftsmen making useful objects. Painters now celebrated as 'geniuses', like Botticelli, were quite happy to design wedding chests and decorate banners – as well as to produce the paintings which later critics have celebrated so differently.

But towards the end of the sixteenth century, culminating in nineteenth-century romanticism, artists began to be credited with rather special powers and were described via some of the assumptions which had previously been reserved for God:

Figure 28.1 Why do you think this logo was chosen for a prestigious television arts programme?

- No longer just an artisan, the artist increasingly had 'gifts' which were attributed to divine inspiration.
- Accordingly, artists were 'like God' in so far as they too were seen to create from the void.
- Flowing from this was an emphasis on the separation of the 'true artist' from his or her social setting, including the other people they worked with and for. All that was of interest was what 'the creative individual' was able to make from nothing, or against all odds, by means of the 'vision' or 'inner promptings' or 'talent' they had been 'blessed with'.

The image in numerous **biopics** is of the artist or author working in the garret, wild-eyed with solitary inspiration, and often hollow-cheeked because of concentration on higher things than how to earn enough to eat. Countless tales, films, television serials on artists such as the Brontës or Van Gogh (three feature films since the 1950s) have emphasised the virtues of unworldliness, solitude, the pre-industrial nature of paint or quill pen, rather than struggles over contracts, or with publishers and exhibitors, let alone existing and powerful conventions in chosen media.

Shakespeare in Love (US 1998) is in this way a refreshing change with its interest in deals, contracts, managers etc.

It's relatively easy to argue for individual inspiration if you're focusing on an apparently lone painter or poet. But, once industrial, technological and mass production of art takes place, such positions become less satisfactory. Typical mass-media products like films, television programmes and CDs are produced by numbers of people often employing complex technology.

The problem of authorship in the mass media has been most substantially confronted in the context of the cinema. In its early history

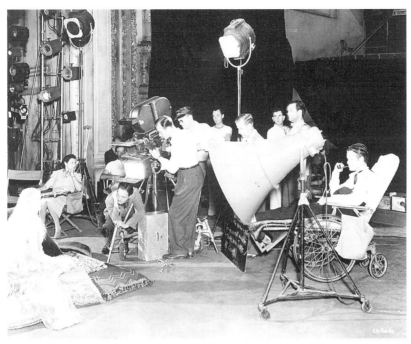

Figure 28.2   Orson Welles (seated in the wheelchair during this set-up for *Citizen Kane* (US 1941))
is a good example of the problem of 'genius' in mainstream production. After the commercial
failure of the expensively shot *Kane*, the major studio RKO cut Welles's next film savagely, and he
left the Hollywood studio system for a career as a maverick director and jobbing actor (and critical
acclaim as an *auteur*)

cinema was dismissed as an art form precisely because films were
produced by groups of people (directors, writers, cinematographers,
editors, sound recordists etc.).

A group of French critics writing in the magazine *Cahiers du Cinéma* in
the 1950s argued that the director was 'the artist' in the film-making
process and suggested that a close scrutiny of the films of directors like
Alfred Hitchcock or Roberto Rossellini revealed that they expressed a vision
of the world in the same way as Shakespeare did in his plays or Jane Austen
in her novels. Directors whose work expressed such a vision deserved to be
called *auteurs*. The championing of Hollywood directors like Hitchcock
was particularly controversial because the Hollywood system was seen as the
least sympathetic to possibilities of individual expression.

However, we'd like to take these terms further. Though the contribution
of a director like Tarantino or Cameron may be key to a film, we feel that
this long-standing emphasis on the separateness or 'outsideness' of 'authors'
and of independent work is not very useful. We want you to look, in
whatever kind of media production, for what it is dependent on, at what
costs, and with what advantages and disadvantages.

See Case study 19 *Pulp Fiction* for
more on Tarantino's status as
author.

ACTIVITY 28.1

The director

Look up some of the Internet websites or magazine articles which focus on a well-known director like James Cameron.

- Is the director treated like a 'sole creator'?
- What words or phrases suggest this?

Independents and finance

The usual definition of 'independent' media industries is very broad, encompassing every unit which is not an industry major. Let's categorise it more carefully.

The vicious circle facing independent producers comes at the stage of distribution. Making a media product is not necessarily a 'megabucks' affair. Modern technology means that a CD, a television programme, a magazine, even a film can be made for the kind of money which could be raised by anyone able to convince a friendly bank manager. But at the stage of distribution (see 'Industries', Chapter 22) money is needed to get the product in front of its intended audience. But this in turn is more likely to be successful if the product has production values – 'stars', special effects etc. – which require a higher production budget.

One possible solution is for independent producers to work in collaboration in networks of various kinds. In this way distribution structures serving several small companies can begin to compete with the majors. In the UK there have been several such independent distribution networks at different times over the last thirty years. Some have catered for film-makers, others for small book publishers, fanzines and specialist magazines, popular music etc.

ACTIVITY 28.2

Independent and mainstream

See 'Making and enjoying global music', Case study 21, for more on 'indie music'.

What is your idea of 'independent' and 'mainstream'? Draw up two lists of films or music acts which you recognise under these headings.

- What were the assumptions behind your allocation of the labels 'independent' and 'mainstream' – effectively the criteria you used to make a selection?

- See whether you can research the current status of your choices. Looking up a website is a useful ploy – there should be clues as to who is supporting distribution of a film or CD.

  You could also try this exercise with specialist magazines.

Mainstream and independent outside the UK and US

The distinction between mainstream and independent is apparent in all the national media industries around the world, but it is difficult to study from a UK perspective. Primarily, but not completely, it is the language difference, which means that any media text in a foreign language is treated as 'alternative'. In practice, distributors often make the assumption that popular 'mainstream' culture does not cross language barriers. So, although you will find the occasional French 'art' film in UK cinemas, you will rarely see a popular French comedy and never one from Italy or Germany. In many parts of the world there is a dominant Anglo-American culture, a national or regional mainstream and a local roots culture (see 'Globalisation', Chapter 20). Where there is a political or artistic resistance to the mainstream, there is the possibility of some recognition; this is taken up later in the chapter and in the case study which follows.

American independent cinema

In America in the 1980s some small independent film distributors were successful in establishing an alternative to Hollywood which became known as *American independent cinema*. Unable to spend enormous sums on publicity and promotion, independent distributors made as much as possible out of the interest they could generate from appearances by films and film-makers at festivals. The festival at Sundance in Colorado, later funded by Robert Redford, became well known for launching 'odd' or 'different' new films. Pierson (1995) dates the era of the independent from the mid-1980s through to *Pulp Fiction* (1994). Pierson points out that what changed in this period was that new film-makers who 'made a splash' at a festival were now much more likely to get a second and a third chance, because there was a structure to support them.

This structure existed partly because in the 1980s money was coming into the film industry in America from other media interests, especially video labels and the music industry. The independents needed exhibition outlets and to a certain extent these were the 'art houses' which had previously shown European films. (In the UK something similar

It's important to note that most of the films discussed in this part of the chapter were perhaps different in subject matter, but not so much in formal terms – see the later section on avant-garde films and Case study 29.

happened, and American independents began to appear in regional film theatres.) They also needed sensitive distributors who would know how to spend small budgets wisely (i.e. to spend enough to reach the target audience, but not to waste money) and to maximise potential revenue. For a time this was the case and the independents flourished.

The majors themselves are aware of the finance problem and they also know that many creative people are worried about being 'taken over' by the industry system. It is the originality and freshness of the independents which attracts interest from the majors, and they have set about recruiting this talent, without appearing to compromise the integrity of the film-makers. All of the Hollywood majors have set up or sometimes simply bought separate **'independent' distribution companies**, so that the 1997 Tarantino film *Jackie Brown*, though still a Miramax film, was marketed with all the muscle of Buena Vista (Disney). The Sundance Festival changed in the late 1990s to become more of a 'spot the next Tarantino' outing for the majors, and 'independent' became something of a marketing ploy.

This process of absorption by the majors can be seen at various times and in different media industries. Something similar has happened several times in the music industry, and the same analysis could be applied to the development of fanzines and the subsequent rise of much glossier 'lifestyle' magazines. However, there will always be a small number of media producers who will be very wary of getting involved with the majors. Film-maker **John Sayles** is a prominent example: 'The strings that come with a studio film usually aren't strings that I want attached to something that I'm going to spend a year of my life working on' (quote from Reuters, reported in *Screen International*, 10 April 1998).

There is more on Sayles in Case study 29, but he is relatively unusual. More common is the media producer who wants to utilise the power of the majors to reach audiences and to resource ambitious production ideas. Sometimes the independent route is the only one open to young creative people who simply want a chance to get started. But it may also be the case that they have specific 'political' or 'personal' concerns which the majors may not consider 'box office'. The decision to compromise or perhaps to try to work 'with and against' the majors is one which has faced several independent producers.

Spike Lee: moving towards the mainstream

Spike Lee is an interesting contrast to John Sayles. Lee produced just one independent film, *She's Gotta Have It* (US 1986), before making deals with the majors in order to get the necessary budgets and distribution for

Other 'independent' distribution companies include New Line (owned by Time Warner), Gramercy (owned by Polygram) and Fox Searchlight (Twentieth Century Fox).

John Sayles (born 1950) Leading American independent film-maker in the fullest possible sense of the word: screenwriter, editor, director, actor and financer, as well as novelist and playwright.

Spike Lee (born 1956) The son of a jazz musician and composer. A multi-talented producer-director and actor (including playing lead roles).

such controversial films as **Do the Right Thing** (US 1988) and *Malcolm X* (US 1992). Lee has embraced the commercialism of Hollywood wholeheartedly, signing up sponsorship deals and publishing through his '40 Acres and a Mule' production company. (Lee's choice of name for his company is significant – the phrase represents the dream (mostly unfulfilled) of the freed slaves after the Civil War.)

The possibility of an African-American writer-director (or for that matter a Native American or Hispanic American) gaining access to the mainstream before the success of Lee's films was slim. Earlier black directors had been confined largely to genre exploitation pictures. Many other African-American film-makers were designated 'independent' whether they wanted to be or not (see Case study 29 for more on this). Lee was criticised from within the black community for his move into the mainstream, but he could reasonably argue that, if he hadn't, such films as *Do the Right Thing* would not have been made or seen by so many people. (See 'Representations', Chapter 10, for further discussion of this issue.) The next generation, led by John Singleton (best known for *Boyz N the Hood* (US 1991)), did not have the same problem in getting mainstream work. Yet, in 1998, with Lee's box office declining and directors like Singleton failing to find big audiences, the majors still seemed to favour African-American *actors* rather than *directors*. How many contemporary African-American film directors can you think of?

Public funding

Independence for American film-makers is primarily a matter of finance, as this observation in a book on black independent film culture makes plain:

> what is really an 'independent film'? Anyone who has made even the simplest super 8 film knows that the phrase is a contradiction in terms. No film-maker is independent in the way that, say, a poet is. Film-making, both capital- and labour-intensive is the most dependent art form. This is both the blessing and the curse of the form. So the question has never been one of 'independence' or 'dependence', but merely the nature of one's dependence. At least in the US, film-making, more than other art forms, operates under Keynesian, or demand-side, economic constraints. Rather than a film being able to seek out and find an audience once made, many films without well-defined markets may simply not get funding in the first place.
>
> (Snead 1994)

Media production in the US does not generally receive public funding (although some forms of 'art production' such as photography are

Do the Right Thing (US 1988) A much discussed film about inner-city racism, based on a true incident, and the first mainstream African-American film to generate massive public interest, Lee's background and assumptions about how he should represent issues were at the centre of debate.

Will Smith, Morgan Freeman and Samuel Jackson are African-American actors whose success in blockbusters has tended to eclipse Spike Lee and the other leading African-American directors.

Independent Film-makers Association Founded in 1974 after a BBC2 executive responded to a group of independent film-makers with the retort 'I'm not having that sort of film on *my* television'. Later to include video, the IFVA played an influential, if controversial, role in developing the independent sector.

supported). Snead makes the point that this is in marked contrast to the UK, where 'black independents' have been able to develop projects funded by Channel 4 and the British Film Institute under the umbrella of **the 1982 Workshop Declaration**.

'The view of artistic production behind the Workshop Declaration is that it takes time and there has to be a space for failure for worthwhile work to be done. "Talent" is a learnt ability. Paradoxically, workshops could be seen to be trying to create the kind of environment the Hollywood studios offered' (Alan Lovell (1990) from the Birmingham Film and Video Workshop, at the time when its contract with Channel 4 was not renewed).

> **The 1982 Workshop Declaration** was made after discussions between the film technicians' union, ACTT (now BECTU), the **Independent Film and Videomakers Association**, (IFVA), the Regional Arts Associations and the British Film Institute.
>
> The declaration made possible 'accreditation' by the union (i.e. professional recognition) for formal production groups who would work together on a non-profit-distributing basis. Each group would have a minimum of four full-time members who would be involved in distribution, exhibition and education and training. This was designed to provide continuity of work for independent film-makers and to make full integration of the production process possible.
>
> As a result of the declaration, by the beginning of 1985, eighteen workshops had been set up under this 'franchise' arrangement and the 'workshop sector' had become an established part of the British production scene. Low-cost film and video productions, many with strong local or regional influences and dealing with issues relevant to 'marginalised communities', were produced on a regular basis in the mid-1980s. Many of them with direct Channel 4 funding were screened as part of the 'Eleventh Hour' programming strand – late-night television for 'difficult material'.

Handsworth Songs A controversial film which excavates the history of black British culture. Winner of the prestigious Grierson Award as 'best British documentary' and acclaimed as well as criticised for its use of sound, archive images and editing. As influential in its own way as *Do the Right Thing*.

The higher-profile black workshops such as Black Audio and Film Collective, Ceddo and Sankofa made a series of programmes including *Handsworth Songs* (UK 1986), *Passion of Remembrance* (UK 1986) and *Looking for Langston* (1989), which were widely seen and much discussed, both in the UK and internationally. Other franchised workshops with notable productions included Amber in the north-east, Leeds Animation Workshop, Retake (an Asian group in London), and Newsreel Collective and Cinema Action (both based in London). Some workshops were not formally constituted under the Declaration but were still able to get sufficient local funding to develop community-based production and training.

Independent film and video in the UK

The second half of the 1980s in the UK saw a public profile, via Channel 4 in particular, for what might be called the 'independent film and video sector'. The sector developed in the 1970s when the students who had been in further and higher education in the late 1960s and had been politicised by the Vietnam War demonstrations and the events of Paris 1968 began to look for jobs in arts administration, education and media production. They were not prepared to work in the mainstream environment which they had criticised as students and they attempted to set up a new environment. In doing so they took advantage of a relatively well-resourced (by 1990s standards) education system and arts-funding policy and linked up with groups representing a long history of 'independence' in British cinema.

The independent sector might be seen to be variously concerned with all of the following:

- 'democratic' ways of working – in opposition to the hierarchised 'division of labour' found in mainstream production (independent film production groups emphasised this aspect of their work by calling themselves collectives)
- use of non-**narrative** and other distancing techniques in their films so that audiences would have to work at producing meaning and not be passive consumers (see 'Narratives', Chapter 3).
- general critique of capitalist ideologies (the groups tended to share a political commitment to left politics)
- a resistance to traditional stereotyping (many groups were specifically formed to produce work attacking mainstream representations of gender, race and class)
- a recruitment policy aimed at creating opportunities for disadvantaged people to gain production experience
- support for an alternative distribution system, to ensure that the films produced were made available to exhibitors
- support for alternative exhibition venues
- an educative role, whereby the ideology of the sector could be introduced to larger audiences – groups would often attend screenings and talk about their work.

These shared aims were all achieved to a certain extent – sometimes by indirect means. Because independent film-makers earned very little, if anything, from their production work, many worked on a part-time basis in education or training or community work. In this way the movement became wider and an audience, although small, was developed. Alternative distribution and exhibition was possible for a time, particularly as the major funding agencies, the Arts Council and the British Film Institute, were committed to ensuring that a wide range of production opportunities and films was available, not only in London but also in the regions.

Co-ops One alternative to capitalist production models is the co-operative. In the UK the Co-operative Retail Movement in the 1930s recognised the importance of cinema, for both entertainment and education. It opened its own cinemas (often in the same buildings as its retail outlets) and made films. See Burton (1994).

Workers' films A wide range of groups was active in the 1930s, making films from within the labour movement, often inspired by the works of Soviet cinema imported by film societies. These were 'political' in content and sometimes 'experimental' in form. See Macpherson (1980).

ACTIVITY 28.2

Regional workshops and resources

Nearly twenty years after the Workshop Declaration, the UK production environment has changed, but the need for local facilities and resources is still there. How could you get involved in film and video production? Where would you start looking? Use the *BFI Handbook* (look under Workshops), or ask for information from your regional arts board, to find your nearest independent production resource centre and check out the following:

- Is it a membership organisation? If so, what does it offer to members?
- Does it charge differential rates to hire equipment and facilities? Can you get a Rate Card?
- Are there any grant schemes or special funds to help new film-makers?
- What else does the centre offer – training courses, links with broadcasters, community projects etc.?

The Lottery has given a new lease of life to some workshops and several can now offer exciting new opportunities for production experience.

During this period the flagship of the independent distribution and exhibition circuit was The Other Cinema, which was able to maintain an exhibition presence at various venues in central London and run a distribution company which handled not only UK independents but also similar work from around the world. Some of the people working for The Other Cinema then set up the Metro in the West End, a more commercially orientated, but still 'independent' cinema. Outside London the opportunity for audiences to see independent cinema was largely dependent on the existence of a regional film theatre (sometimes associated with a university). These venues, like much else in the independent sector, depended on the support of the British Film Institute.

It isn't possible to understand the development of the independent sector without recognising the role of the BFI. Other countries have similar institutions, usually funded by the state, and charged with promoting and maintaining film culture, but few are as instrumental as the BFI has been in ensuring that an 'independent' film culture survives. Refer back to the list of shared aims above. The BFI has at various times operated a production board, an education service, a distribution service and a regional unit with support for exhibition, publications, etc. BFI funds have gone to small magazines, adult education courses and conferences and a range of other activities, all of which supported the independent sector over a period of a dozen years in the 1970s and 1980s.

INDEPENDENTS AND ALTERNATIVES

Funding was so important (few independent films made a profit) that the sector was also known as the 'grant-aided sector'. Funding was both the saviour of the sector and its biggest problem. As the Snead quote above makes clear, if you need money, then you are 'dependent'.

Dependence on funders was a major source of concern and a source of 'institutional conflict'. Even if individual staff members at the BFI might share the ideological viewpoint of the independent film-makers, the BFI as an institution, incorporated by charter and accountable to government for its own funds, could not be expected to act like a workers' collective. Equally, the collectives found it difficult to fulfil some of the funding requirements. The consequence was a sequence of public and private arguments. More seriously, the independent sector was financially dependent on funders who themselves were under pressure, first to cut public expenditure and then to move towards a more market-orientated funding system.

Funding   The British Film Institute's responsibilities are related to film and television culture. The Arts Council(s) and the network of regional arts bodies have some responsibility for film and television, but also for radio, music production, photography and community publishing. See References section.

The independent sector in the contemporary environment

The new funding regimes which began to appear towards the end of the 1980s stressed 'performance outcomes' rather than experimentation and diversity. Take training, for instance. Previously, workshops might have received **revenue funding** on an annual basis, which enabled them to run a course or workshop without constraints, as long as they could show that they were developing access to media production and education in their region. Under the new regime they receive **outcome funding**. This money comes only if they successfully train somebody who achieves a recognised qualification. The latter method forces a greater conformity on the way the course or workshop is run. Similar changes in funding in relation to other activities also curtail the freedom of independent groups.

Independent production groups have also been persuaded into more mainstream production activities by the deregulation of UK television and the consequent development of an 'independent production sector' based on the definition of independence which we gave at the beginning of this chapter. Instead of producing work that might be screened in the early hours of the morning on Channel 4, the independent groups can now submit proposals for programme commissions in more mainstream slots. Other groups have stayed outside broadcast television, but have moved into 'full-cost', commercial work for clients like charities or trade unions or other public sector organisations. This is more 'mainstream' work, but still with a potentially radical edge. Finally, some groups have turned their attention to production of 'new media' such as CD-ROMs, multimedia presentations and website design.

See 'Institutions', Chapter 26, and references to the 25 per cent production quota for independents commissioned by broadcasters.

There are now many 'production courses' in higher education, and the industry has begun to promote 'on the job' training approved by the National Training Organisation for film, video and broadcast, Skillset, and recognised as NVQs (National Vocational Qualifications). Access to these courses is restricted to freelances already working in the industry and in 1998 the relationship between training in colleges and workshops and the industry NVQs had not been fully resolved. Skillset has been influential in analysing the UK industry in terms of employment and demonstrating the need for greater access by 'minorities'. See References section for Skillset contact details.

The independent film and video sector of the 1970s and 1980s provides an institutional case study, demonstrating the difficulties of what we might call '**oppositional** practice' — trying to set up an *alternative* to mainstream production, distribution and exhibition. It could be argued that, from the funders' point of view, the development of the sector was a success in that it helped to create a pool of freelances with experience gained through 'grant-aided' productions at a time when the mainstream British film industry was collapsing. Without these experienced film- and video-makers, the British film and television industry might have been more vulnerable to domination by overseas producers. In the contemporary environment the expansion of more formal education and training courses might now be seen to fill this particular role.

A second success might be seen in terms of the participation and representation of disadvantaged groups in UK media. Whether or not the numbers of women and ethnic minority entrants to the industry would have been less had there never been an independent sector is something that can't be proved either way. Nevertheless, it was an aim of the sector and there has been some success. (It is also a continuing feature of training programmes, especially those supported by the European Social Fund (ESF).) What is most difficult to determine is the extent to which the independent sector contributed to a change in the formal operation of films and television programmes. We noted above that some (but not all) groups were keen to experiment with non-narrative techniques, and an overall aim for those groups working with Channel 4 was to produce new forms of television. To discuss this we need to place the UK independent sector in the context of wider, international, arts movements which have been termed '**avant-garde**'.

Avant-garde film

The nearest direct translation of this term in English is 'vanguard' or 'in the front – leading'. Every art form has an avant-garde, a group of artists deliberately intending to break all the rules or conventions and to shock audiences into acceptance of something new. Gradually, aspects of the avant-garde are absorbed into the mainstream or the conditions that encouraged the specific avant-garde change. Later, other avant-garde groups emerge and so the cycle goes on (see 'Postmodernisms', Chapter 18, for a different view). The cinematic avant-garde is generally recognised as emerging in Berlin and Paris during the 1920s when various modernist groups, including the Surrealists, produced a variety of short features. Many of these artists fled to America in the 1930s to

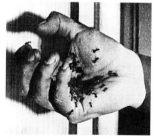

Figure 28.3 A famous image from *Un chien andalou* (France 1928), a Surrealist film by Luis Buñuel and Salvador Dali

escape fascism, and the American avant-garde has its beginning in the early 1940s, becoming a major movement during the 1950s and surviving through to the 1980s.

It is this American movement, especially in the 1950s and 1960s, which brought the idea of avant-garde film to a wider audience as part of a general appreciation of modern art. The American film-makers carried on a tradition from the European pioneers of attacking ideas about conventional narratives. One approach was to explore, through symbolism and disjointed time, the dream-like qualities of film. This approach was heavily influenced by Freud's work on dreams. A good example from the early period is **Maya Deren**'s first feature, *Meshes of the Afternoon* (US 1943), in which the simple actions of a young woman become imbued with violence and violation by the use of specific camera movements and framings and unconventional editing techniques. Deren wrote that the film concerned 'the interior experiences of an individual' and that 'it does not record an event which could be witnessed by another person' (Sitney 1979).

A different approach to film emphasises the physical properties of the medium in relation to the possibilities of narrative – the so-called 'structural film'. **Michael Snow**'s *Wavelength* (US 1967) is one of the most famous (or notorious) of these films which severely tested the audience's staying power. In *Wavelength* a fixed camera very slowly zooms in on an object 80 feet away in a New York loft. This takes forty-five minutes. Things happen in front of the camera and on the soundtrack (and with the film stock), but it is the tension created for an audience, used to editing and movement, by the fixed frame, which gives the film its power and fascination.

British avant-garde film-makers can be related to the overall history of the avant-garde, with examples of work influenced by both the European and American movements and also by what Peter Wollen in a famous essay (Wollen 1976) described as 'The Two Avant-gardes'. He argued that there was a second avant-garde tradition which derives from the experimental cinema of the Soviet Union in the 1920s. The difference between these two traditions according to Wollen (1976) and Petley (1978) is that the French, German and, later, American groups were generally 'painterly', interested in film as an artistic medium, allowing opportunities to explore the physical properties of film and light sensitivity, as well as the time and space dimensions of cinema – a formalist approach. This painterly group included photographers as well as painters (e.g. Man Ray, **Moholy-Nagy** and Dali) and emphasised the 'personal expression' of individual artists. Wollen suggested that the second group were interested in 'contentism' and how to present a

Figure 28.4 **Maya Deren** (1917–61) shown here in *Meshes of the Afternoon*, made with her first husband, Alexander Hammid (already a documentary film-maker). In subsequent films she drew upon her interest in modern dance and ritualistic behaviour. Her influence spread through writings and lectures on the avant-garde

Michael Snow A Canadian, working out of New York, Snow gained the reputation as the 'dean of structural film' during the 1960s. His work represents one of the most sophisticated attempts to explore film-making as an intellectual activity.

Laszló Moholy-Nagy 'Theorist, teacher, photographer, designer, painter and filmmaker, one of the most important modernist figures' (Petley 1978). Best known for *Lichtspiel* (Germany 1930).

Dziga Vertov Russian experimental documentarist. Best known for *The Man with a Movie Camera* (USSR 1929), a film about how to construct documentary reality, full of camera tricks and experiments. Vertov was in charge of the entire news and propaganda service throughout the USSR at the time.

political argument. These Russians generally came from experimental theatre (Eisenstein) or documentary film (**Vertov**). Although they adopted new approaches to editing and to camerawork, the Russians kept within the confines of a photographic realism and a recognisable, even if revolutionary, narrative structure.

The Russian tradition was revived by Jean-Luc Godard and Jean-Pierre Gorin in the early 1970s when they called themselves the 'Dziga Vertov Group'. Much of the interest in the work of Jean-Luc Godard can be explained by the way in which he appears to span both avant-garde traditions and the mainstream. In his first feature, *A bout de souffle* (France 1959), Godard pays homage to the American B picture in what at first appears to be a simple genre film but then erupts into a fractured and playful narrative reminiscent of the Surrealists in the 1920s (Figure 28.5). During the next decade Godard's films moved increasingly towards a more sustained critique of traditional forms of narrative, and Petley (1978) discusses *Une femme marie* (France 1964) under the heading 'The Avant-garde Feature Film'. By the end of the decade, Godard and his new partner, Gorin, had moved towards a more overtly political kind of film-making ('making films politically, not making political films'). In effect, what was being created, not just by Godard and Gorin, was a new cinematic institution, formulated to be the exact opposite of Hollywood: 'counter-cinema'.

Figure 28.5   Using a hand-held camera in a confined space, cinematographer Raoul Coutard invented a new way of representing the affair between Jean Seberg and Jean-Paul Belmondo in *A bout de souffle*

Counter-cinema

Thirty years on, the politics of 1968 seem very distant, but during a distinct period in the history of 'independent production' the work of the Dziga Vertov Group stands as a specific example of practice complemented by a theoretical project. From a Maoist base (attacking the 'imperialism' of both the West and the Soviet Union), Godard and Gorin set out to 'counter the hegemony of Hollywood'. After one of the most widely discussed examples of this counter-cinema, *Vent d'est* (France 1972), in which Godard and Gorin examined imperialism using characters and narrative ideas taken from the Western, Peter Wollen formulated a useful checklist of the different ways in which classic Hollywood could be 'countered'.

Godard and Gorin challenged the idea of **stars** in *Tout va bien* (France 1972). Jane Fonda and Yves Montand play central roles in a narrative, but are also foregrounded as 'stars' who are needed to ensure distribution. This is perhaps the best example of the questions posed by counter-cinema.

Classic Hollywood	Counter-cinema
Coherent, linear narrative	Disrupted, non-linear narrative
Identification with characters	Estrangement from characters
Transparency	Foregrounding (making clear the image is constructed)
Single theme or main story	Multiple themes and stories
Narrative 'closure' or resolution	No resolution
Fiction	Reality
Pleasure	Work
	(Adapted from Wollen 1972)

You will need to look at 'Narratives' and 'Realisms' (Chapters 3 and 16) to get a full sense of what these 'oppositions' mean in practice. Let's concentrate on the last pair. Did counter-cinema really mean a denial of pleasure? Many critics would argue that it did. If you take away all the glamour of Hollywood (including 'Technicolor, CinemaScope and Stereophonic Sound') with its stars and easy storylines, what is left? For the politically committed in the 1970s what was left was ideas – difficult ideas in many cases. But there was a pleasure and an interest in political ideas at the time and there were other pleasures; even when Godard was trying not to create visual effects, he still produced arresting and pleasurable images, as well as witty sketches and dramatic moments. If, however, an audience was not already committed to the politics of counter-cinema (which would include a commitment to new forms of cinema), there was little chance that it would remain with many of these films all the way through.

The Dziga Vertov Group were not the only practitioners of 'counter-cinema', although they were perhaps the most adventurous in opposing Hollywood. Film-makers around the world were influenced by the politics of the Vietnam War, by the protest movements of 1968 and later by feminism. **Dusan Makavejev** made *The Diary of a Switchboard Operator* (Yugoslavia 1967) with a primary aim of opposing the hegemony of Soviet Cinema rather than Hollywood. Other examples of counter-cinema can be found in the work of film-makers in Germany, Italy, Latin America, Japan and the United States.

The influence of 'counter-cinema' is also evident in the work of the independent film and video sector in the UK as we discussed above. Many film-makers would have studied both the avant-garde traditions as cinema history and as contemporary practice. Many would also have been involved in the theoretical discussions promoted by *Screen* magazine (which provided translations of international work on counter-cinema). Black British film-makers were particularly influenced by counter-cinema in relation to what came to be known as 'Third Cinema' – i.e. neither mainstream commercial nor 'art house' cinema, neither Hollywood nor Europe, a political term used to describe cinema movements in Africa and Latin America.

Independence now

The work of all the film-makers we have discussed and of similarly 'independent artists' in photography, music and video, has provided the foundation for contemporary independents. Even film-makers like Quentin Tarantino and David Lynch, apolitical and intent on commercial success, will admit to influences from the movements we have described. The 1990s might have seemed a particularly bad time for avant-garde or alternative work (see 'Postmodernisms', Chapter 18 for arguments as to why this might be so). But look more closely, and experimental work is continuing in video and in digital formats associated with multimedia and computer graphics. In animation there is a particularly strong British, Irish and European industry, partly connected to the rebirth of commercial animation under Disney and screenings on MTV, and partly the result of support from the workshops and screening policies by Channel 4.

In the 1990s the claymation techniques which have brought acclaim to the Aardman company, with films such as *The Wrong Trousers* (UK 1993) have raised the profile of what was previously a relatively unknown independent sector, financed by work for commercial advertising and public information films. If you are interested in

Dusan Makavejev Yugoslav film-maker (born Belgrade 1932) who acknowledged the influence of Vertov and Godard. His radical approach to sexuality caused controversy in the West after his departure from Yugoslavia and he has been able to make only a few films, usually poorly received.

Len Lye (1901–80) British animator (originally from New Zealand) working in the 1930s who used experimental techniques such as painting directly on film stock on a series of abstract advertisements (e.g. *The Birth of the Robot* (UK 1936) for Shell).

Norman McLaren (1914–87) British animator, influenced by Len Lye, who combined radical politics and experimental animation in the 1930s and went on to achieve international fame on productions for the National Film Board of Canada.

animation, you will find it worthwhile to look back at similarly important British animation teams who worked in the 1930s, in particular **Len Lye** and **Norman McLaren**.

ACTIVITY 28.3

Countering the mainstream

The best way to test your understanding of independent and alternative film-making is to view some films advertised as independent and see whether they meet your expectations. Another possibility is to consider how you would set out to 'counter the mainstream' if you were invited to tender a proposal:

- What would you want to challenge in relation to contemporary mainstream cinema?
- Are there any specific camera or sound techniques which could distinguish your work from the mainstream (and work on a low budget!)?
- How could you best expose the way in which Hollywood blockbusters work to offer entertainment?
- What kind of audiences do you think are most likely to be attracted to independent films? What would you offer them as an inducement to see your film?

References

Burton, Alan (1994) *The People's Cinema, Film and the Co-operative Movement*, London: BFI (National Film Theatre).

Lovell, Alan (1990) 'That Was The Workshop, That Was', *Screen*, vol. 31, no. 1 (spring), p. 107.

Macpherson, Don (ed.) (1980) *British Cinema, Traditions of Independence*, London: BFI.

Murdock, G. (1986) 'Authorship and Organisation', *Screen Education*, no. 35.

Petley, Julian (1978) *BFI Distribution Library Catalogue*, London: BFI.

Pierson, John (1995) *Spike, Mike, Slackers & Dykes*, London: Faber & Faber.

Sitney, P. Adams (1979) *Visionary Film: The American Avant-Garde 1943–1978*, New York: Oxford University Press.

Snead, James (1994) in Colin MacCabe and Cornel West (eds) *white screens/black images*, New York: Routledge.

Wollen, Peter (1972) 'Counter-cinema: *Vent d'est*', *Afterimage*, no. 4.
Wollen, Peter (1975) 'The Two Avant-gardes', *Studio International* (November/December).

Further reading

Balio, Tino (1998) 'The Art Film Market in the New Hollywood', in Geoffrey Nowell-Smith and Steven Ricci (eds) *Hollywood in Europe*, London: BFI.

Bordwell, David and Thompson, Kristin (1994, 5th edition) *Film History: An Introduction*, New York: McGraw-Hill.

Georgakas, Dan and Rubenstein, Lenny (1984) *Art, Politics, Cinema: The Cineaste Interviews*, London: Pluto.

Hill, John and Church Gibson, Pamela (eds) (1998) *The Oxford Guide to Film Studies*, Oxford: Oxford University Press.

Hillier, Jim (1993) *The New Hollywood*, London: Studio Vista.

Lott, Tommy L. (1998) 'Hollywood and Independent Black Cinema', in Neale and Smith, *Contemporary Hollywood Cinema*.

Milne, Tom (1972) *Godard on Godard*, London: Secker & Warburg.

Neale, Steve and Smith, Murray (eds) (1998) *Contemporary Hollywood Cinema*, London: Routledge.

Ray, Robert B. (1998) 'Impressionism, Surrealism and Film Theory', in Hill and Church Gibson, *The Oxford Guide to Film Studies*.

Reid, Mark A. (ed.) (1997) *Spike Lee's 'Do the Right Thing'*, Cambridge and New York: Cambridge University Press.

Schamus, James (1998) 'To the Rear of the Back End: The Economics of Independent Cinema', in Neale and Smith, *Contemporary Hollywood Cinema*.

Schatz, Thomas (1993) 'The New Hollywood', in J. Collins, H. Radner and A. P. Collins (eds) *Film Theory Goes to the Movies*, London: Routledge.

Wyatt, Justin (1998) 'The Formation of the 'Major Independent': Miramax, New Line and the New Hollywood', in Neale and Smith, *Contemporary Hollywood Cinema*.

29 / Case study: Making films outside the mainstream

Making feature films outside the mainstream usually means working with lower budgets and little support if anything goes wrong. On the positive side it means at least the possibility of more creative control and the opportunity perhaps to say something different, in a different way.

There are different forms of independence (or 'dependence') and the kinds of decisions which film-makers have to make vary in different cultural contexts. This case study draws on the experiences of five different contemporary film-makers, all of whom have films available on videotape.

Self-financing

Amazingly, there are film-makers who can finance themselves, or more accurately can raise the money themselves. John Sayles is a remarkable film-maker, who writes, directs, edits and sometimes acts in his own films (and others). He is also a gifted novelist.

Sayles wants to make his own films and he is prepared to work for the major studios as a scriptwriter to earn the money he needs to finance them. He first worked for Roger Corman (the producer of 'exploitation films' with a radical edge), transferring *The Seven Samurai* (Japan 1954) into a space adventure in the *Star Trek* mode (*Battle Beyond the Stars*, US 1980) and introducing *Piranha* and *Alligator* to follow *Jaws*. The budget for his first 'independent feature', *The Return of the Secaucus Seven* (1980), came out of the fees he earned: 'I had $40,000 dollars in my pocket.'

Although he doesn't make overt political statements, Sayles is very much on the left in an American context, and his own films (i.e. as director) display a concern with social and political issues and a perspective on them rarely, if ever, found in Hollywood features. *Lianna* (US 1983) is a non-sensational story about a lesbian relationship; *Matewan* (US 1987) centres on a miners' strike played out as a Western; and *City of Hope* (US 1991) dissects the interrelationships in an urban community beset by corruption in local politics.

None of these is a 'difficult' film in formal or narrative terms, and all have the witty dialogue and narrative surety you would expect from a successful writer of genre exploitation films. They are, however, not the films that the majors would make or would support through distribution. Some critics have suggested that Sayles's films are too long for their dramatic subject matter – that they need the tighter editing a mainstream editor might offer. Their length could also be a deliberate attempt to give depth to the subject.

Being labelled as an 'independent' might be seen as a constraint on Sayles's ambitions. His only film for a major so far ('it cost ten times my usual budget') was *Baby It's You* (US 1983), a familiar 'rich girl/poor boy, growing-up' melodrama with a 1960s soundtrack. It sounded like, and indeed proved to be, a mainstream picture of some potential, yet it was initially shelved by its distributors and finally released in the UK on the 'art house' circuit.

The subject matter and the budget of Sayles's films mark him as an independent and so too do his working practices. His partner, Maggie Renzi, acts in his films and, crucially, as his producer. He has built up a stock company of actors and collaborators and has worked hard to create working-class roles in dramas which grow from his own sense of community.

Sayles is unusual in surviving as an independent for so long and seemingly wishing to stay within that definition. He recognises that trends and fashions in cinema change. In the early 1990s two of his best films, *City of Hope* and *Passion Fish* (US 1992), although made expansively for the big screen, were mostly seen on video and without video pre-sales they would not have been made at all. But his next film, the gentle fantasy *The Secret of Roan Inish* (US/Ireland 1994), made $6 million and *Lone Star* (US 1996) over $12 million, which for an independently produced film was good money. During this period Sayles also worked as uncredited script doctor on *Apollo 13* and the Sharon Stone Western *The Quick and the Dead*.

Lone Star was distributed by Sony Classics (one of the new 'independent divisions' of a major), and Sayles clearly had the chance again to work for the studios, but he typically turned away to make a film in Spanish, centred on a doctor in Central America – *Men With Guns* (US 1998).

Details of Sayles's career can be found on the website, 'John Sayles Border Stop' at:

`http://www-scf.usc.edu/~rskelley/`

(this is a personal page on a university site and may move – use a search engine if necessary).

Self-financing and public finance: America

Sayles's ability to generate income from his 'commercial' writing projects is not open to everyone (and many independents would not necessarily want to do it). Some film-makers have a tough time getting money together. Others are also more closely identified with specific projects.

Julie Dash (born 1952) (Figure 29.1) is an African-American film-maker who took several years to put together her cherished project, *Daughters of the Dust* (US 1992). This film was never going to interest a major studio

Figure 29.1   Julie Dash

because of its refusal to conform to a mainstream narrative structure. It deals with the events of a single day, but moves backwards and forwards in time to explore the history of a special African-American community on an island off the coast of South Carolina at the start of the twentieth century. The events of the day are not dramatic – a photographer arrives and records the celebrations as some of the community take their leave before starting a new life on the mainland. The stories the characters tell and the discussion of identity is the central interest.

This project was very much a part of what was happening in African-American scholarship and literature at the time. But despite the budgets Spike Lee was able to negotiate and despite Steven Spielberg's adaptation of Alice Walker's *The Color Purple* (US 1985), black independent film-makers like Dash, Haile Gerima and Charles Burnett had to search widely for their small budgets. Dash directed music videos to finance her preparation and the budget finally came from a combination of sources, including American Playhouse (public service television).

Julie Dash has said this about her work:

My films are about women at pivotal moments in
their lives; enigmatic women who are juggling
complex psyches; who speak to one another in
fractured sentences, yet communicate completely
through familiar gestures and stances; women who
remind me of my old neighborhood and the women
who raised me.

(Dash 1992)

Her films are not just *about* women, they are made for
women (and primarily, black women). This targeting of
specific audiences is a feature of independent film-making
which does not aspire to the revenue-maximising appeal
of the mainstream with its universal narratives. *Daughters
of the Dust* had a specific audience, described here by
John Pierson:

the college-educated, black, middle-class, female,
Toni Morrison-reading audience would line up
for her feature … its $2 million box office gross
with almost no paid advertising support was a
genuine triumph.

(Pierson 1995)

Audiences who did not understand the history and the
culture of the characters in the film found it difficult to
follow, even though the visual style was familiar and the
cinematography sumptuous. Those who did understand
found the film moving and deeply rewarding.

There are other aspects of Dash's career which mark
her out as of particular interest as an independent film-
maker. She was a film school graduate, but unlike the
'movie brats' generation (Spielberg, Scorsese, Coppola,
Lucas) her interest lay in the cultural aspects of film. She
studied at the American Film Institute and made
important links with black film-makers in Britain (see
'Independents and alternatives', Chapter 28) and took
her work on a tour of Africa.

Julie Dash also worked specifically to challenge
representations, and in her 1983 short film *Illusions* she
explores the lives of two young black women who work
in the Hollywood of the 1940s – one who must 'pass for
white' and the other who lip-syncs a white starlet's
singing. This compares with some of the British work of

the period, but Dash has not had the public support that
the British groups of the 1980s found. Since 1992 she
has continued to direct music videos for black
performers and has contributed to an anthology of
television short dramas, *Subway Stories* (1997). Julie Dash
has her own multimedia production company called
Geechee Girls which runs an informative website at:
`http://www.geechee.com`.

Self-financing and public finance: Britain

An interesting film-maker to compare with Julie Dash is
Sally Potter. Born in 1949 and roughly the same age as
Dash, Potter also began with films which specifically
addressed a feminist agenda and a female audience with
Thriller (UK 1979) and *Gold Diggers* (UK 1983). The first
of these investigated the narrative of the opera *La
Bohème*, asking why the oppressed woman should die.
The second is perhaps best remembered as a film with a
big star (Julie Christie) and an all-female crew who all
worked for the same flat fee. Christie's support is worth
noting, since the support of a mainstream star, or indeed
the development of an 'art house' or independent star
like Harvey Keitel can be important for the profile and
recognition of an independent film.

During the 1980s Potter was one of the group of
British independents who were able to get commissions
from Channel 4. As well as *Gold Diggers*, she made a
television programme about the female stars of Soviet
cinema. This work with Channel 4 and the research she
did in Russia were useful in setting up her big
international success, *Orlando* (UK 1992). This visually
splendid adaptation of Virginia Woolf's novel explored the
construction of masculinity and femininity and also poked
fun at costume dramas and ideas of national heritage.

Orlando is a good example of the potential for a
'European' independent film, which is able to
demonstrate what appear to be high production values
through the use of careful location shooting and the
support of several different funding agencies. The film
was shot in Britain and in both European and Asiatic
parts of the old Russian Empire.

This approach was also followed with Potter's next feature, *The Tango Lesson* (UK 1997) which was filmed in Britain, France and Argentina and was funded by the Arts Council and British Screen and Eurimages (an EU fund). This public money was augmented by BSkyB and other public and private moneys from France, Germany and the Netherlands.

Sally Potter originally trained as a dancer, as well as a choreographer and a musician. In *The Tango Lesson* (which had a mixed reception, from the ecstatic to the damning), Potter directs herself as a film director who takes lessons from and falls in love with a star tango dancer. The film works on many levels but at its centre is the question of fiction and reality. All the major characters in the film are played by the people who inspired these fictional constructions.

Part of the narrative of *The Tango Lesson* deals with the film director's failed attempt to close a deal with a Hollywood studio, after which she decides to make a film with the tango dancer. This is in fact what happened to Potter in 'real' life. The success of *Orlando* had prompted that process of absorption into the mainstream, which Potter resisted. The appearance of *The Tango Lesson* possibly confused some critics by its refusal to conform to mainstream conventions.

Sally Potter has managed to work in the 'joint-production' world of European film-financing, and this has possibly given her some creative freedom and a reasonable budget, which might be more difficult to find in an American context. *The Tango Lesson* has several specialist markets in which to recoup its costs, but it remains to be seen whether Potter can repeat the trick. Compared to the output of John Sayles (a dozen features in eighteen years), Julie Dash and Sally Potter have made only a handful of films. Perhaps those films were more challenging for audiences (and distributors), perhaps they have not wanted to make films so frequently, perhaps it is just more difficult for women to get the money?

The Tango Lesson has a website at: `http://www.spe.sony.com/Pictures/SonyClassics/tango`

Self-financing and public finance: France

In 'Independents and alternatives', Chapter 28, we make a reference to the concept of an *auteur* cinema which was recognised and promoted by the critics of *Cahiers du Cinéma* in the 1950s and early 1960s. We suggested that while the concept of the *auteur* – the single author of a film text – had been important in the development of Film Studies, it had later been superseded by approaches drawn from structuralism.

'Authorship' has survived as a means of marketing films made by 'name' directors, and you might feel that our discussion of Sayles, Dash and Potter is a contribution to that trend. However, what interests us about them is their ways of working and their means of funding and developing projects. Independent cinema is partly defined by a more 'personal' attention to the production process, even where this is related to the tortuous process of funding and organising the shoot.

In France the concept of the *auteur* is not dead, indeed it is enshrined within the institution of French cinema and within a structure of public funding. Film is an important part of French cultural life and the *auteur* is validated as an artist. The French film industry during the 1990s maintained a relatively high level of feature production (over a hundred features annually – many co-produced with Italy, Spain or Germany) divided between relatively big-budget (by French standards)

Figure 29.2   Sally Potter in a dance sequence in *The Tango Lesson*

mainstream comedies and thrillers and smaller-budget *auteur* pictures.

A small subsidy has been made possible for *auteur* pictures under a scheme set up by the Ministry of Culture of the socialist government of the late 1980s and early 1990s. One of the beneficiaries of this supportive structure was *Mathieu Kassovitz*. Kassovitz (born 1968) (Figure 29.3) has developed a career as both an actor and director and his major success as a director, *La Haine* (France 1995), led to his title as *l'enfant terrible* of French cinema.

La Haine is a 'youth picture' – the story of three young men and what happens to them in the twenty-four hours following a riot on their housing estate in the outer suburbs of Paris. (The English translation of the title is 'Hate'.) In France the film was a major box-office success and a major talking-point. Kassovitz himself is Jewish and his three protagonists are African-French, Arab and Jewish. The spark for the riot in the film is the attitude of the police towards the youth on the estate. The story was based on a riot which Kassovitz and his lead actor Vincent Cassell witnessed.

The film so effectively captured the imagination of French youth that a chain store brought out a brand of *La Haine* clothing and the French cabinet were shown the film as an insight into the feelings on the street. The successful box office run (close to two million admissions in France) prompts the question: was this in any way an 'independent' film?

In the UK and the US the film also did good business, but like all subtitled films it was presented not in multiplexes but art cinemas (the monochrome cinematography would also be a problem for the mainstream, although it is becoming more common for American independents). Released the summer before the arrival of *Trainspotting*, *La Haine* was bracketed with the British film, which also seemed to hover between independent and mainstream status. But *Trainspotting* was in English (or, more correctly, Edinburgh Scots) and therefore could make it to the multiplex.

Critics attempted to explain Kassovitz by reference to other film-makers, and the two immediate examples were Spike Lee and John Singleton, the makers of *Do the Right Thing* and *Boyz N the Hood*. The first had *La Haine*'s concern for violence and racial conflict, the second the combination of youth and guns. Kassovitz himself preferred to name Ken Loach (see 'Realisms', Chapter 16), who is well-known in France, as an inspiration, and to talk about the time he spent in preparation on the estate where much of the film was shot. *La Haine* certainly shows the commitment of Loach, but the camerawork by Pierre Aïm is much more expressive and self-conscious.

Kassovitz had made only one feature before *La Haine*. *Metisse* (France 1993) is an interracial love triangle involving Kassovitz the actor and Hubert Kounde, who is one of the leads in *La Haine*. An earlier short film was the basis for *Assassins* (France 1997). This attacked the media, rather than the police, for their attitudes towards violence. This time Kassovitz was not able to use the Cannes Film Festival to his advantage as he had with his previous appearances as director or actor (Cannes can help launch a European or world cinema art picture just as well as Sundance can launch an American independent). The critics turned on him and the film suffered at the French box office after great expectations (it was not released in America or the UK).

Jodie Foster, a maverick star in the Hollywood system and an independent producer/director in her own right, was impressed by *La Haine* and has talked about becoming Kassovitz's producer. In early 1998 rumours

Figure 29.3 Mathieu Kassovitz

circulated suggesting that Kassovitz would follow an earlier *auteur* turned mainstream producer, Luc Besson, and make a French film in English with a blockbuster budget.

Kassovitz may provide us with an example of an independent absorbed into the mainstream – perhaps like Tarantino? Yet, *La Haine* is far removed from a conventional mainstream film. Kassovitz measures up to our other examples in writing, directing and co-editing as well as acting. The acting gives him a further link to *auteur* cinema, with two of his starring roles being for parts in 'small' but critically regarded and relatively very successful films directed by Jacques Audiard: *Regarde les hommes tomber* (France 1994) and *Un héros très discret* (France 1996), both of which did reach the UK.

It is well worth searching for websites featuring Mathieu Kassovitz. The majority are currently in French but *La Haine* is featured on several English language sites.

Independent and mainstream in Hong Kong

Wong Kar-Wai (born 1958) is a graduate of one of the most commercial film industries in the world, but by 1998 he had become known as one of the hottest directors in 'world cinema'.

So far we have been careful to distinguish between mainstream and independent in America, Britain and France. These are all major national cinemas and also major exporters of films worldwide. There are bigger film industries in India and China, which have regional export markets and then there are countries where only a handful of films are made, but there has been a possibility of some of those films being elevated to have an international profile by screenings at International Film Festivals. Each year the major festivals – Berlin, Cannes, Venice, Toronto – throw up a handful of prizewinners which go on to international box office success (i.e. measured in terms of non-mainstream film).

Fashions in world cinema change, partly because of changes in audiences in New York, Paris and London, partly because of local changes in the producing countries. Japanese films were widely praised in the 1950s and 1960s, Latin American in the 1960s and 1970s, African in the 1980s. In the late 1980s and early 1990s Chinese films gained centre stage.

Several languages or dialects are spoken in China, but one of the most influential in cinema terms is Cantonese – the language of Shanghai and south China, including Taiwan and Hong Kong. It is also an important language of the Chinese **diaspora** throughout south-east Asia generally.

The cinema in China itself re-emerged from the isolation of the Cultural Revolution in 1984 with *Yellow Earth*, the first film to be seen in the West from the so-called 'Fifth Generation' of new young film-makers. Hong Kong and Taiwan have very different cinema experiences. Hong Kong developed one of the most successful commercial cinemas in the world, which at times spilled over and dominated cinema in Taiwan. Martial arts films gained a profile in America and Europe and were exported successfully around the world in the 1970s. In the 1980s new genres developed including comedies and police thrillers. Size for size, Hong Kong could rival Hollywood in genre production and studio structure.

But this mainstream cinema also generated its independent sector – young directors who enjoyed the rising affluence and greater educational opportunities, gaining access to films from around the world. From the late 1970s a 'New Wave' developed and produced directors recognised in world cinema – Ann Hui, Allen Fong and Stanley Kwan. Similar developments in Taiwan produced Edward Yang and Hou Hsiao-Hsien.

In the mid-1990s Hong Kong film-makers were successful in the West commercially (John Woo, Jackie Chan) and at festivals in the shape of Wong Kar-Wai. Born in Shanghai and the son of a sailor, Wong moved to Hong Kong aged five – a family history very similar to many Chinese in the diaspora and a recurring influence in his films. He began his career in Hong Kong television after studying graphic design and moved into cinema as a scriptwriter. His films, beginning with *As Tears Go By* in 1988, have ranged across genres, but have used an array of popular young stars including Leslie Cheung, Maggie Cheung and Andy Lau (see 'Making and enjoying global music', Case study 21) and a very important production team comprising art director William Chang and Australian cinematographer Chris Doyle.

The films have not always been great box office in Hong Kong, but they have all achieved critical acclaim and, following the overseas success of *Chungking Express* in 1994 (promoted in America by Quentin Tarantino), Wong's future seemed assured. He followed this up with two more festival prizewinners, *Fallen Angels* (Hong Kong 1995) and *Happy Together* (Hong Kong 1997).

Wong's success in the West is not so surprising. He is well versed in European cinema – the 'youth melodrama' *Days of Being Wild* (Hong Kong 1991) is a fascinating study of a doomed romance in the Hong Kong of 1960 which feels very close to work of the celebrated German director Rainer Werner Fassbinder. It is deliberately slow, moody and atmospheric, which makes more startling the brief snatches of violence with their genre references.

Chungking Express (Figure 29.4) is by contrast a modern urban film with exciting and innovative camerawork. Wong appears to be interested in Hong Kong and China *and* in the wider world – *Happy Together* was filmed in the waterfront district of Buenos Aires. The intriguing biographical details (e.g. the sailor/exile motif) also encourage the notion of Wong as an *auteur* with something personal to say. His interests and approach to film-making mark him out as fascinating for postmodernists (see 'Postmodernisms', Chapter 18) as well as traditional art cinema audiences.

Figure 29.4 Chungking Express

But part of Wong's success is also attributable to the general interest in Chinese language cinema and the willingness of its leading stars and film-makers to make films in the international environment. This applies to many of Wong's collaborators including Maggie Cheung, now working in France, and Chris Doyle and Leslie Cheung working with Fifth Generation Chinese director Chen Kaige (*Farewell My Concubine* and *Temptress Moon*). Significantly, since Hong Kong has returned to China, films are being produced in Mandarin Chinese – the language of Beijing.

The work of Wong Kar-Wai raises many of the issues we have discussed. Is he independent because of the subjects he chooses, or the way he approaches them (with Chang and Doyle) in terms of design, camerawork and direction? Or is he simply different because the language and the cultural content is unfamiliar – and therefore consigns the films to art house cinemas in the West? Is his independence undermined by a background in commercial work in Hong Kong?

There are many websites discussing Wong Kar-Wai, but a good starting point is this (English-language) site in the Netherlands: `http://www.xs4all.nl/ %7Echinaman/`.

Conclusion

This case study has offered a range of film-makers all of whom you are most likely to encounter in relation to ideas of 'independence from the mainstream'. Their cases are quite different and serve to demonstrate that once we have defined the central mainstream, which in cinema means Hollywood, we define everything else as non-mainstream, often without giving weight to the real differences.

The way to think about it may be to imagine international cinema as a stellar structure. At its centre is the largest star – Hollywood. Orbiting this star and attracted by its gravitational pull are clusters of smaller planets – national cinemas and independent movements. Sometimes these smaller bodies will feed on

Hollywood's energies and grow, sometimes they will burn up and be absorbed.

ACTIVITY 29.1

Defining 'independent'

Check the new cinema releases listed in the press or television over a few weeks. Note the coverage each film receives and where the films are screened.

- Do they all come to your local cinemas?
- Which would you term 'independent' in terms of distribution?

Select one or more of the film-makers represented here (or others whom you think fit the criteria), study some of their work and what critics and audiences have said about them. Decide for yourself what the distinction between mainstream and independent means and satisfy yourself that you can point to evidence which demonstrates your understanding.

Further reading and viewing

All the film-makers discussed here have work available on video, as well as screenings at regional film theatres of new releases and revivals.

Videotapes

John Sayles   Amongst Sayles's films in circulation are: *Passion Fish* G0049, *The Secret of Roan Inish* TVT1270 and *Lone Star* CVR 84310

Julie Dash   *Daughters of the Dust* CR134

Sally Potter   *Orlando* EP0034, *The Tango Lesson* ART151

Mathieu Kassovitz   *La Haine* TVT1239

Wong Kar-Wai   *As Tears Go By* HK015, *Days of Being Wild* HK005, *Chungking Express* ICAV1019, *Fallen Angels* PG0563043

Books and articles

Bordwell, David and Thompson, Kristin (1994) *Film History: An Introduction*, New York: McGraw-Hill.

Dash, Julie with Bambara, Tonu Cade and hooks, bell (1992) *'Daughters of the Dust', The Making of an African-American Woman's Film*, New York: The New Press.

Donahue, Walter (1993) 'Immortal Longing' (*Orlando*), *Sight and Sound*, vol. 3, no. 3 (March).

Felperin, Leslie (1996) 'Walking Alone' (*Lone Star*), *Sight and Sound*, vol. 6, no. 9 (September).

Gross, Larry (1996) 'Nonchalant Grace' (Wong Kar-Wai), *Sight and Sound*, vol. 6, no. 9 (September).

hooks, bell (1996) *reel to reel: Sex and Class at the Movies*, New York: Routledge.

Johnston, Trevor (1993) 'Sayles Talk: Interview with John Sayles', *Sight and Sound*, vol. 3, no. 9 (September).

Pierson, John (1996) *Spike, Mike, Slackers & Dykes*, London: Faber & Faber.

Reader, Keith (1995) 'After the Riot' (*La Haine*), *Sight and Sound*, vol. 5, no. 11 (November).

Romney, Jonathan (1995) 'La Haine', *Short Orders*, London: Serpent's Tail.

Sayles, John (1987) *Thinking in Pictures: The Making of the Movie, 'Matewan'*, Boston: Houghton Mifflin.

30 Advertising and marketing

To advertise means 'to draw attention to something' or to notify or inform someone of something (Dyer 1982). It is now the media form most often encountered, most of the time: on urban billboards; on the Internet; on commercially funded television; in magazines and newspapers; pushed through front doors and even in movies. The sum of $200 billion was spent worldwide on advertising in 1995, funded, of course, by consumers, through the cost of the goods we bought.

ACTIVITY 30.1

How many forms of advertising have you encountered this week?

- Jot down where you encountered them – as brochures in the middle of a magazine? In the middle of a television programme? On the Net?
- What difference did their location make to the ads, and to your engagement with them?
- Have you ever advertised? Where: 'free' or other local paper? local cable television? the Internet? postcards in a shop window?

(According to CIA MediaLab, April 1998, people are increasingly purchasing via computer, fax or telephone, while direct mail and catalogue shopping are becoming less popular.)

Advertising has drawn the attention of generations of analysts, especially in work on the effects of mass commercial culture. Objections to it have included the following allegations:

- It brainwashes its audience with base, deceptive promises and appeals, designed to promote materialism, waste, hedonism and envy.
- It acts as an unnecessary business expense, which adds significantly to the costs of goods for customers. Large monopolies such as Proctor & Gamble spend millions advertising their own products (such as soap powders) against their own subsidiaries.

- It leads to barriers to competition and to oligopolies because young companies cannot afford the huge costs needed to break into markets.
- Its glamorous body images lead to ideological conformity, especially in relation to already powerfully stereotyped areas such as gender, class, ethnicity and age.

Histories of gender and advertising

Advertising can arguably be found as far back as Greek and Roman public criers, shouting the wares of local traders. But its recognisable modern form appears with the nineteenth-century Industrial Revolution and the over-production of goods through new manufacturing techniques. In the 1850s, after Prime Minister Gladstone removed regulations and taxes on advertising, manufacturers were able to appeal to consumers over the heads of retailers, through the media.

In the USA, with its huge capitalist economy, consumers began to be educated (informally, by ads) into the possibilities and attractions of mass consumption. For many years ads were described as though they operated in a trivial and irrational way, and as though that was why they had a 'brainwashing' effect on women (because femininity is often constructed as irrational and as bound up with consumption (shopping) not production or work).

In fact the effects of advertising cannot be understood outside other powerful contexts. In the nineteenth century real gains and freedoms for women were represented by these new products, both by saving labour in the home and in the pleasures of the new shops where they were sold. They were displayed, at fixed prices, in large, attractively laid out department stores in safe shopping districts ('factories for selling' in Rachel Bowlby's words, and see also Pumphrey 1984). The attractions were rather like those of early picture palaces: attention paid to opulent visual display and comfort, with rest rooms, restaurants and polite service from assistants. Later came supermarkets, which introduced the revolutionary idea that shoppers need not wait for, and deal through, a shop assistant when choosing goods. Decisions to buy were usually far from irrational, and far from being prompted only by ads. Such developments also brought women increased work opportunities, though unionisation for working rights was slow and they often found themselves in low-skilled, low-paid jobs.

ACTIVITY 30.2

Find some writings on advertising which put a heavy emphasis *on its power alone* to influence people into buying certain goods.

ADVERTISING AND MARKETING

- How would you want to qualify them?
- Note when you next visit your local supermarket what we might call its careful **mise en scène**. (Slightly pink lighting over the meats? Smell of bread enticing you through the store? 'Dump bins' full of goodies, like a kids' party? Sweets for tired children at checkout? Muzak pacing your visit, its rhythm depending on time of day?)
- Think how you would relate its attractions, and the way it invites you to buy certain goods at certain points in your trip, to the power of ads.

By the end of the 1920s US advertisers, consciously or unconsciously, began to try to transform the buying habits of a national audience of consumers (largely women). They realised that to do this they could not simply reject traditional assumptions about gender roles. The power of the American government's **propaganda** during the First World War convinced them that they could also use **social psychology** or **behaviourism** as research into human motivation and ways of associating came to be called (see 'Audiences', Chapter 29).

Lifestyle advertising developed, going beyond a simple outline of a product's uses to encouraging potential buyers to associate it with a whole desirable style of life, and to feel that not owning the product would involve personal failure, unpopularity, loneliness. Along with this, the idea of fashion and keeping up with fashion through consuming goods was newly emphasised. This now may seem to have culminated in obsessive and expensive attitudes: even young children have to wear the 'right' trainers or jeans, or have the 'right' body shape. But in the 1920s the positive connotations which fashion gave to change, novelty and youth undermined traditional attitudes (endorsing 'thrift, self-sufficiency, home cooking, family entertainment, hand-made and hand-me-down clothes' (Pumphrey 1984)).

These traditional attitudes often had oppressive consequences for women, generally the ones expected to do the 'making' and the 'handing down'. So the figure of *the Flapper* in films, magazines and books (Figure 30.1) offered a challenge to nineteenth-century constructions of femininity on the level of style, image and consumption rather than in other areas such as conventional politics. The other major figure to which women were invited to relate seemed very different: *the housewife*, constructed as having sole responsibility for keeping the home clean. Yet she too was set up as a modern figure. Ads, even those encouraging the most paranoid levels of anxiety about germs in the home, did not treat their addressees patronisingly. The housewife was constructed as having a

Figure 30.1

The Flapper's 'unencumbered simplified clothing, short hair and boyish figure, rebellious lifestyle and pursuit of pleasure … [along with] her hectic social life' (Pumphrey 1984) made her a key cultural figure, though one raising many questions: Where does she work? Where does her money come from? What will happen when she grows older? What else is she interested in? How does she relate to the 1920s political women's movements?

'Dirt is matter out of place' (Mary Douglas, *Purity and Danger: An Analysis of the Concepts of Pollution and Taboo* (London: Ark, 1996)).

serious responsibility (keeping the home clean and safe); and as democratically joining 'hundreds of thousands of American women' said to have also benefited from this or that product. She was therefore encouraged to think of herself as, in a way, both a private *and* a public figure, who was being offered the opportunity to take advantage of modern, labour-saving devices; in other words to be connected with technological advances.

Figure 30.2

ADVERTISING AND MARKETING

As with the Flapper, though, there are gaps in this construction. Why should such labour-saving devices actually mean more work for women, via the much higher standards of cleanliness expected of them? If women's work in the home is so important, why is it not counted or paid as work? Why cannot men, or some children, share responsibility for this work within the family?

For both these mythical figures, advertisers constructed a kind of *self-surveillance* in which women were repeatedly invited to take part, asking questions about how clean, how safe was their bathroom/kitchen/cutlery/ toilet, and how appealing was their hair/skin/figure/personal aroma.

'A woman … is almost continually accompanied by her own image of herself … She has to survey everything she is and everything she does because how she appears to others, and ultimately how she appears to men, is of crucial importance for what is … thought of as the success of her life' (John Berger, *Ways of Seeing* (Harmondsworth: Penguin, 1972)).

ACTIVITY 30.3

Look through television ads during programmes which might be assumed to attract audiences of mainly women (e.g. morning or afternoon television).

- Do you think such self-surveillance is still invited? How can you tell?
- How does the camera position viewers in relation to the women in the ads?
- Are there any ads addressing men in ways that encourage self-surveillance?
- How are they similar or different to those addressing women?
- What kinds of questions are women shown putting to themselves in ads for cosmetics, clothes, household cleaners?
- Are the two kinds of ads significantly different in their use of fantasy situations, irony, wit, playfulness?

Hollywood movies from early on (there was alarm in England and Germany as early as 1912) were an important arm of American exports. Fashions, up-to-the-minute kitchen technology and furnishings were showcased in 'women's films', establishing **tie-ins** with manufacturers. In the mid-1930s sketches of styles to be worn by specific actresses in films were sent to merchandising bureaux, which produced them in time for the film's release, then sold them in Macy's Cinema Fashions Shops, among others (see Eckert 1990 and LaPlace 1987). The cigarette industry regularly lobbied performers to smoke on screen. These tie-in products were controversial as early as the 1920s. By the late 1930s Hollywood occupied a privileged position in the advertising industry.

'In post-war West Germany, women were constrained to search beyond national boundaries for female cultural forms untainted by aftertastes of Nazism. To don the accoutrements of an American female ideal – nylon stockings, scarlet lipstick, narrow skirts and high-heeled shoes – was in part to register a public disavowal of fascist images of femininity: scrubbed faces shining with health, sturdy child-bearing hips sporting seamed stockings and sensible shoes.'

(Carter 1984)

See also Hebdige (1988, chs 3–5) on the 'threat' of American style in Britain of the 1950s, also treated in 'Genres', Chapter 8.

Synergy is often taken to be a very modern term, referring to the **marketing** across different media of figures such as Batman or the *Friends* characters by **conglomerate** corporations like Warner and Disney (in cards, toys, T-shirts, theme parks, mugs and so on, sold in worldwide chains of shops). Today it is a highly focused part of the film industry. Companies like Coca-Cola and Pepsi have their own in-house divisions dedicated to **product placement**, including the influencing of scripts (see Wasko 1994). The history of advertising, fashion and Hollywood suggests that such link-ups have been around for some time – and that the 'escapism' of media is often into worlds which have very recognisable products in them.

ACTIVITY 30.4

Watch for product placement in the next movie you see.
- What do you think the product owners hoped to get from the placement?

Branding involves persuading customers of a product's quality prior to purchase or experience, usually by the reputation or image of the producing company, as in 'it must be all right if it's Marks and Spencer' – an interesting example since until very recently M&S engaged in hardly any advertising yet is Britain's strongest brand. Film studios, especially in the days of the studio system, tried to act as brands, guaranteeing certain kinds of expectations. The Blair government currently talks of 're-branding Britain'.

Marketing

Such histories make visible the close connection between advertising and marketing, as well as the surrounding fantasies into which, say, the latest Nike ad fits.

Marketing can be defined as the sum of the ways in which a product is positioned in its particular market. This includes pricing, physical availability in shops, by mail order etc., and often the '**brand**' image of

Figure 30.3 1949 tie in between film star Esther Williams and swim wear advertising. Compare the marketing of Una Thurman's nail varnish in *Pulp Fiction* (Vogue May 1949)

the product's makers. This may be constructed by the brand name's placement in movies, pop videos, television serials, or in association with stars or sponsorship deals (such as that of *Friends* star Jennifer Aniston with Wella products, or athletes' deals with Nike). It is argued that the versatility of modern capitalism means that products (e.g. a bar of chocolate) are not unique for very long: product specifications can be copied by rivals often in a few days. Brands, however (e.g. Rowntree), are less volatile, and a focus on a brand also cuts marketing and advertising expenses. Virgin is the best example of 'brand extension': from records to air travel to finance and railways.

Public relations or PR is a related area, involving the selling of persons or companies, using many of same techniques as advertising: competitions, free offers, but also arranging incidents, 'spontaneous' happenings, dates, even staged relationships to be reported by the media as news (see the career of publicist Max Clifford). Video PR companies for example will often scan their sales data bases for names of customers for, e.g., science fiction videos (which in 1997 accounted for only 9 per cent of the total market, but has many 'hard core' fans). The PR agency may then set up fan clubs for particular films (by mailing purchasers) which can act as a further publicity mechanism. All of these activities can overlap with those of the **advertising agencies** who make ads and manage campaigns, 'placing' or buying space for ads in particular media.

Such processes of **commodification** have never been as powerful as they are now. MTV, VH1 and many other programmes use music videos which are themselves

- an ad (for particular albums)
- a product (a purchasable video) as well as
- television (selling audiences' attention to more advertisers).

In many cases tie-ins (such as Michael Jackson's $15m deal with Pepsi on the 'Bad' album) further commoditise the whole operation.

The effects of advertising

How do these areas work together? Many accounts of advertising analyse particular ads outside the full marketing and indeed cultural context in which they 'work'.

Huge powers are then attributed to the ads themselves, and teaching can lead to the satisfying (but illusory) feeling that the class can coolly examine the ways that advertising works *on the rest of* its audience, while they personally 'stay above all that'.

Even in the 1980s, when study of the media included broader histories of advertising, there was still a tendency to assume the **effects** of

---

Commodification: a *commodity* is anything which can be bought and sold within a capitalist market; *commodification* and the idea of *commodity fetishism* are often used to argue the *undue* spread of services, items, values which can be bought and sold in this way. 'The commodification of messages [and stories, images etc.] is facilitated by the fact that they are *reproducible*, that is, fixed in a medium which enables them to be produced in multiple copies for sale and distribution' (John B. Thompson in O'Sullivan et al. 1998, p. 32).

An example: the fascination with **subliminal advertising**, associated with hypnosis and said to work by flashing barely perceptible messages to audiences in between frames of a film or ad. Slender evidence came from the USA in the (Cold War) 1950s (flashing images of ice cream during a film encouraged sales of ice cream in the interval) but the stories persisted much longer. See Packard 1979, pp. 41–2.

individual ads. To some extent such work was swayed by the well-established hype of advertising itself which in the 1950s, for example, had often succeeded in taking credit for stimulating British consumer demand after the Second World War. Actually the welfare state was at least as crucial in this change, giving millions of ordinary people proper health care, pensions and education for the first time. By 1989 the advertising bubble had burst and recessionary times, including a tighter market for advertising, set in (see Brierley 1997). This has had formal effects on the ways ads will try to address their viewers (**intertextual** reference to other products, ads, films; the use of deliberately puzzling 'messages' to draw the viewer in and identify the product, and themselves, as 'smart' etc.). We need now to try to understand both the *limits of ads as individual texts* and the *extent of the powers of advertising as a system of representation*.

ACTIVITY 30.5

Have you ever seen a major ad (with prime-time placement on television, for example) for a product which it has been difficult to obtain? Choose a prime-time television ad and research in your local supermarket:

- How easy is it to find the product?
- How does its pricing relate to its marketing, its position in the store etc.? Is it on special offer while being intensively advertised?

You don't have to share the extreme global pessimism of the **Frankfurt School** and its successors to argue for some key influence to the advertising system:

See Chapter 32 'Audiences'.

- the power of the identities which advertising (and other forms) invites us into
- the consequences of increasingly ad-funded cultures, from television to schools and colleges
- the persistence of older-style advertising in some parts of the world. Despite the ironic self-awareness and regulation of western advertising, many older-style ads and marketing ploys are still used in the 'Third World' and Eastern Europe, as well as in poorer areas of the 'First World'.

Cigarette companies, for example, are rushing to ensure that their brands are known in Russia and China before health restrictions are imposed. New mothers in 'developing' countries are often encouraged in hospital to begin the habit of buying expensive packeted baby food instead of learning, like western women, the advantages of breastfeeding as a

'[In India] television has brought the lifestyle of the urban middle class – with its electric kitchen gadgets, motor scooters and fancy furnishings – to villages where women still collect cow dung to fuel their cooking fires … Though [washing machines and fridges] have little practical use in a farm hamlet with no running water and only a few hours of electricity each night, they have become status symbols in one of the world's fastest growing consumer markets' (*Guardian*, 4 January 1995).

Figure 30.4   Old-style, macho, no-health-warning cigarette ad, Mauritius, 1997

cheaper and healthier practice. However, even the biggest brands still face inescapable contradictions.

Example: Nike

Nike in the summer of 1998 faced huge falls in its share prices and shoes piling up in its warehouses. After phenomenally high-profile advertising

'Basketball prince Michael Jordan earned more ($20m) in 1992 for endorsing Nike's running shoes than Nike's entire 30,000 Indonesian workforce did for making them' (Ross 1997, p. 9). The poor performance of Ronaldo in the 1998 World Cup final was constructed by some sports journalists as involved with the pressures of Nike's rumoured $125m ten-year deal with Brazil, giving it control over where and when the team plays friendly matches.

Figure 30.5   Ronaldo of the Brazilian World Cup team (1998) 'practising' for Nike ad

from 1988 to 1998, using celebrities such as Michael Jordan, Tiger Woods and Spike Lee, and hiring the entire Brazilian football team and Eric Cantona for just one commercial, Nike seemed in trouble. Even before the defeat of 'its' team, Brazil, in the 1998 World Cup by the rival Adidas/France squad:

- The patent on Nike Air, its phenomenally successful brand, ran out in 1997.
- Adidas, a rival brand, had staged a very successful comeback, especially in Europe.
- There had been a successful campaign for reform of working conditions in Nike's sweatshop factories in the 'tiger economies' of south-east Asia.
- Fashion was said to be turning from sports shoes to 'browns', or outdoor shoes like Timberlands.
- Most interestingly, for this chapter, it was proving hard to carry on as a 'just do it', young irreverent brand, with a 'swoosh' logo, when you were an established market leader.

Nike retaliated by selling its own 'browns'; cutting $100m off its $890m annual advertising budget; diversifying into clothing and developing a new 'I can' advertising strategy, designed to respond to 1990s perceptions that using sports shoes is now about health, companionship etc. rather than the aggressive 'just do it' slogan coined in 1988.

ACTIVITY 30.6

- Collect all the Nike ads you can over the next week.
- Make notes on: where they are placed; how big they are; what slogans are being used; what expense seems to have gone into them (star names, production values etc.); whether stories of the Nike and other garment workers' campaigns for fair wages are circulated around them.
- Read *Campaign*, or the financial pages of the press, for news of Nike's fortunes.
- From this evidence, how successful would you say Nike seems to be in regaining its market lead? Why?

(See *Campaign* magazine, 3 April 1998.)

Identities and advertising

Advertising has always been keen to locate and profit from the cutting edge of cultural fashions and change. Since the 1960s this has involved processes like **focus groups**. Advertisers have also learnt from developing knowledge and discussions about the media. Media Studies, after all,

Focus groups are small groups of consumers of a product, usually chosen to be representative in terms of age, class etc. They are assembled together to take part in guided discussion of the product, usually taped for later close analysis, so as to help producers assess the likely success of changes to that product (see Stoessl, in Briggs and Cobley 1997).

started some fifty years ago, and many of its assumptions are embedded in journalistic and other popular discourses.

Agencies do achieve successes like those of the BBH (Bartle, Bogle and Hegarty) campaigns for Levi's 501 jeans, 'relaunched' in 1982 via a change in image from 'the sort of thing bank clerks would wear – middle-aged ones, at weekends'. This was done partly by tapping into changes in riskable attitudes, that 'edge' cultural activity we sometimes call 'fashion' or 'trend'. One 1996 Levi's ad featured a transvestite wearing the jeans, a daring move, but also part of many advertisers' attempts to steer between the lucrative 'pink pound' (the gay community's spending power) and the possible distaste of other consumers. The processes of advertising's necessary attempts to keep up to the minute means that it has to take such risks, which many would applaud as giving visibility to identities whose very existence has previously been censored. Likewise, as the Nike example above suggests, a brand which sells itself to a youth market on street cred and rebelliousness can end up in trouble when it is perceived as too established and powerful.

Yet all these ideological processes within ads inevitably address us as shoppers, as consumers, promising to solve all the cutting-edge dilemmas and imagery they evoke simply by acts of shopping. In the process some rich contradictions are thrown up. Magazines often produce challenging articles and even campaigns around topics like date rape; women's guilt at their supposed inadequacy as mothers, wives, home-makers; child abuse; the dangers of sexualising very young girls in advertising imagery and so on. For it's precisely on such topicality that they sell their space to advertisers.

But the bulk of those very ads will appeal to readers on the basis of feelings like guilt about weight or housework, images of sexualised toddlers, of 'perfect' bodies, hair, kitchens, relationships, even if many of these are dealt with ironically and with a sense of humour.

To take a few specific examples of the possible influence of advertising:

- Research into anorexia suggests that young women's understandable absorption into representations of fashion can very easily lead to dissatisfaction with, and an inability to imagine as desirable, any but the most conventional (usually thin or at least adolescent) body.
- Research into housewives' attitudes to their work quickly reveals enormous amounts of guilt about the cleanliness or tidiness of their homes, even if they laugh at, or with, individual ad representations.
- Many men feel that the most compelling advertising representations of masculinity are ones that produce real levels of anxiety and inadequacy, even if male culture, with its emphasis on strong silences or loud camaraderie, makes it difficult to talk about or explore such feelings.

Summer 1998: it is being reported that denim jeans are also suffering sales slumps, now too 'cosy' in image, seen as being worn by ageing pop stars. Of course firms as big as Levi's are also 'major players' in the lucrative replacement chinos markets.

- The tobacco industry spends scores of millions of pounds a year on posters which, with their huge health warnings against using the product, embody the contradictions of this deadly and addictive commodity, and of advertising itself.

References

Bowlby, Rachel (1985) *Just Looking*, Basingstoke: Macmillan.

Brierley, Sean (1995) *The Advertising Handbook*, London and New York: Routledge.

Briggs, Adam and Cobley, Paul (eds) (1997) *The Media: An Introduction*, Harlow: Longman.

Carter, Erica (1984) 'Alice in the Consumer Wonderland', in A. McRobbie and M. Nava (eds) *Gender and Generation*, London: Macmillan.

Cubitt, Sean (1986) 'Reply to Robins and Webster', *Screen*, vol. 27, nos 3–4.

Eckert, Charles (1990) 'The Carole Lombard in Macy's Window', in J. Gaines and C. Herzog (eds) *Fabrications Costume and the Female Body*, London: Routledge.

LaPlace, Maria (1987) 'Producing and Consuming the Woman's Film', in Christine Gledhill (ed.) *Home Is Where the Heart Is*, London: BFI.

Pumphrey, Martin (1984) 'The Flapper, the Housewife and the Making of Modernity', *Cultural Studies*, vol. 1, no. 2 (May).

Ross, Andrew (ed.) (1997) *No Sweat: Fashion, Free Trade and the Rights of Garment Workers*, London and New York: Verso.

Slater, Don (1997) *Consumer Culture and Modernity*, Cambridge: Polity.

Wasko, Janet (1994) *Hollywood in the Information Age: Beyond the Silver Screen*, London: Polity.

Further reading

Barthes, Roland (1972) *Mythologies*, London: Paladin.

Coward, Ros (1984) *Female Desire: Women's Sexuality Today*, London: Paladin.

Goffman, Erving (1976) *Gender Advertisements*, London: Macmillan.

Hebdige, Dick (1979) *Subcultures: The Meaning of Style*, London: Methuen.

Hebdige, Dick (1988) *Hiding in the Light*, London: Routledge.

Lee, Martyn (1993) *Consumer Culture Reborn*, London: Routledge.

Leiss, W., Klein, S. and Jhally, S. (1986) *Social Communication in Advertising*, London: Marion Boyars.

Marcuse, Herbert (1964) *One Dimensional Man*, London: Routledge & Kegan Paul.

Mattelart, Armand (1991) *Advertising International*, London: Routledge.

Mort, Frank (1996) *Cultures of Consumption: Masculinities and Social Space in Late Twentieth Century Britain*, London and New York: Routledge.

Myers, G. (1995) *Words in Ads*, London: Edward Arnold.

Myers, Kathy (1986) *Understains: The Sense and Seduction of Advertising*, London: Comedia.

Packard, Vance (1979) *The Hidden Persuaders*, London: Penguin.

Williamson, Judith (1978) *Decoding Advertisements: Ideology and Meaning in Advertising*, London: Marion Boyars.

Williamson, Judith (1985) *Consuming Passions*, London: Marion Boyars.

31 / Case study: Local newspapers and advertising

In one sense a local paper is a public service. How else is a small community to discuss issues and exchange useful information? (Local radio could provide discussion space, but not the range of information.) Without a commercial newspaper the community would have to finance some form of newsletter. In practice most communities find that there is enough advertising revenue available locally to support a regular paper. In small communities this will be a weekly, in larger areas a daily evening and in one or two large cities a morning daily and possibly a Sunday paper.

This chapter looks at an example of local advertising: you should read it in conjunction with 'Advertising and marketing', Chapter 30.

Background to the *Keighley News*

Keighley is a small town in West Yorkshire which, with its surrounding rural areas, has a population of around seventy thousand. It supports a weekly newspaper, the *Keighley News*, which sells 16,500 copies a week. Each paper is read by two or three people, and total readership is 38,000. Within Keighley itself 67 per cent of adults see the paper – a very high **market penetration**. The next small town, 9 miles away, is Skipton, also with a weekly paper which overlaps the potential circulation area slightly. During the week Keighley readers receive up to two free papers (depending on the efficiency of delivery) and many residents also buy an evening paper, most likely a local edition of the *Bradford Telegraph and Argus*, which circulates throughout the whole metropolitan district of nearly five hundred thousand, Monday to Saturday. A small proportion of Keighley residents buy the *Yorkshire Evening Post*, published in Leeds (15 miles away) and again with a series of local editions. There is also a 'regional morning daily' from the *Yorkshire Post*.

In this fairly saturated media market, keeping a weekly newspaper afloat is difficult. So, how does the Editor of the *Keighley News* (*KN*) face his task and what kind of publication does he produce?

The 'spec' for the **Keighley News**

The *KN* is a **broadsheet** paper with two main parts plus at least one and sometimes two half-size supplements. The issue published on Friday 24 April 1998, which we will analyse here, comprised a total of 32 full pages (two 16-page main sections) including five pages of colour (the outside covers plus one inner page). The half-size *Homes & Gardens* supplement had 12 pages, with colour on the outside covers and the centre page spread (four pages).

ACTIVITY 31.1

Paper requirements

From these descriptions can you calculate the paper requirements at the printworks? Assume that a double spread of broadsheet pages is printed at one pass (and that they are cut in half to produce pages for the half-size supplements).

- How many double sheets are required altogether?
- How does this affect the choice for the number of pages in each part?

- What would be the problem in having a supplement with 14 pages or 15 pages?

The production of pages with colour is more complicated because it requires the application of three separate inks.

- What is odd about producing 5 pages of colour?

The contents of the paper can be roughly divided up into **editorial** – news and feature material written by the local team or bought in – and two forms of advertising: **display** and **classified**. A quick count is possible by scanning each page and estimating the amount of advertising in units of a quarter of a broadsheet page. For this issue of the *KN* it works out like this:

Editorial	44%
Display	25%
Classified	31%

To make the calculation simpler these figures assume that all motor vehicle and house purchase advertising is 'classified' (even though it includes a number of larger 'display' ads). We consider the different forms of advertising below, but here it is worth noting that the advertising revenue is what supports the paper. The ratio of 'cover price' to 'advertising' revenue for local newspapers has remained fairly constant for the last decade and the national figure is 1:5 (see Franklin and Murphy 1998). Survival for a local newspaper means selling advertising in a competitive market.

The task of the Editor now begins to get clearer – produce enough interesting material to attract readers at a set price (in this case 40p – an increase of a third on the 1995 price) and sell enough space to balance the production costs when taken in conjunction with the revenue from sales.

Producing the editorial material

Page 2 of the *KN* lists fifteen editorial staff (complete with photos – a nice touch which emphasises the 'open' nature of the organisation). This is a relatively high number for a paper of this size (some may have wider responsibilities in the 'group' of associated papers which operates in Bradford).

The *KN* is published by Bradford and District Newspapers, which also publishes the *Telegraph & Argus*, the local free sheets and, like most regional groupings, the other smaller papers in the district as well. The *KN* competitors are therefore mostly papers within the group. Printing takes place in Bradford, saving the cost of a dedicated printworks. Keighley is the 'backup' base for the group, with modern accommodation and extra staff.

Bradford and District Newspapers is owned by Newsquest, one of the five major regional newspaper groups in the country. Newsquest is a relatively new company formed by a 'management buy-out' (using American venture capital) of the holdings of the former Reed Elsevier Group. The new company then bought the Westminster Press (including Bradford and District) from the Pearson Group. This was part of a whole series of changes in 1996–7 when many of the big media corporations such as Reed, Pearson and EMAP moved out of local newspapers.

Ownership of local newspapers

Who owns your local newspaper? Fifty-one per cent of all local newspapers sold come from five companies: Trinity International, Northcliffe (*The Daily Mail* group), Newsquest, United Provincial (*The Daily Express* etc.) and Johnston Press (see details in Franklin and Murphy 1998).

The job roles of some of the staff give a clue to the nature of the editorial material used by the *KN*. A *business editor* is essential. Keighley is still very much a manufacturing town and every week there are enough small news items to justify a business page. This week's big story celebrates the success of O&K Escalators in supplying major items of equipment to the New York Transit Authority. Keighley has strong links with America, in both business and tourism, and the *KN* is diligent in promoting and using these links.

Every local paper has a *sports correspondent* responsible for a considerable amount of sports news – in Keighley all the local amateur teams plus the town's professional rugby league team are featured. Sport provides guaranteed copy week in, week out (four pages this week). One of the editorial team is responsible for entertainment, covering cinema, local theatre and music, and another for co-ordination of reports from 'village correspondents' – these are essential in an area with a large number of small communities which, although close to each other, are also proud of their separate identities and keen to find news about themselves in the local paper (two pages this week).

In the centre pages are a number of features which you will certainly find in your local paper. The Editorial column includes a statement about the independence of the paper and its proud tradition (the paper started in 1862, when there was a growing band of newspaper readers – Charlotte Brontë came down from Haworth to collect the papers in Keighley in the early part of the nineteenth century). 'Local independence' is an important feature. Although many local papers will actually have quite evident political party leanings, expressing them too clearly might backfire in a small community and prevent the paper following up important stories or alienating a proportion of readers.

The 'leader' in this issue picks up on the front-page picture celebrating the success of the Town Centre Management Group, who have won a national award for improving the town centre environment. This might not sound like a very 'sexy' story, but the decline of town centres is an important issue for readers of all ages, for different reasons. You might want to reflect on the listing of 'news values' in 'Selecting and constructing news', Case study 13, and consider what makes important 'local' news.

Alongside the Editorial are three 'columns' by local writers. These often revolve around nostalgia (one is written here by a retired local librarian who has become the recognised archivist for the town and seems to have an endless supply of vintage photographs) or something 'folkloric' or dialect-based – ruminations on the world from the perspective of a local person. Where the national columnist is urbane and sophisticated, local columnists must to some extent cater for the sensibilities of local culture. On this occasion the two other *KN* columnists are both dealing with universal issues but there have been occasions when a traditional Yorkshire influence was evident in their stance. (Interestingly, one of the major reasons, revealed by **reader research**, for residents not buying the paper was that they were 'not from Yorkshire' – so a local identity cuts both ways.)

Opposite the columnists is the *letters page,* the source of passionate interest in both short-term and long-term debates. The major issue in Keighley, as throughout Bradford, in 1998 is school re-organisation. The change from 'first', 'middle' and 'upper' schools to 'primary' and 'secondary' affects every family with children at school in the district. This one, as they say, will 'run and run'. At the time of writing, tempers are high and the *KN* is being accused of 'taking sides' – the paper is going to be criticised whatever it does, but everyone will want to buy it.

Education is crucially important to all local newspapers, and the *KN* is no exception. A relatively recent innovation is a youth page called *wired*, which invites contributions from local schools and often carries reports by students on work experience at the *KN*, both from schools and colleges and from the journalism degree courses in the region. The *KN* is well known as a good place to learn about the industry. Many other local papers have similar spaces for student writing, but not all are so willing to offer placements. There are many benefits to the paper in this section, not least the interest of younger readers, some of whom will become future regular purchasers. It is worth noting that the *wired* pages (one and a half) shown in Figure 31.2 use a more 'modern' layout and typography. This makes the pages distinctive and perhaps introduces the idea of a gradual change into the rest of the paper.

Masthead

Publishing information (blue)

'Puff' or 'blurb' for advertising features

Lead story

Secondary leads

Banner

Website address

Colour photograph

Menu for news 'around the district'

Barcode

Display ad (colour)

Blue strip (advert)

Small display ads (colour)

Figure 31.1   Keighley News front page, 24 April 1998

Analysis of front page

You can tell a great deal about a newspaper by looking carefully at its front page and in particular at the design features. We've identified a number of specific features in our example issue of the *KN*.

Masthead   The *KN* has a simple and straightforward title, KEIGHLEY NEWS in a traditional serif typeface. It is an old-fashioned name, but also blunt and Yorkshire. Beneath, in the same upper-case serif, is the **banner** 'THE PAPER THAT PAYS FOR ITSELF' – suggesting the value-for-money philosophy, popular in the town. Nothing else appears in the masthead. This is unusual. A common practice is to include a small ad in each corner, known as 'earpieces' or 'title-corners'. These are usually taken by a well-known local company and can carry a very high ad rate. The argument is that, when the newspaper is folded for display on the shelves, these ads will always be showing. They are more common on daily and evening papers. Check your own paper. Beneath the title a blue band carries the date, issue number, price and contact telephone number, plus the recent addition of the web address – a neat presentation of all the necessary cover information.

Puffs   Underneath the masthead in a prominent position is a set of 'puffs' – promotions for what is inside. In this issue they include two competitions, one sponsored by Marks & Spencer, and the *Homes & Gardens* supplement.

Lead story   The main story is usually placed on the left-hand side of the page, where we tend to look first. It carries a headline in the same size as the masthead (about 62 points).

This particular story is a good example of a new angle on a continuing story. The long-running school re-organisation story refers this week to two small first schools and the intervention of an American businessman who has bought himself the title of 'Lord of the Manor' and is attempting to prevent the closure of one of the schools.

Main photograph   The lead photograph, one of four on the broadsheet page, refers to the Town Centre Award and shows the civic team holding the trophy aloft in much the same manner as a victorious sports team. The high angle on the photo makes for a slightly unusual image and it works well as a composition when the paper is folded for display at the newsagent. Of the other three photos, the kestrel on the wrist works quite well but the bus station image is cluttered and poorly composed and the school is similarly unattractive as a result of the cropping. On a more positive note, the headline of 'Yeehaa!' on the lead story has been 'filled' with a stars and stripes pattern in red, white and blue which works well to give life to the story.

Secondary leads   As well as the Town Centre story, there are two other stories. The kestrel story has human (and avian) interest and allows the paper to pat itself on the back for helping to find the bird. Without the image it could only be justified as 'filler'. The taxi story at the foot of the page is potentially a more serious story. Would a photograph of the rogue cars have helped? Overall, the Editor must achieve balance on the front page with important news and something more light-hearted perhaps. What do you think of the mix here?

Filler   This refers to a non-essential story which can be cut to any length to fill a hole in the page. This is especially important when the 'hole' might be only a couple of paragraphs. On this occasion there is no need for filler as such, but editors always need a stock of filler stories available.

Menu   Most publications carry some form of index or menu on the front page. This serves a different purpose to the puff. None of the items in the menu is likely to persuade the casual reader to buy the paper, but the information is helpful in locating items (and it also acts as another front page filler). In this case the menu refers to specific local community items.

Display ads   The bottom corners and strip of the front page are sold as display advertising. The main design feature here is the use of the second colour, blue. The strip at the foot of the page matches that at the top which neatly frames the whole page. The colour is also the dominant colour in the display ads, improving their visibility, but building them into the page.

Barcode   This is an important item and is a sign of the increasing importance of sales through supermarkets, garages etc.

Design of the front page

The *KN* is a traditional broadsheet. There is a basic eight-column grid across the paper, but this is very often replaced with a mixture of columns of different widths as on the front page. This gives the benefit of flexibility but compromises the overall look of the publication.

How many typefaces are used? Most of the headlines and body text use a serif face in two weights, plain and bold. The puffs, reporters' by-lines and information in the coloured bars are all presented in a standard sans-serif face (see 'Production techniques', Chapter 5).

By modern standards the *KN* presents a traditional-looking local paper with splashes of colour and quite a 'clean' and open presentation. Total control over layout has only been possible locally fairly recently – previously some of the make-up decisions were taken in Bradford.

Sans-serif faces are thought to suggest a more modern, 'younger' look to a paper and we might expect to see more of them in use on the *KN* (as on the youth page, *wired*). However, the Editor knows his market and he doesn't want to move too fast. The readership profile and reader research suggests that too much change could alienate readers. (The sister paper in Skipton has a very 'old-fashioned' look and it is extremely healthy.) Overall, the 'look' of the *KN* probably suits its readership – a balanced age-profile, cautious about change but not uninterested and expecting value for money and open, honest comment.

What does your local paper look like? Do you think it matches the expectations of its readers?

Figure 31.2   Typography for the *wired* pages of the *KN*

In section two of the *KN* the editorial content comprises the television listings, entertainment coverage and wedding photographs plus advertising features and one extra page of news. The rest of section two is taken up by ads.

Many parts of the paper are 'pre-determined' each week. Out of sixteen pages in section one, six are for 'general news' and the other ten are concerned with business, sport, letters, education or village news etc. The reporters have all week to collect news stories. 'News' will last that long if no one else reports it, and so getting the editorial material together is not really like the frantic rush of the daily paper (although it can be with decisions over schools or with the rugby league team) – it is more a question of getting the details right and making sure that all parts of the community are properly covered.

ACTIVITY 31.2

Structure and content of the paper

Analyse your local paper and divide the news and features up as we have done above.

- Does your paper work in the same way?
- Do you have any particular local features not commonly found?
- What kinds of issues feature in the letters page and Editorial?
- What is the difference (if any) in terms of 'news values' between these issues in your local paper and those commonly found in national newspapers?

Selling advertising

There are a number of separate issues to consider in selling advertising. How do you produce high-quality editorial material, and present it attractively, without raising costs too much? How do you increase advertising revenue without deterring readers who don't want to feel overwhelmed by the ads? There is nothing worse than the publication which seems to be all ads and no news or features (unless of course it is *Exchange & Mart*). It is worth noting here, though, that resistance to advertising is probably less in local papers, because all ads are relevant in the sense that they are targeted much more precisely than in national newspapers.

Advertising and editorial are interdependent. Advertising space sells because of the promise to reach the readers. If the editorial quality falls and circulation falls with it, advertising revenue will also fall. If advertising revenue falls, the cover price must rise, but this in turn will drive more readers away and so on. This is the vicious whirlpool of decline every publisher dreads. Get

it right and it works the other way. New readers mean more advertising revenue and in turn more resources for editorial. The *KN* appears to have managed to increase its price dramatically while retaining roughly the same editorial to advertising ratio during the changes of the last three years.

Display advertising

Most of what we think of as advertising is display advertising, although in the second section of the *KN* as in many papers, local and national, the majority of space goes to classified ads. The easiest way to distinguish between the two is to remember that classifieds are usually just a few lines of text in a tiny standard print size, whereas display ads can be any size, but will be in their own, separate, space and may use any typeface or graphics they choose in order to stand out or 'display' on the page.

The most obvious users of display space (i.e. the biggest ads) in local papers tend to be local supermarkets, furniture warehouses, garden centres etc. In this issue, the *Homes & Gardens* supplement is sponsored by Morrisons Supermarkets, which has a half-page display ad on the back page. Display ads cost a great deal and therefore in order to justify their cost they must reach a high proportion of potential buyers of the products being advertised. This explains why nationally available products are rarely advertised in local papers. There is little point in advertising a particular brand of car in a local paper since the ad would be seen by only a small fraction of the potential national market. Advertising in every local paper would not be as good value as advertising in one or two national papers. However, advertising a car as part of an ad for a local garage makes sense in a local paper, if 'two out of three' potential buyers at that garage get to see the ad.

Classified advertising

Hundreds of tiny two-line ads don't sound very glamorous, and 'selling classifieds' might be thought of as a very routine job. In fact, a successful classified section is often the basis for overall success on a newspaper (the *KN* has five dedicated classifieds staff). This is true of local and national papers. One of the strengths of the *Guardian* is its different specialist classified section for each day of the week. Classifieds offer a very important service, and they may be the sole reason some people buy the paper.

We can split the classified section in a local paper into different functions. First there are 'official announcements' – public announcements which must be made by law such as planning notices, licence applications etc. Then there are the more personal announcements, the 'hatched, matched and dispatched' as they are often known (births, marriages and deaths). We are all interested in what happens to friends and neighbours, and these are often the most eagerly scrutinised part of the paper. In Keighley, the convention has grown up whereby, when someone has a birthday such as a fortieth or fiftieth, friends or relatives will put in a photograph of said person at five or fifteen. This increases the fun and the interest and is the kind of custom warmly encouraged by the paper.

The third function of the classified section is to advertise local products and services, and here again there are strong links to the local community. The local council is likely to be a big advertiser in relation to job vacancies, and this may create difficulties if the paper is also running investigative stories on the council. There have been several instances, especially in London and other large cities, where paper and council have fallen out so badly that the council has refused to advertise in the local paper. Both sides suffered badly in such disputes. The paper lost advertising revenue and the council found recruitment much more difficult. This is a good example of how commercial necessity might constrain (or help maintain) local press relations.

A successful classified section will generate good business for the paper if it convinces readers that the goods and services on offer are worth pursuing, i.e. that everyone offering something uses the classifieds to sell it. The Classifieds Manager dreams of the situation where

eager punters are waiting for the paper to appear so they can be the first to apply for the job, bid for the second-hand car etc. It might not be such a rush on a weekly paper like the *KN*, but in big cities, where the evening paper may have several editions starting at around 11 or 12 noon, the first edition is likely to be bought either by people chasing jobs or flats or by gamblers checking the afternoon racing.

Advertising features

Part way between advertising and editorial copy is the *advertising feature* or *advertorial*. This material is designed to attract advertising *directly*. The newspaper produces a general article, usually with an aim of giving information about a particular topic, and invites businesses with some link to the topic to advertise on a special deal basis. There are a number of standard ploys. For instance, when a new restaurant opens or is refurbished a piece may be written about the opening and advertisements sought from the drinks suppliers, builders, furnishings suppliers etc. associated with the opening. Most of the parties concerned benefit from the arrangement. The paper sells space, the advertisers get a good deal and a little extra attention because of the focus on the page, the restaurant gets free publicity and even the reader gets useful information in terms of knowledge about a new facility. In order to preserve its ethical position the paper will print 'Advertising Feature' at the head of the piece to signify that what follows is not a news report or a food and drink 'review'. The reader must then accept that the information in the piece, though not factually inaccurate, will not be as objective as in other parts of the paper.

This issue of the *KN* has a number of such features. One is a 'news special' feature with the companies in the town centre congratulating the Town Centre Management Group (see above). Another is titled 'Women of Today', with editorial on fashion, exercise etc., and the whole *Homes & Gardens* supplement comprises a single advertising feature.

A comprehensive advertising sales and promotion policy

You will have noted that many aspects of selling advertisements are, like the news itself, relatively fixed. Many of the classifieds and even some of the regular display ads are placed week in week out. However, in order to maintain a high level of ad revenue and to deter competitors (see below), it is important for the paper to be 'selling' space and not just 'renting' it out. In other words the paper must employ people to contact firms and persuade them of the value of advertising. The *KN* has several regular advertising supplements such as 'The Class of 98' which is little more than a collection of group photographs from local schools. This ensures that all those featured will buy the paper as a souvenir, but also gives an opportunity for schools outfitters, local newsagents etc. to advertise to parents and friends.

ACTIVITY 31.3

Developing an ad feature

The advertising feature can be planned well in advance since retailers themselves recognise certain times of the year when particular shopping needs are paramount. Christmas, holidays, 'back to school' are obvious subjects for features.

- Draw up a schedule of twelve possible advertising features, one a month throughout the year. There are several ideas listed here, but you'll need to consider others suitable for less obvious months, like October or March.
- Go to your local library (or direct to the paper itself) and check back to see what your local paper actually carried at different times.

The most competitive area of advertising is in the classifieds, and here the paper must be sure that it is efficient (and accurate) in taking copy, i.e. it provides a good service to users, but also it must sell new ideas and new deals to business users of classifieds like the estate agents and motor dealers. A new deal such as discounts for long 'runs' over several weeks or for bigger displays within the classified section can make a dramatic impact. There is also a 'production constraint' factor.

Selling advertising space

Imagine you are the editor of a local paper and you plan a 40-page issue with 18 pages of classifieds. The deadline for copy to go to the printers arrives and you have all the editorial material sorted out, but you only have seventeen pages of classified ads. What do you do?

There are a number of options, but you certainly can't leave the page blank. You can't drop the page because pages come in fours, at least. You could spread the material more widely and lose the space, but this will mean that you have lost potential revenue. The best move is to phone round your regular advertisers and offer them lower and lower rates until you persuade them to buy the remaining space.

Q Can you see any drawbacks in this?

A If you do it too often, the advertisers may start to think you are in some kind of trouble – or they might decide to withhold their ads until your prices fall.

Selling advertising space (and from the other side buying space – known in the industry as **media buying**) requires specialist knowledge and skills. A whole separate industry has grown up which supports the process, and you can get a good flavour of the business if you read the trade publication *Media Week*, which carries advertisements by newspapers themselves targeting media buyers and presenting information about their circulation figures (usually as audited by the Audit Bureau of Circulation – **ABC**) and their reader profile (i.e. the percentage of AB, C1 etc.). You may also come across reports from organisations who log the effectiveness of advertising campaigns in different media. Local newspapers want to show that they offer better

ACTIVITY 31.4

Market research

Find out how people use your local newspaper. Create a questionnaire designed to address the following issues:

- How long do they spend reading the paper?
- How long do they keep the paper in the house?
- How reliable and accurate do readers feel local news is compared to national or regional news?
- Why do they read the paper? Why do some people not read it?
- What kind of research findings would be most useful in persuading advertisers that local newspapers offer a good deal? Try to mock up an ad for the group which owns your local newspaper, to appear in *Media Week*.

value to advertisers, and they may commission research to prove it. This wouldn't normally be done by a single title, but may be undertaken by a newspaper group as a whole. The *KN* receives material produced by a national market research organisation commissioned by the group. This is followed up with local **reader panels**.

The nature of media research is such that what may appear insignificant details can be crucial in persuading advertisers. For instance the *KN* has a relatively balanced readership in terms of **age profile** (i.e. the same percentage of each age group reads the paper).

Advertising managers need to be constantly up-to-date in terms of how advertising is changing and what kinds of new products are being sold. A new arrival in 1995 was the National Lottery, and many newsagents took to buying small display ads to let local residents know that they were selling tickets. Figure 31.3 shows the readership profile for the *KN*. A significant factor for advertisers is the bias towards the C2DE group. Keighley

ADWEB Newspaper Readership Report (JICREG DATA)
for

Keighley News

NS DATA

This newspaper has **MODELLED** data.

Newspaper Readership Demographic Profile

Adult (15+) readership : 38869				Readership by Demographics					
Total men	Total women	Total aged between 15 and 24	Total aged between 25 and 34	Total aged between 35 and 44	Total aged between 45 and 54	Total aged between 55 and 64	Total aged 65 or more	Total of social class ABC1	Total of social class C2DE
18886	19983	5224	7477	7196	6699	4890	7383	15622	23247

Readership by Location

Location Name	Population	Households	ADULTS	MEN	WOMEN	ABC1	C2DE	15-24	25-34	35-44	45-54	55-64	65+
BINGLEY	20847	10796	1300	629	672	683	617	146	214	248	256	177	261
BRADFORD	239929	122412	594	296	298	268	326	66	136	114	116	69	94
HAWORTH	9607	5145	4942	2423	2519	2268	2672	530	933	980	1005	663	831
KEIGHLEY	32024	16825	20825	10170	10656	7185	13641	3226	4351	3733	3176	2476	3862
SILSDEN	26700	13781	9616	4614	5000	4554	5062	1048	1594	1843	1871	1299	1962
SKIPTON	22748	12165	1591	753	838	663	928	207	249	278	276	208	372

Figure 31.3   Readership details, published by JICREG for the *KN*

is a working-class town and will not attract some of the advertising which goes to middle-class Ilkley a few miles away. On the other hand, the high penetration will attract volume advertising for lower-priced goods.

The saturated media market and advertising spend

So far we have discussed only newspaper advertising and noted the different types of newspaper circulating in a local area. We have also made the point that the total 'advertising spend' in any locality is probably relatively fixed, i.e. there is a limit to how much businesses or individuals are prepared to spend on advertising at any one time. If a new medium or a new competitor in the same medium comes along, the same spend will be spread further and divided up between a greater number of media products. (There may be an increase in overall advertising spend during an economic 'boom', but similarly advertising spend can fall during a recession.) If this is the case, it means that the new media products (e.g. the programmes on digital television) will be relatively cheap productions, because there is no guarantee that the advertising revenue will support bigger budgets for them.

So what competition might a local newspaper be afraid of? The obvious threat is a free newspaper, which in some parts of the country has taken away sufficient advertising business to cause the collapse of a 'paid-for' rival. Since Newsquest is the largest free paper publisher in the country, it is unlikely to threaten its own paid-for titles. The other two obvious contenders in the current climate are local radio and cable television. Radio stations have been opening in several new localities recently, and cabling of much of the country is either completed or under-way at the time of writing. The threat from radio is immediate, but in a small town like Keighley the impact has not been great so far. The local commercial station in Bradford broadcasts across the whole metropolitan district and tends to compete with the *Bradford Telegraph and Argus*. Keighley is also on the edge of the new Dales Radio station's coverage, but again other newspapers are

going to be more affected. Nevertheless, the *KN* is watching the franchises on offer carefully.

Broadcast radio can't target small districts directly, but cable can. The local franchise-holder, Yorkshire Cable, does not carry local advertising, but other cable companies have experimented with very local schemes. It is possible for a cable company to send advertising material down the cable to just a handful of streets. This could be highly attractive to supermarkets, i.e. they could promote a special offer at a local store at a very low cost to just a few people who live close by, while a different ad went out to customers on the other side of town. Such ads would obey our rule of reaching a very high percentage of the target group. At one point the *KN* worked closely with Yorkshire Cable, who sponsored the television listings supplement. Reader research discovered this was not valued, so it was dropped, but the *KN* Editor is well aware of the need to keep ahead of the market.

The *KN* can't act unilaterally, and decisions about the relationship with other media are taken at group level. Local papers may be one of the oldest media, but they have survived by adapting to new conditions. The *KN* is already stored on CD-ROM and is prepared to offer new services to businesses and individual readers when the market is proved to be there. Who knows, in a few years' time local newspapers may act as 'network servers', distributing business information down ISDN lines and providing everyone in the neighbourhood with up-to-date listings of events and a library of local history

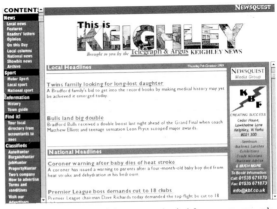

Figure 31.4 The *KN* website at **www.keighleynews.co.uk**

information for schools. The newspaper's website was launched last year and is gradually developing its range of information, as part of Newsquest's ambitious Internet presence. In 1998 the paper also introduced Internet connection services (see 'Digital publishing and the Internet', Case study 15) – if this is successful, it will probably help to sell advertising space on the *KN* site. Has your local paper got a website? What is it like and what kinds of services are being offered?

The local newspaper business had a traumatic time in the 1980s with titles down by nearly 50 per cent and circulation down by a third (see Franklin and Murphy 1998). The changes in this period meant that many local papers began to downplay news reporting at the expense of (cheaper) feature writing. In this regard the *KN* may be different in stressing its community news (which is emphasised in its trade announcements).

The industry has stabilised somewhat in the 1990s and looks set to make a challenge for the advertising spend of the future, when the media environment may look very different. But no doubt readers will still want to know who has been 'hatched', 'matched' and 'dispatched'.

References and further reading

The most useful source is the spread of local newspapers in your area, and, if possible, some contact with the people who produce them.

Most text-books and manuals are geared more towards the national press:

Evans, Harold (1978) *Pictures on a Page: Photojournalism, Graphics and Picture Editing*, London: Heinemann.

Keeble, Richard (1998, 2nd edition) *The Newspapers Handbook*, London: Routledge.

An excellent new book covering the local media is:

Franklin, Bob and Murphy, David (1998) *Making the Local News: Local Journalism in Context*, London: Routledge, in particular the opening essay by Franklin and Murphy: 'Changing Times: Local Newspapers, Technology and Markets'. A slightly earlier version of the same article is published as 'The Local Rag in Tatters', in Bromley, Michael and O'Malley, Tom (eds) (1997) *A Journalism Reader*, London: Routledge.

The front page analysis exercise in this chapter is based on Ben Moore, 'Hold the Front Page!', in *In the Picture*, no. 17 (summer 1992).

32 Audiences

Ways of thinking about 'audiences'

In Media Studies *audience* refers to the groups and individuals addressed and often partly 'constructed' by media industries. Research into audiences has been far from straightforward: the same issues and concerns recur as each new medium arrives. But it has two poles between which assumptions have occurred: the **effects model** and the **uses and gratifications model**.

The effects model (also called the **hypodermic model**) is the name given to approaches that emphasise what the media do *to* their audiences. Power lies with the message here. The media in such work are often called 'the mass media' or 'mass communications' so as to emphasise the size and scale of their operations.

The language used in such writing will often imply that meanings are 'injected' into this mass audience's minds by powerful, syringe-like media. The next step is often to describe the media as working like a drug, and then to suggest that the audience is drugged, addicted, doped or duped.

On the other hand, the uses and gratifications model emphasises what the audiences and readerships of media products do *with* them. Power here is often argued to lie with the individual consumer of media, who is imagined as consciously using particular programmes, films or magazines to gratify certain needs and interests. Far from being duped by the media, the audience here is seen as made up of individuals free to reject, use or play with media meanings as they choose. The needs to be gratified, following Maslow (1970) and McQuail et al. (1972), would include those for diversion and escapism, for information, for comparing relationships and lifestyle of characters with one's own, or for sexual stimulation.

More recent theories have explored ways in which the cultures which both audiences and 'texts' are part of might enter into thinking about both particular audiences and particular media forms (see 'Genres', Chapter 8).

'There are in fact no "masses" but only ways of seeing people as masses' (Raymond Williams, *Culture is Ordinary*, 1958).

'In 1976, a group of friends from Los Angeles who often gathered together in order to indulge in hours long sessions of television viewing, decided to call themselves "couch potatoes". With tongue in cheek publications such as *The Official Couch Potato Handbook* ... and *The Couch Potato Guide to Life* ... they started a mock-serious grassroots viewers' movement' (Ang 1991).

The effects model

The Frankfurt School was set
up in 1923, mostly composed of
left-wing German, Jewish
intellectuals. Key members were
Theodor Adorno (1903–70), *Herbert
Marcuse* (1898–1973) and *Max
Horkheimer* (1895–1973). After
Nazism consolidated its power in
1933 the group worked in exile in
the US.

Let's look in more detail at some effects approaches:

- The **Frankfurt School** theorised the possible effects of modern media,
especially in response to German fascism's use of radio and film for
propaganda purposes and later to the experience, in exile, of the early
power of US media, including advertising. Its members developed a
variant of Marxism known as *critical theory* at a time when 'it seemed as
though the possibility of radical social change had been smashed
between the twin cudgels of concentration camps and television for the
masses' (quoted in Strinati 1995). They emphasised the power of
corporate capitalism, owning and controlling new media, to restrict
and control cultural life in unprecedented ways, creating what they
called a 'mass culture' of stupefying conformity, with no space for
innovation or originality.

- A slightly different emphasis on effects was developed by researchers
into what was then the new phenomenon of television in the US in
the 1950s and 1960s. They were alarmed by a perceived increase in
violent acts and their possible relationship to violence represented on
television, though uninterested in linking these to a critical analysis
of late capitalist society, as the Frankfurt School had attempted.
Again, though, they focused on the power of television to do things
to people – or rather, to *other* people. Self-styled 'moral majority'
movements like the National Viewers' and Listeners' Association
(NVLA) in Britain or parental movements in the US try to have
television and other media more closely censored, on the assumption
that they are the most important causes of a society perceived as
increasingly violent.

- Other 'effects' researchers from the 1940s on were interested in issues
such as whether or not television affected people's political attitudes, as
measured in acts like voting in elections.

Many researchers, especially those studying the effects of media on
children, were influenced by the work of **behavioural** scientists who
tried to understand human *social* behaviour by modifying the *laboratory*
behaviour of animals. **B. F. Skinner** is one of the most famous
behaviourists. You have probably also heard of Pavlov's dogs, laboratory
animals whose feeding times were accompanied by a bell ringing, until
eventually they would salivate whenever the bell rang, with or without
the food. Clearly their laboratory behaviour had been violently modified,
and scientists working on such experiments hoped that control by
reinforcement could be applied to human behaviour – though in different
ways. American advertisers were interested, and some media researchers

Burrhus Frederic Skinner
(1904–90), US behaviourist
scientist, argued that all behaviour
is explainable solely in terms of
genetic dispositions interacting
with 'reinforcements' or rewards.

felt that there might be similarities in the 'repeated messages' or 'reinforcement' of television and their effects on audiences.

A now much-criticised piece of research was called the 'Bobo doll experiment' (Bandura and Walters 1963). It showed children some film of adults acting aggressively towards a 'Bobo doll', then recorded children acting in a similar way later when left alone with it. The implication was then extended to violent media content, which was asserted to have similar effects on children.

Of course there are problems in trying to transfer findings from (unfortunate) laboratory animals to human beings:

- People (a group which includes children!) are often very willing to please those conducting experiments, and also have a shrewd sense of what responses are required to do this – or entertainingly to mess it up.

- A simple, controlled laboratory experiment has very limited application to the complicated conditions under which we interact with the various media in our social lives.

- If people are seen as being like laboratory animals, they will be assumed to be empty vessels, passively absorbing simple television messages. **Cognitive psychologists** have argued instead that children actively construct, rather than passively receive, meanings from the media, and that these interpretations are affected by prior knowledge and experience.

- Entertainment and fiction forms, involving fantasy, group and 'cult' viewings, and 'trying out' identifications are more complex 'messages', and near impossible to fit into the model.

- The 'effect' of watching even factual television may not be shown in our measurable *outward* behaviour, such as voting, or shopping – or violent acts.

'As she entered a laboratory, one small four-year-old girl was heard to say "Look, Mummy, there's the doll we have to hit" ' (Root 1986 on the Bobo doll work).

Other problems with the effects model

The effects of the media, especially television, are usually assumed to be negative, never positive. For example, if you look closely at the kinds of writing (e.g. **tabloid** editorials) that urge censorship, they often fall into one of two apparently contradictory positions, sometimes called **moral panics**:

- The media produce inactivity, make us into 'couch-potatoes', into students who won't pass their exams or unemployed box-watchers who make no effort to get a job.

- The media produce activity, but of a bad kind, such as violent 'copycat' behaviour, or mindless shopping in response to advertisements.

Moral panic term first used by Stanley Cohen (1972) for a process whereby 'a condition, episode, person or group ... emerges to become defined as a threat to societal values and interests; its nature is presented in a stylised and stereotyped fashion by the media, the moral barricades are manned by editors, bishops, politicians' etc. See Thompson 1998.

Of course the media can have effects of a quite simple, though immediate kind: a weather forecast may encourage you to put a coat on; the flashings of strobe lighting in films can be dangerous for epileptics. But usually the word 'effects' is claiming broader, less manageable influence for the media.

ACTIVITY 32.1

Take any recent panic over media effects. Make notes on the language of the pro-censorship writers, including:

- the tell-tale use of 'them' rather than any admission of the researchers' or campaigners' own involvement in media
- implications that 'things were all right' in some earlier age, often thirty years or so ago
- visual stereotyping or stylisation of the group or person being panicked over.

'Let us go into the houses of the poor, and try to discover what is the effect on the maiden mind of the trash the maiden buys ... the ... pretensions of the young girls of the period, their dislike of manual work and love of freedom, spring largely from notions imbibed in the course of a perusal of their penny fiction' (Edward Salmon 1888).

'thousands of children in this country with fathers they never see and mothers who are lazy sluts ... sniff glue on building sites, scavenge for food and, until now, they were free to watch increasingly horrific videos' (Linda Lee Potter, *Daily Mail* 1997).

'The mass audience' as they or we figure in such discourses is usually assumed to consist of the 'weaker' members of society such as women, and children, especially of the 'lower orders'. In the nineteenth century, novels were thought to be potentially harmful for such women; in our century there have been similar fears that romantic novels, and then **soaps**, render women passive, helpless, drugged with trivia.

Children also feature in such discourses: worried over in the 1950s because of the supposed harm done by American comics, then in the 1980s and 1990s in relation to 'video nasties', computer games and even Teletubbies (Figure 32.1). Such worries are usually strikingly isolated from other factors affecting children's use of media, such as:

- underfunded or uninteresting childcare, school and leisure activities
- children's awareness of the conventions and special effects of horror movies
- children's awareness that the computer skills acquired through playing games are highly job-marketable as well as entertaining

Thinking about the models underlying different approaches makes it easier to see when the logic of a particular model has led researchers to 'throw out the baby with the bathwater', as has happened with some effects work. More sophisticated research into broader *influences* of the media emphasise the capacity of television to affect our *perceptions* of violence, politics, strikes etc.:

Figure 32.1   Hard to believe that debates on child audience effects could rage over such characters as BBC's Teletubbies

- Gerbner and Gross (1976) produced work in the US which suggested that the more television you watch, the more likely you are to have a fearful attitude to the world outside the home. (These questions have been revived recently around British television programmes such as *Crimewatch*.)
- Lazarsfeld et al. (1944) explored, over six months, the influence exerted on voters by the media during an American presidential campaign. They concluded that voters were very resistant to media influence since individual predispositions or political preference influenced which media they consulted. The term *two-step flow* was coined to describe the important influence of opinion leaders, whose views often mediated those offered by the media. Media effect began

When the coal strike was over, the National Council for Civil Liberties reported that 'contrary to the impression created by the media, most of the picketing during the strike has been orderly and on a modest scale'.

to be seen as one of reinforcement and *intervening variables* rather than radical change, or brainwashing.

● Greg Philo's (1990) work some years after the British coal strike of 1984–5 suggested another form of effect. Over a period of time audiences tended to forget details of news reporting but to remember key themes and phrases, such as 'picket line violence'. These, through repetition, became part of popular consciousness, and even memory about the strike, even if it could be shown at the time that they were mythical or exaggerated.

The uses and gratifications model

Figure 32.2 The uses and gratifications audience?

Jane Feuer, speaking at a conference in 1997, suggested that for some lesbian fans of the US sitcom *Ellen*, the 'coming out' of the main character, while politically admirable, deprived them of the pleasures of making their own, secret readings of phrases etc. in the programme, which could be assumed to be not 'seen' by the rest of the mass audience.

The uses and gratifications model first found expression in the US in the 1940s (see Moores 1993). It seemed like a breath of fresh air, resisting the easy pessimism and crudely behaviourist emphases of some effects work. It saw the media as functioning in an 'open' way, with personality types in the audience giving rise 'to certain needs, some of which are directed to the mass media for satisfaction' (Morley 1991).

Unlike the Frankfurt School, this was not a position interested in critiquing capitalist mass culture. Indeed some of its extreme adherents came close to denying *any* influence for the media. Just as metaphors of drugs, addiction, passivity characterise the 'effects' tradition, so 'uses' traditions buzz with words like 'choice', 'consuming', 'users' and 'activity'. Of course, this has one big attraction: we're much more likely to *want* to identify ourselves as active readers, zap-happy operators of the television remote control than as the passive dupes of some brainwashing media corporation.

Later writers within cultural studies (see Lewis 1992 and Barker and Brooks 1998) explored the activity of fans and 'cult' viewers, whose pleasure in certain texts could be miles away from either the meaning intended by their makers or the meaning produced by most other viewers.

ACTIVITY 32.2

Take any advert, from television or the press, and say what reading might be made of it by (a) an extreme 'effects' critic and (b) an extreme 'uses and gratifications' critic.

● Which kind of reading seems to you more convincing?
● Why? What does each leave out?
● If you are a fan of any series or star, try to jot down how that produces special audience pleasures and meanings for you.

Recent developments in audience research

A few more approaches need to be outlined here:

- **content analysis**
- **semiotic** approaches
- the broader contexts of cultural understandings.

Media texts are still most likely to be approached through content analysis. This looks for the frequency with which an element in a media text occurs (such as 'violent acts' or 'images of women in the kitchen'), counts them, and implies or suggests as a result what might be the effect on audiences (see 'Representations', Chapter 10). The **violence debate** is full of such 'countings', in themselves useful, but here often part of a disastrously narrowed **agenda**. Rightly concerned when horrible murders or other acts of violence take place, campaigners then argue that they might be prevented by censoring 'violence on television', meaning countable 'acts of violence'. This ignores:

- the problem of defining the violence that is to be counted. It may seem quite a simple thing to decide to count 'violence' or 'violent acts' on television or in computer games and then to conclude they are affecting audiences. Yet the question of what, in our culture, gets perceived as 'violence' is a huge one. Some kinds of activity are labelled 'violent' and others aren't: the latter are sometimes called 'keeping the peace' or 'war heroism'.
- the differences between the many kinds of representations of violence that get counted. A familiar example: is the 'violence' in a Tom and Jerry cartoon, or a Nintendo game the same as the violence in a news bulletin?

As with any media text, *the counting of elements that can be counted* is a circular process, which usually ignores the ways codes and resonances of meaning are combined. If researchers talked about 'counting combinations', it might be clearer what a complex business this would be. In the case of film/television, for instance, it would have to combine the 'act of violence' with

- its place in the narrative
- the stance the audience is invited to take up in relation to it by camera movement, positioning, editing, costume, lighting and other elements of the **mise en scène**
- casting (is a sympathetic star involved?)
- intertextual reference (is a joke being made about another text?)
- the historical stage of its genre (is it a Western at a stage when audiences are likely to be very familiar with special effects of violent death?) as well as the conventions of that genre and so on.

Quantitative analysis (involving the counting of quantities: of hours of television output; or of numbers of women appearing in television news etc.) is popular partly because numbers, unlike languages, form a universal 'currency', and can be read even when their author is not there to explain them. What matters is the quality of the questions asked.

'Since the late '20s an entire research tradition (on violence and media) whose total expenditure must run into hundreds of millions of dollars and pounds, and which has been guaranteed serious political reception and "front page" media coverage …, has dominated the media research agenda – and achieved nothing' (Martin Barker, letter to *Sight and Sound*, August 1995).

'It is the height of hypocrisy for Senator Dole [powerful US republican politician], who wants to repeal the assault weapons ban, to blame Hollywood for the violence in our society' (Oliver Stone, June 1995).

ACTIVITY 32.3

Take a recent film or television programme which was called violent and go through the above list.

- What would you say is its 'message' about violence?
- How might this strike: (*a*) an audience experienced in its genre? (*b*) an audience inexperienced in its genre?

Finally, it's perhaps worth noting that some representations of violence may have not negative but positive effects in the revulsion they invite us to feel, for example at certain kinds of assault, or military power, or bullying.

ACTIVITY 32.4

Think back to the most horrifying or frightening moment in a media text that you have ever experienced.

- How does it fit into the discussion above?
- Why was it so horrifying for you?
- Did anyone else share your feeling?
- What kind of text, what kind of genre was it part of? Fairy tale? Cartoon? News?
- Did this make a difference to how you understood it?
- How would you relate this to any current panic about the effects of media texts?

Semiotics and audience theory

Semiotic and structuralist approaches to meaning (see 'The languages of media', Chapter 1) were applied in Britain from the 1960s onwards, especially in the journal *Screen*. Questions such as

- How does this programme or ad or movie produce meaning?
- With what codes and conventions is it operating?

promised to understand the making of meaning as a much more mediated, active and social process than the counting of elements in, for example, violence and media debates.

But the theories, along with speculation from psychoanalytic approaches, were often applied in extremely text-isolated ways (notably to films in *Screen* in the 1970s, and later to television by others). One example was an emphasis on the assumed powers of the Hollywood editing system (and later television) to 'suture' (stitch) or position 'the spectator' in certain ways, making only one reading possible, however unconscious readers were of that position. Most influential was Laura Mulvey's 1975 argument, heavily couched in psychoanalytic terms (*fetishism*, *voyeurism*, *scopophilia*), that audiences were put into masculine, and therefore inevitably **voyeuristic** positions by Hollywood films through the ways that women on screen are rendered 'to-be-looked-at' (by lighting, editing, positioning as well as narrative placement) while it is usually the male characters who are doing that looking and have control over it, and the narrative. Key questions later put to this immensely influential position, by writers who included the later Mulvey herself, included:

- How do women in the audience respond to such moments? Is there no escape from this predetermined 'position'?

- What of lesbian viewers, who might be reluctant to go along with such attacks on taking pleasure in the female image?

- What happens in genres which try to address a female audience directly (e.g. the 'woman's film' or romantic comedies)?

- Can the theory be applied to television, with its very different, less compelling screen size, its more 'open' unending soap narratives, its more fluid invitations to identify (e.g. the 'in and out' of trying to guess the answers to game shows) and its invitation to a glancing rather than gazing 'look'?

Despite using the language of revolution (with terms such as *regime*, *subversion*, *radical*), *Screen* theory was often almost totally uninterested in what actual audiences might be doing with these 'texts'. A key, though slippery, distinction began to be made. These '*ideal spectators*' (or 'subject-positions created by the text', and by such theories) could be distinguished from the *social audience* for those texts at any given period in time (e.g. groups of women Second World War cinemagoers, interviewed, and therefore constructed by a more **empirical** approach). Methods of investigating them (textual analysis; interviews) were very different and recently people working in each field have felt the need to integrate the approaches of the other.

Voyeurism the pleasure of looking while unseen (here accounted for in Freudian terms), used in thinking about male pleasure in the ways cinema constructs women as 'objects of the gaze'.

Gay and lesbian viewing responses would produce a quite different sense of such images (see Medhurst, cited in 'Representations', Chapter 10).

'In the 1970s the feminist slogan "Who does this ad think you are?" pasted across street advertisements, sought to expose the hidden power of address to position women as subordinate' (Gledhill 1997, p. 370).

The *Nationwide* work

At the same time, during the 1970s, the Centre for Contemporary Cultural Studies (**CCCS**) at Birmingham, under Stuart Hall, worked with a combination of semiotic and more sociological approaches. David Morley's *The Nationwide Audience* (1980), working on an early evening magazine news programme, argued that audiences worked at **decoding** media texts. Though this used a semiotic model of audience activity, it broadened it into study of its relation to:

- power structures *outside* the text which shape audience members: class, gender, ethnicity, age and so on
- power structures *within* the text and media institutions. These mean that such programmes try to promote a 'preferred reading' which was argued to be in line with the 'dominant ideology' (see 'Ideologies and discourses', Chapter 11).

This broadly Gramscian model of hegemonic power in the media (power which was constantly having to work to win consent, rather than just being imposed from above) worked with Stuart Hall's 'encoding–decoding' model of three types of audience readings:

- **dominant**, or *dominant hegemonic*, where the reader recognises what a programme's 'preferred' or offered meaning is and broadly agrees with it
- **oppositional**, where the dominant meaning is recognised but rejected for cultural, political or ideological reasons
- **negotiated**, where the reader accepts, rejects or refines elements of the programme in the light of previously held views.

Questions were later raised about this work, not least by David Morley:

Q Does it see language and media as a kind of conveyor belt for pre-made (especially ideological) meanings or messages?

Q Does it blur together a number of processes? Are viewers' activities better thought of as 'comprehension/incomprehension' rather than 'agreement/disagreement' or 'decoding'?

Q How is class defined in this context of 'dominant/oppositional'? Is it equated too easily with occupation? What of age, gender, ethnicity, sexual orientation for example?

Q What about *entertainment* forms? This, and much other audience work, had stayed with news and documentary. Where pleasure and play seem central, can we still use the idea of a single preferred meaning?

Q Questioning people about videotaped programmes in a college setting is fine. But how likely would they be to watch those kinds of programmes outside that setting? This leads to considerations of **genres**, **discourses** and *domestic contexts for viewing* (see below).

Overall, however, the *Nationwide* work, though drawing on semiotics, opened up interest in more empirical studies of television audiences, increasingly in relation to entertainment and fiction forms and to the domestic contexts in which viewing usually takes place. Before we move to this though, one more text-centred emphasis deserves explanation.

Mode of address

The idea of **mode of address** comes out of linguistics. It refers to the ways a text 'speaks to' its audience, 'who it thinks we are'. A good comparison might be with how, in everyday encounters, our way of addressing a friend, a teacher, a bank manager will each be slightly different. It will also incorporate a position for that person, and his or her status, within what we are saying: as someone being treated respectfully, with intimacy, or with caution (see 'Ideologies and discourses', Chapter 12). The further implication is that when we are addressed in certain ways (as naughty children; as newly 'grown up' etc.) we 'play along' and may partly assume the identity thus constructed for us, at least temporarily.

If your course involves practical work you will be expected to think carefully about how to *address* your audience. In academic work you will have to learn how to address an essay to an imagined audience: how much knowledge are you supposed to assume they have? How much 'proof' (references etc.) do they need of statements in the essay?

Example

The Clothes Show (BBC) addressed its audience as being interested in fashion and in buying clothes, and (often though not always) as being quite young. This can be argued on the basis of the kinds of cultural references made in it, such as the easy use of designers' names; the display of prices and shop names (an openly consumerist mode of address); the high-tech effects, use of pop music, joky presenters' style etc.

ACTIVITY 32.5

Take a current affairs programme and make notes on its mode of address, e.g. *Newsnight*, *World In Action*. Look at such signifiers as title sequence; studio set-up, if any; voices, accents, dress of presenters; whether the programme takes a position on its subject; use or avoidance of 'you', 'us' etc. by the presenter. How would you describe its mode of address overall? Respectful? Boisterous and irreverent?

ACTIVITY 32.6

Watch a cross-examination in a televised law court (or 'courtroom drama' story). How are identities constructed by the ways that lawyers address witnesses, judges, each other?

'Social identity depends … on the recognition by others, formally or informally, that one has indeed a certain identity, and not just on self-recognition' (Andermahr et al. (1997) *A Concise Glossary of Feminist Theory*).

ACTIVITY 32.7

Take a tabloid and a broadsheet newspaper and compare their modes of address. Look at such signifiers as: headline and typeface size; kind of language used (is slang or racy abbreviation present?); the proportion of the page taken up by photographs; any use of 'we' or 'you' especially in the Editorial slot where the paper 'speaks its mind'; adverts and how they seem to be addressing their audience.

Figure 32.3 How does this cover address its audience?

Such textual work suggests that modes of address:

- are linked to assumptions about audiences, and the desire to attract or maximise them or perhaps to target specialised ones
- may also reinforce or even help to create these assumed identities, and to define or informally 'teach' them.

Audience ethnographies

More recently there has been a turn to **audience ethnographies**, or fieldwork research, largely derived from **anthropology**, where the researcher attempts to enter intensively into the culture of a particular group and provide an account of its meanings and activities 'from the inside'. He or she will often employ *participant observation* methods, participating in the lives of the groups to be studied for an extended period of time, asking questions and observing what goes on. When the research is written up, it often tries to show a respect for the group studied by providing life histories, case studies and verbatim quotes from them. Problems remain:

- How can the observer ever know the extent to which their questions, presence even, have affected the group 'under observation'?
- Have questions, and what the researcher hears in the answers to them, been selected to fit his or her pre-existing agenda or theory?
- There is usually an imbalance in power between researcher and researched. How might this affect the findings?

Nevertheless, it seems likely that more can be learned from careful ethnographic accounts than from the assertions of theory on its own, or from simple, number-crunched questionnaires alone. The key areas which recent media ethnographic work has investigated include:

- the domestic contexts of reception
- genre and cultural competence
- technologies and consumption.

The domestic contexts of reception

Morley (1986), Gray (1992) and others (see Geraghty 1998) have explored ways in which the home, or rather, different homes – the domestic context for most television viewing – affects and structures those viewings.

Such research suggests that the home, 'the private sphere', our 'retreat from the world', is in fact as cross-cut by social power as anywhere else. In particular, television viewing is structured by gender and age power relations. A few examples:

- For men, often coming home after work or a day spent outside it, viewing can be a very different experience than it is for women who, whether or not they work outside the home, are likely to see it as a place of (house)work. It's much easier for men to watch in an uninterrupted way than it is for women, who are often expected to manage the interruptions and disputes that break out among children.
- Because women's (house)work is always there, in the home, women have spoken of their pleasure in carving out time for themselves to refuse their domestic duties for a while and enjoy a video, or a novel.
- The remote control, and who wields it, is a key symbol of power within families (and other groups).

Williams argued, on the basis of his first experience of US television, that television and radio are not experienced as composed of separate items or programmes. More often they are experienced as a **flow** of similar segments ('watching television'). If you have seen any US television in the US you will know how confusingly adverts often flow into and through programmes, without any separation.

All this has powerful implications for theories such as those of decoding, which imply a very concentrated relationship of viewer or text. Television viewing doesn't feel like that a lot of the time, partly because of the **flow** which Williams (1974) and others have suggested is the characteristic experience of television, especially in commercially funded systems, keen to keep fingers off channel buttons so as to sell more audience attention to advertisers.

ACTIVITY 32.8

Interview other students on the following questions :

- How many televisions do you have in your household? Where are they? Are they all colour sets? Who uses which?
- Have you ever successfully waged a struggle for the remote control? How?
- Do you watch any programmes because you know you'll disagree with them, or enjoy ridiculing them?
- Do you have 'special occasion' viewing? If so, what arrangements do you make? Does this make television viewing more like cinemagoing?
- Do you use television as part of a relationship – to mend it, or help begin one, or even to avoid conversation?

Discuss your findings, then answer the following questions:

- Which of the answers supported a 'uses and gratifications' and which an 'effects' model of the audience?
- If most supported a uses and gratifications model, did you feel there was any case to be made for television having any effects which are beyond your control?

Genres and 'cultural competences'

Pierre Bourdieu (b. 1930), French sociologist who began ethnographic work after being conscripted into the French army during the Algerian War of 1958. His book *Distinction: A Social Critique of the Judgement of Taste* (1984) explored how the supposedly natural, universal quality of 'taste' is actually formed along class and educational lines.

Bourdieu's concept of **cultural competence** is useful in understanding the pleasures which particular audiences or readerships take in different media forms. It suggests that the media/art forms we feel easy and familiar with will be related to our social class position via the cultural competences we have acquired (competence here does not mean correctness or efficiency, but shared knowledge and perspectives). A good example would be women's magazines and romance fiction, or soap operas, especially in the period before the mid-1980s when television companies tried to attract larger male audiences by means of the kinds of 'serious', 'tough' themes now found in *EastEnders* or *Brookside*.

Until then, it was assumed that women's soaps and magazines were an inferior media form, which anyone could understand, though in which only a rather stupid or **trivial**-minded audience would be interested. **Feminist** critics, however, pointed out that fans of such genres will have the competences needed to engage with the themes of personal, domestic life and intimate, often family relationships. For example, they need to know the significance of certain kinds of looks between characters, or to feel easy with a lot of talk in soaps ('yakkety yak' to those hostile to the form). They need to have an interest in the domestic, in the personal experiences dealt with in those genres, so as to read certain small-scale gestures, silences and so on as having meanings for the narrative. Women are argued to have easy access to such competences through years of informal training for their presumed future role as caring mothers; or as carers in jobs like nursing, or teaching; or through their confinement to the home, except in periods of high male unemployment.

Bourdieu further suggested that in capitalist societies there is an analogy or likeness between the ways that access to capital (economic power) is differently distributed between different classes and groups, and the ways that some groups will have access to cultural competences that have higher status than others (such as knowledge of literary allusions, or of computers). Some theorists of **cult** forms (such as 'trash television' or movies) have suggested that fans have the privilege of 'double access' to both 'naive' enjoyment of the form and a knowing humour at its codes. We don't want to argue that no male viewers ever come upon, or have developed, the competences to enjoy romances or soaps, nor that some women may not be irritated by those forms. But informal gender training from early on means that certain responses to some genres (like the sad-ending romance) are from very early on made unacceptable for some groups ('big boys don't cry') and natural-seeming for others.

From the male side of *gendered competences* it's been argued that boys are socialised from early on into acting tough in the face of 18-rated videos and horror films, which they sometimes find hard to stomach. Our culture still expects men, in the end, to differentiate themselves from women along the lines of 'toughness'. Young men are encouraged not to cry, not to explore feelings, and to try to appear as decisive and hard as the heroes of action adventures.

Trivial 'From the Latin "tres" = three, and via = way, "trivia" originally referred to the place where three roads met ... The modern sense of trivial – commonplace, ordinary, of small account, trifling ... – may have been influenced by the crossroads being a place where women met to exchange news' (Jane Mills, *Womanwords*, London: Virago, 1991).

'So what was the significance of that little look then?' (much-used male query on soaps and everyday interactions within them).

'When I was 3 or 4 my mother was already teaching me to see dust and other people's feelings' (woman interviewed by Shere Hite 1988).

The Simpsons often operates a 'double mode of address', using 'adult' allusions and jokes, which may fly 'over the head' of the main, child audience. *Xena: Warrior Princess* has likewise been said to produce the possibility of a 'parallel' lesbian reading alongside the 'children's adventure story' of its main marketing.

ACTIVITY 32.9

To explore the relative status of cultural competences in your household, jot down whether

- certain people seem to find some genres difficult to follow and have to have help in finding out 'what's going on'. Does this relate to what might be called 'cultural competences' in some genres and not others?

- any of your viewing choices are ever ridiculed by other members of your household.
- If so, in what terms, and about what kinds of programmes?
- How insistent or lighthearted or serious is the ridiculing?
- Does it ever prevent you from watching the programme?

ACTIVITY 32.10

- Do you ever describe yourself as an 'addict' of a media form (programme, magazine, novel)?
- Do you think this is a way of apologising for your interest in it?
- Find a news report of 'Internet addiction' and explore how this is treated: as serious or trivial?

'Western heroes have usually restricted themselves to a pitiably narrow range of activities. They can't daydream, or play the fool, or look at flowers, or cook ... or ... make mistakes' (Jane Tompkins, *West of Everything: The Inner Life of Westerns*, Oxford and New York: Oxford University Press, 1992).

Such cultural approaches to genres are interested in the intimate relationships between audiences and the ways they fit media forms with the rest of their lives.

- Do young men absorb a sense of how to be Really Cool or (in more old fashioned terms, a Real Man) from action thrillers or Westerns, or young women learn how to enjoy certain kinds of power over men (another kind of cool) from romance forms?
- Do the repetitions within certain genres, and the imaginings they exclude, as well as the ones they encourage, reinforce dominant and sometimes oppressive sets of values?

On the other hand it's been argued that men's enjoyment of (even addiction to) news and documentary forms has related to the assumption that their lives, more than women's, will take place within the world of public rather than domestic events, which they get to 'catch up on' and feel part of through news media.

Technologies and consumption

'According to the Sixth World Wide Web User Survey, almost 70% of users are male ... Alan Durndell [a researcher] found that by the time they were 15 or 16, when important career choices were being made, girls were turned off by "violent and immature" computer games' (*Guardian*, 21 December 1996).

A more recent development has been an interest in the 'double' character of the media. Media consist of both

- the programmes, music, etc. which are brought to us, and
- media technologies themselves, which work both through their cultural status as objects (the attempts to disguise or conceal the satellite dish, or to show off the mobile phone) and through gendered differences in attitudes to technology. Ann Gray (1992) interviewed women and asked them to colour-code technologies and activities on a

scale from pink to blue, depending on whether they found them intimidating or friendly. She cites 'pink' irons and 'blue' electric drills, with interesting mixes such as the video recorder's 'lilac' controls, but 'pink' 'record', 'rewind' and 'play' controls, and 'blue' timer switch.

Others have researched the reasons for young women's reluctance to use computers and have suggested not that they are incapable of using machines or technology, but that they resist, or feel ill at ease in, the world of the 'computer virtuosos', the 'technoheads' – young men who seem to be involved in an intimate relationship with their machines, one which is often strongly competitive and macho – 'mine's bigger and faster than yours' – and centred on very masculine genres such as the action adventure and science fiction and skills such as decisiveness.
Q Do you experience such gender contrasts?

Attempts are being made to counter such perceptions, both in TV programmes and in schools, since a very real fear is that the 'information-rich' and 'information-poor' distinction predicted will work along the lines not simply of class, and the world's North–South divide, but also of gender.

Figure 32.4 Lara Croft, the Tomb Raider: empowering girls or reinforcing male dominance and 'look' in PC games?

ACTIVITY 32.11

Collect some recent images of scientists and computers in PC magazine advertising and television programmes such as *The Net* or *Tomorrow's World*.

- How far do they conform to the suggestions above? How do they represent machines? Is the setting in the home?
- What efforts seem to be being made to change the gender balance of such images? In the image of someone like Carol Vorderman for example?

Finally, audiences in the media ...

Access has traditionally meant programme-making where power, including editorial control, is handed over to a group or individual outside the broadcasting institutions. The BBC's *Open Space* slot, or Channel 4's *Right to Reply* are examples. These question old ideas of 'balance between two sides' in broadcasting, and instead try to represent a plurality of voices, especially those from outside television's often cosy world where professionals are often said to make programmes partly for each other's approval.

The audience-in-the-media can also be thought of in the expansion of (cheap) daytime television shows and interactive computer technologies (and indeed the potential merging of the two in digital television). Radio and television phone-ins, magazines, access television and chat shows routinely allow parts of the audience 'into' the media, though on rather special terms.

See 'Selecting and constructing news', Case study 13 for discussion of the increasing replacement of (expensive) reporters by columnists and (cheap) audience-centred chat shows.

ACTIVITY 32.12

Take your favourite radio phone-in or television chat show and examine on what terms members of the audience manage to get a hearing. Look at the following:

- What does the title sequence promise?
- How is the studio set up, both visually and aurally?
- How does the host organise things such as interruptions, noise levels, 'expert' contributions, escalation of conflict?
- How is the show concluded?
- What kinds of ideas and positions can be circulated through such shows?
- Try to list expert fields which might have been consulted for the programme you watch. What seem to have been the criteria for choosing the actual experts used in it?
- What is the most surprising or unfamiliar position you have ever heard voiced on such shows? How was it treated?

References

Ang, I. (1991) *Desperately Seeking the Audience*, London: Routledge.

Bandura, A. and Walters, R. (1963) *Social Learning and Personality Development*, New York: Holt, Rinehart & Winston.

Barker, Martin and Brooks, Kate (1998) *Knowing Audiences 'Judge Dredd': Its Friends, Fans and Foes*, Luton: University of Luton Press.

Barker, Martin and Petley, Julian (eds) (1997) *Ill Effects: The Media/Violence Debate*, London and New York: Routledge.

Cohen, S. (1972) *Folk Devils and Moral Panics*, Oxford: Martin Robertson.

Geraghty, Christine (1991) *Women and Soap Opera: A Study of Prime Time Soaps*, London: Polity.

Geraghty, Christine (1998) 'Audiences and "Ethnography": Questions of Practice', in C. Geraghty and D. Lusted (eds) *The Television Studies Book*, London and New York: Arnold.

Gerbner, G. and Gross, L. (1976) 'Living with Television: The Violence Profile', *Journal of Communication*, no. 28.

Gledhill, Christine (1997) 'Genre and Gender: The Case of Soap Opera', in Stuart Hall (ed.) *Representation: Cultural Representations and Signifying Practices*, London, Thousand Acres and New Delhi: Sage.

Gray, Ann (1992) *Video Playtime: The Gendering of a Leisure Technology*, London: Routledge.

Hite, Shere (1988) *The Hite Report on Women and Love: A Cultural Revolution in Progress*, London: Viking.

Lazarsfeld, P., Berelson, B. and Gaudet, H. (1944) *The People's Choice*, New York: Duell, Sloan and Pearce.

McQuail, D., Blumler, J. and Brown, J. R. (1972) 'The Television Audience: A Revised Perspective', in D. McQuail (ed.) *Sociology of Mass Communications*, Harmondsworth: Penguin.

Maslow, A. (1970) *Motivation and Personality*, New York: Harper & Row.

Modleski, T. (1982) *Loving with a Vengeance*, New York: Methuen.

Moores, Sean (1993) *Interpreting Audiences: The Ethnography of Media Consumption*, London: Sage.

Morley, David (1980) *The Nationwide Audience*, London: BFI.

Morley, David (1986) *Family Television: Cultural Power and Domestic Leisure*, London: Comedia.

Morley, David (1991) 'Changing Paradigms in Audience Studies', in E. Seiter, H. Borchers, G. Kreutzner and E. Warth (eds) *Remote Control Television, Audiences and Cultural Power*, New York and London: Routledge.

Pearson, Geoffrey (1984) 'Falling Standards: A Short, Sharp History of Moral Decline', in M. Barker (ed.) *The Video Nasties*, London: Pluto.

Philo, Greg (1990) *Seeing and Believing: The Influence of Television*, London: Routledge.

Radway, Janice (1984) *Reading the Romance: Women, Patriarchy and Popular Literature*, Chapel Hill: University of North Carolina Press.

Root, Jane (1986) *Open the Box*, London: Comedia.

Thompson, Kenneth (1998) *Moral Panics*, London and New York: Routledge.

Williams, Raymond (1958) 'Culture is Ordinary', in *Resources of Hope: Culture, Democracy, Socialism*, London and New York: Verso, 1988.

Williams, Raymond (1974, 2nd edition 1990) *Television: Technology and Cultural Form*, London: Fontana.

Further reading

Lewis, L. (ed.) (1992) *The Adoring Audience Fan Culture and Popular Media*, London: Routledge.

Staiger, Janet (1992) *Interpreting Films: Studies in the Historical Reception of American Cinema*, Princeton: Princeton University Press.

Strinati, Dominic (1995) *An Introduction to Theories of Popular Culture*, London: Routledge.

33 / Case study: Selling audiences

Academic research is a tiny body of work compared to advertising research. Remember, as you study contemporary advertising :

- The **effects model** of readers' engagement with the media is alive and well in this media sector. Indeed **advertising agencies**, whatever the playfulness and irony of their products, still need to persuade companies using them that they will have some kind of effect on buying habits: in a sense they sell audiences to their clients.

- Yet oddly enough much contemporary **marketing** talk sounds innocent of any desire to affect people. Terms like 'level playing field', 'the market', 'the discriminating consumer' attribute power to the picking and choosing consumer from the **uses and gratifications model**. This is somewhat surprising given that the biggest change in modern advertising has been from working on the product's brand image to researching the audience to be 'targeted'.

- Whatever the arguments about the *effects* on our immediate buying habits, ads are argued to have other, broader *influence* (see 'Advertising, marketing and fashion', Chapter 30). The very act of targeting audiences contributes towards their creation and consolidation. The previously unknown concept of 'the teenager' was by the late 1950s an accepted part of advertising (and political) rhetoric, one that confirmed and actually helped to create a new identity for people in a certain age range.

Advertising agencies

These are businesses that exist to devise, produce and place ads for their customers, the manufacturers of products. They are usually divided into departments specialising in ad design (the 'creative' team), those buying 'suitable' spaces on television etc. (media buyers) and those who oversee the operation (account managers).

> When *South Park*, a cartoon series described as 'Peanuts on acid', was launched on Sky One in April 1998 six advertisers appeared in the expensive 'centre break': Ford Ka, COI World Cup tickets, Oxy On the Spot, a trailer for Tarantino's *Jackie Brown*, Oasis (the drink) and Levi's 501s, who also sponsored the programme. '*South Park* reflects Levi's brand values: male, rebellious and youthful' said the buyer.

Advertisers in newspapers and magazines still use the **JICNARS** (Joint Industry Committee for Newspaper Advertising Research) scales (culled from the NRS or National Readership Surveys: see Stoessl), originally designed to investigate magazine and newspaper sales distribution. But though such indicators of class are important, several objections have been made to such occupation-based surveys of readerships, which indicate how complex now are questions of class.

The **JICNARS scale** divides audiences into:
Group A: upper middle class, e.g. successful business or professional

Group B:	middle class, e.g. senior business or professional, but not at the top of their business etc.	
Group C1:	white-collar, lower-middle-class consumers, e.g. small tradespeople and non-manual workers	
Group C2:	blue-collar, skilled working class	

Group D:	semi- or unskilled manual workers
Group E:	those at the lowest levels of subsistence, 'casual workers or those who, through sickness or unemployment, are dependent on social security schemes'.

THE MOST IMPORTANT GAP IN YOUR MARKET PLACE

We can target your leaflets one of three ways, making sure that your advertising message is delivered to the heart of your market. Our professional sales team will help you to plan your campaign. You can select by demographical breakdown, geographical area or by postcode areas.

DEMOGRAPHICAL BREAKDOWN

To make sure that your message reaches exactly the right target you can plan your campaign by demographical breakdown ie: distributing to terraced housing only. You can also use this type of targeting in conjunction with either geographical area or postcodes.

Have a look at the demographical breakdown below to see which category would suit your campaign.

CATEGORY DESCRIPTION

A Affluent Suburban Housing
B Modern Housing Higher Income
C Older Housing Intermediate Status
D Terraced Housing
E Better Off Council
F Less Well Off Council
G Poorest Council

GEOGRAPHICAL AREA

Plan your campaign by geographical area, just select the towns or villages you wish to target, i.e. West Cross, Skewen and Trallwn and we can let you know how many leaflets are needed to cover those areas. This can also be used with the demographical breakdown i.e. targeting B type households only within those areas.

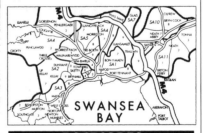

POSTCODES

You can plan your campaign by postcode areas and sectors. Just consult the map and select the sectors you wish to reach i.e. SA3 Sector 5 and we can let you know how many leaflets are required to cover your selected area. This can also be used with the demographical breakdown i.e. private housing in SA3 Sector 5.

CONTACT LORNA DAVIES

OR CONTACT NICHOLA LEWIS

Herald Direct Distribution, Cambrian House, Cambrian Place, Swansea SA1 1RH Telephone (0792) 468833 Ext 3540/3600 Fax No. (0792) 472208

Figure 33.1   Herald Direct distribution ad

423

- The NRS questions rely on the occupation of the 'head of the household' and assume that to be a man. In many households the main wage-earner is a woman, or the income is made up of part-time work by both partners.
- They see the family as a single, uncontradictory consuming unit, without generational or life-stage distinctions.
- They underestimate the ways in which a 'flexible labour market' has brought about rapid changes of occupation, and kinds of work that no longer smoothly fit the scales used.

'40% of the population no longer has a job that fits the system at all.' This statement is from a *Guardian* report (17 July 1995) on the government's decision to change the way class is measured by the Office of Population Censuses and Surveys.

From the 1970s onwards agencies began to use new categories, aimed at specific audience groups, by means of **demographics** (see Figure 33.2) which 'measured the population in terms of occupational class, age, sex and region to read off certain values and assumptions about spending' (Brierley 1998). These often divide potential buyers by geographical location (using postcodes or national census returns). Figure 33.1 shows the kind of research offered by ACORN (A Classification of Residential Neighbourhoods).

Psychographic profiles are another, very different approach to occupational and geographical models. They use questionnaires mailed to members of a panel who are invited to respond to statements like: 'A woman's place is in the home' or 'The use of marijuana should be made legal'. On the basis of the replies, consumers are classified as belonging to a number of lifestyle categories. There are various models competing for manufacturers' and agencies' fees, but a typical one would be the

Information supplied by *JICREG Ltd* . Copyright © 1998 JICREG Ltd and *ADWEB Ltd.*
ALL RIGHTS RESERVED

ADWEB Newspaper Readership Report (JICREG DATA)
for

CARDIFF POST

NS DATA

This newspaper has **ACTUAL** data.

Newspaper Readership Demographic Profile

Adult (15+) readership : 146109				Readership by Demographics					
Total men	Total women	Total aged between 15 and 24	Total aged between 25 and 34	Total aged between 35 and 44	Total aged between 45 and 54	Total aged between 55 and 64	Total aged 65 or more	Total of social class ABC1	Total of social class C2DE
64302	81809	15524	19588	27370	22293	17171	44174	91979	54132

Readership by Location

Location Name	Population	Households	ADULTS	MEN	WOMEN	ABC1	C2DE	15-24	25-34	35-44	45-54	55-64	65+
CAERPHILLY BEDWAS	42606	20494	10013	4497	5517	5340	4673	1025	1205	2048	1788	1322	2624
CARDIFF	273351	126824	118834	52273	66562	75009	43823	12958	16556	22136	17416	13633	36135
PENARTH	30328	15364	17264	7531	9732	11630	5634	1543	1819	3185	3087	2214	5415

Figure 33.2

CASE STUDY: SELLING AUDIENCES

American VALS (Values and Lifestyles) system which classifies people into four groups: needs-driven, outer-directed, inner-directed and integrated.

Agencies may also research consumers' feelings about a product using **focus groups** (see 'Advertising and marketing', Chapter 30) of a few selected consumers presented with an issue to work on, or asked about the image a particular product has for them.

You are being targeted! A one-day marketing conference (admission £450–£500) in June 1998 on students is advertised thus: 'Love 'em or hate 'em – they're a valuable consumer group spending over £5bn per annum and that's before they've left college. Catch them now and they're yours for life' (*Campaign* magazine, 3 April 1998).

The availability of remote controls, video and more television channels and radio stations for advertising also mean that audiences' habits have become less easy to predict. Media buyers in the agencies are specialists who know the most effective medium, and the best vehicle in that medium to carry a specific campaign. They are also hired for their skills in negotiating the best price for their ads. They were active, for example, in pressurising **BARB** to investigate the effect of video playback on ad consumption.

Television and advertising

Commercial or 'independent' television is funded by the sale of advertising space by the television companies, also described as selling audiences to advertisers. Actually it is audiences' attention which advertisers hope to purchase.

This system of buying and selling produces, and is the result of, the commercial logic for ITV funding, the opposite of the notion of public service at work within the early years of the BBC. It began in the US during the Depression of the 1930s, when radio proved the perfect medium for advertisers wanting access to audiences who were confined to the home, for a variety of reasons. The huge success of soap-company-funded serials (soaps) soon went along with a construction/selling of housewives' attention during the day and that of men still in employment and some children during the evening. Scheduling, and the selling of advertising space in programmes likely to attract particular groups, took off, determining, and not simply following, the programmes themselves.

'If television buyers think ITV is driving a hard bargain in its World Cup negotiations, they should ask NBC the price of a 30-second spot in *Seinfeld*. Advertisers … will have to pay as much as $2m [for a slot in the final episode].'

(*Campaign* magazine, 3 April 1998)

Commercial television and radio programmes are made to attract audiences, so that advertisers can buy time or 'slots' (and more recently sponsorship deals) to catch their attention. Sometimes a guaranteed-numbers audience will be 'purchased', spread across a number of slots. Interestingly, it has been suggested that advertisers sometimes prefer programmes that are not too involving and so do not detract from attention to the ads (Curran and Seaton 1991, p. 223). This has important implications for the future of what can be called totally commercial broadcasting ecologies.

ACTIVITY 33.1

Record or take notes on four or five advertising or sponsorship slots from commercial radio and television across the day, e.g. one from early morning, another from 9 am or so, through to late night or early morning.

- What does this suggest about the kinds of audiences advertisers expect to be watching or listening?
- How do the surrounding programmes relate to these ads?

● Why do you think these sponsors want these slots? Repeat the activity for **broadsheet** and **tabloid** newspapers. Look especially at the difference between 'small ads' and whole-page ones.

In paying out these huge sums of money, companies hope to reach the kind of people who will buy their products. Indeed, they check that broadcasters do in fact put out the ads at the times they contracted to do, and even check the whole range of output and criticise the ITV Network Controller in general terms if audiences slip.

Since the 1990 Broadcasting Act, sponsorship has also become a part of UK television. (It was deliberately not chosen as the funding mechanism in the Television Act of 1954 which established commercial television.) The head of sponsorship for the J. Walter Thompson ad agency, which oversees Kellogg's sponsorship of *Gladiators*, is quoted on ways of catching the zapping viewer with a sponsor's credit rather than (or rather, as well as) ads during programmes:

> Your brand is closer to the programme and is a message before other advertising cuts in ... It obviously reinforces other brand advertising, but ... allows the advertiser to build a closer relationship with a consumer ... it's like saying 'We know what you're into and we support it too.'
>
> (*Observer*, 8 January 1995)

Regions and audience size

One of the arguments for the ITV system of regionally based companies was that they would serve and sustain local identities. In fact the 'Big Five' companies dominate

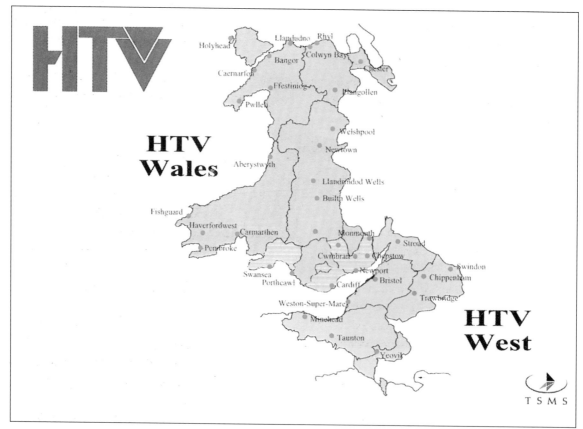

Figure 33.3   HTV area

> '"Granada has the skilled workers: surveys prove it!" read an advertisement in a 1959 trade magazine. "Westward where women cook," read another in *Campaign* in 1962.'
>
> (Curran and Seaton 1991)

programming; only rarely does a programme from HTV get on to **prime-time** commercial television. Though it's been argued that Border Television may have strengthened a sense of local identity, the regional companies' main logic is a commercial one. HTV consists of HTV West and HTV Wales, because Wales on its own is not considered advertiser-lucrative enough to sustain major programming (Figure 33.3). Additionally, the regional nature of commercial television allows additional advertising pressure to be applied in any region where sales are slumping.

It is not the case, if it ever was, that advertising simply seeks to reach the largest possible audience. At both national and global level, regional differences are carefully studied and 'pitched' to. Products are test-marketed in particular areas, for example, and some magazines produce London supplements to try to catch the attention of a concentrated and relatively affluent, young audience.

Television and radio **ratings** work within an advertising industry which segments or divides up its **target audiences**, or readerships, whatever the medium. It is within these groups that ads hope to reach as many people as possible; in fact magazines and television companies trying to reach advertisers will talk of **CPT**s, or 'Costs Per Thousand' (consumers reached).

Another example of ways in which such 'mass media' do not in fact always seek to reach 'the masses' occurred in 1986. British advertising agencies succeeded in persuading BARB, who used to measure social groups D and E together in viewing figures, to separate them out. This was because the 'E's (those 'on the lowest level of subsistence' like retired working-class people and the unemployed) are of little interest to advertisers, yet are heavy consumers of media because they have so much spare time. They were said to be distorting the viewing figures by suggesting that programmes had huge audiences of people itching to spend the pounds in their pockets. It's likely that there will be an increasing tendency to ignore such large but unattractive-to-advertisers audiences if cultural activities continue to be funded mostly by commercial advertising. As with the press, what's often sought are more specific, affluent viewing and buying audiences.

Relatedly, the ability of advertisers to shape broadcasting by **niche marketing**, encouraging the making of certain television genres and seeing others as unprofitable or even undesirable (especially in the US), has been, and should be, cause for concern. Wasko (1994) argues that it is even spreading to cinema, in the form of advertiser-preferred projects with 'placement' potential.

Huge amounts of money, time and energy are invested in audience measurement, especially in the US, as competition between the television networks and the cable companies intensifies. In Britain, where similar trends are visible, research bodies compile 'ratings' of programmes which suggest how many, and what kinds of, viewers are watching them. These are made up for

Key terms in this research include:	
TV ratings	A percentage: the number of viewers of a programme is divided by the number of people in the target audience for that region.
Audience share	If all the people watching any television at any one time are added together, the share for one programme is its audience divided by all viewers.
Reach	The reach to a series, e.g., is the percentage who watched a part of any episode in a series for at least a predetermined time (e.g. ten minutes).

(adapted from Stoessl 1998)

TSMS NATIONAL 30" RATES

RATES EFFECTIVE FROM 1ST JANUARY 1998

PREMIER RATES

Rate Code	Anglia 30 Sec £	Grampian 30 Sec £	HTV 30 Sec £	Meridian 30 Sec £	Scottish 30 Sec £	S4C 30 Sec £	UTV 30 Sec £
P6	42,500	9,000	32,500	60,000	30,000	3,250	9,000
P5	35,000	7,500	27,500	45,000	22,500	2,750	7,500
P4	28,500	6,000	20,000	40,000	20,000	2,150	6,000
P3	25,000	5,000	17,500	35,000	16,500	1,750	5,000
P2	21,500	4,250	15,000	30,000	14,250	1,500	4,250
P1	18,000	3,750	13,250	25,000	12,250	1,350	3,750

STANDARD RATES

Rate Code	30 Sec £	30 Sec £	30 Sec £	30 Sec £	30 Sec £	30 Sec £	30 Sec £
SR	15,000	3,000	11,000	21,000	10,200	1,100	3,000
10	13,500	2,700	9,900	18,900	9,180	990	2,700
20	12,000	2,400	8,800	16,800	8,160	880	2,400
25	11,250	2,250	8,250	15,750	7,650	825	2,250
30	10,500	2,100	7,700	14,700	7,140	770	2,100
40	9,000	1,800	6,600	12,600	6,120	660	1,800
50	7,500	1,500	5,500	10,500	5,100	550	1,500
60	6,000	1,200	4,400	8,400	4,080	440	1,200
65	5,250	1,050	3,850	7,350	3,570	385	1,050
70	4,500	900	3,300	6,300	3,060	330	900
75	3,750	750	2,750	5,250	2,550	275	750
80	3,000	600	2,200	4,200	2,040	220	600
85	2,250	450	1,650	3,150	1,530	165	450
90	1,500	300	1,100	2,100	1,020	110	300
93	1,000	200	733	1,400	680	73	200
95	750	150	550	1,050	510	55	150
97	500	100	367	700	340	37	100
98	300	60	220	420	204	22	60
99	150	30	110	210	102	-	30

Subject to campaign requirements a variable spot rate may be made available

Figure 33.4 Selling audiences to advertisers?

BARB by recording the viewing habits of a sample of viewers. (The size varies depending on how much the television company will spend on such research.) Machines called People Meters are attached to these viewers' television sets, and record, every five seconds, which channel the set is tuned to and which members of the household are watching. In addition the amount of VCR recording is measured, the playback of broadcast programmes which carry an electronic code, and playback of 'non-coded', bought or hired videos, in an attempt to chart audiences who are now partly freed from the schedules (see Stoessl 1998 for fuller detail).

> 'last week … the advertising agency Lowe Howard-Spink Lowe … found that at least one third of the audience "vigorously and continuously" tries to escape TV commercials. And the most zealous practitioners of this "ad avoidance" are that most desirable group, "young and early middle-aged fully employed males".'
>
> (*Observer*, 21 May 1995)

Scheduling

Scheduling is choosing where to put a programme on radio or television, usually with a competitor's programming in mind. Broadcasters have traditionally worked with ideas such as prime time, the period from around 19.30 to 22.30, when large and relatively affluent audiences are watching. The division of schedules into such viewing periods enables a scale of the commercial value of audiences to be calculated. Because all British broadcasting is partly public-service-regulated, though, both ITV and BBC have also worked with the regulated Family Viewing Policy which, drawing on effects approaches, has responded to lobbying groups such as the NVLA (National Viewers' and Listeners' Association). The FVP constructs profiles of audience availability and type, and then an image of Family Life from which is prescribed what should be viewable at particular times:

- 16.15 to 17.15 on weekdays is 'children's hour'.

- 17.15 to 19.30 is presumed to be family viewing time, but with all material broadcast suitable for children to view alone.
- 19.30 to 21.00 is when no material unsuitable for children viewing with the family is broadcast.
- 21.00 onwards: it is assumed that parents are responsible for any children who may still be watching. This relates to the so-called 'nine o'clock watershed', a barrier to certain kinds of language and violent or sexual imagery. Interestingly, it does not exist for radio broadcasting. (The audience survey board for radio is called **RAJAR** (Radio Joint Audience Research), owned jointly by the BBC and the commercial radio stations.)

Schedulers also use the following terms:

- **pre-scheduling**   Starting a programme five minutes before its rival programme on the other channel
- **inheritance factor**   Some audiences seem to 'trust' and watch one channel for most of the evening, so programmes of lesser appeal are put on after popular ones, in the hope that the audience will continue watching
- **pre-echo**   Audiences watch part of the programme before the one they want so they don't miss the beginning. This may be used as a strategy for building up an audience for the less popular programme
- **common junction points**   Where two programmes start at the same time on BBC1 and 2, for example, the chance for cross-trailing arises: 'And now a choice of viewing on BBC …'

ACTIVITY 33.2

Watch a few hours of television on BBC or ITV at the weekend.

- What scheduling decisions seem to have been made?
- Which programmes are pitched 'against' each other?
- Are there any cable programmes which you think BBC and ITV may have an eye on?
- How do the programmes connect to the ads being shown during them?

- About how much time is spent per hour advertising forthcoming programmes on the channel you are watching?
- How far might scheduling practices be considered as part of the spectrum of censorship processes, in their ability to make easily available, or unavailable, certain kinds of material?

Ratings-consciousness does not only apply to commercial broadcasting, trying to convince advertisers of its desirability. The BBC equally needs to justify the licence fee (as well as to provide a satisfying environment for its programme-makers). An important marker of such success is judged to be how many people are watching or listening to its programmes. Hence ratings and scheduling battles exist even where sales of audiences' attention are not involved.

There is now much emphasis on the difficulty of scheduling. Video, cable, digital and other multi-channel developments as well as '**zapping**' and the fragmentation of older 'certainties' like family structure, all make it seem a more volatile process than previously. Yet it still seems wrong to argue that viewers are completely unpredictable, too busy 'surfing' the networks, 'grazing' across channels to be drawn in by ads, if only because:

- Programme-makers and advertisers still battle for 'good' slots, i.e. regular ones, and ones within prime time. Programmes (such as the controversial US sitcom *Ellen)* can be effectively stopped not at the production level but by constantly moving them around the schedules so that viewers can't find them.
- Effective schedulers are highly sought-after within television and radio. Witness the careers and salaries of people like Michael Grade, renowned for his scheduling skills at BBC1 and Channel 4.
- Some audiences do graze, at certain times of the day, but most need to have fixed viewing or listening slots in their routines which schedulers are keen to discover, and to target.

Nevertheless, ratings figures are not transparent in their meanings. High ratings for various programmes may be due to a number of factors, including curiosity, the weather, the fact that there was little on other channels. Ambiguity is built into the process.

A note on the reporting of television controversies

It is worth remembering in current debates led by the press about deregulation, the selling off of the BBC, its ratings, etc. that the press also lives largely by advertising revenue. The position taken by particular newspapers on television controversies has to be understood in relation to often contradictory drives, in addition to the ideological positions of those with power and ownership positions in these industries:

- *Deregulation*   How far would the extension of television advertising (for example, if the BBC were to be completely commercialised) undercut newspaper advertising revenues by bringing down costs and widening the pool of media available to advertisers?
- *Ownership*   Who owns the paper which is arguing against the BBC? Is it News Corporation which owns a large share of the British press and broadcasting, and has a particular interest in acquiring more?

References

Ang, Ien (1991) *Desperately Seeking the Audience*, London: Routledge.

Brierley, Sean (1998) 'Advertising and Marketing: Advertising and the New Media Environment', in Adam Briggs and Paul Cobley (eds) *The Media: An Introduction*, Harlow: Longman.

Curran, James and Seaton, Jean (1997) *Power without Responsibility: The Press and Broadcasting in Britain*, London: Routledge.

Myers, Kathy (1986) *Understains: The Sense and Seduction of Advertising*, London: Comedia.

Stoessl, Sue (1998) 'Audience Feedback: Administrative Research of Audiences', in Briggs and Cobley, *The Media: An Introduction*.

Wasko, Janet (1994) *Hollywood in the Information Age: Beyond the Silver Screen*, London: Polity.

Further reading

Braithwaite, Brian (1998) 'Magazines', in Briggs and Cobley, *The Media: An Introduction*.

Brierley, Sean (1995) *The Advertising Handbook*, London and New York: Routledge.

Kent, R. (1994) *Measuring Media Audiences*, London: Routledge.

Paterson, Richard (1990) 'A Suitable Schedule for the Family', in Andrew Goodwin and Gary Whannel (eds) *Understanding Television*, London and New York: Routledge.

Names of useful journals are given on p. 457. You might also try approaching an ad agency and asking for a back copy of *BRAD* (*British Rates and Data*) which will give you the current rate in every UK publication, including broadcasting. You may even find that your school or college has a staff member responsible for publicity, who can lend you one.

ɔssary of
ʌey terms

Listed below are some of the key terms we have used, and which you will need to know, with short 'thumbnail' definitions. Some common words are referenced only when they have special meanings in Media Studies. Use this glossary in conjunction with the index, contents page and chapter 'menus' to find the material you want.

180° rule   narrative continuity 'rule' on the placement of the camera in film-making (also known as 'not crossing the line')

25% production quota   requirement for British broadcasters to commission 25 per cent of programmes from 'independents'

'A' picture   during the studio period, the main feature in a double bill at the cinema

A&R   'Artists and Repertoire' represent the main assets of companies in the music industry. Performers are signed on contract and rights are held on recordings

ABC   Audit Bureau of Circulation – independent body which provides circulation figures of newspapers and magazines for advertisers

Academy ratio   the traditional cinema screen shape before the coming of widescreen

access   the possibility that audiences can either become producers or have some form of right to reply to dominant media

acoustics   the science of sound – here, a consideration of the environment for sound recording

actuality   term used in early cinema to describe recording of 'real events' – tended to be replaced by 'documentary' in the 1920s

Adobe Photoshop   industry standard computer software used to manipulate a visual image

ADR   Automatic Dialogue Replacement – a process during feature film production, also known as 'looping', which allows actors to re-record dialogue for greater clarity while watching themselves on screen

advertising agencies   organisations which create and manage advertising campaigns, from conception to placement

aesthetics   relating to a sense of beauty, or of form in a text

age profile   the audience for a particular media text, classified according to age group

GLOSSARY OF KEY TERMS

agenda prioritised list of items dealt with by a media text – powerful media producers are 'agenda setters'

analogue any device which represents a quality or value by a physical change in a measuring agent, e.g. the silver nitrate on photographic film which changes colour in response to light

anamorphic lens distorting lens which 'squeezes' an image – used in widescreen film projection

anchoring as used in semiotics – written text (e.g. caption) used to control or select a specific reading of a visual image

anthropology study of the human species – applied in audience studies

anti-realism an aesthetic based on denying any attempt to represent surface reality

anti-trust legislation US government action taken to break up the monopoly power of large producers, e.g. the Paramount decision in 1948 forcing Hollywood studios to sell their cinema chains

arbitrary signifiers term used in semiotics; signifiers with no resemblance to the referent or the signified; see **iconic**, **indexical** and **symbolic**

archive any collection of similar material which can be used in future media productions, e.g. a film archive

articulation term developed to think how elements of social orders or media messages are connected, suggesting not a direct or inevitable link but a process working like a complicated joint; also used of the ways genre elements are mixed

artwork term used in printing to describe any material which will be used to make a printing plate – could be text or illustrations

ASA Advertising Standards Authority: regulator of advertising in newspapers and magazines

aspect ratio the ratio of height to breadth of a cinema screen, or breadth to height of a television screen

audience ethnographies research using ethnographic approaches; joining a specific audience group and working from the inside

auteur/**auteurist** French term for author, used in *la politique des auteurs* (see **authorship**)

authorship approach to film studies which places emphasis on an individual author (usually the director); see *auteur*

avant garde an artistic movement which is 'ahead of the mainstream' and usually experimental

AVID name of the market leader in provision of non-linear editing equipment. Often used as a generic term for computer editing of video or film

'B' picture in the studio era, the shorter and less important feature in a cinematic double bill

Baby Bells American telecommunication companies formed from the forced break-up of the giant Bell Telephone Company

banner slogan used by a newspaper, immediately below the title

BARB Broadcasters' Audience Research Board, the body in Britain which produces television viewing figures

base–superstructure   critical term from early Marxism referring to the economic base on which is built the superstructure of cultural and ideological institutions

behaviourism/behaviourist   movement in psychology which sees human behaviour as something which can be moulded by punishment and reward

bias/biased   ideological 'slant' in debates around factual reporting

bi-media journalism   a BBC policy to train journalists for television and radio under the same scheme

binary oppositions   sets of opposite values said to reveal the structure of media texts; see structuralism

biopics   'biographical pictures' – a traditional Hollywood film genre

bit   corruption of 'binary digit', the '0' or '1' in a stream of binary data. Often used as an indicator of 'quality' or 'resolution', e.g. '24 bit colour image' implies a palette of millions of colours described by different combinations of primary colours, whereas a '1 bit' image can be only black and white

bitmap   an image stored on a computer in the form of a matrix of 'bits' (*qv*). Bitmaps cannot be enlarged without losing quality

branding   persuading consumers of a product's quality prior to purchase or experience, usually by the reputation or image of the producing company

bricolage   French term for 'putting together different articles', as in punk fashion

broadband cable   modern telecommunications and television cable which allows more separate signals (channels) to be transmitted

broadsheet   type of 'serious' newspaper with larger, less square pages than **tabloids** (see Chapter 5)

browser   computer software used to look at pages on the World Wide Web

burden of representation   argument that, when a previously under- or misrepresented group begins to be imaged in the media, those few characters have to bear the burden of being seen to represent the whole group as 'positive role model' etc.

byte   computer term (not the same as bit (*qv*)), referring to the basic unit of data storage for characters. File sizes and the capacity of computer memory is measured in kilobytes (a thousand bytes – KB), megabytes (MB) or gigabytes (GB)

camera obscura   literally a 'dark room', the precursor of the modern camera

camp   a sensibility, emerging from male gay culture, which revels in surface, style, theatricality, and exaggeration or parody of 'straight' forms of life

capitalism   a competitive social system, emerging in the seventeenth century in Europe, based on **commodification** and the drive of the owners of the means of production to maximise the profits of their companies

cartel   a group of organisations in an industry which secretly agree on maintaining high prices and effectively killing competition; see also **oligopoly**

CCCS   Centre for Contemporary Cultural Studies at Birmingham University

CD   compact disc (or disk), a digital data storage medium. **CD-ROM** is a 'read-only' disk. **CD-R** is 're-writable'

censorship   decisive acts of forbidding or preventing publication or distribution of media products, or parts of those products, by those with the power, either economic or legislative, to do so

CGI   (1) Computer Generated Imagery, a term sometimes used for digital special effects; (2) Common Gateway Interface, an agreed standard that defines how a web page can allow users interactivity with an external program, e.g, using a search engine or shopping over the Internet

cinéma vérité   literally 'cinema truth' – an approach to documentary film-making aiming to get as close to events as possible, often producing very high shooting ratios of footage shot to that used in the final edit. Sometimes describes fiction narratives which attempt to resemble documentaries through use of hand-held cameras etc.

CinemaScope   trade name for the anamorphic widescreen process introduced by Twentieth Century Fox in 1953

cinematography   the art of lighting the set and photographing a film

class   (1) one of the groups into which people are divided as a result of socio-economic inequality; (2) a specific group of consumers as recognised by advertisers, six classes now usually grouped into ABC1 ('upmarket') and C2DE ('downmarket'); (3) one of the groups assigned to occupational categories for statistical purposes as defined by the UK Registrar-General, changed in 1998 from six to eight categories

classical   reference to the art and style of Greek and Roman civilisation; used to describe the Hollywood cinema of the studio system, which had developed into a form generally accepted as 'mature' and 'stable'. Contemporary forms which have changed this form radically are thus 'post-classical'

classified advertising   advertising expressed in a few lines of text, also known as 'small ads'

clipart   commercially produced artwork, available at low cost to enhance business and semi-professional print and electronic publications

closed   term used of a narrative which is 'resolved' or comes to a conclusion as opposed to an '**open**' or more ambiguous set of signs

codes   the systems of meaning production recognised by semiotics

cognitive psychology   movement in psychology (opposed to **behaviourism**) which argues that human behaviour is changed by appeals to thought processes

colour grading   final process in preparing a feature film print for screening

colour temperature   a measure of the lighting source on a film or video shoot, which affects the colour cast of white parts of the image and needs correction via filters (see **white balance**)

commodification   a **commodity** is anything which can be bought and sold, usually within capitalist relations; **commodification** and the idea of **commodity fetishism** are terms used, often in Marxist theory, to draw attention to what is argued as the *undue* spread and valuation of services, items, values which can be bought and sold

in Marxist theory, to draw attention to what is argued as the *undue* spread and valuation of services, items, values which can be bought and sold

common sense in discussions of ideology, a set of assumptions that the world's meanings are obvious and can be understood without recourse to theory or analysis

commutation test a critical test used in semiotics, involving the substitution of one element in a complex sign

conglomerate large industrial corporation, usually involved in several different industries

connote/connotation in semiotics, the meanings interpreted from a sign which link it to other concepts, values, memories

construct/construction semiotic term used to emphasise that media texts are 'made' and not simply 'taken from the real world'

consumers term for media audiences which emphasises the commercial aspects of distribution and exhibition, thus production and **consumption** of media texts

content analysis media research technique, counting the number of times an item appears in a media text

content provider media companies who produce programme material for specific delivery or distribution systems, especially cable, satellite and Internet

continuity editing editing techniques which are said to disguise the filmic construction of the narrative. Sometimes called the 'continuity system' or 'continuity rules'

conventions 'un-written rules' in the production of mainstream texts. Conventions are the dominant codings in any media

convergence describes the 'coming together' of previously separate industries (computing, printing, film, audio etc.) which increasingly use the same or related technology and skilled workers. A feature of contemporary media environment, convergence is a product of mergers between companies in different sectors as well as a logical outcome of technological development

copy (1) text written to support an advertisement; (2) the 'raw material' for journalism

copy editing checking the accuracy and legality of text intended for publication and its adherence to house style

CPT advertisers' term standing for 'Cost Per Thousand' or the cost of reaching each thousand people in the target audience

critical pluralism a theoretical approach which acknowledges the co-existence of different sets of ideas (as in pluralism) but recognises that some are more powerful than others, and that they are in a struggle for ascendancy

cropping cutting parts from an image

cross-cutting technique of sequencing images from different narrative spaces so that stories run in parallel, e.g. 'meanwhile, back at the ranch ...'

crossing the line 'rule' for ensuring narrative continuity – 'not crossing the line (of action)' (also known as the **180° rule**)

crossover a media text which gains acceptance in a different genre market

cultural codes meanings derived from cultural differences; see **codes**

cultural competence from Bourdieu, the idea that ease of access to media texts depends on cultural difference and experience

cultural imperialism much-debated position that the globalisation of communication has been driven, particularly since the Second World War, by the commercial interests of the large US-based corporations, often acting in collaboration with American political and military interests. Sometimes used interchangeably with 'media imperialism'. Can also refer to other dominant cultures, especially European

cut a transition between two different visual or audio images in an edited sequence in which one image is immediately replaced by another (see **fade, dissolve, wipe**)

cutaway an extra shot inserted between two visual images in a sequence which prevents a jarring transition (see **jump cut**)

DAT Digital Audio Tape. Compact cassette housing tape suitable for digital recording. Used for some forms of professional audio recording and also for computer data storage

decoding semiotic term for 'reading' the codes in a media text

deconstruction a means of analysing media texts

deep-focus technique in photography or cinematography, producing 'depth of field' – everything in shot in focus

demographics measurement of a population (from Greek *demos* = people) in terms of occupational class, age, sex and region (usually to ascertain their values and assumptions about spending)

denote/denotation in semiotics, the work of that part of the sign (the signifier) which is immediately recognisable to the reader and which has a direct relationship to a real world entity (the referent)

deregulation removal of government restrictions on media industries

design grid the page layout design in a magazine

development media media production associated with aid programmes (in ex-British colonies especially)

dialectical montage juxtaposition of sequences in Soviet cinema representing the 'struggle' of opposing ideas

dialectics Marxist term to describe the process of change: the struggle of opposing ideas (thesis and antithesis) produce synthesis

diaspora dispersal, often forced, across the globe of peoples who originated in a single geographical location, e.g. the dispersed communities formed as a result of the European slave trade with the Americas

diegesis the time and space of the world of the audiovisual narrative. Most useful in distinguishing between diegetic and non-diegetic sound

difference key part of structuralist and semiotic emphases, arguing that meaning is produced largely in the difference between units, rather than what they have in common. Has important (often destructive) consequences for thinking about struggles for equal rights; political and emotional identification with 'sameness' etc.

differential pricing means of accumulating maximum profit on a product by differentiating its price depending on what different markets (i.e. the wealth of potential consumers) will allow

digital based on numerical information, distinguished from **analogue**

digital editing   editing using audio and/or video images which have been **digitised** (converted into computer data). Digital audio editing is sometimes called 'hard disk recording'. Digital video editing is usually termed **nonlinear** editing

digital imaging   used to describe 'photography' which involves capture, manipulation or exhibition of images using a computer or other digital device. Some critics argue that this term should replace photography altogether

Direct Cinema   documentary movement in 1960s US

disc   English spelling used here to refer to analogue recording devices

discourse   term from linguistics, meaning any regulated system of statements or language use which has rules, and therefore exclusions and assumptions. For media it is extended to include visual as well as verbal languages, and also Foucault's work on discourses' different connections to power

disk   American spelling used here to refer to digital (computer) devices

display advertising   advertising using a substantial area of a newspaper page (including graphics)

dissolve   film term for the transition between two images in which one fades out as the other fades up (usually called a **mix** in television)

division of labour   work organised in specialist roles – traditional in the Hollywood studio system

docudrama   fiction narrative using documentary techniques

documentary   media text dealing with 'real world' events; see also **actuality**

dominant   referring to the most powerful ideas in society at any time – expressed in **discourse** and **ideology**

dominant discourses   see **discourse**

dominant ideology   see **ideology**

DP   Director of Photography – the person responsible for camerawork and lighting on a film shoot. British term used instead of *cinematographer*

drama-documentary   documentary which uses techniques from fiction drama (also *dramadoc*)

duopoly   an industry in which two companies control the market

DVD   Digital Video Disc. A storage device for digital data which through **MPEG** compression allows video copies of feature films to be carried on a single 'compact' disc. Also used as a removable storage device for computer data. Attempts have been made to market DVD as 'Digital Versatile Disc' to emphasise the different uses

dystopia   term used in science fiction; a dreadful future society, the opposite of utopia

economic determinist   theory in political economy which looks for economic conditions as the basis for explanations of the social, cultural etc.

economies of scale   cost savings which can be made by large organisations on the basis of the size of the operation, e.g. 'bulk buying'

editing   sequencing of text, images and sounds; see **continuity editing**

editorial   either a statement in a publication by the editor or any feature material (i.e. not advertising)

effects model   model concerned with how the media 'does things to' audiences

empirical   relying on observed experience as evidence for positions. A controversial term, often caricatured by opponents to imply an approach opposed to any kind of theory and relying on sense experience or simplistic facts alone

EPS   encapsulated Postscript – a computer image format used for placement of images in print documents

equilibrium   the initial status quo which is 'disrupted' in a narrative

escapist   'seeking escape, especially from reality', a term used disparagingly of mass cultural forms. Often used as synonymous with 'entertainment'

establishing shot   the opening shot of a conventional visual narrative sequence showing the geography of the narrative space

ethnography   a method of deep research, involving spending considerable periods of time with a particular community or group of people. Audience ethnography was important in establishing Cultural Studies and has been important in developing work on audiences within Media Studies

expressionism   aesthetics in which ideas and feelings are shown through exaggerated elements in the image (lighting, decor, sound etc.)

fabula   term in narrative theory – Russian for 'story'

fade   a production direction in audio and video editing in which an image gradually disappears

feminist   belonging to movements and ideas which advocate the rights of women to have equal opportunities to those possessed by men

fibre optic   technology using glass fibres to carry data

fill light   one of three lighting sources on a film **set-up**, used to 'fill' shadows created by the **key light**

flow   term coined by Raymond Williams, after his first experience of US television, to suggest that broadcast media are experienced not as separate items but as a flow of similar segments

focal length   the distance between the lens and the sensing device in a camera

focus groups   method of audience research involving assembling small, representative groups, e.g. of television viewers whose fairly informal discussions are taped and analysed by, e.g., the producers of a television series seeking guidance on how to increase viewing figures

Foley   refers to technology used in feature film production to create sound effects. **Foley artists** work with a variety of materials to produce sounds mixed by a **Foley editor**

Fordism   ideas about industrial production derived from the concentrated large-scale assembly line established by Henry Ford in Detroit and then internationally from the 1920s

formal   referring to the characteristics of a media text concerned with shape, colour, length etc., rather than content

formalist   theoretical approach which privileges form over content

formats   different size or shape of common media products (videotapes, films etc.)

framing   referring to an image selected to show a person or object. Various framings from 'long shot' to 'extreme close-up' are defined by the size of the human body in the frame. Framing forms part of the process of composition of the image

Frankfurt School   German theorists of mass culture in the 1920s and 1930s

ftp   Internet **protocol** controlling file transfers between computers

gatekeeping   process of choosing certain items for inclusion in news programmes and rejecting others

GATT   General Agreement on Trade and Tariffs. International round of agreements, a site for battles between European (especially French) and American media interests

genre   theoretical term for classification of media texts into type

globalisation   a process in which activities are organised on a global not national scale, in ways which involve some interdependence, and which are often instantaneous around the world

grid   basic design of a 'page' in a print or electronic publication, showing columns, margins etc.

gutter   distance between two columns of print on a page

hardware   the physical equipment used to produce, distribute and exhibit media products

HDTV   High Definition Television. Standard for video images with a resolution in 'lines' which is roughly double current norms (i.e. 1250 lines in the UK, 1050 lines in Japan and US). More likely to be introduced with digital broadcasting

hegemony, hegemonic   concept from Gramsci suggesting that power is achieved by dominant groups through successful struggles to persuade the subordinate that arrangements are in their interest

high-concept movie   the modern high-budget Hollywood film, based on a single strong idea which is easily 'pitched' and can be effectively marketed

hitting the mark   process by which actors in film and television are helped to position themselves correctly for filming by means of marks on the floor

homophobia   fear of homosexuality, expressed in a spectrum of activities from hostile or demeaning vocabulary and images to discriminatory legislation

horizontal integration   when an organisation takes over its competitors in the same industry

hybrid, hybridity   combination of differences, often styles, or technologies or cultural forms

hypertext   computer language allowing readers options to read documents in any order, hypertext markup language (**html**) is used to write pages on the **World Wide Web**

hypodermic model   model of media effects on audiences, imaged as being drug-like

iconic   resembling real-world objects (of signs) – see also **arbitrary**, **indexical** and **symbolic**

GLOSSARY OF KEY TERMS

iconography   art history term, used to describe the study of familiar iconic signs in a genre

ident   a logo or sound image used on television or radio to identify the station

identity   the characteristics of an individual human being which are most central to that person's self-image and self-understanding; see **difference**

identity politics   the values and movements which have developed since the 1960s around issues of identity, in particular gender, race, sexuality and disability. Class is not usually included as one of these key identities

Ideological State Apparatus (ISA)   term from Althusser to describe education, judicial system, church etc.

ideology, ideological complex term relating to ideas and understanding about the social world and how these ideas are related to the distribution of power in society; also about how ideas and values are posed as 'natural'

image   a 'representation' of something expressed in visual or aural terms

imperfect competition   in economics, any 'market' in which a group of buyers or sellers are able to influence market forces; the basic condition for **oligopoly**. The term implies (like 'level playing field') that there could be such a thing as 'perfect competition'

indexical   (in semiotics) referring to concepts via causal relationships (e.g. heat signified by the reading on a thermometer)

infotainment   new genre of media texts which combine information programmes and light entertainment

institution   complex term, used in Media Studies to refer to the social, cultural and political structures within which media production and consumption is constrained

institutional documentary   common genre type, a documentary about school, hospital life etc.

Internet   the global 'network of networks' offering a range of services governed by different protocols, such as the World Wide Web, e-mail, IRC etc.

intertextuality   the variety of ways in which media and other texts interact with each other, rather than being unique or distinct

IRC   Internet Relay Chat. Software which allows Internet users to join 'conversations' organised in an ad hoc way around particular topics

ISDN   Integrated Services Digital Network – a high-speed digital version of the familiar telephone system

ISP   Internet Service Provider. A company that provides access to Internet services through a telephone 'dial-up' link

Italian neo-realism   national film movement of 1940s and 1950s

jargon   derogatory word for terms with strict definitions within a subject discipline

JICREG   Joint Industry Committee of Regional Newspapers – industry body researching readership of the regional press in the UK

JPEG   Joint Photographic Experts Group. A standard for compression of data in a computer image file. JPEGs use 'lossy' compression – some quality is lost. Used for photographic images on the Internet

jump cut   a very noticeable edit between two images with the same subject and roughly the same framing. Can be avoided by use of cutaways

justification   in typesetting, alignment of text to right or left or both ('flush'). Text which is not justified right is known as 'ragged'

key light   the main light source in a film **set-up**, a bright hard light producing deep shadows

leader   (1) another name for the main editorial statement in a newspaper; (2) coloured tape at the beginning of an audio tape reel

leading   the space a typesetter creates between lines of text, derived from strips of lead placed on the frame when text was set in trays of metal type

light touch regulation   a loosening of regulatory controls associated with 'free market' policies in the 1980s and 1990s

long shot   shot size or framing which shows the full human figure

long take   shots lasting twenty seconds or more

MAI   Multilateral Agreement on Investment, currently being negotiated by the OECD (the twenty-nine richest nations on earth) to regulate world trade and investment in the interests of the multinational conglomerates

mainstream   that area of media production in which dominant cultural and industrial values operate

majors   the most powerful producers in any media industry, e.g. the Hollywood studios

market   the total of all the potential sellers and buyers for a particular product (and the number of products likely to be exchanged)

market penetration   the extent to which a product captures the potential sales in a market – expressed as market share

marketing   the process of presenting a product to its target audience; the ways in which it is positioned in its particular market

media buying   the function of an advertising agency in buying 'space' in a media product in which to place an advertisement

media imperialism   the idea that rich and powerful countries dominate poorer countries through control of international media industries

mediate, mediation   changing the meaning of any 'real' event through the application of media technology

melodrama   a particular kind of drama, developing an elaborate language of gesture and spectacle as a result of emerging from underground theatre, banned from using language, in the seventeenth century. Often used in very approximate ways as a term meaning 'exaggerated' or 'hysterical'

mid-market   in classifications of media texts (especially newspapers), the middle position between **tabloid** and **quality**

Mini-Disc   format designed by Sony to provide both a smaller CD for consumer playback and a recording medium for the audio industry. Only the latter use has been taken up widely

mise en scène   literally 'putting together the scene'; in textual analysis, how we read the actions of the creative personnel in a film crew who visualise a script

mix   in video, a transition between scenes in which one image fades up as another fades down; see **dissolve**

mode of address   the way a text 'speaks' to its audience

model   in social sciences, a way of imagining how a system might work

modernism   innovative artistic movements which ran roughly from the 1920s to the 1970s

modernity   (1) in postmodern theory such 'pre-contemporary' processes as Fordism (*qv*) and values such as belief in progress, rationality etc.; (2) in sceptical accounts of postmodernism, a means of describing the 'contemporary'

monopoly   any market situation where one seller controls prices and the supply of product

moral panics   a sudden increase in concern about the possible 'effects' of media products, e.g. 'video nasties' in the 1980s

morphing   the process of presenting a change in shape from one object to another as a single, continuous movement. Achieved by computer software, e.g. the shape-changing Terminator in *Terminator 2* (US 1991)

MPAA   Motion Picture Association of America is the trade association formed by the major Hollywood studios to protect their interests. The Motion Pictures Association (MPA) is the international arm of the organisation which has successfully defended the studios' rights to free trade and exploitation of international markets

MPEG   Motion Picture Experts Group. A standard for compressing video data for editing and playback

multimedia   referring to several traditionally separate media being used together, e.g. sound, image and text on computers

multiplex   (1) multi-screen cinemas which have resuscitated cinema exhibition; (2) in digital broadcasting, the capacity for several different television or radio channels to be broadcast in the same waveband width as a single analogue channel

myths   traditional stories through which societies reinforce and explore their beliefs about themselves; in Media Studies, associated with the work of Lévi-Strauss

narration   the process of telling a story, the selection and organisation of the events for a particular audience

narrative   complex term referring to a sequence of events organised into a story with a particular structure

national identity   in terms of representation, the set of ideas constructed around the concept of 'nation' and the ways in which individuals and groups relate to them

negotiated   in audience theory, the idea that a meaning is arrived at as a result of a process of give and take between the reader's assumptions and the text

news agencies   organisations which gather news stories and sell them to broadcasters and newspaper publishers

news professionals   the media workers who are trained to process news stories according to institutional constraints

news values   the criteria used by editors to select and prioritise news stories for publication

niche marketing   the idea that there are very small, but highly profitable markets which could support specialist advertising-led media products

nonlinear editing (NLE) film and video editing performed wholly on a computer. Video and audio images are digitised and can be sequenced in a script. Several different scripts can be compiled for playback from the computer, before a final version is 'printed' to film or tape. Analogue video and audio editing are 'linear'. Film editing has always been 'nonlinear'

NRS National Readership Survey is the organisation supplying information on readership of national newspapers and magazines

objectivity an idealist aim for journalists – to report events without becoming involved in them (i.e. not being 'subjective')

oligopoly an industry controlled by a small number of producers

oppositional actively opposed to the dominant

option in Hollywood, a purchased right to develop a property such as a novel for a new film

outcome funding media training which must lead to a qualification for funding purposes

outline (1) term for an idea forming the basis for negotiating a production commission; (2) a drawing or a font used in desktop publishing based on a mathematical formula describing the shape, also sometimes known as 'vector graphics' (cf. **bitmap**). Outline drawings and fonts maintain the same quality if enlarged

package unit system the basis for Hollywood film production which replaced the studio system in the 1950s. Each film is treated as a 'one-off' and a package of director, stars and crew brought together for a specific production

PageMaker computer software used for desktop publishing. An industry standard, along with Quark Xpress

pan and scan technique for showing widescreen films on a standard-shape television set

paradigm in structuralist analysis, a class of objects or concepts

paradigmatic a relationship 'across' a set of elements of the same type; compare to syntagmatic, a relationship 'down' or 'up' a sequence of different elements

permissions agreements to film on specific locations or by rights holders that images, sounds and text may be used in a media production

persona the constructed image of a 'star', originally the mask which Roman actors wore

perspective a drawing convention which suggests depth in a flat image. Often associated with the Renaissance and the growth of individualism since it suggests a single viewpoint on a scene

PhotoCD process for recording photographic images on CD, invented by Kodak

photographic truth the belief that photography can produce documentary 'evidence' – now challenged by **digital imaging**

photorealistic referring to the realist effect achieved by photography

PhotoShop computer software used for image manipulation

plot defined in relation to 'story' as the events in a narrative which are presented to an audience directly (see also **fabula** and **syuzhet**)

pluralist   of a political position which allows for several competing ideologies to be accepted as valid

point size   measure of the size of text characters in typesetting: 72 points is roughly one inch

political economy   a theoretical approach which emphasises the importance of combining political and economic analysis in understanding a media text

politically correct   term, usually hostile, for attempts to implement non-discriminatory language, imagery, working practices etc.

polysemic   literally 'many-signed', an image in which there are several possible meanings depending on the ways in which its constituent signs are read

popular   widely used term, literally meaning 'of the people'. Negatively, in contrast to 'high culture', 'art', etc. and as synonymous with 'mass'

post-feminism   position which argues that the condition of women 'after' the successes of the 1960s and 1970s wave of feminist struggles means they can take for granted respect and equality and enjoy the pleasures and playfulness around traditional 'femininity'

post-Fordism   method of commodity production which subcontracts part of the production process to a number of firms and uses new technology to make production more responsive to consumer demand

postmodernism   complex term used with several meanings, usually a contemporary

movement in the arts or, more widely, a set of attitudes to the contemporary world

Postscript   'page description language' used in print publishing which is 'platform free' – not dependent on the type of computer used

PPV   Pay Per View. Method of charging television viewers for a single viewing of a programme, rather than subscribing to a channel for a set period. Used first for sports events and concerts, now also for film screenings

pre-sale   the possibility of selling the distributions rights to a product before production is completed, giving some security to the production

Press Complaints Commission   newspaper industry body set up to monitor the publication of unethical material

primary research   research into the original source of a media story – an interview, personal letters or government records

prime time   that part of a radio or television schedule expected to attract the biggest audience, i.e. 19.30 to 22.30 hours

principal photography   the production phase on a film shoot

privatisation   process by which public services or utilities are transferred to private ownership

producer choice   BBC policy encouraging producers to consider less expensive non-BBC facilities

product placement   an unofficial form of advertising in which branded products feature prominently in films, etc.

production cycle   in the Hollywood studio system, the constant film production process involving strict division of labour

progressive aesthetic, representations   an approach to presentation of images which seeks to promote change in society

proofing   process of checking the text in the final version of a media product before publication for errors in placement, spelling etc.; test printing a colour image on paper (because colours on a computer screen are not reliable guides)

propaganda   any media text which seeks openly to persuade an audience of the validity of particular beliefs

property   any original story the rights to which have been acquired by a production company

proposal   idea for a new media product submitted speculatively by a freelance to a major producer, including an outline and an argument that a market exists

protocol   software controlling the interface between computers in a network. Protocols cover every aspect of using the Internet

public domain   describes any media product for which copyright has expired, or has never been claimed, implying that no payment to a rights holder is required. This applies only to the work itself and not a particular publication of it – i.e. the text of a Dickens novel, but not the Penguin printed version

public relations   professional services in promoting products by arranging opportunities for exposure in the media

public service broadcasting (PSB)   regulated broadcasting which has providing a public service as a primary aim

qualitative research   audience research based on discussion groups or one-to-one interviews with interaction between researcher and subject

quality document   an audit document showing how an organisation maintains the integrity of its administration systems

quality press   the 'serious' newspapers – in the UK synonymous with **broadsheet** (but not in Europe)

quantitative analysis   method of analysis involving the counting of quantities: of hours of television output; or of numbers of women appearing in television news. Popular partly because numbers, unlike languages, form a universal 'currency', and can be read even when their author is not there to explain them. What matters is the quality of the questions asked

quantitative research   audience research based on anonymous data with **samples** constructed to represent larger populations of viewers, listeners and readers

Quark Xpress   industry standard computer software used in page layout

quota   a designated amount of production, minimum or maximum, which is specified for purposes of regulation or to protect specific producers from competition e.g. attempts to limit Hollywood's share of film markets by insisting that cinemas show 'home' product

racism   the stigmatising of difference along the lines of 'racial' characteristics in order to justify advantage or abuse of power, whether economic, political, cultural or psychological

RAJAR Radio Joint Audience Research, the industry body which collects and publishes data on radio audiences in the UK

ratings viewing and listening figures presented as a league table of successful programmes, depending on audience size

reader panels groups of readers who can be questioned about their responses to a media product

reader research research into who 'reads' a media product

real time time taken for an event in an audio-visual text which exactly matches the time taken for the same event in the real world

realism a fiercely contested term which emphasises taking seriously the relationship between media texts and the rest of the 'real world'

realism effect the appearance of a realist image, achieved through artifice

realist aesthetic an approach to presenting an image which seeks to achieve realism

ream standard measure of paper – 500 sheets

recce 'reconnoitres' – part of pre-production, checking out venues for performances or locations for recording

recto the right-hand page in a print publication

referent in semiotics, the 'real world' object to which the sign refers

regional press newspapers (morning or evening dailies and/or Sundays) with a regional circulation

release patterns the geographical patterns of the release of media texts, especially feature films

repertoire of elements the fluid system of conventions and expectations associated with genre texts

repetition and difference the mix of familiar and new characteristics which offer pleasures and attract audiences to generic media texts

revenue funding public funding of media organisations which covers aspects of day-to-day expenditure (distinguished from capital funding)

right of reply the idea that persons who feel that they have been misrepresented should have the right to challenge media producers on air or in a newspaper

romance fiction genre in which intimate personal relationships related to love and marriage are the central focus

samples (1) in digital audio production, sounds or sequence of sounds 'captured' by a computer for use in future productions; (2) carefully selected groups of people chosen in audience research to represent larger populations

sans-serif any typeface or font 'without a **serif**'

schedule as in 'production schedule', the careful planning of the production process

scheduling strategies adopted to place programmes in radio and television schedules to most effect

script (1) dialogue and production directions for a radio, film or television production; (2) arrangement of sounds, images and effects placed in sequence on a computer for presentation; (3) a typeface designed to resemble handwriting

search engine computer software used to find a specific word or phrase in a database or across a network like the Internet

secondary image   the image of a film star used in another, 'secondary' medium such as television or magazine publishing

secondary research   research using reference books or previously annotated or published sources (cf. **primary research**)

segment   (verb) to divide up a target audience into even more specialised groups which can be addressed by advertisers

self-reflexive   applied to texts which display an awareness or a comment on their own artificial status as texts

semiotics/semiology   the study of sign systems

serif   the bar across the ends of the main strokes of a text character in a typeface

service provider   see **ISP**

set-top box   computer which sits on top of a television set and controls the variety of possible incoming signals

set-ups   term for the separate camera, lighting and sound positions necessary for shooting a feature film

shot   the smallest element in any film sequence, a single 'take' during shooting which may be further shortened during editing

shot/reverse shot   term for the conventional way of shooting an exchange between two characters in a film or television programme

signified/signifier   the components of a sign

slate   film industry term for the list of major features to be produced during a production period

soap, soap opera   the radio and television multi-strand continuous serial narrative form originally designed as a vehicle for sponsorship by soap powder manufacturers

social psychology   the study of human behaviour

socialist realism   the prescribed realist form forced on Soviet film-makers by the Stalin regime in the 1930s – featuring romanticised heroic workers

sociobiology   theory that social behaviour can be explained by recourse to explanations from genetics or natural history

software   the programs written for computers, or the films, music etc. which could be played on them

sound effect   frequently used to refer to artificially created 'sounds' produced for audiovisual texts; also could be extended to refer to all aural material in a production apart from dialogue and music

sound image   term used to emphasise the possibility of analysing or reading sounds in the same way as 'pictures'

sound stages   term describing the individual buildings available for shooting in a film studio – the name implies that they could be used for recording sound

spaghetti Westerns   a cycle of films made in Italy and Spain in the 1960s and 1970s, drawing on the Hollywood Western for inspiration

spin doctor   press or PR officer employed to put a positive 'spin' or angle on stories about their employer. The term suggests an unjustifiable degree of intervention in the construction of news

standardisation   has a double meaning: it can signify 'sameness'; but can also denote the maintenance of standards, in the sense of quality

star   actor whose image, via accumulated publicity, debate etc. is strong enough to be seen as an added component of any performance and acts as a specific attraction for audiences

star image   the constructed image of the star, usually in relation to film and associated 'secondary circulation'

Steadicam   trade name for a stabilising device allowing a camera operator to move freely without jerking the image

stereotypes, stereotyping   originally a term from printing, literally a 'solid' block of metal type; then, a representation of a type of person, without fine detail

story   all of the events in a narrative, those presented directly to an audience and those which might be inferred – compare with **plot**

structuralism   an approach to critical analysis which emphasises universal structures underlying the surface differences and apparent randomness of cultures, stories, media texts etc.

structuring oppositions   see **binary oppositions**

studio system   Hollywood factory-like production system from about 1930 to 1950

sub-editing   process late in the production of a newspaper in which stories are shortened or re-written to fit the space available and headlines and picture captions are written

subliminal advertising   associated with hypnosis and said to work by flashing barely perceptible messages to audiences in between frames of a film or advertisement

superstructure   ideological structures built on an 'economic base' according to certain Marxist theories

symbolic   used in semiotics of a sign which has come to stand for a particular set of qualities or values, e.g. the cross for Christianity; see **arbitrary, iconic** and **indexical**

synergy   produced by combining two separate products, so that they 'feed' each other, e.g. a film and a video game using the same characters

syntagmatic   term used in semiotics of the way certain elements are ordered in particular sequences, e.g. narrative (see **paradigmatic**)

syuzhet   term in narrative theory – Russian for 'plot'

tabloid   the size of a newsprint page, half that of the 'broadsheet'; by extension: sensationalist media form (television and radio as well as the press)

talent   anyone appearing in front of the camera or microphone, the performers

target audiences   the specific audiences to be addressed by a particular media text

Technicolor   colour film process developed for cinema in the 1930s

technophobia   fear of machines or technology, especially in science fiction narratives

telephoto   long camera lens which enables distant objects to be shown in close-up –– has the effect of 'flattening' the image

telnet   Internet **protocol** software which enables a user to control a host computer elsewhere on the network

tentpole movie   a major film which a studio hopes will provide the support for its annual slate and almost guarantee box-office returns

territories   geographical areas for which the rights to a media product are negotiated

text   any system of signs which can be 'read' – a poster, photograph, haircut etc.

tie-ins   products which accompany and help publicise a major film or television release, e.g. the publication of a 'novelisation' of the script

transparency   the way in which media texts present themselves as 'natural'; their construction is invisible to casual readers

treatment   document in the pre-production process for television and video which describes how the ideas in the outline will be developed into a programme, referring to genre, style etc.

turn-around   film industry term for a script dropped by one studio and waiting for another to pick it up

type/typical   classification of characters in a narrative according to selected common features; see **stereotype**

typeface   a complete set of text and numeric characters plus symbols and punctuation marks with common design features. A typeface may be available in different weights (bold, light etc.) or styles (italic, condensed etc.)

typesetting   now completely computerised, the process of arranging text in precise positions on the page

unit production system, unit-based production   way of organising production under the Hollywood studio system

universal service   (in relation to public service broadcasting) a service available to everyone at the same price

uses and gratifications model   'active' model of audience behaviour, emphasising the uses to which audiences put even the most unlikely texts

Utopian   associated with an ideal, if not impossible, social world

vector graphics   see **outline** (2)

verisimilitude   quality of seeming like what is taken to be the real world of a particular text

verso   left-hand page in a print publication

vertical integration   business activity involving one company acquiring others elsewhere in the production process

violence debate   recurring debates over audience behaviour, focusing on the possible 'effects' of representations of violence

virtual   something which is a representation rather than the 'real' thing, thus 'virtual reality'

voyeurism   the pleasure of looking while unseen; used in thinking about male pleasure in the ways cinema, especially, constructs women as 'objects of the [male] gaze'

white balance   the process of correcting the sensitivity of a video camera to match a specific lighting source (see **colour temperature**)

white space   the blank spaces on a printed page – considered to be an important component in the overall design and 'look' of the page

wide angle   camera lens which is used with the subject close to the camera, but with the whole scene shown – can lead to distortion of objects very close to the camera

wipe transition in video editing in which one image replaces another according to a specific pattern such as the appearance of a page being turned

word-of-mouth informal way in which media products become known about by audiences

Workshop Declaration an agreement by independent video production groups to work according to a set of guidelines – allowing union members to work at lower rates of pay on 'non-broadcast' jobs

World Wide Web the network of 'pages' of images, texts and sounds on the Internet which can be viewed using browser software

wrap industry jargon for the completion of a film shoot

zapping the technique of rapidly cutting between television channels using a remote control device

zoom an arrangement of camera lenses, allowing the operator to change the focal length and move between **telephoto** and **wide angle** settings

Select bibliography and resources

For detailed lists of sources and ideas for further reading on specific topics, see individual chapters. The titles below provide general introductions to the major debates in the book. You can use them as starting points for background reading and consult their bibliographies for further ideas.

Abercrombie, Nicholas (1996) *Television and Society*, Cambridge: Polity.

Allen, Robert C. (ed.) (1987) *Channels of Discourse*, Chapel Hill and London: University of North Carolina Press.

Andermahr, Sonya, Lovell, Terry and Wolkowitz, Carol (1997) *A Concise Glossary of Feminist Theory*, London and New York: Arnold.

Ang, Ien (1991) *Desperately Seeking the Audience*, London: Routledge.

Baehr, Helen and Dyer, Gillian (eds) (1987) *Boxed In: Women and Television*, London: Pandora.

Barker, Chris (1997) *Global Television: An Introduction*, Oxford: Blackwell.

Barker, Martin and Beezer, Anne (eds) (1992) *Reading Into Cultural Studies*, London and New York: Routledge.

Barker, Martin and Brooks, Kate (1998) *Knowing Audiences 'Judge Dredd': Its Friends, Fans and Foes*, Luton: University of Luton Press.

Barker, Martin and Petley, Julian (eds) (1997) *Ill Effects: The Media/Violence Debate*, London and New York: Routledge.

Barthes, Roland (1972; first published 1957) *Mythologies*, London: Paladin.

Barthes, Roland (1977) *Image-Music-Text* (trans. Stephen Heath), London: Fontana/Collins.

Berger, Arthur Asa (1995) *Essentials of Mass Communication Theory*, London: Sage.

Berman, Edward S. and McChesney, Robert W. (1997) *The Global Media: The New Missionaries of Corporate Capitalism*, London and Washington, DC: Cassell.

Bignell, Jonathan (1997) *Media Semiotics: An Introduction*, Manchester: Manchester University Press.

Bogle, Donald (1994, 2nd edition) *Toms, Coons, Mulattoes, Mammies and Bucks: An Interpretative History of Blacks in American Films*, New York: Continuum.

Bordwell, David and Carroll, Noël (eds) (1996) *Post-theory: Reconstructing Film Studies*, Madison and London: University of Wisconsin Press.

Bordwell, David and Thompson, Kristin (1997, 5th edition) *Film Art: An Introduction*, London and New York: McGraw-Hill.

Brierley, Sean (1995) *The Advertising Handbook*, London and New York: Routledge.

Briggs, Adam and Cobley, Paul (eds) (1998) *The Media: An Introduction*, Harlow: Longman.

Bromley, Michael and O'Malley, Tom (eds) (1997) *A Journalism Reader*, London: Routledge.

Carter, Cynthia, Branston, Gill and Allan, Stuart (eds) (1998) *News, Gender and Power*, London: Routledge.

Cohen, Stan (1972) *Folk Devils and Moral Panics*, Oxford: Martin Robertson.

Corner, John (1996) *The Art of Record: A Critical Introduction to Documentary*, Manchester: Manchester University Press.

Corner, John (1998) *Studying Media: Problems of Theory and Method*, Edinburgh: Edinburgh University Press.

Crisell, Andrew (1994, 2nd edition) *Understanding Radio*, London: Routledge.

Crisell, Andrew (1997) *An Introductory History of British Broadcasting*, London: Routledge.

Curran, James and Gurevitch, Michael (eds) (1991) *Mass Media and Society*, London: Arnold.

Curran, James and Seaton, Jean (1997) *Power without Responsibility: The Press and Broadcasting in Britain*, London: Routledge.

Dimbleby, Nick, Dimbleby, Richard and Whittington, Ken (1994) *Practical Media*, London: Hodder & Stoughton.

Dunant, Sarah (ed.) (1994) *The War of the Words: The Political Correctness Debate*, London: Virago.

Dyer, Gillian (1983) *Advertising as Communication*, London: Methuen.

Dyer, Richard (1973) *Only Entertainment* (1992), London: Routledge.

Dyer, Richard (1997) *White: Essays on Race and Culture*, London: Routledge.

Dyer, Richard (1998, 2nd edition) *Stars*, London: BFI.

Eagleton, Terry (1983) *Literary Theory: An Introduction*, Oxford: Blackwell.

Ellis, John (1982, 2nd edition 1992) *Visible Fictions*, London: Routledge.

Evans, Harold (1978) *Pictures on a Page: Photojournalism, Graphics and Picture Editing*, London: Heinemann.

Franklin, Bob and Murphy, David (1998) *Making the Local News: Local Journalism in Context*, London: Routledge.

Frith, Simon and Goodwin, Andrew (eds) (1990) *On Record*, London: Routledge.

Gamman, Lorraine and Marshment, Margaret (eds) (1998) *The Female Gaze: Women as Viewers of Popular Culture*, London: Women's Press.

Geraghty, Christine (1991) *Women and Soap Opera: A Study of Prime Time Soaps*, London: Polity.

Geraghty, Christine and Lusted, David (1998) *The Television Studies Book*, London and New York: Arnold.

Glasgow University Media Group (1976) *Bad News*, London: Routledge & Kegan Paul.

Glasgow University Media Group (1993) *Getting the Message: News, Truth and Power*, London: Routledge.

Gledhill, Christine (ed.) (1987) *Home Is Where the Heart Is*, London: BFI.

Gledhill, Christine (1991) *Stardom: Industry of Desire*, London: Routledge.

Gledhill, Christine and Williams, Linda (2000) *Reinventing Film Studies*, London and New York: Arnold.

Goffman, Erving (1976) *Gender Advertisements*, London: Macmillan.

Golding, Peter and Elliott, Philip (1979) *Making the News*, London: Longman.

Gomery, Douglas (1992) *Shared Pleasures*, London: BFI.

Goodwin, Andrew and Whannel, Gary (eds) (1990) *Understanding Television*, London: Routledge.

Hall, Stuart (ed.) (1997) *Representation: Cultural Representations and Signifying Practices*, London: Thousand Oaks and New Delhi: Sage.

Hartley, John (1982) *Understanding News*, London: Routledge.

Hawthorn, Jeremy (1998) *A Glossary of Contemporary Literary Theory*, London and New York: Arnold.

Hill, John (1999) *British Cinema in the 1980s*, Oxford: Oxford University Press.

Hill, John and Church Gibson, Pamela (eds) (1998) *The Oxford Guide to Film Studies*, Oxford and New York: Oxford University Press.

Hillier, Jim (1993) *The New Hollywood*, London: Studio Vista.

Holland, Patricia (1997) *The Television Handbook*, London and New York: Routledge.

Hood, Stuart and Tabary-Peterssen, Thalia (1997, 4th revised edition) *On Television*, London: Pluto.

Jenkins, Tricia (ed.) (1997) *GNVQ Advanced Media: Communication & Production*, Oxford: Focal Press.

Keeble, Richard (1998, 2nd edition) *The Newspapers Handbook*, London: Routledge.

Langham, Josephine (1996, 2nd edition) *Lights, Camera, Action!: Careers in Film, Television and Radio*, London: BFI.

Lewis, Justin (1991) *The Ideological Octopus: The Exploration of Television and Its Audience*, New York and London: Routledge.

Lister, Martin (ed.) (1995) *The Photographic Image in Digital Culture*, London: Routledge.

Lull, James (1995) *Media, Communication, Culture: A Global Approach*, Cambridge: Polity.

Lusted, David (ed.) (1991) *The Media Studies Book*, London: Routledge.

McDonald, Myra (1995) *Representing Women: Myths of Femininity in the Popular Media*, London and New York: Arnold.

McGuigan, Jim (1992) *Cultural Populism*, London: Routledge.

McGuigan, Jim (1999) *Modernity and Postmodern Culture*, London: Open University Press.

Maltby, Richard and Craven, Ian (1995) *Hollywood Cinema*, Oxford: Blackwell.

Masterman, Len (1984) *Television Mythologies: Stars, Shows and Signs*, London: Comedia.

Medhurst, Andy and Munt, Sally R. (eds) (1997) *Lesbian and Gay Studies: A Critical Introduction*, London: Cassell.

Moores, Sean (1993) *Interpreting Audiences: The Ethnography of Media Consumption*, London: Sage.

Morley, David and Chen, Kuan-Hsing (eds) (1996) *Stuart Hall: Critical Dialogues in Cultural Studies*, London: Routledge.

Myers, Kathy (1986) *Understains: The Sense and Seduction of Advertising*, London: Comedia.

NCVQ (1996) *Working in Print*, London: NCVQ.

Neale, Steve (1985) *Cinema and Technology: Image, Sound, Colour*, London: BFI/Macmillan.

Neale, Steve (1990) 'Questions of Genre', *Screen*, vol. 31, no.1.

Neale, Steve and Smith, Murray (eds) (1998) *Contemporary Hollywood Cinema*, London: Routledge.

Newbold, Chris et al. (1996) *GNVQ Media: Communication & Production Advanced*, London: Longman.

Nowell-Smith, Geoffrey and Ricci, Steven (eds) (1998) *Hollywood and Europe: Economics, Culture, National Identity 1945–1995*, London: BFI.

O'Malley, Tom and Treharne, Jo (1993) *Selling the Beeb*, London: Campaign for Press and Broadcasting Freedom.

O'Sullivan, Tim, Dutton, Brian and Rayner, Philip (1998, 2nd edition) *Studying the Media: An Introduction*, London, New York, Melbourne and Auckland: Arnold.

O'Sullivan, Tim, Hartley, John, Saunders, Danny, Montgomery, Martin and Fiske, John (1994, 2nd edition) *Key Concepts in Cultural and Communication Studies*, London: Routledge.

O'Sullivan, Tim and Jewkes, Yvonne (eds) (1997) *The Media Studies Reader*, London and New York: Arnold.

Philo, Greg (1990) *Seeing and Believing: The Influence of Television*, London: Routledge.

Pines, Jim (ed.) (1992) *Black and White in Colour: Black People in British Television since 1936*, London: BFI.

Pirie, David (ed.) (1981) *Anatomy of the Movies*, London: Windward.

Pumphrey, Martin (1987) 'The Flapper, the Housewife and the Making of Modernity', *Cultural Studies*, vol. I, no. 2 (May).

Root, Jane (1986) *Open the Box*, London: Comedia.

Ross, Andrew (ed.) (1997) *No Sweat: Fashion, Free Trade and the Rights of Garment Workers*, London and New York: Verso.

Schatz, Thomas (1989 and 1998) *The Genius of the System: Hollywood Filmmaking in the Studio Era*, London: Faber & Faber.

Schlesinger, Philip (1987) *Putting Reality Together*, London: Methuen.

Schlesinger, Philip et al. (1992) *Women Viewing Violence*, London: BFI

Shohat, Ella and Stam, Robert (1994) *Unthinking Eurocentrism: Multiculturalism and the Media*, London and New York: Routledge.

Slater, Don (1997) *Consumer Culture and Modernity*, Cambridge: Polity.

Sreberny-Mohammadi, Annabel, Winseck, Dwayne, McKenna, Jill and Boyd-Barrett, Oliver (eds) (1997) *Media in Global Context*, London and New York: Arnold.

Stacey, Jackie (1993) *Star Gazing: Hollywood Cinema and Female Spectatorship*, London: Routledge.

Strinati, Dominic (1995) *An Introduction to Theories of Popular Culture*, London: Routledge.

Strinati, Dominic and Wagg, Stephen (eds) (1992) *Come on Down: Popular Media Culture in Post-war Britain*, London: Routledge.

Thompson, John B. (1997) *The Media and Modernity: A Social Theory of the Media*, Cambridge: Polity.

Thompson, Kenneth (1998) *Moral Panics*, London and New York: Routledge.

Thompson, Kristin and Bordwell, David (1994) *Film History: An Introduction*, New York and London: McGraw-Hill.

Tolson, Andrew (1996) *Mediations: Text and Discourse in Media Studies*, London and New York: Arnold.

Turner, Graeme (1993) *Film as Social Practice*, London: Routledge.

Van Zoonen, Lisbet (1994) *Feminist Media Studies*, London: Sage.

Wasko, Janet (1994) *Hollywood in the Information Age: Beyond the Silver Screen*, London: Polity.

Wells, Liz (ed.) (1996) *Photography: A Critical Introduction*, London and

Williams, Granville (1996) *Britain's Media: How They Are Related*, London: Campaign For Press and Broadcasting Freedom.

Williams, Kevin (1998) *Get Me a Murder a Day!*, London: Arnold.

Williams, Raymond (1976) *Keywords: A Vocabulary of Culture and Society*, London: Fontana/Croom Helm.

Williams, Raymond (1979) *Politics and Letters: Interviews with New Left Review*, London: Verso.

Williams, Raymond (1990, first published 1974) *Television: Technology and Cultural Form*, London: Fontana.

Williamson, Judith (1978) *Decoding Advertisements: Ideology and Meaning in Advertising*, London: Marion Boyars.

Winston, Brian (1998) *Media Technology and Society*, London: Routledge.

Wollen, Tana and Hayward, Philip (eds) (1993) *Future Visions: New Technologies of the Screen*, London: BFI.

Young, Lola (1996) *Fear of the Dark, 'Race', Gender and Sexuality in the Cinema*, London: Routledge.

There are no texts referring to media production techniques in this list. For specific technical manuals, please see the catalogues published by Focal Press, Linacre House, Jordan Hill, Oxford OX2 8DP; and by BBC Training, BBC Elstree Centre, Clarendon Road, Borehamwood, Herts WD6 1JF.

Resources

Magazines

The following magazines are very useful sources of specialist material on the industries concerned. The American magazines are all available in the UK, although outside major city centres they would need to be ordered. Trade magazines are expensive, but access to only one or two copies can give you a valuable insight into industry concerns, unavailable elsewhere.

Billboard, American music and related entertainment industry trade paper.

Broadcast, the trade magazine for the UK broadcasting industry.

Campaign, the trade magazine for the UK advertising industry.

Free Press, magazine of the Campaign for Press and Broadcasting Freedom (CPBF) available from 8 Cynthia Street, London N1 9JF.

Hollywood Reporter, American film industry paper.

The Journalist, magazine of the National Union of Journalists.

Marketing Week, the trade magazine for the UK marketing industry.

Media Week, the trade magazine for UK media buyers.

Music Week, trade paper of the UK music industry.

Screen, academic journal for film and television studies in higher education.

Screen Digest, monthly international television industry news magazine.

Screen Finance, fortnightly news and financial analysis of UK and European film and television.

Screen International, the trade magazine for film production, distribution and exhibition (includes video and television films).

Sight & Sound, monthly magazine from the British Film Institute, giving details of film and video releases plus critical writing and features.

Stage, Screen and Radio, journal of the media union BECTU.

UK Press Gazette, trade paper of the UK Press.

Variety, the American trade paper for the entertainment industry generally.

Yearbooks

BFI Film and Television Handbook.
Guardian Media Guide.
The Writers' and Artists' Year Book, London: A. C. Black.
Writers Handbook, London: Macmillan.

Doing your own research

To assist in your own research for essays, projects and seminars, we have listed organisations which offer useful advice and information for media students. We have included e-mail and website addresses where these are available but do check these since they may change after publication. Below the organisations is a list of magazines which are very useful sources of specialist material on the industries concerned. The American magazines are all available in the UK, although outside major city centres they would need to be ordered. Trade magazines are expensive, but access to only one or two copies can give you a valuable insight into industry concerns, unavailable elsewhere.

Useful addresses

The following organisations all offer advice and information which may be useful for media students.

Advertising Standards Authority (ASA)

2 Torrington Place
London WC1E 7HW ☎ 0171 580 5555

Arts Council of England

14 Great Peter Street
London SW1P 3NQ ☎ 0171 333 0100

(Contact the Arts Council for details of your own
Regional Arts Board.)

e-mail: Information.ace@artsfb.org.uk
web site: www.artscouncil.org.uk

Arts Council of Northern Ireland

77 Malone Road
Belfast BT9 5DU ☎ 01232 385200

Arts Council of Wales

9 Museum Place
Cardiff CF1 3NX ☎ 01222 394711

BBC

Television Centre
Wood Lane
London W12 7RJ ☎ 0181 743 8000

web site: www.BBC.co.uk

Broadcasting House

Portland Place
London W1A 1AA ☎ 0171 580 4468

Bartle Bogle Hegarty

24 Great Pulteney Street
London W1R 4LB ☎ 0171 734 1677

British Board of Film Classification (BBFC)

3 Soho Square
London W1V 6HD ☎ 0171 439 7961

web site: www.bbfc.co.uk

British Film Institute (BFI)

21 Stephen Street
London W1P 2LN ☎ 0171 255 1444

web site: www.BFI.org.uk

Broadcasting, Entertainment, Cinematograph and Theatre Union (BECTU)

111 Wardour Street
London W1V 4AY ☎ 0171 437 8506

Broadcasting Standards Commission

7 The Sanctuary
London SW1P 3JS ☎ 0171 233 0544

web site: www.bsc.org.uk

Campaign for Press and Broadcasting Freedom

8 Cynthia Street
London N1 9JF ☎ 0171 278 4430

Channel 4 Television

124 Horseferry Road
London SW1P 2TX ☎ 0171 396 4444

web site: www.channel4.com

CIC Video

4th Floor
Glenthorne House
5–7 Hammersmith Grove
London W6 0ND ☎ 0171 563 3500

Community Radio Association

5 Paternoster Square
Sheffield S1 2BX ☎ 0114 279 5219

Film Education

Alhambra House
27–31 Charing Cross Road
London WC2H 0AU ☎ 0171 976 2291

web site: www.filmeducation.org

Independent Television Commission (ITC)

33 Foley Street ·

London W1P 7BL ☎ 0171 255 3000

Institute of Practitioners in Advertising (IPA)

44 Belgrave Square

London SW1 8QS ☎ 0171 235 7020

Mechanical Copyright Protection Society (MCPS)

Elgar House

41 Streatham High Road

London SW16 1ER ☎ 0181 664 4400

Media Education Wales

Cardiff Institute of Higher Education

Cyncoed Road

Cardiff CF2 6XD ☎ 01222 689101/2

National Union of Journalists

314 Gray's Inn Road

London WC1X 8DP ☎ 0171 278 7916

Northern Ireland Film Commission

21 Ormeau Avenue

Belfast BT2 8HD ☎ 01232 232444

Performing Rights Society (PRS)

29–33 Berners Street

London W1P 4AA ☎ 0171 580 5544

Press Complaints Commission

1 Salisbury Square

London EC4Y 8AE ☎ 0171 353 1248

web site: www.pcc.org.uk

Radio Authority

Holbrooke House

Great Queen Street

London WC2B 5DG ☎ 0171 430 2724

web site: www.radioauthority.gov.uk

Royal Photographic Society

Milsom Street

Bath

Avon BA1 1DN ☎ 01225 462841

Scottish Arts Council

12 Manor Place

Edinburgh EH3 7DD ☎ 0131 226 6051

e-mail: administrator.sac@artsfb.org.uk

web site: www.sac.org.uk

Scottish Screen

Dowanhill

74 Victoria Crescent Road

Glasgow G12 9JN ☎ 0141 302 1700

e-mail: info@scottishscreen.demon.co.uk

web site: www.scottishscreen.demon.co.uk

Sgrin (Media Agency for Wales)

Screen Centre

Ty Oldfield

Llantrisant Road

Llandaff

Cardiff CF5 2PU ☎ 01222 578370

Skillset

124 Horseferry Road

London SW1P 2TX ☎ 0171 306 8585

Index

This index lists page references to four different kinds of information: key terms, media organisations, people and titles of films, radio and television programmes etc. It isn't exhaustive, but used in conjunction with the Glossary, should help you find out what you want. Many definitions are signalled by **bold numbers**, illustrations by *italic numbers* and margin entries by '(m)'.